Recent Advances in Data Mining of Enterprise Data: Algorithms and Applications

Series on Computers and Operations Research

Series Editor: P. M. Pardalos *(University of Florida)*

Published

Vol. 1 Optimization and Optimal Control
eds. P. M. Pardalos, I. Tseveendorj and R. Enkhbat

Vol. 2 Supply Chain and Finance
eds. P. M. Pardalos, A. Migdalas and G. Baourakis

Vol. 3 Marketing Trends for Organic Food in the 21st Century
ed. G. Baourakis

Vol. 4 Theory and Algorithms for Cooperative Systems
eds. D. Grundel, R. Murphey and P. M. Pardalos

Vol. 5 Application of Quantitative Techniques for the Prediction of Bank Acquisition Targets
by F. Pasiouras, S. K. Tanna and C. Zopounidis

Vol. 6 Recent Advances in Data Mining of Enterprise Data: Algorithms and Applications
eds. T. Warren Liao and Evangelos Triantaphyllou

Vol. 7 Computer Aided Methods in Optimal Design and Operations
eds. I. D. L. Bogle and J. Zilinskas

Series on Computers and Operations Research **Vol. 6**

Recent Advances in Data Mining of Enterprise Data: Algorithms and Applications

T Warren Liao

Evangelos Triantaphyllou

Louisiana State University, USA

World Scientific

NEW JERSEY • LONDON • SINGAPORE • BEIJING • SHANGHAI • HONG KONG • TAIPEI • CHENNAI

Published by

World Scientific Publishing Co. Pte. Ltd.
5 Toh Tuck Link, Singapore 596224
USA office: 27 Warren Street, Suite 401-402, Hackensack, NJ 07601
UK office: 57 Shelton Street, Covent Garden, London WC2H 9HE

British Library Cataloguing-in-Publication Data
A catalogue record for this book is available from the British Library.

RECENT ADVANCES IN DATA MINING OF ENTERPRISE DATA: Algorithms and Applications
Series on Computers and Operations Research — Vol. 6

ISBN-13 978-981-277-985-4
ISBN-10 981-277-985-X

Printed in Singapore by World Scientific Printers (S) Pte Ltd

I wish to dedicate this book to my wife, Chi-fen, for her commitment to be my partner and her devotion to assist me developing my career and becoming a better person. She is extremely patient and tolerant with me and takes excellent care of our two kids, Allen and Karen, while I am too busy to spend time with them, especially during my first sabbatical year and during the time of editing this book. I would also like to dedicate this book to my mother, Mo-dan Lien, and my late father, Shu-min, for their understanding, support, and encouragement to pursue my dream. Lastly, my dedication goes to Alli, my daughter's beloved cat, for her playfulness and the joy she brings to the family. — *T. Warren Liao*

I gratefully dedicate this book to Juri; my life's inspiration, to my mother Helen and late father John (Ioannis), my brother Andreas, my late grandfather Evangelos, and also to my immensely beloved Ragus and Ollopa ("Ikasinilab, Shiakun"). Ollopa was helping with this project all the way until the very last days of his wonderful life, which ended exactly when this project ended. He will always live in our memories. This book is also dedicated to his beloved family from Takarazuka. This book would have never been prepared without Juri's, Ragus' and Ollapa's continuous encouragement, patience, and unique inspiration. — *Evangelos (Vangelis) Triantaphyllou*

ヴァン は じゅぽい の ことを 愛して います。

Contents

Foreword

The confluence of communication systems and computing power has enabled industry to collect and store vast amounts of data. Data mining and knowledge discovery methods and tools are the only real way to take full advantage of what those data hold. The lack of available materials and research in data mining as it is applied to the manufacturing and industrial enterprise only came to my attention in the spring of 2004.

At that time, I was Program Officer of the Manufacturing Enterprise Systems program in the Division of Design, Manufacture and Industrial Innovation at the National Science Foundation (NSF), Arlington, Virginia, USA. The two editors of this book, Drs. Liao and Triantaphyllou, proposed a Workshop on *Data Mining in Manufacturing Systems* to be held in conjunction with the Mathematics and Machine Learning (MML) Conference in Como, Italy, June 23-25, 2004 (http://www.mold.polimi.it/MML/Location.htm). At that point, I had funded two or three proposals in the area.

The workshop highlighted for me the need for a more focused effort in data mining research in applications of enterprise design and control, reliability, nano-manufacturing, scheduling, and technologies to reduce the environmental impacts of manufacturing. The trend in modeling and analysis of the manufacturing enterprise is becoming increasingly complex. The interaction between an enterprise and other intersecting systems significantly adds to the difficulty of this task. Mining data related to these interactions and relationships is an essential aspect of the process of understanding and modeling. This workshop also emphasized the need for expanding the community of users who are knowledgeable and have the capability of applying the tools and techniques of data mining.

I would like to congratulate the two editors of this book for filling a critical gap. They have brought together some of the most prominent researchers in data mining from diverse backgrounds to author a book for researchers and practitioners alike. This volume covers traditional topics and algorithms as well as the latest advances. It contains a rich selection of examples ranging from the identification of credit risk to maintenance scheduling. The theoretical developments and the applications discussed in this book cover all aspects of modern enterprises which have to compete in a highly dynamic and global environment.

For those who teach graduate courses in data mining, I believe that this book will become one of the most widely adopted texts in the field, especially for engineering, business and computer science majors. It can also be very valuable for anyone who wishes to better understand some of the most critical aspects of the mining of enterprise data.

Janet. M. Twomey, PhD
Industrial and Manufacturing Engineering
Wichita State University
Wichita, KS, USA

July 2007

Preface

The recent proliferation of affordable data gathering and storage media and powerful computing systems have provided a solid foundation for the emergence of the new field of data mining and knowledge discovery. The main goal of this fast growing field is the analysis of large, and often heterogeneous and distributed, datasets for the purpose of discovering new and potentially useful knowledge about the phenomena or systems that generated these data. Sources from which such data can come from are various natural phenomena or systems. Examples can be found in meteorology, earth sciences, astronomy, biology, social sciences, etc. On the other hand, there is another source of datasets derived mainly from business and industrial activities. This kind of data is known as "enterprise data." The common characteristic of such datasets is that the analyst wishes to analyze them for the purpose of designing a more cost-effective strategy for optimizing some type of performance measure, such as reducing production time, improving quality, eliminating wastes, and maximizing profit. Data in this category may describe different scheduling scenarios in a manufacturing environment, quality control of some process, fault diagnosis in the operation of a machine or process, risk analysis when issuing credit to applicants, management of supply chains in a manufacturing system, data for business related decision-making, just to name a few examples.

The history of data mining and knowledge discovery is only more than a decade old and its use has been spreading to various areas. It is our assertion that every aspect of an enterprise system can benefit from data mining and knowledge discovery and this book intends to show just that. It reports the recent advances in data mining and knowledge discovery of enterprise data, with focus on both algorithms and applications. The intended audience includes the practitioners who are interested in knowing more about data mining and knowledge discovery and its potential use in their enterprises, as well as the researchers who are attracted by the opportunities for methodology developments and for working with the practitioners to solve some very exciting real-world problems.

Data mining and knowledge discovery methods can be grouped into different categories depending on the type of methods and algorithms used. Thus, one may have methods that are based on artificial neural networks (ANNs), cluster analysis, decision trees, mining of association rules, tabu search, genetic algorithms (GAs), ant colony systems, Bayes networks, rule induction, etc. There are pros and cons associated with each method and it is well known that no method dominates the other methods all the time. A very critical question here is how to decide which method to choose for a particular application. We do hope that this book would provide some answers to this question.

This book is comprised of 16 chapters, written by world renowned experts in the field from a number of countries. These chapters explore the application of different methods and algorithms to different types of enterprise datasets, as depicted in Figure 1. In each chapter, various methodological and application issues which can be involved in data mining and knowledge discovery from enterprise data are discussed.

The book starts with the chapter written by Professor Liao from Louisiana State University, U.S.A., who is also one of the Editors of this book. This chapter intends to provide an extensive coverage of the work done in this field. It describes the main developments in the type of enterprise data analyzed, the mining algorithms used, and the goals of the mining analyses. The two chapters that follow the first chapter describe two important service enterprise applications, i.e., credit rating and detection of insolvent customers. The following eight chapters deal with the mining of various manufacturing enterprise data. These application chapters are arranged in the order of activities carried out by each functional area of a manufacturing enterprise in order to fulfill customers' orders; that is, sales forecasting, process engineering, production control, process monitoring and control, fault diagnosis, quality improvement, and maintenance. Each covered area is important in its own way to the successful operation of an enterprise. The next two chapters address two unique data: one on workflow and the other on images of cell-based assays. The remaining three chapters focus more on the methodology and methodological issues. A more detailed overview of each chapter follows.

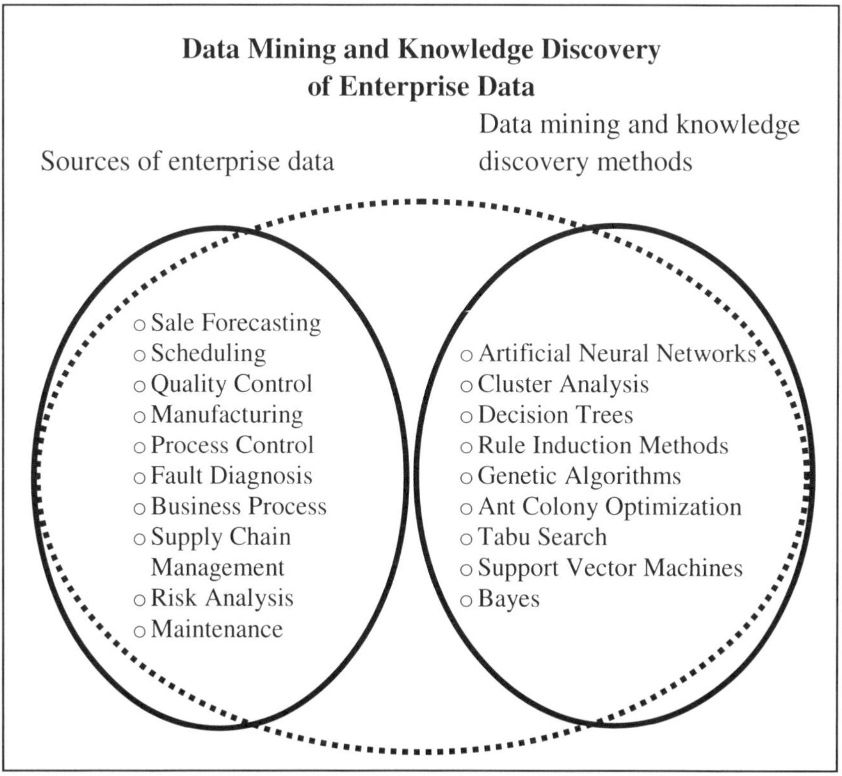

Figure 1. A sketch of data mining and knowledge discovery of enterprise data.

In particular, the second chapter is written by Professors Yu and Chen and their associates from Tsinghua University in Beijing, China. It studies some key classification methods, including decision trees,

Bayesian networks, support vector machines, neural networks, *k*-nearest neighbors, and an associative classification method in analyzing credit risk of companies. A comparative study on a real dataset on credit risk reveals that the proposed associative classification method consistently outperformed all the others.

The third chapter is authored by Professors Daskalaki and Avouris from University of Patras, Greece, along with their collaborator, Mr. Kopanas. It discusses various aspects of the data mining and knowledge discovery process, particularly on imbalanced class data and cost-based evaluation, in mining customer behavior patterns from customer data and their call records.

The fourth chapter is written by Professors Chang and Wang from Yuan-Ze University and Ching-Yun University in Taiwan, respectively. In this chapter, the authors study the use of gray relation analysis for selecting time series variables and several methods, including Winter's method, multiple regression analysis, back propagation neural networks, evolving neural networks, evolving fuzzy neural networks, and weighted evolving fuzzy neural networks, for sale forecasting.

The fifth chapter is contributed by Professor Jiao and his associates from the Nanyang Technological University, Singapore. It describes how to apply specific data mining techniques such as text mining, tree matching, fuzzy clustering, and tree unification on the process platform formation problem in order to produce a variety of customized products.

The sixth chapter is written by Dr. Min and Professor Yih from Sandia National Labs and Purdue University in the U.S.A., respectively. This chapter describes a data mining approach to obtain a dispatching strategy for a scheduler so that the appropriate dispatching rules can be selected for different situations in a complex semiconductor wafer fabrication system. The methods used are based on simulation and competitive neural networks.

The seventh chapter is contributed by Professor Last and his associates from Ben-Gurion University of the Negev, Israel. It describes their application of single-objective and multi-objective classification algorithms for the prediction of grape and wine quality in a multi-year agricultural database maintained by Yarden – Golan Heights Winery in

Katzrin, Israel. This chapter indicates the potential of some data mining techniques in such diverse domains as in agriculture.

The eighth chapter is written by Professor Chien and his associates from the National Tsing Hua University, Taiwan. This chapter aims at describing characteristics of various data mining empirical studies in semiconductor manufacturing, particularly defect diagnosis and yield enhancement, from engineering data and manufacturing data.

The ninth chapter is contributed by Professors Porzio and Ragozini from the University of Cassino and the University of Naples in Italy, respectively. This chapter aims at presenting their data mining vision on Statistical Process Control (SPC) analysis and to describe their nonparametric multivariate control scheme based on the data depth approach.

The tenth chapter is written by Professor Jeong and his associates from the University of Tennessee in the U.S.A. This chapter addresses the problems of fault diagnosis based on the analysis of multi-dimensional function data such as time series and hyperspectral images. It presents some wavelet-based data reduction procedures that balance the reconstruction error against the reduction efficiency. It evaluates the performance of two approaches: partial least squares and principal component regression for shaft alignment prediction. In addition, it describes an analysis of hyperspectral images for the detection of poultry skin tumors, focusing in particular on data reduction using PCA and 2D wavelet analysis and support vector machines based classification.

In the eleventh chapter, Professor Khoo and his associates from the Nanyang Technological University in Singapore describe a hybrid approach that is based on rough sets, tabu search and genetic algorithms. The applicability of this hybrid approach is demonstrated with a case study on the maintenance of heavy machinery. The proposed hybrid approach is shown to be more powerful than the component methods when they are applied alone.

The twelfth chapter describes some recently proposed techniques of high potential for optimizing business processes and their corresponding workflow models by analyzing the details of previously executed processes, stored as a workflow log. This chapter is authored by

Professor Gunopulos from the University of California at Riverside and his collaborator from Google Inc. in the U.S.A.

The thirteenth chapter, contributed by Dr. Perner from the Institute of Computer Vision and Applied Computer Science in Germany, presents some intriguing new intelligent and automatic image analysis and interpretation procedures and demonstrates them in the application of HEp-2 cell pattern analysis, based on their *Cell_Interpret* system. Although bio-image data are mined in this chapter, the described system can be extended to other types of images encountered in other enterprise systems.

The fourteenth chapter is written by Professor Trafalis and his research associate from the University of Oklahoma in the U.S.A. The main focus of this chapter is the theoretical study of support vector machines (SVMs). These optimization methods are in the interface of operations research (O.R.) and artificial intelligence methods and seem to possess great potential. The same chapter also discusses some application issues of SVMs in sciences, business and engineering.

The fifteenth chapter, written by Professor Huo and his associates from Georgia Tech in the U.S.A., discusses some manifold-based learning methods such as local linear embedded (LLE), ISOMAP, Laplacian Eigenmaps, Hessian Eigenmap, and Local Tangent Space Alignment (LTSA), along with some important applications. These methods are relatively new compared to other methods and their potential for enterprise data mining is thus relatively unexplored.

The sixteenth chapter describes mining methods that are based on some statistical approaches. It is written by Professor Feng and his research associate from the Bradley University in the U.S.A. The statistical methods studied in this chapter include regression analysis, bootstrap, bagging, and clustering. It is shown how these methods could be used together to build an accurate model when only small datasets are available. This chapter is thus particularly relevant when there is a lack of data due to high cost or other reasons.

Each chapter is self-contained and addresses an important issue that is related to data mining methods and the analysis of enterprise data. Each chapter provides a comprehensive treatment of the topic it covers.

Furthermore, when all the chapters are considered together, they cover all aspects of crucial importance to any modern enterprise in today's increasingly competitive world.

This book is unique in that it focuses on the key algorithmic and application issues in the mining of enterprise data. Instead of discussing a particular software environment, which may become obsolete when the new version becomes available, it studies the fundamental issues related to the mining of enterprise data. A few chapters present new methodologies that are not even available in commercially available software packages at all. Thus, this book can definitely be very valuable to researchers and practitioners in the field. It can also be used by graduate students in computer science, business, or engineering schools as well.

T. Warren Liao, Ph.D.
Evangelos Triantaphyllou, Ph.D.
Louisiana State University
Baton Rouge, LA, U.S.A.

July of 2007

Acknowledgements

The two editors wish to express their sincere gratitude to all authors who have contributed to the writing of the chapters, for the quality of their work, for the effort spent, and for their great patience which had been challenged many times during the course of this project.

The editing of this book would never have been accomplished without the support from a number of people to which ***T. Warren Liao*** is deeply indebted. First and foremost his thank goes to the former NSF Program Director, Professor Janet Twomey from Wichita State University. Without her support for the International Workshop on Data Mining in Manufacturing Enterprise Systems, this book might not be materialized. He would also like to thank his good colleague and dear friend, Professor E. Triantaphyllou, for his willingness to collaborate in this area of research and his total dedication to this edited book. Dr. Liao is also very grateful to his friends at the Intelligent Systems Branch of the Army Research Laboratory (ARL). His one-year sabbatical at ARL has definitely enriched his research experience and had served quite well as the launch pad for his research in the mining of time series data. Furthermore, Dr. Liao would like to acknowledge the support of his research collaborators as well as the assistance of his graduate students in carrying out various research projects and ideas. It is this experience of exploring and learning together through research that he really relishes.

Evangelos Triantaphyllou is always deeply indebted to many people which have helped him a tremendously during his career and beyond. He always recognizes with immense gratitude the very special role his math teacher played in his life; Mr. Leuteris Tsiliakos and his UG Advisor at the National Technical University of Athens; Dr. Luis Wassenhoven. His most special thanks go to his first M.S. Advisor and Mentor, Professor Stuart H. Mann, currently the Dean of the W.F. Harrah College of Hotel Administration at the University of Nevada. He would also like to thank his other M.S. Advisor Distinguished Professor Panos M. Pardalos currently at the University of Florida and his Ph.D. Advisor Professor Allen L. Soyster, former IE Chair at Penn State and former Dean of Engineering at the Northeastern University for his inspirational advising and assistance during his doctoral studies at Penn State. Special thanks also go to his great neighbors and friends; Janet, Bert, and Laddie Toms for their multiple support during the development of this book and for taking such a good care of Ollopa during his last days in the summer of 2007. Also, for allowing him to work on this book in their amazing Liki Tiki study facility. Many special thanks are also given to Steven Patt, Editor at World Scientific, the publisher of this book, for his encouragement and great patience.

Most of the research accomplishments on data mining and optimization by Dr. Triantaphyllou would not had been made possible without the critical support by Dr. Donald Wagner at the Office of Naval Research (ONR), U.S. Department of the Navy. Dr. Wagner's contribution to this success is greatly appreciated.

Many thanks go to his colleagues at LSU. Especially to Dr. Kevin Carman; Dean of the College of Basic Sciences at LSU for his leadership and support to all of us especially during the challenging times when Hurricanes Katrina and Rita hit our area in the fall of 2005, Dr. S.S. Iyengar; Distinguished Professor and Chairman of the Computer Science Department at LSU, and Dr. T. Warren Liao; his good neighbor, friend and distinguished colleague at LSU, and last but not least to Dr. Janet Twomey from the NSF and Wichita State University.

Dr. Triantaphyllou would also like to acknowledge his most sincere and immense gratitude to his graduate and undergraduate students, which have always provided him with unlimited inspiration, motivation, pride, and **joy**.

Chapter 1[1]

Enterprise Data Mining: A Review and Research Directions

T. Warren Liao
Construction Management and Industrial Engineering Department
Louisiana State University, CEBA Building, No. 3128, Baton Rouge, LA 70803, U.S.A.
Email: ieliao@lsu.edu

Abstract: Manufacturing enterprise systems and service enterprise systems carry out the bulk of economic activities in any country and in the increasingly connected world. Enterprise data are necessary to ensure that each manufacturing or service enterprise system is run efficiently and effectively. As it becomes easier to capture and fairly inexpensive to store, digitized data gradually overwhelms our ability to analyze in order to turn them into useful information for decision making. The rise of data mining and knowledge discovery as an interdisciplinary field for uncovering hidden and useful knowledge from large volumes of data stored in a database or data warehouse is very promising in many areas, including enterprise systems. Over the last decade, numerous studies have been carried out to investigate how enterprise data could be mined to generate useful models and knowledge for running the business more efficiently and effectively. This chapter intends to provide a comprehensive overview of previous studies on enterprise data mining. To give some idea about where the research is heading, some on-going research programs and future research directions are also highlighted at the end of the chapter.

***Key Words*:** Data mining, Knowledge discovery from enterprise data, Enterprise data mining.

---

[1] Liao, T.W. and E. Triantaphyllou, (Eds.), **Recent Advances in Data Mining of Enterprise Data: Algorithms and Applications**, *World Scientific*, Singapore, pp. 1-109, 2007.

1. Introduction

According to the Merriam-Webster Online Dictionary, enterprise is a unit of economic organization or activity. In the context of this edited book, enterprise is defined as a business organization that exists either to produce some products, or to provide some kinds of service as part of their profit seeking activities. The products can be agricultural, textile, houseware items, transportation related, sports goods, and any other engineered artifacts. The service provided can be healthcare, finance, utility, telecommunication, transportation, maintenance, sanitary, etc. The enterprise in the business of producing some products is a manufacturing enterprise and the enterprise in the business of providing service is a service enterprise.

A manufacturing enterprise system exists to produce an array of parts, subassemblies, and/or products of its own design or of others. On the other hand, a service enterprise system exists to provide necessary service to their clients. To be competitive, an enterprise system must be lean, able to produce good quality parts/subassemblies/products or service, and responsive to customers needs/demands. A lean, quality, and responsive enterprise system cannot be achieved without good engineering and management practices in all aspects of system operations including marketing, sales, product design, purchasing and supplier management, process development, task execution, process monitoring, process control, troubleshooting, process improvement, warehouse management, quality control, logistics management, customer relationship management, and so on. Good engineering and management practices in turn rely a great deal on excellent human resources, great work knowledge, sound business processes, timely reliable data, and necessary hardware and software tools and systems.

Over the years, every unit of a manufacturing or service enterprise system has been gradually adopting computer hardware and software to assist their operation in a way consistent with the general trend of digital revolution, which has made digitized information easy to capture and fairly inexpensive to store. For example, forecasting software is used by the Sales Department to generate sales forecast based on historical data gathered over the years. Also, computer-aided design/computer aided engineering (CAD/CAE) systems are used by the Product Engineering Department to analyze engineering designs, to prepare engineering drawings, and to manage product data.

Many manufacturing processes in a manufacturing enterprise system, especially those located in highly industrialized nations where labor cost is high, are mostly automated and computerized in order to ensure product quality and to minimize production cost. A computerized process is often instrumented with sensors that record streams of data during its functioning. This real-time sensory data constitutes the bulk of manufacturing enterprise data, which is recorded mainly for on-line process monitoring and control and to ensure the ability to trace production steps. Such data can definitely also be used off-line for process development, troubleshooting, optimization, and improvement. However, such usage has been limited except in the semiconductor industry where the potential benefit is higher than in other industries. Generally speaking, operational data relevant to current and near-term future operations are kept in the database and past operational data are archived in the data warehouse. As the result of having available today more affordable digital storage devices, more data are archived for longer periods of time.

The rise of data mining and knowledge discovery as an interdisciplinary field for uncovering hidden and useful knowledge from such large volumes of data in the database and/or data warehouse is very promising in many areas, including enterprise systems. Due to its gaining popularity, several books have been written on the subject of data mining and knowledge discovery and more books are due to be out. Zhou (2003) reviewed three data mining books written from different perspectives, i.e., databases (Han and Kamber, 2001), machine learning (Witten and Frank, 2000), and statistics (Hand *et al.*, 2001). The book edited by Triantaphyllou and Felici (2006) focused on rule induction techniques. Regular data mining related meetings are also held each year to report new progress made in advancing this research area.

Theoretically speaking, data mining and knowledge discovery can be applied to any domain where data is rich and the potential benefit of uncovered knowledge is high, including enterprise systems of concern in this book. Actually many efforts have been made by some to this effect. For example, Berry and Linoff (1999) presented several examples and applications of data mining in marketing, sales, and customer support. Chen *et al.* (2000a) gave a comprehensive view of data mining methods, support tools, and applications in various industries. Hamuro *et al.* (1998) discussed how the data mining system of Pharma, a drugstore chain in Japan, produces profits and how the system is constructed to increase its effectiveness and efficiency. Hormozi and Giles (2004) discussed how banking and retail industries have been effectively utilizing data mining in marketing, risk management, fraud detection, and customer acquisition and retention.

McDonald (1999) considered data mining as one of the new tools that have accelerated the pace of yield improvement in IC (Integrated Circuit) manufacturing. One data mining application is in "low yield analysis", which is the investigation of samples of low yield wafers to determine priorities for improvement. Kittler and Wang (1999) described possible uses of data mining in semiconductor manufacturing, which include process and tool control, yield management, and equipment maintenance. Büchner *et al.* (1997) described four areas of data mining applications, including fault diagnosis, process and quality control, process analysis, and machine maintenance. The book edited by Braha (2001) focused on design and manufacturing applications. Kusiak (2006) presented examples of data mining applications in industrial, medical, and pharmaceutical domains and proposed a framework for organizing and applying knowledge for decision-making in manufacturing and service applications. Most recently, Harding *et al.* (2006) reviewed applications of data mining in manufacturing engineering, in particular production processes, operations, fault detection, maintenance, decision support, and product quality improvements.

Using the results of an Internet survey with a total of 106 responses (59% response rate), Nemati and Barko (2002) elaborated on the purpose, utility, and industrial status of organizational data mining (ODM) and how service organizations are benefiting through enhanced enterprise decision-making. They defined organizational data mining as leveraging data mining tools and technologies to enhance the decision-making process by transforming data into valuable and actionable knowledge to gain a strategic competitive advantage. To remain competitive, there is a need for service organizations to build a holistic view of their customers through a mass customization marketing strategy, which drives the growing popularity and adoption of customer relationship management (CRM) projects within the industry. The ODM techniques including decision trees, clustering, and market-basket analysis are popular to support these applications. Yada *et al.* (2005) introduced a data mining oriented CRM system, named C-MUSASHI, which can be constructed at very low cost by the use of the open-source software MUSASHI. C-MUSASHI consists of three components, which include basic tools for customer analysis, store management systems, and data mining oriented CRM systems and it has been applied to a large amount of customer history data of supermarkets and drugstores in Japan to discover useful knowledge for marketing strategy.

This chapter first surveys the enterprise data mining practices and studies, which were reported in the open literature, then summarizes and discusses what has been done, and finally identifies some research directions undertaken by major players in this research area. Through this review, we hope to generate more interest on this topic for both researchers and practitioners alike. The remainder of this chapter is organized as follows. The next section introduces the basics of data mining and knowledge discovery, followed by the description of the main types and characteristics of enterprise data. The fourth section provides an overview of research activities related to the use of data mining and knowledge discovery in enterprise systems. These contributions from the literature are grouped into seven categories: customer related, sales related, product related, production planning and control related, logistics related, process related, and others. A discussion is given in Section 5. The last section highlights some research directions currently pursued by some researchers working in the area of enterprise data mining.

2. The Basics of Data Mining and Knowledge Discovery

This section describes the data mining and knowledge discovery process, major data mining methodologies, commercial software programs developed for data mining and knowledge discovery, and data mining system architectures.

2.1 Data Mining and the Knowledge Discovery Process

The overall knowledge discovery process was outlined by Fayyad *et al.* (1996) as an interactive and iterative process involving, more or less, the following steps: understanding the application domain, selecting the data, data cleaning and preprocessing, data integration, data reduction and transformation, selecting data mining algorithms, data mining, interpretation of the results, and using the discovered knowledge. According to Han and Kamber (2001), data mining tasks can be generally classified into two categories: descriptive and predictive. The former characterizes the general properties of the data in the database. The latter performs inference on the current data in order to make predictions.

Using finer categorization than Han and Kamber, Hand *et al.* (2001) group data mining into five types of tasks: (a) exploratory data analysis (EDA) to explore the data without having a clear idea of what we are looking for; (b) descriptive modeling to describe all of the data (or the process generating the data); (c) predictive modeling including classification and regression to build a model that will permit the value of one variable to be predicted from the known values of other variables; (d) discovering patterns and rules that concern with pattern detection without model building, and (e) retrieval by content to find similar patterns in the dataset given a known pattern of interest. They make a distinction between models and patterns. A model is a high-level, global description of a dataset whereas a pattern is a local feature of the data which holds perhaps for only a few records or a few variables or both.

Büchner *et al.* (1997) presented a generic data mining process starting from the identification of a problem requiring information technology (IT) support for decision-making. The process that follows begins with the identification of the human resources required to carry out the data mining process that normally include domain experts, data experts, and data mining experts. Problem specification is the second step of the process, which involves the identification of (i) those tasks that can be solved using a data mining approach and (ii) the ultimate user of the knowledge discovered. The third step is data prospecting, which consists of analyzing the state of the data required for solving the problem with four major considerations, i.e., identification of relevant attributes, accessibility of data, population of required data attributes, and distribution and heterogeneity of data. The fourth step is domain knowledge elicitation. The domain knowledge must be verified for consistency before proceeding to the next step – methodology identification. The main task of methodology identification is to find the best data mining methodology for solving the specified problem.

The next step is data preprocessing, which involves removing outliers, filling in missing values, noise modeling, data dimensionality reduction, data quantization, transformation, coding, and heterogeneity resolution. The data preprocessing step is followed by pattern discovery, which consists of using some algorithms to automatically discover patterns from the pre-processed data. The last step is knowledge post-processing, which involves both knowledge filtering by ranking and knowledge validation by using techniques such as holdout sampling, random re-sampling, *n*-fold cross-validation, and bootstrapping. The knowledge discovered is finally examined by the domain expert(s) and the data mining expert(s) together. This examination of knowledge may lead to the refinement process of data mining. Refinement could take different forms which might include redefining the data, changing the methodology used, refining the parameters of the mining algorithm, etc. Figure 1 summarizes the two processes mentioned above for ease of comparison.

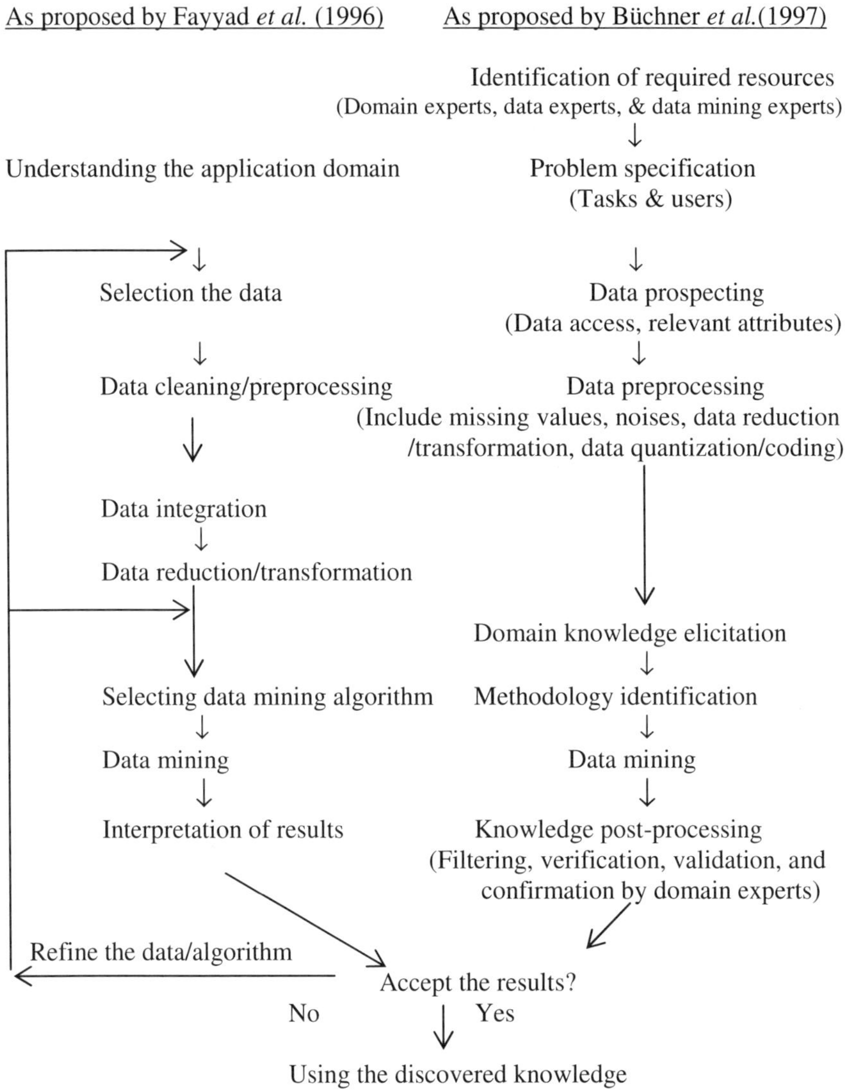

Figure 1. Summary of two KDD processes.

2.2 Data Mining Algorithms/Methodologies

Methodologies are necessary in most steps of the data mining and knowledge discovery process. Numerous algorithms/techniques have been developed for both descriptive mining and predictive mining. Descriptive mining relies much on descriptive statistics, the data cube (or OLAP; short for On-Line Analytical Processing) approach, and the attribute-oriented induction approach.

The OLAP approach provides a number of operators such as roll-up, drill-down, slice and dice, and rotate in a user-friendly environment for interactive querying and analysis of the data stored in a multi-dimensional database. The attribute-oriented approach is a relational database query-oriented, generalization-based, on-line data analysis technique. The general idea is to first collect the task-relevant data using a relational database query and then perform generalization either by attribute removal or attribute aggregation based on the examination of the number of distinct values of each attribute in the relevant set of data.

On the other hand, the purpose of predictive mining is to find useful patterns in the data to make nontrivial predictions on new data. Two major categories of predictive mining techniques are those which express the mined results as a black box whose innards are effectively incomprehensible to non-experts and those which represent the mined results as a transparent box whose construction reveals the structure of the pattern. Neural networks are major techniques in the former category. Focusing on the latter, the book of Witten and Frank (2000) includes methods for constructing decision trees, classification rules, association rules, clusters, and instance-based learning; the book edited by Triantaphyllou and Felici (2006) covers many rule induction techniques; and the recent monograph by Triantaphyllou (2007) is mostly devoted to the learning of Boolean functions.

Hand *et al.* (2001) discussed regression models with linear structures, piecewise linear spline/tree models that represent a complex global model for nonlinear phenomena by simple local linear components, and nonparametric kernel models. The spline/tree models replace the data points by a function which is estimated from a neighborhood of data points. Kernel methods and nearest neighbor methods are alternative local modeling methods that do not replace the data by a function, but retain the data points and leave the estimation of the predicted value until the time at which a prediction is actually required. Kernel methods define the degree of smoothing in terms of a kernel function and bandwidth whereas nearest neighbor methods let the data determine the bandwidth by defining it in terms of the number of nearest neighbors. Two major weaknesses of local methods are that they are poorly scaled to high dimension and the lack of interpretability of models built by local methods.

Soft computing methodologies such as fuzzy sets, neural networks, genetic algorithms, rough sets, and hybrids of the above are often used in the data mining step of the overall knowledge discovery process. This consortium of methodologies works synergistically and provides, in one form or another, flexible information processing capability for handling real-life ambiguous situations. Mitra *et al.* (2002) surveyed the available literature on using soft computing methodologies for data mining, not necessary related to enterprise systems.

Support vector machines (SVMs), originally designed for binary classification (Corts and Vapnik, 1995) and later extended to multi-class classification (Hsu and Lin, 2002), have gained wider acceptance for many classification and pattern recognition problems due to their high generalization ability (Burges, 1998). SVMs are known to be very sensitive to outliers and noise. Hence, Huang and Liu (2002) proposed a fuzzy support vector machine to address the problem. The central concept of their fuzzy SVM is not to treat every data points equally, but to assign each data point a membership value in accordance with its relative importance in the class.

A high degree of interactivity is often desirable, especially in the initial exploratory phase of the data mining and knowledge discovery process. This emphasis calls for the visualization of data as well as the analytical results. Visual exploration techniques are thus indispensable in conjunction with automatic data mining techniques. Oliveira and Levkowitz (2003) surveyed past studies on the different uses of graphical mapping and interaction techniques for visual data mining of large datasets represented as table data.

Keim (2002) proposed a classification of information visualization and visual data mining techniques based on the data type to be visualized, the visualization technique, and the interaction and distortion technique. The data type to be visualized may be one dimensional, two dimensional, or multidimensional, text or hypertext, hierarchies or graphs, and algorithms or software. The visualization techniques used may be classified into standard 2D/3D displays, geometrically transformed displays, icon-based displays, dense pixel displays, and stacked displays. The interaction and distortion techniques may be classified into interactive projection, interactive filtering, interactive distortion, and interactive linking and brushing.

One of the challenges to effective data mining is how to handle vast volumes of data. One solution is to reduce data for mining. Data reduction can be achieved in many ways: by feature (or attribute) selection, by discretizing continuous feature-values, and by selecting instances. Feature selection is the process of identifying and removing irrelevant and redundant information as much as possible. Feature selection is important because the inclusion of irrelevant, redundant, and noisy attributes in the model building process can result in poor predictive performance as well as increased computation. Hall and Holmes (2003) presented a benchmark comparison of six attribute selection methods for supervised classification using 15 standard machine learning datasets from the widely known UCI collection (http://kdd.ics.uci.edu/). Since some attribute selection methods only operate on discrete-valued features, numeric-valued features must be discretized first, using a method such as the one developed by Fayyad and Irani (1993). Liu and Motoda (2001) edited a book on instance selection and construction, which include a set of techniques that reduce the quantity of data by selecting a subset of data and/or constructing a reduced set of data that resembles the original data. Jankowski and Grochowski (2004a, b) compared several strategies to shrink a training dataset using different neural and machine learning classification algorithms. In their study, nearly all tests were performed on databases included in the UCI collection (Merz and Murphy, 1998).

Scaling up the data mining algorithms to be run in high-performance parallel and distributed computing environments offers an alternative solution for effective data mining. Darlington *et al.* (1997) presented preliminary results on their experiments in parallelizing C4.5, a classification-rule learning system that represent the learned knowledge in decision trees. Pizzuti and Talia (2003) described the design and implementation of P-AutoClass, which is a parallel version of the AutoClass system based upon the Bayesian model for determining optimal classes in large datasets. Anglano *et al.* (1999) presented G-Net, which is a distributed algorithm able to infer classifiers from pre-collected data. G-Net was implemented on Networks of Workstations (NOWs) and it incorporated a set of dynamic load distribution techniques to profitably exploit the computing power provided. Hall *et al.* (2000) discussed a three-step approach for generating rules in parallel: first creating disjoint subsets of a large training set, then allowing rules to be created on each subset, and finally merging the rules. An empirical study showed that good performance can be achieved but performance could degrade as the number of processors increased. Johnson and Kargupta (2000) presented the Collective Hierarchical Clustering (CHC) algorithm for analyzing distributed, heterogeneous data.

2.3 Data Mining System Architectures

In a large enterprise system, not only datasets can be very large, data from numerous sources might need to be accessed and combined to perform comprehensive analyses, and groups of data miners might require access to the same data and results. Chattratichat *et al.* (1999) stated that an enterprise data mining architecture should be flexible enough to scale well in all of the three areas mentioned above and thus proposed a three-tier client/server architecture, which includes client, application server, and third-tier servers. They described the Kensington enterprise data mining system that was designed using the Enterprise JavaBeans (EJB) component architecture and implemented in Java.

The Kensington system integrates parallel data mining functions written in C and MPI via a Common Object Request Broker Architecture

(CORBA) interface and provides an interface to any statistical functions in S-plus. Databases anywhere on the Internet can be accessed via a Java Database Connectivity (JDBC) connection. The client is built as a highly interactive Java application using JavaBeans to provide two main capabilities, i.e., interactive visual programming of data mining tasks, and three-dimensional visualization of data and analytical models. To evaluate the performance of such a distributed, three-tier, client-server architecture, Harrison and Lladó (2000) developed an analytical queuing network model for the central schedulers and validated that the theoretical results of their model attain good accuracy compared with those obtained from simulation.

Prodromidis *et al.* (2000) first described meta-learning, a technique that seeks to compute high-level classifiers that integrate multiple classifiers, which computed separately over different databases. Then they presented the Java Agents for Meta-learning (JAM) system, which is an agent based metal-learning system for large-scale data mining applications. In their paper, Klusch *et al.* (2003) briefly reviewed existing approaches to agent-based distributed data mining, presented a novel approach to distributed data clustering based on density estimation, and discussed some issues involved in agent-oriented implementation.

Coppola *et al.* (2004) described a parallel KDD architecture in the framework of the SAIB industrial research project that brings together several Italian academic institutions and industrial partners in an effort to produce a flexible, open-source based customer relationship management system for Internet Banking and Insurance. Their KDD architecture is based on four main modules providing data management functionalities (the Data Repository), knowledge and metal-data management (the Knowledge Repository), a set of mining algorithms including a decision tree induction algorithm, an Apriori-like association rule algorithm, filters, and a control interface called the Activity Scheduler.

The Knowledge Grid (Cannataro and Talia, 2003) provides a middleware for knowledge discovery services for a wide range of high performance distributed applications. The Knowledge Grid architecture is composed of a set of services resided in two layers: the core K-Grid layer that interfaces the basic and generic Grid middleware services and the High-Level K-Grid layer that interfaces the user by offering a set of services for the design and execution of knowledge discovery applications. A knowledge discovery process is represented as a workflow composed using a visual interface that shows the available resources (data, tools, and hosts) to the user and offers mechanisms for integrating them in a workflow. Both the resources and workflows are stored using an XML-based notation. The Visual Environment for Grid Applications (VEGA) is a software prototype that implements the main components of the Knowledge Grid environment, which comprises services and functionalities ranging from information and discovery services to visual design and execution facilities (Cannataro *et al.*, 2002). Zhang *et al.* (2003) briefly described the Jilin University Grid and implemented two programs for parallel association rule mining on it.

2.4 Data Mining Software Programs

A comprehensive data mining software program should provide multiple and/or integrated data mining functionalities and techniques that support the entire data mining and knowledge discovery process. In addition a data mining system should be integrated with a database or a data warehouse system, as argued by Han and Kamber (2001).

They classified the coupling schemes between a data mining system with a database/data warehouse system into four kinds, which includes no coupling, loose coupling, semi-tight coupling, and tight coupling. Tight coupling is most desirable but its implementation is nontrivial and more research is still needed.

Han and Kamber (2001) briefly described five commercial data mining systems that provide multiple data mining functions and techniques. They are Intelligent Miner, Enterprise Miner, MineSet, Clementine, and DBMiner. Each one of them has its own distinctive features as briefly summarized below.

- o Intelligent Miner - the scalability of its mining algorithms and its tight integration with IBM's DB2 relational database.
- o Enterprise Miner - its variety of statistical analysis tools, built on SAS's strength.

- MineSet – a set of robust graphics tools using powerful graphics feature of SGI computers.
- Clementine - its object-oriented, extended module interface, which allows users to add their own algorithms and utilities to Clementine's visual programming environment.
- DBMiner – its data-cube-based online analytical mining.

Haughton *et al.* (2003) presented an overview of five data mining packages with the intent of leaving the reader with a sense of their different capabilities, ease of use, and user interface of each package. The five packages reviewed include the Enterprise Miner by SAS, Clementine by SPSS, XLMiner, Quadstone, and GhostMiner and they were compared in the areas of descriptive statistics and graphics, predictive models, and association (market basket) analysis. For the descriptive and modeling analysis, the dataset contains 19,185 observations with nearly 200 candidate predictor variables, which was derived from the Direct Marketing Educational Foundation dataset #2 merged with Census geo-demographic variables from dataset #6. For association analysis, they used the Direct Marketing Educational Foundation's Bookbinders Club Case dataset, which includes data from 1,580 customers.

Adams (2002) described a number of commercial data mining programs including *STATISTICA Data Miner*, *Qualtrend*, and *SAS Decision Trees and Tree Viewer*. *STATISTICA Data Miner* offers the most comprehensive selections on the market to uncover hidden trends, explain known patterns, and predict the future. It comes in two versions. The desktop version of *STATISTICA Data Miner* is designed for the Windows environment. The client-server version of *STATISTICA Data Miner* is platform independent. Its client side features an Internet browser-based user interface whereas its server side works with all major Web server operating systems (e.g., UNIX Apache) and Wintel server computers. The icon-based design of *STATISTICA Data Miner* creates an extremely easy-to-use user interface.

QualTrend® is a cost-effective web-based manufacturing intelligence solution. It first extracts plant-floor data from diverse systems and then applies extensive analytics to transform these data into business context information for production, plant and quality management (http://www.carlisletechnology.com/2003cd/qualtrend/qualtrendtop.htm). *SAS Decision Trees and Tree Viewer* is one of the analysis models included in the Enterprise Miner.

Yield Dynamics, Inc. developed a decision tree-based Yield Mine software module as part of its larger Genesis Enterprise software suite. The Yield Mine module allows engineers to find relationships in the data and to relate different device characteristics affecting the performance or speed of a microprocessor to its manufacturing history (check also http://www.ydyn.com/products/genesis_enterprise.htm). The company VTT Information Technology developed the X-proFiles software to improve paper runability by means of data mining (Parola *et al.*, 2000). X-proFiles is based on multivariate methods (multiple linear regression and principal component regression) using a stepwise interactive interface. By using the software to effectively process and make detailed analyses of large amounts of measured 3-D data in the machine direction (MD) and the cross-machine direction (CD), a diminish of 50% in the web break rate was reported.

Recently, several commercial data mining tools have been developed based on soft computing methodologies. These include Data Mining Suite, using fuzzy logic, Braincell, Cognos4Thought and IBM Intelligent Miners for Data, using neural networks; and Nuggets, using GAs. Much more information can be found on the KDnuggets web site (http://www.kdnuggets.com), including some free data mining software. Generally speaking, most existing software programs run on workstation platforms such as Windows, while most large commercial programs were designed to run on client-server systems.

It is essential that an organization considering the purchase of a data mining package carefully evaluates all possible options and chooses the one that fits the best with its particular needs. Commercially available data mining systems do not guarantee success and a specialized method might have to be developed for a specific application; the study by Bertino *et al.* (1999) is a case in point.

3. Types and Characteristics of Enterprise Data

A manufacturing enterprise system exists to fulfill its mission, i.e., to produce an array of products to satisfy the requirements of their customers in a profitable fashion. To carry out this mission, a typical organization as shown in Figure 2 is put in place. Through this organization, sales are forecasted; products are designed; the manufacturing procedure and processes are engineered; the facility is set up; equipment is acquired; operators are hired and trained; and suppliers are identified to provide the necessary materials, parts, and subassemblies. Once getting them into the enterprise system, all the above necessary resources must be maintained, managed, and improved continuously to tap their full potential.

To successfully support its operation in producing some specific products of good quality at specific time, the process of planning, execution, feedback, and correction must be followed in every function of the manufacturing enterprise system. To this end, data is created, stored, accessed, and processed at various points of operating the manufacturing enterprise. Poor planning and lousy execution should be avoided because they often lead to undesirable consequences. Quick evaluation and feedback is important in order to detect undesirable situations early and to give more time for taking corrective actions. Coming up with an appropriate corrective action relies on good knowledge about the operations. Problems are often cross functional. For their solution, good communication, coordination, and cooperation to overcome the functional barriers across the enterprise system is critical.

Marketing and Sales are responsible for understanding and fulfilling the needs of customers, directly and/or indirectly through designated distributors, sales people, and marketing surveys. The sales forecast provides the key input to product development and production planning.

The rush orders, created by the need to fulfill the order of a customer in an unplanned manner, should be kept to the minimum because they undesirably disturb the normal production. A data mining system capable of generating more accurate forecasts could cut down the need for re-planning and rush orders, which often lead to smoother operation.

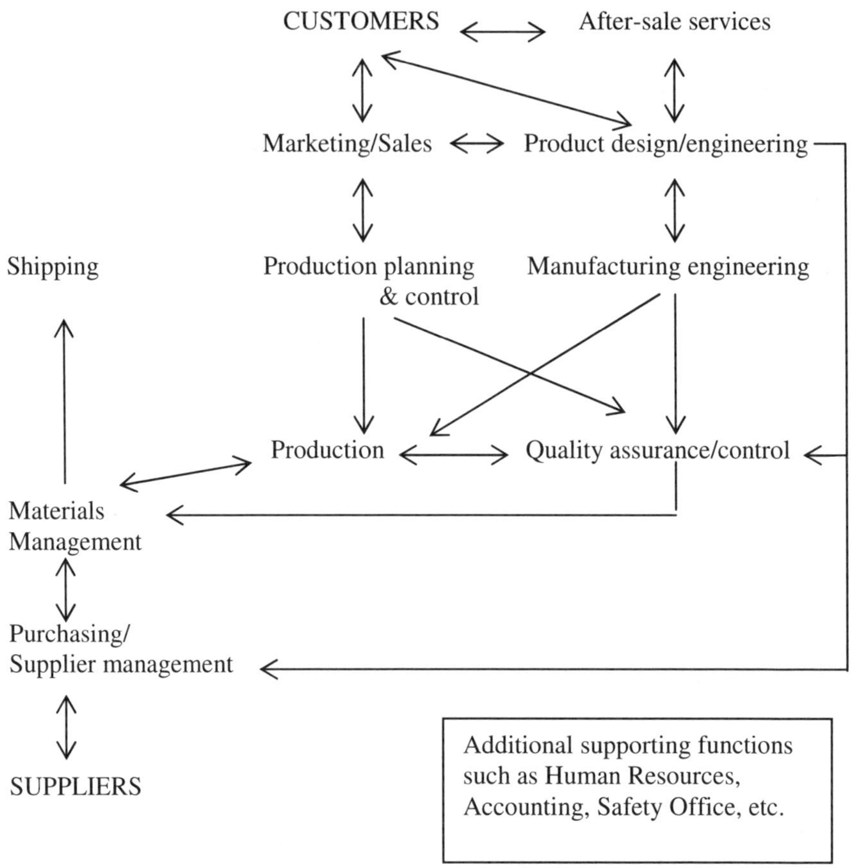

Figure 2. Functions of a typical manufacturing enterprise system.

The Product Design/Engineering Department produces the details of product data that are necessary for engineering analysis, purchasing, material management, manufacturing engineering, production, quality control, quality assurance, marketing and sales, end users, and after-sale services. Since every product takes some shape, the product geometry data is an important part of the product's details. The product design process is iterative in nature. Thorough engineering analyses are required to verify a product design and to determine key parameters before the product design details can be finalized.

In contrast to the serial engineering practice, the concurrent engineering concept calls for the consideration of all phases of the product life cycle in the early product design stage. This implies that other than the product performance data, additional data and information coming from manufacturing, inspection, services, etc. must all be processed and analyzed together in order to reach a product design decision. Such data and information, most likely derived from the experience gained in designing previous products, is often kept in different forms.

Product engineers are often tempted to create new designs without due consideration of reusing an old design, which often lead to a proliferation of parts/products, at least in the eyes of the production people who often need to deal with the consequences. A data mining system that can retrieve old designs might be helpful here. What complicates the matter is that legacy systems that keep the product details designed in different periods are most likely incompatible.

The Manufacture Engineering Department engineers and produces the details of production and inspection processes necessary to produce products at some specified rates in good quality according to the engineering specifications. The process details include facility layout, equipment configuration, tooling/molds, jigs/fixtures, route sheets, and operation details that are necessary information for production, facility service, production planning and control, tool crib, and machine shop. Other than maintaining the current processes in good working condition and training the operators for good workmanship, manufacturing engineers are constantly searching for ways to reengineer the process in order to produce better quality products at higher rates and lower costs. To this end, manufacturing engineers must keep up with new developments in the manufacturing technologies, get to know each individual process better, and be innovative. Manufacturing engineers are key players in the design, modeling, control, troubleshooting, improvement, and optimization of their processes. Many of theses tasks rely heavily on the process feedback provided by production, quality control, and sensors. They maintain records of process details, including maintenance and improvement activities. They also issue reports of manufacturing concerns, which often call for product design modifications and improvements.

The Material Management Department plans for material acquisition, keeps the inventory records of raw materials, parts, subassemblies, and final products, and is responsible for storing them physically in the warehouse, controlling their access, replenishing the production with required materials, and loading the trucks with shipping orders. The material acquisition plan is needed for purchasing. The inventory records are necessary for marketing, sales, production control, production, purchasing, and top management. Since it is equivalent to idle money, inventory should be kept to the minimum for a short duration. On the other hand, material shortfall should be avoided because it leads to production disruption. To maintain a good balance between these two conflicting goals, a concerted effort from marketing, sales, production planning and control, production, and purchasing is important. Good warehousing design, planning, and control are critical for efficient and accurate operations. Nearly every company experiences receiving wrong parts from their suppliers and is guilty in shipping incorrect products to their customers as well.

The Purchasing Department identifies, selects, and works with vendors to acquire the necessary materials, parts, and subassemblies required for production. Purchasing keeps a database of vendors and tracks their performance.

The Production Planning and Control Department produces long-term production plans and short-term production schedules in order to satisfy the forecasted demands and/or sale orders on hand. The production plans and schedules are used to orchestrate activities such as manufacture engineering, purchasing, production, material management, facility service, and quality control. Due to the complexity and dynamic nature of the system operation, unforeseen factors often trigger unexpected events, which in turn may throw the system operation off. Depending upon the seriousness of an upset, re-planning or some reactive measures might be necessary. For example, Product Engineers are asked to find substitute parts for some period of time in the case that the specified part is not available to sustain the production for whatever reasons. A breakdown in one key component of the process triggers a quick response to remedy the situation and re-planning might be necessary if a quick fix is not possible. Due to the high degree of the involved uncertainty, re-planning and rescheduling might have to be repeated many times. System operations tend to be chaotic whenever a schedule is rendered useless the minute it is issued. In such cases, the causes of the instability must be rooted out.

The Production Department executes the production schedule with the support of facility service, manufacture engineering, material management, quality control, and human resources. Production keeps records of the quantity and quality of the parts/subassemblies/products produced.

The Quality Control Department develops and executes quality control plans, works with suppliers to ensure the quality of the supplied parts and subassemblies, monitors the quality performance of key parameters important to product quality, and is given the authority to stop the production if poor quality is rampant and going out of control. Quality Control produces reports flagging quality concerns and rallies product engineering, manufacture engineering, production, purchasing, and material management all together to tackle quality problems.

The Human Resource Department is in charge of various aspects of the data related to the human resource in the enterprise system, which include workforce planning, hiring, training, promotion and raises, employee benefits and compensation, employee records and personnel policies, etc.

Based on the above description, numerous types of manufacturing enterprise data are possible as listed below.

- Tabulated data – Examples are engineering analysis results, production plans, materials requirements, inventory, cross-sectional product quality, warranty data, and information about the suppliers, customers, and employee.
- Hierarchical data – Examples are product structure, organization structure, equipment structure, and operations sequence.
- Spatial and spatial-temporal data – Examples are sales in different regions over time, distribution of defects on products as a function of time, and the distribution network.

- o Time-dependent data – Examples are sales over time, inventory over time, manpower over time, production schedules, production data, sensory data, and quality related data.
- o Image data – Examples are part/product quality characteristics and pictures of important assets such as employees, facilities, machinery, and instruments.
- o Video data – Examples are training materials, and process operations.
- o Geometry data – Examples are product, facility layout, equipment/ tool configuration, and workstation design.
- o Text data – Examples are product specifications, route sheets, operation instruction details, purchasing orders, shipping orders, manufacturing orders, product failure and repair reports.

In a similar manner, a service enterprise exists to provide some necessary service to its customers. Modern service enterprises depend more and more on computer-processed transactions. To improve their organization's effectiveness, efficiency, and prospects, these companies like to find ways to provide better service than their competitors to win over more customers. This explains why customer relations management is extremely important to any service organization. Data mining from customer, transaction, and survey data, possibly collected through e-commerce would play a key role in customer relations management. Common data types include numerical, categorical, text, web logs, and reports with some of them time stamped.

It shall be noted that an enterprise is an evolving entity that changes with time. Thus, the data that supports its activities will also be dynamically changing. Ideally, for data mining purposes all enterprise data should be made available on line through the Internet and intranets with adequate security and access control. There is also an economic issue as to how often data mining shall be carried out to best serve an enterprise.

4. Overview of the Enterprise Data Mining Activities

4.1 Customer Related

Hamuro *et al.* (1998) discussed how point-of-sale data could be mined with association rule algorithm to uncover interesting patterns of buying behavior that in turn has been applied to produce profits at Pharma, a drugstore chain in Japan. Chen *et al.* (2000) showed how a scalable data warehouse/online application processing (OLAP) framework can handle high data volumes and data flow rates for customer profiling and pattern comparison. In addition they described how to automate the whole operation chain, including data capture, filtering, loading, and incremental summarization and analysis, in order to enable the analysis of transaction records continuously. They developed a formalism for defining and computing multi-dimensional and multi-level similarity measures, and showed how the calling patterns that represent customers' calling behaviors can be compared using these similarity measures. They have actually implemented the whole application through "OLAP programming", i.e., as programs written in the scripting language supported by the OLAP server.

Cox (2002) described how to apply data mining and modeling methods to learn predictive models of customer behaviors from survey and behavioral data. In turn, these models can be used to prescribe actions to maximize the economic value of a company's customer base or of individual customers, based on what is known about them. They showed that classification trees can be used to test conditional independence relations among variables, which allow them to be used to help implement causal graph modeling methods and to develop predictably useful definitions of states to use in state look up tables and state transition models. A causal graph has been constructed to satisfy the Markov property, i.e., the probability distribution of each node (variable) in it depends only on the values of its immediate parents.

Ha *et al.* (2002) proposed a dynamic customer relations management (CRM) model utilizing data mining and a monitoring agent system to extract longitudinal knowledge from the customer data and to analyze customer behavior patterns over time for a retailer. A self-organization map (SOM) neural network clustered the retailer's customers into a set of segments with similar customers. The results from the Markov chain analysis was shown to provide a general impression on their customers' behaviors over time and help improve the effectiveness of marketing strategies.

Kuo *et al.* (2002) proposed a 2-stage method for market segmentation, which first uses a SOM to determine the number of clusters and the starting point, and then employs the *k*-means algorithm to find the final solution. The targeted customers are those visited the 3C stores located in Kaohsiung, Taiwan. The data were collected through 240 questionnaires with three categories of attributes: (1) customer experience attributes, (2) benefit attributes that the 3C stores can provide, and (3) demographic information attributes. Factor analysis was carried out to form a six-dimensional structure from the original 20 benefit attributes. The best cluster number selected is the one that has the most significant difference in the variables of demographic information and customer experience, or the one with the most significant difference according to the chi-square test results. The reason is that each segment can be better explained and the researcher can easily determine the marketing strategy for every segment. Kuo *et al.* (2006) proposed a similar market segmentation method that replaces the *k*-means algorithm in the second stage with genetic *k*-means.

Wang *et al.* (2005a) proposed an approach to select a set of valuable customers for direct marketing. The overall algorithm has three main steps: rule generation to find a set of good rules that capture features of responders called focused association rules (FAR), model building to combine rules into a prediction model, and model pruning to prune overfitted rules that do not generalize to the whole population. They validated the proposed method using the standard split of the KDD98-learing-set (95,412 records) and KDD98-validation-set (96,367 records) used by the KDD competition. Compared to the KDD-CUP winner, they generated 41% more profit by predicting less than half of the contacts. Crespo and Weber (2005) presented a 5-step methodology for dynamic data mining based on fuzzy *c*-means and applied it to customer segmentation, which is an important requirement for improved CRM. The five steps are: (1) identifying objects that represent changes, (2) determining changes in the class structure, (3) changing the class structure by moving and/or creating classes, (4) identifying the trajectories of classes, and (5) eliminating the unchanged classes.

Recognizing the importance of web mining for e-Business, Zhang *et al.* (2004) mined customer behavior patterns from web logs, sales, and customer information gathered in e-commerce web sites. Web logs were first filtered and categorized based on a semantic taxonomy. Specifically, they discovered association rules related to the visited web pages, sequential patterns of visiting tracks, clusters of web users, a decision tree with the class label being the buyer-flag, and an RBF neural network prediction model for predicting customers' revenue. Kohavi *et al.* (2004) briefly reviewed the architecture of Blue Martini software's e-commerce suite and discussed the many lessons learned over the past four years from mining retail e-commerce data for more than 20 clients and the challenges that still need to be addressed.

Customer churn, a term used to indicate the propensity of customers to cease doing business with a company, is a major concern for many service providers. Two major characteristics of the customer churn prediction problem are the relatively few negative examples (churn customers) and the economic impact of prediction accuracy. Various data mining techniques have been applied to predict customer churn. Mozer *et al.* (2000) explored techniques from statistical machine learning including logit regression, decision trees, neural networks, and boosting to predict churn and, based on these predictions, to determine what incentives should be offered to subscribers to improve retention and maximize profitability to the carrier. Ng and Liu (2000) proposed a solution that integrates various data mining techniques such as feature selection via induction, deviation analysis, and mining multiple concept-level association rules to form an intuitive and novel approach to gauging customer loyalty and predicting their likelihood of defection.

To predict the likelihood of a subscriber to churn, Au *et al.* (2003) proposed an algorithm called data mining by evolutionary learning (DMEL). DMEL encodes a complete set of rules in a single chromosome and begins the evolutionary process by generating a set of first-order rules, R_1, (a rule with one condition only) by probabilistic induction. Based on these rules, it then discovers a set of second-order rules, R_2, in the next iteration and based on the second-order rules, it discovers third-order rules, etc. The iterative process goes on uninterrupted until no more interesting rules in the current population can be identified. To determine the fitness of a chromosome that encodes a set of l-th order rules, DMEL uses a performance measure defined in terms of the probability that the value of an attribute of a tuple can be correctly predicted based on the rules in $R = R_1 \cup \ldots \cup R_{l-1} \cup$ (rules encoded in the chromosome being evaluated). DMEL is capable of mining rules in large databases without any need for user-defined thresholds or mapping of quantitative attributes into binary attributes. However, it requires quantitative attributes to be transformed to categorical attributes through the use of a discretization algorithm. It was shown that DMEL was able to predict churn accurately under different churn rates when applied to 100,000 real telecom subscriber records. The experimental results showed that DMEL outperformed neural networks, which in turn outperformed C4.5.

Hung *et al.* (2006) compared various data mining algorithms that can assign a 'propensity-to-churn' score periodically to each subscriber of a mobile operator. The results indicate that both decision tree (with and without customer segmentation by k-means) and neural network techniques can deliver accurate churn prediction models by using customer demographics, billing information, contract/service status, call detail records, and service change log. Qian *et al.* (2006) used a functional mixture model to profile customer behavior in order to identify and capture churn activity patterns. Based on the model, a five-step procedure was proposed, which includes the following: (1) standardizing profiles, (2) screening out uninterested (flat) profiles, (3) projecting profiles into a feature space represented by a set of basis functions (B-splines were chosen), (4) applying clustering algorithms to the resultant coefficients in the feature space, and (5) identifying interesting profiles.

Black and Hickey (2003) described the application of the CD3 decision tree induction algorithm (Black and Hickey, 1999) to telecom customer call data presented in batches to obtain classification rules. CD3 is robust against drift in the underlying rules over time: it detects drift and protects the induction process from its effects. The central idea is that a time-stamp is associated with examples and treated as an attribute during the induction process. This attribute is used to differentiate between those parts of the data which have been affected by drift from those that have not. A removal technique called purging is applied to the knowledge base following the concept drift to extract the now out-of-date examples thus maintaining an up-to-date version of the database. Real world call data of 1,000 customers over a period of twenty seven months was presented to the algorithm in five batches to locate the drift and highlight the changing properties within the customer profiles.

Daskalaki *et al.* (2003) described the process of building a predictive model of customer insolvency through knowledge discovery and data mining techniques in vast amounts of heterogeneous as well as noisy data for a large telecommunication company. The data mining algorithms they used were discriminant analysis, decision trees, and back-propagation neural networks. The decision tree classifier produced the best result in terms of the highest accuracy of detecting insolvent customers and the lowest false alarms. Readers are referred to Chapter 3 for more details. Kim *et al.* (2006) carried out the association analysis for a telecommunication service provider to determine the associations for the services that enterprise customers are using.

Kim *et al.* (2005) investigated the effectiveness of an SVM approach in detecting the underlying data pattern for the credit card customer churn analysis. The results demonstrated that SVM outperformed back-propagation neural networks. Zhao *et al.* (2005) introduced an improved one-class support vector machine and applied it to a dataset provided by a wireless telecom company which includes more than 150 variables describing more than 100,000 customers. A comparison with other methods such as ANN, decision trees, and naïve Bayesian was also made. Morik and Köpcke (2004) presented a complete knowledge discovery process applied to insurance data and showed that better results in terms of accuracy, precision, and recall could be obtained by using the

TF/IDF (term frequency/inverse document frequency) representation from information retrieval for compiling time-related features.

Lariveère and Van den Poel (2005) used random forests techniques to investigate the effects of a broad set of explanatory variables, including past customer behavior, observed customer heterogeneity and some typical variables related to intermediaries on three measures of customer outcome: next buy, partial-defection, and customers' profitability evolution. They analyzed a real-life sample of 100,000 customers taken from the data warehouse of a large European financial services company using two types of random forests techniques: random forests for binary classification and regression forests for the models with linear dependent variables. It was shown that both techniques offered better fit to the estimation and validation samples compared with ordinary linear regression and logistic regression models.

For a financial institution, customer credit is of much concern due to the high risks associated with inappropriate credit decisions. Therefore, credit scoring is gaining more and more attention as the industry can benefit from reducing possible risks. Credit scoring can be cast as a classification problem in order to assign credit applicants to either a "good credit" group that is likely to repay financial obligation or a "bad credit" group which has high possibility of defaulting on the financial obligation. After examining a set of behavior data from a large UK bank related to the status of current accounts over a twelve month period, Adams *et al.* (2001) showed how conventional clustering approaches (specifically the clustering algorithm *clara* in the S-plus language was used) could be used to define broad categories of behavior, whereas pattern search could be used to find small groups of accounts that exhibit distinctive behavior.

Shi *et al.* (2002) described a data mining approach to classify the credit cardholders' behavior into two groups (good and bad) and three groups (good, normal, and bad) through multiple criteria linear programming implemented with SAS. Ong *et al.* (2005) employed genetic programming (GP) to build credit scoring models. Continuous attributes were discretized with a Boolean reasoning algorithm before GP was applied. Whittaker *et al.* (2005) presented a statistical analysis of a bank's credit card database, focusing on those accounts that miss a single payment on a certain month but subsequently recover. They introduced a neglog transformation to highlight features that are hidden on the original scale and to improve the joint distribution of the covariates. Quantile regression, a novel methodology to the credit scoring industry, was used as it is relatively assumption free and it is suspected that different relationships might be manifest in different parts of the response distribution.

To discriminate good creditors from bad ones, Wang *et al.* (2005) proposed a fuzzy support vector machine that treats each sample as both of positive and negative classes with different memberships based on the argument that one customer cannot be absolutely good or bad. They reformulated the fuzzy SVM training problem into a quadratic programming problem. Memberships were generated from the credit scores obtained by other methods such as linear regression, logistic regression, and a BP-network. A major issue in its application to solve high dimensional quadratic programming is the computational complexity. Lee *et al.* (2006) explored the performance of credit scoring on one bank credit card dataset using two commonly discussed data mining techniques, i.e., classification and regression tree (CART) and multivariate adaptive regression splines (MARS). The results indicated that CART and MARS outperformed traditional discriminant analysis, logistic regression, neural networks, and support vector machine approaches in terms of credit scoring accuracy and misclassification costs. Sexton *et al.* (2006) applied a GA-based algorithm called the Neural Network Simultaneous Optimization Algorithm to a credit approval dataset. The algorithm not only finds good solutions for estimating unknown functions, but also correctly identifies those variables that contribute to the model.

Loss of revenue due to fraud is a major concern to some service enterprises. Fraud involves the use of false representation to gain an unjust advantage. Fraud exhibits in a variety of different forms. Among them, credit card fraud, ATM card fraud, mobile telecommunications fraud, and computer intrusion tops the list of concern. Prevention measures are often taken to prevent fraud from occurring; but they are not perfect. Thus, fraud detection is necessary to identify fraud as quickly as possible once it has been perpetrated. Of course, it takes effort and cost to detect fraud. In practice, some compromise has to be reached between the cost of detecting a fraudulent case and the savings to be made by detecting it. Bolten and Hand (2002) described the tools available for statistical fraud detection and the areas in which fraud detection technologies are most used. Fraud detection methods can be supervised or unsupervised. Major considerations in building a supervised tool for fraud detection include those of uneven class sizes and different costs of different types of misclassification. Phua *et al.* (2006) proposed a fraud detection method that uses a BP network, together with naïve Bayesian and C4.5 algorithms, on data partitions derived from minority over-sampling with replacement. Table 1 summarizes most of the customer related data mining studies reviewed above. In this table and hereafter, the items highlighted include data mining goal, data sources and data type actually analyzed, data preprocessing operations, data mining algorithms chosen, and software programs used.

4.2 Sales Related

Bansal *et al.* (1998) used neural network based techniques to predict demands more accurately in order to solve the problem of inventory (set at three-weeks of supply) in a large medical distribution company. To handle the data scarcity problem for items sold infrequently, a data transformation was carried out to compute the new time series $X[i]'$ from old ones $X[i]$ as $X[i]'=X[i]+uX[i-1]$, where u is some numerical factor. The transformation enables the retention of non-zero sales items for a longer period of time. A trial and error process was followed to find the best neural network configuration based on three coefficients: *Pearson Correlation Coefficient, Normalized Mean Square Error,* and *Absolute Error.*

Table 1. Summary of customer related data mining studies.

Reference	**Goal**	**Databases/Data Description**	**Data size actually used**	**Preprocessing**	**Data Mining Algorithm**	**Software**
Au *et al.* (2003)	To predict the likelihood of a subscriber to churn	Telecom subscriber data	100,000 subscribers	Discretization	Evolutionary computation (DMEL)	
Black and Hickey (2003)	To determine the change of customer profiles	Telecom customer and call data	1,000 customers over a period of 27 months	Attribute selection and discretization	CD3 decision tree induction algorithm	
Chen *et al.* (2000b)	To discover calling patterns	Call records			OLAP	Oracle Express
Cox (2002)	To learn the predictive model of customer behaviors over time	Survey data and customer data		Stepwise variable selection	Regression models, classification trees, and causal graph models	The Knowledge -Seeker
Crespo and Weber (2005)	To segment customers	CoIL Challenge 2000 (5,822 customers with each described by 86 features)	5-feature data		Fuzzy *c*-means based dynamic clustering	

Table 1. Summary of customer related data mining studies (cont'd).

Reference	Goal	Databases/Data Description	Data size actually used	Preprocessing	Data Mining Algorithm	Software
Daskalaki *et al.* (2003)	To classify customers into solvent and insolvent classes	Static customer data and call detail records	2,066 cases with 46 attributes each	Synchronization of data, elimination of records, stepwise feature selection	Discriminant analysis Decision trees Backpropagation neural networks	
Ha *et al.* (2002)	To analyze customer behavior patterns	Customer data (RFM values) over time of a retailer	2,036 customers		SOM and Markov chain analysis	
Hung *et al.* (2006)	To predict a subscriber's 'propensity to churn'	Wireless telecom data	160,000 subscribers	Variable selection by interviewing human experts	C5.0 and BP neural network	
Kim *et al.* (2005)	To classify whether a customer will churn or not	Credit card data	4,650 customers with each having 7 predictors and one binary response variable	Missing values filtered	SVM	
Lariveère and Van den Poel (2005)	To investigate the effect of variables on customer outcome	Financial service customer data	100,000 customers		Random forest and regression forest	

Table 1. Summary of customer related data mining studies (cont'd).

Reference	Goal	Databases/Data Description	Data size actually used	Preprocessing	Data Mining Algorithm	Software
Lee *et al.* (2006)	To classify credit applicants	Bank credit card dataset	8,000 customers with 9 inputs and one output		CART 4.0 and MARS 2.0	Salford Systems
Morik and Köpcke (2004)	To predict churn of insurance policies	Insurance policy and customer data	10-fold cross-validation on 10,000 examples	Variable selection and transformation	Apriori, J48, and Naïve Bayes	
Mozer *et al.* (2000)	To predict churn and offer incentive for maximum profitability	Wireless telecom customer and call data	46,744 primarily business subscribers, all of which had multiple services	Data standardized. Feature representation with expert's input	Logit regression, decision tree, neural network, and boosting	
Ng and Liu (2000)	To predict customer loyalty and their likelihood of defection	Transactional database	More than 40 attributes and 60,000 periodical records	Feature selection	Association rules	
Ong *et al.* (2005)	To build credit scoring models	UCI data bases	Australian credit scoring data and German credit data	Discretization	Genetic programming	

Table 1. Summary of customer related data mining studies (cont'd).

Reference	Goal	Databases/Data Description	Data size actually used	Preprocessing	Data Mining Algorithm	Software
Qian *et al.* (2006)	To detect churn activity patterns	Telecom customer data over time	1,787 customers over 24 months	Standarized to the range	Gaussian mixture model with number of clusters determined by BIC	
Phua *et al.* (2006)	To detect fraud	Auto insurance data	11,338 examples with 6% fraudulent	Deriving new attributes from existing ones	BP, Naïve Bayesian, C4.5	
Sexton *et al.* (2006)	To classify whether to grant a credit card	UCI credit screening dataset	690 records with 51 inputs and 2 outputs		A GA-based algorithm	
Wang *et al.* (2005a)	To select a subset of customers for direct marketing	KDD98 competition data	95,412 records for learning and 96,367 records for validation	Discretization of continuous variables	Association rules	
Wang *et al.* (2005b)	To discriminate good creditors from bad ones	Credit card applicants data	3 datasets. The largest contains 1,225 applicants with 12 variables each		Fuzzy SVM	

Table 1. Summary of customer related data mining studies (cont'd).

Reference	Goal	Databases/Data Description	Data size actually used	Preprocessing	Data Mining Algorithm	Software
Whittaker *et al.* (2005)	To retain existing customers	Bank's credit card database	150,000 clients with 30 or so variables	Variable selection, data transformation	Quantile regression	
Zhang *et al.* (2004)	Mining of customer behavior patterns	Web logs, sales, and customers		Web logs are filtered and categorized	Clustering, decision tree, and RBG neural network	IBM DB2 Intelligent Miner
Zhao *et al.* (2005)	To predict whether a customer will churn	Customer data (normal and churn) with 171 predictor variables	Training (2,134 normal and 152 churn), Testing (824 normal and 67 churn)		One-class support vector machine	

By deploying the neural network based models (multi-layer perceptron and time delay neural network), the inventory could be reduced by 50% while maintaining the original customer satisfaction level (at 95% availability level). The models were trained with two methods: the standard method and the rolling method. The rolling method produces more training examples, but is more difficult to train due to the close similarity between examples. To better handle the promotion effect on sales, Kuo (2001) proposed an intelligent forecasting system that consists of four parts: (1) data collection, (2) general pattern model implemented by a feed forward neural network, (3) special pattern model implemented as a fuzzy neural network with initial weights generated by genetic algorithm, and (4) decision integration by another feed forward neural network. Sales data from a convenience store were used to evaluate the performance of the proposed system, an ARMA model and a single ANN for comparison purpose.

Kuo *et al.* (2006) proposed a 2-stage method for market segmentation, which first uses a SOM to determine the number of clusters and the starting point, and then uses a genetic *k*-means algorithm to find the final solution. A real world market segmentation problem of the freight transport industry was tested. A questionnaire was first designed and surveyed. Factor analysis was then performed to extract the factors from the questionnaire items as the basis of market segmentation. Finally, the proposed method was used to cluster the customers.

Chang *et al.* (2005) presented a method to forecast monthly PCB production demand using four categories of data: time series data, macroeconomic data, downstream production demand data, and industrial production data. Gray relation analysis was first used to choose the data most related to the demand. The forecast model is then built using an evolutionary neural network (see also Chapter 4 for more details on their work). Lee and Lee (2004) proposed a method to mine seasonal patterns using a SOM. Real world data from stationary stores in Indonesia were tested to show its effectiveness. To handle the problem of discontinuities, daily sales were aggregated into monthly sales. The monthly sales were then divided by the average monthly sales in a year to derive the seasonality index. They measured the similarity between two time series using the Euclidean distance. The trained SOM of size 16×20 was used to visually identify patterns in the dataset. To obtain a finer clustering result, the prototype vectors from the map were clustered using the *k*-means algorithm. Twelve clusters were found to be the best clustering result based on the Davies-Bouldin index.

Tong and Li (2005) proposed a data mining forecasting method that combines wavelet, neural networks, and ARMA modeling. The method has three phases: (i) wavelet decomposition, (ii) model building for the decomposed time series (with ARMA for the final transformation and BP neural networks for all other decomposition levels), and (iii) final forecasting based on wavelet reconstruction. A time series of 1,344 points (2 weeks with 15 minutes interval) was modeled and the model was then used to predict 96 points for the next day. The proposed method was shown to yield lower mean square errors than using BP or ARMA alone. Table 2 summarizes all of the sales related studies reviewed above.

4.3 Product Related

Adams (2002) discussed two case studies of industrial data mining. The first case study is how Intuitive Surgical used the Datasweep Advantage software to detect any trend in both manufacturing history and field uses for a given subassembly or unit of their product, i.e., the da Vinci system that is the most technologically sophisticated robotic assisted surgery system on the market today. The company is regulated by the U.S.'s Food and Drug Administration (FDA) and is required to track the manufacturing history in detail for every unit shipped. The second case study involves how Cymer used Statserver to analyze shop floor and field data in order to uncover problems associated with critical components (called consumables) of their exciter laser, which is the essential light source for a deep ultraviolet photolithography system used in manufacturing semiconductors. Data analysis operations include using Pareto, Shewhart, and CuSum Charts to check whether data are within the specified standards, regression analysis and variance analysis to uncover problems.

Table 2. Summary of sales related data mining studies.

Reference	Goal	Databases/Data Description	Data size actually used	Preprocessing	Data Mining Algorithm	Software
Bansal *et al.* (1998)	To minimize inventory level	Historical weekly sales data	2 years for training and 1 year for testing	Data transformation	MLP and Time Delay Neural Networks	SNNS Version 4
Chang *et al.* (2005)	To forecast sales	Historical monthly production, macroeconomic, downstream production, and industrial production data	60 monthly demand data and 15 items of related indexes	Variable selection by gray relation analysis	Evolutionary neural network	
Kuo (2001)	To forecast sales	Sales from a convenience store	379 data points of a product		Neural networks and fuzzy neural networks with initial weights generated by GA	
Lee and Lee (2004)	To mine seasonal patterns	2-year stationery sales of 1.5 millions transactions for 17,836 products	572 with 12 dimensions (months)	Aggregation and normalization	Self-organizing map	SOM Toolbox 2.0
Tong and Li (2005)	To predict future data values	Time series data	A series of 1,344 data points	Wavelet decomposition and normalization	Wavelet, BP neural network, ARMA	

Their CymerOnline is an e-diagnostic system that provides light source performance monitoring capabilities, stores data to enable data mining, and delivers easy-to-interpret charts and reports.

Buddhakulsomsiri *et al.* (2006) presented a rough set theory-based association rule generation algorithm to uncover the relationships between product attributes and causes of failure from warranty data. They applied the algorithm to an automotive warranty dataset collected over 2 years. To simplify the product quality evaluation process, Zhai *et al.* (2002) proposed an integrated feature extraction approach based on rough set theory and genetic algorithms. Using the historical data gleaned from the manufacturer of an electronic device, the prototype system was able to identify significant attributes for product quality evaluation, leading to a 58% cost reduction. Strobel and Hrycej (2006) presented a framework for the association analysis of quality data, with the goal to find relationships between the assembly and testing process and the failures in the field. They performed a case study on quality control of electronic units in automotive assembly with 3,789 field failures and 3,310 process attributes.

Menon *et al.* (2004) presented two successful implementations of text data mining for the purpose of quality and reliability improvement in the product development process within two large multi-national companies. The first case study involved the use of association analysis to analyze a service center database. This database contained records of the repair actions, customer complaints and individual product details of inkjet printers. The database was a hybrid of fixed format fields and free-form text fields. The fields relevant to the analysis were first extracted from the database before applying association analysis. Classification analysis was performed in the second case on a collection of 'voice of the customer' data from call centers using SVMssupport vector machines. Preprocessing the text was undertaken to remove "unwanted" text, stop words, and stemming words.

It is important to consider the relationship between the product market and technical diversity early in the product life cycle, ideally at the product development stage. To this end, Agard and Kusiak (2004a) developed a 3-step methodology for the design of product families based on the analysis of customers' requirements using a data mining approach. In the first step, data mining algorithms were used for customer segmentation. Once a set of customers was selected, an analysis of the requirements for the product design was performed and association rules were extracted. The second step created a functional structure that identifies the source of the requirements' variability. The last step elaborated on a product structure and distinguished modules to support the product variability. Agard and Kusiak (2004b) discussed the selection of subassemblies for manufacturing by a supplier based on customers' requirements. A data mining algorithm together with an integer programming model were used to determine a candidate set of modules and options to be considered for building subassemblies. Cunha *et al.* (2006) presented a data mining approach based on the learning and inference of association rules to determine the sequence of assemblies that minimizes the risk of producing faulty products.

Shao *et al.* (2006) proposed an effective architecture to discover customer group-based configuration rules in configuration design. Fuzzy clustering and variable precision rough sets were integrated to analyze the dependency between customer groups and product specification clusters. The Apriori algorithm was implemented as the mining method to obtain configuration association rules between clusters of product specifications and configuration alternatives.

To explore the opportunity for Taiwan's hi-tech industry to penetrate into a new market, in particular the automobile telematics computer market, Su *et al.* (2006) proposed an E-CKM model with a methodology for precisely delineating the process of customer knowledge management (CKM). In the E-CKM model, the CKM process is comprised of four stages: identification of product features, categorization of customers' needs, segmenting the markets, and extracting patterns of customers' needs, which are supported by the applications of different methods in information technology. After data cleaning, 1,472 effective questionnaires with each having 29 attributes were obtained through a survey posted on a website. Three clustering methods including *k*-means, SOM, and FuzzyART were applied for segmenting the markets with the number of 'natural' clusters determined by locating the 'elbow' point in the plot of R-squared values versus the number of clusters.

Many engineering artifacts such as space shuttle fuel tanks and off-shore drilling plate forms are joined by welding. Perner *et al.* (2001) empirically compared the performance of neural nets and decision trees based on a dataset for the detection of defects in welding seams. Each digitized weld image was decomposed into various ROIs (Region of Interest) of 50×50 pixel size and for each ROI 36 features were computed. A parameter significance analysis was used for feature selection to reduce the number of features to seven before training four neural nets (BP, RBF, fuzzy ARTMAP, and LVQ). Numerical attribute discretization was done before inducing decision trees using Decision Master. BP and RBF were found to produce lower error rates but they are not comprehensible by humans.

On the other hand, Liao (2003) reported that a GA-enhanced fuzzy rule approach outperformed both fuzzy k-nearest neighbors and MLP neural networks when all three methods were tested with 147 records of six different weld flaw types with each characterized by 12 numeric features. Ceramics have been chosen as the material of choice for many applications such as cutting tools due to their desirable properties; but they are known to be brittle. Dengiz *et al.* (2006) investigated the effects of three ceramic powder preparation methods for ceramics manufacturing on the growth and characteristics of microstructure flaws and damage on the ceramic surface, using a two-stage procedure. In the first stage, digital microstructural images are mined to characterize the flaws and surface damage. In the second stage, an extreme value probability distribution was fitted using the information from the first stage.

Hsu and Wang (2005) applied decision tree-based approaches to develop systems for sizing pants for soldiers in Taiwan. Samples that contain missing or abnormal data were first deleted. Domain experts were consulted to determine eight anthropometric variables that are strongly associated with garment production. Factor analysis was performed to select waist girth and outside leg length as the two most important sizing variables. Finally, taking the body mass index as the target variable, the CART technique was used to model the data.

Romanowski *et al.* (2006) developed a similarity measure that can be used to cluster bills of materials (BOMs) into product families and subfamilies. In their formulation, each BOM was depicted as a rooted, unordered tree. They argued that different engineers may build completely identical end items with very different BOM structures. They distinguished three ways that BOM trees may differ: (i) structural differences such as the number of intermediate parts, parts at different levels, and parts with different parents, (ii) differences in component labels, and (iii) differences in both components and structures. Computing the similarity of BOMs was formulated as an NP-hard tree bundle matching problem and for its solution some possible heuristic approaches were suggested. In (Romanowski and Nagi, 2005), 75 BOMs with known product family classifications were collected from an electronic manufacturer and the Decomposition and Reduction (DeRe) algorithm was used to compute the pairwise distances between them. A *k*-medoid clustering algorithm, CLARANS, was used to group similar BOMs into product families.

Product portfolio planning has far reaching impact on the company's business success in competition. In general, product portfolio planning has two major stages: portfolio identification and portfolio evaluation and selection. Portfolio identification aims to capture and understand customer needs effectively and accordingly to transform them into specification of product offerings. Portfolio evaluation and selection deals with the determination of an optimal configuration of these identified offerings with the objective to achieve best profit performance for the company. Jiao and Zhang (2005) developed explicit decision support to improve product portfolio identification by efficient knowledge discovery from past sales and product records using an association rule mining system. The system involves four consecutive stages, data preprocessing, functional requirements clustering, association rule mining, and rule evaluation and presentation, which interact with one another to achieve the goals. They applied the methodology and system to a consumer electronics company in order to generate a vibration motor portfolio for mobile phones.

To tackle the problem of product assortment analysis, Brijs *et al.* (2004) introduced a microeconomic integer programming model for product selection called the PROFSET model based on the use of frequent itemsets. The objective was to maximize the overall profitability of the hit list of products. Basic products can be specified by forcing the model to select certain products. The size of the hit list was also specified as a constraint. They carried out an empirical study based on some sales data. The study involved two phases: discovery of the frequent sets of the products and selection of a hit list of products using the PROFSET model.

Wong *et al.* (2005) studied the problem of Maximal-Profit Item Selection (MPIS) with cross-selling effect, which involved finding a set of items in consideration of the cross-selling effect such that the total profit from the item selection is maximized. They modeled the cross-selling factor with a special kind of association rules called loss rules. The rules take the form I -> $\Diamond d$, where I is an item and d is a set of items, and $\Diamond d$ means the purchase of any items in d. Such a rule is used to estimate the loss in profit of item I if all items in d are missing after the selection. The rule corresponds to the cross-selling effect between I and d. They proposed a quadratic programming method, a heuristics method called MPIS_Alg and a genetic algorithm approach to solve the problem. A comparison was also made with a naïve approach that simply calculates the profits generated by each item for all transactions and selects the J items with the greatest profit, and the HAP approach that applied the "hub-authority" profit ranking. Table 3 summarizes all of the product related data mining studies reviewed above.

4.4 *Production Planning and Control Related*

Sun and Kuo (2002) proposed a visual exploration approach for mining abstract, multi-dimensional data stored in a relational database and applied it to generate visual images from which users could quickly and easily compare the machine idle cost performance of alternative master production plans. Their approach used the small multiples design and automatically generated a non-uniform color mapping.

Table 3. Summary of product related data mining studies.

Reference	Goal	Databases/Data Description	Data size actually used	Preprocessing	Data Mining Algorithm	Software
Adams (2002)	To uncover problems related to critical components of products	Shop floor and field use data			Control chart monitoring, regression analysis, and variance analysis	Datasweep Advantage and Statserver
Agard and Kusiak (2004a)	Customer segmentation and to associate customers' requirements	Customers' requirements over time			Clustering and association rules	
Brijs *et al.* (2004)	To select a list of products with cross-selling effects for maximum profit	Sales transaction data over 5.5 months from a convenience store	27,148 transactions of 206 different items		Integer programming	CPLEX 6.5
Buddha-kulsomsiri *et al.* (2006)	To associate product attributes with failure causes	Warranty data	684,038 records of 88 attributes each + vehicle-problems represented by 2,238 different labor codes	Removal of attributes, missing values, and discretization of continuous variables	Rough set based association rules and statistical analysis	

Table 3. Summary of product related data mining studies (cont'd).

Reference	**Goal**	**Databases/ Data Description**	**Data size actually used**	**Preprocessing**	**Data Mining Algorithm**	**Software**
Cunha *et al.* (2006)	To associate the sequence of assemblies with faulty products	Product routings	250,000 routings	Data are filtered and transformed	Association rules	TANAGRA
Dengiz *et al.* (2006)	To model the effect of processing on product flaws	Microstructural images of ceramic flaws	Images (28 internal flaw and 18 surface)		Regression analysis and extreme value probability	
Hsu and Wang (2005)	To classify body shape patterns for sizing pants	610 soldiers and 265 static variables each	590 records of 8 variables	Factor analysis to identify the most important variables	CART	
Jiao and Zhang (2005)	To identify product portfolio	Past sales and product records	30 records of customer needs and functional requirements	Feature weighting using the AHP method and data normalization	Fuzzy clustering and association rule mining	Magnum Opus
Menon *et al.* (2004)	To improve product quality and reliability	A service center database and a call center database		Decoding fixed-format fields, adding derived fields, & transforming free-form fields into fixed-format fields. Removing unwanted text, stop words, and word stemming	Association analysis and SVM	SAS Enterprise Miner

Table 3. Summary of product related data mining studies (cont'd).

Reference	Goal	Databases/Data Description	Data size actually used	Preprocessing	Data Mining Algorithm	Software
Perner *et al.* (2001)	To select a data mining algorithm for defect detection	Welding seams images	1,924 ROIs of 50×50 pixel size (1,024 good, 465 cracks, and 435 undercuts)	Feature selection and discretization	Neural nets and decision trees	Decision Master
Romanowski *et al.* (2006)	To cluster bills of materials (BOMs) into product families and subfamilies	Bills of materials (BOMs)	75 BOMs from an electronic manufacturer		CLARANS, Heuristic for tree bundle matching	
Shao *et al.* (2006)	To discover product configuration rules	Target transaction data acquired from the sales records in CRM and PDM	Hundreds of transaction data of electrically powered bicycles	Data standardization	Fuzzy clustering, variable precision rough sets, and association rules	ARMiner
Strobel and Hrycej (2006)	To uncover the relationships between the assembly/testing process and field failures	Electronic units in automotive assemblies	3,789 field failures and 3,310 process attributes		Association rules	

Table 3. Summary of product related data mining studies (cont'd).

Reference	Goal	Databases/ Data Description	Data size actually used	Preprocessing	Data Mining Algorithm	Software
Su *et al.* (2006)	To extract customer knowledge for product development	Questionnaires	1,472 records with each having 29 attributes about the product	Data cleaning	*k*-means, SOM, and FuzzyART	SAS, NeurolShell 2, and ART GALLERY
Wong *et al.* (2005)	To select items with cross-selling effects for maximum profit	Drug store transaction data over 3 months	26,128 items and 193,995 transactions		Quadratic programming, a heuristic, and GAs	
Zhai *et al.* (2002)	To simplify product quality evaluation	Historical product test data	170 records with 12 condition attribute of continuous value and one decision attribute of binary value	Continuous-valued attributes were discretized into binary intervals	Rough set theory and genetic algorithms	

Koonce and Tsai (2000) used an attribute-oriented induction methodology to extract a set of rules from data generated by a genetic algorithm (GA) that was implemented to perform a scheduling operation. Specifically the GA was designed to solve a 6×6 benchmark job shop scheduling problem and run 1,000 times. Of all 1,000 optimal sequences, 264 were unique and mined together with some operations' characteristics using attribute-oriented induction to determine a set of 24 distinct characteristic rules, which duplicate the GA's performance. Before the induction, GA sequences were mapped into a relation and numerical attributes were divided into a number of intervals.

Kwak and Yih (2004) presented a data-mining-based production control approach, called the competitive decision selector (CDS), for the testing-and-rework cell in a dynamic and stochastic computer-integrated manufacturing (CIM) system. For the construction of CDS, the training data were generated by simulation models developed using SIMAN. Features were selected through the iterative process of a hybrid feature-selection approach, which involves using the filter approach to prescreen promising features and the wrapper approach to determine the final set of features. The data were then transformed and partitioned according to the system congestion level. A knowledge base was constructed by using a decision tree algorithm, specifically C4.5, within each sub-partition. The proposed CDS is comprised of two algorithms. It observes the status of the system and jobs at each decision point and makes its decision on job preemption and dispatching rules in real time by activating the corresponding group of knowledge bases. The CDS dynamic control was shown to perform better than static control rules, particularly when static control rules are competing with each other. Readers are referred to Chapter 6 for other related work by Yih and her associates.

Li *et al.* (2006) proposed a hybrid approach that combined metal-fuzzification, data trend estimation, and ANFIS to learn FMS scheduling rules from a small dataset. The predictor attributes used were size of the input/output buffers of each machine, arrival rate of parts, and speed of AGV. The dispatching rules considered include first come first served, shortest processing time, and earliest due date. Li and Olafsson (2005) introduced a framework for using data mining, specifically decision tree models, to discover dispatching rules from production data. They also developed methods for using frequent item set generation to construct composite attributes which in combination with attribute selection improve the performance of the predictive models.

Estimating the cycle time for a product in a factory, especially one with complicated processes such as semiconductor manufacturing is necessary to assess customer due dates, schedule resources and actions to anticipated job completions, and to monitor the operation. To forecast the cycle time of a lot or a product, Yu and Huang (2002) proposed a production learning system based on the tool model. The tool model attempts to divide the flow of a lot or a product into the basic elements, or steps, rather than stages. The tool model concept involves building a model to determine the time required for a step for a lot being processed. At each step, the tool model can be divided into two parts: the waiting part and the processing part, thus both the waiting time and the processing time are involved in each step. The cycle time of a lot is the summation of both waiting time and processing time at each step. To estimate the (waiting or processing) time, a backpropagation neural network was used to establish the relationship between the input and output (time) of the model.

Sha and Liu (2005) presented a rule based total work content model (RTWK) which incorporated a decision tree for minimizing the knowledge of job scheduling about due date assignment in a dynamic job shop environment. The decision tree induced by C4.5 was able to adjust an appropriate allowance factor *k* according to the condition of the shop at the instant of a job arrival, thereby reducing the due date prediction errors of the TWK method. Simulation results showed that the proposed RTWK model was significantly better than its static and dynamic counterparts (i.e., TWK and dynamic TWK methods). Several studies seek to predict individual lot cycle time by comparing key characteristic of a lot in progress to lots that have completed the target operation for which predictions are to be made. The assumption is that the production process is approximately constant over the time frame of prediction. Öztürk *et al.* (2006) explored the use of data mining for lead time estimation in make-to-order manufacturing. They chose the regression tree approach as the data mining method. To select a small subset of features with high predictive power, they also devised an empirical attribute selection procedure, which starts with the set of all attributes and then eliminates attributes based on a criterion called the weighted attribute usage ratio (WAUR).

Chang *et al.* (2002, 2005b) applied a partition-based fuzzy modeling method to build a prediction model for estimating the flow time for an order by taking into account a number of dynamic characteristics of a wafer fabrication factory. The number of fuzzy terms for each attribute is optimized by a genetic algorithm. Test results of data generated from a simulated wafer factory showed that the proposed method outperformed both case based reasoning and back-propagation neural networks. In another study, Chang and Liao (2006) showed that even higher prediction accuracy could be achieved by combining SOM with fuzzy rules. Backus *et al.* (2006) compared three data mining methods (*k*-nearest neighbors, neural networks, and regression trees, with and without clustering first) to learn a predictive model for cycle time from historical manufacturing data. CART with clustering was found to build the best predictive model. The residuals were checked to monitor the model to signal whether the process has changed from the conditions used to build the model.

Last and Kandel (2001) applied an information theoretic fuzzy approach, the Information-Fuzzy Network (Maimon and Last, 2000), to a real-world dataset provided by a semiconductor company. The dataset contains about 110,000 records with each characterized by 8 attributes. A set of 58,076 records related to a product family were selected for the study. The objective was to predict the yield and the flow time of each manufacturing batch. The method produced a compact and reasonably accurate prediction model, which could be converted into a small set of interpretable rules.

Subsequently, they presented a novel, perception-based method, called the Automated Perceptions Network (APN), for the automated construction of compact and interpretable models from highly noisy datasets (Last and Kandel, 2004). They evaluated the method on yield data of two semiconductor products. The accurate estimation of the actual yield is of interest to planning personnel because an "optimistic" estimate would cause delays in the delivery of a customer order and a "pessimistic" estimate would lead to a waste of precious resources. Readers are referred to Chapter 7 for a recent data mining project carried out by Dr. Last and his associates on the prediction of wine quality based on agricultural data. Table 4 summarizes all of the production planning and control related data mining studies reviewed above.

4.5 Logistics Related

Logistics activities mainly consist of transportation, inventory management, warehousing, and order fulfillment. To assist transportation providers in assessing the condition of their assets and efficiently focusing on their maintenance, Brence and Brown (2002) described the discovery and comparison of empirical models from eddy current non-destructive test data to predict corrosion damage.

To improve inventory management for a small UK chemical company, Garcia-Flores *et al.* (2003) reported on a project carried out by a multidisciplinary team of academic researchers and company managers to categorize stocks and to set ordering policies to optimize inventory costs under a continuous review inventory policy. In some cases, sophisticated data mining techniques were replaced by relatively simple rules. For example, stocks were classified using the one-feature-at-a-time approach instead of a genetic-based classification algorithm called GAMIC. The Croston's method for intermittent demand was found to predict finish products better than ARIMA (Autoregressive Integrated Moving Average). The inventory policy parameters were determined with a decision tree and the procedure was captured with IDEF0 diagrams.

Chen *et al.* (2005) presented an association rule based clustering procedure for an order batching problem in a distribution center with a parallel-aisle layout. Order batching is considered as one of several approaches to reduce travel distance, and thus to attain higher order picking efficiency. Orders with more similar product items are expected to have higher associations. Six test problems were used to evaluate the performance of their method in comparison with existing heuristics.

Table 4. Summary of production planning and control related data mining studies.

Reference	Goal	Databases/Data Description	Data size actually used	Pre-processing	Data Mining Algorithm	Software
Backus *et al.* (2006)	To estimate cycle time	Historical lot cycle time data		Outlier detection	Three methods: *k*-nearest neighbors, neural network, CART with or without clustering	
Chang and Liao (2002)	To predict flow time for due date assignment	Simulated wafer factory data	241 records of simulated data with each having 6 inputs (job and shop characteristics) and 1 output (flow time)		GA-enhanced fuzzy modeling	
Koonce and Tsai (2000)	To extract a set of scheduling rules	Operation's characteristics and sequences generated by a GA performing a scheduling operation	1,000 GA solutions of a test case with 6 jobs, 6 operations and 6 machines	Map GA sequence into a relation and divide numerical attributes into discrete intervals	Attribute oriented induction	
Kwak and Yih (2004)	To construct a competitive decision selector	Simulated data		Feature selection, data partition and transformation	Decision trees (C4.5)	

Table 4. Summary of production planning and control related data mining studies (cont'd).

Reference	Goal	Databases/Data Description	Data size actually used	Preprocessing	Data Mining Algorithm	Software
Last and Kandel (2001)	To predict the yield & flow time of each batch	110,000 records with each having 8 attributes	58,076 records related to a product family	Data selection, discretization	Info-Fuzzy Network	
Last and Kandel (2004)	To predict the yield				Automated Perceptions Network (APN)	
Li and Olafsson (2005)	To learn dispatching rules	Production data	7,140 to 19,900 instances, 8 basic attributes plus the class attribute	Data integration, attribute construction and selection	Decision trees	
Li *et al.* (2006)	To learn FMS scheduling rules	Simulated data of an FMS system	200 data records		A hybrid approach that combines metal-fuzzification, data trend estimation, and ANFIS	
Öztürk *et al.* (2006)	To estimate lead time	Simulation data	4 job shops with about 38,000 records each	Attribute selection	Regression trees	See5 & Cubist

Table 4. Summary of production planning and control related data mining studies (cont'd).

Reference	Goal	Databases/Data Description	Data size actually used	Preprocessing	Data Mining Algorithm	Software
Sha and Liu (2005)	To learn due date assignment model	Simulation data	10,000 records with each having 6 input variables and a due date allowance factor *k*	Discretize the due date allowance factor	Decision trees (C4.5)	See5 package
Yu and Huang (2002)	To predict the flow time	Data collected from a real wafer fab			BP neural network	

Wu (2006) proposed a novel approach based on frequent itemset mining to identify all the small subsets of items that can satisfy a large percentage of orders. By assigning a small subset of items identified this way to a highly automated order completion zone, one can improve the warehousing performance. They used a real order database provided by a warehouse of a large local snack company to test the proposed approach and the item order completion distribution approach for comparison. Table 5 summarizes all of the logistics related data mining studies reviewed above.

4.6 Process Related

Manufacturing process related documents exist in various formats according to different sources, such as documents in digital text, paper, and audio formats. Huang *et al.* (2006) proposed a rough-set-based approach to improve document representation and to induce classification rules. It was shown that the proposed approach achieved higher user satisfaction than the vector space method. Other process related data mining studies are reviewed by industry area in the following subsections.

4.6.1 For the Semi-Conductor Industry

Saxena (1993) described how Texas Instruments isolated faults during semiconductor manufacturing using automated discovery from wafer tracking databases. Associations were first generated based on prior wafer grinding and polishing data to identify interrelationships among processing steps. To reduce the search space of the discovered associations, domain filters were incorporated. In addition, the interestingness evaluator tried to identify patterns such as outliers, clusters, and trends; only those patterns with interestingness value higher than a set threshold were generated.

Table 5. Summary of logistics related data mining studies.

Reference	Goal	Databases/Data Description	Data size actually used	Preprocessing	Data Mining Algorithm	Software
Brence and Brown (2002)	To predict corrosion damage	Eddy current non-destructive test data	160,608 observations (75% for training and 25% for testing)	Data selection	Multiple linear regression, regression trees, polynomial networks, and ordinal logistic regression	
Chen *et al.* (2005)	To identify batch of orders	Six test problems			An association rule based clustering procedure	
Garcia-Flores *et al.* (2003)	To optimize inventory costs	Inventory data			Decision trees	
Wu (2006)	To identify a small subset of items that can satisfy a large percentage of orders	Order data	172 items and 9,436 orders		Association rule mining based	

Bertino *et al.* (1999) reported their experience in the use of data mining techniques, particularly association rules and decision trees, for analyzing data concerning the wafer production process with the goal to determine possible causes for errors in the production process in less time (from several days to a few hours). They showed that two commercial tools, i.e., Mineset and Q-Yield, were inadequate to solve the fault detection problem and thus developed a new graph-based algorithm. Significant combinations of process attributes and the interest order are represented as a directed graph, called the interest graph. As a result of the interest order, the visit to nodes corresponds to a slightly modified breadth search of the graph. The algorithm returns a set of certain causes. It is thus not always easy to determine right away which data mining technique works best for the problem at hand.

Chen *et al.* (2004) proposed an integrated processing procedure RMI (Root cause Machine Identifier) to discover the root cause of defects. The procedure consists of three sub-procedures: data preprocessing to transform raw data into the records to be considered, Apriori-based candidate generation, and interestingness ranking based on a newly proposed measure called *continuity*. This is a measure used to evaluate the degree of continuity of defects in the products in which a target machine-set is involved. A higher value of *continuity* means that the frequency of defect occurrence in the involved products is higher and the corresponding machine-set has higher possibility to be the root cause.

Karim *et al.* (2006) proposed some modifications to the original growing self-organizing map for manufacturing yield improvement by clustering. The modifications include introduction of a clustering quality measure to evaluate the performance of the program in separating good from faulty products and a filtering index to reduce noise from the dataset. To investigate the huge amount of semiconductor manufacturing data and infer possible causes of faults and manufacturing process variations, Chien *et al.* (2007) developed a data mining and knowledge discovery framework that consists of the Kruskal-Wallis test, *k*-means clustering, and the ANOVA F-test as the variance reduction splitting criterion for building a decision tree. The viability of the proposed framework was demonstrated using a case study, which involved the analysis of some low CP yield lots in order to find the root causes of a low yield problem. Readers are referred to Chapter 8 for another work of Dr. Chien and his associate.

Cunningham and MacKinnon (1998) discussed statistical methods used to distill large quantities of defect data into relevant information important for a quick understanding of low yield. In particular, they proposed a spatial pattern recognition algorithm that employs defect parsing and data transformation by the Hough transformation for detecting collinear spatial patterns.

Gardner and Bieker (2000) presented three case studies of Motorola semiconductor wafer manufacturing problems. Self-organizing neural networks and rule induction were used together, implemented in CorDex developed by Motorola in house, to identify the critical poor yield factors from normally collected wafer manufacturing data, to explain the wild variation in transistor beta of the bipolar devices manufactured for an automotive application, and to find the cause of intermittent yield problem in a high yield wafer line that manufactures discrete powers used in automobile ignition applications. Using the data mining technology, wafer yield problems were solved ten times faster than using the standard approach; yield increases ranged from 3% to 15%; and endangered customer product deliveries were saved. Li *et al.* (2006b) presented a genetic programming approach for predicting and classifying the product yields and for uncovering those significant factors that might cause low yield in semiconductor manufacturing processes. They tested their approach using a DRAM fab's real dataset in comparison with C4.5.

Chen and Liu (2000) used an adaptive resonance theory network (ART1) to recognize defect spatial patterns on wafers. This information could then be used to aid in the diagnosis of failure causes. Because the total number of dies for this wafer product was 294, the number of input nodes was 294 in the ART1 network. The numbers of outputs were seven corresponding to the numbers of defect patterns. A self-organizing map (SOM) was also used for comparison. The training data used was 35 wafers with 5 for each defect pattern. The results showed that ART1 could recognize similar spatial defect patterns more easily and correctly.

Han *et al.* (2005) described the decision tree technique to automatically recognize and classify a failure pattern using a fail bit map.

Wang *et al.* (2006) proposed an on-line diagnosis system based on denoising and clustering techniques to identify spatial defect patterns for semiconductor manufacturing. First, a spatial filter was used to determine whether the input data contained any systematic cluster and to extract it from the noisy input. Then, an integrated clustering scheme which combined fuzzy *c*-means with hierarchical linkage was applied to distinguish different types of defect patterns. Furthermore, a decision tree based on two cluster features (convexity and eigenvalue ratio) was applied to a separate pattern to provide decision support for quality engineers. Hsu and Chien (2007) proposed a framework that integrated spatial statistics, ART1 networks, and domain knowledge to improve the efficiency of wafer-bin-map clustering.

Lee *et al.* (2001) applied data mining techniques, which include a SOM neural network for clustering, a statistical homogeneity test to merge clusters, and interactive explorative data analysis of SOM weight vectors, to wafer bin map data in order to design an effective in-line measurement sampling method. Rietman *et al.* (2001) presented a large system model capable of producing Pareto charts for several yield metrics by sensitivity analysis for a fab devoted to the manufacturing of a transistor structure known as gate. These Pareto charts were then used to target specific processes, among twenty-two of them, for improvement of the yield metrics.

Bergeret and Le Gall (2003) proposed a Bayesian method to identify the process stage where there is a yield drift as seen at electrical or class-probe tests. The approach is based only on the process dates of all the process stages. They demonstrated the efficiency of their approach by using two real yield issues where the defective stage is known. Note that this method requires sufficient lot mixing along the process flow and some minimal number of defective lots. Besse and Le Gall (2005) used two change detection methods to identify a defective stage within a manufacturing process. One was a Bayesian method with the use of a reversible Markov Chain Monte Carlo computation (Green, 1995) and another was based on an optimal segmentation of a random process

(Lavielle, 1998). To prevent false alarms, two complementary approaches were used with one based on the theory of shuffling a deck of cards and another based on bagging and hypothesis testing. Three examples with known solutions were presented to show that the Bayesian method was efficient in highlighting the defective stage but more likely to involve false alarms. Optimal segmentation was also efficient but it required more parameters to be fixed than the Bayesian method did.

Last and Kandel (2002) presented a novel, fuzzy-based method for automating the cognitive process of comparing frequency histograms obtained from an engineering experiment for process improvement at a semiconductor factory. The method involves first calculating the membership grades of per-interval proportion differences in the "small" and the "bigger" fuzzy sets and then evaluating the overall shift between the compared distributions with three possible outcomes: positive shift, negative shift, and no shift. The method was found to provide a more accurate representation of the experts' domain knowledge than several statistical tests.

Considering time series to be composed of segments between change points, Ge and Smyth (2000) formulated the problem of change point detection in a segmental semi-Markov model framework where a change-point corresponds to state switching. This segmental semi-Markov model is an extension of the standard hidden Markov model (HMM), from which learning and inference algorithms are extended. The semi-Markov part of the model allows for an arbitrary distribution of the location of the change point (equivalently, state duration) whereas the segmental part allows for flexible modeling of the data within individual segments. The proposed method was shown to be useful to detect the end of the plasma etch process which is quite important for reliable wafer manufacturing.

Braha and Shmilovici (2002) applied three classification-based data mining methodologies to better understand the laser cleaning mechanisms for removing micro-contaminants harmful to wafer manufacturing, and to identify the attributes that are significant in the cleaning process. Two groups of input variables were considered: energy factors with 7 variables and gaseous flow factors with 4 variables. The performance of the cleaning process was measured by percentage of particles moved from the original location (%Moval) and percentage of particles removed from the target wafer (%Removal). The two performance indices were continuous and were converted into a finite number of discrete classes before applying the three methodologies: decision trees, neural networks, and composite classifiers. Some experimental data were used in the study and the results indicated that the strategy of building a diverse set of classifiers from different model classes performed better than other strategies.

Braha and Shmilovici (2003) performed an exploratory data mining study of an actual lithographic process, which was comprised of 45 sub-processes. Based on the records of 1,054 unique lots of 13 different 0.7-micron products, a decision tree induction algorithm called C4.5 implemented in the KnowledgeSEEKER environment was employed to enhance the understanding of the intricate interactions between different processes, and to extract high-level knowledge that can be used to enhance the overall process quality. Given a historical dataset of wafer input variables and their corresponding critical dimension (CD) classes, a decision tree was induced that could identify the CD class to which a new set of input variables is most likely to fit. Braha *et al.* (2007) developed a model for evaluating classifiers in terms of their value in decision-making. Based on the decision-theoretic model, they proposed two robust ensemble classification methods that construct composite classifiers, which are at least as good as any of the component classifiers for all possible payoff functions and class distributions. They showed how these two robust ensemble classification methods could be used to improve the prediction accuracy of yield and the flow time of every batch in a real-world semiconductor manufacturing environment.

Lada *et al.* (2002) proposed a general procedure for detecting faults in a time-dependent rapid thermal chemical vapor deposition (RTCVD) process based on a reduced-size dataset, which had the following steps: (a) data reduction; (b) construction of the nominal (in-control) process data model; (c) development of the process fault detection statistic; and (d) application of the test statistic to detect potential process faults. Furthermore, the data reduction step is consisted of two sub-steps: (1) selecting wavelet coefficients by working with a single dataset based on a method that effectively balances model parsimony against data reconstruction error; and (2) deciding on a data-reduction strategy for all replicates, where each replicate is a different set of signals collected form an independent, identically distributed instance of the same in-control process. The nominal process model is approximated by using the selected coefficients. If the original data are normally distributed, a variant of the classical two-sample Hotelling's T^2-statistic adapted to the reversed jackknife sampling scheme is used to test whether the estimated wavelet coefficient vector for the new process is in control. A nonparametric procedure is applied when the original datasets are non-normal; interested readers are referred to the original paper for more details.

Jeong *et al.* (2006) experimented with a tree-based classification procedure, CART, for identifying process fault classes from semiconductor fabrication data, reduced with a new data reduction method based on the discrete wavelet transform to handle potentially large and complicated non-stationary data curves. Their data reduction method minimized an objective function which balances the trade-off between data reduction and modeling accuracy.

Gibbons *et al.* (2000) discussed research involving the implementation of data mining techniques to achieve a greater level of process control using a predictive model. They first carried out principal component analysis on over one hundred wafer process parameters and then built a predictive model using partial least squares regression and a feed-forward backpropagation three layer neural network. For fault detection and operation mode identification in processes with multimode operations, Chu *et al.* (2004b) proposed a method which employed a SVM as a classification tool together with an entropy-based variable selection method. They gathered a dataset of 1,848 batches from a rapid thermal annealing process in which a wafer is processed for about 2 minutes. To monitor the process condition, seven process variables were measured once every 3 seconds (the number of measurement in one batch run was 43), resulting in 301 total numbers of variables. Sixty-two variables were selected to build 3 SVM classifiers with 1,000 batch data (one for each mode). Considerably lower errors than that of the traditional PCA-based fault detection method were reported.

Kot and Yedatpre (2003) described how e-diagnostics capabilities combined with proven enterprise data mining technology could help pinpoint the specific critical process conditions and variables that affect process control.

Kusiak (2001) presented a rough set theory based rule-restructuring algorithm to extract decision rules from datasets of different types generated by different sources, in support of making predictions in the semiconductor industry. The structural quality of extracted knowledge was evaluated with three measures. They are: (1) a decision support measure (DSM), (2) a decision redundancy factor (DRF), and (3) a rule acceptance measure (RAM). DSM is the total number of rules or the number of objects from the training set supporting a decision. DRF is the number of mutually exclusive feature sets associated with the same decision. RAM reflects the user confidence in the extracted rules. The prediction quality such as classification accuracy of a rule set was evaluated with one of the following three methods: partitioning, bootstrapping, and cross validation. Table 6 summarizes all of the process related data mining studies for the semiconductor industry reviewed above.

4.6.2 For the Electronics Industry

Apté *et al.* (1993) employed five classification methods (*k*-nearest neighbors, linear discriminant analysis, decision trees, neural networks, and rule induction) to predict defects in hard drive manufacturing. Error rates at a critical step of the manufacturing process were used as input to identify knowledge of two classes (fail or pass) for providing further assistance to engineers. Büchner *et al.* (1997) described three case studies of successful use of data mining in fault diagnosis. The first study involved building a model using the C4.5 algorithm from process data in order to identify a lapse in the production of recording heads. The second and third studies were identical to those reported by Saxena (1993) and Apté *et al.* (1993), respectively.

Table 6. Summary of process related data mining studies for the semi-conductor industry.

Reference	Goal	Databases/Data Description	Data size actually used	Preprocessing	Data Mining Algorithm	Software
Bergeret & Le Gall (2003)	To identify the process stage related to yield drift	Process dates of all process stages			A Bayesian method	
Bertino *et al.* (1999)	To detect the certain or uncertain causes of failure	Process database with each tuple containing info about a given process step	80-90 lots of process data		Graph-based algorithm	ESQL/C of Informix data management system
Besse & Le Gall (2005)	To detect a defective stage				Bayesian and optimal segmentation	
Braha *et al.* (2007)	To predict yield and flow time	Semiconductor manufacturing batches	1,378 batches of yield data and 1,635 batches of flow time data	Discretization of real values	Nine classifiers with five composite ones	
Braha & Shmilovici (2002)	To identify significant attributes in a cleaning process	Process data with each record having 11 inputs and 2 outputs		Real-valued responses converted into discrete numbers	C4.5, BP network, and composite classifiers (stacked-generalization and Adaboost)	

Table 6. Summary of process related data mining studies for the semi-conductor industry (cont'd).

Reference	Goal	Databases/Data Description	Data size actually used	Preprocessing	Data Mining Algorithm	Software
Braha and Shmilovici (2003)	To discover complex interactions among the inputs and outputs	Lithography process data with each having 9 inputs and a few outputs	1,054 lots of 13 different 0.7-micron products	Missing data treatment and discretization of numeric values	Decision trees (C4.5)	Knowledge -SEEKER
Chen and Liu (2000)	To identify spatial patterns of wafer defects	Each wafer is a vector of 294 binary features indicating a defect die or not.	35 wafers for training and 35 simulated for testing	Transformation of data coordinates	ART1 and SOM	
Chen *et al.* (2004)	To discover the root cause of defects (the machine-set correlated to defects)	Wafer manufacturing data	Nine datasets with varying products, stages, and machines	Transform raw data into a manufacturing process relation	Association rule mining and interestingness measure	
Chien *et al.*(2007)	To find the root causes of low yield	Wafer manufacturing data	CP test data of 77 lots	Data integration, cleaning, and transformation	K-W test, *k*-means, and decision trees	
Chu *et al.* (2004b)	To detect fault and operation mode	1,848 batches of 7-variate process data	1,000 batches for training and 848 for testing	Entropy-based variable selection	SVM	

Table 6. Summary of process related data mining studies for the semi-conductor industry (cont'd).

Reference	**Goal**	**Databases/Data Description**	**Data size actually used**	**Preprocessing**	**Data Mining Algorithm**	**Software**
Cunninghm & MacKinnon (1998)	To detect collinear spatial wafer defect patterns			Hough transformation	Statistical	
Gardner and Bieker (2000)	To identify critical poor yield factors	Wafer manufacturing data	17,246 entries of 133 parameters		SOM and rule induction	CorDex (Motorola internal)
Ge and Smyth (2000)	To detect change points in a process	Single channel spectrometer output	One run with one change point		Sequential semi-Markov model	
Gibbons *et al.* (2000)	To achieve a greater level of process control	Inputs include process parameters, two plasma machine measurements, and output is the test result		Principal component analysis	Partial least square regression and BP neural networks	Unscrambler
Han *et al.* (2005)	To classify failure patterns	Chip level wafer data		Adjusting the grade of unit block	C4.5 (with the entropy index)	SAS E-Miner
Hsu and Chien (2007)	To cluster defect patterns	Wafer bin maps	138 maps	Data integration, cleaning, transformation; Denoising	Spatial statistics & ART1	

Table 6. Summary of process related data mining studies for the semi-conductor industry (cont'd).

Reference	Goal	Databases/Data Description	Data size actually used	Preprocessing	Data Mining Algorithm	Software
Jeong *et al.* (2006)	To detect faults	Rapid thermal chemical vapor deposition process data		Discrete wavelet transform based data reduction	CART	
Karim *et al.* (2006)	To differentiate good and faulty products	Wafer data	133 parameters by 16,381 entries	Noise reduction, data transformation from categorical to numerical, variable removal	Growing self-organizing map	
Kusiak (2001)	To extract meaningful rules from data	Data containing numerical and categorical attributes	2 small examples		Rough set based rule restructuring algorithm	
Lada *et al.* (2002)	To detect faults in a time-dependent RTCVD process	Numerical data collected by sensors or product testing devices over time	21 in-control runs and 421 in-control runs and 4 induced-fault runs	Discrete wavelet transform for data reduction	Hypothesis testing	
Lee *et al.* (2001)	To design an in-line sampling method for process monitoring	200 wafers with 431 locations within the wafer and 11 probe test bins	431 records of 11-dimensional vectors	Data normalization	SOM, followed by statistical test, and visualization of SOM weight vectors	

Table 6. Summary of process related data mining studies for the semi-conductor industry (cont'd).

Reference	Goal	Databases/Data Description	Data size actually used	Preprocessing	Data Mining Algorithm	Software
Rietman *et al.* (2001)	To identify processes to increase yield	Wafer production data	111,117 records each with 181 fields	Data preprocessed normalized for some fields	Neural network with forward gating and backward gating	
Saxena (1993)	Fault diagnosis	Wafer tracking databases			Association rules, domain filters, interestingness evaluator	
Wang *et al.* (2006)	To identify spatial defect patterns	Real and synthetic wafer samples of DRAM		Denoising	Fuzzy *c*-means, hierarchical linkage, decision trees	

Kusiak and Kurasek (2001) used rough set theory to identify the causes of soldering defects in a printed-circuit board assembly process. Special attention was paid to feature selection, data collection, extraction of three rule sets (rules for defect occurrence, rules for defect non-occurrence, and approximate rules for the occurrence of ambiguous outcomes under the same set of conditions), and knowledge validation. The presence of approximate rules indicates that the feature set considered was insufficient and additional features were needed to be defined.

Tseng *et al.* (2004) presented a new heuristic algorithm, called extended rough set theory, for identifying the most significant features and deriving a set of decision rules simultaneously that explain the cause of soldering ball defects. Zhang and Apley (2003) proposed an MLPCA (maximum-likelihood principal component analysis) logistic regression clustering algorithm and applied it to identify the two underlying variation sources which govern the variation pattern among more than 3,000 soldering joints in a selected region of printed circuit boards (PCBs).

Maki and Teranishi (2001) developed an automated data mining system designed for quality control in manufacturing and discussed three characteristic functions of the system: (a) periodical data feeding and mining involving data transformation, discretization, and rule induction by the CHRIS algorithm; (b) storage and presentation of data mining results through the Web on the factory intranet; and (c) extraction of temporal variance of data mining results, which involves comparing the rank of each rule in the newer rule lists with that of the corresponding rule in the older lists in terms of their u-measure values and recognizing a change in rank as a “rise”, a “fall”, or a “stay”. The u-measure evaluated the significance of each rule. The system was applied to liquid crystal display fabrication to show its usefulness for rapid recovery from problems of the production process. Table 7 summarizes most of the process related data mining studies for the electronics industry reviewed above.

Table 7. Summary of process related data mining studies for the electronics industry.

Reference	Goal	Databases/Data Description	Data size actually used	Preprocessing	Data Mining Algorithm	Software
Apté *et al.* (1993)	To predict processing defects	Error rates of processing steps			*k*-nearest neighbors, linear discriminant analysis, decision trees, neural networks, and rule induction	
Büchner *et al.* (1997)	To uncover the causes of a lapse in the production of recording heads	Production process data		Converting date/time fields into numerical values	C4.5	
Kusiak and Kurasek (2001)	To identify the cause of soldering defects in a circuit board	PCB assembly process data with 14 input variables, and binary output (soldering balls present or absent)	2,052 PCBs out of which 89 are defective		Rough set theory	

Table 7. Summary of process related data mining studies for the electronics industry (cont'd).

Reference	**Goal**	**Databases/Data Description**	**Data size actually used**	**Preprocessing**	**Data Mining Algorithm**	**Software**
Maki and Teranishi (2001)	To cue engineers in finding the causes of problems	Records of the events occurred in a LCD manufacturing process		Data transformation and discretization of numerical values	Characteristic rule induction by subspace search (CHRIS)	
Tseng *et al.* (2004)	To identify the causes of soldering ball defects				Extended rough sets	
Zhang and Apley (2003)	To identify the underlying variation sources	Soldering joints on PCBs			A MLPCA (maximum-likelihood principal component analysis) logistic regression clustering algorithm	

4.6.3 For the Process Industry

Milne *et al.* (1998) described a data mining application that used an induction method to build a decision tree model from average process data for predicting paper defects. Wang *et al.* (1997) reported an application of probabilistic networks and decision trees (C5.0) for learning about failure diagnosis of process units in the process industry by extracting knowledge in the form of rules from databases made up of previous cases. The extracted rules can be used either by human experts or in building expert systems. Each historical case is comprised of a number of binary attributes.

To explore the applicability of data mining techniques to computer-aided process decision support, Wang and McGreavy (1998) employed a Bayesian unsupervised classification method, i.e. AutoClass, to automatically cluster the data into classes corresponding to various operational modes. Forty two cases were generated. For each case, six process parameters were chosen and for each parameter 60 data points were recorded in a single run. The data were thus formulated as a 360×42 matrix. The clustering results of five classes were obtained by AutoClass and were discussed.

Sebzalli and Wang (2001) presented an industrial case study which used principal component analysis (PCA) and fuzzy *c*-means clustering to identify operational spaces and develop operational strategies for manufacturing desirable products. Analysis of 303 records of 14-variate data collected from a refinery fluid catalytic cracking process revealed that the data could be projected to four operational zones in the reduced 2-dimensional plane, with three corresponding to three different product grades and the fourth to a changeover zone. The most important variables responsible for the observed operational spaces were identified and accordingly some strategies were developed for monitoring and operating the process in order to be able to move the operation from producing one product grade to another, with minimum time delays.

Singhal and Seborg (2002) proposed a pattern matching methodology to locate periods of historical data similar to the snapshot data, without the knowledge of starting and ending times of the various operating conditions in the historical database. A window of the same size as the snapshot data was moved through the historical data by *w* observations at a time. Setting *w* to be equal to a range, from 1/10 to 1/5, of the snapshot data was found to provide a satisfactory tradeoff between accuracy and computational load. Historical data windows with the largest values of the similarity factors were collected in a candidate pool for further inspection by a person familiar with the process. For dataset comparison a distance similarity factor was defined as the probability that the center of the historical dataset is at least some distance away from the snapshot dataset. The distance was computed using singular value decomposition. An average of two metrics, the pool accuracy that characterizes the accuracy of the candidate pool and the pattern matching efficiency that characterizes how effective a pattern matching technique has been in locating similar records in historical database, was used as a measure of the overall effectiveness of pattern matching.

Meel *et al.* (2003) employed the Gustafson-Kessel fuzzy clustering algorithm to classify step-like disturbances in a dynamic space. For the rejection of unmeasured disturbances, they proposed deploying composite controllers that were built by fuzzy aggregation of the individual controller actions. The methodology was validated using close-loop simulation involving a nonlinear, multivariate continuous stirred tank reactor process in normal and four measured disturbance modes.

For dynamic event recognition and fault diagnosis, Roverso (2002) described the ALADDIN methodology which combined techniques such as recurrent neural network ensembles, wavelet on-line pre-processing, and autonomous recursive task decomposition in an attempt to improve the practical applicability and scalability of this type of system to real processes and machinery. Srinivasan *et al.* (2004) proposed a two-step clustering method for efficient and automatic identification of different process states using large historical datasets. The method first involved classifying process states into modes corresponding to quasi-steady states and transitions by using a PCA-based Hamming distance. Dynamic PCA-based similarity measures were then used in the second phase to compare the different modes and the different transitions, and to cluster them separately by thresholding. Dynamic PCA consists of applying traditional PCA to the extended data matrix that augments the original data matrix with time-lagged variables to account for the autocorrelation.

To analyze multi-variate process data, Aboyni *et al.* (2005) proposed a clustering algorithm for the simultaneous identification of local probabilistic PCA models, used to measure the segment homogeneity, and fuzzy sets, used to represent the segments in time. The proposed clustering-based segmentation algorithm has the following steps:

(1) Uniformly segment the data into a large number of segments and determine the number of principal components based on the analysis of the eigenvalues of these segments.
(2) Set the appropriate parameters.
(3) Execute the clustering algorithm. The cluster merging must be evaluated after a predefined number of iteration steps. The algorithm stops if the termination tolerance is reached and additional cluster merging is not necessary.

It was shown that the proposed algorithm could be applied to extract useful information from temporal databases, e.g. the detected segments could be used to classify typical operational conditions and to analyze product grade transitions.

To uncover possible causes for major problems occurring in the quality of the product produced in a batch drying process, multivariate statistical methods were used (García-Muñoz *et al.*, 2003). The batch data included three sets of variables: (a) initial product condition including 10 chemical variables and the weight, (b) 10 process variable trajectories, and (c) 11 product quality variables. They first built a PCA model on the final product properties to classify product quality. Before further analysis, the trajectories were first aligned using prior knowledge of the process. Then, they built partial least squares (PLS) regression models to relate final product quality to the aligned process trajectories and initial condition variables. The results of the analysis were shown to be useful for suggesting process improvements.

Chu *et al.* (2004a) proposed a bootstrapping-based variable selection method for the improvement of the quality estimation performance and knowledge extraction in a batch process. The variable selection method was performed with a search algorithm, i.e., sequential forward floating selection, based on a selection criterion. To evaluate its performance, the proposed method was applied to an industrial polymerization process for producing PVC and was compared with an existing multi-way partial least squares (MPLS) method. The results showed that the proposed method required much higher computational cost than MPLS. Therefore, the proposed method is effective only when a more accurate prediction performance is required.

To develop a better Operator Support System (OSS), Pach *et al.* (2006) proposed the integration of heterogeneous historical data taken from various production units into a data warehouse, designed the data warehouse based on the synchronization of the events related to the heterogeneous information sources, and showed that the designed data warehouse could be used not only for generating reports and executing queries, but also for supporting the analysis of historical data, process monitoring, and data mining applications. This process-focused data warehouse is called process data warehouse. It differs from the traditional data warehousing strategy in that not only historical data are integrated but also real-time data that represent the current status of the process are effectively handled. Multivariate statistical-based approaches, such as PCA and PLS, are incorporated into the OSS to reduce the dimensionality of the correlated process data by projecting them down onto a lower dimensional latent variable space where the operator can be easily visualized. They illustrated the concept by an industrial case study, where OSS was designed for the monitoring and control of a high density polyethylene plant with nonlinear processes modeled by the first principle and by neural networks for product quality estimation. Table 8 summarizes all of the process related data mining studies for the process industry reviewed above.

Table 8. Summary of process related data mining studies for the process industry.

Reference	Goal	Databases/Data Description	Data size actually used	Pre-processing	Data Mining Algorithm	Software
Aboyni *et al.* (2005)	To analyze historical multi-variate process data	10-variate polymerization reactor data	160 hours operational data that include three product transitions	Principal component analysis	Fuzzy clustering (modified Gath-Geva)	
Chu *et al.* (2004a)	To improve the performance of quality estimation	40-batch of PVC process data	30 different sets of bootstrap data generated from the 40 samples	Normalization to zero mean and unit variance	Partial least squares via bootstrapping-based generalized variable selection	
García-Muñoz *et al.* (2003)	To uncover possible reasons for quality problems	Initial product condition (11 chemical variables + weight), 10 process variable trajectories, and 11 final chemical properties		Alignment of trajectories by using prior knowledge	PCA model for product quality classification and PLS regression models to relate quality to process variables and initial condition	MACSTAT v4 and BatchSPC v2 (MATLAB tool boxes)
Meel *et al.* (2003)	To classify process disturbances	A multivariate continuous stirred tank reactor process	2,500 data points (5 modes with 500 data points each. Five modes (normal + four disturbances)		Gustafson-Kessel fuzzy clustering	

Table 8. Summary of process related data mining studies for the process industry (cont'd).

Reference	Goal	Databases/Data Description	Data size actually used	Pre-processing	Data Mining Algorithm	Software
Milne *et al.* (1998)	To predict paper defects	Process data			Rule induction	
Pach *et al.* (2006)	To develop a better Operator Support System	Heterogeneous historical production data		Dimension reduction	Process data warehouse, multivariate statistical-based approaches such as principal component analysis (PCA) and partial least square (PLS)	
Roverso (2002)	Dynamic event recognition and fault diagnosis				The ALADDIN methodology that combines techniques such as recurrent neural network ensembles, wavelet on-line pre-processing, and autonomous recursive task decomposition	
Sebzalli and Wang (2001)	To identify operational zones	Data from a refinery fluid catalytic cracking process	303 records with each having 14 variables	Dimension reduction by PCA	Fuzzy *c*-means	

Table 8. Summary of process related data mining studies for the process industry (cont'd).

Reference	Goal	Databases/Data Description	Data size actually used	Pre-processing	Data Mining Algorithm	Software
Singhal and Seborg (2002)	To generate a candidate pool of similar periods of operation	Continuous stirred tank reactor process operation simulated for 463 operation periods (409 abnormal) over 39 days.	14-variate time series with each snapshot of 1024 samples. A set of 28 snapshots was used for pattern matching.		Multivariate statistical techniques such as PCA and SVD and unsupervised clustering	
Srinivasan *et al.* (2004)	To identify different process states	Multivariate process data (fluidized catalytic cracking & Tennessee Eastman)		Normalization of each variable	PCA and dynamic PCA	
Wang *et al.* (1997)	Mining of failure diagnosis rules	Compressor and process failure cases with each having 12 and 13 binary attributes, respectively	356 compressor failures with 12 attributes and 864 patterns of a fluid catalytic cracking process		Probabilistic networks and decision trees (C5.0)	
Wang and McGreavy (1998)	To identify process upsets	Process operational data	42 cases of 6-variate profiles with 60 points each (360×42 matrix)		Bayesian clustering	AutoClass

4.6.4 For Other Industries

Kusiak (2002) used rough set theory to derive associations among control parameters and the product quality in the form of decision rules for a metal forming process. He also developed an integer programming model for the selection of control signatures that lead to good quality products, for the cases involving large numbers of rules and features. For in-process diagnosis of a stamping process, Jin and Shi (1999) developed a methodology for automatic wavelet-based feature extraction and feature subset selection based on a criterion of class separatability. A two-step analysis was proposed to enable the knowledge accumulation of process faults whenever a new process fault was identified. Their two-step analysis first involved the identification of the closest cluster for a newly detected fault using a piecewise linear classifier, then testing to determine whether a new fault cluster needed to be formed or not.

The dimensional quality of a sheet metal assembly is commonly represented by 150-300 dimensional characteristics measured by a coordinate measuring machine. Lian *et al.* (2002) proposed a data mining driven decision support system, with which the dimensional variation causes could be identified quickly. The system used correlation analysis and maximal tree methods to extract large variation groups, principal component analysis to discover principal variation patterns, and a decision tree for variation cause reasoning. The main variation causes considered include failure of a welding fixture, variation of stamping parts, variation of process parameters, and poor workmanship.

Porzio and Ragozini (2003) proposed a visual data mining strategy to mine large and high-dimensional off-line datasets. Their strategy allows users to achieve a deeper understanding of the process through a set of linked interactive graphical devices, which include: (1) an rCUSUM chart for the identification of retrospective rational subgroups, (2) a Subgroup Mean chart to aid in the evaluation of differences among the means of each retrospective rational subgroup, (3) a Subgroup Interquartile chart to graphically compare the variability among groups, and (4) a correlation Pareto chart to visually identify the variables that mainly lead to the decay of process quality. The strategy was illustrated with an industrial process case study, in which data are real-time measurements on 68 key points of the surfaces of bodies of vehicles, taken from a production plant of a European car industry. Readers are referred to Chapter 9 for a nonparametric multivariate control chart that these authors recently developed.

By transforming the change-point problem into building a supervised learner with time as the output and process characteristics as inputs, Li *et al.* (2006) proposed a tree-based supervised learner, specifically a random forest, to detect change points caused by mean-shift in a multivariate distribution without assumptions regarding the form of the distribution and the number of change points.

Peng (2004) presented a fuzzy induction learning method (a fuzzy decision tree) and applied it to generate fuzzy rules for diagnosing the conditions of a tapping process. Five classes of tapping process conditions were distinguished. Eight features were generated from data collected from the sensors of thrust force and torque. A 3-fold cross-validation study was carried out based on a total of 120 data records (24 records for each class) to show that the proposed method fairs better than C5.0. Hur *et al.* (2006) presented an intelligent manufacturing process diagnosis system that was built using a hybrid data mining method and proposed it for a coil-spring manufacturing process as a case study. The hybrid learning method had two parts: a decision tree (DT) and an evolutionary strategy (ES). The initial cause-and-effect rules for the manufacturing process condition were inferred by the DT. ES learning was carried out with the dataset belonging to the lead node which had an accuracy rate lower than the overall accuracy rate of the DT.

Gertosio and Dussauchoy (2004) described how a French truck manufacturer used the KDD method to exploit the datasets of measures recorded during the test of diesel engines manufactured on their production lines. The goal was to discover "knowledge" in the data of the test engine process in order to significantly reduce (by about 25%) the processing time. To build a regression model with the data, the software LPSTAT developed by the Renault Research Department was used.

Shi *et al.* (2004) presented two case studies to illustrate the concurrent application of artificial neural networks and a virtual design of experiments to quality improvement. One case was related to a chemical manufacturing process and the other involved the machining of PCB slots by a milling cutter. A neural model was built for each individual response of interest in either case. Therefore, their models failed to capture the functional relationships between process parameters and multiple responses, rendering them inadequate to identify factors for simultaneously achieving multiple objectives. Huang and Wu (2005) used a decision tree to analyze the factors that affect the percentage of defectives in the ultra-precision manufacturing industry.

Yu *et al.* (2003) developed an online imaging system for monitoring and controlling product quality (specifically coating concentration and distribution) of several industrial snack food processes. The methodology first extracted feature information from color images (32 features were extracted from each image) using multivariate image analysis based on principal component analysis. The extracted features were then used to develop partial least squares models for predicting the coating content and coating distribution on the products. To illustrate the methodology, 110 images of one product and 180 images of the other product were collected and analyzed.

Hou and Huang (2004) presented a fuzzy variable precision rough set approach for mining the causal relationship rules from the database of a remote monitoring manufacturing process. The proposed fuzzy rough set approach was shown to perform better than the original rough set approach based on a dataset of 27 records with 8 attributes each, collected from a process of manufacturing industrial conveyor belts. Tsai *et al.* (2006) proposed a knowledge discovery model for the monitoring of the process of manufacturing industrial conveyor belts that achieves even higher classification accuracy than the fuzzy rough set approach proposed by Hou and Huang. Their model contained an algorithm for correlation-based feature selection, a modified minimum entropy principle algorithm for defining membership functions and a variable precision rough set model.

Ho *et al.* (2006) proposed an intelligent production workflow mining system, which contained three main modules: measurement, prediction, and improvement that employ OLAP, ANNs, and fuzzy rule sets, respectively. The system was developed using Visual Basic 6.0, Microsoft SQL Server 7.0, MATLAB Fuzzy Logic Toolbox and Qnet for Windows, and was applied to slider manufacturing with the objective to minimize the defects of the finished goods.

Povinelli and Feng (2003) introduced a method for analyzing time series data, which employed time-delayed embedding and identified temporal patterns in the resulting phase spaces by a genetic algorithm. The method was applied to the characterization and prediction of the release of metal droplets from a welder, in comparison with a Time Delay Neural Network and the C4.5 decision tree algorithm.

To meet the increasing demand for maintaining the network proactively, Sasisekharan *et al.* (1996) examined how to warehouse data about faulty network behavior for a large-scale telecommunication network such as that of AT&T and how to later mine them to find trends and patterns that characterize current and future network behavior. They presented an approach to systematically and exhaustively search time-varying, diagnostic data using machine learning for non-transient faults and correlation techniques for transient faults. Their machine learning approach involved a series of steps as described below. The first step was to define and extract features from time-varying diagnostic data and to transform these data into a standard classification format. The next step was to determine which features can be used as class labels. Next, a classification method was applied to the set of cases to see if there are patterns that differentiate one class from other classes. The final step was to repeat the classification process at regular time intervals. They also discussed how to correlate problems that have similar behavior patterns by exhaustively searching historical and network topological data using the Scout approach which is an AT&T system developed to improve network reliability.

Sterritt *et al.* (2000) proposed a hybrid data mining architecture and a parallel genetic algorithm applied to the mining of Bayesian Belief Networks for fault identification and management from

Telecommunication Management Network data. Table 9 summarizes all of the process related data mining studies for other industries reviewed above.

4.7 Others

Absenteeism due to medical reasons causes great losses to both individual employees and their companies. Decreasing sickness absence is thus a concern in the occupational healthcare field and to any enterprise system. Sugimori *et al.* (2003) used data mining methods such as Association Rule Analysis, Correlation Coefficient Analysis, and Risk Ratio Analysis, to elucidate interrelationships in sickness absences, lifestyle, medical findings, and present illness of 6,010 Japanese male employees in a large telecommunication telephone company which they surveyed consecutively from 1991 to 1998. The sickness absence in 1998 was maximally associated with sickness absence in 1997. It was also found that secular trend of risk ratio showed different patterns according to present illness category (seven were assessed, which included hypertension, heart disease, respiratory disease, hyperuricemia, diabetes, mellitus, gastroduodenal ulcer and liver disease).

Selecting a good supplier is critical to financial success of any enterprise since supply chain management (SCM) focuses on the development of cooperation and trusting relationships between supply chain suppliers. To analyze the suppliers' data for extracting useful information to assist supplier selection is critical to the success of SCM. Tseng *et al.* (2006) presented a methodology for selecting preferred suppliers for a video game company. The methodology employed two main algorithms. One was called the rough-set-based Weight Incorporated Rule Identification (WIRI) algorithm. The other was named the Negative Data Driven Compensation Algorithm (NDDCA) algorithm. The WIRI algorithm was used to derive high-accuracy decision rules and to identify significant features. The NDDCA algorithm was used to improve the learning algorithm performance through compensating the base hypothesis by using the negative training dataset.

Table 9. Summary of process related data mining studies for other industries.

Reference	**Goal**	**Databases/Data Description**	**Data size actually used**	**Preprocessing**	**Data Mining Algorithm**	**Software**
Gertosio and Dussauchoy (2004)	To discover knowledge to reduce processing time	Product test data of 20-30 attributes recorded every second (more than 30,000 measures)		Data selection by prior classification	Regression model	LPSTAT developed by Renault
Hou and Huang (2004)	To extract process diagnosis rules	Manufacturing process parameters	27 records with 8 attributes and 4 types of faulty product		Fuzzy rough set based rule induction	
Huang and Wu (2005)	To identify defect influencing factors				Decision tree (CART)	
Huang *et al.* (2006)	To retrieve manufacturing process document	Document term table	50 documents		Rough set theory	
Hur *et al.* (2006)	To infer cause-and-effect rules	Data collected from a coil-spring manufacturing process	Each record has 12 inputs and one output class		Decision trees and evolutionary strategy	Enterprise-Miner
Jin and Shi (1999)	To identify process faults in-line	Stamping process data		Wavelet-based feature extraction and subset selection	A piecewise linear classifier followed by testing	

Table 9. Summary of process related data mining studies for other industries (cont'd).

Reference	**Goal**	**Databases/Data Description**	**Data size actually used**	**Pre-processing**	**Data Mining Algorithm**	**Software**
Jin and Shi (1999)	To identify process faults in line	Stamping process data		wavelet-based feature extraction and subset selection	A piecewise linear classifier followed by testing	
Kusiak (2002)	To produce control signatures that lead to quality products	Metal forming process data	93 records with each has 82 features plus product quality		Rough set theory	
Li *et al.* (2006)	To detect change points	Simulated multivariate process data	Five case with each having 500 vectors		Random forest	
Lian *et al.* (2002)	To identify causes of dimensional variation	CMM data			correlation analysis, maximal tree methods, PCA, & decision trees	
Peng (2004)	To classify process conditions	Sensory data (thrust force and torque) from tapping process	120 records	Feature extraction (8 features from sensory data)	Fuzzy decision trees	

Table 9. Summary of process related data mining studies for other industries (cont'd).

Reference	Goal	Databases/Data Description	Data size actually used	Preprocessing	Data Mining Algorithm	Software
Porzio and Ragozini (2003)	To achieve a deeper process understanding	Real-time measurements of 68 locations on the surfaces of vehicles			Visual data mining via various charts	
Povinelli and Feng (2003)	To predict the release of metal droplets in welding				A method that employs time-delayed embedding and GA	
Sasisekharan *et al.* (1996)	To identify faults in a telecom network	Historical data for several months		Feature extraction	Correlation & rule based classification	AT&T's Scout
Tsai *et al.* (2006)	To extract diagnostic rules	Process data of manufacturing industrial conveyor belt	27 records of 5 classes of belt with 8 variables each	Correlation based feature selection	Modified minimum entropy principle and variable precision rough sets	
Yu *et al.* (2003)	To monitor product quality variables	Snack food images	110 images for one and 180 images for another	PCA based feature selection	Partial least squares	

4.8 Summary

Tables 1-9 have summarized the previous data mining studies with highlights on their data mining goals, data sources, size of the processed data, data preprocessing performed, data mining algorithms and software programs used. This section elaborates more on data sources, size of the processed data, in Section 4.8.1, and on data preprocessing performed, in Section 4.8.2.

4.8.1 Data Type, Size, and Sources

Most studies focus on relational (table) data. Lee *et al.* (2001) used the historical wafer bin map data as input for the analysis of the spatial patterns of all defective chips on all of the wafers. Lian *et al.* (2002) used a high-dimensional dimension data taken from sheet metal assemblies. Au *et al.* (2003) mined 100,000 telecom subscriber data records. Last and Kandel (2004) used two sets of yield data: one having 1,378 records with 6 input and 1 output attributes, and another having 816 records with 5 input and 1 output attributes.

Chen *et al.* (2004) used nine real datasets of semiconductor fabrication, provided by Taiwan Semiconductor Manufacturing Company. The number of products range from 53 to 484, the number of processing stages from 1,176 to 1,734, and the number of machines from 2,004 to 4,437. Tseng *et al.* (2004) used 3,568 records of data containing features related to PCB manufacturing. The credit approval dataset used by Sexton *et al.* (2006) included 690 observations with 51 inputs and two outputs.

Time series data were used by Bansal *et al.* (1998) and Tong and Li (2005) to forecast demands, by Lee and Lee (2004) to mine seasonal patterns in sales, by Ge and Smyth (2000) to detect change points in a plasma etching process, by Wang and McGreavy (1998) to identify process upsets, by Jin and Shi (1999) for in-process diagnosis of faults in a stamping process, and by Lada *et al.* (2002) and Jeong *et al.* (2006) to detect faults in a time-dependent RTCVD process. Multivariate time series data were used by Sebzalli and Wang (2001) to identify operational zones, by Singhal and Seborg (2002) in their pattern matching study in order to generate a candidate pool of similar periods of operation from the historical data, by Roverso (2002) in identifying the state and dynamics of plant operation, by Abonyi *et al.* (2005) for the fuzzy segmentation of large multivariate time series, and by Li *et al.* (2006) for change-point detection.

Image data were used in (Perner *et al.*, 2001) and (Liao, 2003) for welding flaw identification, in (Brence and Brown, 2002) for predicting corrosion damages, and in (Wang *et al.*, 2006) and (Hsu and Chien, 2007) for identifying spatial defect patterns on wafer bin maps.

Menon *et al.* (2004) mined text data collected in a service center database and a call center database. Huang *et al.* (2006) focused on the retrieval of manufacturing process documents. The data processed by Romanowski *et al.* (2005) were bills of materials, which were depicted as rooted, unordered trees.

4.8.2 Data Preprocessing

Most commonly used data preprocessing operation is data normalization to unit intervals so that the effect of magnitude is removed.

Missing values are also common problems. Some studies simply remove records with missing values. Some use the average value to fill in while others fill in all possible values, which have the drawback of exploding the number of records. Some algorithms such as the DMEL algorithm developed by Au *et al.* (2003) require the discretization of numeric variables into some categorical vales.

Last and Kandel (1999) used the concepts of fuzzy set theory to automate the process of human perceptions for three tasks: evaluating data reliability, comparing frequency distributions, and detecting outliers in discrete attributes. These tasks are useful for finding unreliable data recordings, for comparing data distribution before and after a process change, and for cleaning the data with outliers to prevent causing a bias in the results of the data mining process, respectively. Gibbons *et al.* (2000) carried out an in-depth analysis of over one hundred parameters using the principal component analysis technique.

To handle the data scarcity problem for items sold infrequently, a data transformation was carried out by Bansal *et al.* (1998) to compute the new time series $X[i]'$ from old ones $X[i]$ as $X[i]'=X[i]+uX[i-1]$, where u is some numerical factor. Mozer *et al.* (2000) imposed lower and upper limits on the variables to suppress irrelevant variation. In their study, Chen *et al.* (2004) transformed raw data into a relation form based on a schema $(PID, S_1, S_2, \ldots, S_l, D)$ to record the sequential processing procedure for each product, including the machine in each stage and its finally testing result. In this scheme PID is an identification attribute used to uniquely label the product; $S_i = <m_{ij}, t_i>$, where $1 \leq i \leq l$, is a context attribute used to record the pair of processing machine in the ith stage and the timestamp after this stage; and D is a class attribute used to represent whether the product is defective or not.

Preprocessing of the texts was required before implementing the algorithms for text mining. In their study, Menon *et al.* (2004) performed the following preprocessing steps: decoding fixed-format fields; adding derived fields; and transforming free-form fields into fixed-format fields in their first case study and removing 'unwanted' text; stop words; and word stemming in their second case study.

To handle the high dimensionality of data/signals, Jin and Shi (1999) developed an automatic feature extraction and selection methodology for in-process diagnosis of a stamping process. Jeong *et al.* (2006) presented new data reduction methods based on discrete wavelet transform to handle potentially large and complicated non-stationary data curves. Their methods minimize objective functions to balance the trade-off between data reduction and modeling accuracy. To improve the model quality of 'fat' data (i.e., data with higher numbers of variables than samples), Chu *et al.* (2004) proposed a bootstrapping-based generalized variable selection method that employs a sequential forward floating selection algorithm.

Before clustering, the wafer-bin-map data were preprocessed in three stages in Hsu and Chien (2007): data integration, data cleaning, and data transformation. The wafer-bin-map data had to be integrated with process data such as tools, dates, and operators into a lot-based map to support analysis with lot-based process data. Missing data were deleted;

thus any position on a map with missing data was not analyzed. For a different analysis, a wafer-bin-map was transformed into either a binary map or a binary vector.

5. Discussion

There is a gap between the amount of data actually used in most studies and the amount of data that data mining and knowledge discovery is intended for. Several explanations are possible. First is the access issue. An enterprise will not easily open up its data bases or data warehouse to any researcher, unless there is an established good relationship which usually takes time to develop. Two common approaches to get around this data access problem are either using the open source data available in various repositories, such as the UCI Repository, or generating the data by building a simulation model. Soares (2003) argued that data repositories are indeed representative of KDD dataset for the purpose of supporting the algorithm selection step.

Secondly, there is the data preprocessing issue. The amount of effort required to put the data together in a form ready for data mining is too great and not justifiable in terms of research value for a researcher to spend much time on. Thirdly, even if there exist neither access problem nor data preprocessing issue, the time required to run a data mining algorithm on a large dataset is simply too long for a desktop computer and the access to more sophisticated computing platforms such as a supercomputer, distributed computer network, or grid is not always available.

Analysis of text data is common in information retrieval but is not frequently done within the manufacturing/engineering discipline. This may largely be due to a lack of know-how within the manufacturing/ engineering community. Thus, there is an opportunity for the information retrieval community to offer enterprise systems their expertise in the mining of text data. It was pointed out in Section 3 that there is a vast amount of heterogeneous data in an enterprise. However, most studies focus on only one data type. This deficiency might be related to the lack of access issue discussed above. To facilitate the mining of heterogeneous data, a data warehousing technology should be implemented first, which usually implements the process to access heterogeneous data sources: first clean, filter, and transform the data, and then store the data in a structure that is easy to access, understand, and use.

In a more and more customer driven economy, each enterprise has to be flexible, agile, and reconfigurable in order to meet the high variety of customer demands. As the number of products and processes increase, the complexities of the enterprise system increases as well. This is compounded by the high data collection frequency for some part of the enterprise operation. The higher the system complexity and data acquisition frequency are the data supporting the operation are expected to change more quickly. How to conduct data mining in such an environment is the focus of dynamic data mining, but it is rarely addressed by most researchers. Koonce *et al.* (2000) pointed out that future research should incorporate incremental learning into the mining process to allow for multiple schedule scenarios in the datasets. Lee *et al.* (2001) indicated that they plan to extend their work to dynamic process data sampling. Few exceptions that have considered dynamic data mining are Maki and Teranishi (2001), Ha *et al.* (2002), Black and Hickey (2003), and Crespo and Weber (2005).

6. Research Programs and Directions

Based on the above review, it is easy for readers to find the researchers who have worked on the data mining and knowledge discovery of enterprise data. In this section, the author attempts to highlight a few selected areas, apparently biased by the available information.

6.1 On E-commerce and Web Mining

Kohavi and his associates continue working on data mining of retail e-commerce data. In Kohavi *et al.* (2004), three top challenges were identified as follows:

1) To translate business questions to the desired data transformations.
2) To design efficient data mining algorithms whose output is comprehensible for business insight, and which can handle multiple data types (dates, hierarchical attributes, and data of different granularity).
3) To integrate workflow to enable tracking of the progress for tasks requiring multiple people and processes.

As web sites become more and more sophisticated, a possible future work is to automatically feed acquired models and rules of web customers' behaviors to a personalization or recommendation engine to navigate web visitors online (Zhang *et al.*, 2004).

6.2 On Customer-Related Mining

To improve the quality of customer profiling and churn prediction, Qian *et al.* (2006) plan to extend their research in two directions by considering multiple profiles rather than univariate profiles and by incorporating other data such as customer contracts and competitors. Working on the insolvency problem facing the telecommunication industry, S. Daskalaki from the University of Patras, Greece, and her collaborators focus their attention on several aspects of the knowledge discovery process such as class imbalance, cost-based evaluation, combination of classifiers, and the use of discovered knowledge in building a decision support system.

G. Chen and his colleagues from the Tsinghua University, China, continue to work on using data mining to control credit risk, especially on the subject of enhancing the performance of classification methods with feature selection.

The challenges in fraud detection are both formidable and intriguing. First and foremost is the peculiar non-stationary nature of the problem. A fraud detection tool must adapt to the changing behavior of fraudsters to ensure its continued effectiveness. The analysis must deal with a large number of problems simultaneously and also with diverse data records. The speed of detection is important too. Thus, the objective function must weight the value of detection as a function of time. There is also a need to have a precise definition of classes of fraud detection problems.

Many of the problems are not near solution in terms of satisfactory false alarm and detection rates. Fraud detection is very much an open field for the exercise of ingenuity, algorithm creation, and data snooping. It is also a field worth millions if not billions of dollars. One research group that is actively pursuing this area of research is comprised of C. Phua and his collaborators at Monash University, Australia.

6.3 On Sales-Related Mining

Lee and Lee (2004) planned to work on combining the clustering results of seasonal sales patterns with the association rules that are discovered from a dataset. The reason for doing so is because items with different seasonal patterns that were frequently sold together can be put together as a sales promotional package.

Several researchers are working on the association rule-maximal profit item selection problem. Wong *et al.* (2005) particularly considered the cross-selling effect. They plan to enhance their heuristic method with known methodologies such as hill climbing and to study the switching behavior of customers when some items are missing.

Since sale forecasting drives the planning of enterprise operations, the more accurate the sale forecasting is the smoother the enterprise operates. The research by many people, including P. C. Chang from the Yuan Ze University, Taiwan, and his colleagues, indicates that soft computing techniques are quite effective for sale forecasting compared to traditional statistical approaches.

6.4 On Product-Related Mining

R. Nagi from the University of Buffalo, SUNY, have worked on developing data mining algorithms in the engineering design environment – an area that generates large amounts of heterogeneous data for which suitable mining methods are not readily available. Data mining methods are applied to extract the relevant design information and to improve its accessibility to design engineers. Working in the area of mass customization manufacturing, J. Jiao from the Nanyang Technological University, Singapore, and his collaborators have applied association rule mining to identify product portfolios and have developed a tailored methodology to solve the process platform formation problem, specifically the development of generic routings, in order to support the fulfillment of product families identified in the portfolios. Currently, the similarity in operations and similarity in precedence are considered of equal importance. They plan to carry out another study to investigate cases with unequal importance.

Since the field and service data keep a good track of the product performance and related problems over time, data mining researchers start to tap into these data in order to uncover potential product design and fabrication flaws linked to their product in order to make their products more competitive.

6.5 On Process-Related Mining

Many researchers in Taiwan, such as C.-F. Chien from the National Tsing Hua University, are working closely with Taiwan's semiconductor industry to develop and apply all kinds of data mining techniques to help better analyze their process data, understand their processes, identify the root causes of problems, and hopefully to improve the production yield. This is supported by the numerous papers published on this subject.

False alarms should be minimized in any fault detection problem because they generate useless work loads for engineers, and a loss of time to solve the real problems. Not to forget that false alarms diminish the confidence of users on a system. Therefore, there is a need to develop data mining methods that are able to highlight false alarms without excluding actual detections. Bergeret and LeGall (2003) are interested in this particular research issue among many other researchers. Braha and Shmilovici (2003) take another big step further and set their ultimate research goal on developing an integrated yield management system, which can utilize data mining methodologies as a supportive vehicle for closed-loop system-level control.

To increase the applicability of the ALADDIN system for real world dynamic event recognition and fault diagnosis, Roverso (2002) continues to improve the ALADDIN methodology: (1) by the inclusion of input dimensionality reduction techniques such as feature selection and nonlinear PCA and (2) by adding a new validation methodology based on first principle physical models. M. K. Jeong from the University of Tennessee, U.S.A., has worked together with his collaborators extensively on the mining of multi-functional data such as time series data and images for fault diagnosis. They plan to extend their work into quality improvement and SPC areas.

With multi-variate process monitoring and control applications in mind, G. Porzio from the University of Cassino, Italy, and G. Ragozini from the University of Naples, Italy, have proposed approaches to address the issues involved with large datasets. They have explored the power of some visual data mining techniques for retrospective analysis and present a nonparametric approach based on the data depth notion for multi-variate process control as discussed in Chapter 9 of this book.

6.6 On the Use of Text Mining in Enterprise Systems

Though rough-set-based document retrieval achieved higher user satisfaction, it is quite time consuming. Therefore, Huang *et al.* (2006) plan: (1) to investigate a hybrid approach by combining rough set theory with vector space methods, (2) to develop a weighting scheme for premise terms and documents, (3) to derive a user query weight using a pairwise comparison method through domain experts, and (4) to incorporate the appropriate ontologies in practical applications.

Acknowledgements

This chapter is an extension of the presentation given by the author at the International Workshop for the Mining of Enterprise Data, which was held on June 23, 2004 at Como, Italy, as part of the Mathematics and Machine Learning (MML) Conference. The author acknowledges the support provided by National Science Foundation for the Workshop (DMI-0437734).

References

Abonyi, J., Feil, B., Nemeth, S., and Arva, P. (2005). Modified Gath-Geva clustering for fuzzy segmentation of multivariate time series, *Fuzzy Sets and Systems*, **149**, 39-56.

Adams, L., (2002). Mining factory data, May 2002, Business News Publishing Company (www.bnp.com).

Adams, N.M., Hand, D. J., and Till, R. J. (2001). Mining for classes and patterns in behavioral data, *Journal of the Operational Research Society*, **52**, 1017-1024.

Agard, B. and Kusiak, A., (2004a). Data mining based methodology for the design of product families, *Int. J. Production Research*, **42**(15), 2955-2969.

Agard, B. and Kusiak, A. (2004b). Data mining for subassembly selection, *J. Manufacturing Science and Engineering*, **126**, 627-631.

Anglano, C., Giordana, A., and Bello, G. L. (1999). High-performance data mining on networks of workstations, *Proc. 11th Int. Symposium on Intelligent Systems*, Warsaw, Poland, June 1999, 520-528.

Apté, C., Weiss, S., Grout, G. (1993). Predicting defects in disk drive manufacturing: a case study in high-dimensional classification, *Proc. 9th Conf. Artificial Intelligence on Applications*, 212-218.

Au, W.-H., Chan, K. C. C., and Yao, X. (2003). A novel evolutionary data mining algorithm with applications to churn prediction, *IEEE Trans. On Evolutionary Computation*, **7**(6), 532-545.

Backus, P., Janakiram, M., Movzoon, S., Runger, G., and Bhargava, A. (2006). Factory cycle-time prediction with a data-mining approach, *IEEE Trans. On Semiconductor Manufacturing*, **19**(2), 252-258.

Bansal, K., Vadhavkar, S., Gupta, A. (1998). Neural network based forecasting techniques for inventory control applications, *Data Mining and Knowledge Discovery*, **2**, 97-102.

Bergeret, F. and Le Gall C. (2003). Yield improvement using statistical analysis of process dates, *IEEE Trans. On Semiconductor Manufacturing*, **16**(3), 535-542.

Berry, M. J. A. and Linoff, G. (2004). *Data Mining Techniques: For Marketing, Sales, and Customer Support*, Wiley: New York, NY, U.S.A.

Bertino, E., Catania, B., and Caglio, E. (1999). Applying data mining techniques to wafer manufacturing, *Technical Report*, University of Milan, Italy, 1999 (http://citeseer.nj.nec.com/context/1457533/377982).

Besse, P. and Le Gall, C. (2005). Application and reliability of change-point analyses for detecting a defective stage in integrated circuit manufacturing (http://www.lsp.ups-tlse.fr/Recherche/Publications/2005/bes02.pdf).

Black, M. and Hickey, R. (1999). Maintaining the performance of a learned classifier under concept drift, *Intelligent Data Analysis*, **3**, 453-474.

Black, M. and Hickey, R. (2003). Learning classification rules for telecom customer call data under concept drift, *Soft Computing*, **8**, 102-108.

Bolton, R. J. and Hand, D. J. (2002). Statistical fraud detection: a review, *Statistical Science,* **17**(3), 235-255.

Braha, D. (Ed.) (2001). *Data Mining for Design and Manufacturing: Methods and Applications*, Kluwer: New York, NY, U.S.A.

Braha, D., Elovici, Y., and Last, M. (2007). Theory of actionable data mining with application to semiconductor manufacturing control, *Int. J. Production Research*, **45**(13), 3059-3084.

Braha, D. and Shmilovici, A. (2002). Data mining for improving a cleaning process in the semiconductor industry, *IEEE Trans. On Semiconductor Manufacturing*, **15**(1), 91-101.

Braha, D. and Shmilovici, A. (2003). On the use of decision tree induction for discovery of interactions in a photolithographic process, *IEEE Trans. Semiconductor Manufacturing*, **16**(4), 644-652.

Brence, J. R. and Brown, D. E. (2002). Data mining corrosion from eddy current non-destructive tests, *Computers & IE*, **43**, 821-840.

Brijs, T., Swinnen, G., Vanhoof, K., and Wets, G. (2004). Building an association rules framework to improve product assortment decisions, *Data Mining and Knowledge Discovery*, **8**, 7-23.

Buddhakulsomsiri, J., Siradeghyan, Y., Zakarian, A., and Li, X. (2006). Association rule-generation algorithm for mining automotive warranty data, *Int. J Production Research*, **44**(14), 2749-2770.

Büchner, A. G., Anand, S. S., and Hughes, J. G. (1997). Data mining in manufacturing environments: goals, techniques, and applications, *Studies in Informatics and Control*, **6**(4), 319-328.

Burges, J. C. (1998). A tutorial on support vector machines for pattern recognition, *Data Mining and Knowledge Discovery*, **2**, 121-167.

Cannataro, M., Congiusta, A., Talia, D., and Trunfio, P. (2002). A data mining toolset for distributed high-performance platforms, *Proc. 3rd Int. Conf. Data Mining*, Bologna, Italy, September, 41-50.

Cannataro, M. and Talia, D. (2003). The Knowledge Grid, *Communications of the ACM*, **46**(1), 89-93.

Chang, P. C., Hsieh, J.C., and Liao, T. W. (2005b). Evolving fuzzy rules for due date assignment problem in semiconductor manufacturing factory," *J. of Intelligent Manufacturing*, **16**(4-5), 549-557.

Chang, P. C. and Liao, T. W. (2002). Generation of fuzzy due-date assignment rules, *FSKD'02, Proc. 1st Int. Conf. on Fuzzy Systems and Knowledge Discovery, Vol. II,* Nov. 18-22, 2002, Orchid Country Club, Singapore, 611-615.

Chang, P. C. and Liao, T. W. (2006). Combining SOM and fuzzy rule base for flow time prediction in semiconductor manufacturing factory," *Applied Soft Computing*, **6**(2), 198-206.

Chang, P. C., Wang, Y.-W., and Tsai, C.-Y. (2005a). Evolving neural network for printed circuit board sales forecasting, *Expert Systems with Applications*, **29**, 83-92.

Chattratichat, J., Darlington, J., Guo, Y., Hedvall, S., Köhler, M., and Syed, J. (1999). An architecture for distributed enterprise data mining, *Lecture Notes of Computer Science 1593*, 573-582.

Chen, F.-L. and Liu, S.-F. (2000). A neural-network approach to recognize defect spatial pattern in semiconductor fabrication, *IEEE Transactions on Semiconductor Manufacturing*, 13(3), 366-373.

Chen L.-D., Sakaguchi, T., and Frolick, M. N. (2000a) Data mining methods, applications, and tools, *Information Systems Management*, Winter 2000, 65-70.

Chen, M.-C., Huang, C.-L., Chen, K.-Y., and Wu, H.-P. (2005). Aggregation of orders in distribution centers using data mining, *Expert Systems with Applications*, **28**, 453-460.

Chen, Q., Dayal, U., and Hsu, M. (2000b). OLAP-based data mining for business intelligence applications in telecommunications and e-commerce, S. Bhalla (Ed.): DNIS 2000, LNCS 1966, 1-19.

Chen, W.-C., Tseng, S.-S., and Wang, C.-Y. (2004). A novel manufacturing defect detection method using data mining approach, *IEA/AIE 2004, LNAI 3029*, 77-86.

Chien, C.-F., Wang, W.-C., and Cheng, J.-C. (2007). Data mining for yield enhancement in semiconductor manufacturing and an empirical study, *Expert Systems with Applications*, **33**, 192-198.

Chu, Y.-H., Lee, Y.-H., and Han, C. (2004a). Improved quality estimation and knowledge extraction in a batch process by bootstrapping-based generalized variable selection, *Ind. Eng. Chem. Res.*, **43**, 1680-1690.

Chu, Y.-H., Qin, S. J., and Han, C. (2004b). Fault detection and operation mode identification based on pattern classification with variable selection, *Ind. Eng. Chem. Res.*, **43**, 1701-1710.

Coppola, M., Pesciullesi, P., Ravazzolo, R., and Zoccolo, C. (20204). A parallel knowledge discovery system for customer profiling, M. Danelutto, D. Laforenza, M. Vanneschi (Eds.): Euro-Par 2004, LNCS 3149, 381-390.

Corts, C. and Vapnik, V. N. (1995). Support vector networks, *Machine Learning*, **20**, 273-297.

Cox, L. A., Jr. (2002). Data mining and causal modeling of customer behavior, *Telecommunication Systems*, **21**(2-4), 349-381.

Crespo, F. and Weber, R. (2005). A methodology for dynamic data mining based on fuzzy clustering, *Fuzzy Sets and Systems*, **150**, 267-284.

Cunha, C. D., Agard, B., and Kusiak, A., Data mining for improvement of product quality, *Int. J. Production Research*, **44**(18-19), 4027-4041.

Cunningham, S. P. and MacKinnon, S. (1998). Statistical methods for visual defect metrology, *IEEE Transactions on Semiconductor Manufacturing*, **11**(1), 48-53.

Darlington, J., Guo, Y., Sutiwaraphum, J., and To, H. W. (1997). Parallel induction algorithms for data mining, *Proc. 2nd Int. Symposium on Intelligent Data Analysis (IDA '97)*, London, U. K., August 4-6, 1997, 437-445.

Daskalaki, S., Kopanas, I., Goudara, M., and Avouris, N. (2003). Data mining for decision support on customer insolvency in telecommunications business, *European J. of Operational Research*, **145**, 239-255.

Dengiz, R., Smith, a. E., and Nettleship, I. (2006). Two-stage data mining for flaw identification in ceramics manufacture, *Int. J. Production Research*, **44**(14), 2839-2851.

Fayyad, U. M. and Irani, K. B. (1993). Multi-interval discretization of continuous-valued attributes, *Proc. 13th Int'l Joint Conf. Artificial Intelligence*, 1993, 1022-1027.

Fayyad, U., Shapiro, G. P., and Smyth, P. (1996). The KDD process for extracting useful knowledge from volumes of data, *Commun. of the ACM*, **39**, 27-34.

Garcia-Flores, R., Wang, X. Z., and Burfess, T. F. (2003). Tuning inventory policy parameters in a small chemical company, *Journal of the Operational Research Society*, **54**, 350-361.

Garcia-Munos, S., Kourti, T., McGregor, J. F., Mateos, A. G., and Murphy, G. (2003). Troubleshooting of an industrial batch process using multivariate methods, *Ind. Eng. Chem. Res.*, **42**, 3592-3601.

Gardner, M. and Bieker, J. (2000). Data mining solves tough semiconductor manufacturing problems, *Proc. KDD 2000*, Boston, MA, U.S.A., 376-383.

Ge, X. and Smyth, P. (2000). Segmental semi-Markov models for change-point detection with applications to semiconductor manufacturing, *Technical*

Report UCI-ICS 00-08, Department of Information and Computer Science, University of California, Irvine, March 2000.

Gertosio, C. and Dussauchoy, A. (2004). Knowledge discovery from industrial databases, *Journal of Intelligent Manufacturing*, **15**, 29-37.

Gibbons, W.M., Ranta, M., Scott, T. M., and Mantyla, M. (2000). Information management and process improvement using data mining techniques, R. Loganantharaj et al. (Eds.): IEA/AIE 2000, LNAI 1821, 2000, 93-98.

Green, P. J. (1995). Reversible jump Markov chain Monte Carlo computation and Bayesian model determination," *Biometrika*, 82, 711-732.

Grochowski, M. and Jankowski, N. (2004). Comparison of instances selection algorithms II. Results and comments, ICAISC 2004, LNAI 3070, L. Rutkowski *et al.* (Eds.), 580-585.

Ha, S. H., Bae, S. M., and Park, S. C. (2002). Customer's time variant purchase behavior and corresponding marketing strategies: an on-line retailer's case, *Computers & IE*, **43**, 801-820.

Hall, L. O., Chawla, N., Bowyer, K. W., and Kegelmeyer, W. P. (2000). Learning rules from distributed data, *Large-Scale Data Mining*, LNAI 1750, M. J. Zaki and C.-T. Ho (Eds.), Springer-Verlag, 211-220.

Hall, M. A. and Holmes, G. (2003). Benchmarking attribute selection techniques for discrete class data mining, *IEEE Trans. On Knowledge and Data Engineering*, **15**(6), 1437-1447.

Hamuro, Y., Katoh, N., Matsuda, Y., Yada, K. (1998). Mining pharmacy data helps to make profits, *Data Mining and Knowledge Discovery*, 2, 391-398.

Han, J. and Kamber, M. (2001). *Data Mining: Concepts and Techniques*, Morgan Kaufmann: San Francisco, CA, U.S.A.

Han, Y., Kim, J., and Lee, C. (2005). Automatic detection of failure patterns using data mining, R. Khosla et al. (Eds.), KES 2005, LNAI 3682, 1312-1316.

Hand, D., Mannila, H., and Smyth, P. (2001). *Principles of Data Mining*, MIT Press: Cambridge, MA, U.S.A.

Harding, J. A., Shahbaz, M., Srinivas, S., and Kusiak, A. (2006). Data mining in manufacturing: a review, *Journal of Manufacturing Science and Engineering*, **128**, 969-976.

Harrison, P. G. and Lladó, C. M. (2000). Performance evaluation of a distributed enterprise data mining system, *TOOLS 2000, LNCS 1786*, 2000, 117-131.

Haughton, D., Deichmann, J., Eshghi, A., Sayek, S., Teebagy, N., and Topi, H. (2003). "A review of software packages for data mining," *The American Statistician*, **57**(4), 290-309.

Ho, G. T. S., Lau, H. C. W., Lee, C. K. M., Ip, A. W. H., and Pun, K. F. (2006). An intelligent production workflow mining system for continual quality enhancement, *Int. J. Adv. Manuf. Technol.*, **28**, 792-809.

Hormozi, A. M. and Giles, S. (2004). Data mining: a competitive weapon for banking and retail industries, *Information Systems Management*, Spring 2004, 62-71.

Hou, T.-H. and Huang, C.-C. (2004). Application of fuzzy logic and variable precision rough set approach in a remote monitoring manufacturing process for diagnosis rule induction, *J. of Intelligent Manufacturing*, **15**, 395-408.

Hsu, C. W. and Lin, C. J. (2002). A comparison of methods for multi-class support vector machines, *IEEE Trans. On Neural Networks*, **13**(2), 415-425.

Hsu, C.-H. and Wang, M.-J. J. (2005). Using decision tree based data mining to establish a sizing system for the manufacture of garments, *Int. J. Advanced Manufacturing Technology*, **26**, 669-674.

Hsu, S.-C. and Chien, C.-F. (2007). Hybrid data mining approach for pattern extraction from wafer bin map to improve yield in semiconductor manufacturing, *Int. J. Production Economics*, **107**, 88-103.

Huang, C.-C., Tseng, T.-L., Chuang, H.-F., and Liang, H.-F. (2006). Rough-set-based approach to manufacturing process document retrieval, *Int. J. Production Research*, **44**(14), 2889-2911.

Huang, H. and Wu, D. (2005). Product quality improvement analysis using data mining: a case study in ultra-precision manufacturing industry, L. Wang and Y. Jin (Eds.), FSKD 2005, LNAI 3614, 577-580.

Huang, H.-P. and Liu, Y.-H. (2002). Fuzzy support vector machines for pattern recognition and data mining, *Int. J. Fuzzy Systems*, **4**(3), 826-835.

Hur, J., Lee, H., and Baek, J.-G. (2006). An intelligent manufacturing process diagnosis system using hybrid data mining, ICDM 2006, LNAI 4065, P. Perner (Ed.), 561-575.

Jankowski, N. and Grochowski, M. (2004). Comparison of instances selection algorithms I. algorithms survey, ICAISC 2004, LNAI 3070, L. Rutkowski *et al.* (Eds.), 598-603.

Jeong, M. K., Lu, J.-C., Huo, X., Vidakovic, B., and Chen, D. (2006). Wavelet-based data reduction techniques for process fault detection, *Technometrics*, **48**(1), 26-40.

Jiao, J. and Zhang, Y. (2005). Product portfolio identification based on association rule mining, *Computer-Aided Design*, **37**, 149-172.

Jin, J. and Shi, J. (2001). Automatic feature extraction of waveform signals for in-process diagnostic performance improvement, *J. of Intelligent Manufacturing*, **12**, 257-268.

Johnson, E. L. and Kargupta, H. (2000). Collective, hierarchical clustering from distributed, heterogeneous data, *Large-Scale Data Mining*, LNAI 1750, M. J. Zaki and C.-T. Ho (Eds.), Springer-Verlag: Berlin Heidelberg, Germany, 221-244.

Karim, M. A., Halgamuge, S., Smith, A. J. R., and Hsu, A. L. (2006) Manufacturing yield improvement by clustering, ICONIP 2006, Part III,

LNCS 4234, I. King et al. (Eds.), Springer-Verlag: Berlin Heidelberg, Germany, 526-534.

Keim, D. A. (2002). Information visualization and visual data mining, *IEEE Trans. On Visualization and Computer Graphics*, **8**(1), 1-8.

Kim, S., Shin, K.-S., Park, K. (2005). An application of support vector machines for customer churn analysis: credit card case, L. Wang, K. Chen, Y. S. Ong (Eds.): ICNC 2005, LNCS 3611, 636-647.

Kim, S.-J., Yun, D.-S., and Chang, B.-S., Association analysis of customer services from the enterprise customer management system, ICDM 2006, LNAI 4065, P. Perner (Ed.), 279-283.

Kittler, R. and Wang, W. (1999). The emerging role for data mining, *Solid State Technology*, **42**(11), 1-11.

Klusch, M., Lodi, S., and Moro, G. (2003). Agent-based distributed data mining: the KDEC scheme, *Intelligent Information Agents*, LNAI 2586, M. Klusch *et al.* (Eds.), Springer-Verlag, 104-122.

Kohavi, R., Mason, L., Parekh, R., and Zheng, Z. (2004). Lessons and challenges from mining retail e-commerce data, *Machine Learning*, **57**, 83-113.

Koonce, D. A. and Tsai, S.-C. (2000). Using data mining to find patterns in genetic algorithm solutions to a job shop schedule, *Computers & Industrial Engineering*, **38**, 361-374.

Kot, V. and Yedatore, M. (2003). The next step in e-diagnostics: mining the tool sensors, *Semiconductor International*, Oct 2003, 45-48.

Kuo, R. J. (2001). A sales forecasting system based on fuzzy neural network with initial weights generated by genetic algorithm, *European J. of Operational Research*, **129**, 496-517.

Kuo, R. J., An, Y. L., Wang, H. S., and Chung, W. J. (2006). Integration of self-organizing feature maps neural network and genetic K-means algorithm for market segmentation, *Expert Systems with Applications*, **30**, 313-324.

Kuo, R. J., Ho, L. M., and Hu, C. M. (2002). Integration of self-organizing feature map and K-means algorithm for market segmentation, *Computers & OR*, **29**, 1475-1493.

Kusiak, A. (2001). Rough set theory: a data mining tool for semiconductor manufacturing, *IEEE Transactions on Electronics Packaging Manufacturing*, **24**(1), 44-50.

Kusiak, A. (2002). A data mining approach for generation of control signatures, *J. Manufacturing Science and Engineering*, **124**, 923-925.

Kusiak, A. (2006). Data mining: manufacturing and service applications, *Int. J. Production Research*, **44**(18-19), 4175-4191.

Kusiak, A. and Kurasek, C. (2001). Data mining of printed-circuit board defects, *IEEE Transactions of Robotics and Automation*, **17**(2), 191-196.

Kwak, C. and Yih, Y. (2004). Data-mining approach to production control in the computer-integrated testing cell, *IEEE Transactions on Robotics and Automation*, 20(1), 107-116.

Lada, E. K., Lu, J.-C., and Wilson, J. R. (2002). A wavelet-based procedure for process fault detection, *IEEE Trans. On Semiconductor Manufacturing*, 15(1), 79-90.

Larivière, B. and Van den Poel, D. (2005). Predicting customer retention and profitability by using random forests and regression forests techniques, *Expert Systems with Applications*, 29, 472-484.

Last, M. and Kandel, A. (1999). Automated perception in data mining, *Proc. IEEE Int. Fuzzy Systems Conf.,* Part I, Seoul, Korea, Aug. 1999, 190-197.

Last, M. and Kandel, A. (2001). Data mining for process and quality control in semiconductor industry, in *Data Mining for Design and Manufacturing: Methods and Applications*, D. Braha (Ed.), Kluwer Academic Publishers: Boston, MA, U.S.A.

Last, M. and Kandel, A. (2002). Perception-based analysis of engineering experiments in the semiconductor industry, *Int. J. Image and Graphics*, **2**(1), 107-126.

Last, M. and Kandel, A. (2004). Discovering useful and understandable patterns in manufacturing data, *Robotics and Autonomous Systems*, **49**, 137-152.

Lavielle, M. (1998). Optimal segmentation of random process, *IEEE Transactions on Signal Processing*, **46**(5), 1365-1373.

Lee, D. and Lee, V. C. S. (2004). An alternative methodology for mining seasonal pattern using self-organizing map, *PAKDD 2004, LNAI 3056*, H. Dai, R. Srikant, and C. Zhang (Eds.), 424-430.

Lee, J. H., Yu, S. J., and Park, S. C. (2001). Design of intelligent data sampling methodology based on data mining, *IEEE Transactions on Robotics and Automation*, **17**(5), 637-649.

Lee, T.-S., Chiu, C.-C., Chou, Y.-C., and Lu, C.-J. (2006). Mining the customer credit using classification and regression tree and multivariate adaptive regression splines, *Computational Statistics & Data Analysis*, **50**, 1113-1130.

Li, D.-C., Wu, C.-S., Tsai, T.-I., and Chang, F. M. (2006). Using mega-fuzzification and data trend estimation in small dataset learning for early FMS scheduling knowledge, *Computers & OR*, **33**, 1857-1869.

Li, F., Runger, G. C., and Tuv, E. (2006a). Supervised learning for change-point detection, *Int. J. Production Research*, **44**(14), 2853-2868.

Li, T.-S., Huang, C.-L., and Wu, Z.-Y. (2006b). Data mining using genetic programming for construction of a semiconductor manufacturing yield rate prediction system, *J. Intelligent Manufacturing*, **17**, 355-361.

Li, X. and Olafsson, S., Discovering dispatching rules using data mining, *J. of Scheduling*, **8**, 515-527.

Lian, J., Lai, X. M., Lin, Z. Q., and Yao, F. S. (2002). Application of data mining and process knowledge discovery in sheet metal assembly and dimensional variation diagnosis, *J. Materials Processing Technology*, **129**, 315-320.

Liao, T. W. (2003). Classification of welding flaw types with fuzzy expert systems, *Expert Systems with Applications*, **25**, 101-111.

Liu, H. and Motoda, H. (Eds.) (2001). *Instance Selection and Construction for Data Mining*, Kluwer Academic Publishers: Boston, MA, U.S.A.

Maimon, O. and Last, M. (2000). *Knowledge Discovery and Data Mining, the Info-Fuzzy Network Methodology*, Kluwer Academic Publishers: Boston, MA, U.S.A.

Maki, H. and Teranishi, Y. (2001). Development of automated data mining system for quality control in manufacturing, *DaWaK 2001, LNCS 2114,* Y. Kambayashi, W. Winiwarter, and M. Arikawa (Eds.), 93-100.

McDonald, C. J. (1999). New tools for yield improvement in integrated circuit manufacturing: can they be applied to reliability? *Microelectronics Reliability*, **39**, 731-739.

Meel, A., Venkat, A. N., and Gudi, R. D. (2003). Disturbance classification and rejection using pattern recognition methods, *Ind. Eng. Chem. Res.*, **42**, 3321-3333.

Menon, R., Tong, L. H., Sathiyakeerthi, S., Brombacher, A., and Leong, C. (2004). The needs and benefits of applying text data mining within the product development process, *Quality and Reliability Engineering International*, **20**, 1-15.

Merz, C. J. and Murphy, P. M. (1998). UCI repository of machine learning databases, http://www.ics.uci.edu/~mlearn/MLRepository.html.

Milne, R., Drummond, M., and Renoux, P. (1998). Predicting paper making defects on-line using data mining, *Knowledge-Based Systems*, **11**, 331-338.

Mitra, S., Pal, S. K., and Mitra, P. (2002). Data mining in soft computing framework: a survey, *IEEE Transactions on Neural Networks*, 13(1), 3-14.

Morik, K. and Köpcke, H. (2004). Analyzing customer churn in insurance data – a case study, J.-F. Boulicaut et al. (Eds.): KPDD 2004, LNAI 3202, 325-336.

Mozer, M.C., Wolniewicz, R., Grimes, D. B., Johnson, E., and Kaushansky, H. (2000). Predicting subscriber dissatisfaction and improving retention in the wireless telecommunications industry, *IEEE Trans. On Neural Networks*, 11(3), 690-696.

Nemati, H. R. and Barko, C. D. (2002). Enhancing enterprise decisions through organizational data mining, *Journal of Computer Information Systems*, Summer, 21-28.

Ng, K. and Liu, H. (2000). Customer retention via data mining, *Artificial Intelligence Review*, **14**, 569-590.

Oliveira, M. C. F., and Levkowitz, H. (2003). From visual data exploration to visual data mining: a survey, *IEEE Trans. On Visualization and Computer Graphics*, **9**(3), 378-394.

Ong, C.-S., Huang, J.-J., and Tzeng, G.-H. (2005). Building credit scoring models using genetic programming, *Expert Systems with Applications*, **29**, 41-47.

Öztürk, A., Kayaligil, S., and Özdemirel, N. E. (2006). Manufacturing lead time estimation using data mining, *European J. of Operational Research*, **173**, 683-700.

Pach, F. P., Feil, B., Nemeth, S., Arva, P., and Abonyi, J. (2006). Process-data-warehousing-based operator support system for complex production technologies, *IEEE Transactions on Systems, Man, and Cybernetics-Part A: Systems and Humans*, **36**(1), 136-153.

Parola, M., Sundell, H., Virtanen, J., and Lang, D. (2000). Web tension profile and gravure parts runability, *Pulp & Paper Canada*, **101**(2), T35-T39.

Peng, Y. (2004). Intelligent condition monitoring using fuzzy inductive learning, *Journal of Intelligent Manufacturing*, 15, 373-380.

Perner, P., Zscherpel, U., and Jacobsen, C. (2001). A comparison between neural networks and decision trees based on data from industrial radiographic testing, *Pattern Recognition Letters*, **22**, 47-54.

Phua, C., Alahakoon, D., and Lee, V. (2006). Minority report on fraud detection: classification of skewed data, *Sigkdd Explorations*, 6(1), 50-59.

Pizzuti, C. and Talia, D. (2003). P-AutoClass: scalable parallel clustering for mining large datasets, *IEEE Trans. On Knowledge and Data Engineering*, **15**(3), 629-641.

Porzio, G. C. and Ragozini, G. (2003). "Visually mining off-line data for quality improvement," *Quality and Reliability Engineering International*, **19**, 273-283.

Povinelli, R. J. and Feng, X. (2003). A new temporal pattern identification method for characterization and prediction of complex time series events, *IEEE Transactions on Knowledge and Data Engineering*, **15**(2), 339-352.

Prodromidis, A. L., Chan, P. K., and Stolfo, S. J. (2000). Meta-learning in distributed data mining systems: issues and approaches, in *Advances in Distributed and Parallel Knowledge Discovery*, H. Kargupta and P. K. Chan (Eds.), AAAI Press/MIT Press: Boston, MA, U.S.A., 81-87.

Qian, Z., Jiang, W., and Tusi, K.-L. (2006). Churn detection via customer profile modeling, *Int. J. Production Research*, **44**(14), 2913-2933.

Rietman, E. A., Whitlock, S. A., Beachy, M., Roy, A., and Willingham, T. L. (2001). A system model for feedback control and analysis of yield: a multistep process model of effective gate length, polyline width, and IV parameters, *IEEE Transactions on Semiconductor Manufacturing*, **14**(1), 32-47.

Romanowski, C. J. and Nagi, R. (2005). On comparing bills of materials: a similarity/distance measure of unordered trees, *IEEE Trans. On Systems, Man, and Cybernetics-Part A: Systems and Humans*, **35**(2), 249-260.

Romanowski, C. J., Nagi, R., and Sudit, M. (2006). Data mining in an engineering design environment: OR applications from graph matching, *Computers & OR*, **33**, 3150-3160.

Roverso, D. (2002). Plant diagnostics by transient classification: the ALADDIN approach, *Int. J. Intelligent Systems*, **17**, 767-790.

Saxena, S. (1993). Fault isolation during semiconductor manufacturing using automated discovery from wafer tracking databases, *Proc. Knowledge Discovery in Databases Workshop*, 81-88.

Sasisikharan, R., Seshadri, V., and Weiss, S. M. (1996). Data mining and forecasting in large-scale telecommunication networks, *IEEE Experts*, Feb, 37-43.

Sebzalli, Y. M. and Wang, X. Z. (2001). Knowledge discovery from process operational data using PCA and fuzzy clustering, *Engineering Applications of Artificial Intelligence*, **14**, 607-616.

Sexton, R. S., McMurtrey, S., and Cleavenger, D. J. (2006). Knowledge discovery using a neural network simultaneous optimization algorithm on a real world classification problem, *European J. Operational Research*, **168**, 1009-1018.

Sha, D. Y. and Liu, C.-H. (2005). Using data mining for due date assignment in a dynamic job shop environment, *Int. J. Adv. Manuf. Technol.*, **25**, 1164-1174.

Shao, X.-Y., Wang, Z.-H., Li, P.-G., and Feng, C.-X. J. (2006). Integrating data mining and rough set for customer group-based discovery of product configuration rules, *Int. J. Production Research*, **44**(14), 2789-2811.

Shi, X., Schillings, P., and Boyd, D. (2004). Applying artificial neural networks and virtual experimental design to quality improvement of two industrial processes, *Int. J. Production Research.*, **42**(1), 101-118.

Shi, Y., Peng, Y., Xu, W., and Tang, X. (2002). Data mining via multiple criteria linear programming: applications in credit card portfolio management, *Int. J. of Information Technology & Decision Making*, **1**(1), 131-151.

Singhal, A. and Seborg, D. E. (2002). Pattern matching in multivariate time series databases using a moving-window approach, *Ind. Eng. Chem. Res.*, **41**, 3822-3838.

Soares, C. (2003). Is the UCI repository useful for data mining? F. M. Pires and S. Abrue (Eds.), *EPIA 2003 LNAI 2902,* 209-223.

Srinivasan, R., Wang, C., Ho, W. K., and Lim, K. W. (2004). Dynamic principal component analysis based methodology for clustering process states in agile chemical plants, *Ind. Eng. Chem. Res.*, **43**, 2123-2139.

Sterritt, R., Adamson, K., Shapcott, C. M., and Curran, E. P. (2000). Parallel data mining of Bayesian networks from telecommunications network data, J. Rolim et al. (Eds.): IPDPS 2000 Workshops, LNCS 1800, 415-422.

Strobel, C. M. and Hrycej, T. (2006). A data mining approach to the joint evaluation of field and manufacturing data in automotive industry, PKDD

2006, LNAI 4213, J. Fürnkranz et al. (Eds.), Springer-Verlag: Berlin Heidelberg, Germany, 625-632.

Su, C.-T., Chen, Y.-H., and Sha, D. Y. (2006). Linking innovative product development with customer knowledge: a data mining approach, *Technovation*, **26**, 784-795.

Sugimori, H., Iida, Y., Suka, M., Ichimura, T., and Yoshida, K. (2003). Data mining for seeking relationships between sickness absence and Japanese worker's profile, V. Palade, R. J. Howlett, and L. C. Jain (Eds.), *KES 2003, LNAI 2774,* 410-416.

Sun, T.-L. and Kuo, W.-L. (2002). Visual exploration of production data using small multiples design with non-uniform color mapping, *Computers & IE,* **43**, 751-764.

Tong, W. and Li, Y. (2005). Wavelet method combining BP networks and time series ARMA modeling for data mining forecasting, L. Wang, K. Chen, and Y. S. Ong (Eds.): *ICNC 2005, LNCS 3611*, 123-134.

Tsai, Y.-C., Cheng, C.-H., and Chang, J.-R. (2006). A new knowledge discovery model for extracting diagnosis rules of manufacturing process, *Materials Science Forum*, Vols. **505-507**, 889-894.

Tseng, T.-L., Huang, C.-C., Jiang, F., and Ho, J. C. (2006). Applying a hybrid data-mining approach to prediction problems: a case of preferred suppliers prediction, *Int. J. Production Research*, **44**(14), 2935-2954.

Tseng, T.-L., Jothishankar, M. C., and Wu, T. (2004). Quality control problem in printed circuit board manufacturing-an extended rough set theory approach, *J. Manufacturing Systems*, **23**(1), 56-72.

Triantaphyllou, E. (2007). Data Mining and Knowledge Discovery via a Logic-Based Approach (a monograph), Springer: Boston, MA, U.S.A., Massive Computing Series, 420 pages, in print.

Triantaphyllou, E. and Felici, G. (Eds.) (2006). *Data Mining and Knowledge Discovery Approaches Based on Rule Induction Techniques*, Springer: Boston, MA, U.S.A.

Wang, C.H., Wang, S.-J., and Lee, W.-D. (2006). Automatic identification of spatial defect patterns for semiconductor manufacturing, *Int. J. Production Research*, **44**(23), 5169-5185.

Wang, K., Zhou, S., Yang, Q., Yeung, J. M. S. (2005a). Mining customer value: from association rules to direct marketing, *Data Mining and Knowledge Discovery*, **11**, 57-79.

Wang, X. Z., Chen, B. H., and McGreavy, C. (1997). Data mining for failure diagnosis of process units by learning probabilistic networks, *Trans. IChemE*, **75**, Part B, 210-216.

Wang, X. Z. and McGreavy, C. (1998). Automatic classification for mining process operational data, *Industrial Engineering Chemical Research*, **37**, 2215-2222.

Wang, Y., Wang, S., and Lai, K. K. (2005b). A new fuzzy support vector machine to evaluate credit risk, *IEEE Transactions on Fuzzy Systems*, **13**(6), 820-831.

Whittaker, J., Whitehead, C., and Somers, M. (2005). The neglog transformation and quantile regression for the analysis of a large credit scoring database, *Appl. Statist.*, **54**(5), 863-878.

Witten, I. H. and Frank, E. (2000). *Data Mining: Practical Machine Learning Tools and Techniques with Java Implementations*, Morgan Kaufmann: San Francisco, CA, U.S.A.

Wong, R. C.-W., Fu, A. W.-C., and Wang, K. (2005). Data mining for inventory item selection with cross-selling considerations, *Data Mining and Knowledge Discovery*, **11**, 81-112.

Wu, C. (2006). Applying frequent itemset mining to identify a small itemset that satisfies a large percentage of orders in a warehouse, *Computers & OR*, **33**, 3161-3170.

Yada, K., Hamuro, Y., Katoh, N., Washio, T., Fusamoto, I., Fujishima, D., and Ikeda, T. (2005) Data mining oriented CRM systems based on MUSASHI: C-MUSASHI, S. Tsumoto et al. (Eds.), *AM 2003, LNAI 3430*, 152-173.

Yield dynamics turns to data mining for semiconductor yield management, *Data Mining News*, **2**(15), March 29, 1999.

Yu, C.-Y. and Huang, H.-P. (2002). On-line learning delivery decision support system for highly product mixed semiconductor foundry, *IEEE Trans. On Semiconductor Manufacturing*, **15**(2), 274-278.

Yu, H., MacGregor, J. F., Haarsma, G., and Bourg, W. (2003). Digital imaging for online monitoring and control of industrial snack food processes, *Ind. Eng. Chem. Res.*, **42**, 3036-3044.

Zhai, L.-Y., Khoo, L.-P., and Fok, S.-C. (2002). Feature extraction using rough set theory and genetic algorithms-an application for the simplification of product quality evaluation, *Computers & IE*, **43**, 661-676.

Zhang, F. and Apley, D. (2003). MLPCA based logistical regression analysis for pattern clustering in manufacturing processes, J. Liu et al. (Eds.): IDEAL 2003, LNCS 2690, 898-902.

Zhang, X., Gong, W., and Kawamura, Y. (2004). Customer behavior pattern discovering with web mining, *APWeb 2004,* LNCS 3007, J. X. Yu, X. Lin, H. Lu, and Y. Zhang (Eds.), Springer-Verlag: Berlin Heidelberg, Germany, 844-853.

Zhang, X.-B., Li, X.-F., Zhao, K., and Guan, X. (2004). A data mining algorithm based on grid, FCC 2003, LNCS 3033, M. Li *et al.* (Eds.), 807-810.

Zhao, Y., Li, B., Li, X., Liu, W., and Ren, S. (2005). Customer churn prediction using improved one-class support vector machine, X. Li, S. Wang, and Z. Y. Dong (Eds.), ADMA 2005, LNAI 3584, 300-306.

Zhou, Z.-H. (2003). "Three perspectives of data mining," *Artificial Intelligence*, **143**, 139-146.

Author's Biographical Statement

T. Warren Liao graduated with a BS degree in Industrial Engineering (IE) from the National Taipei University of Technology, Taiwan, in 1977. He received his MS and Ph.D. degrees also both in IE from Lehigh University, U.S.A. in 1984 and 1990, respectively. Since 1990, he has been with Louisiana State University, U.S.A. Dr. Liao's research started in the area of creep feed grinding of ceramics with diamond wheels. Since then, he has diversified his research portfolios to include cellular manufacturing, intelligent manufacturing, automated inspection, applied soft computing, and data mining. His research has been supported by private industries, Louisiana's Board of Regents, U.S. Army Research Laboratory, Oak Ridge National Laboratory, and the National Science Foundation.

Dr. Liao has more than 60 refereed journal publications. He has served as a Guest Editor for several journals. He together with Dr. E. Triantaphyllou organized the International Workshop on "Data Mining in Manufacturing Enterprise Systems", as part of the Mathematics and Machine Learning (MML) Conference, held on June 23, 2004 at Como, Italy. He was a Research Fellow with the U.S. Army Research Laboratory from September 2001 to August 2002 and also a Visiting Professor at the Yuan Ze University, Taiwan, in the summer of 2004.

Chapter 2[1]

Application and Comparison of Classification Techniques in Controlling Credit Risk

Lan Yu[1], Guoqing Chen[2,3], Andy Koronios[4], Shiwu Zhu[2], Xunhua Guo[2]
[1]Department of Computer Science and Technology
[2]School of Economics and Management
[3]Research Center for Contemporary Management,
Tsinghua University, Beijing 100084, China.
[4]School of Computer and Information Science, University of South Australia, Australia.

Abstract: Credit rating is a powerful tool that can help banks improve loan quality and decrease credit risk. This chapter examines major classification techniques, which include traditional statistical models (LDA, QDA and logistic regression), *k*-nearest neighbors, Bayesian networks (Naïve Bayes and TAN), decision trees (C4.5), associative classification (CBA), a neural network and support vector machines (SVM), and applies them to controlling credit risk. The experiments were conducted on 244 rated companies mainly from the Industrial and Commercial Bank of China. The receiver operating characteristic curve and the Delong-Pearson method were adopted to verify and compare their performance. The results reveal that while traditional statistical models produced the poorest outcomes, C4.5 or SVM did not perform satisfactorily, and CBA seemed to be the best choice for credit rating in terms of predictability and interpretability.

***Key Words*:** Classification, credit risk, ROC curve, Delong-Pearson method.

---

[1] Liao, T.W. and E. Triantaphyllou, (Eds.), **Recent Advances in Data Mining of Enterprise Data: Algorithms and Applications**, *World Scientific*, Singapore, pp. 111-145, 2007.

1. Credit Risk and Credit Rating

In a broad sense, credit risk is the uncertainty or fluctuation of profit in credit activities. People pay high attention to the possible loss of credit assets in the future. In other words, the credit risk is the possibility that some related factors change and affect credit assets negatively, thus leading to the decline of the whole bank's value (Yang, Hua & Yu 2003).

Credit activity in a commercial bank is strongly influenced by the factors from outside as well as inside, such as macro-economic status, industrial situation and internal operations. For example, the credit assets may suffer a loss because of an undesirable movement in interest rates, exchange rates or inflation. Management problems and inappropriate operations in commercial banks may also result in the loss of credit assets. Furthermore, a contractual counterpart may not meet its obligations stated in the contract, thereby causing the bank a financial loss. It is irrelevant whether the counterpart is unable to meet its contractual obligation due to financial distress or is unwilling to honor an unenforceable contract. This chapter focuses on the last kind of risk, i.e., the risk of breaching contracts.

A commercial bank is requested to evaluate the credit level of clients when extending credit to them. Evaluation may not always be correct and these clients' credit level may vary all the time for miscellaneous reasons. If there is a lack of objectivity during the audit process, the loan quality may deteriorate and the bank has to seriously face the risk of losing credit assets. An effective instrument in decreasing credit risk is to use a credit rating system, which is of extraordinary concern in China these years.

Credit rating is a qualified assessment and formal evaluation of a company's credit history and capability of repaying obligations by a credit bureau. It measures the default probability of the borrower, and its ability to repay fully and timely its financial debt obligations (Guo 2003). The credit ratings of these companies are expressed as letter grades such as AAA, A, B, CC, etc. The highest rating is usually AAA, and the lowest is D. '+' and '-' can be attached to these letters so as to make them more precise. Credit rating provides an information channel for both the borrower and the lender, making the capital market to work more effectively. Commercial banks can control their credit risk with the powerful support from credit ratings. If there is no credit rating, the commercial bank has to increase the charge so as to cover the extra risk due to information asymmetry. Therefore, these companies benefit from credit ratings too.

However, to obtain a company's credit rating is usually very costly, since it requires credit bureaus to invest large amounts of time and human resources to perform a deep analysis of the company's risk status based on various aspects ranging from strategic competitiveness to operational level details (Huang, Chen, Hsu, Chen &Wu 2004). This situation may consequently lead to at least two major drawbacks that exist in credit rating. First of all, it is not possible to rate all companies. The number of companies applying for credit rating is too large and rating all of them is intolerable. In addition, rating companies, such as Moody's and Standard & Poors which rate other companies, will not rate companies that are not willing to pay for this service. Secondly, credit rating cannot be performed frequently, so it cannot reflect timely the credit level of companies applying for loans. Usually, the rating work is implemented twice a year and not all companies can afford rating themselves very often. Therefore, intelligent approaches based on data mining are considered to support the credit activities of commercial banks. Such approaches have their own learning mechanisms and become intelligent after they have been trained on historical rating data. They can alarm the bank as soon as they determine that a new client has high risk of breaching a contract.

In past years, quantitative models such as linear discriminant analysis and neural networks have been applied to predict the credit level of new clients and achieved satisfactory performance results (Baesens 2003; Galindo &Tamayo 2000; Huang, Chen, Hsu et al. 2004; Pinches &Mingo 1973). For example, Pinches and Mingo employed discriminant analysis to bond rating data in 1973 (Pinches &Mingo 1973). A logistic regression technique was also applied in this area (Ederington 1985). In addition to these traditional statistical methods, artificial intelligence techniques, such as case based reasoning systems and neural networks, were adopted to improve the prediction ability in credit ratings. Investigations of neural networks and numerous experiments revealed that such methods can normally reach higher accuracy than traditional statistical methods (Dutta & Shekhar 1988; Singleton & Surkan 1990; Moody & Utans 1995; Kim 1993; Maher & Sen 1997). Shin and Han proposed a case based reasoning approach, enhanced with genetic algorithms (GAs) to find an optimal or near optimal weight vector for the attributes of cases in case matching, to predict bond rating of firms (Shin &Han 1999). A good literature review can be found in (Huang, Chen, Hsu et al. 2004; and Shin &Lee 2002).

This chapter endeavors to make a much more comprehensive application of classification techniques in credit rating. More specifically, it applies seven types of classification models that include traditional statistical models (LDA, QDA and logistic regression), *k*-nearest neighbors, Bayesian networks (Naïve Bayes and TAN), a decision tree (C4.5), associative classification (CBA), neural networks, and SVM.

Though the total accuracy is a commonly used measure for classification, in the credit ratings context the cost of rating a bad client as good one is much more expensive than that of rating a good client as a bad one. Thus, in this chapter the receiver operating characteristic (ROC) curve analysis, which takes misclassification error into account, is considered. The value of AUC (area under the receiver operating characteristic curve) is taken as the performance evaluation criterion. The Delong-Pearson method is applied to test if there is a statistically significant difference between each pair of these classification techniques.

Furthermore, our study is to use credit data from China, collected mainly by the Industrial and Commercial Bank of China. The rest of this chapter is organized as follows. The second section describes the data and index used to train the models. Seven types of classification techniques are discussed in the third section, where the principle and characteristics of each technique are elaborated. The experimental settings, the classification performance and a statistical comparison are presented in the fourth section.

2. Data and Variables

In this chapter, the training data are derived from 140 companies that were granted loans from the Industrial and Commercial Bank of China between 2000 and 2002. These companies are described in detail by their financial records and corresponding credit rating. Another 104 companies with similar data are used to derive the test data, while they are mainly the clients of the Bank of Communications, the Bank of China and the CITIC Industrial Bank.

It is difficult to set a crisp criterion to discriminate high risk from low risk. In this chapter, all companies with their credit rating equal to or lower than grade CCC are classified as group 1, which indicates that there is a high possibility of breaching the contract in the future. The rest of the companies constitute group 0. Thus, the training data includes 34 companies from group 1 and 106 from group 0. For the test data, 22 companies were taken from group 1 and 82 companies were taken from group 0.

In this chapter, 18 financial indexes are chosen as the criteria for the credit rating, according to the expertise from the credit bureau of the Industrial and Commercial Bank in Shanghai. These indexes are summarized by means of their financial structure, their ability of paying debt, the management's ability and the operations profitability, as listed in Table 1.

3. Classification Techniques

Classification is a type of data analysis which can help people predict the class labels of the samples to be classified. A wide variety of classification techniques have been proposed in fields such as machine learning, expert systems and statistics. Normally, classification models are trained first on a historical dataset (i.e., the training set) with their class labels already known. Then, these trained classifiers are applied to predict the class labels of new samples.

Table 1. Financial variables for credit rating.

Financial Structure	Net asset/loan ratio	r1
	Asset/liability ratio	r2
	Net fix asset/fix asset book value ratio	r3
	Long-term asset/shareholder equity ratio	r4
Ability of paying debt	Current ratio	r5
	Quick ratio	r6
	Non-financing cash inflow/liquidity liability ratio	r7
	Operating cash inflow/liquidity liability	r8
	Interest coverage	r9
	Contingent debt/net asset ratio	r10
Management Ability	Cash revenue/operating revenue ratio	r11
	Account receivable turnover ratio	r12
	Inventory turnover ratio	r13
	Fix asset turnover ratio	r14
Operation Profitability	Gross profit margin	r15
	Operating profit ratio	r16
	Return on equity	r17
	Return on assets	r18

3.1 Logistic Regression

Logistic regression (LOG) extends the ideas of multiple linear regression to the situation where the dependent variable, y, is discrete. In logistic regression (Hosmer & Lemeshow 2000) no assumptions are made concerning the distribution of the independent variables. Given are a set of N samples (x_i, y_i) with $x_i \in R^d$, where d is the number of dimensions and its corresponding class label $y_i \in \{1, 2, \ldots, K\}$. Then, logistic regression tries to estimate the posterior probability of a new sample x as follows:

$$p(y=k \mid x) = \frac{\exp(-(w_{k_0} + w_k{}^{\mathrm{T}} x))}{1 + \sum_{l=1}^{K-1} \exp(-(w_{l_0} + w_l{}^{\mathrm{T}} x))}, \ k = 1, \ldots, K-1, \tag{1}$$

and

$$p(y=K \mid x) = \frac{1}{1 + \sum_{l=1}^{K-1} \exp(-(w_{l_0} + w_l{}^{\mathrm{T}} x))}. \tag{2}$$

The maximum likelihood procedure can be adopted to obtain the parameters. Given the N samples and their observed class labels, the log-likelihood function is shown below and can be maximized using the Newton-Raphson algorithm (Hastie, Tibshirani & Friedman 2001).

$$LL = \sum_{i=1}^{N} \ln p_{y_i}(x_i;\theta) \tag{3}$$

where $p_k(x_i;\theta) = p(y_i = k \mid x_i;\theta)$ and θ denotes all these parameters to be estimated above. Normally, logistic regression is applied in binary classification problems, with $y \in \{0, 1\}$. Then the posterior probability of a sample x can be calculated as follows:

$$p(y=0 \mid x) = \frac{\exp(-(w_0 + w^{\mathrm{T}}x))}{1+\exp(-(w_0 + w^{\mathrm{T}}x))}, \tag{4}$$

and

$$p(y=1 \mid x) = \frac{1}{1+\exp(-(w_0 + w^{\mathrm{T}}x))} \tag{5}$$

The variable for observing either class is supposed to obey the Bernoulli distribution:

$$p(y \mid x) = p(y=1 \mid x)^{y}(1-p(y=1 \mid x))^{1-y} \tag{6}$$

If it is assumed that these samples are drawn independently, then the likelihood of observing such a dataset D is given by:

$$\prod_{i=1}^{N} p(y_i = 1 \mid x_i)^{y_i}(1-p(y_i = 1 \mid x_i))^{1-y_i} \tag{7}$$

Its corresponding log-likelihood function then becomes:

$$LL = \sum_{i=1}^{N} \{y_i \log(p(y_i = 1 \mid x_i)) + (1-y_i)\log(1-p(y_i = 1 \mid x_i))\} \tag{8}$$

3.2 *Discriminant Analysis*

Discriminant analysis uses Bayes' theorem to compute the posterior probability of a sample x.

$$p(y \mid x) = \frac{p(x \mid y)p(y)}{p(x)} \tag{9}$$

The sample x is then assigned to the class label with the largest posterior probability. The discriminant function is defined as any of the following three forms (Johnson &Wichern 2002; Hastie, Tibshirani & Friedman 2001):

$$g(x) = p(y = i \mid x) - p(y = j \mid x) \tag{10}$$

$$g(x) = p(x \mid y = i)p(y = i) - p(x \mid y = j)p(y = j) \tag{11}$$

$$g(x) = \ln \frac{p(x \mid y = i)}{p(x \mid y = j)} - \ln \frac{p(y = j)}{p(y = i)} \tag{12}$$

where i, j denote the possible class label. According to the Bayesian classification rule, sample x belongs to class i if $g(x) > 0$, otherwise it belongs to class j. Assuming that the samples in class i obey the Gaussian distribution,

$$p(x \mid y = i) = \frac{1}{(2\pi)^{n/2}|\Sigma_i|^{1/2}} \exp\{-\frac{1}{2}(x-\mu_i)^{\mathrm{T}}\Sigma_i^{-1}(x-\mu_i)\} \tag{13}$$

where μ_i denotes the mean vector and Σ_i the covariance matrix of samples in class i. Then, the discriminant function $g(x)$ becomes:

$$\begin{aligned} g(x) = {} & (x-\mu_j)^{\mathrm{T}}\Sigma_j^{-1}(x-\mu_j) - (x-\mu_i)^{\mathrm{T}}\Sigma_i^{-1}(x-\mu_i) \\ & + 2(\log(p(y=i)) - \log(p(y=j))) + \log|\Sigma_j| - \log|\Sigma_i| \end{aligned} \tag{14}$$

The quadratic terms $x^{\mathrm{T}}\Sigma_i^{-1}x$ and $x^{\mathrm{T}}\Sigma_j^{-1}x$ in $g(x)$ indicate that the decision boundary is quadratic and therefore this classification technique is called quadratic discriminant analysis (QDA). When it satisfies $\Sigma_i = \Sigma_j = \Sigma$, the function $g(x)$ can be simplified as:

$$g(x) = (\mu_i - \mu_j)\Sigma^{-1}(x-\mu) + \ln(p(y=i)) - \ln(p(y=j)) \tag{15}$$

where $\mu = (\mu_i + \mu_j)/2$. Therefore, the function $g(x)$ is a linear function on x and the corresponding classification technique is called linear discriminant analysis (LDA).

3.3 K-Nearest Neighbors

The methodology of the k-nearest neighbor algorithm (KNN) is very intuitive. It considers the k labeled samples nearest to sample x to be classified and assign x to the most common class of these k neighbors (Aha & Kibler 1991; Han & Kamber 2001). An appropriate k value can be determined by using k-fold cross validation. The parameter k is supposed to be odd in order to avoid ties. This algorithm can produce non-linear classification boundaries, while it is very computationally expensive and may have the effect of overtraining when the samples are overlapping.

Let $P_N(e)$ be the average probability of the error for k-nearest neighbors on N labeled samples. If

$$P = \lim_{N \to \infty} P_N(e) \tag{16}$$

then we can obtain the bound of P in terms of Bayes rate P^*(Duda, Hart & Stork 2001):

$$P^* \le P \le 2P^*(1 - P^*) \tag{17}$$

The Bayes rate P^* is computed as follows:

$$P^*(e \mid x) = 1 - \max_m [p(y = m \mid x)] \tag{18}$$

where m is the possible class label for sample x. When applying the KNN algorithm on practical problems, how to define an appropriate similarity measure between samples becomes the crucial step. A very common similarity measure is the Minkowski distance:

$$d_M(x_i, x_j) = \left(|x_{i1} - x_{j1}|^p + |x_{i2} - x_{j2}|^p + \cdots + |x_{id} - x_{jd}|^p \right)^{\frac{1}{p}} \tag{19}$$

where p is a positive integer and d is the number of dimensions. The Minkowski distance is normally called the L_k norm and it turns into the Euclidean distance when p equals 2.

3.4 *Naïve Bayes*

The Naïve Bayes technique (NB) is one simplified form of the Bayesian network for classification. A Bayes network can be seen as a directed acyclic chart with a joint probability distribution over a set of discrete and stochastic variables (Pearl 1988). It has the advantage of incorporating domain knowledge and prior distribution information of the observed samples. A sample x is assigned to the class label with the largest posterior probability. The structure of the Bayesian network has to be settled or learned before estimating the parameters. By assuming that the variables are conditionally independent given the class label, as shown in Figure 1, the posterior probability of a sample x can be computed as follows (Han &Kamber 2001; Langley, Iba & Thompson 1992):

$$p(y \mid x) = \frac{p(y)p(x \mid y)}{p(x)} = \frac{p(y)\prod_{j=1}^{n} p(x_j \mid y)}{p(x)} \tag{20}$$

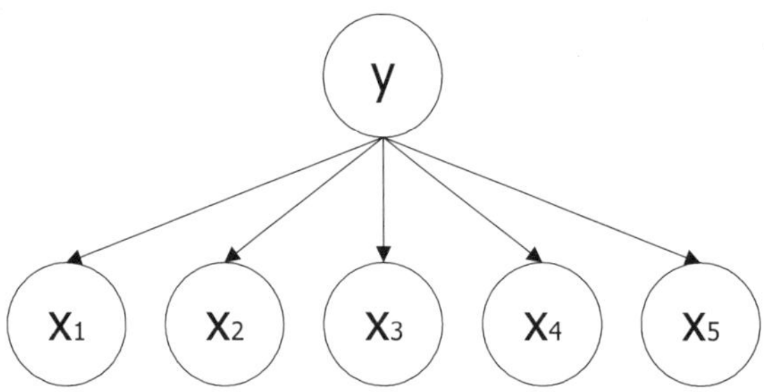

Figure 1. Variable relationship in Naive Bayes.

It is not necessary to estimate $p(x)$ since it is the same for all possible class labels. Frequency statistics are calculated to estimate $p(x_j|y)$ for discrete variables. Any continuous variable needs to be discretized first or is supposed to obey some type of a continuous distribution such as the normal distribution.

3.5 *The TAN Technique*

The tree augmented naïve (TAN) Bayes technique is an extension of the NB approach. Since the conditional independence of variables might be unrealistic in real-life, TAN relaxes the assumption by allowing dependence between condition variables. From a tree-diagram viewpoint, as shown in Figure 2, the class variable has no parents and the condition variable has the class variable and at most one other variable as parents. Friedman et al. (1997) have presented an algorithm to learn the structure of a TAN and its corresponding parameters.

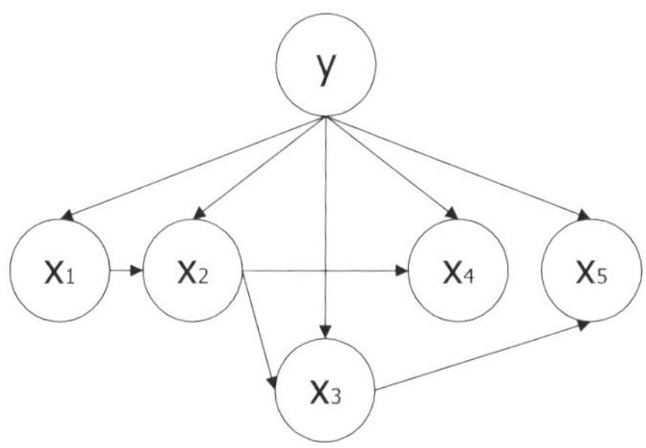

Figure 2. Variable relationship in TAN.

This algorithm uses conditional mutual information between attributes given the class variable. The function is defined as follows:

$$I(x_i;x_j \mid y) = \sum_{x_i, x_j, y} p(x_i, x_j, y) \log \frac{p(x_i, x_j \mid y)}{p(x_i \mid y) p(x_j \mid y)}, \tag{21}$$

which measures the information that x_i (x_j) provides about x_j (x_i) when the class variable y is known. The construction of a TAN consists of five main steps as follows:

- Compute $I(x_i;x_j|y)$ between each pair of attributes, $i \neq j$;
- Build a complete undirected graph in which the vertices are the attributes, $x_1, x_2, \dots x_d$;
- Build a maximum weighted spanning tree;
- Transform the resulting tree to a directed one by choosing a root variable and setting the direction of all edges to be outward from it;
- Construct a TAN model by adding a vertex labeled by y and adding an arc from y to each x_i.

3.6 *Decision Trees*

A decision tree (DT) classifier has a tree-like structure, which contains two types of nodes – internal nodes and leaf nodes. An internal node corresponds to a test for samples on individual or several attributes and a leaf node assigns class labels to samples based on the class distribution it records. A decision tree classifies samples in a top-down manner, starting from the root node and keeping moving according to the outcome of the tests at internal nodes, until a leaf node is reached and a class label is assigned (Breiman, Friedman, Olshen & Stone 1984). Figure 3 shows how a decision tree can help analyze labor negotiation data.

The construction of a decision tree is based on splitting internal nodes recursively. The selection of split attributes on internal nodes is extremely important during the construction process and determines to a large extent the final structure of the decision tree. Many efforts have been made on this aspect and a set of split criteria, such as the Gini index (Breiman, Friedman, Olshen et al. 1984), the information gain (Quinlan 1993) and the Chi-Square test (Biggs & Ville 1991; Kass 1980), are available. Entropy theory is adopted to select the appropriate split attribute by the well-known C4.5 algorithm (Quinlan 1993). Let N be the size of the dataset D and N_j the number of samples in class j. Assuming that there are K class labels, the entropy theory states that the average amount of information needed to classify a sample is as follows:

$$Info(D) = -\sum_{j=1}^{K} \frac{N_j}{N} \log_2\left(\frac{N_j}{N}\right) \tag{22}$$

When the dataset D is split into several subsets $D_1, D_2, \ldots, D_n$ according to the outcomes of attribute X, the information gain is defined as:

$$Gain(X, D) = Info(D) - \sum_{i=1}^{n} \frac{N^i}{N} Info(D_i) \tag{23}$$

where N^i is the number of samples in subset D_i. ID3, the forerunner of C4.5, favors all attributes with the largest gain, which is biased towards those attributes that have a lot of outcomes. C4.5 thus applies *Gain_ratio*, instead of *Gain*, as the criterion:

$$Gain\_ratio(X, D) = Gain(X, D) / \left(-\sum_{i=1}^{n} \frac{N^i}{N} \log_2\left(\frac{N^i}{N}\right)\right) \tag{24}$$

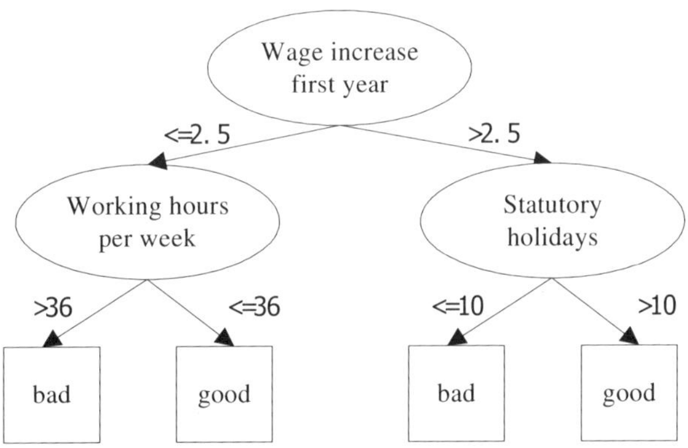

Figure 3. Decision tree for the labor negotiation data.

C4.5 greedily partitions nodes until a trivial value of the *Gain_ratio* is achieved. A prune procedure is then performed in order to avoid generating a complex tree that overfits the data. For a leaf node with N samples, E of which are misclassified, C4.5 estimates the classification error rate p under the assumption of the binomial distribution:

$$CF = \sum_{i=0}^{E} C_N^i p^i (1-p)^{N-i} \tag{25}$$

where CF is the confidence factor and normally is set at 0.25. C4.5 then substitutes a subtree with a leaf node or branch if p is decreased so as to improve the prediction ability for new samples. Although these N samples that arrive at a leaf node are not drawn independently, which violates the assumption of the binomial distribution, this kind of pruning strategy achieves excellent performance as shown empirically.

3.7 Associative Classification

Deriving association rules were first proposed by Agrawal and his associates in order to discover the concurrence of items in transaction datasets (Agrawal & Srikant 1994; Agrawal, Imielinski & Swami 1993). Let $I = \{i_1, i_2, \ldots, i_n\}$ be the set of items (attributes). A typical association rule is of the form $X \Rightarrow Y$, where $X \subset I$, $Y \subset I$, and $X \cap Y = \varnothing$. The support of an association rule is the probability that a sample containing both X and Y occurs, and it can be calculated as follows:

$$support(X \Rightarrow Y) = \frac{|\{T : X \cup Y \subseteq T, T \in D\}|}{|D|} \tag{26}$$

The confidence of an association rule is the probability that a sample containing X will contain Y, and it can be calculated as follows:

$$confidence(X \Rightarrow Y) = \frac{|\{T : X \cup Y \subseteq T, T \in D\}|}{|\{T : X \subseteq T, T \in D\}|} \tag{27}$$

These two measures indicate the coverage and accuracy of the rule separately. To make association rules suitable for classification tasks, associative classification focuses on a special subset of association rules, i.e. the rules with consequents limited to class label values only (so-called class association rules). Thus only those rules of the form $X \Rightarrow C_i$, where C_i is the possible class, are generated. Normally, association rule approaches search globally for all rules that satisfy some pre-specified minimum support and minimum confidence thresholds. The richness of the rules gives this technique the potential to uncover the true classification structure of the data.

One of the most popular associative classification techniques is CBA (Liu, Hsu & Ma 1998). It first generates, by using an adapted Apriori algorithm (Agrawal & Srikant 1994), all class association rules that satisfy minimum support and confidence. These rules are then ranked and sorted in descending sequence. The ranking is as follows: given two rules r_i and r_j, then we order them as $r_i > r_j$ (or r_i is said to have higher rank than r_j), if

(i) confidence (r_i) > confidence (r_j); or
(ii) confidence (r_i) = confidence (r_j), but support (r_i) > support (r_j); or
(iii) confidence (r_i) = confidence (r_j) and support (r_i) = support (r_j), but r_i is generated before r_j.

Each training sample is classified by the rule with the highest ranking among those rules that cover the sample. These sorted rules are then pruned to obtain a compact and accurate classifier. The pruning procedure tries to select a subset of the rule set, each of which correctly classifies at least one training sample, to cover the training dataset and to achieve the lowest empirical error rate. The default class is set as the majority class among these remaining samples that are not covered by any rule in the final classifier.

Associative classification has attracted significant attention in recent years and has proved to be intuitive and effective in many cases. Another associative classifier is ADT (Wang & Zhou 2000) and it organizes the rule sets in the tree structure according to its defined relations. The decision tree pruning technique is then applied to remove rules which are too specific.

The algorithms CAEP (Dong, Zhang, Wong & Li 1999), CMAR (Liu, Han & Pei 2001) and CPAR (Yin & Han 2003) are three of the most recent associative classification algorithms. They propose expected accuracy, weighted chi-square and growth rate, respectively, as the rule interestingness measures, and all perform classification based on multiple rules that the new sample fires. That is, instead of building a decision list (i.e., a set of rules in sequence) as CBA does, these associative classifiers pick out all rules that the new sample fires and apply a certain strategy, such as voting or weighted sum, to assign the new sample a class label. Moreover, another new approach to associative classification is GARC (Chen, Liu, Yu, Wei & Zhang 2005), which incorporates information gain, excluded sets, and certain redundancy/conflict resolution strategies into the classification rule generation process, so as to significantly reduce the number of rules generated while keeping the accuracy satisfactory.

3.8 Artificial Neural Networks

Artificial neural networks (ANN) are mathematical representations based on the understanding of the structure and mechanism of the human brain (Ripley 1996; Haykin 1998). The characteristics of ANN are subject to their topologies and corresponding weights. The learning procedure in an ANN is to tune weights intelligently after their topologies are designed. This chapter concentrates on the popular Multilayer Perception (MLP) structure and the back-propagation learning algorithm (BP).

As shown in Figure 4, an MLP is typically composed of an input layer, one or more hidden layers and an output layer, each containing several neurons. Each neuron processes its input and transmits its output to the neurons at the next layer, and finally to the output layer. A number of activation functions are available: sigmoid, hyperbolic tangent, sine and others.

Without loss of generality, consider the jth neuron at some layer. Let subscript i denote the ith neuron of its antecedent layer and k the kth neuron of its subsequent layer. Furthermore, let O_j denote the jth neuron's output and w_{ij} the weight between these two neurons. Each neuron generates the output net_j as follows:

$$net_j = \sum_i w_{ij} O_i + b_j \tag{28}$$

$$O_j = f(net_j) \tag{29}$$

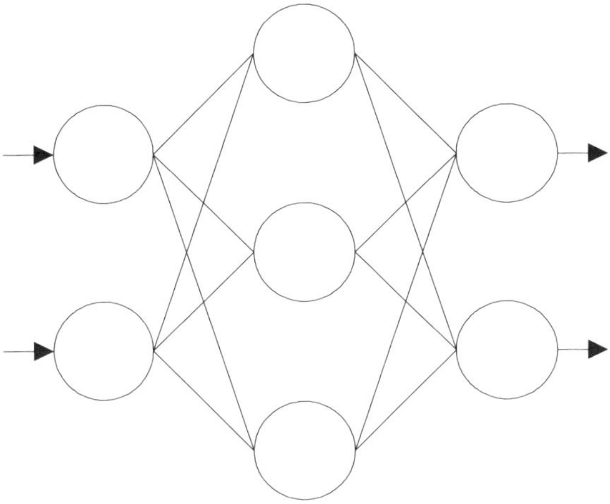

Figure 4. Model of the MLP.

where $f(\bullet)$ is the activation function and b_j is the bias. The sigmoid activation function is adopted in our experiments, which is defined as follows:

$$f(x) = \frac{1}{1+e^{-x}} \tag{30}$$

For neurons in the output layer, $\hat{y}_j = O_j$ is the actual output. Let y_j denote the class label. The BP algorithm uses the following objective function to be minimized:

$$E = \frac{1}{2}\sum_j \left(y_j - \hat{y}_j\right)^2 \tag{31}$$

The gradient descent method is applied to adjust the weights of the neural network. Define the local gradient:

$$\delta_j = \frac{\partial E}{\partial net_j} \tag{32}$$

Next consider the impact of weight w_{ij} on the objective function:

$$\frac{\partial E}{\partial w_{ij}} = \frac{\partial E}{\partial net_j}\frac{\partial net_j}{\partial w_{ij}} = \delta_j O_i \tag{33}$$

The weights are then tuned as follows in order to decrease the error:

$$\Delta w_{ij} = -\eta \delta_j O_j \tag{34}$$

$$w_{ij}(t+1) = w_{ij}(t) + \Delta w_{ij}(t) \tag{35}$$

If this neuron belongs to the output layer, then

$$O_j = \hat{y}_j \tag{36}$$

$$\delta_j = \frac{\partial E}{\partial \hat{y}_j}\frac{\partial \hat{y}_j}{\partial net_j} = -(y_j - \hat{y}_j)f'(net_j) \tag{37}$$

Otherwise, this neuron impacts all neurons in the next layer. Thus

$$\delta_j = \frac{\partial E}{\partial net_j} = \sum_k \frac{\partial E}{\partial net_k}\frac{\partial net_k}{\partial O_j}\frac{\partial O_j}{\partial net_j} = \sum_k \delta_k w_{jk} f'(net_j) \tag{38}$$

The parameter b_j can be tuned in a similar way since

$$\frac{\partial E}{\partial b_j} = \frac{\partial E}{\partial net_j}\frac{\partial net_j}{\partial b_j} = \delta_j \tag{39}$$

The error E of the network is thus back propagated through the network and can be minimized in a gradient descent way. As mentioned above, the chain rule is applied to compute the changes on the network weights and biases. The parameter η in Equation (34) denotes the learning rate and normally is assigned a value between 0 and 1. In previous studies, η was usually set as $1/t$, where t is the number of iterations the program has already executed, in order to favor both training speed and convergence.

A great deal of effort has been made to improve the performance of the BP algorithm, such as applying the Levenberg-Marquardt or the Quasi-Newton optimization method in order to speed up the training procedure (Bishop 1995), or incorporating a regularization method to avoid fitting noise in the training dataset (Haykin 1998).

3.9 Support Vector Machines

A support vector machine (SVM) is based on the statistical learning theory (SLT) and structural risk minimization (SRM) developed by Vapnik and his co-workers since the 1960's (Burges 1998; Cristianini & Shawe-Taylor 2000; Vapnik 1995). It exerts a deliberate trade-off between complexity and accuracy of the classifier on the training set in order to achieve better generality ability.

Given a set of training samples (x_i, y_i), i = 1, 2,…,N, $x_i \in R^d$, $y_i \in \{1, -1\}$, a typical SVM is designed to find the optimal separating hyperplane which has the maximal margin. In order to handle the linearly non-separable situation, a slack variable ξ and penalty factor C are introduced into the SVM model. This leads to the following convex quadratic programming (QP) problem:

$$\min_{w,b,\xi} J(w,b,\xi) = \frac{1}{2} w^{\mathrm{T}} w + C \sum_{i=1}^{N} \xi_i \tag{40}$$

subject to:

$$\begin{cases} y_i \left[w_i \varphi(x_i) + b \right] \geq 1 - \xi_i & i = 1,\ldots,N \\ \xi_i \geq 0 & i = 1,\ldots,N \end{cases}$$

where $\Phi(x_i)$ denotes the function that maps samples from the input space into a high dimensional feature space. The decision function is

$$y(x) = sign\left[w^{\mathrm{T}} \varphi(x) + b \right] \tag{41}$$

The Karush-Kuhn-Tucker conditions play a central role in solving this QP problem and convert it into its dual formulation as follows:

$$\max_{\alpha} Q(\alpha) = \sum_{i=1}^{N} \alpha_i - \frac{1}{2} \sum_{i,j=1}^{N} \alpha_i \alpha_j y_i y_j K(x_i, x_j) \tag{42}$$

subject to:

$$\begin{cases} \sum_{i=1}^{N} \alpha_i y_i = 0 \\ 0 \le \alpha_i \le C \qquad i = 1,\ldots,N \end{cases}$$

The decision function becomes:

$$y(x) = sign\left[\sum_{i=1}^{N} \alpha_i y_i K(x_i, x) + b\right] \tag{43}$$

where $K(x_i, x_j)$ is a kernel function that satisfies the Mercer theory and is applied to replace the dot products of x_i and x_j in the feature space. There are several choices for kernel functions, such as linear kernel, polynomial kernel and RBF kernel. The RBF kernel, which is applied in this chapter, is defined as follows:

$$K(x_i, x_j) = \exp\left(-\left\|x_i - x_j\right\|_2^2 / \sigma^2\right) \tag{44}$$

where σ is the kernel parameter.

The kernel techniques have solved the non-linear problem as well as controlled the high dimension problem elegantly. Furthermore, an SVM model can avoid being trapped into a local optimum, which may occur with neural networks, since it is convex quadratic. However, SVM still have some difficulties in model selection. Although previous studies have endeavored to estimate the generality ability of SVM with respect to parameter selection, there is a lack of theory that can efficiently guide users to choose a fitting penalty factor C or an appropriate kernel with its parameters for a specific problem. In addition, though there are numerous optimization algorithms to solve convex quadratic programming problems, the optimization might be extraordinarily slow or unstable when a huge number of samples are to be used for training. Several techniques, such as chunking (Vapnik 1995), decomposition (Osuna, Freund & Girosi 1997) and SMO algorithms (Platt 1998; Keerthi, Shevade, Bhattacharyya & Murthy 1999), have been introduced to alleviate such problems.

Basically two alternatives can be employed in extending this SVM model to a multi-class situation. The first one is to consider all class labels in a single model, whose mechanism is similar to the binary one (Weston & Watkins 1999):

$$\min_{w,b,\xi} J(w,b,\xi) = \frac{1}{2}\sum_{m=1}^{K} w_m^{\mathrm{T}} w_m + C\sum_{i=1}^{N}\sum_{m\neq y_i}\xi_i^m \tag{45}$$

subject to:

$$w_{y_i}\Phi(x_i) + b_{y_i} \geq w_m\Phi(x_i) + b_m + 2 - \xi_i^m$$

$$\xi_i^m \geq 0, \quad i = 1,\ldots,N \quad m \in \{1,\ldots,K\}\setminus y_i$$

and its corresponding decision function becomes:

$$f(x) = \arg\max_i [w_i\Phi(x) + b_i], \quad i = 1,\ldots,K \tag{46}$$

Another choice is to decompose the multi-class problem into several binary class problems. There are three main methods: one against one, one against the rest, and a directed acyclic graph (DAG) approach (Platt, Cristianini & Shawe-Taylor 2000). Experiments in (Hsu & Lin 2002) reveal that one-against-one and DAG are more preferable in practice.

4. An Empirical Study

4.1 Experimental Settings

Since these classification models stem from diverse technical contexts and no integrated data mining platform is available so far, various software toolboxes were utilized in our experiments. In particular, the LDA and QDA were programmed in SAS code. SPSS/Clementine was applied to carry out logistic regression and neural networks. Naïve Bayes and TAN algorithms were implemented by using the jNBC toolbox (Sacha 1999). The authors of the C4.5 decision tree and the CBA algorithms have published their corresponding software on the web. To implement support vector machines, the well-known LIBSVM system (Chang &Lin 2003) was employed.

LDA, QDA, logistic regression, C4.5 and CBA require no parameter tuning, while model selection is necessary for the *k*-nearest neighbors (by using the Euclidean distance), neural networks (using only one hidden layer and the sigmoid activation function) and support vector machine (using the RBF kernel). For the neural network approach, we used financial variables as the input nodes and only one node at the output layer. The 10-fold cross validation on the training dataset was applied to select their appropriate parameters, i.e., the *k* value, the number of neurons in the hidden layer, the penalty factor *C* and the kernel parameters.

All these classifiers are supposed to output the posterior probability for further analysis. LDA, QDA, logistic regression, Naïve Bayes and the TAN algorithms generate directly the posterior probability of a new sample. For the *k*-nearest neighbor classifier, the posterior probability is computed as *m*/*k* if *m* numbers of *k* nearest neighbors vote for this class. The class distribution proportion in the leaf node, where the sample arrives at, is used to estimate its posterior probability. The confidence of a class association rule that the sample first fires is taken as the posterior probability. With neural networks, the output of the neurons in the output layer is regarded as the probability when the sigmoid activation function is applied. It is a bit complex for an SVM to compute the posterior probability. LIBSVM provides this function, which is an improvement of Platt's previous work (Platt 2000).

For the missing values in our dataset, we replace them with the average attribute values of the samples with the same class label. Regularization of attributes is performed to make them obey a standard normal distribution, in order to avoid the negative impacts from different measurements and outliers. Entropy-based discretization (Fayyad & Irani 1993) was employed when needed. We applied ANOVA on this dataset and selected those features with large F values as inputs, while it did not bring improvements to these classification algorithms' prediction ability. Principal Component Analysis (PCA) has the same problem. Feature selection/transformation in this case seems to cause information loss and all these 18 indexes are consequently kept as the input variables.

4.2 The ROC Curve and the Delong-Pearson Method

There are two assumptions to be made when taking classification accuracy as a measure of a model's discriminatory performance. First, the class distribution keeps constant over time and is relatively balanced. Second, the misclassification costs are the same for false positive and false negative predictions. Since the class distribution in the credit rating dataset was skewed and it costs much more when the bank predicts a bad client as good than a good client as bad, the receiver operating characteristic (ROC) curve was adopted to evaluate the discriminatory performance from a comprehensive perspective.

The ROC curve is a graphical illustration of the discriminant ability and normally is applied to binary classification problems (Swets & Pickett 1982; Provost & Fawcett 1997). Suppose that the class label $y \in \{+,-\}$ and there is a threshold τ. The sample is classified as positive if the output (posterior probability of being high risk in this chapter) is larger than τ, otherwise it is negative. A confusion matrix is then obtained on the test result, as shown in Table 2.

Table 2. The confusion matrix for binary classification.

	Actual	
Predicted	+	-
+	True Positive (TP)	False Positive (FP)
-	False Negative (FN)	True negative (TF)

Define sensitivity as TP/(TP+FN) and specificity as TF/(FP+TF). Sensitivity (specificity) measures the proportion of positive (negative) samples that are classified correctly and they vary with the threshold τ. The ROC curve can then be plotted with sensitivity as the vertical axis and 1-specificity as the horizontal axis. Each point on the ROC curve corresponds to a specific threshold value.

The area under the ROC curve (AUC) was computed to measure the discriminatory performance. From a statistical viewpoint, it estimates the probability that the output of a randomly selected sample from the negative population will be less than or equal to that of a randomly selected sample from the positive population. The larger AUC, the more powerful the classifier is.

Long and his associates proposed a nonparametric approach to compare the areas under two or more correlated receiver operating characteristic curves (Long, Long & Clarke-Pearson 1988). Suppose that there are K classifiers to be compared and the outputs of the rth classification algorithm on positive samples are $X_i^r, i = 1,2,\ldots,m$, and the outputs on negative samples are Y_j^r, $j = 1,2,\ldots,n$. The AUC value of the rth classifier can be evaluated as:

$$\hat{\theta}^r = \frac{1}{mn}\sum_{j=1}^{n}\sum_{i=1}^{m}\psi\left(X_i^r, Y_j^r\right) \tag{47}$$

where:

$$\psi(X,Y) = \begin{cases} 1 & Y < X \\ \frac{1}{2} & Y = X \\ 0 & Y > X \end{cases} \tag{48}$$

For the statistic $\hat{\theta}^r$, the X-components and Y-components are defined as follows, respectively:

$$V_{10}^r(X_i) = \frac{1}{n}\sum_{j=1}^{n}\psi\left(X_i^r, Y_j^r\right) \quad i = 1,2,\ldots m \tag{49}$$

$$V_{01}^r(Y_j) = \frac{1}{m}\sum_{i=1}^{m}\psi\left(X_i^r, Y_j^r\right) \quad j = 1,2,\ldots n \tag{50}$$

Also define the $K \times K$ matrices S_{10} and S_{01}. The $(r,s)^{th}$ element of each matrix is:

$$s_{10}^{r,s} = \frac{1}{m-1}\sum_{i=1}^{m}\left[V_{10}^r(X_i) - \hat{\theta}^r\right]\left[V_{10}^s(X_i) - \hat{\theta}^s\right] \tag{51}$$

$$s_{01}^{r,s} = \frac{1}{n-1}\sum_{j=1}^{n}\left[V_{01}^r(Y_j) - \hat{\theta}^r\right]\left[V_{01}^s(Y_j) - \hat{\theta}^s\right] \tag{52}$$

Thus the covariance matrix for the vector $\hat{\theta} = \left(\hat{\theta}^1, \hat{\theta}^2, \ldots \hat{\theta}^k\right)$ equals

$$S = \frac{1}{m} S_{10} + \frac{1}{n} S_{01} \tag{53}$$

Long *et al.* then designed a standard normal distribution statistic:

$$\frac{L\hat{\theta}^T - L\theta^T}{\left[L \left(\frac{1}{m} S_{10} + \frac{1}{n} S_{01} \right) L^T \right]^{1/2}} \tag{54}$$

where L is the row vector of coefficients. For instance, when only two classifiers are compared, L is set at (1, -1) and θ^1 is assumed to be equal to θ^2. The corresponding value of equation (54) shows whether these two AUC values are statistically different.

4.3 Experimental Results

Table 3 summarizes the accuracy and AUC value of each classifier on the test dataset. Their ROC curves are plotted in Figures 5, 6, 7 and 8.

Table 3. Accuracy and AUC values of classifiers.

	LDA	QDA	LOG	KNN	NB
Accuracy	86.5%	74.0%	82.7%	92.3%	90.4%
AUC	0.860	0.881	0.828	0.967	0.974
	TAN	C45	CBA	NN	SVM
Accuracy	92.3%	92.3%	93.3%	93.3%	84.6%
AUC	0.956	0.918	0.970	0.967	0.933

In order to test whether the difference between two classifiers is significant, the non-parametric Delong-Pearson statistical method (Long, Long & Clarke-Pearson 1988) was employed. The comparison results are described in Table 4 in terms of one-tail P values.

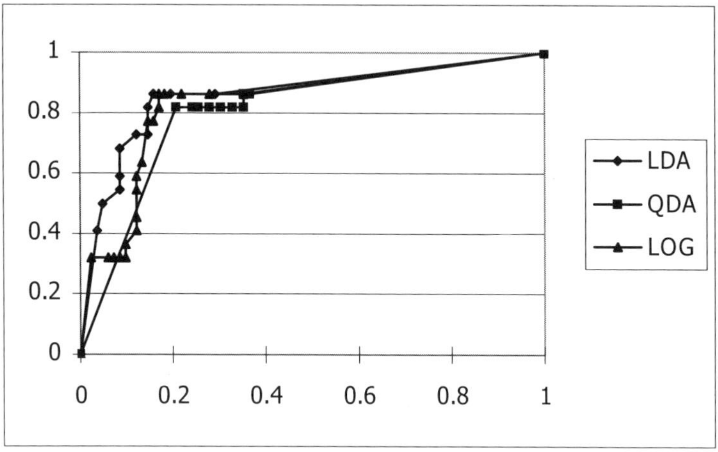

Figure 5. ROC for LDA, QDA and LOG.

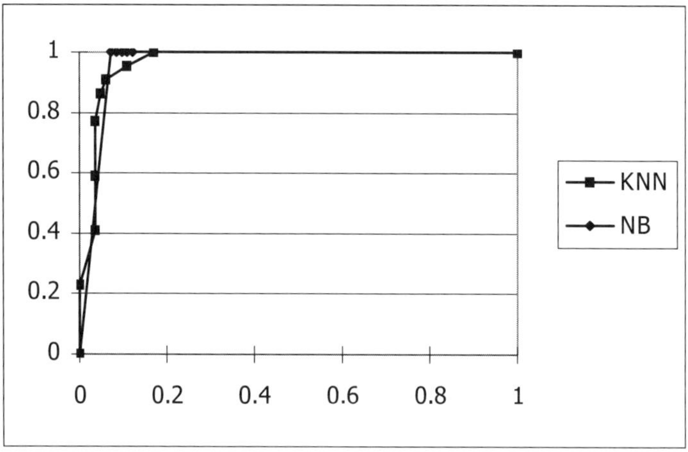

Figure 6. ROC for KNN and NB.

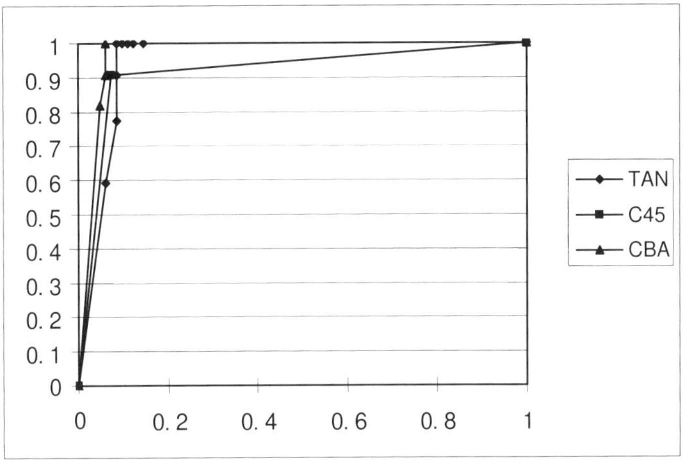

Figure 7. ROC for TAN, C4.5 and CBA.

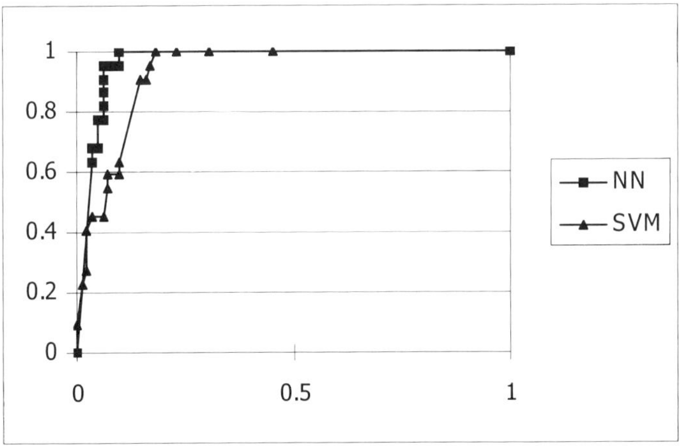

Figure 8. ROC for Neural network and SVM.

Table 4. The Delong-Pearson comparison result.

	LOG	LDA	QDA	C4.5	SVM	TAN	KNN	NN	CBA	NB
LOG	-	0.125	0.245	0.082	0.032	0.015	0.008	0.010	0.009	0.007
LDA	0.125	-	0.394	0.179	0.076	0.042	0.023	0.024	0.025	0.018
QDA	0.245	0.394	-	0.268	0.149	0.062	0.046	0.045	0.038	0.026
C4.5	0.082	0.179	0.268	-	0.337	0.154	0.054	0.074	0.066	0.052
SVM	0.032	0.076	0.149	0.337	-	0.104	0.015	0.021	0.030	0.007
TAN	0.015	0.042	0.062	0.154	0.104	-	0.264	0.251	0.242	0.062
KNN	0.008	0.023	0.046	0.054	0.015	0.264	-	0.5	0.413	0.295
NN	0.01	0.024	0.045	0.074	0.021	0.251	0.5	-	0.401	0.298
CBA	0.009	0.025	0.038	0.066	0.03	0.242	0.413	0.401	-	0.390
NB	0.007	0.018	0.026	0.052	0.007	0.062	0.295	0.298	0.39	-

The AUC value of a classifier on the ith row is less than or equal to that of the classifier on the jth column when $i < j$. According to the above table, the performance of these classifiers can be grouped into three categories. The traditional statistical methods, such as LOG, LDA and QDA, resulted in the poorest performance. The C4.5 and SVM methods did not achieve the satisfactory results as expected. The ROC values of the rest of the five classifiers are higher and have no significant differences among them. The CBA algorithm is preferred in this experiment because of its powerful classification ability as well as understandable rule sets for decision makers.

Our research results are consistent with prior research studies indicating that machine learning techniques, such as decision trees and neural networks, can normally provide better prediction outcomes than traditional statistical methods. This is probably the case because traditional statistical methods require researchers to impose specific structures and assumptions to different models and then to estimate parameters in them so as to fit these training data. Machine learning techniques, however, are free of structural assumptions that underlie statistical methods, and can extract knowledge from a dataset directly. For example, the structure of a decision tree is never determined before being trained, while it can be recursively split, from a root node, and pruned later in order to fit the training data as well as to obtain good prediction ability. The most surprising result is that the popular SVM method did not achieve outstanding performance no matter what penalty factor and kernel parameters were selected. This result disagrees with previous work regarding the application of SVM to the analysis of credit data. The mechanism behind this phenomenon deserves more exploration and analysis in the future.

The associative classification techniques, such as CBA, have not been emphasized in previous credit rating research work. As mentioned above, associative classifiers search globally for all class association rules that satisfy given minimum support and minimum confidence thresholds. The richness of the rules gives this technique the potential to uncover the true classification structure of the data. Compared with decision tree based techniques, associative classification is more flexible because a decision tree is generated in a recursive way, which may prevent it from discovering a better classification strategy. For example, once the first split of the root node is performed, it will affect all subsequent split choices, which appears to be a bit rigid in this sense. As long as class association rules are pruned and organized appropriately, associative classification techniques can probably yield good performance.

Although the experiments in this chapter indicate that CBA (or associative classification methods in general) has its advantage and might be a proper choice when rating the risk of an applicant, it is worthy of mentioning that these techniques are heuristic and data driven, and it is impossible for one algorithm to outperform all others in all situations. Users or decision makers are expected to be cautious in selecting appropriate classification tools and their corresponding parameters if they try to extract knowledge of high quality in enterprise data.

5. Conclusions and Future Work

Controlling credit risk is crucial for commercial banks to identify the clients that will probably breach their contracts in the future. Although the credit rating system provides an effective tool, it is not possible to rate all the clients and repeat the rating frequently. Data mining and computational intelligence, especially classification techniques, can be applied to learn and predict the credit rating automatically, thus helping commercial banks detect the potential high-risk clients in an accurate and timely manner.

A comprehensive examination of several well-known classifiers is described in this chapter. All these classifiers have been applied to 244 rated companies mainly from the Industrial and Commercial Bank of China. The results revealed that traditional statistical models had the poorest outcomes, and that C4.5 and SVM did not achieve a satisfactory performance as expected. On the other hand, CBA, an associative classification technique, seemed to be the most appropriate choice.

Future work may focus on collecting more data for experiments and applications, particularly with more exploration of Chinese credit rating data structures. In this chapter, feature selection/transformation methods such as ANOVA or PCA analysis are found independent of these classification methods and did not lead to improvements of their prediction abilities. An investigation in the future might be to apply another type of feature selection methods, which are dependent on the classification algorithms, in order to find out the best feature combination for each classifier.

Acknowledgements

The work was partly supported by the National Natural Science Foundation of China (79925001/70231010/70321001), and the MOE Funds for Doctoral Programs (20020003095).

References

Agrawal, R., Srikant, R. (1994). A fast algorithm for mining association rules. The 20th International Conference on Very Large Data Bases, Santiago, Chile.

Agrawal, R., Imielinski, T., Swami, A. (1993). Mining association rules between sets of items in large databases. The ACM SIGMOID Conference on Management of Data, Washington, D.C. U.S.A.

Aha, D., D. Kibler. (1991). Instance-based learning algorithms, *Machine Learning*, **6**, 37-66.

Baesens, B. (2003). Developing intelligent systems for credit scoring using machine learning techniques. Department of Applied Economic Sciences. Leuven, Belgium, Leuven University**:** 221.

Biggs, D., Ville, B. (1991). A method of choosing mulitway partitions for classification and decision trees, *Applied Statistics*, **18**, 49-62.

Bishop, C.M. (1995). Neural networks for pattern recognition, Oxford University Press.

Breiman, L., Friedman, J., Olshen, R., Stone, C. (1984). Classification and Regression trees. Wadsworth and Brooks: Monterey, CA, U.S.A.

Burges, C. J. C. (1998). A tutorial on Support Vector Machines for pattern recognition, *Data Mining and Knowledge Discovery*, **2**(2), 121-167.

Chang, C. -C., Lin, C.-J. (2003). LIBSVM: a library for support vector machines, (URL: http://www.csie.ntu.edu.tw/~cjlin/papers/libsvm.pdf).

Chen, G. Q., Liu, H. Y., Yu, L., Wei, Q., Zhang, X. (2007). A New Approach to Classification Based on Association Rule Mining. Decision Support Systems, (to appear).

Cristianini, N., Shawe-Taylor, J. (2000). An Introduction to Support Vector Machines, Cambridge University Press.

Dong, G., Zhang, X., Wong, L., Li, J. (1999). CAEP: Classification by aggregating emerging patterns. 2nd International Conference on Discovery Science,(DS'99), Lecture Notes in Artificial Intelligence 1721, Tokyo, Japan, Springer-Verlag.

Duda, R. O., Hart, P. E., Stork, D. G. (2001). *Pattern Classification*, John Wiley and Sons.

Dutta, S., S. Shekhar. (1988). Bond rating: a non-conservative application of neural networks. *IEEE International Conference on Neural Networks.*

Ederington, H. L. (1985). Classification models and bond ratings, *Financial Review*, **20**(4): 237-262.

Fayyad, U. M., and Irani, K. B. (1993). Multi-interval discretization of continuous valued attributes for classification learning. the *Thirteenth International Joint Conference on Artificial Intelligence* (IJCAI), Morgan Kaufmann: Chambery, France.

Friedman, N., Geiger, D., Goldszmidt, M. (1997). Bayesian network classifiers. *Machine Learning*, **29**, 131-163.

Galindo, J., and Tamayo, P. (2000). Credit risk assessment using statistical and machine learning: basic methodology and risk modeling applications, *Computational Economics*, **15**(1-2), 107-143.

Guo, M. H. (2003). *Credit rating*, China Renmin University Press, China.

Han, J., and Kamber, M. (2001). *Data Mining: Concepts and Techniques*, Morgan Kaufmann: San Francisco, CA, U.S.A.

Hastie, T., Tibshirani, R. and Friedman, J. (2001). *The Elements of Statistical Learning, Data Mining, Inference, and Prediction*, Springer.

Haykin, S. (1998). Neural networks: a comprehensive foundation, Prentice Hall.

Hosmer, D. W., and Lemeshow, S. (2000). *Applied logistic regression.* Wiley: New York, NY, U.S.A.

Hsu, C. -W., and Lin, C.-J. (2002). A comparison of methods for multi-class support vector machines, *IEEE Transactions on Neural Networks*, **13**(2), 415-425.

Huang, Z., Chen, H. Hsu, C.-J., Chen, W.-H., and Wu, S. (2004). Credit rating analysis with support vector machines and neural networks: a market comparative study, *Decision Support Systems*, **37**(4), 543-558.

Johnson, R. A., and Wichern, D. W. (2002). *Applied multivariate statistical analysis*. Prentice Hall: Upper Saddle River, N.J., U.S.A.

Kass, G. V. (1980). An exploratory technique for investigating large quantities of categorical data, *Applied statistics*, **29**, 119-127.

Keerthi, S., Shevade, S., Bhattacharyya, C., and Murthy, K, (1999). Improvements to Platt's SMO algorithm for SVM classifier design. Banglore, India, Dept. of CSA.

Kim, J. W. (1993). Expert systems for bond rating: a comparative analysis of statistical, rule-based and neural network systems, *Expert Systems*, **10**, 167-171.

Langley, P., Iba, W., Thompson, K. (1992). An analysis of Bayesian classifiers, the *tenth National Conference on Artificial Intelligence* (AAAI'92), San Jose, CA, U.S.A, AAAI Press.

Liu, B., Hsu, W., Ma, Y. (1998). Integrating classification and association rule mining, the *4th International Conference on Discovery and Data Mining*, New York, NY, U.S. A.

Liu, W., Han, J., Pei. J. (2001). CMAR: Accurate and efficient classification based on multiple class-association rules, *ICDM'01*, San Jose, CA, U.S.A.

Long, E. R. D., Long, D. M. D., and Clarke-Pearson, D. L. (1988). Comparing the areas under two or more correlated receiver operating characteristic curves: a nonparametric approach, *Biometrics*, **44**, 837-845.

Maher, J. J., and Sen, T. K. (1997). Predicting bond ratings using neural networks: a comparison with logistic regression, *Intelligent Systems in Accounting, Finance and Management*, **6**, 59-72.

Moody, J., and Utans, J. (1995). Architecture selection strategies for neural networks application to corporate bond rating, *Neural Networks in the Capital Markets*, 277-300.

Osuna, E., Freund, R. and Girosi, F. (1997). Improved training algorithm for Support Vector Machines, *Proc. IEEE NNSP '97*.

Pearl, J. (1988). *Probabilistic reasoning in Intelligent Systems: networks for plausible inference*, Morgan Kaufmann: San Francisco, CA, U.S.A.

Pinches, G. E., and Mingo, K. A. (1973). A multivariate analysis of industrial bond ratings, *The journal of finance*, **28**(1): 1-18.

Platt, J. (1998). Fast training of support vector machines using sequential minimal optimization, in *Advances in Kernel Methods - Support Vector Learning*, B. Scholkopf, C. Burges and A. J. Smola (Eds.). The MIT Press: Cambridge, MA, U.S.A.

Platt, J. (2000). Probabilistic outputs for support vector machines and comparison to regularized likelihood methods, in *Advances in Large Margin*

Classifiers, A.J. Smola, P.L. Bartlett, B. Scholkopf and D. Schuurmans (Eds.), The MIT Press: Cambridge, MA, U.S.A.

Platt, J. C., Cristianini, N. and Shawe-Taylor, J. (2000). Large margin DAGs for multiclass classification, *Advances in Neural Information Processing Systems*, **12**, 547-533.

Provost, F., and Fawcett, T. (1997). Analysis and visualization of classifier performance: Comparison under imprecise class and cost distributions. 3rd International Conference on Knowledge Discovery and Data Mining, AAAI Press: Huntington Beach, CA, U.S.A.

Quinlan, J. R. (1993). *C4.5 programs for machine learning*, Morgan Kaufmann: San Francisco, CA, U. S. A.

Ripley, B. D. (1996). *Pattern Recognition and Neural Networks*, Cambridge University Press.

Sacha, J. (1999). jBNC: Bayesian Network Classifier Toolbox. (Online Version: http://jbnc.sourceforge.net/).

Shin, K.-S., and Han, I. (1999). Case-based reasoning supported by genetic algorithms for corporate bond rating, *Expert Systems with Applications*, **16**, 85-95.

Shin, K.-S., and Lee, Y. J. (2002). A genetic algorithm application in bankruptcy prediction modeling, *Expert Systems with Applications*, **23**, 321-328.

Singleton, J. C., and Surkan, A. J. (1990). Neural networks for bond rating improved by multiple hidden layers, in *Proc. Of IEEE International Conference on Neural Networks*.

Swets, J. A., and Pickett, R.M. (1982). *Evaluation of Diagnostic Systems: Methods from Signal Detection Theory*. Academic Press: New York, NY, U. S. A.

Vapnik, V. (1995). *The nature of statistical learning theory*, Springer-Verlag, New York, NY, U.S.A.

Wang, K., and Zhou, S. (2000). Growing decision trees on support-less association rules, in *KDD'00*, Boston, MA, U. S. A.

Weston, J., and Watkinsm C. (1999). Multi-class support vector machines, in the *7th European Symposium on Artificial Neural Networks*, Brussels, Belgium.

Yang, L., Hua, L. and Yu, W. B. (2003). *Credit risk management in Bank: Theory, Technology and Practice*, Economic Management Press.

Yin, X., and Han, J. (2003). CPAR: Classification based on predictive association rules, in the *2003 SIAM International Conference on Data Mining (SDM'03)*, San Francisco, CA, U.S.A.

Authors' Biographical Statements

Lan Yu graduated from the School of Economics and Management, Tsinghua University (Beijing, China), in 2006 with a doctoral degree in management. In recent years he has been doing research on data mining, focusing on the improvement and application of classification techniques. His research publications have appeared in several international journals including *Decision Support Systems*, and *Expert Systems with Applications*. Dr. Yu is currently working as a post-doctoral researcher at Tsinghua University's Department of Computer Science and Technology, in expanding the business intelligence knowledge to the banks in China.

Guoqing Chen received his PhD from the Catholic University of Leuven (K.U. Leuven, Belgium), and now is the EMC^2 Chair Professor of information systems at the School of Economics and Management, Tsinghua University (Beijing, China). His research interests include information systems management, business intelligence and decision support, and soft computing.

He has published internationally and served as area editor/associate editor/editorial board member for international journals such as *Information Sciences, Information Processing & Management*, *Journal of Strategic Information Systems, Information & Management, Fuzzy Sets and Systems, etc.* Prof. Chen is the founding president of Association for Information Systems (AIS) China Chapter (CNAIS), and served as chair/co-chair for several international conferences including IFSA2005 World Congress, IEEE ICEBE2005, IESM2007, etc.

Andy Koronios earned his PhD from the University of Queensland (Brisbane, Australia), and now is a professor of information systems at the School of Computer & Information Science, University of South Australia (Adelaide, Australia).

His research interests include electronic commerce, data quality and security, multimedia and online learning systems. He has a major role in the CRC for Integrated Engineering Asset Management (CIEAMP) as a research program leader in the area of systems integration and IT for assets management. Professor Koronios has numerous publications in international journals, edited volumes and conference proceedings.

Shiwu Zhu received his PhD from the Shanghai University of Finance and Economics (Shanghai, China), and currently is an associate professor of finance at the School of Economics and Management, Tsinghua University (Beijing, China). His research interests include fixed income, risk management, credit derivative pricing, and financial database. Dr. Zhu has been the Principal Investigator for a number of research grants including the research grant awarded by the National Natural Science Foundation of China (NSFC).

Xunhua Guo received his doctoral degree from Tsinghua University (Beijing, China) in 2005, and currently he is an assistant professor of information systems at the School of Economics and Management, Tsinghua University. His research interests include information systems and organizational evolution, systems analysis and design, and data management. His academic publications have appeared in international journals such as *Communications of the ACM*, *Information Sciences, Journal of Enterprise Information Systems etc.* He has co-authored books on information systems management, and co-developed a case recently on Digital China published by Harvard Business School in 2007. Dr. Guo has served as a Co-Chair for the International Conference on Industrial Engineering and Systems Management (IESM2007).

Chapter 3[1]

Predictive Classification with Imbalanced Enterprise Data

Sophia Daskalaki
Dept. of Engineering Sciences, University of Patras, Greece, sdask@upatras.gr
Ioannis Kopanas
OTE S.A, Hellenic Telecommunications Organization, Patras, Greece, ikopanas@ote.gr
Nikolaos M. Avouris
Dept. of Electr. and Computer Engin., University of Patras, Greece, avouris@upatras.gr

Abstract: Enterprise data present several difficulties when are used in data mining projects. Apart from being heterogeneous, noisy and disparate, they may also be characterized by major imbalances between the different classes. Predictive classification using imbalanced data necessitates methodologies that are adequate for such data, and particularly for the training of algorithms and evaluation of the resulting classifiers. This chapter suggests to experiment with several class distributions in the training sets and a variety of performance measures, especially those that are known to better expose the strengths and weaknesses of classification models. By combining classifiers into schemes that are suitable for the specific business domain, may improve predictions. However, the final evaluation of the classifiers must always be based on the impact of the results to the enterprise, which can take the form of a cost model that reflects requirements of existing knowledge. Taking a telecommunications company as an example, we provide a framework for handling enterprise data during the initial phases of the project, as well as for generating and evaluating predictive classifiers. We also provide the design of a decision support system, which embodies the above process with the daily routine of such company.

***Key Words*:** Predictive classification, Knowledge discovery from data, Imbalanced datasets, Performance measures, Voting schemes.

---

[1] Liao, T.W. and E. Triantaphyllou, (Eds.), **Recent Advances in Data Mining of Enterprise Data: Algorithms and Applications**, *World Scientific*, Singapore, pp. 147-188, 2007.

1. Introduction

Continuous advances in the digitization and processing of information as well as in storage technology have altered considerably common practices in most business environments. The ubiquitous computer support and the automation of enterprise activities have resulted in the collection of tremendous amounts of data on a daily basis. These data, which can be stored and processed in very high speeds, are potentially a valuable source of knowledge and an important asset for the companies concerned. For this reason, competitive companies attempt to exploit the data they own with the ultimate goal to gain advantage in the market they belong to.

In order to facilitate the extraction of knowledge, several Data Mining and Knowledge Discovery tools and techniques have been developed during the last years. However, some key questions are associated with such an objective. For instance: How easy is to extract and operationalize the knowledge that is hiding in the data? Can we expect that the process of extracting knowledge from the enterprise data will be fully automated in the near future? What form may the extracted knowledge take? Will it be simply a Study Report identifying trends and patterns in the data along with some recommendations for future actions? Alternatively, can it take the form of a Decision Support System (DSS) that will aid humans in their daily decision making process? When is the decision of building such a system going to be made during the knowledge discovery process and on what criteria should it be based?

In order to build a DSS that is based to a great extent on knowledge extracted from large amounts of data, it is certain that one has to go through a typical Knowledge Discovery from Data (KDD) process. KDD was initially defined as the "nontrivial process of identifying valid, novel, potentially useful, and ultimately understandable patterns in data" (Frawley et al., 1991). In other words, KDD is the multi-step process that involves understanding the domain, preparing the data, identifying the function to be applied, choosing the right algorithms, searching for patterns, evaluating and interpreting the revealed knowledge and finally incorporating it into the decision making process (Fayyad et al., 1996). There have been many attempts to describe this process beyond Fayyad's original nine-step model (e.g. Cabena et al., 1998; Wirth and Hipp, 2000; Cios and Kurgan, 2005), while Brachman and Anand (1996) discuss the process from an analyst's perspective.

The common aspects of all these models are: (1) the phase of understanding the domain, where the business objectives are determined; (2) the collection, preparation and analysis of enterprise data; (3) the data mining phase, which refers to the application of algorithms for the extraction of patterns[2]; (4) the evaluation of the discovered knowledge, and finally (5) the use of knowledge (Figure 1). Fayyad et al. (1991) further divide Phase 2, where most of the effort of the KDD research is placed, as well as Phase 3, the actual heart of the process. Instead, little attention has been placed on Phase 4 and particularly on the decision to proceed or not with the operationalization of the acquired patterns. However in business environments, it is this phase that will probably yield results worth the effort of the whole KDD exercise and permit re-use of the acquired knowledge beyond the simple description of the identified patterns. It is often argued that it is only in this latter case that any knowledge is obtained. For instance, Wilson (2002) has commented, that knowledge is a term highly misused, often taking the meaning of derived facts (data) or information, when these facts are embedded in a context of relevance to the recipient. Conversely, knowledge is directly related to the mental process of comprehension, understanding and learning. So, one may argue that only when the discovered patterns are inserted in the business process and take the form of operational tools that can be applied in every day situations, real knowledge has been extracted from the original data.

In this chapter, we review the process of Data Mining and Knowledge Discovery in large enterprise datasets and focus on the phase of evaluating the discovered knowledge in order to decide whether it is worth proceeding with the development of a DSS based on the discovered knowledge. It is our goal to demonstrate the complexity of this phase in connection to the typical decisions that need to be made.

---

[2]Since the term Data Mining (DM) is often used in the literature to describe the whole KDD process, a proposal has been made to use the term Data Mining and Knowledge Discovery (DMKD) instead, in order to avoid confusion (Cios and Kurgan, 2005).

Our proposal is based on previous experience and lessons learned from a Data Mining and Knowledge Discovery (DMKD) project that had the objective to manage customer insolvency in the telecommunications industry (Daskalaki et al., 2003). We further provide the architecture and the main functionalities of a DSS which will be built when a decision that it is worth proceeding with the operationalization of the discovered patterns is made.

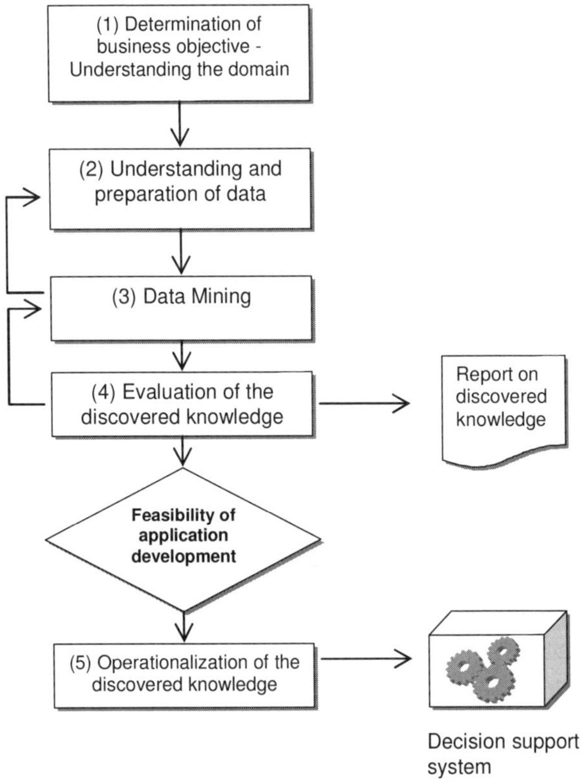

Figure 1. An abstract model of the process of Knowledge Discovery from Data (KDD).

2. Enterprise Data and Predictive Classification

Telecommunications companies are typical examples of enterprises that accumulate large amounts of data on a daily basis. For this matter they take advantage of the new developments on technology, which continues to provide faster storage devices with higher capacity and lower costs. However, despite the modern techniques in database management systems and data warehouse systems, in most real-world problems, the data is almost never ready for knowledge extraction and the stages of data cleaning, pre-processing and formatting require a considerable amount of effort. Blind application of data mining methods to unprocessed data may result in patterns that are not valid, leading to improper interpretations and wrong conclusions. It is therefore important that the DMKD process, when applied to a certain problem, is characterized by many loops that connect the middle and final steps with earlier ones. The iterative character of the DMKD process has been stressed by many researchers (Brachman and Anand, 1996), while it is estimated that only a small portion (15-25%) of the total effort needs to be devoted to the actual application of data mining algorithms (Brachman et al., 1996, Zhang et al., 2003).

Real world data are often of low quality, due to incompleteness, noise, inconsistencies, etc. This may result in distortion in the patterns that are hidden in the data, lower performance of the algorithms and in outputs of poor quality. From our experience with the customer insolvency problem in telecommunications and several other classification problems, the following characteristics are known to cause the majority of the technical difficulties in the DMKD process:

(a) *Noise*: Noise in data is a well documented characteristic for certain real-world problems. In a study on the sensitivity of machine learning algorithms in noisy data, Kalapanidas et al. (2003) report that decision trees performed better than other classification algorithms. Several techniques have been proposed as a remedy for the problem of noise, including the wavelet denoising (Li et al., 2002). However, it is almost certain that noise cannot be completely eliminated. For the telecommunications industry, for example, it is known that a case of insolvency may be the result of a fraudulent act or due to factors that the customer cannot control (health problems, personal bankruptcy, etc.). The success of predicting insolvency is based on the premise that customers change behavior during a certain period, therefore the second group of customers will add noise to the first group, unless they are distinguished. Most companies, however, will not carry such information; therefore any classification effort cannot be expected to achieve high scores of accuracy.

(b) *Missing Data*: This is another well known problem that appears extensively in real-world datasets. Missing values in data is related to non-applicability of a specific data field, unavailability of a value, data corruption or delayed insertion of the value (the well known semantics of the "NULL" value in data bases). Machine learning algorithms, with a few exceptions (for example, C4.5), cannot tackle datasets with missing values. Therefore, various techniques need to be applied for filling the empty fields. These include replacing the "NULL" value with a default value or with the mean value of the specific characteristic over the whole dataset or the mean value of the specific characteristic over a given class. Recent efforts in treating the problem of missing data suggest more elaborate techniques, for example a Naïve Bayesian classifier supported by the concept of information gain (Liu et al., 2005).

(c) *Limited and distorted view of the world*: In any data mining project the available datasets represent the real world entities (for example, the individual customer of the enterprise) in a limited and distorted way. In our case, the source of our information was exclusively the telecommunication company and the information that this company can maintain on its customers. Due to various ethical and legal reasons, this information cannot be inter-related to other sources of information; so for instance, the customer is represented as a user of the particular service, with no means of revealing other social or financial aspects that might had influenced the individual's behavioral patterns and might had strong impact towards an insolvent behavior.

(d) *Overwhelming amount of secondary characteristics*: In the usually very large datasets involved in a DMKD project, often deduced from transactional data or other sources that register interaction of the company with its clients, many parameters may be defined. In a modern telecommunications company this data may very well characterize the behavior of customers. Selection of only relevant parameters for the problem of interest is a tedious process that can be partly based on statistical analysis tools and techniques and partly on understanding the significance of the parameters in the problem by the analysts involved. Therefore, identifying a subset of these parameters, and subsequently using adequate tools for selecting the most relevant ones is a crucial and important phase, often directly related to the particular problem and not easily reproducible.

Apart from these well documented characteristics, in classification problems data may exhibit additional and more subtle deficiencies. These include:

- Uneven distribution of the cases among different classes.
- Rarity of the events of interest, for example only a very small number of cases of insolvent customers (minority class) in the dataset.
- Different and often unknown misclassification costs for the two classes.

The detection of oil spills from satellite radar images (Kubat et al., 1998), the detection of fraud in mobile communications (Fawcett and Provost, 1997) or in the use of credit cards (Chan et al., 1999), the customer insolvency problem (Daskalaki et al., 2003), the prediction of failures in some manufacturing processes (Riddle et al., 1994) and the diagnosis of rare diseases (Laurikkala, 2001), are problems that exhibit at least one of these characteristics. The presence of such characteristics influence adversely the predictive classification and turn the data mining stage into a much more difficult task than it usually is. Several remedies have been suggested including modification of the dataset by under sampling or over sampling methods, considering other than the usual performance measures and of course combining classifiers with techniques like bagging or stacking.

3. The Process of Knowledge Discovery from Enterprise Data

As already mentioned in the introduction of this chapter, the KDD or DMKD process has been modelled in various ways. The 9-step framework according to Fayyad et al. (1996), presented in Figure 2, was found most suitable for describing our experience with the customer insolvency problem and is used in this section as a frame for reviewing the process. Since our final goal was to develop a knowledge-based DSS for managing insolvency, the suggested process was applied first to confirm the hypothesis that prediction of customer insolvency is possible by studying patterns in the data provided by the telecommunications company. Although researchers aspire to fully automated processes for all steps involved, the discovery of knowledge with little intervention or support from domain experts cannot be achieved (Kopanas et al., 2002). In fact, in (Brachman and Anand, 1996) it is admitted that the domain knowledge should lead the process.

```
(1) Learning the application domain
(2) Creating a target dataset
(3) Data cleaning and preprocessing
(4) Data reduction and projection
(5) Choosing the function of data mining
(6) Choosing the data mining algorithm(s)
(7) Data Mining
(8) Interpretation
(9) Use of the discovered knowledge
```

Figure 2. The 9-step framework of the KDD process according to Fayyad et al., 1996.

Taking one step at a time, we briefly describe the actions that need to be taken at each phase of the process. We enrich the description with our experiences from the insolvency prediction problem. Emphasis is given to the role of the domain expert throughout the whole project. From the early stages, it was well understood that a number of domain experts and several sources of data had to be involved in the process. Domain experts, including executives involved in handling the problem of customer insolvency and salespersons who deal with the problem on a day-to-day basis, were interviewed during the problem formulation phase. Their views on the problem and its attributes were recorded and used suitably throughout. An investigation of the available data was also performed and this involved executives of departments like information systems and corporate databases. They were able to provide an early indication on the sources but most importantly on the quality of the data. Other key players for this project were the data analysts, who were also involved together with the knowledge engineers and the data mining experts.

3.1 Definition of the Problem and Application Domain

During this initial phase of each project, specific characteristics for the problem need to be defined and objectives or goals for the whole project need to be set. The role of the domain experts during this phase is evident and very important.

For our project, for example, we had to define the term "insolvency prediction" in a way that made sense to the telecommunications company. In practice, this means that the prediction should take place early enough, when there is still time for preventive and possibly aversive measures. The billing process of the company, the rules concerning overdue payments and the currently applied measures against insolvent customers had to be explicitly described by the domain experts. Moreover, the project objectives had to be defined with the help of decision makers or domain experts. Setting objectives in a given project is a very important task and influences heavily the selection of performance measures to be set later in the data mining phase. Furthermore, the performance measures play a decisive role for the evaluation of classifiers. For our problem, three objectives were set as prevailing for the company:

1. Detection of as many insolvent customers as possible.
2. Minimal number of false alarms, i.e. the number of good customers that are falsely classified as insolvent, should be as low as possible.
3. Timely warning for possible insolvencies, so that prediction can be useful in business terms.

The first objective is evident, given that insolvent customers cause loss of revenue for the company; therefore detection of as many as possible of them is of prime importance. However, an even more important objective is to maintain a good relationship with the good customers (second objective). In other words, the company should take action against a suspected insolvency if and only if a given customer is classified as insolvent with high certainty. Otherwise, the company takes the risk of loosing good customers. It turns out that these two objectives are conflicting, thus reducing false alarms causes further reduction to the number of customers predicted to become insolvent after the next due date for payment. Lastly, the third objective partly determined the data that were collected from the corporate data sources. Our experiment investigated the hypothesis that in the case of customer insolvency, calling habits and phone usage in general change during a critical period just before and right after termination of the billing period. Therefore, this objective indicated the need for data that exhibit the usage of the service in regular intervals much shorter than the billing periods.

3.2 Creating a Target Dataset

During this phase, the data to be analyzed throughout the project are determined. It is an important stage because critical decisions must be taken. The decisions concern the type of data that are needed to fulfill the objectives, the timeframe during which data will be collected and the subset of the actual population on which the study will take place. The role of domain and business knowledge at this stage concerns the structure of the available information and its semantic value. The key players for this stage come from the data processing department, i.e. employees mainly involved in the data entry and processing activities for the corporate information systems.

Customer behavior, in particular, may be described by numerous characteristics, most of them not readily available. For our research purposes, two groups of data were requested. The first referred to detailed customer information (such as name, occupation, address, etc.) and were derived from the contract files and phone directory entries. The second group of data referred to time-dependent attributes. They provided information about the telephone usage (from the so-called CDRs, i.e. Call Detail Records) and the financial transactions (such as bills and payments) of the customers. Unfortunately, there was no additional information on the credit condition of individual customers in the corporate databases; neither could become available from outside sources.

In order to make this study more representative, a cross-section of the population was used. The data concerned 100,000 customers and were collected from three different geographic areas: one rural, one small tourist town and one major urban centre. In terms of time, the data in the target dataset covered a span of 17 months. Moreover, as often occurs in DMKD projects, the data came from several different sources (databases) of the organization. In our premises, they were integrated and kept in a suitably designed data warehouse built for this project. For confidentiality purposes and protection of customer privacy, the data were codified in a secure way. As an indication for the size of the data warehouse built, the collected data were over 10 GB in raw form.

3.3 Data Cleaning and Preprocessing

At this stage, it is essential to test the quality of the collected data, to inter-relate the heterogeneous data items in the data warehouse, and to filter out information of no significance. Data cleaning is a tedious process. However if not performed it is impossible to proceed to the data mining phase, where the data is assumed to be of good quality and very relevant. During the cleaning and preprocessing phase, domain knowledge is again very important and the role of domain experts is very critical.

Since the size of the collected data in a data mining project is usually very large, it is helpful to reduce it, if possible. In our study, for example, a 50% decrease in the data volume was achieved by eliminating all calls that were charged for less than 0.3 €. The elimination of such data items did not affect the final goal for insolvency prediction. This is the case because a company was interested in detecting mainly the patterns of those expensive calls placed from customers with the ultimate goal not to disburse their charges.

Decisions and actions like the reduction of data just described are extremely important since they manage to purify the data towards the upcoming application of the data mining algorithms and the domain experts should be consulted for them. In fact, all data cleaning and preprocessing activities that take place during this phase should be guided by domain experts emanating from the departments that are involved with the underlined procedures. Furthermore, using domain knowledge, elimination of certain irrelevant attributes is also possible at this stage, before the actual feature selection in the data mining phase. For example, in our case, the attribute "amount charged" in each bill was considered irrelevant, since it is known that not only insolvent customers relate to high bills, but also solvent and very good customers. Instead, large fluctuations of the amounts charged in consecutive bills were considered as more relevant to insolvency. Thus, such fluctuations were calculated and taken into consideration.

In addition, certain error correction procedures may need to be applied at this stage, in order to sanitize the data from missing or erroneous values. Such problems are unavoidable with real data and in most cases are due to the dispersion of data sources and the lack of consistency among information systems within the organizations that provide the data. Accordingly, data synchronization is a very important and tedious procedure during this step. For our project, it was necessary to study the calling habits of all customers during a period starting several weeks before a billing period expires. However, different customers belong to different pre-set billing periods, thus the full set of customers forms several "groups of phone accounts". According to these groups, insolvencies may appear at varying points of time within a period of study. In order to study the behavioral patterns of insolvent customers it was necessary to place the events in a time scale relative to the end of a billing period.

3.4 Data Reduction and Projection

The cleaning and pre-processing tasks during the previous phase usually expose for the first time the problems that may exist with the collected data. Therefore at this stage, the data are further reduced, if necessary, while new features may be added following actions of data transformations. Such decisions are usually based on methods of statistical inference applied to the primary data. For the transformations or projections of data, the project objectives and domain knowledge should be again the actual guides.

For the customer insolvency problem, the pre-processing task revealed a number of instances among customers with insufficient historical data. These customers eventually had to be eliminated from the dataset. On the contrary, new attributes had to be created using transformations of the original data, in order to detect fluctuations in the telephone usage or exhibit the overdue payments. The study period for the insolvent customers' behavior was set to be approximately seven months before the actual disconnection of their phone. The decision on the length of the study period was based on data analyses and business requirements. Within the seven-month study period, all statistics regarding the call transactions made by each customer were aggregated in two-week periods, according to certain aggregation functions (sum, count, average, standard deviation, etc.). This procedure generated several new attributes which were calculated for all customers, solvent and insolvent.

In addition, with the help of statistical inference at this point, a number of features were tested and those that did not provide any valid or useful information in distinguishing solvent from insolvent customers were eliminated. For example, a chi-square test was performed to test whether solvent and insolvent customers were distributed with the same proportion across the twenty-three different categories of telephone accounts that existed at the time. Similarly, using chi-square homogeneity tests it was checked whether certain customer attributes, such as the "average extra charges in the bill", the "average amount owed" and "payments by installments" appeared in significantly different proportions for the two classes of customers. All tests were performed in the original dataset. However, in order to create customer profiles, and even more so in order to study the phone usage for customers of both classes, it was important to create a smaller and more manageable dataset. The new dataset ought to project all customer characteristics just like in the original one. In our case, the new dataset was comprised of 28,220 customers out of which only 196 were the insolvent ones. For each customer the data included: (i) two attributes for the customer's profile (static information), (ii) sixty-six attributes for the usage of the phone over fifteen consecutive two-week periods, and (iii) four attributes for the financial transactions of the customer (payment and agreements for payment with instalments). Therefore, in total seventy-seven attributes were collected for each customer in the dataset.

3.5 Defining the Data Mining Function and Performance Measures

During this phase, the purpose of the knowledge to be derived from data mining is defined and this in turn defines the data mining function and the performance measures to be used for evaluating the function. The data mining function can be classification, clustering, regression, association rules, etc.

In many projects, the data mining function is defined at an earlier stage. In other projects, however, the analysts may initially define a set of possible functions and it is only after the data preparation and pre-processing tasks that any decision about the function is finalized.

The problem of predicting customer insolvency was viewed as a *two-class classification problem*, where each customer could be classified in one of the two classes: *most possibly solvent* or *most possibly insolvent*. As a classification problem, it carried some of the characteristics discussed earlier:

1. In the dataset that resulted from the pre-processing stage, approximately 99.3% were solvent (negative) and 0.7% insolvent (positive) cases. Thus, the distribution between the two classes was very uneven.

2. The absolute number of insolvent cases in the data set was very small. This happened because only a few, if any at all, insolvencies arise in every billing period.
3. The misclassification costs for the two classes of customers, although unknown, were not the same.

Classification problems with such characteristics are particularly difficult to solve. As suggested in (Weiss and Provost, 2001; Chan and Stolfo, 1998) new training datasets have to be created, where the distribution of cases between classes is altered by either under sampling or over sampling the majority class. For our work, the new datasets were achieved by under sampling, i.e. maintaining all insolvent cases as in the original dataset, while taking only a sample from the solvent cases. For the sampling technique, a stratified sampling procedure was performed while the sample size was determined each time by the corresponding desired distribution. Our goal was to create a representative sample of the solvent customers, so that the algorithms could be trained sufficiently well. Therefore, the triad of characteristics *geographic area*, *type of phone connection*, and *bill group* were used as sampling strata. These three characteristics had to be carried in the sample with the same proportions as in the original dataset, in order: (a) to maintain the three previously mentioned distinct geographic areas in the reduced dataset; (b) to represent the different types of phone connections; and (c) to eliminate the seasonality which may be associated with the billing periods. Using under sampling several datasets were created, each with a different class distribution, which were further used for experimentation with machine-learning algorithms.

As mentioned earlier, the class distribution in the dataset was highly imbalanced (1:142), while this ratio may vary with time and geographic area. As for the misclassification costs, it is known that companies are interested in predicting as many insolvent-to-be customers as possible. However, they also rather prefer to miss a portion of "bad" customers than to hassle a large number of "good" customers (Ezawa and Norton, 1996; Daskalaki et al., 2003). In technical terms, this means that false alarms (falsely predicting a solvent customer as insolvent) are highly undesirable, because companies do not want to put at risk their relation with good customers. This information, which originated from the decision makers in the company, defined the *business objectives* for our study. Even though it would had been of some help, the objectives were not quantified further, so our effort was mainly to match the business objectives with the performance measures to be used in the evaluation process.

For classification problems with high imbalance in class distribution as well as for problems with unknown class distribution, the *Average Accuracy Rate* is not an appropriate performance measure (Provost and Fawcett, 1997). This can be explained in datasets with two classes, out of which one is rare, because the error that stems from the minority cases is disproportionally larger compared to the error that stems from the majority cases. Thus even accuracy rates close to 100% may not be satisfactory (Weiss and Provost, 2003). Alternative measures and evaluation strategies have been suggested and these include the *ROC analysis* (Provost et al., 1998), the *Area under Curve (AUC)* (Chawla, 2003), and the *Geometric Mean* (Kubat and Matwin, 1997) or the *F-measure* (Lewis and Gale, 1994) of the accuracy rates for the majority and the minority classes. All these measures calculate accuracy rates for the two classes separately and then attempt to combine them in a way that both rates can play some significant role. An additional performance measure, which may incorporate objectives (1) and (2) set forth earlier (i.e. high True Positive and low False Positive), is the *Precision rate* (*PR*) for the positive class. This measure, which is calculated as:

$$PR = Pr\{\text{actually P} \mid \text{predicted as P}\} = \frac{TP\text{ cases}}{TP\text{ cases}+FP\text{ cases}} \tag{1}$$

gives the percentage of the correctly predicted minority cases out of the total number of cases classified to the minority class. The precision rate measures the ability of a classifier to be more "precise" with its predictions, instead of just achieving a high percentage of correct predictions in a given class. In our case, we were primarily interested in maximizing both the precision and true positive rates and secondarily the true negative rate.

3.6 Selection of Data Mining Algorithms

At this stage of the KDD process, the data mining algorithms are selected. For each data mining function, the fields of statistics and machine learning provide many alternative algorithms, which differ quite a lot in terms of their model representation. Selecting the data mining algorithms depends on several factors including the type of data, the analyst's preferences and competences, and also the availability and popularity of certain computational tools.

We experimented with several alternative classification algorithms for testing our hypothesis. The algorithms used initially in our study were: *Linear Discriminant Analysis* (Johnson and Wichern, 1998), *Decision Trees* (DT) trained with the C4.5 pruning algorithm (Quinlan, 1992), and *Multilayer Perceptron Neural Networks* (NN) using for training the backpropagation algorithm. Later during a broader experimentation, we additionally used: *Linear Logistic Regression* (LLR) equipped with the LogitBoost bias reduction algorithm and simple regression functions as base learners for fitting the logistic models, *Multinomial Logistic Regression* (MLR) with a ridge estimator (le Cessie and van Houwelingen, 1992), *Bayesian Networks* (BN), using a simple estimator for finding the conditional probability tables of the network and using a hill-climbing search algorithm with initial network for structure learning a Naive Bayes Network, and a *Support Vector Machine* (SVM) classifier with a linear polynomial kernel, trained using the Sequential Minimal Optimization algorithm (Platt, 1999). Each one of them gives a different classifier, for example, a linear one is produced by the Discriminant Analysis, a non-linear by the Neural Network, and a rule-based by the Decision Tree.

These algorithms were initially applied to the dataset that carried 196 cases of insolvent and 28,024 cases of solvent customers (a proportion of 1:142) and the results are shown in Table 1. As one may see, not all algorithms managed to accurately train classifiers when applied to such an extremely imbalanced dataset. In fact, only the Discriminant Analysis (with a 30.77 % for TP rate) and the Bayes Networks (with a 64.29% for TP rate) appeared to overcome this problem successfully, while the Multilayer Perceptron Neural network and the Multinomial Logistic

Regression exhibited only a very low performance for the minority class (2.04% and 1.53%, respectively). The other three algorithms treated insolvent customers completely as noise and classified all cases of the test sets in the 10-fold cross validation procedure to the majority class. In order to overcome the problem caused by the "natural" distribution, datasets with the artificial distributions 1:100, 1:50, 1:25, 1:15, 1:10, 1:5 and 1:1 were constructed. For this purpose, the original dataset was split into a testing set (using 25% of the data) and training set (with the remaining 75% of the data). The new datasets were built using the stratified random sampling procedure discussed earlier for constructing the new training sets.

Table 1. Classification results when the "natural" distribution is used for training.

Classification Algorithm	True Positive Rate	True Negative Rate	Precision Rate
Discriminant Analysis	0.3077	0.9864	0.1402
Neural Network	0.0204	0.9998	0.4444
Decision Tree	0.0000	0.9999	0.0000
Bayes Network	0.6429	0.9259	0.0572
M/mial Logistic Regression	0.0153	0.9998	0.3750
Linear Logistic Regression	0.0000	1.0000	N/D
Support Vector Machine	0.0000	1.0000	N/D

3.7 *Experimentation with Data Mining Algorithms*

At this stage, the actual search for patterns of interest takes place with the help of the chosen data mining algorithms. Particularly for predictive classification, the results are summarized in confusion matrices, which provide the true and false positives, and true and false negatives. In order to test and compare the performance of the aforementioned classification algorithms for our project, several experiments were realized using a 10-fold validation procedure and splitting the data in training and testing data, as discussed in Section 3.6. For performance criteria, initially, three simple measures were used (the two accuracy rates and the precision rate) and in the sequel three composite ones, the *AUC*, the geometric mean, and the *F*-measure. In this chapter, we provide a summary of our experimental results (Table 2), while more details can be found in (Daskalaki et al., 2006).

Table 2. Simple and composite performance measures from a 10-fold validation classification procedure.

		DT	LLR	NN	BN	MLR	SVM
TP	**1:142(N)**			0.061	0.673	0.020	
	1:100	0.020		0.102	0.673	0.020	
	1:50	0.204	0.061	0.306	0.673	0.082	0.041
	1:25	0.367	0.224	0.551	0.694	0.245	0.082
	1:15	0.469	0.347	0.469	0.755	0.347	0.245
	1:10	0.469	0.408	0.592	0.735	0.469	0.347
	1:5	0.653	0.694	0.755	0.837	0.714	0.674
	1:1(B)	0.816	0.898	0.878	0.878	0.898	0.857
TN	**1:142(N)**			0.998	0.925	0.999	
	1:100	0.999		0.997	0.923	0.999	0.999
	1:50	0.993	0.998	0.991	0.920	0.998	0.997
	1:25	0.984	0.993	0.983	0.920	0.993	0.995
	1:15	0.975	0.987	0.984	0.917	0.985	0.988
	1:10	0.970	0.983	0.968	0.916	0.979	0.980
	1:5	0.957	0.950	0.938	0.910	0.950	0.951
	1:1(B)	0.761	0.812	0.813	0.894	0.804	0.809
PR	**1:142(N)**			0.176	0.059	0.500	
	1:100	0.250		0.217	0.058	0.167	
	1:50	0.167	0.176	0.195	0.056	0.200	0.100
	1:25	0.140	0.190	0.182	0.057	0.194	0.095
	1:15	0.099	0.156	0.173	0.060	0.142	0.121
	1:10	0.116	0.143	0.114	0.058	0.138	0.108
	1:5	0.095	0.088	0.078	0.061	0.091	0.087
	1:1(B)	0.023	0.032	0.032	0.055	0.031	0.030

		DT	LLR	NN	BN	MLR	SVM
AUC	**1:142(N)**	0.500	0.500	0.530	0.799	0.510	0.000
	1:100	0.510	0.500	0.550	0.798	0.510	0.500
	1:50	0.598	0.530	0.649	0.797	0.540	0.519
	1:25	0.676	0.609	0.767	0.807	0.619	0.538
	1:15	0.720	0.667	0.727	0.836	0.666	0.616
	1:10	0.722	0.696	0.780	0.825	0.724	0.663
	1:5	0.805	0.822	0.847	0.873	0.832	0.812
	1:1(B)	0.789	0.855	0.845	0.886	0.851	0.833
GM	**1:142(N)**			0.104	0.200	0.101	
	1:100	0.071		0.149	0.197	0.058	
	1:50	0.184	0.104	0.244	0.194	0.128	0.064
	1:25	0.226	0.206	0.317	0.199	0.218	0.088
	1:15	0.216	0.233	0.285	0.213	0.222	0.172
	1:10	0.233	0.241	0.259	0.206	0.254	0.194
	1:5	0.249	0.248	0.243	0.225	0.256	0.243
	1:1(B)	0.138	0.170	0.167	0.219	0.167	0.161
F	**1:142(N)**			0.091	0.109	0.002	
	1:100	0.038		0.139	0.107	0.003	
	1:50	0.183	0.091	0.238	0.103	0.009	0.058
	1:25	0.202	0.206	0.274	0.108	0.016	0.088
	1:15	0.185	0.215	0.253	0.111	0.017	0.162
	1:10	0.164	0.212	0.191	0.107	0.032	0.165
	1:5	0.166	0.157	0.142	0.113	0.062	0.155
	1:1(B)	0.045	0.062	0.061	0.103	0.187	0.059

Using the simple performance measures it is concluded that the accuracy rate for the minority class (*TP* rate) has the tendency to increase as the proportion of positive examples in the dataset increases. The same is also true for the accuracy rate for the majority class (*TN* rate) and more so the precision rate (*PR*) for the minority decrease. These observations are roughly true for all classification algorithms except of the Bayesian Network. As discussed also previously in (Chan and Stolfo, 1998; Elkan, 2001) the Bayes Network classification algorithm is not sensitive to changes in the class distribution.

Compared to the other algorithms, the Bayes Network algorithm gives the highest values for the *TP* rate but the lowest ones for the *PR* and the *TN* rate for nearly all class distributions. In addition, from the experimental results it is clear that maximizing the *TP* rate conflicts with the maximization of the *PR* or the *TN* rate. Increasing the percentage of the positive cases in the training dataset, the probability of positive prediction from an induced classifier becomes higher too. Thus, both the number of false positive cases and true positive cases are expected to increase. Apparently, the increase in the number of true positive cases is a lower percentage than the corresponding increase of the false positive cases and the *PR* decreases.

The performance of the classification algorithms was additionally evaluated using three composite performance measures, the *AUC* that uses both the *TP* and *TN* ($FP = 1 - TN$) rates, the geometric mean of *TP* rate and *PR* ($GM = \sqrt{TP \cdot PR}$), and the *F*-measure of *TP* rate and *PR*:

$$F = \frac{(\beta^2 + 1) * TP * PR}{\beta^2 * PR + TP} \tag{2}$$

According to our experimental results (Table 2), the *AUC* measure behaves very similarly to the *TP* rate and has the tendency to increase as the proportion of minority cases in the training set increases. Again, the classifiers induced by the Bayes Networks give the highest *AUC* value for all different class distributions. Conversely, the geometric mean and the *F*-measure exhibit approximately concave behavior for most algorithms and attain their “maximum” values when the class distribution is in the range of 1:25 to 1:5. For the *GM*, this is explained because when the number of minority cases in the dataset increases the *TP* rate increases and the *PR* decreases. Thus, an increase of the geometric mean indicates that the achieved improvement in the *TP* rate is beneficial since it is not accompanied by a simultaneous "large" decrease of the *PR*. The *GM* attains a "maximum" at that class distribution where the benefit from the increase in the *TP* rate is larger than the corresponding decrease in the *PR*. Using the *GM* as performance measure, the classifiers induced by the Neural Network algorithm exhibit superior behavior, by achieving its best performance at the 1:25 dataset. The rest of the classification algorithms behave in a comparable fashion and attain best performance either at the 1:10 or 1:5 dataset, while the SVM classifiers exhibit the worst performance. The only exception again is the Bayesian Network algorithm, which as already discussed, is insensitive to changes in the class distribution. Therefore, the values for the *GM* are approximately the same for all class distributions.

The *F*-measure (Lewis and Gale, 1994) also combines the rates *TP* and *PR*. Its value depends on a factor denoted by β (Equation (2)), which takes on values from 0 to infinity and its role is to control the impact of the *TP* rate and the *PR* separately. It is easy to show that if $\beta = 0$ then the *F*–measure reduces to the *PR* and conversely if $\beta \to \infty$ then the *F*–measure approaches the *TP* rate. Based on the *F*-measure, the classifiers induced by the Neural Network prevail by giving the highest values for several datasets followed by the classifiers induced by the Decision Tree and the Linear Logistic Regression algorithms. For all class distributions the Bayesian Network's classifiers achieve approximately the same *F* value (close to 0.1), while the classifiers induced by the Multiple Logistic Regression give the lowest values except only of the dataset 1:1. Lastly, the datasets in the range 1:25 to 1:5 appear to train classifiers in a way that achieves the highest *F* values for all algorithms.

3.8 Combining Classifiers and Interpretation of the Results

At this stage, the results of the experimentation that took place at the previous stage are interpreted and if necessary, certain previous steps are repeated afresh, while ensemble techniques that involve combination of classifiers are used for improving the performance.

For our study, judging from the range of the class distributions we examined (from the set with the "natural" to the set with the "balanced" distribution) using the six classification algorithms, it was concluded that the measures *TP* rate and *PR* are conflicting to each other. On the contrary, the geometric mean $\sqrt{TP * PR}$ and the *F*-measure of *TP* and *PR* combine the two measures in an effective way. As suggested by these two measures, the classifiers induced by the Neural Network algorithm may provide better overall predictions for the insolvent customers. They are followed by the Decision Tree algorithm and the Linear Logistic Regression. For further improving the predictive capability of our classifiers, we decided to compare case-by-case the results of the three best classification algorithms and thus combine them into voting schemes. The goal of this effort was to achieve stronger reassurance for our predictions and an improved basis for an operational decision support system that gives safe predictions on possible customer insolvencies.

Using a case-by-case comparison of the actual classifications of the different classifiers many combinations or voting models are possible to be developed. For our study, three such voting schemes were attempted. Rule #1 (R1) is the democratic rule and any given case is classified to class *i*, if two or more classifiers classify it as *i*. Rule #2 (R2) is a veto rule for the majority class, where any given case is classified to the minority class, if and only if all three classifiers vote for the minority class; otherwise, the case is classified to the majority class. Rule #3 (R3) is also a veto rule but for the minority class, i.e. any given case is classified to the majority class, if and only if all three classifiers vote for this class; otherwise the case is classified to the minority class.

The three voting schemes were applied in conjunction with the classifiers that were induced by the algorithms of Neural Networks, Decision Trees and Linear Logistic Regression for all different datasets (class distributions 1:142 to 1:1). A comparison of their performance (Table 3) shows that R3 gives the highest values for the *TP* rate and *AUC* for nearly all class distributions. At the same time, it gives the lowest values for the *TN* rate and *PR*. Exactly the reverse is observed for rule R2, while the democratic rule R1 is always between the other two. This behavior of the rules was expected since R3 is riskier and R2 is more conservative in classifying an instance to the minority class. Given that apart from the high *TP* rate, in this problem we are also looking for high *PR* rate, it is once more clear that combinations of *TP* and *PR* should be examined for the final decision.

Table 3. Values of simple and composite performance measures for the voting rules.

		R1	R2	R3		R1	R2	R3
TP	1:142(N)				AUC	0.500	0.500	0.500
	1:100	0.020		0.102		0.510	0.500	0.549
	1:50	0.163	0.041	0.367		0.579	0.520	0.677
	1:25	0.388	0.143	0.612		0.690	0.570	0.791
	1:15	0.408	0.163	0.714		0.698	0.579	0.838
	1:10	0.469	0.224	0.776		0.725	0.610	0.860
	1:5	0.714	0.531	0.857		0.837	0.757	0.880
	1:1(B)	0.898	0.755	0.939		0.855	0.836	0.798
TN	1:142(N)				GM			
	1:100	1.000		0.997		0.082		0.137
	1:50	0.996	0.999	0.987		0.183	0.117	0.246
	1:25	0.992	0.998	0.970		0.313	0.209	0.278
	1:15	0.989	0.995	0.962		0.286	0.181	0.288
	1:10	0.981	0.995	0.945		0.264	0.224	0.264
	1:5	0.959	0.983	0.902		0.280	0.310	0.222
	1:1(B)	0.813	0.917	0.656		0.171	0.212	0.133
PR	1:142(N)				F (β=1)			
	1:100	0.333		0.185		0.038		0.132
	1:50	0.205	0.333	0.165		0.182	0.073	0.228
	1:25	0.253	0.304	0.127		0.306	0.194	0.210
	1:15	0.200	0.200	0.116		0.268	0.180	0.200
	1:10	0.148	0.224	0.090		0.225	0.224	0.161
	1:5	0.109	0.181	0.058		0.190	0.269	0.108
	1:1(B)	0.032	0.060	0.019		0.063	0.111	0.037

According to the values presented in Table 3, the geometric mean (*GM*) has the highest value when either rule R2 is used with the 1:5 class distribution or rule R1 with the class distribution 1:25. Rule R3 achieves its best performance with the 1:15 dataset. Similar conclusions are drawn when examining the *F*–measure (for β=1).

Comparing the values of Table 3 with the corresponding ones of Table 2, it is suggested that the voting schemes in most cases outperform the classifiers induced by plain algorithms. Therefore, the collaboration between classification algorithms is proved to be beneficial for problems like the prediction of customer insolvency, where the cost of misclassification for good customers is high and the decision maker requires high degree of assurance prior to adopting the advice of a prediction tool for a possible action. Furthermore, for the *F*–measure we examined more values for the factor β and specifically the values β =1/4, β =1/2, and β =5. The results of these experiments are shown in Table 4.

Table 4. Performance of the three voting rules according to the *F*-measure.

		R1	R2	R3		R1	R2	R3
F (β =1/4)	1:142(N)				F (β =1)			
	1:100	0.175		0.177		0.038		0.132
	1:50	0.202	0.234	0.171		0.182	0.073	0.228
	1:25	0.259	0.285	0.133		0.306	0.194	0.210
	1:15	0.206	0.197	0.122		0.268	0.180	0.200
	1:10	0.155	0.224	0.095		0.225	0.224	0.161
	1:5	0.115	0.188	0.061		0.190	0.269	0.108
	1:1(B)	0.034	0.063	0.020		0.063	0.111	0.037
F (β =1/2)	1:142(N)				F (β =5)			
	1:100	0.082		0.159		0.021		0.104
	1:50	0.195	0.137	0.186		0.165	0.042	0.351
	1:25	0.272	0.248	0.150		0.380	0.146	0.534
	1:15	0.223	0.191	0.140		0.392	0.164	0.596
	1:10	0.172	0.224	0.109		0.433	0.224	0.600
	1:5	0.132	0.208	0.071		0.589	0.494	0.559
	1:1(B)	0.040	0.073	0.023		0.443	0.521	0.325

The conclusion from this table is that for small values of β the *PR* influences more the *F*–measure and the voting rule R2 prevails with its highest value at the 1:25 dataset. As the value for β increases, the influence of the *TP* rate on the *F*–measure increases and the voting rule R1 becomes a better choice. Lastly, when β=5, then the influence of the *TP* rate on the *F*–measure is even higher and R3 dominates by achieving the highest values at the 1:15 and 1:10 datasets.

3.9 Using the Discovered Knowledge

At this stage, the newly discovered knowledge is evaluated from an operationalizational point of view and the focus is on integrating the new knowledge with the existing domain knowledge. In case the enterprise needs a knowledge-based decision support system to aid the execution of certain business activities, this step is very critical. This is true because first one has to justify the cost effectiveness of a suggested classification scheme and this can be done by introducing additional cost criteria for the evaluation of classifiers. Secondly, because the integration of the new knowledge with the existing domain knowledge should be reflected into the design of the suggested decision support system. The following two sections of this chapter are devoted to these two issues. The evaluation of classifiers using cost criteria and the design of an Intelligent Insolvencies Management System intended for the telecommunications enterprise.

4. Development of a Cost-Based Evaluation Framework

Following the evaluation procedure of the induced classifiers in Section 3.8, it is clear that selecting the optimal classifier is not an easy task. Having experimented with several classification algorithms and some combinations of them, trained with a wide range of class distributions and calculating many performance measures, it should be commented that the picture remained still blurred for the decision makers. In reality, the performance measures used are exclusively based on the contents of confusion matrices that count cases of correct and incorrect predictions.

However, for real-world problems and specifically those that concern enterprises, it is necessary to associate performance measures with the economic impact of such predictions. This can be done by defining a cost/gain matrix and a penalty function. Both of them are defined uniquely for a given problem or set of problems and their definition requires the involvement of domain experts. As mentioned earlier, for problems like the fraud detection or the customer insolvency prediction, the objective is to maximize the *TP* rate and minimize the *FP* rate. So the penalty function may be defined as follows:

Total Gain (*TG*) = Gain from Positives (*GP*) – Loss from Negatives (*LN*)

This penalty function is based on the fact that predicting correctly bad customers may be translated into revenue for the company and hassling good customers by mistakenly taking actions against them may result in loss of money. Let us assume the following two cost measures (Table 5): C_P, the expected gain per customer that is correctly classified as insolvent and C_N, the expected cost per customer incorrectly classified as insolvent, respectively. Then the penalty function can be written as follows:

$$TG = a \cdot C_P - c \cdot C_N \tag{3a}$$

where a and c represent the number of true positive and false positive cases, respectively, in the confusion matrix. Moreover, when the class distribution of a given dataset changes by throwing away only majority cases, then the value for c, the number of false positive cases, must be multiplied by a normalizing factor, where N_0 is the population size of the majority class in the original dataset and N_a is the population size of the majority class in the dataset with the artificial distribution. Thus, the penalty function takes the format:

$$TG = a \cdot C_P - c\left(\frac{N_0}{N_a}\right) \cdot C_N \tag{3b}$$

Table 5. The cost/gain matrix used for the customer insolvency problem.

		Predicted	
		Positive (P)	Negative (N)
Actual	Positive (P)	C_P	0
	Negative (N)	C_N	0

Conversely, if the testing set carries the "natural" distribution the normalizing factor N_0/N_a equals to one.

Using non-zero costs only for the true positive and the false positive cases is quite a reasonable structure of the cost/gain matrix for this type of problems (Zadrozny and Elkan, 2001). The meaning of C_P and C_N can be expressed through some functions $f_i(\omega_i, z_i)$, $i=1,2$, where ω_i represent weights with values in [0, 1]. These weights express the percentage of the insolvent-to-be customers that are expected to be turned around and eventually recover or a percentage of the solvent customers characterized as insolvent that may be distressed and cause loss to the company by stepping away. Similarly, z_i may represent the average amount in their monthly bills for each class separately. It is true, however, that the cost coefficients C_P and C_N cannot be calculated using an easily described manner. Fortunately, as will be shown later in this section, it is only the relative gain C_P / C_N that is necessary to indicate whether predictions provided from a classification scheme may result in profitable solutions for the company.

First, we give two conditions that are necessary to hold for a classifier to be of interest.

Proposition 4.1 Given a cost/gain matrix with the structure of Table 5, then any classifier must satisfy the following two conditions:

$$\frac{c_n}{a} < \frac{C_P}{C_N}, \quad \textit{or equivalently for the rates} \quad \frac{FP}{TP} < \frac{C_P}{C_N} \cdot \frac{p(+)}{p(-)} \tag{4}$$

$$\textit{and} \qquad PR_n > \frac{1}{\frac{C_P}{C_N}+1} \tag{5}$$

in order for the penalty function (3) to be greater than zero.

In Equation (4), $c_n = c \cdot (N_0/N_a)$ denotes the normalized value for the number of false positive cases in the confusion matrix, while $p(+)$ and $p(-)$ are the prior probabilities for the positive and negative cases, respectively, in the dataset.

Using Equations (4) and (5), the outcome of a classification algorithm can be related directly with the profitability of a system that potentially will be developed using the results of the algorithm. It is suggested that in order for the penalty function *TG* to be positive, it is necessary for any candidate classifier to provide a value for FP/TP which is smaller than the relative gain per insolvent customer compared to the loss per misclassified solvent customer times the fraction of the prior probabilities in the dataset. Similarly, the precision rate must be quite high if the relative gain C_P / C_N is small. Conversely, if the fraction C_P / C_N is large, then the precision is allowed to take smaller values.

The impact of the fraction C_P / C_N in the total gain becomes more distinct if we write the penalty function as a line equation:

$$\frac{TG}{C_N} = a \cdot \frac{C_P}{C_N} - c_n \tag{6}$$

Given any classifier it is now easy to plot the line represented by Equation (6) for different values of C_P / C_N. Every classifier defines such a line using the information that is provided from its confusion matrix. In case we need to compare a number of classifiers then we have to track the point where each line crosses the horizontal axis (given by c_n/a) and the slope of each line. The former is important because it is from that point on that the total gain takes positive values and the later because it gives the rate of change for the total gain. Thus for our problem even if the relative gain from correct classification is not known, given a large number of classifiers one may still find the set that maximizes the total gain for different values of C_P / C_N.

Let us consider four hypothetical classifiers, which are assumed to have provided the four lines shown in Figure 3. It is clear that there is no classifier that is worth considering if the value for C_P / C_N is less than or equal to x_1. However, if the fraction C_P / C_N is in the interval $(x_1, x_2]$, then classifier 1 is the best choice. This is the case because it crosses first the x-axis and achieves positive values for the penalty function, when all other classifiers still give negative values. For the interval $(x_2, x_3]$ classifier 2 is the best choice, because it promises higher values for the penalty function. For the same reason, when the C_P / C_N takes values larger than x_3 classifier 4 is the best choice. It is obvious that classifier 3 never prevails; therefore, it is never a good classifier for the underlined problem. This procedure is repeated until there are no more classifiers left with any higher slope from the last best. The result is a multi-segment line where each line segment represents the classifier of best choice for some specific interval in the definition set of C_P / C_N.

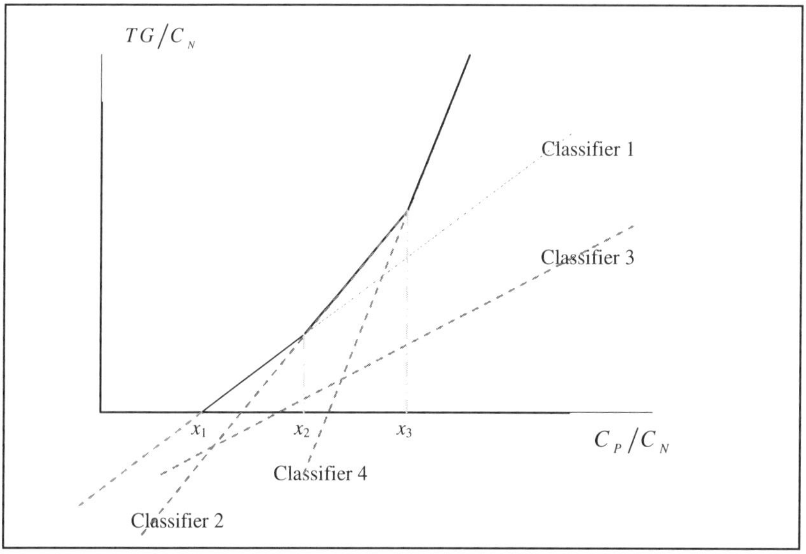

Figure 3. The optimal classifiers for the customer insolvency problem.

The approach just presented was developed in (Daskalaki et al., 2006) to study the economic impact of classification in the customer insolvency problem and bears similarities to the methodology presented in

(Drummond and Holte, 2000b; and Drummond and Holte, 2004), where the normalized cost curves are plotted against the probability cost function. In addition, the normalized cost curves are the duals of certain points in the ROC space (Provost and Fawcett, 2001) and as such the optimal cost curves form the dual representation to the ROC convex hull. The cost curves, however, are more informative because they indicate the range of class distributions and cost fractions where a given classifier dominates over the others.

For the customer insolvency problem, this procedure was applied for all previously mentioned classifiers. The results, which are shown in Table 6, give the set of best classifiers for a large range of values of the relative gain C_P / C_N. Specifically, Table 6 indicates that if the relative gain is less than or equal to 2.0, then it is not profitable obtaining prediction of insolvent customers with any of the available classifiers. If the relative gain takes values in the interval (2.0, 2.4] then the classifier induced by R2 and trained in the dataset with the artificial class distribution 1:50 is the best choice. Similarly, in the interval (2.4, 3.3] the classifier induced again by R2 and trained in the dataset 1:25 is the best choice. Combining this conclusion with the results presented in Tables 2 – 4, it is noted that these two classifiers give the highest value for the *PR* and the F – measure when $\beta = ¼$ for the respective datasets.

Proceeding as previously, in the interval (3.3, 8.1] the classifier induced by R1 in the 1:25 dataset gives the best classifier. Going back to Tables 2, 3, and 4, the chosen classifier gives one of the highest values for the *GM* and the highest for the F – measure when $\beta = ½$ or $\beta = 1$ in the 1:25 dataset. The superior performance of this classifier according to these measures makes it prevail in the examined interval. For larger values of the fraction C_P / C_N, the classifiers induced in turn by the Neural Network in the dataset 1:25, the voting rule R3 in the 1:15, 1:10, and 1:5 datasets and lastly the voting rules R1 and again R3 in the 1:1 dataset are selected as best. These classifiers performed superior according to the measures *GM*. *AUC* and *TP* or according to the F – measure when $\beta = 2$, $\beta = 5$, and $\beta > 5$, respectively.

The conclusion of this procedure is that different classifiers will prevail depending on the value of the relative gain C_P / C_N. These classifiers have been trained using different class distributions in the training dataset and different algorithms or combinations of them. In business terms, our conclusion can be transformed as follows. If predicting insolvent customers and taking actions against them is very risky (i.e., if the fraction of costs C_P / C_N takes *very small* values) it may be wiser not to proceed with any classifications.

For little less risky environments (i.e., if the fraction of costs C_P / C_N takes *small* values) the classifications should be very precise; in order for this to happen the training dataset should be as close to the "natural" distribution as possible and the leading performance measure should be the *PR* or the *F* – measure with small value for β. As the risk level in the business environment decreases, classifiers with better performance according to measures like the geometric mean of *PR* and *TP*, or the *F* – measure with larger values for the β factor and further down the *AUC* or just the *TP* are recommended. Respectively, the class distributions in the training datasets need to be more balanced in order to achieve higher accuracy for the positive cases.

Table 6. Best classifiers for different values of the relative gain C_P/C_N.

C_P/C_N	Classification algorithm	Leading performance measure	Class distribution
2.0 – 2.4	Rule #2	Precision rate or F (β = ¼)	1:50
2.4 – 3.3	Rule #2	Precision rate or F (β = ¼)	1:25
3.3 – 8.1	Rule #1	G. Mean or F (β = ½ or β = 1)	1:25
8.1 – 18.1	Neural Networks	G. Mean or F (β = 2)	1:25
18.1 – 39.7	Rule #3	G. Mean or AUC or TP or F (β = 5)	1:15
39.7 – 75.5	Rule #3	G. Mean or AUC or TP or F (β = 5)	1:10
75.5 – 313	Rule #3	AUC or TP or F (β > 5)	1:5
313 – 547	Rule #1	AUC or F (β > 5)	1:1
> 57	Rule #3	AUC or TP or F (β > 5)	1:1

5. Operationalization of the Discovered Knowledge: Design of an Intelligent Insolvencies Management System

This section touches upon the final stage of the process, which deals with the operationalization of the discovered knowledge in the form of a system that supports decisions for the enterprise. A crucial decision to be made at this stage is related to the feasibility and cost effectiveness of the development of such a system. Moreover, technical and economical factors need to be carefully studied for this matter.

One should take into consideration the fact that the discovered knowledge, even when it is of high relevance to the mission of the enterprise and of high quality in terms of applicability, validity and time invariability, it may still not be directly usable. This is true because a considerable effort may still be needed for this knowledge to take the form of a software component, so that it will integrate satisfactorily with the rest of the informational infrastructure and will adapt the established rules and practices of the specific business process.

For the rest of this section, we outline the characteristics of a DSS (called the *Intelligent Insolvency Management System or IIMS*). This system is intended to operationalize the knowledge discovered through the process discussed in Section 3 for our case study. This process yielded a number of interesting results that will be used for the DSS. In summary, the main results of the process are as follows:

[1] A data model for the insolvency problem, which contains a number of interesting features. This model has been derived either directly from the primary data in the Corporate Information Systems or through certain transformations. The features concern customer characteristics, telecommunication traffic data, billing data etc. During the process, it was found that these features could be used effectively for predicting, with acceptable accuracy and precision, future insolvent customers. However, in order for this data model to be operational for future use, a software component should be built that contains a database implementing the data model and software components that interface with the Corporate Information Systems. This will be called the *Intelligent Insolvency Management System Data Base (IIMS DB).*

[2] A number of classifiers have been developed and tested. They are the products of classification algorithms that have been trained using historical data with different class distributions and techniques and have known performance when tested against subsets of these historical data. The classifiers may take as input new cases of customers and can predict if they are suspect for insolvency or not. In order for these classifiers to become operational, they need to take the form of a set of software components, which will be called the *Insolvency Predictors (IP)*. Meta-data concerning their expected performance should also be stored in the Data Base of the DSS.

[3] A cost model, visually expressed in Figure 3, has been developed; it takes as input the fraction C_P / C_N, where C_P and C_N represent estimates for the expected gain per customer that is correctly classified as insolvent and the expected cost per customer incorrectly classified as insolvent, respectively. Given this ratio, the cost model may decide if the prediction of insolvency can produce financial benefits and in case of a positive answer, to suggest the best classifier to be used from the Insolvency Predictors. This cost model should take the form of a software component (*Cost Model* or *CM*) that controls the selection of the best classifier, given the cost parameters and an error margin.

These components, once developed, need to be integrated in the *IIMS*. The *IIMS* involves two distinct subsystems, one related to the "Insolvencies Prediction" task and the other to the "Preventive Actions" task. A high level architecture of this system is shown in Figure 4. The main players that interact with this system are: (1) the *Executives* of the enterprise, who are mainly involved with the supervision task and are responsible for setting up the parameters of the *Cost Model*, a direct consequence of strategic decisions related to risk, competition, market forces etc.; (2) the *Operators,* who mainly interact with the Preventive Actions Subsystem; they receive lists with suspected customers from the *IP*, customer information from the *IIMS* Data base and through the *Insolvent Customer Visualizer* and recommendations about possible actions from the *Heuristics Knowledge Base* (*HKB*), which contains business rules on preventive actions; lastly, (3) the *Data Mining Experts*, who supervise the Data Mining and Knowledge Discovery Process; this task involves receiving feedback on the performance of the classifiers and when needed proceed with the retraining of the Insolvencies Predictors with recent data from the Corporate Information Systems.

In a typical use of the system, the *Insolvencies Predictor* is triggered by a decision maker who wishes to investigate possible future insolvencies in a set of customers. The best classifier produces a *list of suspected insolvent customers*. This list is presented to the *Operator* for inspection, while it is also fed to the *HKB*. The *HKB* groups the suspected customers in various risk categories, using heuristics derived from business domain knowledge of the customer insolvencies department. Given that specific actions are associated with these risk categories, recommended actions are fed to the Operator. Before any action takes effect, a suggestion for detailed inspection of the customers' characteristics is made to the decision makers and the *Insolvent Customer Visualizer* is the component that supports this activity.

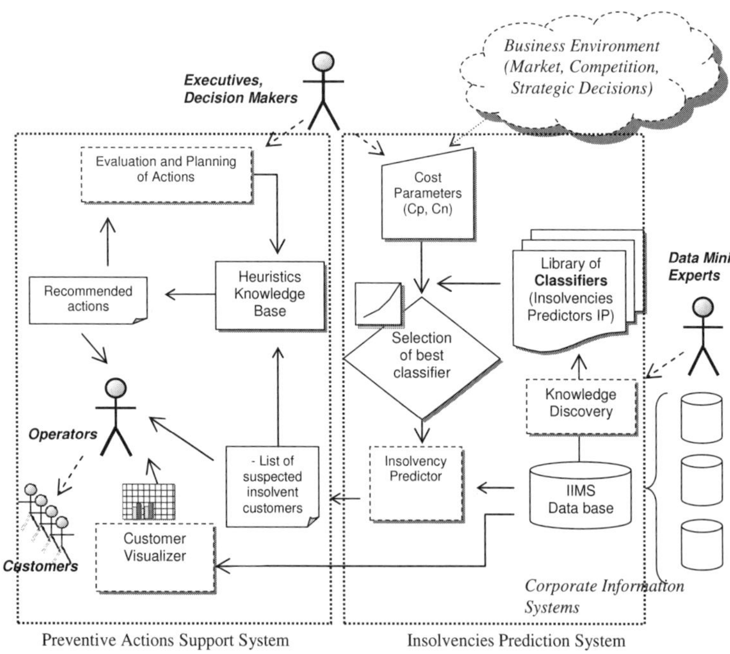

Figure 4. The architecture of the Intelligent Insolvency Management System (IIMS).

The actions may involve a warning to the customers, issue of an interim bill, a request for additional deposit as guarantee, provisional suspension of the service etc. The *Evaluator of Preventive Actions* module records the actions that take effect as well as their impact to the Company. Therefore, the heuristics are constantly updated as a result of this monitoring by the high level decision makers.

In Daskalaki et al. (2004) an example of such use of the *IIMS* prototype is discussed. According to this example, the user defines a new heuristic for grouping the suspected insolvent customers and stores it in the *Heuristic Knowledge Base*. The user through an intuitive interface defines the heuristic rule. An example of such rule is "*Business customers having made telephone calls to "090" numbers to be considered of high risk for insolvency*". This is a heuristic for defining customers of high risk, for which the company would prefer to take certain preventive action. There is a natural language interface for the Operators to express rules of this nature. This is part of the user interface which allows visualization of the user characteristics and definition of rules that recommend preventive actions to different groups of suspected insolvent-to-be customers.

6. Summary and Conclusions

In this chapter, the daunting task of discovering knowledge from enterprise data is reviewed using as an example the problem of predicting customer insolvencies in a telecommunications enterprise. The main conclusion from the initial stages of the DMKD or KDD process is that data handling (including collection, preparation, cleaning and preprocessing, reduction and transformation) can be very strenuous and time consuming. However, these first stages are very important in order for the results of the data mining process to be of any value. The role of domain knowledge during this phase is very critical and the presence of domain experts is extremely valuable.

Through the data mining stage and for several well documented classification problems, it has been found that class imbalance may cause additional challenges in the training of algorithms and in the evaluation of classifiers. Using as an example the customer insolvency problem, it has been argued that the evaluation of classifiers is not possible unless the economic impact of the classification is taken into account. As a result, a set of optimal classifiers can be selected according to the value of the relative gain from correctly classifying positive cases compared to the cost of incorrectly classifying negative cases. The conclusions from the evaluation of classifiers using the proposed cost model are summarized next.

First, combining classifiers induced from different algorithms into voting schemes results in classifiers that perform generally better than single classifiers. Moreover, a veto rule for the majority class has the potential to provide more precise predictions for the minority class (i.e., high precision rate); conversely, a veto rule for the minority or a democratic rule, has the potential to provide more accurate predictions for the minority class (i.e., high true positive rate).

Second, in order for these classifiers to achieve their maximum performance they should be trained using datasets with suitable class distributions. The most precise predictions for the minority class are achieved using datasets with class distributions that are closer to the "natural" distribution, while the most accurate predictions for the minority class are achieved using datasets that are closer to the balanced distribution.

Finally, the performance measures that ought to be used for evaluating classifiers must change according to the value of the relative gain C_P/C_N, where C_P and C_N represent an estimate of the expected gain per customer that is correctly classified as insolvent and the expected cost per customer incorrectly classified as insolvent, respectively. For small values of C_P/C_N the predictions for the minority class must be very precise because it is too risky to misclassify majority cases. In this case, the "precision rate" must be the leading performance measure. Conversely, for large values of C_P/C_N the predictions must be very accurate for the minority class because it is very profitable to detect minority cases and the "true positive rate" is the leading performance measure. For in-between values of C_P/C_N the predictions must be a combination of both performance measures, because it is not so profitable to detect minority cases and not so risky to misclassify majority cases. In such case, the "geometric mean of PR and TP" may be the leading performance measure.

The decision for operationalizing the discovered knowledge is the last most important step in a DMKD project with real enterprise data. This step involves integration of the results of the data mining process with the data available to the operators in the enterprise and the business knowledge that executive members carry, in a way which meets business objectives and supports strategic decisions. Using the design of the proposed architecture for an Intelligent Insolvencies Management System, we conclude that the key components of such a system are the IIMS Data Base, the Insolvency Predictor and the Heuristics Knowledge Base. The IIMS Data Base is built around the data model that results from the DMKD process and incorporates data from the Corporate Information Systems with the discovered knowledge. The Insolvency Predictor is a library of software components that activates the best classifier each time there is a need for predicting insolvency, based on current values of the cost parameters. Lastly, the Heuristics Knowledge Base is the heart of the Preventive Actions Support System that supports the enterprise operators in taking preventive actions against suspected insolvent customers, evaluating previous actions and further filing business rules that have proved their effectiveness.

Overall, despite of the fact that this chapter has been inspired by a specific DMKD project, the conclusions are generic enough and may be applicable to other projects that involve actual enterprise data and similar data mining techniques.

References

Brachman R.J. and Anand T. (1996). The process of Knowledge Discovery in Databases: A human centered approach. In *Advances in Knowledge Discovery and Data Mining*. U. M. Fayyad. G. Piatetsky-Shapiro, P. Smyth, and R. Uthurusamy (Eds). AAAI/MIT Press. 37-57.

Brachman R.J., Khabaza T., Kloesgen W., Piatetsky-Shapiro G., and Simoudis E. (1996). Mining Business Databases. *Communications of the ACM*. **39**(11). 42-48.

Cabena P., Hadjinian P., Stadler R., Verhees J., Zanasi A. (1998). *Discovering Data Mining: From Concepts to Implementation*. Prentice Hall.

Cios K.J. and Kurgan L.A. (2005). Trends in data mining and knowledge discovery. in *Advanced Techniques in Knowledge Discovery and Data Mining*. N.R. Pal, L.C. Jain, and N. Teoderesku. (eds.). Physica-Verlag (Springer): Berlin, Germany. 1-26.

Chan P.K. Wei F., Prodromides A., and Stolfo S. (1999). Distributed Data Mining in credit card fraud detection. *IEEE Intelligent Systems and Their Applications*, **14**(6), 67-74.

Chan P.K. and Stolfo S.J. (1998). Learning with non-uniform class and cost distributions: Effects and a multi-classifier approach. In *Work Notes KDD-98 Workshop on Distributed Data Mining*, August 1998, 1-9.

Chawla N.V. (2003). C4.5 and Imbalanced Data sets: Investigating the effect of sampling method, probabilistic estimate and decision tree structure. *Workshop on Learning from Imbalanced Datasets II. International Conference on Machine Learning*, Washington DC. U.S.A.

Daskalaki S., Kopanas I., Goudara M., and Avouris N. (2003). Data mining for decision support on customer insolvency in telecommunications business, *European Journal of Operational Research*, **145**(2), 239-255.

Daskalaki S., Kopanas I., and Avouris N. (2004). Machine Learning techniques for prediction of rare events in a business environment. In *Proceedings of the 3rd Hellenic Conference on Artificial Intelligence. SETN 2004*, Samos Island, Aegean Sea, Greece, May 2004, 79-88.

Daskalaki S., Kopanas I., and Avouris N. (2006). Evaluation of classifiers for an uneven class distribution problem. *Applied Artificial Intelligence*, **20**, 381-417.

Drummond C. and Holte R.C. (2000). Explicitly representing expected cost: An alternative to ROC representation. In *Proceedings of the sixth ACM SIGKDD International Conference on Knowledge Discovery and Data Mining*, 198-207.

Drummond. C. and Holte R.C. (2004). What ROC curves Can't Do (and Cost Curves Can)? In *Proceedings of the ROC Analysis in Artificial Intelligence, First International Workshop*, Valencia, Spain, August 2004, 19-26.

Elkan C. (2001). The foundations of cost-sensitive learning. In *Proceeding of the 17th International Joint Conference on Artificial Intelligence*, Seattle, WA., U.S.A. August 2001, Morgan Kaufmann Publishers Inc. 973-978.

Ezawa K.J., and Norton S.W. (1996). Constructing Bayesian Networks to Predict Uncollectible Telecommunications Accounts. *IEEE Expert/Intelligent Systems & their Applications*, **11**(5), 45-51.

Fawcett T. and Provost F. (1997). Adaptive Fraud Detection. *Data Mining and Knowledge Discovery*, **1**, 291-316.

Fayyad U.M., Piatetsky-Shapiro G., and Smyth P. (1996). The KDD Process for Extracting Useful Knowledge from Volumes of Data. *Communications of the ACM*, **39**(11), 27-34.

Frawley W.J., Piatetsky-Shapiro G., and Matheus C. (1991). Knowledge Discovery in Databases: An Overview. In *Knowledge Discovery in Databases*. G. Piatetsky-Shapiro and W.J. Frawley (Eds). AAAI Press/The MIT Press: Menlo Park, CA, U.S.A.

Johnson R.A and Wichern D. (1998). *Applied Multivariate Statistical Analysis*. Prentice-Hall. Inc.

Kalapanidas E., Avouris N., Craciun M., and Neagu D. (2003). Machine Learning Algorithms: A study on noise sensitivity. In *Proc. of the 1st Balkan Conference on Informatics*, Thessalonica, Greece, November, 356-365.

Kopanas I., Avouris N., and Daskalaki S. (2002). The role of knowledge modeling in a large scale Data Mining project. In *Methods and Applications of Artificial Intelligence*. I.P Vlahavas. C.D. Spyropoulos (Eds). LNAI 2308, Springer-Verlag: Berlin, Germany, 288-299.

Kubat M. and Matwin S. (1997). Addressing the curse of imbalanced training sets: One-sided selection. In *Proceedings of the 14th International Conference on Machine Learning*, 179-186.

Kubat M., Holte R., and Matwin S. (1998). Machine Learning for the detection of oil spills in satellite radar images. *Machine Learning*, **30**, 195-215.

Laurikkala J. (2001). Improving identification of difficult small classes by balancing class distribution. In *Artificial Intelligence in Medicine*. S. Quaglini, P. Barahona, S. Andreassen (Eds.). LNAI 2101, Springer-Verlag: Berlin, Germany, 63-66.

le Cessie. S. and van Houwelingen. J.C. (1992). Ridge Estimators in Logistic Regression. *Applied Statistics,* **41**(1), 191-201.

Lewis D.D. and Gale W. (1994). A sequential algorithm for training text classifiers. In *Proceedings of the Seventh Annual International ACM-SIGIR Conference on Research and Development in Information Retrieval*, Springer-Verlag, 3-12.

Li Q., Li T., Zhu S., Kambhamettu C. (2002). Improving medical/biological data classification performance by Wavelet preprocessing, In *Proceedings of ICDM 2002*.

Liu P., El-Darzi E., Lei L., Vasilakis C., Chountas P., and Huang W. (2005). An analysis of missing data treatment methods and their application to health care dataset. In *Advanced Data Mining and Applications*. X. Li, S. Wang, and Z.Y. Dong (Eds.). LNAI 3584, Springer-Verlag: Berlin, Germany, 583-390.

Platt J. (1998). Fast Training of Support Vector Machines using Sequential Minimal Optimization. In *Advances in Kernel Methods - Support Vector Learning*, B. Scholkopf, C. Burges, and A. Smola. (Eds.), MIT Press, 185-208.

Provost F. and Fawcett T. (1997). Analysis and visualization of classifier performance: Comparison under imprecise class and cost distributions. In *Proceedings of the Third International Conference on Knowledge Discovery and Data Mining*, AAAI Press: Menlo Park, CA, U.S.A., 43-48.

Provost F., Fawcett T., and Kohavi R. (1998). The case against accuracy estimation for comparing induction algorithms. In *Proceedings of the Fifteenth International Conference on Machine Learning (IMLC-98)*, Morgan Kaufmann: San Francisco, CA, U.S.A., 43-48.

Provost F. and Fawcett T. (2001). Robust Classification for Imprecise Environments. *Machine Learning*, **42**, 203-231.

Quinlan J. (1992). *C4.5: Programs for Machine Learning*. Morgan Kaufmann: San Francisco, CA, U.S.A.

Riddle P., Segal R., and Etzioni O. (1994). Representation design and brute-force induction in a Boeing manufacturing domain. *Applied Artificial Intelligence*, **8**, 125-147.

Weiss G. and Provost F. (2001). The effect of class distribution on classifier learning. *Technical Report ML-TR-43*, Department of Computer Science, Rutgers University, New Brunswick, NJ, U.S.A.

Weiss G. and Provost F. (2003). Learning when training data are costly: The effect of class distribution on tree induction. *Journal of Artificial Intelligence Research*, **19**, 315-354.

Wilson T.D. (2002). The nonsense of 'knowledge management'. *Information Research*, **8**(1), paper no. 144. [Available at http://InformationR.net/ir/8-1/paper144.html]

Wirth R. and Hipp J. (2000). CRISP-DM: Towards a Standard Process Model for Data Mining. In *Proceedings of the Fourth International Conference on the Practical Applications of Knowledge Discovery and Data Mining*, Manchester, UK, 29-39.

Zadrozny B. and Elkan C. (2001). Learning and making decisions when costs and probabilities are both unknown. In *Proceedings of the Seventh ACM SIGKDD International Conference on Knowledge Discovery and Data Mining*, ACM Press: San Francisco, CA, U.S.A., 204-213.

Zhang S., Zhang C., and Yang Q. (2003). Data Preparation for Data Mining. *Applied Artificial Intelligence*, **17**(5-6), 375-381.

Authors' Biographical Statements

Sophia Daskalaki is an Assistant Professor at the Engineering Sciences Department of the University of Patras, Greece. She received her Ph.D. in Industrial Engineering & Operations Research from the University of Massachusetts at Amherst, Massachusetts, USA (1987), her M.Sc. in Statistics & Operations Research from Oregon State University at Corvallis, Oregon, USA (1983) and her University Degree in Mathematics from the Aristotle University of Thessaloniki, Greece (1980).

She joined AT&T Bell Laboratories as a Member of the Technical Staff (1987 - 1991) working on performance evaluation issues of computer systems and networks, intelligent telecommunications services and network management. Her current research interests include data mining techniques, scheduling, timetabling and rostering, as well as stochastic models for systems optimization and queuing networks. Dr. Daskalaki is the author of over 25 research papers. She is a member of INFORMS (Institute for Operations Research and Management Sciences) and the Operational Research Society.

Ioannis Kopanas is working for OTE S.A., the Hellenic Telecommunications Organization since 1977. He has a University Degree in Physics (1984) from the University of Patras, Greece and also a Ph.D in Electrical and Computer Engineering (2004) from the University of Patras.

His current research interests include data mining and data visualisation techniques, data warehousing and applications in telecommunications.

Nikolaos Avouris was born in Zakynthos, Greece (1956). He received his Diploma in Electrical Engineering from NTUA (National Technical University of Athens) in 1979 and his M.Sc. and Ph.D. from the University of Manchester (UMIST), UK in 1980 and 1983, respectively.

He served as a post-doc researcher at UMIST, UK (1983-1984), as Assistant Professor of Computer Science at the Technical Education Institute, Athens, Greece (1985-1986), as Scientific Officer at the Joint Research Centre of the European Commission, at Ispra, Italy, (1986-1993), as Software Engineer at the Public Power Corporation, Athens, Greece (1993-1994). He joined the University of Patras, Greece as Associate Professor (1994-2001) and as Full Professor of Software Engineering, and Human-Computer Interaction (2001-today). He is the founder and head of the Human-Computer Interaction Group (http://hci.ece.upatras.gr) at the Electrical and Computer Engineering Department.

Prof. Avouris' main interests are related to design and evaluation of interactive systems, usability engineering, collaboration technology, context-aware computing systems and analysis and evaluation of collaborative activities. He has published 6 books and over 100 papers in the above fields.

Chapter 4[1]

Using Soft Computing Methods for Time Series Forecasting

Pei-Chann Chang
Department of Information Management, Yuan Ze University
No. 135, Yuan-Tung Rd., Chung-li, Tao-Yuan 32026, Taiwan, R.O.C.
E-mail: iepchang@saturn.yzu.edu.tw
Yen-Wen Wang
Department of Industrial Engineering and Management, Ching-Yun University,
No. 229 Chien-Hsin Rd., Taoyuan 320, Taiwan, R.O.C. E-mail: ywwang@cyu.edu.tw

Abstract: Time series forecasting is one of the important problems in time series analysis. Many different approaches have been developed in this field. Unlike statistical methods, soft computing methods are more tolerant to imprecision, uncertainty, partial truth, and approximation in time series. This chapter addresses two major aspects of time series forecasting: 1) how to identify time series variables including exogenous ones relevant to forecasting future values, and 2) how to build a better forecasting model to improve the forecasting accuracy. Two different models are developed in this research. First, we propose a soft computing based hybrid method to improve the accuracy of a neural network model. Then a sub-clustered rule-based forecasting method, called WEFuNN, is developed to group similar time series data together in order to reduce the computational time and to increase the accuracy of the forecasting method.

***Key Words*:** Time series forecasting, Soft computing, Clustering.

---

[1] Liao, T.W. and E. Triantaphyllou, (Eds.), **Recent Advances in Data Mining of Enterprise Data: Algorithms and Applications**, *World Scientific*, Singapore, pp. 189-246, 2007.

1. Introduction

1.1 Background and Motivation

Forecasting is one of many important problems in time series analysis. Time series forecasting has been a popular research subject for many years because many data are in the form of time series, such as sales data, weather data, stock market data, and traffic flow data. Over the years, several different methods including Moving Average, Box-Jenkins, Winter's method, and Neural Networks have been proposed for time series forecasting. These methods can be roughly grouped into statistical methods and soft computing (SC) methods.

The goal of forecasting research, in general, is to devise a better forecasting method with high accuracy and low complexity. Producing a 100% accurate forecast is impossible because nobody can really foresee the future. However, continuous research is definitely warranted particularly on the following two issues: on the complexity of the forecasting process and on how to capture the relationship between the future values to be forecasted and the variables that should be considered. Reducing the complexity can decrease the computational time of the forecasting process. Finding the relationship between the forecasted future values and the influential variables can help uncover the hidden information from archived historical data, which can be very useful for business modeling and decision-making for either a manufacturing or a service enterprise.

In the business world, sales forecasting plays a very important role. Under the situation of short lifespan of products today, how to accurately predict the product demand has become an emergent issue. Thus, an efficient sales forecasting tool is one of the keys to strengthen a company's survivability in today's competitive business environment.

1.2 Objectives

To improve its effectiveness, this chapter targets at two major aspects of a forecasting system:

- Identify the variables, including those exogenous ones that are relevant to the forecasting of future values.
- Build a hybrid-forecasting model, which applies the concept of clustering to group similar data together in order to reduce the search space and increase the accuracy of forecasting.

Both issues discussed above require that the patterns of observed time series data be identified. The first part of this chapter reviews neural network methods, with focus on how to hybrid the neural network models with other soft computing algorithms to further improve the accuracy of the neural networks, and discusses the relationship between the forecasted future values and the time series variables. An evolving neural network is hence proposed. The second part focuses on a sub-clustered rule-based forecasting method called WEFuNN. It will also be shown later that our proposed approach is able to obtain good forecasting results.

2. Literature Review

2.1 Traditional Time Series Forecasting Research

In the early developments most commonly used forecasting approaches were mainly statistical methods, such as trend analysis and extrapolation. The application of this class of methods is quite simple because complicated calculation is not required. One of the reasons for its popularity is low cost. However, these methods cannot effectively explain factors such as the nature of a tendency, seasonal factors, and changes in the industrial and social structures; thus they quickly became outdated. Thereafter, alternative approaches were developed, often called Time Series Analysis.

The so-called time series analysis refers to the analysis of a collection of serial observation values, which appear in some time order, and how to predict the possible value of the next time point based on these observation values. The advantage is to avoid spending too much time and cost in collecting the data.

Time series forecasting has became a popular research subject because it is relatively easy to observe data in the form of time series, such as sales data, weather data, stock market data, and traffic flow data. Over time, many methods have been developed in this field of time series analysis, which include moving average, the autoregressive moving average model (ARIMA, or Box-Jenkins), Winter's method, Neural Networks, and so on.

2.2 Neural Network Based Forecasting Methods

Recently soft computing methods are found to be more effective than traditional statistical methods when they are applied to forecasting. Among them, Artificial Neural Networks (ANN) is the most commonly used forecasting technique. An ANN is a parallel computing system which uses a large amount of connected artificial neurons to imitate the neural network of a natural creature. After being trained by historical data, an ANN can be used to predict the future values. Because they can be fast and accurate, many researchers use ANN to solve sales forecasting related problems. An ANN is often implemented in software, but it can be implemented in hardware as well if necessary.

Past research that applied ANN to forecasting include Kimoto (1990), Thiesing et al. (1995), Luxhoj et al. (1996), Chow (1996), Kuo (1998), Tawfiq et al. (1999), Chen (2000), Hippert (2001), Chen (2003), Guirelli (2004), Freitas (2005), Chai (2005), Gareta et al. (2005), Wang and Van Gebler et al. (2005), and Barbounis (2006). In the research of ANN-based forecasting, most of the methods focus on the multi-layer perceptron (MLP) neural network model. For learning an MLP network, back-propagation (BP) is the most commonly used training procedure. Therefore, such networks are often called back-propagation networks (BPN).

However, there are two major shortcomings of BPN: First, their method for weight updating is based on gradient descent, which often explores only limited search space and cannot jump out of a local minimum, which in turn causes early convergence. Secondly, their performance relies much on the parameter settings, such as the number of hidden layers, the number of neurons in a hidden layer, the learning rate, and inertia values. Many people have studied the effects of neural network parameters, yet no one has found an optimal network structure and set of parameter values for all problems. For different problems, different parameter settings are often needed to produce better forecasts.

Based on the above two weaknesses of BPN, Chai (2005) reviewed some technologies to improve the structure of ANN. Some researchers suggested using Genetic Algorithms (GAs) to replace the steepest descent method used in BPN, and others proposed to take advantage of the strong searching capability of GAs to find the optimal network structure. The next section will briefly review some articles that applied GAs or other soft computing methods to the forecasting problem.

2.3 Hybridizing a Genetic Algorithm with a Neural Network for Forecasting

GAs were first published by John Holland from the University of Michigan in 1975. A GA imitates the genetic evolution of creatures with three evolution mechanisms: crossover, mutation and reproduction. To take advantage of its superior global search ability, a GA is usually used to improve the performance of other methods. Based on Kim's (2000) research, we can generalize two main improved NN models that make use of GAs:

2.3.1 Using a GA to Design the NN Architecture

As mentioned earlier, specifying a NN topology, including the number of hidden layers, the number of neurons in a hidden layer, the learning rate, and the inertia values, is often a trial-and-error based process. Thus, a GA is sometimes employed to determine the configuration of a NN topology.

Wang and Huang (2005) used GAs to design an NN topology, specifically to determine the optimal parameter settings including the learning rate, the momentum rate, the number of hidden layers, the number of neurons in each hidden layer, etc. However, using a GA to help design an NN topology might increase the complexity of the configuration process; most researchers that applied GAs in NN, hence, focus on the approach to be presented next.

2.3.2 Using a GA to Generate the NN Connection Weights

Sexton et al. (1998) and Kim (2000) pointed out that the gradient descent algorithm might perform poorly in predicting the future data values even for simple problems. Therefore, they suggested that the most promising direction is to use a global search algorithm, instead of a local search algorithm such as gradient descent, to determine the optimal weight vector of the network. For instance, Kuo (2001) used GAs to fine-tune the connection weights of a fuzzy NN (FNN) model, called GFNN, to forecast sales of a well-known convenience store franchise company in Taiwan. In another study, Kuo (2004) also applied his GFNN model to establish an electronic commerce decision support system. In order to improve the performance of GA-based NN, Sexton (2000) has compared the use of BPN and a GA for training NN with five chaotic time series data. Their empirical results showed that the GA approach was superior to BP in effectiveness, ease-of-use, and efficiency for training NN for these problems. Other GA-NN studies include Montana et al. (1989), Srinivasan (1998), and Kim et al. (2000).

2.4 Review of Sales Forecasting Research

In this section, we survey sales forecasting literature published in recent years. These articles are divided into two different types of forecasting concepts.

Similar to the traditional statistical forecasting methods such as exponential smoothing and ARIMA, the first concept usually focuses on how to interpret the natural tendency of past observations for the purpose of forecasting future values. Variables other than the previous observations are not utilized in the forecast process. ANN models are most widely used in this line of research, Alon (2001) compared ANN models with Winter's, ARIMA, and regression models. The test results showed that the ANN models performed better than the traditional methods. The same conclusion was also reported in Chu's (2003) and Thiesing's (1997) studies. Ansuj (1996) and Zhang (2003) combined ANN with traditional methods and they concluded that hybrid models outperformed the individual models. Sexton (2000), Chu (2003), Wang (2005), and Chen (2006) proposed GA-based ANN models and the results of these studies showed that GA-based ANN models offered an excellent means of solving sales forecasting problems. Table 1 summarizes the literature on sales forecasting that considers only historical observations.

The second concept of forecasting models considers other related variables in their forecasting approaches. Kumar (1995) found that ANN models perform quite well in comparison with logistic regression in forecasting in the presence of several independent variables. Thus he concluded that including both time series data and additional exogenous factors in the forecasting model seem to be preferable. Table 2 summarizes some developments from the related literature of sales forecasting that include exogenous variables in their forecasting models.

The second concept of forecasting methods has a problem to be contended with; that is, how to systematically select the related variables to be included in the model. There is no rule to suggest any variable that might influence the observation data, or what factors should be considered in the model. Most variables were collected based on the subjective judgment of researchers. It is very likely that different variables could be considered for the same problem by different researchers.

Even though no systematic method is available to select the variables, the results presented so far nearly all showed that those models that consider related variables other than historical observations performed quite well. The following two research studies did describe a more systematical way of how to select variables as part of their sales forecasting methods. Kuo (2001) proposed an objective procedure for selecting variables, in which all variables that might affect the sales are listed in the questionnaire first, and then used the fuzzy Delphi method to determine which variables should be included in the model based on the returned questionnaires. Luxhoj (1996) used ANN to forecast the total monthly sales of an audio/video manufacturing company in Denmark. His network model considered three kinds of pattern variables: a time series pattern, an economy pattern, and a productivity pattern. Totally 17 variables were considered in his ANN model.

Table 1. Key developments from the literature on sales forecasting that consider historical observations only.

Authors	Methodologies	Method application only	Weights adjustment considered	Network configuration considered
Kong (1995)	ANN	•		
Itsuki (1996)	Regression analysis	•		
Ansuj (1996)	ARIMA+ANN		•	
Thiesing (1997)	Naive, Statistical method, ANN	•		
Yip (1997)	ANN	•		
Sakai (1999)	Fuzzy + regression	•		
Sexton (2000)	GA+ANN		•	
Alon (2001)	ARIMA, Winter's, regression, ANN	•		
Segura (2001)	Holt-Winters	•		
Tseng (2001)	Gray forecasting	•		
Thomassey (2002)	AHFCCX, SAMANN, IDA	•		
Winklhofer (2002)	MIMIC	•		
Zhang (2003)	ARIMA+ANN		•	
Chu (2003)	ARIMA, ANN		•	
Wang (2005)	GA+ANN			•
Chang (2006)	Fuzzy + ANN	•		

Table 2. Key developments from the literature on sales forecasting methods that include exogenous variables.

Authors	Target Area	Methodologies	Variables (factors)
Jagielska (1993)	Lottery sales	ANN	1. Previous sales 2. Draw type (such as special date) 3. Jackpot 4. Division 1 prize 5. Cost of a single bet 6. Cannibalization 7. Economic conditions of CPI 8. Economic conditions of AWE (average weekly earnings) 9. Advertising dollars
Thiesing (1995)	Products in supermarkets	ANN	1. Number of advertising days within a week 2. Sale of article within a week 3. Max sales volume within a period
Luxhoj (1996)	Audio/video equipments	ANN	1. Month corresponding to the sales target 2. Previous years sales 3. Total sales in Denmark / week 4. Total sales in Norway / week 5. Total sales in Sweden / week 6. Total sales in Switzerland / week 7. Exponentially smoothed forecast 8. BNP, CPI, RV 9. Interest 10. Share 11. OIS-Executive optimism index for net sales 12. OIP-Executive optimism index for net profits

Table 2. Key developments from the literature on sales forecasting methods that include exogenous variables (cont'd).

Authors	Target Area	Methodologies	Variables (factors)
Luxhoj (1996)	Audio/video equipments	ANN	13. OISP- Executive optimism index for selling prices 14. OII- Executive optimism index for inventories 15. OIE-Executive optimism index for hiring employees
Bayhan (1997)	Shampoo	Regression	1. Average list price of shampoo in market 2. Average list price of a certain brand of soap in market
Kuo (2001)	Products in a convenience store	Fuzzy NN+GA	1. Promotion methods 2. Advertising media 3. Promotion length 4. Related products with or w/o promotion
Fok (2001)	Market share	Naive method, simulation-based method	1. Own price 2. Own price lagged 3. One-period lagged
Diamantopoulos (2003)	Export sales	Survey	1. Total number of employees 2. Number of years for a firm 3. Export dependence of total sales 4. Export location 5. Turbulence of the export environment

Table 2. Key developments from the literature on sales forecasting methods that include exogenous variables (cont'd).

Authors	Target Area	Methodologies	Variables (factors)
Cao (2003)	Finance price	ANN+SVM	1. Standard & Poor 500 stock index futures 2. US 30-year government bond 3. US 10-year government bond 4. German 10--year government bond 5. French government stock index futures
Cao (2004)	Products in a company	ERFFF	1. Item price 2. Advertising dollars 3. Expense after sales 4. Average income 5. Average deposit
Frees (2004)	Lottery sales	Longitudinal data mixed models	1. Online lottery sales to individual consumers 2. Number of listed retailers 3. Persons per household 4. Median years of schooling 5. Median home value for owner-occupied homes 6. Percent of housing that is renter occupied 7. Percent of population that is 55 or older 8. Household median age 9. Estimated median household income 10. Population

3. Problem Definition

3.1 *Scope of the Research Data*

This chapter mainly deals with the forecasting of monthly production demands for the PCB industry; and the data are from an electronic company in Taiwan for a period of 60 real-world monthly demand data from January of 1999 to December of 2003. In addition, there are 15 items of related production indices taken from the "Yearbook of Industrial Production Statistics", issued by the Department of Statistics, Ministry of Economic Affairs; the "Statistical Yearbook of the Republic of China" and "Indices of Consumer Price", from the Directorate General of Budget Accounting and Statistics, the Executive Yuan, R. O. C. For each of the 15 indices, the corresponding 60 monthly data for the same 5-year period were taken from the data sources.

3.2 *Characteristics of the Variable Considered*

In order to generate more accurate forecasts, the variables that have an influence on the sales amount should all be considered in the forecasting system. In this research, the variables from four different domains were considered. In the following, superscripts represent a domain considered and subscripts specify a variable in the corresponding domain.

3.2.1 Macroeconomic Domain

The main purpose of this domain is to evaluate the current national economic situation by using some quantitative variables such as:

- Gross National Product, GNP (f_1^1)
- Unemployment Rate (f_2^1)
- Consumer Price Index (f_3^1)
- Value of Import Trade (f_4^1) and Export Trade (f_5^1)

3.2.2 Downstream Demand Domain

According to the Materials Research Laboratories, the distribution of PCB usages in Taiwan is shown in Figure 1. Note that about more than 70% of usage falls in the category of computers and peripherals. This means that the demand of computers and peripherals are influential on the demand of PCB.

Our study selected four computer systems with the highest sales amounts: personal computers (f_1^2), notebooks (f_2^2), motherboards (f_3^2) and monitors (f_4^2). Furthermore, our study also investigated the influence of LCD related products (f_5^2) such as liquid crystal devices (LCD), LCD TVs and LCD mobile phones on the demand for PCB. The increased demand for LCD related products is due to the emergence of the liquid crystal monitor (LCM) technology.

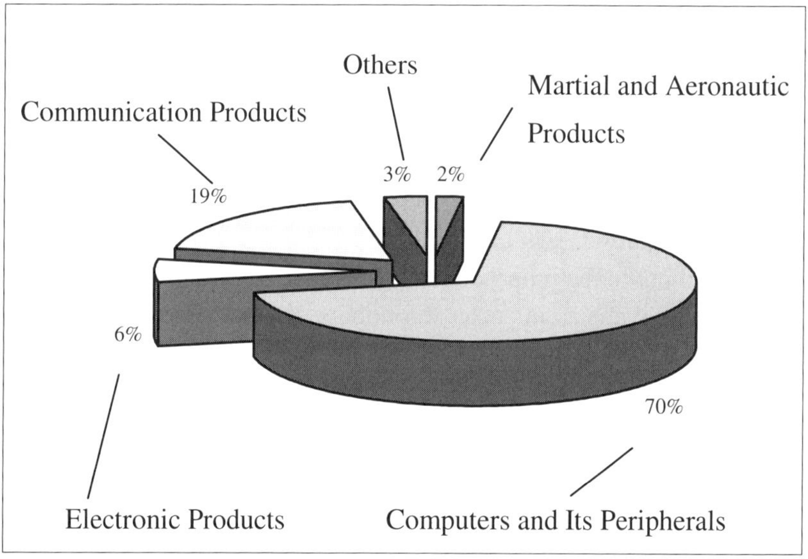

Figure 1. Distribution of PCB application in the Taiwan area (from the Industrial Technology Research Institute.)

3.2.3 Industrial Production Domain

According to the Yearbook of Industrial Production Statistics, Department of Statistics, Ministry of Economic Affairs of R. O. C., the PCB industry is part of manufacturing. Therefore, this study included five indices related to manufacturing as potentially related variables:

- Manufacturing Production Index (f_1^3)
- Manufacturing Sales Index (f_2^3)
- Manufacturing Production Value Index (f_3^3)
- Semiconductor Production Index (f_4^3)
- PCB Production Value (f_5^3)

3.2.4 Time Series Domain

As mentioned before, a total of 60 monthly data collected in this domain are from an electronics company in Taiwan from January of 1999 to December of 2003. Monthly sales and total production are two commonly used measurement units for the general PCB industry and they are highly related. This research focused on the prediction of the production volume rather than the sales amount. Winter's model was selected as the forecasting tool for data in this domain, and the forecasted results serve as part of the input to the proposed hybrid models, to be presented later.

For each domain in macroeconomic, downstream demand, and industrial production; the variable with the highest value was determined based on gray relation analysis. Those selected values served as other parts of the input to the proposed hybrid models.

3.3 The Performance Index

In order to evaluate the accuracy and performance of different forecasting models, this research adopts two evaluation indexes: Mean Absolute Percentage Error (MAPE), and Mean Absolute Deviation (MAD). The formulas for computing these indexes are given below:

$$MAPE = \frac{1}{n}\sum_{t=1}^{n}\frac{|F_t - A_t|}{A_t} \tag{1}$$

$$MAD = \frac{1}{n}\sum_{t=1}^{n}|F_t - A_t| \tag{2}$$

where F_t is the forecasted value for period t, A_t is the actual value for period t, and n is the number of periods. The smaller the values of the above two indexes are, the better the forecasting models will be. Smaller values mean that the forecasts are closer to the actual data.

4. Methodology

Section 4.1 describes the preprocessing of the variables collected from the three different domains mentioned in the previous section. In this section, variables with significant influence on forecasted values are identified among all variables by gray relation analysis and Winter's Exponential Method is used to forecast the PCB production volumes. The proposed Evolving Neural Network (ENN) and Weighted Evolving Fuzzy Neural Network (WEFuNN) are presented in Sections 4.2 and 4.3, respectively. Figure 2 illustrates the framework of the methodology.

4.1 Data Preprocessing

4.1.1 Gray Relation Analysis

An approach to identify the correlations among factors, or to select variables for building forecasting models which is the objective here, is gray system theory (Chang, 1999 and Liang, 1999). The mathematics of gray relation analysis (GRA) is derived from the space theory (Deng, 1988).

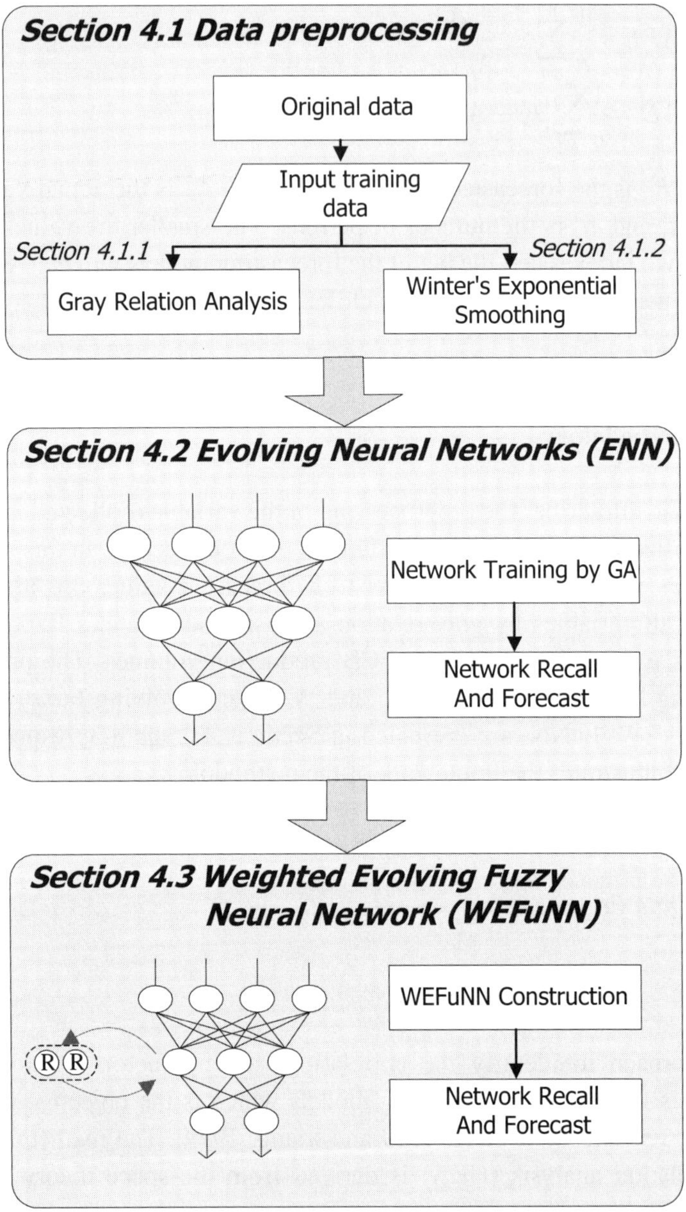

Figure 2. Framework of the methodology.

Using the gray relation grade (GRG), the degree of influence of an index series being compared to the reference series, that is the PCB production volume in this study, can be represented by the relative distance between them in a mapped gray space without making prior assumptions about the data distribution. The smaller the distance is, the larger the influence. The GRG represents the degree that two factors are related to each other. It describes the relative variation in magnitude as well as in trend between the two factors being compared in a given system. If the relative variations of two variables are basically consistent in their development trends, then the GRG between these two variables is large.

The GRG between two series at a certain time point, *k*, is called gray relational coefficient $\xi_{i0}(k)$. Before calculating the gray relational coefficients, some data processing is often needed to transform series of different magnitudes to the same numeric order. Often times each series is normalized by dividing data of the original series by their average. Let the transformed reference sequence be $x_0 = \{x_0(1), x_0(2), \cdots, x_0(n)\}$ and the m sequences being compared to the reference be denoted by $x_i = \{x_i(1), x_i(2), \cdots, x_i(n)\}$, for $i = 1$ to m. The relational coefficient $\xi_{i0}(k)$ between the reference series $x_0(t)$ and the compared series $x_i(t)$ at time $t = k$ can be calculated by the following equation:

$$\xi_{i0}(k) = \frac{\min_i \min_k |x_0(k) - x_i(k)| + \rho \max_i \max_k |x_0(k) - x_i(k)|}{|x_0(k) - x_i(k)| + \rho \max_i \max_k |x_0(k) - x_i(k)|} \quad (3)$$

where $|x_0(k) - x_i(k)|$ denotes the absolute difference between the two transformed sequences. The expression

$$\min_i \min_k |x_0(k) - x_i(k)| \quad (4)$$

is the minimum distance for time point *k* in all compared sequences, which constitute the comparison environment. The maximum distance is defined similarly. Usually, $\min_i \min_k |x_0(k) - x_i(k)|$ equals zero since the transformed series most likely intersect at some particular point in time. The parameter ρ, $(0 < \rho \le 1)$, is a coefficient used to adjust the range of the comparison environment, and to control the level of differences of the gray relational coefficients. When $\rho = 1$, the comparison environment is altered; when $\rho = 0$, the comparison environment disappears. In cases where the data variation is large, ρ usually ranges from 0.1 to 0.5 in order to reduce the influence of extremely large $\max_i \max_k |x_0(k) - x_i(k)|$ values.

The aim of GRA is to measure the geometric relationship between two sets of time series data in the relational space. If the data of two series are the same at all respective time points, then all the relational coefficients equal to one, as does the gray relational grade that is computed as the average of all the relational coefficients. On the other hand, since it is nearly impossible for two transformed series to be perpendicular to one another, the gray relational coefficients are usually greater than zero, as does the gray relational grade.

Fewer indices should be considered in order to increase the efficiency of learning the prediction model. To reduce the number of indices, gray relation analysis (GRA) was used to compute the gray relational grade (GRG) between each index and the monthly PCB production volume. The index with the highest GRG value in each domain is chosen as one of the few input factors to the network. The GRG of each computed factor is shown in Table 3. From this table, the index having the maximum value of GRG in each domain, which represents the biggest influence of each index on the production quantity of PCB, can be easily identified. Accordingly, f_3^1, f_5^2, and f_5^3 are chosen to serve as inputs to the network; they are the Consumer Price Index, Liquid Crystal Element Demand, and PCB Production value, respectively.

Table 3. GRG values of different indices in each domain.

Macroeconomic Domain		Downstream Requirement Domain		Industrial Production Domain	
index	GRG	index	GRG	index	GRG
f_1^1	0.710216	f_1^2	0.757529	f_1^3	0.718227
f_2^1	0.702941	f_2^2	0.664817	f_2^3	0.725007
f_3^1	0.782223*	f_3^2	0.687674	f_3^3	0.720705
f_4^1	0.766208	f_4^2	0.737854	f_4^3	0.717486
f_5^1	0.528671	f_5^2	0.757559*	f_5^3	0.796928*

4.1.2 Winter's Exponential Smoothing

In order to consider the effects of seasonality and trend, Winter's exponential smoothing is used to derive the preliminary forecast of the quantity of PCB production. This method attempts to fit a model with three major components: a permanent component, a trend, and a seasonal component. Each component is continuously updated using a smoothing constant applied to the most recent observation and the last estimate. In Winter's model, it is assumed that each observation is the sum of a deseasonalized value and a seasonal index:

$$S_t = \alpha(X_t - I_{t-L}) + (1-\alpha)(S_{t-1} + b_{t-1}) \tag{5}$$

$$b_t = \gamma(S_t - S_{t-1}) + (1-\gamma)b_{t-1} \tag{6}$$

$$I_t = \beta(X_t - S_t) + (1-\beta)I_{t-L} \tag{7}$$

and forecasts are computed based on:

$$F_{t+m} = S_t + mb_t + I_{t-L+m} \tag{8}$$

where α, β and γ are the general smoothing, seasonal smoothing and trend smoothing coefficients, respectively, with values ranging between 0 and 1; L is the length of seasonality; b_t is the trend component; I is the seasonal adjustment factor; S_t is the smoothed series that does not include seasonality; and F_{t+m} is the forecast value for m periods ahead.

The best combination of these three coefficients, α=0.1, β=0.1, and γ=0.9, were found through a trial-and-error process. Table 4 lists the mean absolute percentage error of Winter's exponential smoothing for each year predicted. These values were obtained by setting $L = 1$, $m = 1$, $b_0 = 0$, $I_0 = 0$, and $S_0 = X_1$.

From Table 4 we can see that the yearly forecasting error by Winter's exponential smoothing ranges from 4.36% to 12.08%. The average error percentage is 7.64%, which might be too high to ignore. Nevertheless, this result undeniably provides a forecasting outcome with the effects of seasonality and trend being taken into account. Thus, the predicted result of Winter's exponential smoothing is used as an input value to the network to represent the effects of seasonality and trend.

Table 4. The Error Percentage of Winter's Exponential Smoothing.

Year	*MAPE*
1999	6.13%
2000	4.36%
2001	12.08%
2002	6.45%
2003	9.17%
Avg.	7.64%

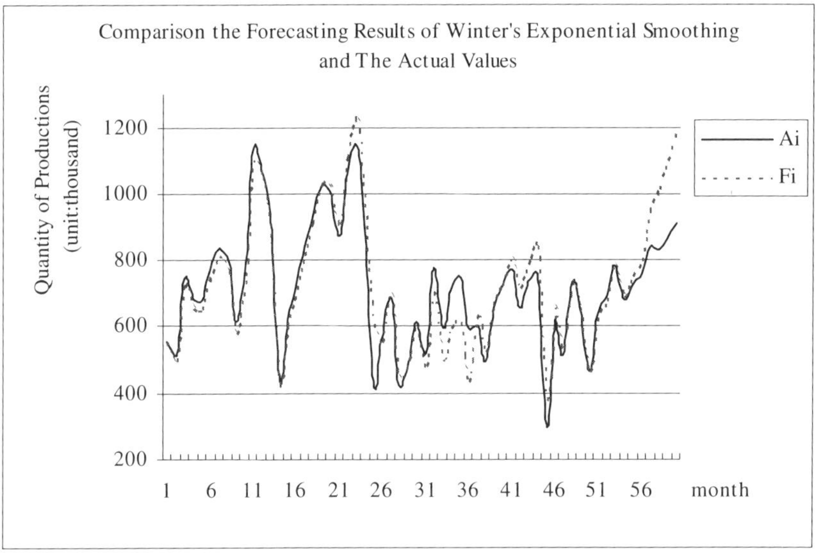

Figure 3. Comparison of the forecasting results from Winter's method and real data.

4.2 Evolving Neural Networks (ENN)

4.2.1 ENN Modeling

In this research, we apply GAs to evolve the weights of the links connecting the neurons in different layers of the neural network. The structure of ENN is discussed in this section. Figure 4 shows the framework of our evolutionary neural network (ENN):

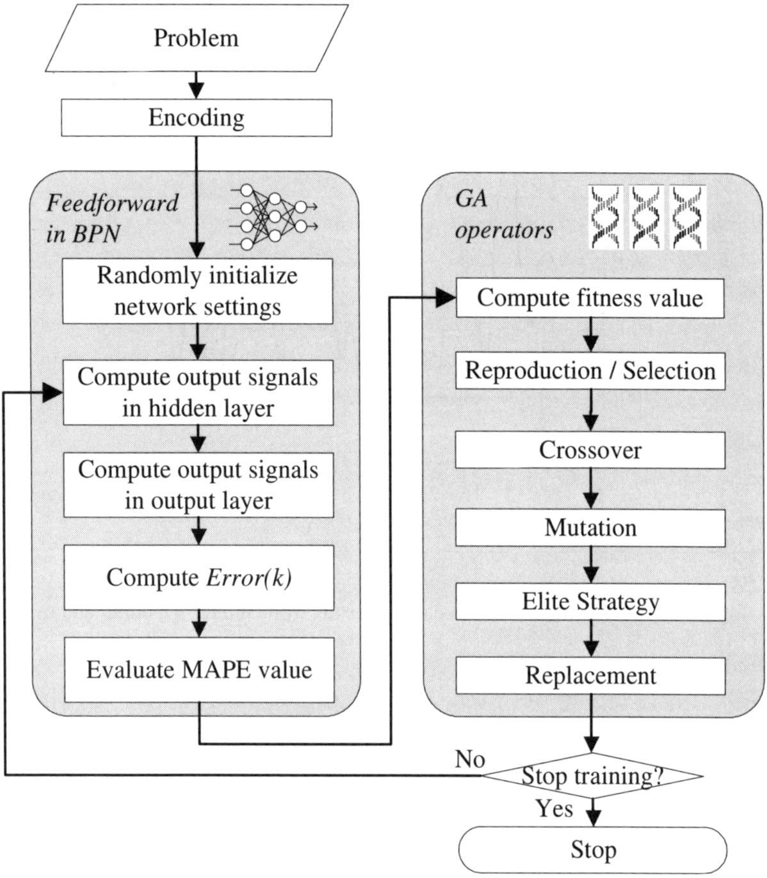

Figure 4. The structure of ENN.

The ENN modeling process is described in the following steps:

Step 1. Encoding

Each gene represents the weight between two neurons at different layers. A chromosome is constructed from a series of genes as shown in Figure 5.

For example, the first gene in the chromosome is the weight between neuron 1 and neuron 5, i.e., W_{15}. The second gene is the weight between neuron 1 and neuron 6, i.e., W_{16}. We use a real value to represent each connection weight.

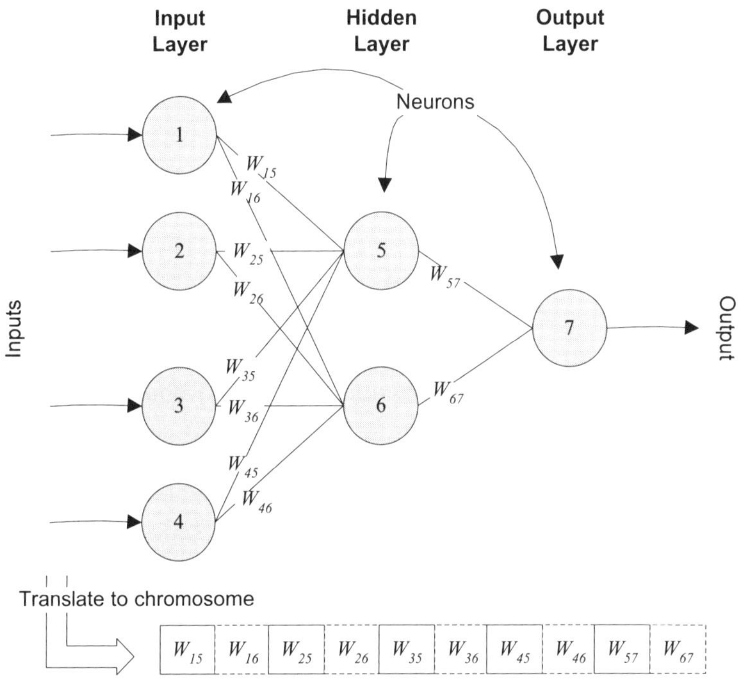

Figure 5. Chromosome encoding.

Step 2. Generate the initial population of chromosomes

The initial weights are randomly generated between 0 and 1. These initial solutions form the first population. The weights in the chromosomes will be evaluated by GA operators in the following steps.

Step 3. Compute the objective value of each chromosome

In this research, MAPE is used as the objective function to evaluate the deviation of the training data during the training process, which is computed as follows:

(1). Each hidden unit Z_j sums its weighted (V_{ij}) input signals(X_i),

$$Z\_in_j = V_{0j} + \sum_{i=0}^{p} V_{ij} * X_i \tag{9}$$

then applies its activation function to compute the output signal,

$$Z_j = f(Z\_in_j) \tag{10}$$

and sends this out signal to all the units in the output layer.

(2). Each output unit Y_k sums its weighted input signals,

$$Y\_in_k = W_{0k} + \sum_{j=0}^{p} W_{jk} * Z_j \tag{11}$$

and applies its activation function to compare the output signal,

$$Y_k = f(Y\_in_k) \tag{12}$$

(3). Compute an error value $Error(k)$ between each output value Y_k and the actual value A_k.

$$Error(k) = |Y_k - A_k| \quad (13)$$

(4). Compute the objective $g(s)$ of each chromosome s.

$$g(s) = MAPE = \sum_{k=1}^{12} \frac{Error(k)}{12}, \quad s = 1, 2, \ldots, N_{pop} \quad (14)$$

Step 4. Compute the fitness function

The original concept of fitness is "the larger the better", because solutions with larger fitness value tend to propagate to the next generation. This chapter considers the minimization of objectives; hence it contradicts the original idea of fitness. Therefore, a transformation should be made to reverse the minimization to maximization. For a solution *g(s)*, its fitness equals to 1 minus itself. The formula is listed as follows:

$$fit(s) = 1 - g(s) \quad (15)$$

Step 5. Reproduction / Selection

After the parameter design (please find details in the next section), the roulette wheel selection approach (Goldberg, 1989) is applied. The probability $p(s)$ of each chromosome s chosen to reproduce is defined below:

$$p(s) = \frac{fit(s)}{\sum fit(s)}. \quad (16)$$

Step 6. Crossover

After the parameter design, the two-point crossover method (Goldberg, 1989) is applied.

Step 7. Mutation

The one-point mutation method (Goldberg, 1989) is also applied as a finer search for the optimal solution.

Step 8. Elite Strategy

The elite strategy selects the top 50% solutions in order to retain the quality solutions obtained in each generation.

Step 9. Replacement

The new population generated by the previous steps updates the old population.

Step 10. Stopping criteria

If the number of generations equals to the maximum value, then stop; otherwise go to Step 3.

Step 11. Forecast and recall

In this step, two measures, MAPE and MAD, are used to evaluate the accuracy of each forecast generated by the ENN model.

4.2.2 ENN Parameters Design

The performance of BPN and GAs depends not only on the input variables but also on the network size. An insufficient network size and poor GA parameter settings will affect the speed of convergence and the quality of predictions. Thus, an appropriate selection of these parameter settings is required. Many parameters have to be chosen and set before learning.

They are described as follows:

1) Activation function

The sigmoid function $f(x)$ denoted as

$$f(x) = \frac{1}{1+e^{-x}}, \text{ where } x \in [-\infty, +\infty] \tag{17}$$

is selected as the activation function between the input layer and the hidden layer. The scaled load output is obtained by simple addition of the scaled output from the hidden layer.

2) Experimental structure design for BPN

The model proposed for the PCB production forecasting problem is a three- or four-layered back-propagation network, including an input layer, an output layer and one or two hidden layers. There are four input factors which include three input indices each selected from each domain and the forth factor is the preliminary forecast of Winter's exponential smoothing model. Our experimental design involved the following combinations of "number of hidden layers" and "number of neurons":

Number of hidden layers: 1~2
Number of neurons: 1~5

The final result is shown in Figure 6. Based on the results, it can be observed that the network structure configured with one hidden-layer and two neurons in the hidden-layer has the minimum MAPE, which is equal to 4.2%.

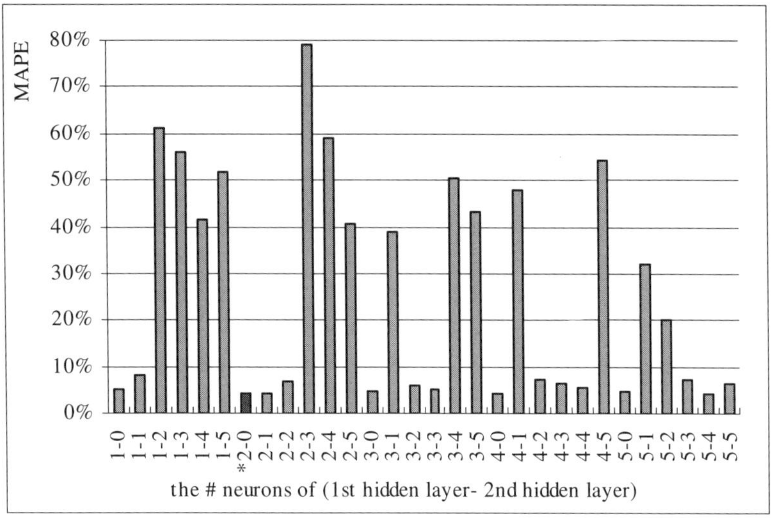

Figure 6. BPN structure design.

3) GA operator related parameters

Five GA operators/parameters are set using the Taguchi experiment design. The Taguchi experiment design is a useful tool for setting parameters. A higher Signal-to-Noise (S/N) ratio as defined below corresponds to a better parameter combination.

$$S/N = -10 \times \log\left(\frac{1}{n} \times \sum_{i=1}^{n} y_i^2\right) \tag{18}$$

where n is the total number of experiments; y_i is the result of the i-th test, $y_i \in (0,1)$, $\forall i = 1,2,\cdots n$. Table 5 lists the levels and codes of each factor.

Table 5. Signal levels and codes of factors.

Factor/code	Level 1	Level 2	Level 3	Level 4
Crossover/(A)	One point crossover	One point crossover	Two-point crossover	Two-point crossover
Mutation/(B)	One point mutation	One point mutation	Shifted mutation	Shifted mutation
Replacement/(C)	Total replacement	Total replacement	Elitist strategy	Elitist strategy
Crossover rate/(D)	0.2	0.4	0.6	0.8
Mutation rate/(E)	0.1	0.3	0.5	0.7

The convergence profiles shown in Figure 7 indicate that the system can converge after 2,000 generations even for small population size such as 10. However, for a quick and smooth convergence population size of 50 is necessary, which converges to a steady state after approximately 300 generations. Therefore, the population size of 50 was used in the following experiments.

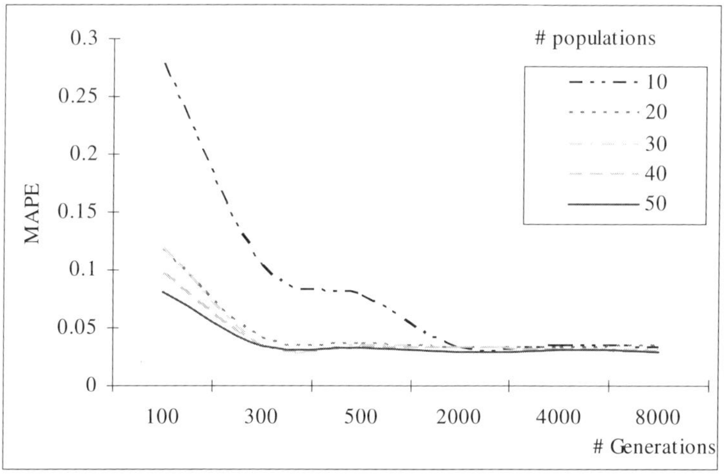

Figure 7. The convergence of different population sizes and generation numbers.

We repeated the experiment three times and computed the average S/N ratio of each factor level. The results are shown in Table 6. From this table, the best combination of parameter settings can be found as (A)3-(B)1-(C)4-(D)4-(E)2 (as highlighted in bold). These codes represent two point crossover, one point mutation, elitist strategy replacement, crossover rate=0.8, and mutation rate=0.3.

Table 6. The S/N ratios.

Factors	(A)	(B)	(C)	(D)	(E)
Level 1	12.19	**24.00**	12.15	14.31	14.79
Level 2	12.98	23.47	13.02	14.40	**15.14**
Level 3	**17.60**	5.91	11.78	14.96	14.36
Level 4	16.51	5.91	**16.99**	**15.62**	15.05

4.3 Weighted Evolving Fuzzy Neural Networks (WEFuNN)

4.3.1 Building of the WEFuNN

Evolving Fuzzy Neural Networks (EFuNN) were first proposed by Kasabov in 1998. In our research, an EFuNN is modified to become a WEFuNN by using a weighted Euclidean distance instead of Kasabov's fuzzy distance function. Both of them are used to forecast the demand of the PCB product. Basically, a WEFuNN is a five-layer network, as shown in Figure 8.

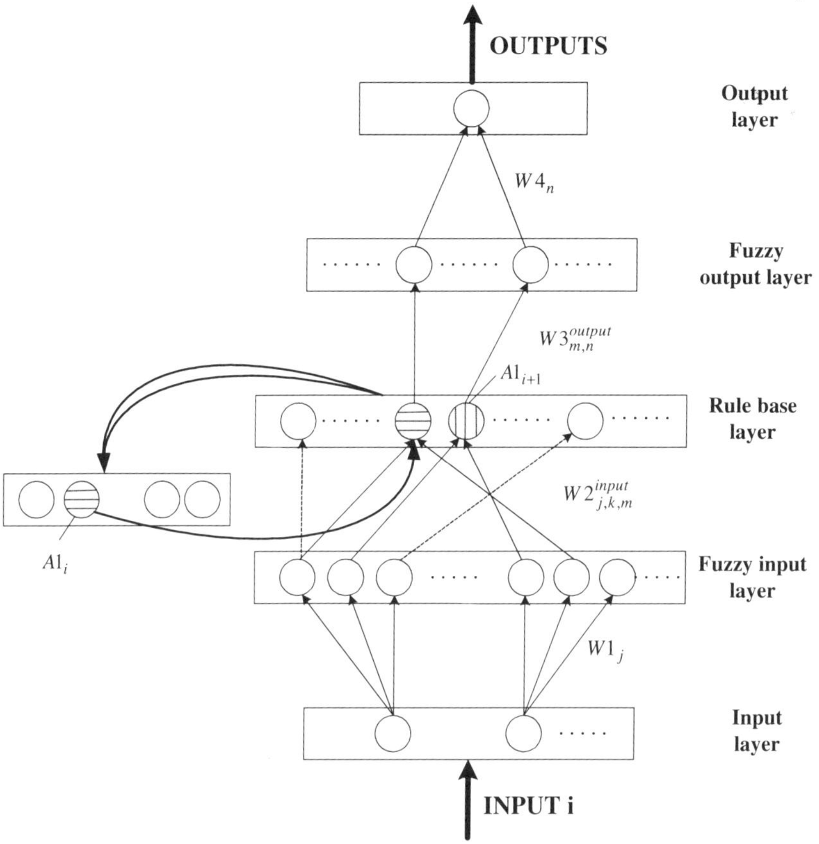

Figure 8. An architecture for WEFuNN (Kasabov, 1998).

The first (input) layer represents the input variables. The second layer of nodes (fuzzy input neurons, or fuzzy inputs) represents the fuzzy quantization of each input variable, different membership functions (MF) can be attached to these neurons. The third layer contains rule nodes. A rule node represents prototypes of the input/output data associations that can be graphically represented as associations of hyper-spheres between the fuzzy input space and the fuzzy output space. The fourth layer of neurons represents fuzzy quantization of the output variables, similar to the input fuzzy neuron representation. The fifth layer represents the values of the output variables. Here an activation function is used to calculate the defuzzified values for the output variables.

Two phases are involved in using WEFuNN are the learning phase and the forecasting phase. The steps of each phase are described next:

4.3.1.1 The feed-forward learning phase

Each training case is processed by using the following steps:

Step 1: Data Fuzzification

Triangular membership functions $\tilde{\mu}_x$ (Equation 19 and Figure 9) were used to fuzzify each input feature (or variable) value. The number of fuzzy regions for each feature is predetermined as part of the parameter design.

$$\tilde{\mu}_x = \begin{cases} 0, x < a \\ \dfrac{x-a}{b-a}, a \le x < b \\ \dfrac{c-x}{c-b}, b \le x < c \\ 0, x \ge c \end{cases} \tag{19}$$

In this research, the dynamic weight ($W1_j$) for feature j between the 1st layer and the 2nd layer was considered and was added to the learning process. For the first training data, $MF_{j,k}^{input}(1)$ was its input fuzzy membership value for the j-th feature in the k-th region, $MF_n^{output}(1)$ is its output fuzzy membership value in the n-th fuzzy region.

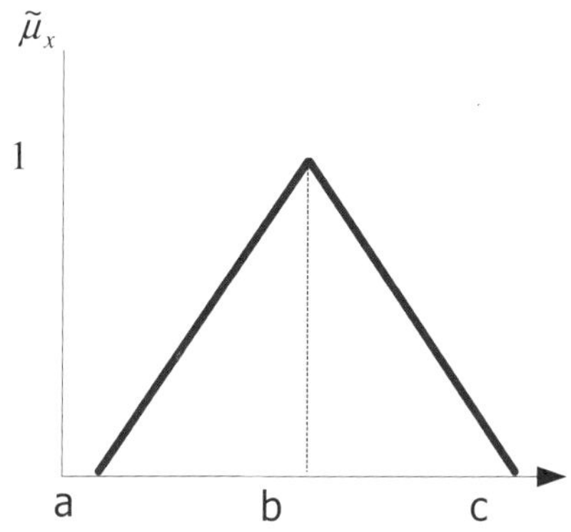

Figure 9. A triangular membership function.

Step 2: Initial Network Setting

In the beginning, there are no fuzzy rules in the network. Thus, the first rule should be built by the first training datum. The connection weights between the 2nd layer and the 3rd layer are $W2_{j,k,m}^{input}$; between the 3rd layer and the 4th layer are $W3_{m,n}^{output}$; between the 4th layer and the output layer are $W4_n$, where m is the number of rules. All connection weights are non-fuzzy and are initialized as 1 with the network started fully connected.

Step 3: Network Construction

In order to construct the fuzzy rules and to learn the weights of the network, all of the training data must be processed by the following sub-steps:

Step 3.1. Computation of Similarity

Instead of using Kasabov's fuzzy distance function, a weighted Euclidean distance $D_{i,m}$ is proposed to compute the distance between the i-th datum and the m-th rule, which is defined as:

$$D_{i,m} = \sqrt{\sum_j \sum_k W1_j \times [MF_{j,k}^{input}(i) - W2_m]^2} \tag{20}$$

The weights $W1_j$ were taken into account in this study in an effort to express the relative degree of importance between features. Moreover, to represent the relation between distance and similarity, an exponential transfer function was used to transfer a distance value to the corresponding similarity. That is,

$$A_{i,m} = \exp(-D_{i,m}) \tag{21}$$

Comparing with linear transfer functions, a much larger similarity for a closer distance and a much smaller similarity for a larger distance can be obtained from this nonlinear function.

Step 3.2. Determination of the Rules

Find the rule most similar to the training datum i, where

$$A1_i = \max(A_{i,m}).$$

If $A1_i > S$, where S is the similarity threshold, then it indicates that the datum has to be merged into this rule. Otherwise, create a new fuzzy rule, generate the associated connection weights $W2^{input}_{j,k,m}$ and $W3^{output}_{m,n}$, and set their initial values to 1, then go to Step 4.

Step 3.3. Computation of the Output Transfer Function

In this sub-step, a saturation linear transfer function is used to convert the fuzzy membership function of case i to a crisp value output as follows:

$$A2_{i,n} = Satlin(W3^{output}_{m,n} \times A1_i) = Satlin(MF^{output}_n(i) \times A1_i) \tag{22}$$

The saturation linear transfer function is shown in Figure 10.

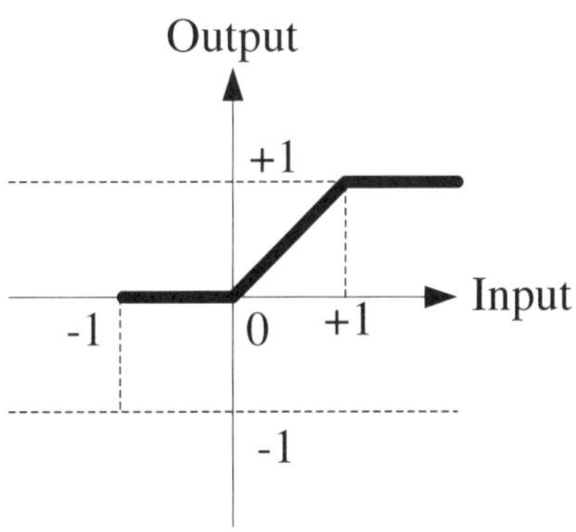

Figure 10. Saturation linear transfer function.

Step 3.4. Computation of the Errors

Compute the error between the output of the training datum i and its actual demand A_i as follows:

$$Err_i = \sum_n | A2_{i,n} - A_i | \tag{23}$$

If $Err_i < E_{thr}$, retain this forecasting result, where E_{thr} is the error threshold. Otherwise, create a new fuzzy rule, generate the corresponding connection weights $W2_{j,k,m}^{input}$ and $W3_{m,n}^{output}$, set their initial values to 1, and then go to Step 4.

Step 3.5. Computation of the Output

The forecasting result of each case is compiled to derive a forecast output as follows:

$$O_i = \sum_n (W4_n \times A2_{i,n}) \tag{24}$$

Step 3.6. Updating of the Weights

For merging a training example i into an existing rule, the connection weights $W2_{j,k,m}^{input}$ and $W3_{m,n}^{output}$ are updated as follows:

$$dist = [MF_{j,k}^{input}(i) - W2_{j,k,m}^{input}(old)] \tag{25}$$

$$W2_{j,k,m}^{input}(new) = W2_{j,k,m}^{input}(old) + \alpha_1 \times dist \tag{26}$$

$$W3_{m,n}^{output}(new) = W3_{m,n}^{output}(old) + \alpha_2 \times (Err_i) \times (A1_i) \tag{27}$$

where α_1 is the learning rate of $W2$ and α_2 is the learning rate of *W3* or $MF_n^{output}(i)$. The diagram of the weight updating process is presented in Figure 11.

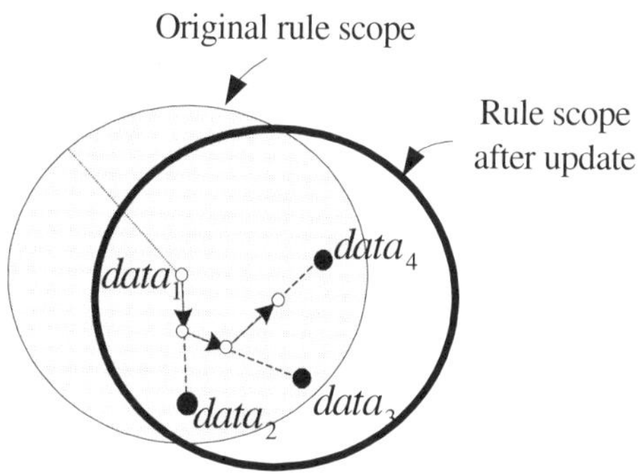

Figure 11. Diagram of rule scope before and after an update.

Step 4: Generation of the Network

For each training data, repeat Step 3 to learn the network model which includes the connection weights and fuzzy rules.

According to Step 3.2., past cases that are similar would be gathered together as a single rule. The diagram of the rules generated from the set of data is illustrated in Figure 12. These rules can be treated as different clusters of past cases. After the network feed-forward training phase, we can obtain a set of fuzzy rules from these training data. These fuzzy rules will be used to generate the forecasting data during the forecasting phase.

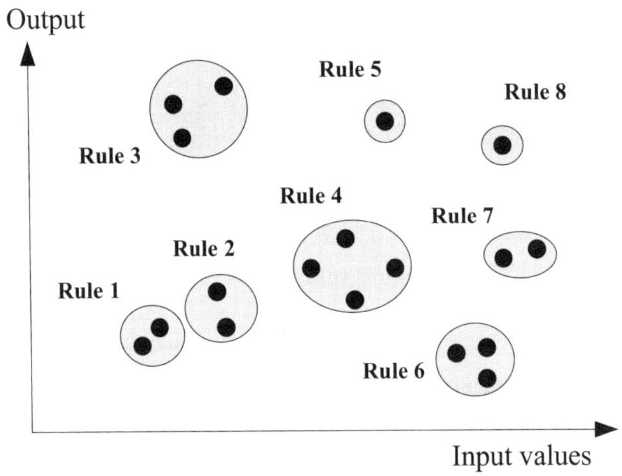

Figure 12. The Diagram of the generated fuzzy rules.

4.3.1.2 The forecasting phase

Generally speaking, for each testing datum the most similar rule to it can be retrieved from the rule base according to the similarity $A_{i,m}$. The fuzzy output of this most similar rule can be treated as the fuzzy forecast of this testing data. This is nothing but the 1-NN rule. After defuzzification, the forecast demand can then be derived. However, the concept of k-NN with $k \geq 1$ has also been utilized to find the forecast. In this case, for each testing datum the k most similar rules are considered; the distances between each of the k-nearest rules and the testing datum are used to compute the ratios for summarizing the forecasts of these k rules.

This approach has the advantage of getting the combined result from many different rules. By doing so, we expect to obtain more accurate forecasting results. In the problem of PCB sales forecasting, there are only 60-period data points in the history, thus, we used $k=1$ in our network as the output result was the best after many trails. The reason for doing so is because WEFuNN gathers similar cases as a simple rule and the generated rules can successfully represent these reference data in the forecasting process. Possibly, different numbers for k may be needed in other problems if there are large numbers of reference data.

4.3.2 WEFuNN Parameters Design

Similar to Section 4.2.2, the Taguchi method was also used to determine the best combination of WEFuNN parameters. A total of 13 factors were considered. The details of these factors and experimented levels are given in Table 7.

Table 7. Factors and their test levels in the Taguchi experimental design.

Code	Factors	Level 1	Level 2	Level 3
A	The no. of fuzzy regions in X_1	8	9	10
B	The no. of fuzzy regions in X_2	3	4	5
C	The no. of fuzzy regions in X_3	3	4	5
D	The no. of fuzzy regions in X_4	8	9	10
E	The no. of fuzzy regions in Y_1	3	4	5
F	Weight of X_1	0.25	0.275	0.3
G	Weight of X_2	0.20	0.25	0.3
H	Weight of X_3	0.15	0.20	0.25
J	Weight of X_4	0.25	0.3	0.35
K	Threshold of error	0.1	0.2	0.3
L	Threshold of similarity	0.7	0.8	0.9
M	Learning rate, α_1.	0.1	0.5	0.9
N	Learning rate, α_2.	0.1	0.5	0.9

In this table as well the Appendix, X_1, X_2, X_3, X_4 and Y represent the index of export trade, liquid crystal element, PCB production value, forecasting value of Winter's exponential smoothing, and the forecasting value of PCB production amount, respectively.

Table 8 shows the S/N ratio computed for each factor in each level, with the highest S/N ratios are highlighted in bold.

Table 8. The S/N ratios.

				Code			
Level	A	B	C	D	E	F	G
1	20.11	20.98	**22.26**	19.97	21.31	**22.67**	**22.76**
2	**23.12**	20.58	21.01	22.06	**22.31**	20.06	21.36
3	21.19	**22.85**	21.15	**22.39**	20.80	21.69	20.29
Level	H	J	K	L	M	N	
1	**22.03**	19.04	21.32	**22.26**	21.18	21.38	
2	21.57	21.47	21.31	21.43	21.22	**21.85**	
3	20.82	**23.90**	**21.79**	20.73	**22.02**	21.19	

The best combination of parameter values is comprised of the largest value in each domain from the above table. Thus, the best parameter combination is (A)2-(B)3-(C)1-(D)3-(E)2-(F)1-(G)1-(H)1-(J)3-(K)3-(L)1 -(M)3-(N)2, as summarized in Table 9.

5. Experimental Results

In this section the performance of WEFuNN in PCB production forecasting is discussed by comparing it with those from other methods, including Winter's Exponential Smoothing, Multiple Regression Analysis (MRA), BPN, EFuNN, and ENN. The total 5-variate 60-period data points collected, given in the Appendix, are divided into two parts: the first 48 periods for training the model and the last 12 periods for testing.

The forecasted results of the last 12-period data were used to evaluate the performance of the forecasting models. Accordingly, 12-period forecasting values and in turn 12 MAPE values of each period were obtained for each model. The average and standard error of MAPE values were also computed. The following subsections give the experimental results obtained by all of the above mentioned forecasting models.

Table 9. Detail parameter settings of WEFuNN.

Code	Factors	Best Setting
A	The no. of fuzzy regions in X_1	9
B	The no. of fuzzy regions in X_2	5
C	The no. of fuzzy regions in X_3	3
D	The no. of fuzzy regions in X_4	9
E	The no. of fuzzy regions in Y	4
F	Weight of X_1	0.25
G	Weight of X_2	0.20
H	Weight of X_3	0.15
J	Weight of X_4	0.35
K	Threshold of error	0.3
L	Threshold of similarity	0.7
M	Learning rate, α_1	0.9
N	Learning rate, α_2	0.5

5.1 Winter's Exponential Smoothing

The development of Winter's Exponential Smoothing was described in Section 4.1.2. Table 10 gives the forecasting results under Winter's method.

Table 10. Forecasting results under Winter's exponential smoothing method.

MAPE of Winter's	
AVE.	9.17%
STD.	11.42%
MAX.	30.45%
MIN.	0.10%

As shown in Table 10, the average MAPE value obtained by Winter's exponential smoothing is 9.17%, the error standard deviation is 11.42%, the maximum percentage error in 12 monthly forecasts is 30.45% and the minimum error percentage in 12 monthly forecasts is 0.1%.

5.2 The BPN Model

The back propagation neural network is the most popular model used for various application domains, such as forecasting of department store sales, bank personal credit rating, and control of manufacturing processes. All of them predict the results with good efficiency. The Neural Network Professional II Plus package was utilized for this study and the Gradient Steepest Descent Method, the popular search method, was employed to learn the weights of BPN.

Here, 4 inputs to the network are the Consumer Price Index, the Liquid crystal element, the PCB Production Value and the forecast result of Winter's exponential smoothing. The output of the network is the PCB sales amount. The Taguchi method was employed by BPN to design other parameters is similar to that used in Section 4.2.4. The best parameters found are presented in Table 11 and the forecasting results are given in Table 12.

Table 11. The best parameter design of BPN.

Parameters	The best setup
The number of hidden layers	1 layer
The number of neurons in the hidden layer	2 neurons
The learning rate	0.4
Momentum coefficient	0.5
The number of learning iterations	100,000 times

Table 12. Forecasting results under BPN.

MAPE of BPN	
AVE.	8.76%
STD.	9.63%
MAX.	25.20%
MIN.	0.49%

5.3 *Multiple Regression Analysis Model*

Multiple regression analysis (MRA) is one of the most popular methods used in statistics. Multiple regression analysis is used for testing the hypothesis with regard to the relationship between a dependent variable (Y) and two or more independent variables (Xs). It is easy to establish a model when there is a linear relationship between the independent variable and the dependent variables. On the other hand, it is very difficult to establish an accurate MRA model when the relation is non-linear.

In this research, the output factor (Y) is forecast of PCB production and the input factors of the linear regression are the Consumer Price Index (X_1), the Liquid crystal element (X_2), the PCB Production Value (X_3), and the forecasting result under Winter's exponential smoothing method (X_4). The regression formula was defined as:

$$Y = a_1 X_1 + a_2 X_2 + a_3 X_3 + a_4 X_4 + b$$

Using the Excel built-in function, a_1, a_2, a_3, a_4, and b were calculated in obtaining the MRA equation as follows:

$$Y = 0.01141 \times X_1 + 0.244169 \times X_2 - 5.91762 \times X_3 + 0.969816 \times X_4 - 13140.4$$

After entering 12-period testing samples into the multiple regression equation the forecasting results were obtained as shown in Table 13.

Table 13. Forecasting results under MRA.

MAPE of MRA	
AVE.	9.88%
STD.	11.03%
MAX.	30.36%
MIN.	0.11%

The forecasting results of MRA are: the average MAPE is 9.88%, the error standard deviation is 11.03%, the maximum percentage error in 12 monthly forecasts is 30.36%, and the minimum percentage error in 12 monthly forecasts is 0.11%.

5.4 Evolving Fuzzy Neural Network Model (EFuNN)

The Taguchi method employed by EFuNN to design the parameters is similar to that used in Section 5.3. The best parameters determined are given in Table 14.

Table 14. The best parameter settings in EFuNN.

Parameter	The best setting
The no. of fuzzy regions for each input feature	2
The no. of fuzzy regions for the output feature	2
The threshold of similarity	0.9
Threshold of error	0.1
Learning rate of W1	0.5
Learning rate of W2	0.5
The number of iterations	1 time

The EFuNN model with the above-mentioned parameter settings learned 38 fuzzy rules during the training stage. The forecasting results generated by the learned model are presented in Table 15.

Table 15. Forecasting results under EFuNN.

MAPE of EFuNN	
AVE.	6.44%
STD.	4.31%
MAX.	13.32%
MIN.	0.66%

The forecasting results of EFuNN are: the average MAPE of EFuNN is 6.44%, the error standard deviation is 4.31%, the maximum percentage error in 12 monthly forecasts is 13.32%, and the minimum percentage error in 12 monthly forecasts is 0.66%.

5.5 *Evolving Neural Network (ENN)*

The weight learning ability of the traditional back-propagation network is always limited by the searching space of the gradient steepest descent method, which in turn can easily affect the speed of convergence.

An ENN could avoid this limitation because the genetic algorithm used has a stronger space searching ability. The best combination of parameter values, which has been detailed in Section 4.2.4, is shown in Table 16, and the forecasting results are shown in Table 17.

Table 16. The best parameter settings of ENN.

Parameter	The best setting
Crossover	Two points
Mutation	Single point
Replacement	Elite strategy
Crossover rate	0.8
Mutation rate	0.3
Hidden layer	2
Generation	300

Table 17. Forecasting results under ENN.

MAPE of ENN	
AVE.	3.06%
STD.	2.61%
MAX.	8.40%
MIN.	0.01%

As shown in Table 17, the ENN is a good forecasting model because its average MAPE is 3.06%, the error standard deviation is 2.61%, the maximum percentage error in 12 monthly forecasts is 8.40%, and the minimum percentage error in 12 monthly forecasts is 0.01%.

5.6 Comparisons

This section focuses on the comparison between WEFuNN and the other forecasting models. As shown in Table 18, both MAPE and MAD were employed to evaluate the degree of prediction accuracy. Among these six forecasting models, WEFuNN is the most accurate forecasting model because of its smallest value of MAPE and MAD, 2.11% and 16,445 square feet, respectively. Therefore, it can be concluded that the WEFuNN forecasting model proposed in this study is considerably more accurate than the other models.

Table 18. The comparison of the forecasting methods.

	WEFuNN	ENN	EFuNN	BPN	Winter's	MRA
MAPE	2.11%	3.06%	6.44%	8.76%	9.18%	9.88%
MAD	16445	23991	47072	72494	78148	82673

According to the above experimental results, several conclusions can be drawn as follows:

(1) The models that take a number of exogenous variables from various domains into consideration rather than just focus on the trend and seasonal factors of the time series produce better prediction accuracy in terms of the average or the standard deviation of the prediction errors. Therefore, taking other domains into account can reduce the prediction errors effectively, mainly due to the increased accuracy and stability of the learned model.

(2) The forecasting model that takes all input factors into account and assigns different weights to these factors produced more accurate results than the forecasting model that treats each factor equally.

(3) In terms of prediction accuracy, the WEFuNN model is superior to other forecasting models because it has the minimum value of MAPE and MAD.

(4) The forecasting ability of MRA is the worst one among all the six forecasting models tested because it is only suitable for modeling linear relations and its forecasting ability for a non-linear system is relatively poor.

6. Conclusions

Taiwan's printed circuit board industry has already become the third largest in the world. The competition is getting more intense as a result of the imbalance between demand and supply, the increase in manpower costs, and over-production in the global market. Therefore, capacity planning becomes an important topic today. If it is possible to control the capacity effectively by using scientific knowledge and modernized management skill to assist the industry, it will not only improve its competitiveness, reduce the cost, control the demand, but also have positive domino effects on related industries and the domestic economy as a whole.

In recent years, the application of soft computing which integrates fuzzy theory and neural networks is getting more and more popular. However, few studies have employed them in PCB sales (or production) forecasting. By employing the WEFuNN model, this study offers the PCB companies in Taiwan a more accurate monthly forecasting method which would facilitate capacity planning, the preparation of material flows, and so on. As can be seen from the experimental results, the MAPE and MAD of the WEFuNN forecasting model are 2.11% and 16,445 square feet, respectively. It also indicates that this highly accurate forecasting model could serve as a scientific basis for capacity planning and could further reduce the extra production costs caused by unfavorable forecasting.

References

Alon, I., Qi, M. and Sadowski, R.J. (2001). Forecasting aggregate retail sales: a comparison of artificial neural networks and traditional methods, *Journal of Retailing and Consumer Services*, **8**, 147-156.

Ansuj, A.P., Camargo, M.E., Radharamanan, R. and Petry, D. G. (1996). Sales forecasting using time series and neural networks, *Computers and Industrial Engineering*, **31**(1-2), 421-424.

Barbounis, T.G. and Theocharis, J.B. (2006). Locally recurrent neural networks for long-term wind speed and power prediction, *Neurocomputing*, **69**(4-6), 466-496.

Bayhan, G. M., and Bayhan, M. (1998). Forecasting using autocorrelated errors and multicollinear predictor variables, *Computers and Industrial Engineering*, **34**(2), 413-421.

Cao, L.J., and Tay, F.E.H. (2003). Support vector machine with adaptive parameters in financial time series forecasting, *IEEE Transactions on Neural Networks*, **14**(6), 1506 – 1518.

Chai, M.L., Song, S., and Li, N.N. (2005). A review of some main improved models for neural network forecasting on time series, *Intelligent Vehicles Symposium*, 6-8 Jun. 2005, 866-868.

Chang, P.C. and Wang, Y. W. (2006). Fuzzy Delphi and back-propagation model for sales forecasting in PCB industry, *Expert Systems with Applications*, **30**(4), 715-726.

Chang, T.C. and Lin, S. J. (1999). Gray relation analysis of carbon dioxide emissions from industrial production and energy uses in Taiwan, *Journal of Environmental Management*, **56**(4), 247-257.

Chelani, A. B. and Devotta, S. (2006). Air quality forecasting using a hybrid autoregressive and nonlinear model, *Atmospheric Environment*, **40**(10), 1774-1780.

Chen, K.Y., and Wang, C. H. (2006). A Hybrid SARIMA and support vector machines in forecasting the production values of the machinery industry in Taiwan, *Expert Systems with Applications*, **32**(1), 254-264.

Chen, S. M., and Hwang, J. R. (2000). Temperature prediction using fuzzy time series, *IEEE Transactions on Systems, Man, and Cybernetics-Part B: Cybernetics*, **30**(2), 263-275.

Chen, T. (2003). A fuzzy back propagation network for output time prediction in a wafer Fab, *Applied Soft Computing,* **2**(3), 211-222.

Chow, T. W. S. and Leung, C. T. (1996). Nonlinear autoregressive integrated neural network model for short-term load forecasting, *IEE Proceedings Online no. 19960600*, 500-506.

Chu, C.W., and Zhang, G. P. (2004). A comparative study of linear and nonlinear models for aggregate retail sales forecasting, *International Journal of Production Economics*, **86**, 217-231.

Contreras, Espinola, J. R., Nogales, F. J., and Conejo, A. J. (2003). ARIMA models to predict next-day electricity prices, *IEEE Transactions on Power Systems*, **18**(3), 1014-1020.

Diamantopoulos, A., and Winklhofer, H. (2003). Export sales forecasting by UK firms: technique utilization and impact on forecast accuracy, *Journal of Business Research*, **56**(1), 45-54.

Doganis P., Alexandridis, A. Patrinos, P. and Sarimveis, H. (2006). Time series sales forecasting for short shelf-life food products based on artificial neural networks and evolutionary computing, *Journal of Food Engineering*, **75**, 196-204.

Fok, D., and Franses, P. H. (2001). Forecasting market shares from models for sales, *International Journal of Forecasting*, **17**(1), 121-128.

Frees, E.W., and Miller, T. W. (2004). Sales forecasting using longitudinal data models, *International Journal of Forecasting*, **20**(1), 99-114.

Freitas, P.S.A., A.J.L. Rodrigues, (2005). Model combination in neural-based forecasting, *European Journal of Operational Research*, **173**(3), 801-814.

Gareta, R., Romeo, L. M., and Gil, A. (2005). Forecasting of electricity prices with neural networks, *Energy Conversion and Management*, **47**(13), 1770-1778.

Guirelli, C.R., Jardini, J. A., Magrini, L. C., and Yasuoka, J. (2004). Tool for short-term load forecasting in transmission systems based on artificial intelligence techniques, *Transmission and Distribution Conference and Exposition: Latin America*, 8-11 Nov. 2004, 243- 248.

Hippert, H.S., Pedreira, C. E., and Souza, R. C. (2001). Neural networks for short-term load forecasting: a review and evaluation, *IEEE Transactions on Power Systems*, **16**(1), 44-55.

Infield, D. G., and Hill, D. C. (1998). Optimal smoothing for trend removal in short term electricity demand forecasting, *IEEE Transactions on Power Systems*, **13**(3), 1115-1120.

Itsuki, R., Yajima, H., Mizuno, H. and Kinukawa, H. (1996). Application and verification of using statistical analysis tool and expert System together in multiple regression analysis, *2nd IEEE Conference on Emerging Technologies and Factory Automation*, 629 – 635.

Jagielska, I., (1993). A neural network model for sales forecasting, *First New Zealand International Two-Stream Conference on Artificial Neural Networks and Expert Systems*, 284 – 287.

Kalpakis, K., Gada, D. and Puttagunta, V. (2001). Distance measures for effective clustering of ARIMA time-Series," *The Proceedings of Data Mining, IEEE International Conference ICDM 2001*, 29 Nov.-2 Dec., 273 – 280.

Kasabov, N. (2001). Evolving fuzzy neural networks for on-line knowledge discovery, *The Information Science Discussion Paper Series.*

Kasabov, N. (1998). Evolving fuzzy neural networks-algorithms, applications and biological motivation, in *Proceedings of Iizuka'98*, Iizuka, Japan, October.

Kim, K. J. and Han, I. (2000). Genetic algorithms approach to feature discretization in artificial neural networks for the prediction of stock price index, *Expert Systems with Applications*, **19**, 125-132.

Kimoto, T. and Asakawa, K. (1990). Stock market prediction system with modular neural network, *IEEE International Joint Conference on Neural Networks*, 1-6, 1990.

Kong, J.H.L. and Martin, G.P.M.D. (1995). A backpropagation neural network for sales forecasting, *Proceedings of* 2nd *IEEE International Conference on Neural Networks*, 1007 – 1011.

Koutroumanidis T., Iliadis, L., and Sylaios, G. K. (2005). Time-series modeling of fishery landings using ARIMA models and fuzzy expected intervals software, Environmental Modelling & Software, **21**(12), 1711-1721.

Kuo, R. J. and Chen, J. Aa. (2004). A decision support system for order selection in electronic commerce based on fuzzy neural network supported by real-coded genetic algorithm, *Expert Systems with Applications*, **26**, 141-154.

Kuo, R. J., and Xue, K. C. (1998). A decision support system for sales forecasting through fuzzy neural networks with asymmetric fuzzy weights, *Decision Support Systems*, **24**, 105-126.

Kuo, R.J. (2001). A sales forecasting system based on fuzzy neural network with initial weights generated by genetic algorithm, *European Journal of Operational Research*, **129**, 496-517.

Liang, R.H. (1999). Application of gray relation analysis to hydroelectric generation scheduling, *International Journal of Electrical Power & Energy Systems,* **21**(5), 357-364.

Luxhøj, James T., Riis, J. O. and Stensballe, B. (1996). A Hybrid econometric-neutral network modeling approach for sales forecasting, *International Journal of Production Economics*, **43**(2-3), 175-192.

Mills, T. C. (1991). *Time Series Techniques for Economists*, Cambridge University Press: Cambridge, UK.

Montana, D. and Davis, L. (1989). Training feed-forward neural networks using genetic algorithms, in *Proceedings of 11th International Joint Conference on Artificial Intelligence*, Morgan Kaufmann: San Mateo, CA, U.S.A., 762-767.

Qi M. and Zhang, G. P. (2003). Trend time series modeling and forecasting with neural networks, *IEEE International Conference on Computational Intelligence for Financial Engineering*, March 20-23, 331-337.

Sadek, N., Khotanzad, A. and Chen, T. (2003). ATM dynamic bandwidth allocation using F-ARIMA prediction model, *Proceedings of the 12th International Conference on Computer Communications and Networks* (ICCCN), 20-22 Oct. 2003, 359-363.

Sakai, H., Nakajima, H., Higashihara, M., Yasuda, M., and Oosumi, M. (1999). Development of a fuzzy sales forecasting system for vending machines, *Computers and Industrial Engineering*, **36**(2), 427-449.

Segura, J.V. and Vercher, E. (2001). A spreadsheet modeling approach to the Holt–Winters optimal forecasting, *European Journal of Operational Research*, **131**(2), 375-388.

Sexton, R.S and Gupta, J. N. D. (2000). Comparative evaluation of genetic algorithm and back propagation for training neural networks, *Information Sciences*, **129**, 45-59.

Sexton, R.S., Alidaee, B., Dorsey, R. E., and Johnson, J. D. (1998). Global optimization for artificial neural networks: a tabu search application, *European Journal of Operational Research*, **106**(2/3), 570-584.

Sisworahardjo, N. S., El-Keib, A. A., Choi, J., Valenzuela, J., Brooks, R., El-Agtal, I. (2006). A Stochastic load model for an electricity market, *Electric Power Systems Research*, 76(6-7), 500-508.

Srinivasan, D. (1998). Evolving artificial neural networks for short term load forecasting, *Neural Computing*, **23**, 265-276.

Tawfiq, A. S. and Ibrahim, E. A. (1999). Artificial neural networks as applied to long-term demand forecasting, *Artificial Intelligence in Engineering*, **13**, 189-197.

Thiesing, F.M. and Vornberger, O. (1997). Sales forecasting using neural networks, *4th International Conference on Neural Networks*, 2125 – 2128.

Thiesing, F.M., Ulrich, M., and Oliver, V. (1995). A neural network approach for predicting the sale of articles in supermarkets, *Third European Congress on Intelligent Techniques and Soft Computing*, 28-31.

Thiesing, F.M., Middelberg, U., and Vornberger, (1995). Short term prediction of sales in supermarkets, *2nd IEEE International Conference on Neural Networks*, 1028 – 1031.

Thornassey, S., Happiette, M. and Castelain, J. M. (2002). Three complementary sales forecasting models for textile distributors, *6th IEEE International Conference on Systems, Man and Cybernetics*, Vol. 6.

Tseng, F.M., Yu, H. C., Tzeng, G. H. (2001). Applied hybrid gray model to forecast seasonal time series, *Technological Forecasting and Social Change*, **67**(2-3), 291-302.

Wang T.Y., and Huang, C. Y. (2007). Applying optimized BPN to a chaotic time series problem, *Expert Systems with Applications*, **32**(1), 193-200.

Wang, W., Van Gelder, P.H.A.J.M., Vrijling, J. K., and Ma, J. (2006). Forecasting daily streamflow using hybrid ANN models, *Journal of Hydrology*, **324**(1-4), 383-399.

Wang, Y., Zhang, X. Zim and Gao, X. J. (2005). A new time-series trend forecasting technique, *Proceedings of 2005 IEEE International Workshop on VLSI Design and Video Technology*, 28-30 May 2005, 403-407.

Winklhofer, H.M and Diamantopoulos, A. (2002). Managerial evaluation of sales forecasting effectiveness: A MIMIC modeling approach, *International Journal of Research in Marketing*, **19**(2), 151-166.

Yip, D.H.F., Hines, E. L., and Yu, W. W. H. (1997). Application of artificial neural networks in sales forecasting, *4th International Conference on Neural Networks*, 2121 – 2124.

Zhang, G.P. (2003). Time series forecasting using a hybrid ARIMA and neural network model, *Neurocomputing*, **50**, 159-175.

Appendix – The data used in this study.

No.	X_1	X_2	X_3	X_4	Y
1	543675	11420838	45501	9252.8	553678
2	491465	10503706	36465	8954.5	515985
3	714565	7616493	40177	10253.2	748610
4	642222	8674804	23527	7609.4	678307
5	638685	10580745	29208	8155.5	678763
6	741159	9102389	36497	8589	793636
7	779432	9357663	30013	8189.7	834252
8	738308	9111833	26029	8302	793293
9	549289	8935974	30963	8555.8	613227
10	723844	9632109	31186	9606.6	797339
11	1059280	9476439	27014	10072.6	1134829
12	1010351	8660979	26876	10938.1	1061306
13	859530	10443753	25853	10130.5	937904
14	405435	9041456	29444	11845.8	437582
15	589368	9799850	34352	11585.7	620259
16	665465	7572281	29350	11172.7	709506
17	795875	10394228	23309	8973.1	842393
18	891553	9149164	39387	12231.9	926282
19	1003783	10327938	37966	11153.6	1029183
20	996677	9846491	39251	10716.6	1005137
21	884111	9957870	42141	11474.2	874773
22	1089077	10705240	43888	12208.2	1057271
23	1194111	9846958	42368	12984	1144526
24	939783	11464267	36933	13049.6	899864

25	590234	11553682	38323	14010.4	420119
26	549685	11025265	37857	14652.6	558776
27	688075	11865047	38336	14753.7	687149
28	444248	9045674	36115	14043.9	422863
29	498017	11949390	29902	10564.8	492605
30	594095	12255430	41972	13957.1	613800
31	480354	13137517	38432	14185.1	519449
32	697069	12391860	43372	15332	779520
33	500890	13573099	43294	15679.2	595869
34	601759	12746544	45183	17849.1	711963
35	613572	12933210	41329	17856.2	744712
36	441666	13657784	36453	17969.7	598816
37	626008	12723275	36087	18737.8	601675
38	516689	12091034	33912	19681.4	494645
39	682209	9827088	29759	17971	666988
40	723786	10126016	26388	13957.3	720610
41	798539	11718515	31541	14032	772659
42	711118	10841181	37485	14848.4	654890
43	799637	10149935	31449	13752.3	740697
44	837546	10327190	30017	13170.5	759466
45	372758	9704380	25954	12590.8	298746
46	651528	9445136	25495	13668.8	612528
47	529568	8854962	28534	14979.2	512144
48	725386	11435107	32410	13972	736557
49	649700	10172510	33092	16063.5	649066
50	465219	10268871	34143	15201.7	466750
51	623542	9682218	33504	12620.4	633615

52	681530	8042396	31840	14072.8	693946
53	783733	11446863	25360	11702.7	785838
54	693935	10858289	39323	15491.4	679312
55	753675	11039892	34471	15182.1	723914
56	800210	11225384	36726	15722.5	757490
57	949143	11141761	31605	14084.9	836846
58	1019900	10887644	35040	14763.8	833012
59	1100546	11251648	33425	14413.6	860892
60	1189945	11483422	34849	14905.8	912182

Authors' Biographical Statements

P.C. Chang received his M.S. and Ph.D. from the Department of Industrial Engineering at Lehigh University in 1985 and 1989, respectively. He is a professor at the Yuan-Ze University in Taiwan. His research fields cover Production Scheduling, Forecasting, Case-Based reasoning, ERP, and Application of Soft-Computing. He has published in several SCI Journals, such as *Expert Systems with Applications*, *European Journal of Operational Research*, *Applied Soft Computing*, *Journal of Intelligent Manufacturing*, *Computers and Industrial Engineering*, *International Journal of Production Economics*, *Computers & Mathematics with Applications*, and *Computers and Operations Research.*

Y.W. Wang received his Ph.D. from the Department of Industrial Engineering and Management at Yuan Ze University, Taiwan. He is currently a Lecturer in the Department of Industrial Engineering and Management at the Ching-Yun University in Taiwan. He is interested in the research of Production Scheduling, Forecasting and Soft Computing and their applications.

Chapter 5[1]

Data Mining Applications of Process Platform Formation for High Variety Production

Jianxin (Roger) Jiao and Lianfeng Zhang
School of Mechanical and Aerospace Engineering
Nanyang Technological University, Nanyang Avenue, Singapore 639798
Email: jiao@pmail.ntu.edu.sg

Abstract: The current intense global competition and diverse customer requirements have been forcing manufacturing companies to produce quickly a high variety of customized products at low costs. The linchpin for companies to achieve efficiency, and thus surviving, lies in the ability to maintain the high variety production as stable as possible. Such stable production can only be achieved by adopting similar production processes to produce the diverse products. Process platforms have been recognized as a promising means for companies to configure optima, yet similar, production processes to fulfill the need for different products. This chapter applies data mining to form process platforms from the existing large volumes of production data in companies' production systems. To meet the challenges encountered in the formation process, more specific data mining techniques, including text mining, tree matching, fuzzy clustering, and tree unification, are incorporated in the proposed methodology. A case study of high variety production of vibration motors for mobile phones is also reported. The results illustrate the feasibility and potential of data mining application in process platform formation.

Key Words: Mass customization, Data mining, Product family, Process configuration, Operations routing, Product variety, Text mining, Tree matching.

---

[1] Liao, T.W. and E. Triantaphyllou, (Eds.), **Recent Advances in Data Mining of Enterprise Data: Algorithms and Applications**, *World Scientific*, Singapore, pp. 247-286, 2007.

1. Background

One of the pressing needs faced by modern manufacturing companies is how to achieve the quick production of a high variety of customized products at low costs. The linchpin for companies to achieve efficiency, and thus surviving, lies in the ability to maintain the production as stable as possible. Such stable production can only be realized through using similar production processes to produce the diverse products. While certain production changeovers resulting from design variations must be implemented when producing the different products, the unnecessary changes caused by improper routings, which are created in traditionally subjective planning, must be eliminated. In traditional routing planning, production engineers develop the routings based on their previous experience, personal skills, individual knowledge and intuition, subjective judgments, etc. There are no well-structured mechanisms available for them to plan routings for new products by taking advantage of existing production knowledge. Consequently, this situation raises the importance of developing a well-structured mechanism for companies to plan similar routings for different products.

Process platforms (Jiao et al., 2007) have been recognized as a promising tool for companies to configure similar and proper production processes for producing customized products while considering a company's existing manufacturing capabilities. The authors provided a rigorous definition of process platforms along with the basic constructs and functionalities. However, they did not discuss further how to form process platforms in current manufacturing environments, where production of customized products generates large volumes of production data.

A process platform entails the conceptual structure and overall logical organization of producing a family of products, thus providing a generic umbrella to capture and utilize commonality, within which each new product fulfillment is instantiated and extends so as to anchor production planning to a common process structure (Martinez et al., 2000). The rationale of such process platforms lies in not only unburdening the knowledge base from keeping variant forms of the same solution, but also in modeling the production of a class of products that can widely variegate the operations and process sequences in accordance with specific design changes within a coherent framework (Meyer and Lehnerd, 1997).

Thanks to the fact that large volumes of production data are available in companies' legacy systems, reusing knowledge from historical data suggests itself as a natural technique to facilitate the handling of process changes and tradeoffs between design variations and process changes. Data mining excels in discovering previously unknown and potentially useful patterns of information, i.e., knowledge, from past data (Chen et al., 1996). Towards this end, this chapter proposes to apply data mining to solve the process platform formation problem. To meet the challenges in forming process platforms, specific data mining techniques, including text mining, tree matching, fuzzy clustering, and tree unification, are incorporated in the proposed methodology.

2. Methodology

A process platform is underpinned by a generic routing of a process family corresponding to a product family (Jiao et al., 2007). The generic routing is common to all individual routings in the process family to produce the corresponding individual products in the product family. Thus the problem of process platform formation can be converted to that of generic routing formation.

The data mining methodology consists of three steps, as shown in Figure 1. In the first step, the similarity of existing routings is measured. Based on the similarity measure results, in the second step, the similar routings are clustered into same families using a fuzzy clustering procedure. In the last step, the generic routings are formed for the corresponding families using a tree unification procedure developed in this research.

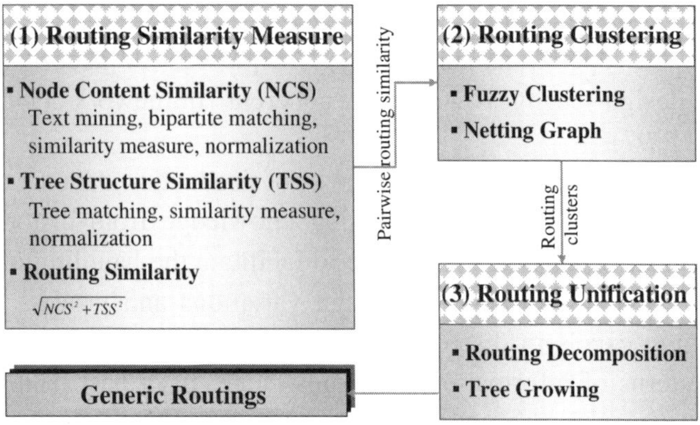

Figure 1. Overview of the data mining methodology for process platform formation.

A routing consists of a number of operations and their precedence relationships. Thus, the similarity of two routings involves two types: operations similarity and precedence similarity. In practice, a routing is represented by a tree precedence graph, in which nodes represent operations and arcs indicate the precedence relationships between two connected operations. Thus, measuring routing similarity can be decomposed into measuring node content similarity and tree structure similarity, which correspond to operations similarity and precedence similarity, respectively. Since node content similarity and tree structure similarity are two independent similarity measures, the Euclidian distance measure is adopted to compute the routing similarity, as shown in Figure 1. In this research, the methodology is applied to the basic representation trees: binary trees, as shown in Figure 2. In a binary tree, the highest number of child nodes of a parent node is 2.

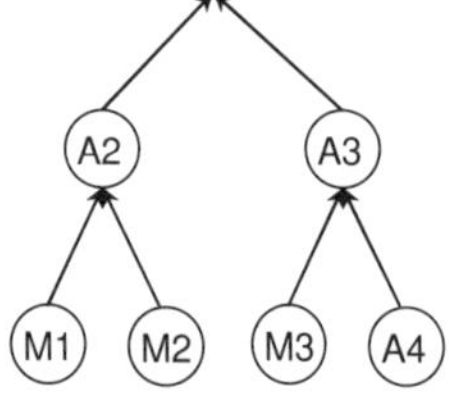

Figure 2. A binary tree representation of a routing.

Besides numerical data, operations are described by categorical data, e.g., specific shapes, materials, pertaining to product and process characteristics. As a result, subjectiveness and imprecision is associated with routings. Thus, fuzzy clustering is adopted to group similar routings into same families by taking its advantage of handling subjectiveness and imprecision inherent in data. In addition, the netting graph method introduced in (Yang and Gao, 1996) is used in the fuzzy clustering of routings. In the last step, a procedure is developed to form the generic routings for the corresponding families identified in the second step. This is accomplished through unifying other trees with an initial tree, i.e., the seed tree, one by one in a process family. The other trees and the seed tree are the sub-common routings in the process family in consideration. Each step of the proposed methodology will be detailed in the following corresponding sections.

3. Routing Similarity Measure

Let $\Omega = \{ROU_1, \cdots, ROU_P\}$ represent a set of routings; S_{rs} for the similarity between two routings, ROU_r and ROU_s; S_{rs}^{NC} for node content similarity; and S_{rs}^{TS} for tree structure similarity.

3.1 Node Content Similarity Measure

A node content similarity measures the degree of approximation of two routings in terms of their operations descriptions. To cope with the textual data, a text mining technique is employed, which performs sentence semantic analysis (Atkinson-Abutridy et al., 2003).

For a set of routings, there are a number of operation types (nodes), $\{o_j\}_N$, from which each individual routing is constituted. Some routings may not assume all these operations types. Thus they may comprise a subset of $\{o_j\}_N$.

Corresponding to P number of routings, each operation type $o_j \in \{o_j\}_N$, assumes a maximum number of P specific variants, $\{o^*_{jk}\}_{N \times P}$. Let $s^{O_j}_{rs}$ be the similarity of two operations variants, o^*_{jr} and o^*_{js}, $\forall r, s = 1, \cdots, P$ and $r \neq s$, corresponding two routings, ROU_r and ROU_s, respectively. Each operation variant is described by materials, $\left\{\Phi^M_{O_j}\right\}$, the product, $\left\{\Phi^P_{O_j}\right\}$, and resources, $\left\{R_{O_j}\right\}$. Accordingly, the operation similarity measure, $s^{O_j}_{rs}$, consists of three elements, namely material similarity, $s^{M_j}_{rs}$, product similarity, $s^{P_j}_{rs}$, and resource similarity, $s^{R_j}_{rs}$.

3.1.1 Material Similarity Measure

The materials of an operation are a set of components. This set is comprised of the type of raw materials, intermediate parts, and/or subassemblies, i.e., $\Phi^M_{O_j} = \{Co^M_{jk} \mid \forall k = 1, \cdots, K_j\}$. For a labeled binary tree, there are at most two material components, i.e., $K_j = 2$. Therefore, $s^{M_j}_{rs}$ of o^*_{jr} and o^*_{js} is calculated based on the similarity of all their material components. Component similarity indicates how similar two components are and to what extent they can be used as an alternative to each other. Since some components may be more important than others for an operation, $s^{M_j}_{rs}$ is computed as a weighted sum of individual material component similarities. The weight of each component, $w^M_{jk} \big| \forall k = 1, \cdots K_j$, indicates the relative importance of $\{Co^M_{jk}\}_{K_j}$ in regard to o_j and $\sum_{k=1}^{K_j} w^M_{jk} = 1$. In practice, the weights are determined based on domain knowledge. Some structured methods, e.g., the analytical hierarchy process (Saaty, 1994), can be employed to obtain weights as well.

Two types of nodes are involved in an *ROU* tree: leaf nodes (noted as *l*-nodes) and intermediate nodes (referred to as *i*-nodes). Each *l*-node represents a machining or assembly operation that consumes at least one primitive component to produce a compound component. Each *i*-node indicates an assembly operation that produces a subassembly or an end product. The materials of an *i*-node are all compound components, i.e., the subassemblies or intermediate parts. For example in Figure 2, operations M1, M2, M3 and A4 are *l*-nodes, whilst operations A1, A2 and A3 are *i*-nodes.

For an *l*-node, the corresponding operation takes at least one primitive component as input materials. If an operation is represented by an *i*-node, its material components are all compound components. Accordingly, the similarity of two component variants, $Co_{jkr}^{M^*}$ and $Co_{jks}^{M^*}$, is computed differently under two situations: (1) Co_{jk}^{M} is a primitive component; and (2) Co_{jk}^{M} is a compound component. Text mining is adopted to compute similarity of primitive components, as shown in Figure 3. The final result is a number of primitive component similarity matrices, each of which is for primitive components of same types. Based on primitive component similarity matrices, the similarity of compound components is computed using bipartite matching, as shown in Figure 3. The procedures of calculating the primitive component similarity and the compound component similarity are detailed in the following:

3.1.1.1 Procedure for calculating similarities between primitive components

The procedure for calculating similarities between primitive components has the following steps:

(1) *Prepare the data files.* Descriptions of all the nodes are extracted from the *P* number of *ROU* representation trees and are organized according to their corresponding operations. All component descriptions of the nodes are further sorted by primitive and compound components, which are saved separately in two text files. One contains the descriptions of all primitive components. The other documents the contents of all compound components.

(2) *Encode semantics.* The primitive component data file needs to be organized in proper formats for text mining tools to work on. A component is generally depicted by some characteristics – more specifically a list of attribute values with respect to descriptive fields. The basic attribute field is the name or ID of the component type. Figure 4 shows an example of attribute descriptions for a specific bracket b variant, called bb. In that figure, four attribute fields are used to describe the component type, including "name/ID", "shape", "color", and "weight". Different bracket variants assume different values of these attribute fields.

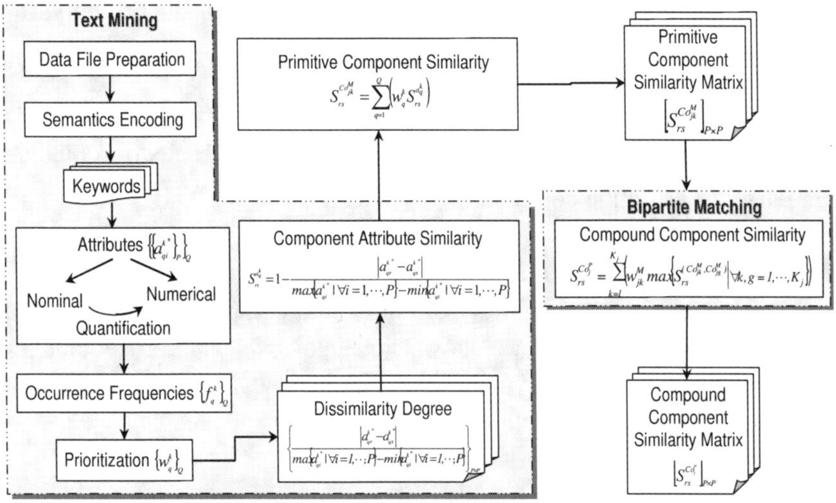

Figure 3. Text mining and bipartite matching for computing material similarity.

Component Description
BRACKET A, SQUARE, BLACK, WEIGHT0.08g

Figure 4. Component description of a "bb" variant.

In general, two types of attributes can be distinguished: nominal and numerical. While a nominal attribute value is in the form of a symbolic text, values of numerical attributes are numbers. In practice, a nominal attribute value itself is meaningful enough for identifying a unique record, e.g., "square shape". However, this is not the case for numerical attributes. A specific numerical value alone cannot suggest which attribute field it pertains to. For example, "10mm" can indicate an instance of "length" or "width". Therefore, rather than by listing single values, numerical attributes are described using attribute-value pairs, for example, "weight0.08g" in Figure 4.

(3) *Extract keywords.* A parser is used to scan the text file related to the primitive components. The result is a list of extracted significant words or phrases. The keywords are generated as separated records in three forms. Single words and word combinations, the first 2 forms, constitute the phrases that represent the values of nominal attributes. Word-number pairs, the 3rd form, are related to numerical attribute fields.

(4) *Derive occurrence frequencies.* All extracted keywords are cataloged according to their corresponding attribute fields. The occurrence of each attribute is counted by the actual values assumed. Suppose that a total number of Q attributes, $\{a_q^k \mid \forall q = 1, \cdots, Q\}$, are used to describe component $Co_{jk}^M \in \{Co_{jk}^M\}_{K_j}$. Dividing the number of occurrence by the total number of records scanned from the text file, $\left\{a_{qi}^{k^*} \mid \forall i = 1, \cdots, P\right\}$, the occurrence frequency, f_q^k, of the q-th attribute of the k-th component, a_q^k, is determined by the count of active instances of a_q^k, c_q^k, and the total number of records contained in the text file, which equals the total number of P routing instances. The occurrence frequencies explicitly suggest how often the attributes are used to characterize individual components of the same type.

(5) *Prioritize attribute fields.* Due to the different contributions to the functions of specific components, an attribute can be found in the descriptions of some component variants rather than others. Therefore, the relative importance of attributes in terms of occurrence frequencies should be introduced to model their relevance to the similarity measure.

This coincides with the common practice that some criteria play more important roles than others in discerning similar entities. The relative importance of these attributes is indicated by their weights as follows:

$$w_q^k = \frac{f_q^k}{\sum_{q=1}^{Q} f_q^k}, \tag{1}$$

where w_q^k denotes the weight of attribute a_q^k and $\sum_{q=1}^{Q} w_q^k = 1$.

(6) *Determine scales for nominal values.* To compare nominal values, a semantic scale is necessary in assessing the corresponding attribute type. Usually a number between 0 and 1 is assigned for a specific nominal value, whereby 0 represents no information content and 1 indicates the maximum amount of information content. For example, the semantic scale for attribute "color" may be established by assigning 0.2, 0.3, 0.4 and 0.6 for "yellow", "green" "red" and "blue", respectively. Usually such scales are determined a priori based on domain knowledge. If no domain experts are available, then simply use 1 for exactly the same nominal values and 0 for different ones, regardless of their proximity. With quantification of nominal attributes, both nominal and numerical values can be processed in the same manner, despite of their origins.

(7) *Compare attributes for their similarity.* For an attribute, $a_q^k \in \{a_q^k\}_Q$, the similarity of its instances is determined by comparing their difference (i.e., dissimilarity) in attribute values, as shown in Figure 3. $s_{rs}^{a_q^k} \in [0,1]$ denotes the similarity of two attribute values, $a_{qr}^{k\,*}, a_{qs}^{k\,*} \in \left\{ a_{qi}^{k\,*} \right\}_P$.

(8) *Calculate the similarity degree.* The similarity of two primitive component variants, $s_{rs}^{Co_{jk}^M}$, is calculated as a weighted sum of similarity measures of all their attributes, as shown in Figure 3. $0 \le s_{rs}^{Co_{jk}^M} \le 1$ and $w_q^k | \forall q = 1, \cdots, Q$ is computed based on Equation (1).

(9) *Construct component similarity matrices.* Repeat steps (7)-(8) for all the instances of this component type recorded in the data file. Then a $P \times P$ matrix, $\left[s_{rs}^{Co_{jk}^M} \right]_{P \times P}$, is constructed to present pairwise similarity

measures for this primitive component type. Enumerating all the primitive components, a number of such $P \times P$ matrices, $\left\{\left[S_{rs}^{Co_{jk}^M}\right]_{P \times P} \mid k = 1, \cdots, K^{\Pr i}\right\}$, are constructed, in accordance with a total number of $K^{\Pr i}$ primitive component types contained in the data file.

3.1.1.2 Procedure for computing similarities between compound components

The procedure of calculating similarities between compound components is summarized as follows:

Each *i*-node operation, o_j, enacts a subtree for producing a compound component, Co_j^P, from primitive components, $\left\{Co_{jk}^M\right\}_{K_j}$. Romanowski and Nagi (2005) demonstrated that when structural differences mean less than content dissimilarity, a bottom-up approach using bipartite matching excels in finding the minimum difference between individual subtrees. Therefore, bipartite matching is applied to derive the compound component similarity based on the similarity of primitive components. Further considering that different primitive components may contribute differently to the compound component, weighted bipartite matching is adopted by introducing different weights to the child nodes. Thus the end result is a weighted sum, as shown in Figure 3. The condition $0 \le S_{rs}^{Co_j^P} \le 1$ suggests the similarity of two compound components of the same type, $Co_{jr}^{P^*}$ and $Co_{js}^{P^*}$. The equation $\sum_{k=1}^{K_j} w_{jk}^M = 1$ indicate the relative importance of $\left\{Co_{jk}^M\right\}_{K_j}$ in regard to o_j and can be determined by, e.g., domain experts, and $S_{rs}^{\left(Co_{jk}^M, Co_{jg}^M\right)}$ denotes the similarity of the paired child nodes, $Co_{jkr}^{M^*}$ and $Co_{jgs}^{M^*}$.

Since the similarity of compound components depends on the similarity of the material components, be primitive components and/or compound components, computing the similarities of compound components should be carried out in a bottom-up approach along with product structures. In other words, the similarity of components at higher levels can only be computed after the similarities of components at lower levels have been obtained. Same as the result of measuring the primitive component similarity, a total number of N compound component similarity matrices, $\left[S_{rs}^{Co_j^P}\right]_{P\times P}$, are constructed.

3.1.2 Product Similarity Measure

Each product component, $\Phi_{O_j}^P = Co_j^P$, is a type of compound components. Thus, the number of N compound component similarity matrices simplifies measuring the similarity of product components of similar types. The data records of product components are extracted from the text file for compound components by identifying those i-nodes. The similarity of the product components is obtained from the corresponding compound component similarity matrices. As a result, a product similarity matrix, $\left[S_{rs}^{P_j}\right]_{P\times P}$, can be constructed for each product component type. By enumerating all the product components contained in the data file, $\left\{Co_j^P\right\}_N$, a total number of N product similarity matrices are constructed.

3.1.3 Resource Similarity Measure

The resource description, R_j, of each operation, $o_j \in \left\{o_j\right\}_N$, includes three attributes: workcenter, W_j, cycle time, T_j, and setup, S_j. While W_j and S_j are nominal attributes, T_j is of the numerical type. Text mining is conducted in a similar fashion as that for the primitive components. Resource descriptions of all operations (both l-nodes and i-nodes) are cataloged in a separate text file. Then text mining is carried out with respect to the three attribute fields and thus similarity measures in terms of workcenter ($S_{rs}^{W_j}$), cycle time ($S_{rs}^{T_j}$) and setup ($S_{rs}^{S_j}$) are derived as follows:

$$S_{rs}^{W_j} = 1 - \frac{\left|W_{jr}^* - W_{js}^*\right|}{\max\left\{W_{ji}^* \mid \forall i = 1, \cdots, P\right\} - \min\left\{W_{ji}^* \mid \forall i = 1, \cdots, P\right\}}, \tag{2}$$

$$S_{rs}^{T_j} = 1 - \frac{\left| T_{jr}^* - T_{js}^* \right|}{\max\left\{ T_{ji}^* \mid \forall i = 1, \cdots, P \right\} - \min\left\{ T_{ji}^* \mid \forall i = 1, \cdots, P \right\}}, \tag{3}$$

$$S_{rs}^{S_j} = 1 - \frac{\left| S_{jr}^* - S_{js}^* \right|}{\max\left\{ S_{ji}^* \mid \forall i = 1, \cdots, P \right\} - \min\left\{ S_{ji}^* \mid \forall i = 1, \cdots, P \right\}}, \tag{4}$$

where $S_{rs}^{W_j}, S_{rs}^{T_j}, S_{rs}^{S_j} \in [0,1]$, W_{ji}^*, T_{ji}^* and S_{ji}^* stand for the specific values of workcenter, cycle time and setup of operation O_j, respectively,

Accordingly, the resource similarity measure of two operation variants, $S_{rs}^{R_j}$, is calculated as a weighted sum of similarity measures regarding all their attributes as follows:

$$S_{rs}^{R_j} = w^{W_j} S_{rs}^{W_j} + w^{T_j} S_{rs}^{T_j} + w^{S_j} S_{rs}^{S_j}, \tag{5}$$

where $0 \le S_{rs}^{R_j} \le 1$, $w^{W_j} + w^{T_j} + w^{S_j} = 1$, and w^{W_j}, w^{T_j} and w^{S_j} denote the relative importance of workcenter, cycle time and setup attributes in regard to operation O_j, respectively. By enumerating all instances of resource description, R_j, a resource similarity matrix, $\left[S_{rs}^{R_j} \right]_{P \times P}$, is constructed to present pairwise resource comparisons of all variants of operation O_j. Similarly, a total number of N resource similarity matrices are constructed for all the operations, $\{O_{jk}^*\}_{N \times P}$.

3.1.4 Operation Similarity and Node Content Similarity Measures

With material similarity, $S_{rs}^{M_j}$, product similarity, $S_{rs}^{P_j}$, and resource similarity, $S_{rs}^{R_j}$, the operation similarity is computed, as shown in Figure 5.

Enumerate the above operation similarity calculation for all operation variants of all operation types. Then present pairwise similarity of same types of operations variants in the same matrices. A total number of N operations similarity matrices are constructed, as shown in Figure 5.

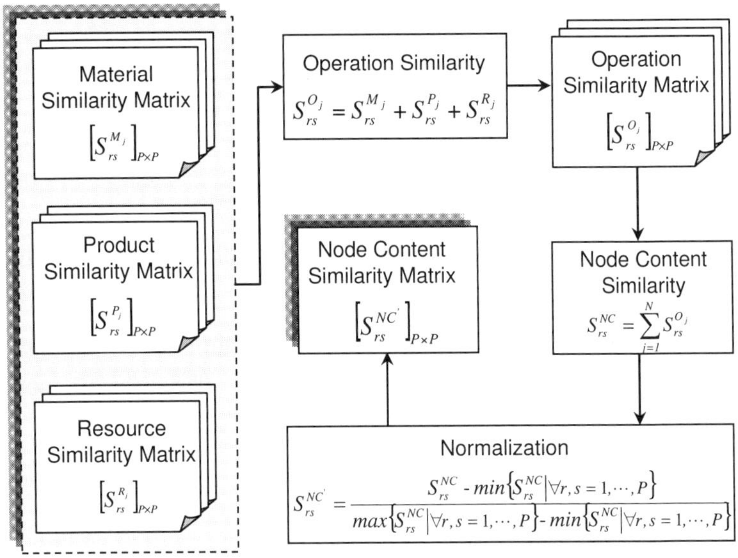

Figure 5. Measuring operation similarity and node content similarity.

The node content similarity, S_{rs}^{NC}, between two routings, ROU_r and ROU_s, is computed as the sum of their operations similarities, as shown in Figure 5.

Enumerate the above node content similarity calculation for all the *ROUs* in the routing set and obtain the pairwise similarity of node content of all routings.

3.1.5 Normalized Node Content Similarity Matrix

Since $0 \le S_{rs}^{M_j}, S_{rs}^{P_j}, S_{rs}^{R_j} \le 1$, $S_{rs}^{O_j}$ and S_{rs}^{NC} may not suggest a relative measure ranging from 0 to 1. They need to be normalized to achieve a consistent comparison. This research adopts the most common approach: the max-min method (Han and Kamber, 2001) to convert the node content similarity to a relative magnitude between 0 and 1, as shown in Figure 5.

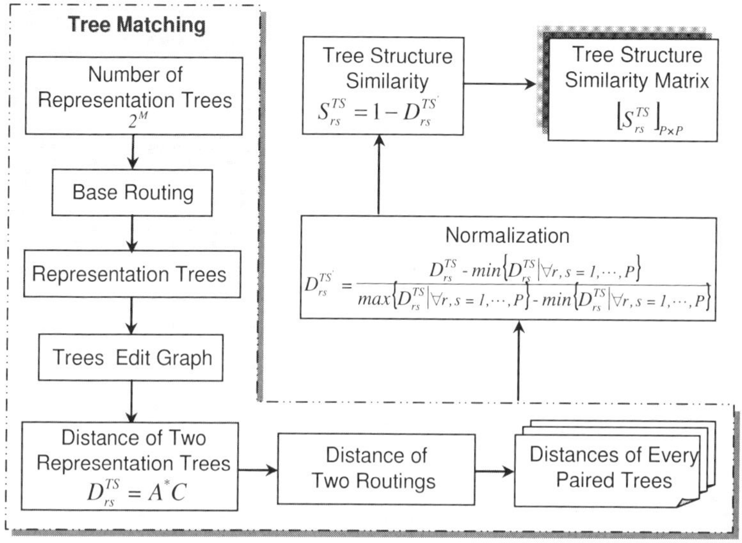

Figure 6. Measuring tree structure similarity.

In this figure S_{rs}^{NC} and $S_{rs}^{NC'}$ denotes the original and normalized node content similarity between ROU_r and ROU_s, respectively. Enumerate the above normalization for all the *ROUs* and then present the result in the form of an *ROU* node content similarity matrix, $\left[S_{rs}^{NC'}\right]_{P \times P}$. Each matrix element indicates the node content similarity of two routing variants corresponding to rows and columns.

3.2 *Tree Structure Similarity Measure*

Tree structure similarity measures the degree of commonality of two routings in terms of their operations precedence. To deal with such structural data, the tree matching technique is applied, which acquires the difference between two trees by finding the likeness of their structures (Valiente, 2002). The procedure, as shown in Figure 6, proceeds as follows:

(1) *Determine a base ROU.* An ROU constitutes a partial order set, in that not all the items in the set follow the same binary relation (NIST, 2004). Since a partial order can be represented by more than one tree (Martinez et al., 2000), each ROU may possess a number of alternative representation trees. The similarity of two $ROUs$ may vary if different representation trees of them are used for the comparison. It is thus necessary to make a decision based on pairwise comparisons of all possible representation trees of two $ROUs$.

Owing to the symmetric property of the distance measure and cyclic representation of a partial order (Martinet et al. 2000), the pairwise comparisons can be simplified to merely compare an arbitrary tree of one of the $ROUs$ (referred to as a base ROU) with all representation trees of the other $ROUs$. To reduce the total number of pairwise comparisons among $ROUs$, the ROU with the most representation trees should be selected as the base ROU. The number of representation trees of an ROU is given as 2^N, where N is the number of nodes with two child nodes.

(2) *Generate representation trees.* For a number of routings, $\{ROU_r \mid \forall r = 1, \cdots, P\}$, each of the first $(P-1)$ routings, $\{ROU_r \mid \forall r = 1, \cdots, P-1\}$, serves as a base ROU for comparison of the tree structure similarity with its immediate next ROU, $\{ROU_{r+1} \mid \forall r = 1, \cdots, P-1\}$. Thus a total number of $P \times (P-1)/2$ pairwise comparisons are needed. Except for the ROU selected to be the first base ROU, ROU_1, all the remaining $ROUs$, $\{ROU_r \mid \forall r = 2, \cdots, P\}$, are compared with their corresponding base $ROUs$, $\{ROU_{r-1} \mid \forall r = 2, \cdots, P\}$. To achieve this, all corresponding representation trees need to be generated for each of these $(P-1)$ $ROUs$.

(3) *Establish a tree edit graph.* The basic principle of tree matching is to compare two trees based on tree transformation – to transform one tree to exactly the same as the other one (Romanowski and Nagi, 2005). To overcome the disadvantage of tree transformation using tree editing operations, the tree edit graph (Valiente, 2002) is adopted in this research to obtain the dissimilarity, and thus the similarity of two trees.

Figure 7 shows a tree edit graph for transformation between two trees, T_1 and T_2. Each vertex indicated by a black dot represents a combination of two paired nodes from two trees, e.g., V_1W_3 meaning V_1 from T_1 and W_3 from T_2. A horizontal arc between two adjacent vertices, e.g., (V_1W_3, V_1W_4), means insertion of a node into the transformed tree, that is, to insert W_4 into tree T_2. A vertical arc, e.g., (V_2W_1, V_3W_1), indicates the deletion of a node from the transforming tree; that is, to delete node V_3 from tree T_1. A diagonal arc, e.g., (V_5W_5, V_6W_6), denotes the substitution of one node in the transformed tree with another node in the transforming tree, that is, to substitute W_6 in T_2 with V_6 in T_1. However, not all arcs in the graph are valid editing operations for tree transformation. The validity of arcs is subject to the following rules: (1) For a valid horizontal arc $\left(V_iW_j, V_iW_{(j+1)}\right)$, $D_{V_{(i+1)}} < D_{V(j+1)}$; (2) For a valid vertical arc $\left(V_iW_j, V_{(i+1)}W_j\right)$, $D_{V_{(i+1)}} > D_{V(j+1)}$; and (3) For a valid diagonal arc $\left(V_iW_j, V_{(i+1)}W_{(j+1)}\right)$, $D_{V_{(i+1)}} = D_{V(j+1)}$, where D_x stands for the depth of node x.

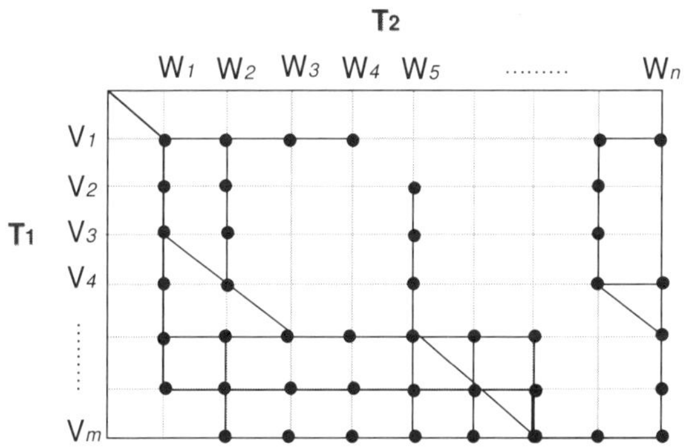

Figure 7. An example of tree edit graph.

The cost of an editing operation is reflected as a value attached to the corresponding arc. To facilitate comparisons based on a consistent common ground, the unit cost values for different types of tree editing operations are assumed to be the same. Therefore, the costs of different editing operations are indicated by the number of operations per se. For the measuring the tree similarity between each ROU with the base ROU, the total number of tree edit graphs needs to be generated is equal to the number of representation trees implied by this ROU.

(4) *Find the shortest path for the distance measure.* In a tree edit graph, there are many paths from the top-left corner to the bottom-right corner. Each such path suggests a possible way of transforming one tree to another, which carries different costs as well. The distance between two trees should be measured according to the shortest path that requires the minimum number of arcs and thus the fewest editing operations. The distance measure between every two trees is determined, as shown in Figure 6. In this figure A^* is the total number of valid arcs in the shortest path and C is a constant indicating the unit cost value associated with each operation, regardless of its type.

Repeat the above procedures for comparing all the representation trees for one ROU with the base ROU. The distance measure between this ROU and the base ROU is determined by the minimum distance among all distance measures between its representation trees and the base ROU. By enumerating all the $(P-1)$ $ROUs$ in the given set, their tree structure distances from the base ROU are reckoned in the same manner.

(5) *Normalize distance data.* The above distance measures are all absolute values instead of relative magnitudes. For consistent comparison, they need to be normalized. The max-min method is adopted to convert the absolute distance measure of each ROU pair to a dimensionless value ranging between 0 and 1, as shown in Figure 6. The variables D_{rs}^{TS} and $D_{rs}^{TS'}$ denote the absolute and normalized distance measures between ROU_r and ROU_s, respectively.

(6) *Calculate the tree structure similarity.* According to the normalized distance measure, the similarity can be calculated, as shown in Figure 6.

(7) *Construct an ROU structure similarity matrix.* Calculate similarity values for all the $ROUs$ in the routing data set. Then present all pairwise similarity measures in a $P \times P$ matrix, $\left[S_{rs}^{TS}\right]_{P \times P}$. Each matrix element indicates the structure similarity between two $ROUs$ corresponding to the respective row and column.

3.3 ROU similarity measure

As the node content similarity, $s_{rs}^{NC'} \in [0,1]$, and the tree structure similarity, $s_{rs}^{TS} \in [0,1]$, are two independent measures, the overall *ROU* similarity, $s_{rs}^{'}$, is composed by an Euclidian distance, as shown in Figure 1.

Repeat the above routing similarity calculation for all *ROUs* in the routing set and obtain the pairwise similarity of all *ROUs*. To convert $s_{rs}^{'}$ to a consistent magnitude for comparison ranging from 0 to 1, the normalization process is applied. The normalized routing similarity value, s_{rs}, is given as follows:

$$S_{rs} = \frac{S_{rs}^{'} - \min\left\{S_{rs}^{'} \middle| \forall r,s = 1,\cdots,P\right\}}{\max\left\{S_{rs}^{'} \middle| \forall r,s = 1,\cdots,P\right\} - \min\left\{S_{rs}^{'} \middle| \forall r,s = 1,\cdots,P\right\}}, \qquad (6)$$

such that $0 \le S_{rs} < 1$.

Repeat the above normalization for all *ROUs*. Then present all the pairwise routing similarities in a $P \times P$ matrix, $[s_{rs}]_{P\times P}$. Each matrix element indicates the normalized similarity between two *ROUs* corresponding to the respective row and column.

4. ROU Clustering

ROU clustering aims to group a set of individual routings into classes of similar routings. An *ROU* cluster is a collection of routings that are similar to one another within the same cluster yet dissimilar to the routings in other clusters. Considering the complex data types, e.g., textual data, involved in routings, this research adopts a fuzzy clustering approach by taking advantage of its ability to handle subjectiveness and impression (Zimmermann, 2001).

The procedure of ROU clustering is as follows:

(1) *Define a fuzzy compatible matrix.* A fuzzy compatible matrix, R, is defined by using the similarity measures for a given set of *ROUs*, $\Omega = \{ROU_1, \cdots, ROU_P\}$. The R is constructed in a matrix form, that is,

$R = [S_{rs}]_{P \times P}$, where $0 \le S_{rs} \le 1$ suggests a pairwise relationship (similarity grade) between any two ROU instances. In R, it holds true that $S_{rr} = 1 | \forall r = 1, \cdots, P$, suggesting that R is reflexive. Also the following condition $S_{rs} = S_{sr}$, $\forall r, s = 1, \cdots, P$, holds suggesting that R is symmetrical. Therefore, the fuzzy compatible matrix $R = [S_{rs}]_{P \times P}$, $S_{rs} \in [0,1]$ is identical to the routing similarity matrix obtained previously.

(2) *Construct a fuzzy equivalence matrix.* A fuzzy equivalence matrix is defined for Ω with transitive closure of a fuzzy compatible matrix (Zimmermann, 2001). The fuzzy compatible matrix R is a fuzzy equivalence matrix if and only if the transitive condition can be met. To convert a compatible matrix to an equivalence matrix, the "continuous multiplication" method, also known as max-min composition, is often used (Lin and Lee, 1996). Let $R(ROU_r, ROU_z)$ and $R(ROU_z, ROU_s)$ be two fuzzy compatible matrices, then $R \circ R = [\max\{\min\{S_{rz}, S_{zs}\}\}]$ is also a fuzzy compatible matrix.

(3) *Determine a λ-cut of the equivalence matrix.* The λ-cut is a crisp set, R_λ, that contains all the elements of the universe, Ω, such that the similarity grade of R is no less than λ, that is,

$$R_\lambda = [\tau_{rs}]_{P \times P}, \tag{7}$$

where $$\tau_{rs} = \begin{cases} 1 & \text{if } S_{rs} \ge \lambda \\ 0 & \text{if } S_{rs} < \lambda \end{cases}, \quad S_{rs} \in [0,1]. \tag{8}$$

Then each λ-cut, R_λ, is an equivalence matrix representing the presence of similarity among routing instances to the degree λ. For this equivalence matrix, there exists a partition on Ω, $\psi(R_\lambda)$, such that each compatible matrix is associated with a set, $\psi(R) = \{\psi(R_\lambda)\}$.

(4) *Identify ROU clusters.* A netting graph method (Yang and Gao, 1996) is applied to identify partitions of routing instances with respect to a given equivalence matrix.

5. ROU Unification

ROU unification attempts to unify all members of each ROU cluster into a generic routing. The major elements of a generic routing, $GROU$, include a set of master routing elements, such as operations and precedence, and a set of selective routing elements.

Built upon the master and selective routing elements, the $GROU$ is formed by maintaining a valid tree structure. The tree structure of a $GROU$, referred to as a generic tree, G, is developed, through a tree growing process, from the general tree structures embedded in individual routings, referred to as basic trees, $\{\mathrm{T}_z\}_Z$, within an ROU cluster. The formation of a $GROU$ involves four major steps, including assorting basic routing elements, identifying master and selective routing elements, forming basic trees, and tree growing, as discussed next.

5.1 Basic Routing Elements

The first step of routing unification is to break down individual routings into operations and precedence elements. For each member of an ROU cluster, $ROU_r \in \{ROU_r \mid \forall r = 1, \cdots, M \le P\}$, the nodes (operations) and arcs (precedence) of the corresponding ROU tree are assorted and categorized by l-nodes or i-nodes. This results in a l-node set, an i-node set, a l-node arc set, and an i-node arc set, corresponding to l-node type $\left\{LN_j\right\}_{N^{LN}}$, i-node type $\left\{IN_j\right\}_{N^{IN}}$, l-node arc type $\left\{LA_j\right\}_{N^{LN}}$, and i-node arc type $\left\{IA_j\right\}_{N^{IN}-1}$, respectively, where $N^{LN} + N^{IN} = N$, $\forall LN_j, IN_j \in \Lambda$, $\left\{LN_j\right\} \cap \left\{IN_j\right\} = \varnothing$, $\forall LA_j, IA_j \in \succ$, and $\left\{LA_j\right\} \cap \left\{IA_j\right\} = \varnothing$.

5.2 Master and Selective Routing Elements

The second step is to generalize each individual routing element (operation or precedence variant) with regard to its original type. This is achieved by replacing the specific name or ID of each specific node or arc with the general name or ID of the operation or precedence class that it belongs to. As a result, each particular routing element is labeled with its class identification.

In turn each operation or precedence class assumes a certain number of occurrences in terms of the number of times individual routing elements are generalized into this class. Such an occurrence count performs as a commonality index revealing to what extent each routing element is reused among individual members of an *ROU* family.

Given an *ROU* cluster, $\{ROU_r\}_M$, if the occurrence count of a precedence class ($O_i \succ O_j$) reaches the maximum number of instances of this class contained in the cluster, i.e., $\varphi_{O_i \succ O_j} = M$, it means that all individual routings in the cluster employ this precedence class. Therefore, this precedence class along with the related operation classes suggest themselves to be the master routing elements, i.e., the master precedence and operation classes, respectively. Should $1 \le \varphi_{O_i \succ O_j} < M$, the related operation and precedence classes are defined as selective operation and precedence classes, respectively, as not all individual variants assume them. In this way, all basic routing elements are grouped into either master or selective routing elements.

5.3 *Basic Tree Structures*

The third step deals with the generalization of basic trees, each of which is common to several members in an *ROU* family. Therefore, a basic tree refers to the common tree structure assumed by certain routing variants. A number of $Z \le M$ basic tree structures, $\{\mathrm{T}_z\}_Z$, are identified from M member trees of an *ROU* family.

While each member tree denotes a specific routing variant, a basic tree represents a class of individual routing variants bearing the same tree structure. To track the commonality of a basic tree with respect to its represented routing variants, each arc of the basic tree is assigned a weight indicating the degree of repetition of this arc among $M_z \le Z$ routings. Initially, the value of such a weight is set to be the same as the occurrence count of each arc, regardless if it is a master or selective precedence. In accordance with the assortment of basic routing elements, a basic tree is specified by a 4-tuple, denoted as:

$$\mathrm{T}_z = \left(\mathrm{L}^N, \mathrm{I}^N, \mathrm{L}^A, \mathrm{I}^A\right), \tag{9}$$

where $L^N(T_z)$, $I^N(T_z)$, $L^A(T_z)$, and $I^A(T_z)$ are sets of basic routing elements, encompassing all *l*-node classes, *i*-node classes, *l*-node arc classes and *i*-node arc classes contained in T_z, respectively.

5.4 *Tree Growing*

The fourth step aims to form the generic tree by pasting all basic trees one by one, that is,

$$G = T_1 \cup T_2 \cdots \cup T_z , \tag{10}$$

where $L^N(G) = L^N(T_1) \cup L^N(T_2) \cdots \cup L^N(T_z)$, $I^N(G) = I^N(T_1) \cup I^N(T_2) \cdots \cup I^N(T_z)$, $L^A(G) = L^A(T_1) \cup L^A(T_2) \cdots \cup L^A(T_z)$, and $I^A(G) = I^A(T_1) \cup I^A(T_2) \cdots \cup I^A(T_z)$.

Tree growing starts with the selection of a seed, i.e., an initial generic tree, G_1. Among basic trees, $\{T_z\}_Z$, the one holding a longest path and possessing the maximum number of *i*-nodes is recognized as the seed. Such a comprehensive tree encompasses most production conditions occurring among the process family members. The initial generic tree, G_1, starts to grow by unifying with the other $Z-1$ basic trees one by one, that is,

$$G_i = G_{i-1} \cup T_i , \tag{11}$$

where G_i is a growing tree. After all basic trees are unified, the growing tree reaches its final form, G_Z, namely, the tree structure of the *GROU*.

Since the structure of a *GROU* includes all operations occurred in the *ROU* cluster, both $L^N(G)$ and $I^N(G)$ are simply the union of all the node sets contained in the basic trees. However, $L^A(G)$ and $I^A(G)$ do not work with simple union operations, because a tree structure has to be maintained throughout the tree growing process. All the master *l*-node arcs and master *i*-node arcs contained in T_i must be added to the respective master *l*-node arc set and master *i*-node arc set of G_{i-1}. However, the selective *l*-node arcs and master *i*-node arcs of T_i may not always contribute to maintaining the generic structure. If adding some arcs of $I^A(T_i)$ to the growing tree may jeopardize the generic tree structure, these arcs are put in an additional arc set, A_{AS}, for further examination with such arcs derived from other tree growing operations. In addition, adding an arc must be conducive to making the generic tree as common as possible to most routing variants. Hence only arcs demonstrating certain commonality (indicated by the recorded weights) are added; otherwise they will be put in A_{AS} for further evaluation.

If an *l*-node arc exists in T_i but not in G_{i-1}, this arc is of selective type, i.e., La_{ij}^S. Such selective arcs, $\{La_{ij}^S\}_{N_i^{LNS}}$, are pasted to G_{i-1} only when their associated operations, i.e., selective *l*-nodes, $\{Ln_{ij}^S\}_{N_i^{LNS}}$, do not exist in G_{i-1} at the same time. Except this situation, to include a selective *l*-node arc of T_i, $La_{ij}^S \in L^A(T_i)$, into G_{i-1} or to put it in A_{AS} depends on the result of comparing its weight, $W_j^{La_{ij}^S}$, with that, $W_j^{La_{(i-1)j}^S}$, of the corresponding arc in G_{i-1}. Whichever assuming a higher weight should be included because a higher weight means a selective arc is more commonly used. Such a weight results from the sum of the occurrence count of this arc in all member trees and the recorded weight of the same arc in A_{AS}, if it is not empty.

In a similar manner, a selective *i*-node arc, $Ia_{ij}^S \in L^A(T_i)$, does not exist in G_{i-1}. Only when the associated parent *i*-node, $PIn_{ij}^S \in I^N(T_i)$, and child *i*-nodes, $CIn_{ij}^S \in I^N(T_i)$, do not exist in G_{i-1} at the same time this *i*-node arc can be added to G_{i-1}. Otherwise, evaluation of its weight is needed. In essence, arc unification aims to combine the arc sets of T_i and G_{i-1} while removing those less common arcs.

Each arc conveys information regarding two operations and the order of their execution. Tree growing is thus performed based on the search and evaluation of arcs. Any change to an *l*-node will propagate upwards in the routing tree until to the root node, thus causing changes to all relevant *i*-nodes and affecting the tree structure as well. Therefore in tree growing, *l*-node arcs are treated first and then *i*-node arcs. Moreover, tree growing first operates on master *l*-node arcs and master *i*-node arcs first, and next on selective *l*-node arcs and selective *i*-node arcs. Figure 8 shows the general procedure for tree growing.

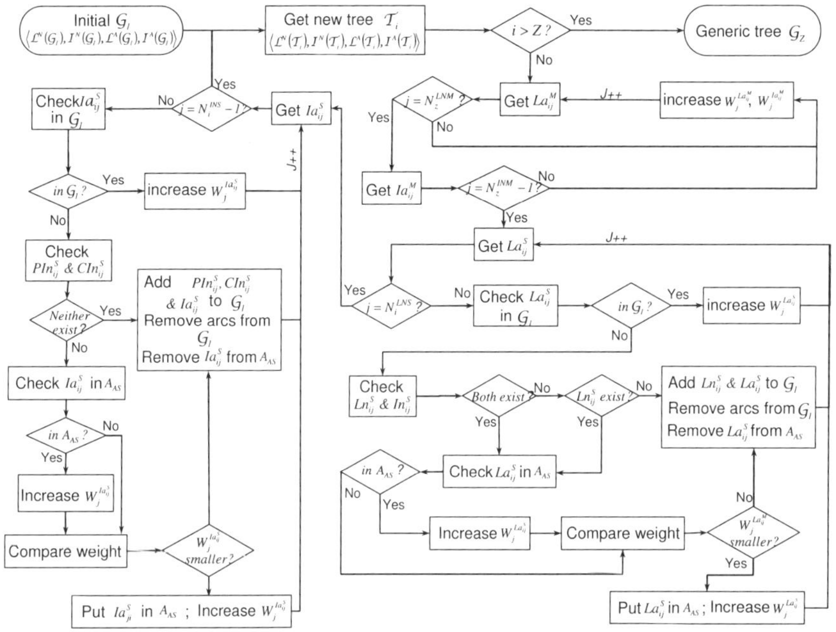

Figure 8. Procedure for tree growing.

For the master l-node and i-node arc sets of T_i, $\left\{La_{ij}^M \middle| \forall La_{ij}^M \in \succ^M\right\}_{N_i^{LNM}}$ and $\left\{Ia_{ij}^M \middle| \forall Ia_{ij}^M \in \succ^M\right\}_{N_i^{INM}-1}$, add their weights, $W_j^{La_{ij}^M}$ and $W_j^{Ia_{ij}^M}$, in G_{i-1} by the corresponding weight values in T_i. For the selective l-node arc set, $\left\{La_{ij}^S \middle| \forall La_{ij}^S \in \succ^S\right\}_{N_z^{LNS}}$ of T_i, if they can be found in G_i, then increase their weights $W_j^{Ia_{ij}^S}$ in G_i by the corresponding weight values in T_i. If they cannot be found in the selective l-node arc list of G_i, it may involve one of the four situations: (a) nonexistence of l-nodes Ln_{ij}^S, (b) nonexistence of i-nodes In_{ij}^S, (c) nonexistence of both, and (d) existence of both but without a single path in between. Figure 9 illustrates these four situations.

As shown in Figures 9(a) and 9(d), both La_{ij}^{S} and Ln_{ij}^{S} are added to the respective arc sets of G_{i-1}. In Figures 9(b) and 9(c), however, the weights of La_{ij}^{S} and $w_j^{Ia_{ij}^{S}}$ need to be compared with those of relevant arcs in G_{i-1}. First, La_{ij}^{S} is searched in A_{AS}. If it exists, then increase $w_j^{Ia_{ij}^{S}}$ by its recorded weight value in A_{AS}. Then use this new weight to compare; otherwise the original weight value of $w_j^{Ia_{ij}^{S}}$ is used. If the weight value of La_{ij}^{S} is smaller, then put La_{ij}^{S} in the A_{AS}; otherwise add it to the selective *l*-node set of G_{i-1} and move relevant arcs from G_{i-1} to A_{AS}.

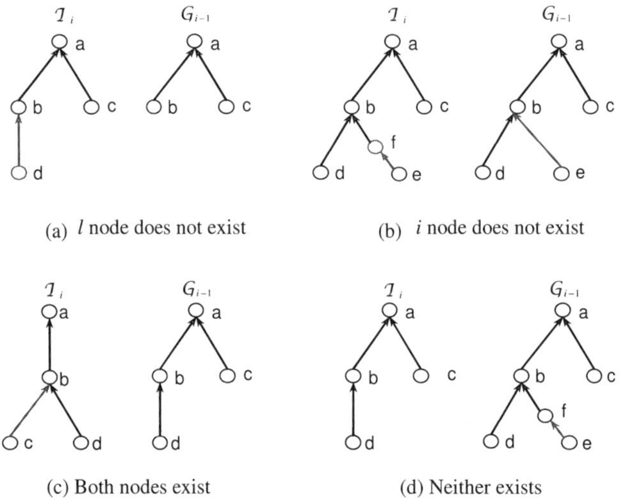

Figure 9. Different situations of an *l*-node arc in the member and generic trees.

For example, in Figure 9(b), arc $e \succ f$ of T_i does not exist in G_{i-1}, and the connected *l*-node *e* exists in both. To determine which arc should be included in the generic structure in order to maintain a valid tree structure, a weight comparison is performed. First check if $e \succ f$ exists in A_{AS} or not. If it can be found in A_{AS}, then increase its weight value by adding up its weight value in A_{AS}. If not, keep the original weight value. Next evaluate arc $e \succ b$ in G_{i-1}. If the weight value of $e \succ f$ is greater than that of $e \succ b$, then $e \succ f$ will be added to the selective *l*-node arc set of G_{i-1}. Meanwhile, the arc $e \succ b$ will be removed from G_{i-1} and it will be added into A_{AS} and arc $e \succ f$ will be removed from A_{AS} if it exists in it. In case that the weight value of $e \succ f$ is smaller, then put it in A_{AS}; otherwise increase the weight value. Similarly in Figure 9(c), the weights of $c \succ b$ in T_i and $c \succ a$ in G_{i-1} need to be compared.

For the selective *i*-node arcs of T_i, $\left\{ Ia_{ij}^S \middle| \forall Ia_{ij}^S \in \succ^S \right\}_{N_i^{INS}-1}$, if they can be found in G_{i-1}, increase their weights in G_{i-1} by the weight values in T_i. Otherwise, there are four possible situations: (a) nonexistence of child *i*-node CIn_{ij}^S, (b) nonexistence of parent *i*-node PIn_{ij}^S, (c) nonexistence of both, and (d) existence of both. In case of both the parent and child *i*-nodes exist, two more cases are further discerned: a single path between the two nodes, or more than one path connecting them.

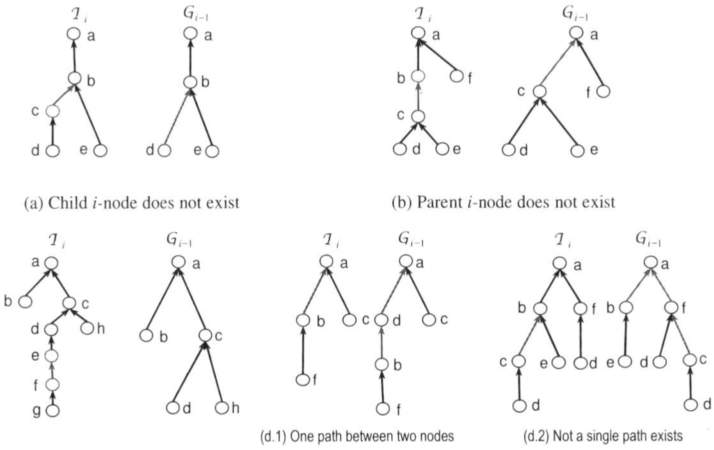

(a) Child *i*-node does not exist

(b) Parent *i*-node does not exist

(c) Neither *i*-node exists

(d.1) One path between two nodes

(d.2) Not a single path exists

(d) Both *i*-nodes exist

Figure 10. Different situations of an *i*-node arc in the member and generic trees.

As shown in Figure 10(c), neither of two nodes of Ia_{ij}^{S} can be found in the selective i-node set of G_{i-1}. In this case, both nodes and arcs are directly added to the i-node set and the selective i-node arc set of G_{i-1}.

Tree unification first checks if Ia_{ij}^{S} is contained in A_{AS}, as shown in Figure 10(d). If it is contained, then its weight is to be increased by its weight value in A_{AS}. The new weight value will be used for comparison with others. If Ia_{ij}^{S} is not contained in A_{AS}, then its original weight value recorded in T_i is to be used. The relevant arcs in G_{i-1} will be compared with Ia_{ij}^{S}, so that relevant arc or node removal and addition operations are carried out.

For example, in Figure 10(d.2), arc $c \succ b$ of T_i does not exist in G_{i-1} while both nodes b and c can be found in the i-node set of G_{i-1}. First $c \succ b$ is searched in A_{AS}. Increase its weight value if it exists; otherwise keep its original weight value. Then compare the weights of $c \succ b$ and $c \succ f$ in G_{i-1}. If the weight value of $c \succ b$ is larger, then add it into the i-node set of G_{i-1}, remove it from A_{AS} in case that it is included, and move $c \succ f$ from the selective arc set of G_{i-1} to A_{AS}. Otherwise, put $c \succ b$ in A_{AS} and increase its weight value if it has already been there. In Figure 10(d.1), weights are compared among arcs $b \succ a$ and $b \succ d$ or $d \succ a$ of G_{i-1}. If the weight of $b \succ a$ is higher, then both $b \succ d$ and $d \succ a$ are moved to A_{AS}. Meanwhile, $b \succ a$ is removed from A_{AS} if it exists in A_{AS}. In Figures 10(a) and 10(b), nodes that cannot be found in G_{i-1} are first added into the corresponding sets. Next operations on arcs proceed in the similar way to that of other situations.

Upon completion of the tree growing process, the formed *GROU* consists of a generic tree structure and an additional arc set. Due to the presence of selective arcs in the generic tree, the *GROU* is by no means the union of all member trees. Addition and removal of certain arcs according to their weights guarantee that the resulted generic structure is the most common to individual routings in an *ROU* family.

6. A Case Study

The proposed data mining methodology for process platform formation has been applied to high variety production of vibration motors for mobile phones in a local electronics company. Due to the many design changes in mobile phones, the orders that the company has received require a large number of different vibration motors. Figure 11 shows the major components of a vibration motor and some motor variants. The company has been struggling to quickly produce the diverse motor variants at low costs. However, handling the frequent production changeovers, most of which are caused by improper routings planned subjectively by production engineers without a well-structured mechanism, becomes the company's major challenge.

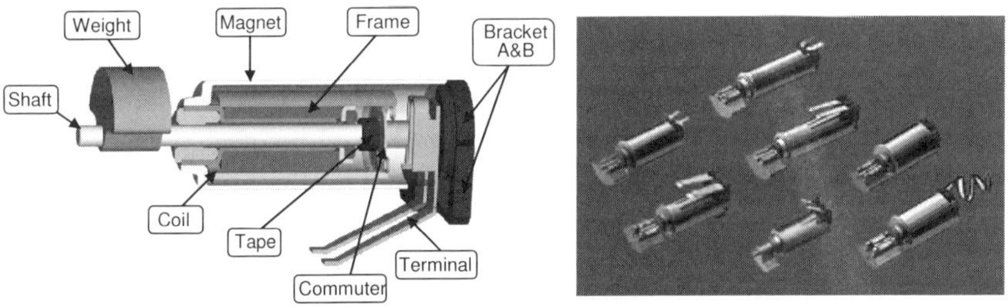

Figure 11. Vibration motors and the major components.

6.1 *The Routing Similarity Measure*

The production data of 30 routing variants for producing 30 motor variants has been used to test the methodology. Figure 12 shows two binary representation trees of routings. In each routing tree, the nodes represent specific operations (machining or assembly). The label of each node indicates the ID of the operation concerned. For example, "F*m*A2" represents a particular assembly operation for producing the final motor product, and "StM3" denotes a specific variant of the shaft machining operation.

The SPSS software package (www.spss.com) was adopted for text analysis due to its powerful capability to analyze textual data. Three attributes were used to describe the characteristics of each operation, including the material, product and resource types. In preparing data files for text mining, raw materials were described as material components of machining operations. An operation description data file was obtained by enumerating all the operations contained in the 30 routings. Assorting all primitive and compound components for each operation, this data file was separated into two text files, one containing all primitive components and the other containing compound components. Next these two files were input into SPSS for text analysis.

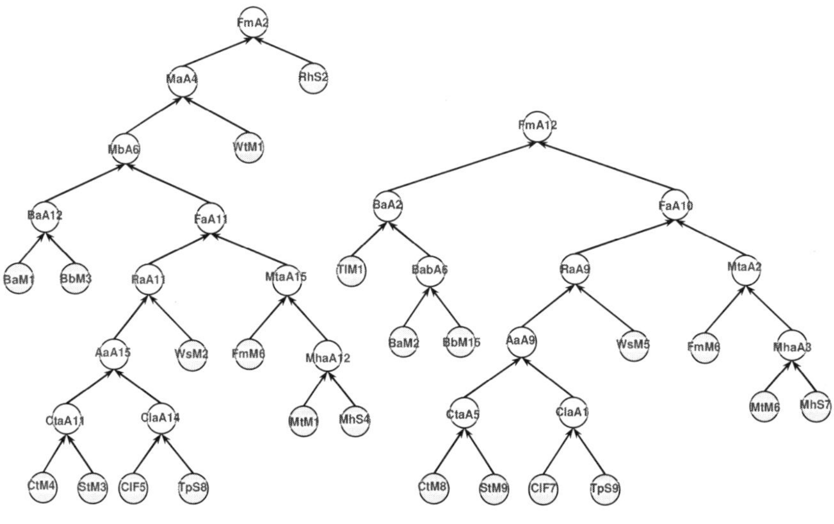

Figure 12. Two routing representation trees.

Figure 13 shows the results of the text analysis. For illustrative simplicity, a type of primitive component: bracket b (referred to as "bb") is used as an example. The result includes the extracted keywords, i.e., attribute values describing "bb" variants, and their respective occurrence counts.

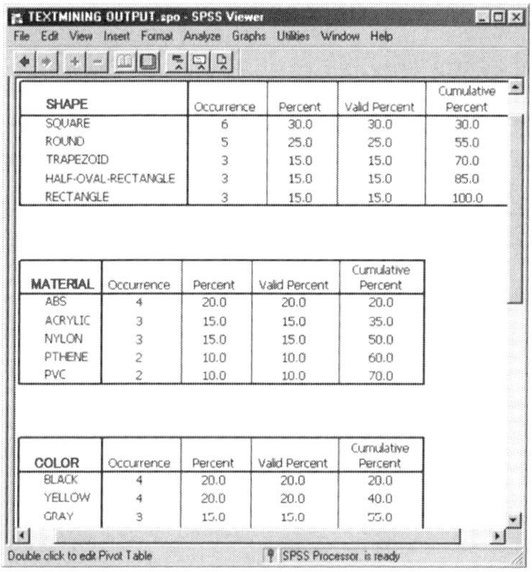

TEXTMINING OUTPUT.spo - SPSS Viewer

SHAPE	Occurrence	Percent	Valid Percent	Cumulative Percent
SQUARE	6	30.0	30.0	30.0
ROUND	5	25.0	25.0	55.0
TRAPEZOID	3	15.0	15.0	70.0
HALF-OVAL-RECTANGLE	3	15.0	15.0	85.0
RECTANGLE	3	15.0	15.0	100.0

MATERIAL	Occurrence	Percent	Valid Percent	Cumulative Percent
ABS	4	20.0	20.0	20.0
ACRYLIC	3	15.0	15.0	35.0
NYLON	3	15.0	15.0	50.0
PTHENE	2	10.0	10.0	60.0
PVC	2	10.0	10.0	70.0

COLOR	Occurrence	Percent	Valid Percent	Cumulative Percent
BLACK	4	20.0	20.0	20.0
YELLOW	4	20.0	20.0	40.0
GRAY	3	15.0	15.0	55.0

Double click to edit Pivot Table | SPSS Processor is ready

Figure 13. Text mining result: extracted keywords and occurrence count.

Based on the extracted information, the relevant attributes were identified and their weights were calculated, as shown in Table 1.

Table 1. Identified attributes and their relative importance.

Attribute	Value Set	Weight
Shape	Square, round, rectangle, trapezoid, half-oval-rectangle	0.235
Color	Black, yellow, gray, white, blue	0.165
Material	ABS, acrylic, pthene, PVC, nylon	0.152
Weight	0.05g, 0.074g, 0.08g, 0.084g, 0.12g	0.224
Thickness	1.52mm, 1.85mm, 2.37mm, 3.04mm, 3.53mm	0.224

For the set of attributes identified in Table 1, shape, color and material are of nominal type whilst weight and thickness are numerical ones. To quantify each nominal attribute, semantic scales were assigned for its specific instances based on domain knowledge. Based on established semantic scales, attribute similarity measures were calculated and the result is shown in Table 2.

Table 2. Attribute similarity measures.

Weight Similarity					Thickness Similarity				
1	0.20	0.25	0.28	0.58	1	0.09	0.24	0.43	0.57
0.20	1	0.05	0.08	0.38	0.09	1	0.14	0.34	0.48
0.25	0.05	1	0.03	0.33	0.24	0.15	1	0.19	0.33
0.28	0.58	0.03	1	0.30	0.43	0.34	0.19	1	0.14
0.58	0.38	0.33	0.30	1	0.57	0.48	0.33	0.14	1
Shape Similarity					**Color Similarity**				
1	0.13	0.02	0.30	0.47	1	0.34	0.32	0.09	0.15
0.13	1	0.15	0.17	0.34	0.34	1	0.66	0.43	0.19
0.02	0.15	1	0.32	0.49	0.32	0.66	1	0.23	0.47
0.30	017	0.32	1	0.17	0.09	0.43	0.23	1	0.23
0.47	0.34	0.49	0.17	1	0.15	0.19	0.47	0.23	1
Material Similarity									
1	0.56	0.27	0.10	0.18					
0.56	1	0.29	0.66	0.39					
0.27	0.29	1	0.37	0.10					
0.10	0.66	0.37	1	0.27					
0.18	0.39	0.10	0.27	1					

When measuring the attribute similarity, 0 is used as the smallest semantic value to indicate nonexistence of an attribute. Based on the results of attribute similarity, the similarity measures of component "bb" among 30 routing variants were derived. The results are presented in a matrix form as shown in Figure 14.

$$\left[\begin{array}{cccccccccccccccccccccccccccccc}
1 & .81 & 0 & .88 & .84 & 1 & .80 & .88 & 1 & .19 & 17. & .13 & 0 & .21 & 0 & .11 & .21 & 0 & .19 & .27 & 1 & .11 & .19 & 0 & .21 & .22 & 0 & .18 & 0 & .15 \\
.81 & 1 & 0 & .83 & .85 & .81 & .89 & .83 & .81 & .10 & .14 & .17 & 0 & .18 & 0 & .13 & .21 & 0 & .10 & .10 & .81 & .20 & .10 & 0 & .18 & .17 & 0 & .21 & 0 & .13 \\
0 & 0 & 1 & 0 & 0 & 0 & 0 & 0 & 0 & 0 & 0 & 0 & 0 & 0 & 0 & 0 & 0 & 0 & 0 & 0 & 0 & 0 & 0 & 0 & 0 & 0 & 0 & 0 & 0 & 0 \\
.88 & .83 & 0 & 1 & .78 & .88 & .82 & .90 & .88 & .17 & .19 & .15 & 0 & .23 & 0 & .11 & .19 & 0 & .17 & .17 & .88 & .13 & .17 & 0 & .23 & .31 & 0 & .20 & 0 & .13 \\
.84 & .85 & 0 & .78 & 1 & .84 & .86 & .85 & .84 & .05 & .19 & .30 & 0 & .15 & 0 & .13 & .15 & 0 & .05 & .13 & .84 & .25 & .12 & 0 & .15 & .14 & 0 & .18 & 0 & .08 \\
1 & .81 & 0 & .88 & .84 & 1 & .80 & .88 & 1 & .19 & .17 & .13 & 0 & .21 & 0 & .11 & .21 & 0 & .19 & .27 & 1 & .11 & .19 & 0 & .21 & .22 & 0 & .18 & 0 & .15 \\
.80 & .89 & 0 & .82 & .86 & .80 & 1 & .82 & .80 & .16 & .15 & .18 & 0 & .19 & 0 & .20 & .20 & 0 & .09 & .09 & .80 & .21 & .09 & 0 & .26 & .18 & 0 & .23 & 0 & .12 \\
.88 & .83 & 0 & .90 & .85 & .88 & .82 & 1 & .88 & .17 & .27 & .23 & 0 & .23 & 0 & .11 & .27 & 0 & .17 & .17 & .88 & .13 & .24 & 0 & .23 & .24 & 0 & .20 & 0 & .13 \\
1 & .81 & 0 & .88 & .84 & 1 & .80 & .88 & 1 & .19 & .17 & .13 & 0 & .21 & 0 & .11 & .21 & 0 & .19 & .27 & 1 & .11 & .19 & 0 & .21 & .22 & 0 & .18 & 0 & .15 \\
.19 & .10 & 0 & .17 & .05 & .19 & .16 & .17 & .19 & 1 & .76 & .73 & 0 & .15 & 0 & .15 & .15 & 0 & .25 & .25 & .19 & .05 & .25 & 0 & .22 & .16 & 0 & .12 & 0 & .12 \\
.17 & .14 & 0 & .19 & .19 & .17 & .15 & .27 & .17 & .76 & 1 & .87 & 0 & .28 & 0 & .12 & .22 & 0 & .11 & .18 & .17 & .19 & .11 & 0 & .21 & .20 & 0 & .17 & 0 & .08 \\
.13 & .17 & 0 & .15 & .30 & .13 & .18 & .23 & .13 & .73 & .87 & 1 & 0 & .17 & 0 & .15 & .18 & 0 & .08 & .08 & .13 & .23 & .15 & 0 & .17 & .24 & 0 & .21 & 0 & .16 \\
0 & 0 & 0 & 0 & 0 & 0 & 0 & 0 & 0 & 0 & 0 & 0 & 1 & 0 & 0 & 0 & 0 & 0 & 0 & 0 & 0 & 0 & 0 & 0 & 0 & 0 & 0 & 0 & 0 & 0 \\
.21 & .18 & 0 & .23 & .15 & .21 & .19 & .23 & .21 & .15 & .28 & .17 & 0 & 1 & 0 & .77 & .84 & 0 & .80 & .87 & .21 & .15 & .15 & 0 & .25 & .24 & 0 & .22 & 0 & .12 \\
0 & 0 & 0 & 0 & 0 & 0 & 0 & 0 & 0 & 0 & 0 & 0 & 0 & 0 & 1 & 0 & 0 & 0 & 0 & 0 & 0 & 0 & 0 & 0 & 0 & 0 & 0 & 0 & 0 & 0 \\
.11 & .13 & 0 & .11 & .13 & .11 & .20 & .11 & .11 & .15 & .12 & .15 & 0 & .77 & 0 & 1 & .80 & 0 & .73 & .73 & .11 & .21 & .08 & 0 & .27 & .11 & 0 & .23 & 0 & .05 \\
.21 & .21 & 0 & .19 & .15 & .21 & .20 & .27 & .21 & .15 & .22 & .18 & 0 & .84 & 0 & .80 & 1 & 0 & .80 & .80 & .21 & .15 & .15 & 0 & .19 & .18 & 0 & .22 & 0 & .15 \\
0 & 0 & 0 & 0 & 0 & 0 & 0 & 0 & 0 & 0 & 0 & 0 & 0 & 0 & 0 & 0 & 0 & 1 & 0 & 0 & 0 & 0 & 0 & 0 & 0 & 0 & 0 & 0 & 0 & 0 \\
.19 & .10 & 0 & .17 & .05 & .19 & .09 & .17 & .19 & .25 & .11 & .08 & 0 & .80 & 0 & .73 & .80 & 0 & 1 & .90 & .19 & .05 & .25 & 0 & .15 & .16 & 0 & .12 & 0 & .12 \\
.27 & .10 & 0 & .17 & .13 & .27 & .09 & .17 & .27 & .25 & .18 & .08 & 0 & .87 & 0 & .73 & .80 & 0 & .90 & 1 & .27 & .05 & .25 & 0 & .15 & .16 & 0 & .12 & 0 & .12 \\
1 & .81 & 0 & .88 & .84 & 1 & .80 & .88 & 1 & .19 & .17 & .13 & 0 & .21 & 0 & .11 & .21 & 0 & .19 & .27 & 1 & .11 & .19 & 0 & .21 & .22 & 0 & .18 & 0 & .15 \\
.11 & .20 & 0 & .13 & .25 & .11 & .21 & .13 & .11 & .05 & .19 & .23 & 0 & .15 & 0 & .21 & .15 & 0 & .05 & .05 & .11 & 1 & .70 & 0 & .88 & .14 & 0 & .26 & 0 & .08 \\
.19 & .10 & 0 & .17 & .12 & .19 & .09 & .24 & .19 & .25 & .11 & .15 & 0 & .15 & 0 & .08 & .15 & 0 & .25 & .25 & .19 & .70 & 1 & 0 & .80 & .16 & 0 & .12 & 0 & .12 \\
0 & 0 & 0 & 0 & 0 & 0 & 0 & 0 & 0 & 0 & 0 & 0 & 0 & 0 & 0 & 0 & 0 & 0 & 0 & 0 & 0 & 0 & 0 & 1 & 0 & 0 & 0 & 0 & 0 & 0 \\
.21 & .18 & 0 & .23 & .15 & .21 & .26 & .23 & .21 & .22 & .21 & .17 & 0 & .25 & 0 & .27 & .19 & 0 & .15 & .15 & .21 & .88 & .80 & 0 & 1 & .24 & 0 & .30 & 0 & .12 \\
.22 & .17 & 0 & .31 & .14 & .22 & .18 & .24 & .22 & .16 & .20 & .24 & 0 & .24 & 0 & .11 & .18 & 0 & .16 & .16 & .22 & .14 & .16 & 0 & .24 & 1 & 0 & .86 & 0 & .85 \\
0 & 0 & 0 & 0 & 0 & 0 & 0 & 0 & 0 & 0 & 0 & 0 & 0 & 0 & 0 & 0 & 0 & 0 & 0 & 0 & 0 & 0 & 0 & 0 & 0 & 0 & 1 & 0 & 0 & 0 \\
.18 & .21 & 0 & .20 & .18 & .18 & .23 & .20 & .18 & .12 & .17 & .21 & 0 & .22 & 0 & .23 & .22 & 0 & .12 & .12 & .18 & .26 & .12 & 0 & .30 & .86 & 0 & 1 & 0 & .77 \\
0 & 0 & 0 & 0 & 0 & 0 & 0 & 0 & 0 & 0 & 0 & 0 & 0 & 0 & 0 & 0 & 0 & 0 & 0 & 0 & 0 & 0 & 0 & 0 & 0 & 0 & 0 & 0 & 1 & 0 \\
.15 & .13 & 0 & .13 & .08 & .15 & .12 & .13 & .15 & .12 & .08 & .16 & 0 & .12 & 0 & .05 & .15 & 0 & .12 & .12 & .15 & .08 & .12 & 0 & .12 & .85 & 0 & .77 & 0 & 1
\end{array}\right]_{30\times 30}$$

Figure 14. Similarity matrix of primitive component "bb".

In the same way, the similarity matrices of other primitive components were constructed. Based on the primitive component similarity matrices, the similarity of compound components, and further the similarity matrices of compound components of same types were obtained. The similarity matrices of compound components provide the similarity of product components. Resource similarity measure proceeded with text analysis in a similar fashion, where workcenter and setup are nominal variables and cycle time numerical. Semantic scales for nominal attributes workcenter and setup were assigned by the company's production engineers. Finally, the resource similarity matrix for "Bracket Assembly" operation was obtained, as shown in Figure 15.

$$
\begin{bmatrix}
1 & .86 & .93 & .35 & .67 & .50 & .68 & .52 & .34 & .48 & .70 & .37 & .48 & .80 & .93 & .94 & .37 & .98 & .50 & .93 & .48 & .39 & .61 & .34 & .49 & .38 & .88 & .54 & .35 & .49 \\
.86 & 1 & .77 & .34 & .65 & .35 & .52 & .53 & .35 & .49 & .82 & .35 & .33 & .78 & .88 & .77 & .37 & .83 & .33 & .69 & .46 & .39 & .47 & .51 & .35 & .48 & .72 & .53 & .45 & .49 \\
.93 & .77 & 1 & .39 & .66 & .48 & .62 & .47 & .36 & .46 & .77 & .37 & .50 & .78 & .95 & .93 & .35 & .95 & .55 & .80 & .48 & .36 & .68 & .34 & .52 & .37 & .83 & .48 & .39 & .53 \\
.35 & .34 & .39 & 1 & .34 & .34 & .37 & .33 & .37 & .33 & .37 & .36 & .47 & .35 & .35 & .35 & .46 & .36 & .39 & .35 & .36 & .63 & .38 & .32 & .36 & .38 & .37 & .38 & .47 & .49 \\
.67 & .65 & .66 & .34 & 1 & .34 & .35 & .53 & .48 & .48 & .66 & .61 & .36 & .84 & .67 & .79 & .35 & .67 & .35 & .77 & .35 & .36 & .36 & .35 & .36 & .36 & .66 & .35 & .36 & .35 \\
.50 & .35 & .48 & .34 & .34 & 1 & .49 & .36 & .36 & .36 & .37 & .36 & .49 & .36 & .50 & .50 & .35 & .49 & .59 & .54 & .38 & .67 & .48 & .45 & .48 & .47 & .50 & .36 & .36 & .35 \\
.68 & .52 & .62 & .37 & .35 & .49 & 1 & .46 & .35 & .46 & .37 & .36 & .51 & .48 & .60 & .60 & .37 & .63 & .50 & .50 & .46 & .38 & .63 & .33 & .50 & .35 & .55 & .55 & .34 & .46 \\
.52 & .53 & .47 & .33 & .53 & .36 & 46 & 1 & .49 & .69 & .38 & .49 & .34 & .65 & .51 & .52 & .35 & .49 & .34 & .41 & .47 & .36 & .45 & .36 & .33 & .35 & .38 & .47 & .34 & .49 \\
.34 & .35 & .36 & .37 & .48 & .36 & .35 & .49 & 1 & .49 & .47 & .50 & .36 & .49 & .36 & .36 & .34 & .37 & .35 & .37 & .36 & .38 & .38 & .35 & .47 & .36 & .47 & .37 & .36 & .35 \\
.48 & .49 & .46 & .33 & .48 & .36 & .46 & .69 & .49 & 1 & .37 & .51 & .34 & .61 & .49 & .47 & .35 & .47 & .36 & .37 & .47 & .36 & .45 & .36 & .33 & .37 & .35 & .47 & .34 & .49 \\
.70 & .82 & .77 & .37 & .66 & .37 & .37 & .38 & .47 & .37 & 1 & .38 & .33 & .68 & .68 & .68 & .35 & .70 & .36 & .69 & .36 & .38 & .35 & .46 & .45 & .53 & .87 & .37 & .48 & .34 \\
.37 & .35 & .37 & .36 & .61 & .36 & .36 & .49 & .50 & .51 & .38 & 1 & .36 & .54 & .39 & .40 & .36 & .36 & .36 & .49 & .40 & .39 & .38 & .36 & .36 & .39 & .36 & .36 & .36 & .37 \\
.48 & .33 & .50 & .47 & .36 & .49 & .51 & .34 & .36 & .34 & .33 & .36 & 1 & .37 & .49 & .50 & .45 & .50 & .50 & .49 & .36 & .46 & .51 & .36 & .52 & .35 & .51 & .35 & .54 & .35 \\
.80 & .78 & .78 & .35 & .84 & .36 & .48 & .65 & .49 & .61 & .68 & .54 & .37 & 1 & .80 & .84 & .34 & .78 & .36 & .68 & .50 & .37 & .49 & .36 & .37 & .39 & .66 & .48 & .36 & .48 \\
.93 & .88 & .95 & .35 & .67 & .50 & .60 & .51 & .36 & .49 & .68 & .39 & .49 & .80 & 1 & .92 & .35 & .96 & .50 & .84 & .55 & .37 & .62 & .36 & .49 & .37 & .84 & .47 & .35 & .49 \\
.94 & .77 & .93 & .35 & .79 & .50 & .60 & .52 & .36 & .47 & .68 & .40 & .50 & .84 & .92 & 1 & .35 & .52 & .90 & .82 & .55 & .37 & .62 & .36 & .50 & .39 & .80 & .47 & .37 & .50 \\
.37 & .37 & .35 & .46 & .35 & .35 & .37 & .35 & .34 & .35 & .35 & .36 & .45 & .34 & .35 & .35 & 1 & .35 & .34 & .36 & .50 & .53 & .36 & .33 & .35 & .34 & .36 & .51 & .45 & .36 \\
.98 & .83 & .95 & .36 & .67 & .49 & .63 & .49 & .37 & .47 & .70 & .36 & .50 & .78 & .96 & .92 & .35 & 1 & .51 & .87 & .47 & .38 & .65 & .35 & .52 & .36 & .93 & .49 & .35 & .46 \\
.50 & .33 & .55 & .39 & .35 & .59 & .50 & .34 & .35 & .36 & .36 & .36 & .50 & .36 & .50 & .50 & .34 & .51 & 1 & .50 & .36 & .36 & .52 & .44 & .50 & .48 & .50 & .36 & .38 & .37 \\
.93 & .69 & .80 & .35 & .77 & .54 & .50 & .41 & .37 & .47 & .69 & .49 & .49 & .68 & .84 & .82 & .36 & .87 & .50 & 1 & .39 & .38 & .50 & .35 & .49 & .37 & .88 & .37 & .35 & .36 \\
.48 & .46 & .48 & .36 & .35 & .38 & .46 & .47 & .36 & .47 & .36 & .40 & .36 & .50 & .55 & .55 & .50 & .47 & .36 & .39 & 1 & .37 & .49 & .36 & .36 & .38 & .35 & .61 & .38 & .48 \\
.39 & .39 & .36 & .63 & .36 & .37 & .38 & .36 & .38 & .36 & .38 & .39 & .46 & .37 & .37 & .37 & .53 & .38 & .36 & .38 & .37 & 1 & .39 & .35 & .37 & .37 & .37 & .41 & .46 & .50 \\
.61 & .47 & .68 & .38 & .36 & .48 & .63 & .45 & .38 & .45 & .35 & .38 & .51 & .49 & .62 & .62 & .36 & .65 & .52 & .50 & .49 & .39 & 1 & .36 & .54 & .37 & .50 & .49 & .36 & .52 \\
.34 & .51 & .34 & .32 & .35 & .45 & .33 & .36 & .35 & .36 & .46 & .36 & .36 & .36 & .36 & .36 & .33 & .35 & .44 & .35 & .36 & .35 & .36 & 1 & .37 & .59 & .32 & .33 & .49 & .38 \\
.49 & .35 & .52 & .36 & .36 & .48 & .50 & .33 & .47 & .33 & .45 & .36 & .52 & .37 & .49 & .50 & .35 & .52 & .50 & .49 & .36 & .37 & .54 & .37 & 1 & .35 & .60 & .36 & .38 & .36 \\
.38 & .48 & .37 & .38 & .36 & .47 & .35 & .35 & .36 & .37 & .53 & .39 & .35 & .39 & .37 & .39 & .34 & .36 & .48 & .37 & .38 & .37 & .37 & .59 & .35 & 1 & .35 & .36 & .50 & .36 \\
.88 & .72 & .83 & .37 & .66 & .50 & .55 & .38 & .47 & .35 & .87 & .36 & .51 & .66 & .84 & .80 & .36 & .93 & .50 & .88 & .35 & .37 & .50 & .32 & .60 & .35 & 1 & .38 & .34 & .34 \\
.54 & .53 & .48 & .38 & .35 & .36 & .55 & .47 & .37 & .47 & .37 & .36 & .35 & .48 & .47 & .47 & .51 & .49 & .36 & .37 & .61 & .41 & .49 & .33 & .36 & .36 & .38 & 1 & .35 & .46 \\
.35 & .45 & .39 & .47 & .35 & .35 & .34 & .34 & .36 & .34 & .48 & .36 & .54 & .36 & .35 & .37 & .45 & .35 & .38 & .35 & .38 & .46 & .36 & .49 & .38 & .50 & .34 & .35 & 1 & .35 \\
.49 & .49 & .53 & .49 & .35 & .35 & .46 & .49 & .35 & .49 & .34 & .37 & .35 & .48 & .49 & .50 & .36 & .46 & .37 & .36 & .48 & .50 & .52 & .38 & .36 & .36 & .34 & .46 & .35 & 1
\end{bmatrix}_{30x30}
$$

Figure 15. Resource similarity matrix for the "Bracket Assembly" operation.

Compiling the results of component and resource similarity measures, the operation similarity is derived. In an analogous manner, similarity matrices of all operations types involved in the 30 routings were obtained. Finally, the normalized node content similarity measures were calculated and are given in Figure 16.

$$
\begin{bmatrix}
1 & .81 & .88 & .84 & .80 & .88 & .81 & .79 & .75 & .89 & .79 & .21 & .84 & .92 & .11 & .87 & .89 & .90 & .18 & .90 & .15 & .83 & .09 & .17 & .77 & .17 & .15 & .23 & .07 & .15 \\
.81 & 1 & .83 & .85 & .89 & .83 & .82 & .76 & .79 & .86 & .81 & .21 & .75 & .75 & .20 & .78 & .86 & .85 & .22 & .88 & .06 & .80 & .13 & .14 & .79 & .36 & .46 & .38 & .34 & .26 \\
.88 & .83 & 1 & .78 & .82 & .90 & .79 & .81 & .77 & .91 & .79 & .19 & .82 & .82 & .13 & .85 & .91 & .99 & .20 & .88 & .13 & .85 & .11 & .19 & .77 & .15 & .13 & .13 & .09 & .13 \\
.84 & .85 & .78 & 1 & .86 & .85 & .67 & .81 & .92 & .83 & .81 & .15 & .70 & .78 & .25 & .80 & .83 & .82 & .18 & .83 & .01 & .85 & .26 & .11 & .79 & .50 & .32 & .48 & .22 & .48 \\
.80 & .89 & .82 & .86 & 1 & .82 & .78 & .77 & .80 & .87 & .88 & .20 & .74 & .74 & .21 & .77 & .94 & .86 & .23 & .87 & .12 & .80 & .14 & .15 & .86 & .36 & .44 & .44 & .36 & .44 \\
.88 & .83 & .90 & .85 & .82 & 1 & .79 & .89 & .84 & .91 & .79 & .27 & .82 & .82 & .12 & .92 & .91 & .92 & .19 & .88 & .13 & .92 & .18 & .19 & .76 & .34 & .52 & .46 & .48 & .34 \\
.81 & .82 & .79 & .67 & .78 & .79 & 1 & .76 & .73 & .79 & .79 & .15 & .90 & .90 & .05 & .90 & .87 & .81 & .11 & .87 & .05 & .85 & .14 & .22 & .75 & .34 & .36 & .36 & .32 & .50 \\
.79 & .76 & .81 & .81 & .77 & .89 & .76 & 1 & .87 & .92 & .76 & .22 & .76 & .83 & .19 & .76 & .85 & .84 & .17 & .82 & .07 & .85 & .24 & .05 & .84 & .44 & .32 & .54 & .48 & .36 \\
.75 & .79 & .77 & .92 & .80 & .84 & .73 & .87 & 1 & .81 & .79 & .18 & .73 & .73 & .22 & .79 & .82 & .89 & .20 & .90 & .05 & .83 & .12 & .12 & .77 & .20 & .18 & .26 & .14 & .08 \\
.89 & .86 & .91 & .83 & .87 & .91 & .79 & .92 & .81 & 1 & .77 & .24 & .80 & .87 & .14 & .75 & .85 & .84 & .21 & .90 & .07 & .80 & .12 & .08 & .90 & .07 & .09 & .08 & .13 & .14 \\
.79 & .81 & .79 & .81 & .88 & .79 & .79 & .76 & .79 & .77 & 1 & .20 & .73 & .73 & .20 & .67 & .86 & .70 & .23 & .83 & .14 & .80 & .04 & .04 & .85 & .28 & .21 & .13 & .17 & .07 \\
.21 & .21 & .19 & .15 & .20 & .27 & .15 & .22 & .18 & .24 & .20 & 1 & .15 & .15 & .90 & .14 & .18 & .17 & .87 & .15 & .89 & .14 & .87 & .84 & .15 & .90 & .78 & .86 & .82 & .72 \\
.84 & .75 & .82 & .70 & .74 & .82 & .90 & .76 & .73 & .80 & .73 & .15 & 1 & .90 & .24 & .90 & .80 & .81 & .11 & .90 & .04 & .87 & .06 & .08 & .81 & .06 & .12 & .06 & .12 & .20 \\
.92 & .75 & .82 & .78 & .74 & .82 & .90 & .83 & .73 & .87 & .73 & .15 & .90 & 1 & .20 & .90 & .80 & .81 & .11 & .90 & .18 & .78 & .09 & .05 & .69 & .08 & .14 & .11 & .14 & .13 \\
.11 & .20 & .13 & .25 & .21 & .12 & .05 & .19 & .22 & .14 & .20 & .90 & .24 & .20 & 1 & .13 & .21 & .13 & .86 & .08 & .75 & .15 & .77 & .89 & .06 & .82 & .74 & .88 & .91 & .83 \\
.87 & .78 & .85 & .80 & .77 & .92 & .90 & .76 & .79 & .75 & .67 & .14 & .90 & .90 & .13 & 1 & .80 & .86 & .11 & .87 & .05 & .84 & .20 & .20 & .75 & .20 & .17 & .32 & .28 & .28 \\
.89 & .86 & .91 & .83 & .94 & .91 & .87 & .85 & .82 & .85 & .86 & .18 & .80 & .80 & .21 & .80 & 1 & .94 & .29 & .87 & .08 & .92 & .16 & .13 & .89 & .05 & .17 & .15 & .12 & .03 \\
.90 & .85 & .99 & .82 & .86 & .92 & .81 & .84 & .89 & .84 & .70 & .17 & .81 & .81 & .13 & .86 & .94 & 1 & .06 & .85 & .05 & .87 & .13 & .13 & .92 & .10 & .12 & .19 & .15 & .11 \\
.18 & .22 & .20 & .18 & .23 & .19 & .11 & .17 & .20 & .21 & .23 & .87 & .11 & .11 & .86 & .11 & .29 & .06 & 1 & .06 & .86 & .12 & .98 & .97 & .22 & .88 & .81 & .86 & .90 & .90 \\
.90 & .88 & .88 & .83 & .87 & .88 & .87 & .82 & .90 & 90 & .83 & .15 & .90 & .90 & .08 & .87 & .87 & .85 & .06 & 1 & .08 & .91 & .10 & .08 & .92 & .10 & .11 & .08 & .11 & .12 \\
.83 & .06 & .13 & .01 & .12 & .13 & .05 & .07 & .05 & .07 & .14 & .89 & .04 & .18 & .75 & .05 & .08 & .05 & .86 & .08 & 1 & .17 & .87 & .88 & .24 & .95 & .86 & .90 & .87 & .91 \\
.15 & .80 & .85 & .85 & .80 & .92 & .85 & .85 & .83 & .80 & .80 & .14 & .87 & .78 & .15 & .84 & .92 & .87 & .12 & .91 & .17 & 1 & .17 & .10 & .90 & .07 & .07 & .13 & .07 & .07 \\
.09 & .13 & .11 & .26 & .14 & .18 & .14 & .24 & .12 & .12 & .04 & .87 & .06 & .09 & .77 & .20 & .16 & .13 & .98 & .10 & .87 & .17 & 1 & .11 & .11 & .75 & .83 & .91 & .77 & .73 \\
.17 & .14 & .19 & .11 & .15 & .19 & .22 & .05 & .12 & .18 & .04 & .84 & .08 & .05 & .89 & .20 & .13 & .13 & .97 & .08 & .88 & .10 & .11 & 1 & .12 & .75 & .83 & .91 & .84 & .73 \\
.77 & .79 & .77 & .79 & .86 & .76 & .74 & .84 & .77 & .90 & .85 & .15 & .81 & .69 & .06 & .75 & .89 & .92 & .22 & .92 & .24 & .90 & .11 & .12 & 1 & .10 & 21. & .14 & .13 & .14 \\
.17 & .36 & .15 & .50 & .36 & .34 & .34 & .44 & .20 & .07 & .28 & .90 & .06 & .08 & .82 & .20 & .05 & .10 & .88 & .10 & .95 & .07 & .75 & .75 & .10 & 1 & .90 & .91 & .77 & .80 \\
.15 & .46 & .13 & .32 & .44 & .52 & .36 & .32 & .18 & .09 & .21 & .78 & .12 & .14 & .74 & .17 & .17 & .12 & .81 & .11 & .86 & .07 & .83 & .83 & .21 & .90 & 1 & .88 & .86 & .83 \\
.23 & .38 & .13 & .48 & .44 & .46 & .36 & .54 & .26 & .08 & .13 & .86 & .06 & .11 & .88 & .32 & .15 & .19 & .86 & .08 & .90 & .13 & .91 & .91 & .14 & .91 & .88 & 1 & .85 & .90 \\
.07 & .34 & .09 & .22 & .36 & .48 & .32 & .48 & .14 & .13 & .17 & .82 & .12 & .14 & .91 & .28 & .12 & .15 & .90 & .11 & .87 & .07 & .77 & .84 & .13 & .77 & .86 & .85 & 1 & .86 \\
.15 & .26 & .13 & .48 & .44 & .34 & .50 & .36 & .08 & .14 & .07 & .72 & .20 & .13 & .83 & .28 & .03 & .11 & .90 & .12 & .91 & .07 & .73 & .73 & .14 & .80 & .83 & .90 & .86 & 1
\end{bmatrix}_{30\times 30}
$$

Figure 16. The node content similarity matrix of 30 routings.

To measure the tree structure similarity, representation trees were generated for each routing and then tree edit graphs were established for every pair of trees in accordance with the number of the *i*-nodes contained in each routing tree. The results of pairwise distance measures of 30 routing trees were obtained. Subsequently, the tree structure similarity matrix was calculated and is given in Figure 17.

$$
\begin{bmatrix}
1 & .43 & 1 & .43 & .43 & .43 & .43 & .43 & .57 & .86 & .57 & .29 & .86 & .86 & .29 & .57 & .86 & .57 & .43 & .71 & .43 & .71 & .71 & .43 & .71 & .57 & .57 & .57 & .57 & .57 \\
.43 & 1 & .43 & .71 & .71 & .71 & .71 & .71 & .86 & .29 & .86 & .57 & .14 & .14 & .57 & .86 & .29 & .86 & .71 & .14 & .71 & .14 & .14 & .71 & .14 & 0 & 0 & 0 & 0 & 0 \\
1 & .43 & 1 & .43 & .43 & .43 & .43 & .43 & .57 & .86 & .57 & .29 & .86 & .86 & .29 & .57 & .86 & .57 & .43 & .71 & .43 & .71 & .71 & .43 & .71 & .57 & .57 & .57 & .57 & .57 \\
.43 & .71 & .43 & 1 & 1 & 1 & 1 & 1 & .86 & .29 & .86 & .86 & .29 & .29 & .86 & .86 & .29 & .86 & .71 & .14 & .71 & .14 & .14 & .71 & .14 & 0 & 0 & 0 & 0 & 0 \\
.43 & .71 & .43 & 1 & 1 & 1 & 1 & 1 & .86 & .29 & .86 & .86 & .29 & .29 & .86 & .86 & .29 & .86 & .71 & .14 & .71 & .14 & .14 & .71 & .14 & 0 & 0 & 0 & 0 & 0 \\
.43 & .71 & .43 & 1 & 1 & 1 & 1 & 1 & .86 & .29 & .86 & .86 & .29 & .29 & .86 & .86 & .29 & .86 & .71 & .14 & .71 & .14 & .14 & .71 & .14 & 0 & 0 & 0 & 0 & 0 \\
.43 & .71 & .43 & 1 & 1 & 1 & 1 & 1 & .86 & .29 & .86 & .86 & .29 & .29 & .86 & .86 & .29 & .86 & .71 & .14 & .71 & .14 & .14 & .71 & .14 & 0 & 0 & 0 & 0 & 0 \\
.43 & .71 & .43 & 1 & 1 & 1 & 1 & 1 & .86 & .29 & .86 & .86 & .29 & ..29 & .86 & .86 & .29 & .86 & .71 & .14 & .71 & .14 & .14 & .71 & .14 & 0 & 0 & 0 & 0 & 0 \\
.57 & .86 & .57 & .86 & .86 & .86 & .86 & .86 & 1 & .43 & 1 & .71 & .43 & .43 & .71 & 1 & .43 & 1 & .86 & .29 & .86 & .29 & .29 & .86 & .29 & .14 & .14 & .14 & .14 & .14 \\
.86 & .29 & .86 & .29 & .29 & .29 & .29 & .29 & .43 & 1 & .43 & .43 & .71 & .71 & .43 & .43 & 1 & .43 & .57 & .86 & .56 & .86 & .86 & .59 & .86 & .71 & .71 & .71 & .71 & .71 \\
.57 & .86 & .57 & .86 & .86 & .86 & .86 & .86 & 1 & .43 & 1 & .71 & .43 & .43 & .71 & 1 & .43 & 1 & .86 & .29 & .86 & .29 & .29 & .86 & .29 & .14 & .14 & .14 & .14 & .14 \\
.29 & .57 & .29 & .86 & .86 & .86 & .86 & .86 & .71 & .43 & .71 & 1 & .14 & .14 & 1 & .71 & .43 & .71 & .86 & .29 & .86 & .26 & .29 & .86 & .29 & .14 & .14 & .14 & .14 & .14 \\
.86 & .14 & .86 & .29 & .29 & .29 & .29 & .29 & .43 & .71 & .43 & .14 & 1 & 1 & .14 & .43 & .71 & .43 & .29 & .86 & .29 & .86 & .57 & .29 & .86 & .71 & .71 & .71 & .71 & .71 \\
.86 & .14 & .86 & .29 & .29 & .29 & .29 & .29 & .43 & .71 & .43 & .14 & 1 & 1 & .14 & .43 & .71 & .43 & .29 & .86 & .29 & .86 & .57 & .29 & .86 & .71 & .71 & .71 & .71 & .71 \\
.29 & .57 & .29 & .86 & .86 & .86 & .86 & .86 & .71 & .43 & .71 & 1 & .14 & .14 & 1 & .71 & .43 & .71 & .86 & .29 & .86 & .29 & .29 & .86 & .29 & .14 & .14 & .14 & .14 & .14 \\
.57 & .86 & .57 & .86 & .86 & .86 & .86 & .86 & 1 & .43 & 1 & .71 & .43 & .43 & .71 & 1 & .43 & 1 & .86 & .29 & .86 & .29 & .29 & .86 & .29 & .14 & .14 & .14 & .14 & .14 \\
.86 & .29 & .86 & .29 & .29 & .29 & .29 & .29 & .43 & 1 & .43 & .43 & .71 & .71 & .43 & .43 & 1 & .43 & .57 & .86 & .57 & .86 & .86 & .57 & .89 & .71 & .71 & .71 & .71 & .71 \\
.57 & .86 & .57 & .86 & .86 & .86 & .86 & .86 & 1 & .43 & 1 & .71 & .43 & .43 & .71 & 1 & .43 & 1 & .86 & .29 & .86 & .29 & .29 & .86 & .29 & .14 & .14 & .14 & .14 & .14 \\
.43 & .71 & .43 & .71 & .71 & .71 & .71 & .71 & .86 & .57 & .86 & .86 & .29 & .29 & .86 & 0.86 & .57 & .86 & 1 & .43 & 1 & .43 & .43 & 1 & .43 & .29 & .29 & .29 & .29 & .29 \\
.71 & .14 & .71 & .14 & .14 & .14 & .14 & .14 & .29 & .86 & .29 & .26 & .86 & .86 & .29 & .29 & .86 & .29 & .43 & 1 & .43 & 1 & .71 & .43 & 1 & .86 & .86 & .86 & .86 & .86 \\
.43 & .71 & .43 & .71 & .71 & .71 & .71 & .71 & .86 & .57 & .86 & .86 & .29 & .29 & .86 & 0.86 & .57 & .86 & 1 & .43 & 1 & .43 & .43 & 1 & .43 & .29 & .29 & .29 & .29 & .29 \\
.71 & .14 & .71 & .14 & .14 & .14 & .14 & .14 & .29 & .86 & .29 & .29 & .86 & .86 & .29 & .29 & .86 & .29 & .43 & 1 & .43 & 1 & .71 & .43 & 1 & .86 & .86 & .86 & .86 & .86 \\
.71 & .14 & .71 & .14 & .14 & .14 & .14 & .14 & .29 & .86 & .29 & .29 & .86 & .86 & .29 & .29 & .86 & .29 & .43 & 1 & .43 & 1 & .71 & .43 & 1 & .86 & .86 & .86 & .86 & .86 \\
.43 & .71 & .43 & .71 & .71 & .71 & .71 & .71 & .86 & .57 & .86 & .86 & .29 & .29 & .86 & 0.86 & .57 & .86 & 1 & .43 & 1 & .43 & .43 & 1 & .43 & .29 & .29 & .29 & .29 & .29 \\
.71 & .14 & .71 & .14 & .14 & .14 & .14 & .14 & .29 & .86 & .29 & .29 & .86 & .86 & .29 & .29 & .86 & .29 & .43 & 1 & .43 & 1 & .71 & .43 & 1 & .86 & .86 & .86 & .86 & .86 \\
.57 & 0 & .57 & 0 & 0 & 0 & 0 & 0 & .14 & .71 & .14 & .14 & .71 & .71 & .14 & .14 & .71 & .14 & .29 & .86 & .29 & .86 & .86 & .29 & .86 & 1 & 1 & 1 & 1 & 1 \\
.57 & 0 & .57 & 0 & 0 & 0 & 0 & 0 & .14 & .71 & .14 & .14 & .71 & .71 & .14 & .14 & .71 & .14 & .29 & .86 & .29 & .86 & .86 & .29 & .86 & 1 & 1 & 1 & 1 & 1 \\
.57 & 0 & .57 & 0 & 0 & 0 & 0 & 0 & .14 & .71 & .14 & .14 & .71 & .71 & .14 & .14 & .71 & .14 & .29 & .86 & .29 & .86 & .86 & .29 & .86 & 1 & 1 & 1 & 1 & 1 \\
.57 & 0 & .57 & 0 & 0 & 0 & 0 & 0 & .14 & .71 & .14 & .14 & .71 & .71 & .14 & .14 & .71 & .14 & .29 & .86 & .29 & .86 & .86 & .29 & .86 & 1 & 1 & 1 & 1 & 1 \\
.57 & 0 & .57 & 0 & 0 & 0 & 0 & 0 & .14 & .71 & .14 & .14 & .71 & .71 & .14 & .14 & .71 & .14 & .29 & .86 & .29 & .86 & .86 & .29 & .86 & 1 & 1 & 1 & 1 & 1
\end{bmatrix}_{30\times 30}
$$

Figure 17. Tree structure similarity matrix of 30 routings.

Finally, compiling node content similarity (Figure 16) and tree structure similarity (Figure 17), the normalized pairwise similarity measures of 30 routings were obtained and are given in Figure 18.

$$
\left[\begin{array}{cccccccccccccccccccccccccccccc}
1 & .65 & .95 & .67 & .64 & .69 & .65 & .64 & .67 & .88 & .69 & .24 & .85 & .90 & .21 & .74 & .88 & .76 & .32 & .82 & .32 & .78 & .51 & .32 & .74 & .42 & .41 & .43 & .40 & .41 \\
.65 & 1 & .66 & .79 & .81 & .78 & .72 & .74 & .83 & .64 & .84 & .43 & .54 & .54 & .42 & .82 & .64 & .86 & .53 & .63 & .50 & .57 & .13 & .51 & .56 & .11 & .03 & .03 & .10 & .03 \\
.95 & .66 & 1 & .63 & .66 & .71 & .64 & .65 & .68 & .89 & .69 & .23 & .84 & .84 & .21 & .73 & .89 & .81 & .33 & .81 & .31 & .79 & .51 & .33 & .74 & .41 & .41 & .41 & .40 & .41 \\
.67 & .79 & .63 & 1 & .94 & .93 & .86 & .92 & .89 & .62 & .84 & .62 & .53 & .59 & .63 & .83 & .62 & .84 & .52 & .59 & .50 & .61 & .20 & .51 & .56 & .07 & .06 & .05 & .14 & .05 \\
.64 & .81 & .66 & .94 & 1 & .92 & .90 & .90 & .83 & .65 & .87 & .62 & .56 & .56 & .62 & .82 & .70 & .86 & .53 & .62 & .51 & .58 & .13 & .51 & .61 & .10 & .03 & .03 & .11 & .03 \\
.69 & .78 & .71 & .93 & .92 & 1 & .91 & .95 & .86 & .68 & .83 & .63 & .62 & .62 & .61 & .90 & .68 & .90 & .52 & .63 & .51 & .67 & .16 & .52 & .55 & .15 & .08 & .08 & .05 & .13 \\
.65 & .72 & .64 & .86 & .90 & .91 & 1 & .89 & .80 & .60 & .83 & .61 & .67 & .67 & .61 & .88 & .65 & .84 & .51 & .62 & .50 & .61 & .13 & .53 & .54 & .09 & .10 & .11 & .08 & .06 \\
.64 & .74 & .65 & .92 & .90 & .95 & .89 & 1 & .87 & .68 & .81 & .63 & .57 & .62 & .62 & .81 & .64 & .86 & .52 & .59 & .51 & .61 & .10 & .50 & .61 & .02 & .08 & .08 & .11 & .05 \\
.67 & .83 & .68 & .89 & .83 & .86 & .80 & .87 & 1 & .65 & .91 & .52 & .60 & .60 & .53 & .91 & .66 & .95 & .62 & .67 & .61 & .62 & .21 & .61 & .59 & .12 & .15 & .20 & .14 & .11 \\
.88 & .64 & .89 & .62 & .65 & .68 & .60 & .68 & .65 & 1 & .62 & .34 & .76 & .80 & .31 & .61 & .93 & .67 & .43 & .89 & .40 & .84 & .61 & .40 & .88 & .51 & .51 & .51 & .51 & .50 \\
.69 & .84 & .69 & .84 & .87 & .83 & .83 & .81 & .91 & .62 & 1 & .52 & .60 & .60 & .52 & .86 & .68 & .87 & .63 & .62 & .61 & .63 & .20 & .61 & .64 & .09 & .17 & .13 & .15 & .10 \\
.24 & .43 & .23 & .62 & .62 & .63 & .61 & .63 & .52 & .34 & .52 & 1 & .13 & .13 & .96 & .51 & .32 & .52 & .87 & .22 & .88 & .22 & .65 & .86 & .22 & .65 & .57 & .62 & .59 & .52 \\
.85 & .54 & .84 & .53 & .56 & .62 & .67 & .57 & .60 & .76 & .60 & .13 & 1 & .96 & .10 & .71 & .76 & .65 & .21 & .89 & .20 & .87 & .40 & .20 & .84 & .50 & .50 & .50 & .51 & .52 \\
.90 & .54 & .84 & .59 & .56 & .62 & .67 & .62 & .60 & .80 & .60 & .13 & .96 & 1 & .10 & .71 & .76 & .65 & .21 & .89 & .23 & .83 & .40 & .20 & .78 & .50 & .51 & .50 & .50 & .50 \\
.21 & .42 & .21 & .63 & .62 & .61 & .61 & .62 & .53 & .31 & .52 & .96 & .10 & .10 & 1 & .50 & .33 & .51 & .86 & .20 & .81 & .22 & .58 & .88 & .20 & .59 & .53 & .63 & .66 & .60 \\
.74 & .82 & .73 & .83 & .82 & .90 & .88 & .81 & .91 & .63 & .86 & .51 & .71 & .71 & .50 & 1 & .64 & .94 & .61 & .65 & .61 & .63 & .24 & .62 & .57 & .17 & .15 & .12 & .10 & .10 \\
.88 & .64 & .89 & .62 & .70 & .68 & .65 & .64 & .66 & .93 & .68 & .32 & .76 & .76 & .33 & .64 & 1 & .73 & .45 & .87 & .40 & .90 & .61 & .41 & .88 & .50 & .52 & .51 & .51 & .50 \\
.76 & .86 & .81 & .84 & .86 & .90 & .84 & .86 & .95 & .67 & .87 & .52 & .65 & .65 & .51 & .94 & .73 & 1 & .61 & .64 & .61 & .65 & .19 & .61 & .69 & .11 & .12 & .16 & .14 & .12 \\
.82 & .53 & .33 & .52 & .53 & .52 & .51 & .52 & .62 & .43 & .63 & .87 & .21 & .21 & .86 & .61 & .45 & .61 & 1 & .30 & .94 & .31 & .77 & .92 & .34 & .66 & .61 & .64 & .67 & .67 \\
.32 & .63 & .81 & .59 & .62 & .63 & .62 & .59 & .67 & .89 & .62 & .22 & .89 & .89 & .20 & .65 & .87 & .64 & .30 & 1 & .30 & .97 & .51 & .30 & .91 & .61 & .61 & .61 & .61 & .61 \\
.32 & .50 & .31 & .50 & .51 & .51 & .50 & .51 & .61 & .40 & .61 & .88 & .20 & .23 & .81 & .61 & .40 & .61 & .94 & .30 & 1 & .32 & .69 & .95 & .34 & .71 & .65 & .67 & .65 & .68 \\
.78 & .57 & .79 & .61 & .58 & .67 & .61 & .61 & .62 & .84 & .63 & .22 & .87 & .83 & .22 & .63 & .90 & .65 & .31 & .97 & .32 & 1 & .52 & .30 & .96 & .61 & .61 & .61 & .61 & .61 \\
.51 & .13 & .51 & .20 & .13 & .16 & .13 & .10 & .21 & .61 & .20 & .65 & .40 & .40 & .58 & .24 & .61 & .19 & .77 & .51 & .69 & .52 & 1 & .31 & .51 & .81 & .85 & .89 & .82 & .80 \\
.32 & .51 & .33 & .51 & .51 & .52 & .53 & .50 & .61 & .40 & .61 & .86 & .20 & .20 & .88 & .62 & .41 & .61 & .92 & .30 & .95 & .30 & .31 & 1 & .30 & .57 & .62 & .68 & .63 & .56 \\
.74 & .56 & .74 & .56 & .61 & .55 & .54 & .61 & .59 & .88 & .64 & .22 & .84 & .78 & .20 & .57 & .88 & .69 & .34 & .91 & .34 & .96 & .51 & .30 & 1 & .61 & .61 & .61 & .61 & .61 \\
.42 & .11 & .41 & .07 & .10 & .15 & .09 & .02 & .12 & .51 & .09 & .65 & .50 & .50 & .59 & .17 & .50 & .11 & .66 & .61 & .71 & .61 & .81 & .57 & .61 & 1 & .96 & .96 & .90 & .91 \\
.41 & .03 & .41 & .06 & .03 & .08 & .10 & .08 & .15 & .51 & .17 & .57 & .50 & .51 & .53 & .15 & .52 & .12 & .61 & .61 & .65 & .61 & .85 & .62 & .61 & .96 & 1 & .95 & .94 & .93 \\
.43 & .03 & .41 & .05 & .03 & .08 & .11 & .08 & .20 & .51 & .13 & .62 & .50 & .50 & .63 & .12 & .51 & .16 & .64 & .61 & .67 & .61 & .89 & .68 & .61 & .96 & .95 & 1 & .94 & .96 \\
.40 & .10 & .40 & .14 & .11 & .05 & .08 & .11 & .14 & .51 & .15 & .59 & .51 & .50 & .66 & .10 & .51 & .14 & .67 & .61 & .65 & .61 & .82 & .63 & .61 & .90 & .94 & .94 & 1 & .94 \\
.41 & .03 & .41 & .05 & .03 & .13 & .06 & .05 & .11 & .50 & .10 & .52 & .52 & .50 & .60 & .10 & .50 & .12 & .67 & .61 & .68 & .61 & .80 & .56 & .61 & .91 & .93 & .96 & .94 & 1
\end{array}\right]_{30\times 30}
$$

Figure 18. Routing similarity matrix of 30 routings.

6.2 *The ROU Clustering*

By its very nature, the routing similarity matrix itself (Figure 18) is a fuzzy compatible matrix. Applying the max-min composition, a fuzzy equivalence matrix was obtained. Based on the domain knowledge on clustering, a threshold level of 0.85 was decided. Accordingly the λ-cut matrix was obtained. Subsequently, the netted graph was developed, as shown in Figure 19, based on which ROU clusters were derived. Table 3 gives the result of ROU clustering with four ROU clusters identified.

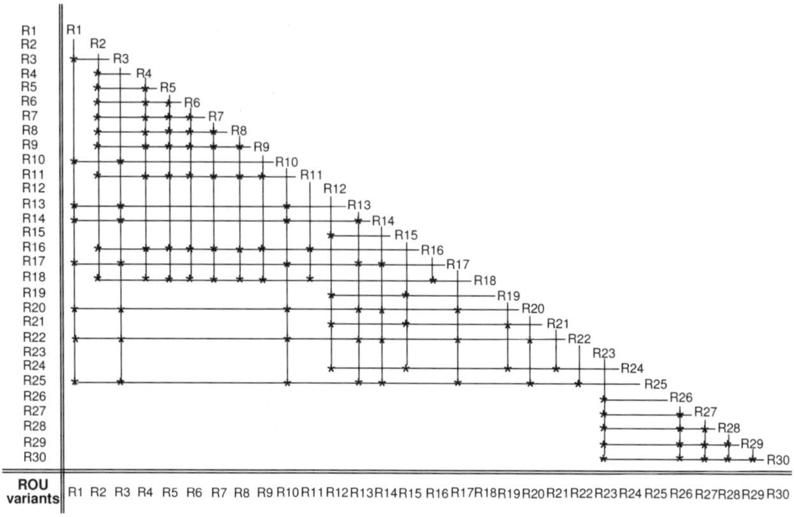

Figure 19. Netting graph for the λ-cut.

Table 3. Result of routing fuzzy clustering.

ROU Cluster	ROU Variants
RC1	R1, R3, R10, R13, R14, R17, R20, R22, R25
RC2	R2, R4, R5, R6, R7, R8, R9, R11, R16, R18
RC3	R23, R26, R27, R28, R29, R30
RC4	R12, R15, R19, R21, R24

6.3 The ROU Unification

For each ROU cluster, one GROU was formed by tree growing. For example, routing cluster "RC1" contains 9 member trees (R1, R3, R10, R13, R14, R17, R20, R22 and R25). The tree structures of these 9 routings were unified as a generic tree. Figure 20 presents the identified GROU for "RC1", which is represented using the unified modeling language (http://www.uml.org).

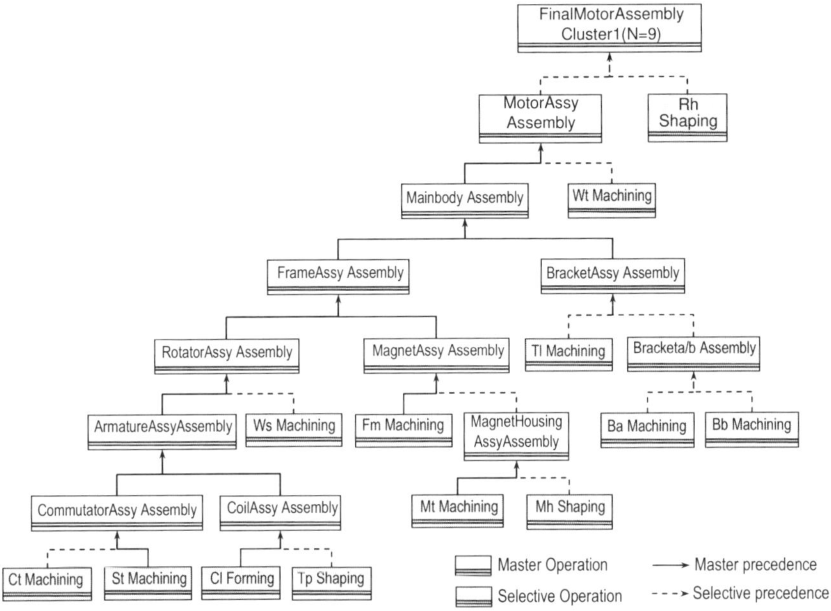

Figure 20. Formed GROU for routing cluster "RC1".

7. Summary

A generic routing essentially performs as a process platform to support the fulfillment of product families. It contributes to the utilization of commonality underlying process variations. The formation of generic routings coincides with the wisdom of knowledge reuse and economy of repetition.

The current approach assumes that operations similarity and precedence similarity are of equal importance. In practice, this may depend on particular production environments. For example, in capital intensive and highly automated industries like automobile or electronics assembly systems, line balancing is an important concern. Their routings sequences are far more important than individual operation characteristics. On the other hand, some labor intensive production systems may not be sensitive to changes in operations sequences, whereas operations characteristics like tooling and setup play a major role. This paves an avenue to further research.

The clustering result depends upon specification of the threshold, which requires intensive collaboration with domain experts and considerations of particular problem contexts. Decisions on the proper similarity threshold may be tricky or complex for enterprise managers. In practice, this can be alleviated through iterative interactions between generic routing identification and evaluation.

Generating generic routings based on knowledge discovery from past data avails to maintain the integrity of existing product and process platforms. In addition, it ensures the continuity of the infrastructure and core competencies, hence leveraging existing design and manufacturing investments. The application of data mining opens opportunities for incorporating experts' experiences into the projection of production planning patterns from historical data, thereby enhancing the ability to explore and utilize domain knowledge more effectively.

References

Atkinson-Abutridy, J., Mellish, C., Aitken, S. (2003). A semantically guided and domain-independent evolutionary model for knowledge discovery from texts, *IEEE Transactions on Evolutionary Computation,* **7**(6), 546-560.

Chen, M., Han, J., Yu, P. (1996). Data mining: An overview from database perspective, *IEEE Transactions on Knowledge and Data Engineering*, **8**(6), 866-883.

Han, J., Kamber, M. (2001). *Data Mining: Concepts and Techniques*, Morgan-Kanfmann: San Mateo, CA, U. S. A.

Jiao, J., Zhang, L., Pokharel, S., (2007). Process platform planning for variety coordination from design to production in mass customization manufacturing, *IEEE Transactions on Engineering Management*, **54**(1), 112-129.

Martinez, M.T., Favrel, J., Ghodous, P. (2000). Product family manufacturing plan generation and classification, *Concurrent Engineering: Research and Applications,* **8**(1), 12-22.

Meyer, M., Lehnerd, A.P., (1997). *The Power of Product Platform – Building Value and Cost Leadership*, Free Press: New York, NY, U.S.A.

NIST, 2004, http://www.nist.gov/dads/HTML/partialorder.html

Romanowski, C.J., Nagi, R. (2005). On comparing bills of materials: A similarity/distance measure for unordered trees, *IEEE Transactions on Systems, Man, and Cybernetics, Part A,* 35(2): 249-260.

Saaty, T. L. (1994). *Fundamentals of Decision Making and Priority Theory with the Analytic Hierarchy Process*, RWS Publications: Pittsburg, PA, U.S.A.

Valiente, G. (2002). *Algorithms on Trees and Graphs*, Springer-Verlag: Berlin, Germany.

Yang, L., Gao, Y. (1996). *Fuzzy Mathematics: Theory and Applications*, ISBN. 7-5623-0440-8.

Zimmermann, H.J. (2001) *Fuzzy Set Theory and Its Applications,* Kluwer Academic Publishers: Boston, MA, U.S.A.

Authors' Biographic Statements

Jianxin (Roger) Jiao is an Associate Professor of Systems and Engineering Management, School of Mechanical and Aerospace Engineering, Nanyang Technological University, Singapore. He received his Ph.D. degree in Industrial Engineering from Hong Kong University of Science & Technology. He holds a Bachelor degree in Mechanical Engineering from Tianjin University of Science & Technology in China, and a Master degree in Mechanical Engineering from Tianjin University in China. He has worked as a lecturer in the Department of Management at Tianjin University. His research interests include mass customization, design theory and methodology, reconfigurable manufacturing systems, engineering logistics, and intelligent systems. He serves as an editorial board member of *Concurrent Engineering: Research and Application* and an Area Editor of manufacturing systems for the *International Journal of Innovation and Technology Management.*

Lianfeng (Linda) Zhang received her PhD degree from the Nanyang Technological University, Singapore, in 2007. Since 2006, she has been working at the Lee Kong Chian School of Business as an adjunct faculty at Singapore Management University, Singapore. Her research focuses on platform-based production configuration, modeling of manufacturing systems, and supply chain configuration.

Chapter 6[1]

A Data Mining Approach to Production Control in Dynamic Manufacturing Systems

Hyeung-Sik Min[1] and Yuehwern Yih[2]
[1]Sandia National Laboratories, Albuquerque, New Mexico, USA
Email: hjmin@sandia.gov
[2]School of Industrial Engineering, Purdue University, West Lafayette, Indiana, USA
Email: yih@purdue.edu

Abstract: This chapter presents a data mining based approach for developing production control strategies under a dynamic and complex manufacturing system. To control such complex systems, it is a challenge to determine appropriate dispatching strategies under various system conditions. Dispatching strategies are classified into two categories: a vehicle-initiated dispatching policy and a machine-initiated dispatching policy. It has been shown that no single strategy consistently dominate the rest. Both policies are important to improve the system performance, especially for the real time control of the system. Focusing on combining them under various situations for semiconductor manufacturing systems, the goal of this chapter is to develop a scheduler for the selection of dispatching rules in order to obtain desired performance given by a user for each production interval. For the proposed methodology, simulation and competitive neural network approaches are used. The test results indicate that applying our methodology to obtaining a dispatching strategy is an effective method given the complexity of semiconductor wafer fabrication systems.

***Key Words*:** Data Mining, Production control, Dispatching rules, Scheduling, Semiconductor wafer fabrication.

---

[1] Liao, T.W. and E. Triantaphyllou, (Eds.), **Recent Advances in Data Mining of Enterprise Data: Algorithms and Applications**, *World Scientific*, Singapore, pp. 287-321, 2007.

1. Introduction

Production control is a very challenging problem for a dynamic manufacturing system, in which there often exists a high degree of uncertainty due to various causes. An order from an important customer is often turned into a rush one for its quick delivery. Unexpected equipment breakdowns are often a norm and the time needed to restore their abilities to serve is very unpredictable, which introduce another facet of uncertainty. Constant design changes exacerbate the problem even more.

Planning and controlling the production of semiconductor wafer fabrication systems is a complicated and difficult task because of their distinguishing characteristics such as reentrant product flow, high uncertainties in operations, and rapidly changing products and technologies. The reentrant product flow is the most distinguishing characteristic, which makes production planning and scheduling of wafer fabrication difficult. Wafers at different stages of their life in a fab have to compete with each other for the same machines. Thus, wafers need to spend a larger amount of their time simply waiting for machines, rather than being processed. The system uncertainties include machine failure, uncertain process yield, and rework. Unreliable machines may disrupt the flow of materials in a fab and cause the cycle time to increase and fluctuate. It is thus a significant challenge to develop effective scheduling methods in a wafer fabrication system. It is desirable to develop a semiconductor wafer fab scheduler that provides real time dispatching decisions and satisfies multiple objectives specified by a user.

To achieve the production goals such as reducing cycle time and its variance, increasing the throughputs, and meeting due dates, previous researchers have developed various scheduling methodologies for semiconductor manufacturing. Two types of scheduling methods have been widely used in both practice and academia: (1) dispatching strategies, which are applied to decide which wafer lot is to be scheduled next when machines or vehicles are becoming available; and (2) input control strategies, which decide the type, amount, and the time to release new wafer lots into a fab. Wein (1988) pointed out that the input control strategy has more significant impact on performances than the dispatching policy does for wafer fabrication. However, later Lu *et al.* (1994), Kumar (1994), Li *et al.* (1996), and Lin *et al.* (2001) showed that a good dispatching policy is also important to improve system performance.

Egbelu and Tanchoco (1984) classified the dispatching policies into two categories: a vehicle-initiated dispatching policy and a machine-initiated dispatching policy. A vehicle-initiated dispatching policy deals with the situation that a vehicle has the choice of a task when multiple lots are waiting for pickup simultaneously at different locations in a facility. A machine-initiated dispatching policy deals with the situation that a machine has a choice of a task when multiple lots are waiting for the process of the same machine simultaneously. These two dispatching policies affect significantly the performance of the whole system. However, there has been little research focusing on combining them under various situations and finding their interactions and effects in a semiconductor manufacturing system. Also, it is shown that no single dispatching strategy consistently dominates others in all situations. In fact, most of the previous scheduling studies only considered the machine initiated dispatching policy (see Section 2). Therefore, we believe that it is more meaningful to identify a combination of policies that give good performance under various situations.

In addition, most studies concerning the scheduling of wafer fabrication systems have been focused on developing scheduling algorithms for a single objective such as reducing cycle time and increasing throughput with a single dispatching decision variable. However, this area of research really needs to consider multiple objectives and multiple decision variables in order to utilize resources efficiently, thereby offsetting the high installation cost of equipment. Thus, in this chapter, the following features will be accommodated in the development of the wafer fab scheduler:

(1) Multiple objectives will be achieved in order to satisfy both customers and the semiconductor company.

(2) The wafer fab scheduler will simultaneously determine multiple decision variables, each of which is assigned an effective rule among candidate rules by considering current system status.
(3) The wafer fab scheduler will be capable of generating the best dispatching rules in real time mode to cope with high uncertainties and frequent configuration changes of a system as much as possible, thereby enhancing productivity and the concept of an agile manufacturing.

The proposed methodology makes use of simulation and a competitive neural network approach in order to realize the wafer fab scheduler described above. First, simulation experiments are conducted to collect the data containing the relationship between changes in the decision rule set and the current system status and performance measures in the dynamic nature of semiconductor manufacturing fab. Then a competitive neural network is employed to classify all the information obtained from the simulation model and produce the scheduling knowledge. In this data mining application, simulation data is preferred over real-world data for two main reasons. First, real-world data is the result of current scheduling practice which might not be perfect. Secondly, simulation data can provide better control in terms of coverage, data distribution, and the kinds of relations to be captured. It goes without saying that the simulation model implemented must be a good approximation to the real-world system. It will be shown that the proposed methodology can help users extract decision rules for multiple dispatching decision variables to achieve the desired system objective in real time.

The remainder of this chapter is organized as follows. Previous approaches to scheduling of wafer fabrication are discussed in Section 2. In Section 3, the simulation model and proposed approaches are described in detail. In Section 4, a simulation-based experiment and its results are presented with an analysis. Other related studies, including those carried out by the second author and her research associates, are summarized in Section 5. Finally, in Section 6, the conclusions of this research are discussed.

2. Previous Approaches to Scheduling of Wafer Fabrication

The dispatching policy has been an important part of scheduling of production systems. It affects significantly the performance of the whole system. There have been many studies to find a good dispatching policy for semiconductor manufacturing systems, in order to meet a system goal such as reducing cycle time and increasing the throughput and so forth. Most methods used for dispatching problems are heuristic in nature.

Li *et al.* (1996) proposed a dispatching rule called the minimum inventory variability schedule rule (MIVS), which keeps a lower Work in Process (WIP) level without sacrificing throughput by decreasing the variability existing in a fab. The method reduces variability by introducing a positive correlation to the arrivals and services of all machines in the product flow. They use the WIP level as the indicator for variability between output rate of a feeder workstation and processing rate of a downstream workstation. A simulation model was used to compare MIVS with five different dispatching rules. The result indicated that MIVS has the least variability of cycle time among the selected dispatching rules. However, this study did not show how to generate an average WIP inventory level profile, which is the prerequisite for applying MIVS.

Lu and Kumar (1991) studied the performance of two classes of dispatching rules: buffer-based and due date-based rules. The buffer-based rules determine which processing step to perform or which buffer to serve based on different criteria. Due date-based policies are the Earliest Due Date and the Least Slack. Their simulation results show that the Last Buffer First Serve policy performs well for reducing mean cycle time, while the Least Slack policy gives good results for minimizing its variance.

Motivated by the work of Lu and Kumar (1991), Lu *et al.* (1994) and Kumar (1994) introduced a new dispatching rule called the fluctuation smoothing (FS) policies, which belongs to the class of least slack policies. FS examines the downstream stations by using iterative simulations in order to estimate downstream delay, and thus the slack available for a lot awaiting processing. This approach focuses on all the flows in a fab as well as a bottleneck machine, whereas many previous approaches to input control and dispatching attempt to deal with bottleneck machines. In their results, FS reduced both mean queuing time and standard deviation of cycle time by 22.4 % and 52.0 %, respectively, over the First-In First-Out (FIFO) policy.

Kim *et al.* (1998) evaluated the effects of input control rules and dispatching rules in a fab producing multiple products with due dates. For their study, different dispatching rules are adapted for photo and non-photo workstations in order to minimize mean tardiness. Results of simulation tests showed that dispatching rules in photo workstations have more effects on the performance than dispatching rules in non-photo workstations. Dispatching rules for non-photo workstations did not have much impact on performance when rules for the other decision problems were given. Also, they found that rules giving smaller mean tardiness are better with respect to average and standard deviation of cycle times.

Baek *et al.* (1998) proposed the Spatial Adaptation Procedure (SAP) which selects the most appropriate dispatching rule for each machine in succession using simulation and the Taguchi experimental design. A suitable dispatching rule for each machine is determined on the basis of the condition of the machine and its related machines through repeated simulation runs, and the Taguchi experimental design finds the set of effective criteria weights. The experimental results showed that the SAP method reduced mean cycle time compared to applying a single decision rule for all machines.

Hung and Chen (1998) developed a simulation-based dispatching rule to reduce cycle time in a fab. The method includes parent and child simulations to predict the waiting times and flow times that lots will encounter in the future. The parent simulation emulates the environment resulting from a simulation-based dispatching rule, while the child simulation aims to predict the consequence of dispatching a particular lot. Thus, in the parent simulation, when a machine becomes idle, a set of child simulations are executed to determine the relative merits of dispatching various lots in the queue of a machine. The simulation experiments were conducted under changing product mix and fixed product mix cases, and its result outperformed other static dispatching rules that use only queue information at the time of dispatch. However, this method requires high computational power since every dispatching decision is based on many simulation runs.

Nakata *et al.* (1999) described a workflow control called JUSTICE/MORAL (just time process control system/method of optimum-buffer restriction and adjustment logic) for a multi-product type fab. The JUSTICE/MORAL method dynamically detects a bottleneck machine and feeds work to the machine at an appropriate time. The method first finds the candidate bottleneck machines and determines their appropriate loads while the product-mix is changed. Then, it calculates the suitable amount of WIP in front of each machine in real time and feeds the appropriate work into the machine. This method synchronizes the bottleneck condition with all the machines in the lines, and controls the progress speed of all lots. The simulation experimental result indicated that cycle time could be reduced by an average of 13% and throughput could be increased up to approximately 10 % compared to using the FIFO rule.

Lin *et al.* (2001) studied the effects of the vehicle dispatching policies in a wafer fab by using simulation. Their simulation model includes a double loop inter-bay automated material handling system (AMHS) in a wafer fab. Their simulation results show that the dispatching policy has a significant impact on average transportation time, waiting time, throughput and vehicle utilization. The combination of the shortest distance with the nearest vehicle and the first encounter first served rule outperformed the other rules. However, their study only focused on the dispatching of transportation systems without considering the dispatching of machines.

From the investigation of previous studies, we found out that most of the scheduling studies only consider the machine initiated dispatching policies. Recently, Lin *et al.* (2001) studied the dispatching policies of a transportation system but they did not consider the machine initiated dispatching.

3. Simulation Model and Solution Methodology

3.1 Simulation Model

The semiconductor fab model in this study imitates a fab of the LG Semiconductor Company in Korea. The fab of the LG Semiconductor Company is divided into the number of bays (aisles) that contain a number of similar or identical processing equipment. This bay configuration creates a large amount of material flow between bays, especially since wafer fabrication processes are highly reentrant. The bay configuration has advantages of maintenance and operation of physical equipment (Cadarelli 1995, Peters 1997). The transport operations in the fab of the LG Semiconductor Company are classified into inter-bay and intra-bay lot transfers. Inter-bay lot transfers are carried out using an overhead monorail system and stockers. The overhead monorails transfer wafer lots using vehicles and they are linked with automated stockers, which are furnished with a device for the lot exchanges with the vehicles. The stockers guarantee the continuous control of lot positions and reduce the chance of wafer contamination. Inside the stocker, a robot called Rack Master transfers the lot between the storage positions and the input-output ports. Intra-bay lot transfers are performed by operators within a bay. Operators transfer wafer lots between the input-output port of a stocker and workstations for specific process steps or deposits of wafer lot to a stocker. Figure 1 shows the layout of the LG semiconductor fab.

The simulation model in this study was developed by using the SLAM II simulation languages with user FORTRAN insert codes. There are 24 multiserver stations which consist of several identical machines in the simulation model of the semiconductor fab. Since operation parameters and process sequences of a fab of the LG Semiconductor Company are confidential, in this study, the basic operation parameters for the simulation model are estimated based on Wein's (1988) paper and are presented in Table 1.

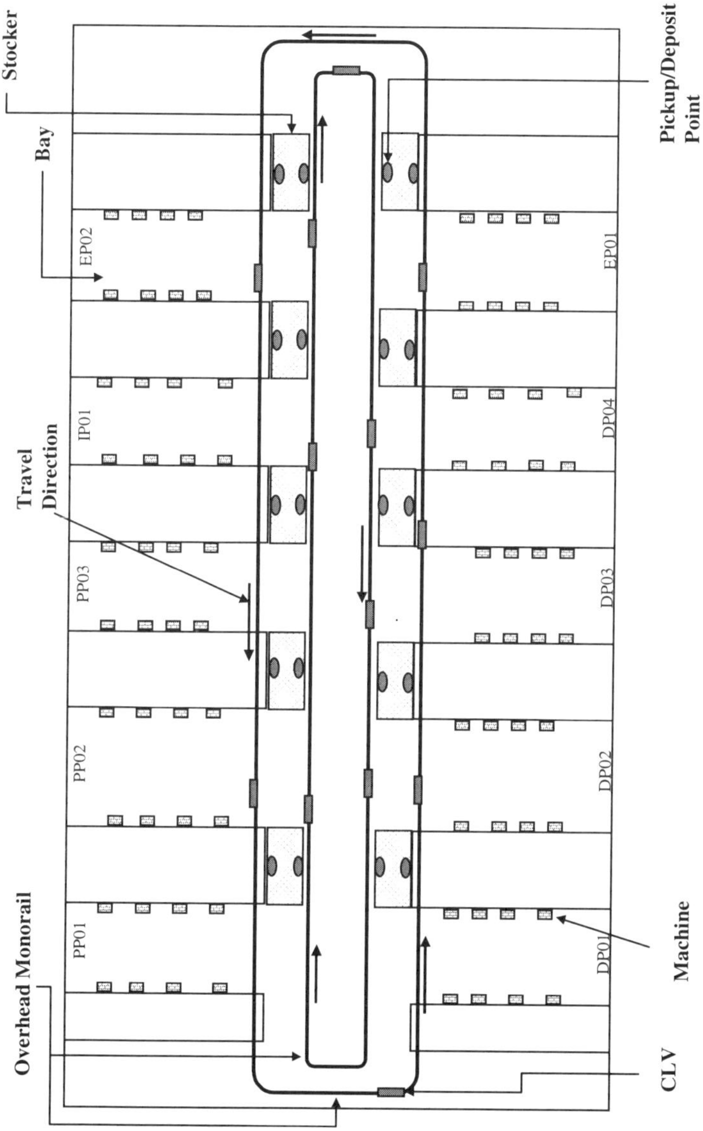

Figure 1. The LG Semiconductor wafer fab model.

Table 1. Workstation descriptions.

Workstations		Type of Operation	NM	Bay #	MPT	MTBF	MTTR
No.	Name						
1	CLEAN	DEPOSITION	4	DP01	0.78	42.18	2.22
2	TMGOX	DEPOSITION	4	DP01	2.49	101.11	10.00
3	TMNOX	DEPOSITION	4	DP02	2.73	113.25	5.21
4	TMFOX	DEPOSITION	2	DP02	2.34	103.74	12.56
5	TU11	DEPOSITION	2	DP02	3.07	100.55	6.99
6	TU43	DEPOSITION	2	DP03	3.88	113.25	5.21
7	TU72	DEPOSITION	2	DP03	3.12	16.78	4.38
8	TU73	DEPOSITION	2	DP03	2.18	13.22	3.43
9	TU74	DEPOSITION	2	DP03	2.36	10.59	3.74
10	PLM5L	DEPOSITION	2	DP04	2.03	47.53	12.71
11	PLM5U	DEPOSITION	2	DP04	3.93	52.67	19.78
12	SPUT	DEPOSITION	2	DP04	3.05	72.57	9.43
13	PHPPS	LITHOGRAPHY	8	PP01	2.12	22.37	1.15
14	PHGCA	LITHOGRAPHY	6	PP02	3.91	21.76	4.81
15	PHHB	LITHOGRAPHY	2	PP02	0.44	387.20	12.80
16	PHBI	LITHOGRAPHY	4	PP03	1.48	No Failures	
17	PHFI	LITHOGRAPHY	2	PP03	0.78	119.20	1.57
18	PHJPS	LITHOGRAPHY	2	PP03	1.80	No Failures	
19	PLM6	ETCHING	4	EP01	6.94	46.38	17.42
20	PLM7	ETCHING	2	EP01	2.71	36.58	9.49
21	PLM8	ETCHING	4	EP02	3.79	36.58	9.49
22	PHWET	ETCHING	4	EP02	0.52	118.92	1.08
23	PHPLO	RESIST STRIP	4	IP01	1.09	No Failures	
24	IMP	IONIMPLANT	4	IP01	3.86	55.18	12.86

⊕ NM = Number of Machines, MPT = Mean Processing Time,
MTBR = Mean Time Between Failures, MTTR = Mean Time To Repair.

We assume that all lots follow exactly the same route presented in Table 2, where the number refers to the workstation number in the first column of Table 1, and all visits by all lots to a specific station have the same processing time distribution. The lot size is 12 wafers per lot and is held constant through the study. Table 2 shows the reentrant characteristics of wafer fabrication where each lot visits the same workstations many times. In Table 2, each lot flows through the photolithography expose station (workstation 14) 12 times. Workstation 14 consists of GCA steppers and is considered as the extreme bottleneck, which is utilized much more than any other workstation. The operation of workstation 14 is referred to as a critical operation in this study. Each workstation and its related bay are also represented in Table 1.

For example, Bay DP01 includes workstations 1 and 2. Our simulation model consists of two opposite directional overhead monorails and ten stockers for transportation and intermediate storage of wafer lots. Each monorail contains ten vchicles with a speed of 70 ft/min for interbay lot transfers. A bay utilizes one or two stockers and also can share a stocker with an adjacent bay. The size of each stocker is varied and dependent on the workloads of the corresponding bays.

Table 2. Process flow.

Enter-1-2-13-14-23-15-20-22-23-22-23-22-17-13-14-15-23-16-24-23-22-17-1-8-4-22-22-1-2-8-13-14-18-23-15-16-23-18-22-1-1-13-14-23-15-16-24-23-22-17-1-2-8-9-21-22-1-4-22-22-1-2-13-14-23-15-16-24-24-23-22-17-24-1-2-7-1-3-22-13-15-23-22-22-22-17-13-14-18-23-15-16-20-23-1-17-1-1-3-13-14-16-24-23-22-17-9-21-1-3-13-14-15-23-15-16-24-23-22-17-1-3-10-22-12-6-22-6-1-1-4-10-19-23-1-10-13-14-16-21-12-13-14-18-23-15-15-15-16-19-23-22-17-11-13-14-15-21-23-5-Exit

3.2 *Development of a Scheduler*

By integrating simulation and a competitive neural network, our study proposes a multi-objective semiconductor fab scheduler that controls the behavior of part flows to accomplish multiple objectives by generating the appropriate decision rules on multiple dispatching decision variables.

A simulation experiment was conducted to collect the data containing the relationship between change of the decision rule set and the current system status and performance measures in the dynamic nature of a semiconductor manufacturing fab. Following the data collection model, the competitive neural network was developed. It classifies all instances obtained from the simulation runs and categorizes them through training of the network. After that, the scheduler has the ability to find a matching instance with expected performance measures most similar with the desired performance measures given by the user. The detailed definition of the decision variables and associated decision rules, and the evaluation criteria will be given first, and then each development procedure will be discussed in the following subsections.

3.2.1 Decision Variables and Decision Rules

In this study, there are four dispatching decision variables. The definition of each decision variable and its associated rules are given as follows (see Table 3).

(1) Selection of a wafer lot by a critical machine (input buffer)

If an input buffer of a critical machine is empty and more than one wafer lot is waiting for the machine in stockers, the machine has to select which wafer lot to be processed next.

(2) Selection of a wafer lot by a non-critical machine (input buffer)

If an input buffer of a non-critical machine is empty and there is more than one waiting wafer lot for the machine in stockers, the machine has to select one wafer lot to be processed next.

Table 3. Decision variables and associated rules.

Decision Variable	Associated rules
Selection of a wafer lot by a critical machine	1. FCFS (First Come First Serve): A wafer lot that comes first is processed first. 2. SRPT (Shortest Remaining Processing Time): A wafer lot that has the shortest processing time is processed first. 3. EDD (Earliest Due Date): A wafer lot that has the earliest due date is processed first. 4. CR (Critical Ratio): A wafer lot that has the smallest critical ratio is processed next. The critical ratio is computed As follows: Critical Ratio = (Due date – Current time – Remaining processing time)/(due date – Current time).
Selection of a wafer lot by a non-critical machine	1. FCFS (First Come First Serve): A wafer lot that comes first is processed next. 2. SRPT (Shortest Remaining Processing Time): A wafer lot that has the shortest remaining processing time is processed next. 3. EDD (Earliest Due Date): A wafer lot that has the earliest due date is processed next. 4. CR (Critical Ratio): A wafer lot that has the smallest critical ratio is processed next. The critical ratio is computed as follows: Critical Ratio = (Due date – Current time – Remaining processing time)/(Due date – Current time).
Selection of a wafer lot by a stocker	1. FRFS (First Request First Serve): The stocker selects the wafer lot that requests it first. 2. IBF (In Bay First): The stocker selects a wafer lot that is waiting in a bay (output buffer of machines) for the stocker. This rule is to avoid the deadlock of a machine where holding an output buffer of a machine blocks the process of a next job. If multiple wafer lots are waiting for the stock in a bay, FRFS is applied to select a lot among them. 3. LRS (Lowest Remaining Spaces In Stocker): The stocker selects a wafer lot in the other stock that has the lowest remaining storage spaces. This rule is to balance the utilization of stockers. If multiple wafer lots are waiting for the stocker in the other stocker, FCFS is applied to select a lot among them. 4. EDD (Earliest Due Date) 5. SRPT (Shortest Remaining Processing Time) 6. CR (Critical Ratio)
Selection of a wafer lot by a vehicle on a monorail	1. FRFS (First Request First Serve) 2. LRS (Lowest Remaining Spaces In Stocker) 3. EDD (Earliest Due Date) 4. SRPT (Shortest Remaining Processing Time) 5. CR (Critical Ratio)

(3) Selection of a wafer lot by a stocker

After finishing an operation in a bay or being transferred from another bay for the next operation, a wafer lot is temporarily stored at a corresponding stocker. However, if the corresponding stocker is full, a wafer lot has to wait until a storage position is available. When a stocker has an empty storage position and there is more than one waiting wafer lot for the stocker available, the stocker has to decide which wafer lot to store next.

(4) Selection of a wafer lot by a vehicle on a monorail

When a vehicle on the monorail finishes its task and more than one wafer lot requests a vehicle, it has to decide which part will be transported next.

3.2.2 Evaluation Criteria: System Performance and Status

Table 4 shows the evaluation criteria of this study. Decision rules for dispatching decision variables are based on system status in the beginning of each production interval and achieve the desired system objectives at the end of each production interval.

Table 4. Evaluation criteria.

System Performance/objective	System status
- Mean of flow time - Mean of slack time - Mean of total remaining processing time	- Total work in process - Total workload of critical machines - Average number of remaining operations of each wafer lot - Mean slack time - Mean remaining processing time

3.2.3 Data Collection: A Simulation Approach

This step gathers unclassified training data by using simulation for training the competitive neural network. To obtain a set of the unclassified training data, the operation of a target semiconductor fab system is simulated for a lengthy period which consists of a sequence of short production intervals $t_1, \ldots, t_i, \ldots, t_n$.

After observing the values of current system status and performance measures at the end of the previous production interval t_{i-1}, a decision rule for each dispatching decision variable for the current production interval t_i is randomly selected. After the current production interval t_i ends, the current system status at the end of the previous interval t_{i-1} and the performance measures at the end of the current interval t_i are collected together with the set of decision rules used for the current interval t_i. Next, this simulation output is fed into the competitive neural network as an input vector for training. The data collection procedure is described graphically in Figure 2 where $s_{j,t}$ is the *j*th current system status value collected at t and $p_{k,t}$ is the *k*th performance measure value collected at time t.

3.2.4 Data Classification: A Competitive Neural Network Approach

Following the data collection phase, a competitive neural network (CNN) approach is applied to group all instances of the simulation outputs. Each instance includes current system status, performance measures and decision rules for the next production interval. Figure 3 shows the framework of data classification where CNN-S is the CNN model using current system status of each instance as an input vector, and CNN-P is the CNN model using performance measures of each instance as an input vector. Through the training of each CNN, each instance is assigned to a certain class with similar values of the current system status and performance measures.

In Figure 3, the training phase of the network consists of two stages. In stage 1, by using current system of an instance as input data of CNN-S, all instances are classified with similar current system status and are assigned to a certain class. In stage 2, each instance in a class of stage 1 are assigned to a certain subclass with similar performance measures from training of CNN-P. Therefore, a final class obtained from stage 2 consists of classified instances with both similar current system status and performance measures.

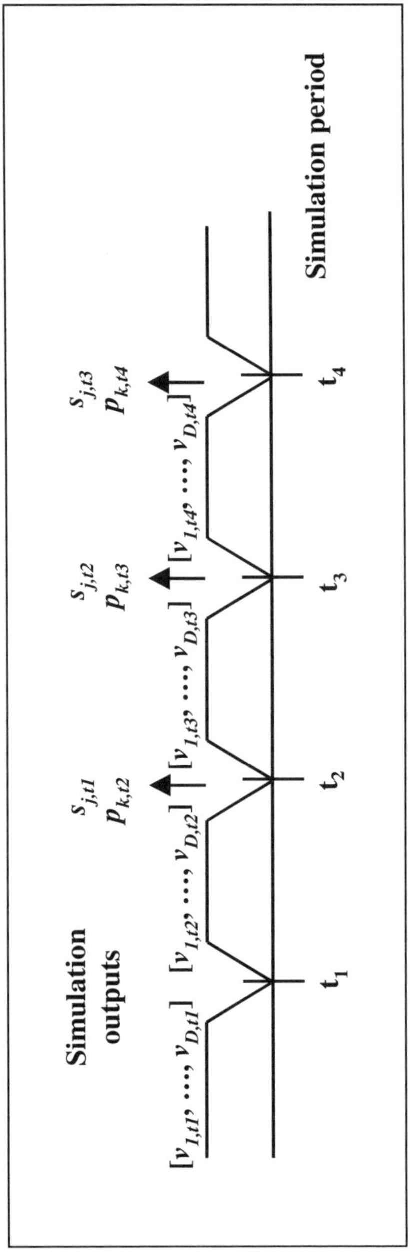

Figure 2. The data collection procedure.

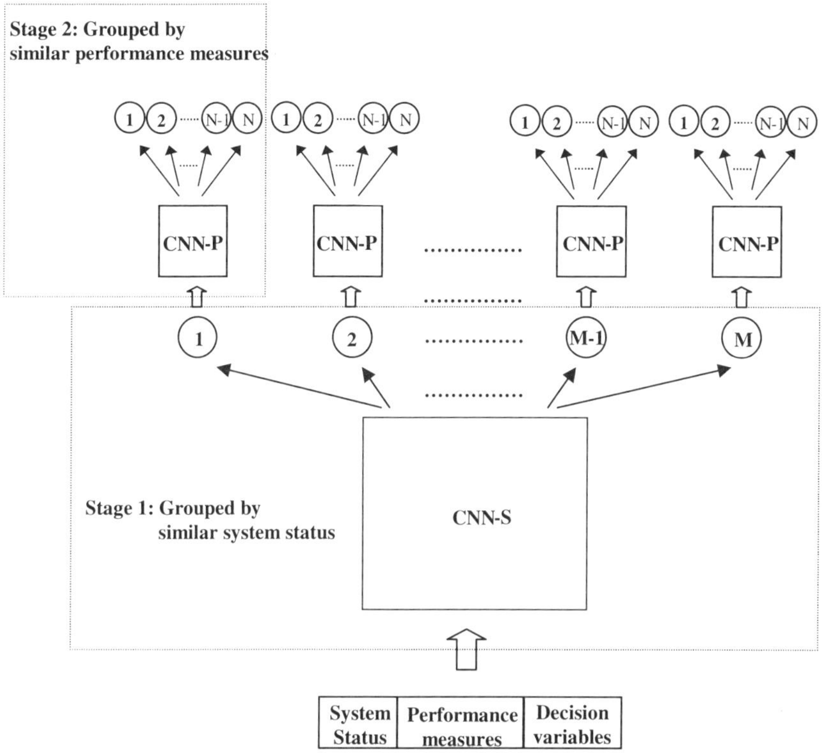

Figure 3. Framework for the data classification.

Each CNN can learn to detect regularities and correlations in its input vectors, and adapt future responses to the input vectors accordingly. The neurons of a CNN learn to recognize the groups of similar input vectors. Figure 4 depicts the architecture of the CNN-S and CNN-P applied to obtain semiconductor fab scheduling knowledge in this study. In Figure 4, n is the size of the input vector, and m or m' is the size of the output vector. Also, x_i indicates the ith input node and y_j or v_j is the jth output node, respectively; w_j is the weighting vector connected to the jth output node from all input nodes.

With a learning rule, the output nodes (classes) of the CNN-S or CNN-P learn to recognize the groups of similar input vectors. In this study, the competitive neural network is trained with the Kohonen learning rule (Demuth and Beale 1998). The Kohonen learning rule is defined as follows:

$$W_{ij}^{new} = W_{ij}^{old} + \Delta w_{ij}$$
$$\Delta w_{ij} = LR \times (x_i - w_{ij}),$$
$$\text{where } LR = \text{learning rate}$$

To reflect the above features, current system status, performance measures and the decision rules for the next decision variables are fed into the neural network as an input vector of CNN-S and CNN-P. In Figure 4, x_1 represents decision rules for the next decision variables. Also, $x_2,\ldots,x_k$ are the current system status, and $x_l,\ldots,x_m$ are the performance measures. In the CNN-S network, only $x_2,\ldots,x_k$ are connected to output nodes through weighting vectors and affect the classification. Other input nodes are not associated with weight vectors and are used for training of CNN-P. The CNN-P network uses classified data from CNN-S as input vectors. For example, classified data of class y_1 from CNN-S are used as input vectors of CNN-P and are divided into subclasses with similarities of performance measures through training of CNN-P. In CNN-P, $x_l,\ldots,x_m$ are connected to output nodes through weight vectors and contribute to the classification. In both CNN-S and CNN-P, x_1 is not connected to output nodes through weight vectors. The x_1 is only included in the input vector to be used in the recall phase.

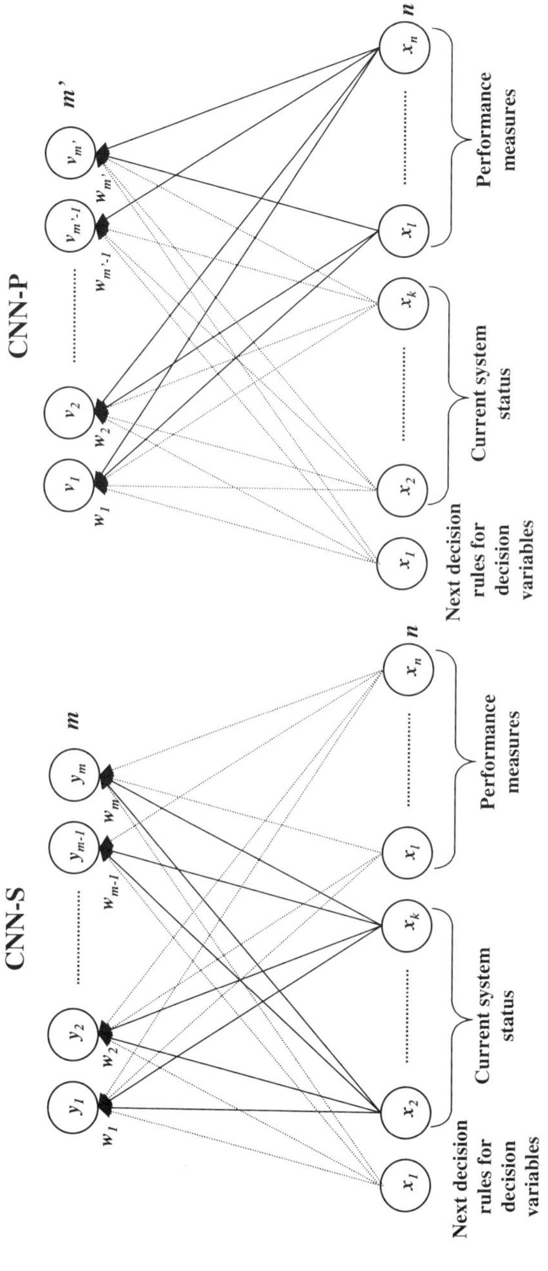

Figure 4. CNN-S and CNN-P.

3.2.5 Selection of Decision Rules for Decision Variables

Figure 5 shows how the proposed scheduler selects the decision rules for the associated decision variables when the desired performance measures and current system status are provided.

The user and semiconductor manufacturing system give the neural network the desired performance measures and current system status, respectively. Then the neural network produces a matching class in which the expected performance measures and current system status of the aggregated instances are similar to desired performance measures and current system status of the input data given by both the manager and the manufacturing system. After this step, the scheduler can obtain the matching instance whose current system status is the most similar to the current system status given by the semiconductor manufacturing system (see the box of Matching Instance Selection in Figure 5). In the matching instance, the user can finally find out decision rules for decision variables for the next production interval.

4. An Experimental Study

4.1 Experimental Design

In this study, three experiments were conducted with three different levels of workloads of critical machine (workstation 14). The workload level was determined by the sum of the remaining processing times at the critical machines for all the lots in the fab. A wafer lot was released into the system when the workload of critical machines falls below a prescribed level. In this study, we conducted experiments in three prescribed workload levels, which are 4,600, 4,800 and 5,000 minutes. As we discussed in Section 3.2, simulation experiments collect the unclassified data by randomly changing decision rules for dispatching decision variables every production interval.

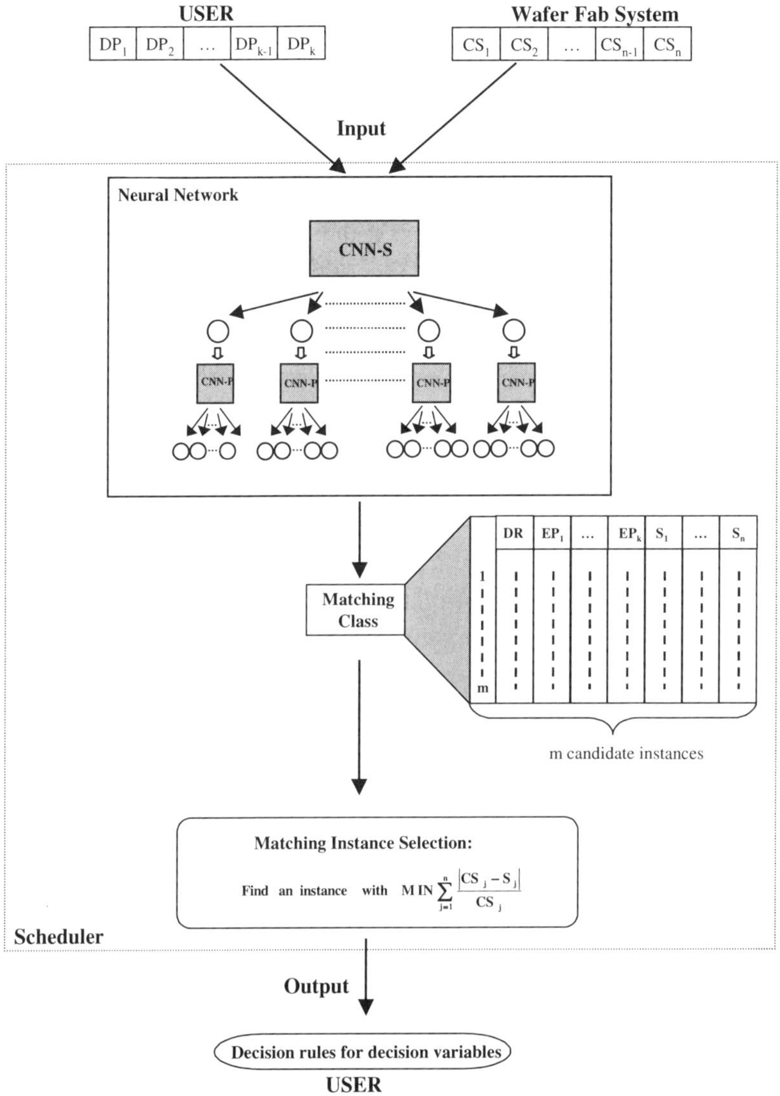

(DP_i: desired performance criterion i, CS_j: Current system status criterion j, DR: Decision rules for decision variables EP_i: Expected performance criterion i, S_j: System status criterion j)

Figure 5. Selection of decision rules for decision variables.

The length of each production interval is set to 480 minutes (1 shift) and 1,500 input data were collected for each experiment. For an experiment, both CNN-S and CNN-P were developed by using the neural network toolbox in Matlab (Demuth and Beale, 1998). CNN-S is a competitive neural network model using the current system status of unclassified simulation data as input vectors. CNN-P is a competitive neural network model using performance measures of unclassified simulation data as input vectors. The 1,500 unclassified data obtained from the simulation were used in the neural networks as the input vectors.

Three methods were used and were evaluated for each experiment. Method 1 is controlled by the proposed methodology, which selects the decision rules to satisfy desired system objectives based on current system status during a production interval (see Figure 5). Method 2 is controlled by the best random decision rules for decision variables among five randomly selected decision rules for decision variables; five simulation runs were performed with randomly generated decision rules for decision variables during the given production interval and the best one is selected among five runs. Method 3 is regulated by fixed decision rules for decision variables at the start of each production interval. The simulation of fixed decision rules for the decision variables uses decision rules [1111], which means FCFS for selection of a wafer lot by a critical machine, FCFS for selection of wafer lots by a non-critical machine, FRFS for selection of a wafer lot by a stocker, and FRFS for the selection of a wafer lot by a vehicle on a monorail. These fixed decision rules are conventionally used in a real semiconductor manufacturing industry. Simulation runs for twenty production intervals for each method in an experiment, then all simulation results are compared with the desired performance values. Each desired performance value of an experiment is set to the average value of 1,500 unclassified data obtained from the simulation data collection.

4.2 Results and Analyses

Each experiment has been conducted to satisfy three desired objectives: mean of flow time, mean of slack time, and mean of total remaining processing time. Table 5 shows the simulation results when workload (WR) of a critical machine is set to 5,000 minutes. The desired objectives are fixed during all production intervals; mean of flow time less than 1,592 minutes, mean of slack time equal to 697 minutes, and the mean of the remaining processing time equal to 153 minutes. Thus, next we will find the best matching decision rules to satisfy the objectives under various current system statuses.

The last three columns in Table 5 indicate the applied decision rules of the three methods for each production interval. For example, the applied decision rules of Method 1 (scheduler) for production period *t1* are [2355], which means using the SRPT rule for selecting a wafer lot by a critical machine, the EDD rule for selecting a wafer lot by a non-critical machine, the SRPT rule for selecting a wafer lot by a stocker, and the CR rule for selecting a wafer lot by a vehicle on a monorail.

Table 6 shows the differences between desired value and actual values by using the three methods. Then Table 7 shows the normalized values of each performance criterion in Table 6. The normalization is done by using the maximum and minimum values of each performance criterion in Table 6. For example, for the criterion of mean of flow time, the maximum value is 124.7 and the minimum value is 0 among the three columns |M1-D|, |M2-D| and |M3-D| under the criterion of mean of flow time. Then each normalized value is calculated as $(p-0)/(124.7-0)$, where p is a value of columns |M1-D|, |M2-D| and |M3-D| under the criterion of mean of flow time. Same calculations are conducted for the normalization of the other two criteria: mean of slack time and mean of total remaining processing time. Using the normalized values of each criterion of performance measure, we obtain the overall performance values, which are the average of the normalized values of the three performance criteria for each method, that is, all three performance criteria are equally weighted. For example, for period *t1*, the overall performance of |M1-D| is calculated as $(0.3653+0.4456+0.0960)/3 = 0.3023$.

Table 5. Actual performance measures (WR = 5,000).

	Mean of flow time			Mean of slack time			Mean of total remaining processing time			Applied decision rules		
	M1	M2	M3	M1	M2	M3	M1	M2	M3	M1	M2	M3
t1	1,637.5	1,649.8	1,716.7	723.0	755.0	697.2	154.5	164.8	147.9	1,452	2,355	1,111
t2	1,465.4	1,521.1	1,640.0	732.9	724.1	668.0	158.1	157.4	143.3	2,114	3,355	1,111
t3	1,630.7	1,626.8	1,688.0	686.4	679.6	654.7	148.8	146.4	140.6	1,135	1,115	1,111
t4	1,567.8	1,602.8	1,675.1	715.2	708.8	680.4	159.7	150.9	145.3	3,452	1,161	1,111
t5	1,622.2	1,614.8	1,657.5	698.5	713.4	679.8	149.8	154.5	145.4	1,415	4,241	1,111
t6	1,546.6	1,619.1	1,664.6	713.1	679.8	671.0	153.7	148.1	144.2	3,211	3,155	1,111
t7	1,551.1	1,555.0	1,664.0	732.0	744.3	651.8	148.8	160.1	140.4	1,251	1,352	1,111
t8	1,513.4	1,552.8	1,680.3	682.4	692.9	680.2	156.1	148.9	145.1	2,313	4,255	1,111
t9	1,609.6	1,646.6	1,657.2	699.4	701.6	646.4	158.3	153.8	138.7	2,223	4,413	1,111
t10	1,593.6	1,602.8	1,670.0	724.6	657.1	664.4	148.9	149.9	142.9	4,314	2,331	1,111
t11	1,605.0	1,713.7	1,668.4	695.9	684.0	685.2	149.4	151.4	146.8	1,452	1,345	1,111
t12	1,601.8	1,601.7	1,672.9	684.4	704.5	652.0	156.8	150.4	139.6	1,421	4,251	1,111
t13	1,604.9	1,611.9	1,676.1	694.1	691.8	675.7	150.8	143.7	145.1	1,421	3,351	1,111
t14	1,597.6	1,585.4	1,673.5	692.2	718.8	659.1	151.3	148.7	141.9	4,132	2,452	1,111
t15	1,619.0	1,574.6	1,663.8	694.3	688.4	675.4	149.4	147.4	145.0	2,325	1,215	1,111
t16	1,625.1	1,626.1	1,654.1	689.4	696.7	679.4	149.3	145.7	145.3	4,225	2,125	1,111
t17	1,599.9	1,592.2	1,661.2	692.8	720.8	674.8	149.5	151.4	144.2	3,113	2,343	1,111
t18	1,607.8	1,567.4	1,649.9	676.9	702.5	676.7	151.0	153.2	145.0	1,133	4,253	1,111
t19	1,617.6	1,661.3	1,671.1	718.7	681.3	655.7	151.3	148.1	141.2	1,422	3,155	1,111
t20	1,531.7	1,586.3	1,669.4	695.1	704.3	670.9	150.9	151.4	144.2	3,331	3,211	1,111

(D= desired values, M1 = actual value (simulation output) by Method 1, M2 = actual value by Method 2, M3 = actual value by Method 3).

Table 6. Differences between actual and desired performance measures (WR = 5,000).

Period	Mean of flow time			Mean of slack time			Mean of total remaining processing time		
	|M1-D|	|M2-D|	|m3-D|	|M1-D|	|M2-D|	|m3-D|	|M1-D|	|M2-D|	|m3-D|
t1	45.5	57.8	124.7	26.0	58.0	0.2	1.5	11.8	5.1
t2	0.0	0.0	48.0	35.9	27.1	29.0	5.1	4.4	9.8
t3	38.7	34.8	96.0	10.6	17.4	42.3	4.2	6.6	12.4
t4	0.0	10.8	83.1	18.2	11.8	16.7	6.7	2.1	7.7
t5	30.2	22.8	65.5	1.5	16.4	17.2	3.2	1.5	7.6
t6	0.0	27.1	72.6	16.1	17.2	26.1	0.7	4.9	8.8
t7	0.0	0.0	72.0	35.0	47.3	45.2	4.3	7.1	12.6
t8	0.0	0.0	88.3	14.6	4.1	16.8	3.1	4.2	7.9
t9	17.6	54.6	65.2	2.4	4.6	50.7	5.3	0.8	14.3
t10	1.6	10.8	78.0	27.6	39.9	32.6	4.1	3.1	10.1
t11	13.0	121.7	76.4	1.1	13.0	11.8	3.6	1.6	6.2
t12	9.8	9.7	80.9	12.6	7.5	45.0	3.8	2.6	13.4
t13	12.9	19.9	84.1	2.9	5.2	21.3	2.2	9.3	7.9
t14	5.6	0.0	81.5	4.9	21.8	37.9	1.7	4.3	11.1
t15	27.0	0.0	71.8	2.7	8.6	21.6	3.6	5.6	8.0
t16	33.1	34.1	62.1	7.6	0.3	17.6	3.7	7.3	7.7
t17	7.9	0.2	69.2	4.2	23.8	22.2	3.5	1.6	8.8
t18	15.8	0.0	57.9	20.1	5.5	20.3	2.0	0.2	8.0
t19	25.6	69.3	79.1	21.7	15.7	41.3	1.7	4.9	11.8
t20	0.0	0.0	77.4	1.9	7.3	26.1	2.1	1.6	8.8
Mean	14.2	23.7	76.7	13.4	17.6	27.1	3.3	4.3	9.4
Max	45.5	121.7	124.7	35.9	58.0	50.7	6.7	11.8	14.3

(D = desired values, M1 = actual value (simulation output) by Method 1, M2 = actual value by Method 2, M3 = actual value by Method 3).

Table 7. Normalized differences between actual and performance measures (WR = 5,000).

	Mean of flow time			Mean of slack time			Mean of total remaining processing time			Overall		
	|M1-D|	|M2-D|	|M3-D|	|M1-D|	|M2-D|	|M3-D|	|M1-D|	|M2-D|	|M3-D|	|M1-D|	|M2-D|	|M3-D|
t1	0.3653	0.4639	1.0000	0.4456	1.0000	0.0000	0.0960	0.8200	0.3458	0.3023	0.7613	0.4486
t2	0.0000	0.0000	0.3849	0.6169	0.4659	0.4983	0.3472	0.2978	0.6768	0.3214	0.2546	0.5200
t3	0.3107	0.2791	0.7704	0.1801	0.2972	0.7281	0.2872	0.4552	0.8659	0.2594	0.3438	0.7881
t4	0.0000	0.0866	0.6664	0.3117	0.1995	0.2842	0.4580	0.1348	0.5300	0.2566	0.1403	0.4935
t5	0.2422	0.1830	0.5253	0.0213	0.2800	0.2937	0.2167	0.0924	0.5272	0.1600	0.1852	0.4487
t6	0.0000	0.2175	0.5824	0.2747	0.2939	0.4470	0.0353	0.3352	0.6076	0.1033	0.2822	0.5457
t7	0.0000	0.0000	0.5777	0.6022	0.8152	0.7788	0.2886	0.4912	0.8793	0.2969	0.4355	0.7453
t8	0.0000	0.0000	0.7080	0.2484	0.0670	0.2868	0.2089	0.2816	0.5434	0.1524	0.1162	0.5127
t9	0.1415	0.4376	0.5231	0.0369	0.0752	0.8731	0.3627	0.0452	1.0000	0.1804	0.1860	0.7987
t10	0.0130	0.0863	0.6258	0.4744	0.6867	0.5603	0.2795	0.2047	0.6994	0.2556	0.3259	0.6285
t11	0.1043	0.9758	0.6131	0.0144	0.2210	0.1999	0.2421	0.1037	0.4234	0.1202	0.4335	0.4121
t12	0.0789	0.0781	0.6492	0.2137	0.1250	0.7757	0.2555	0.1750	0.9365	0.1827	0.1261	0.7871
t13	0.1032	0.1596	0.6744	0.0455	0.0856	0.3653	0.1418	0.6450	0.5455	0.0969	0.2967	0.5284
t14	0.0448	0.0000	0.6536	0.0798	0.3731	0.6528	0.1094	0.2922	0.7749	0.0780	0.2217	0.6937
t15	0.2167	0.0000	0.5762	0.0421	0.1451	0.3696	0.2428	0.3818	0.5561	0.1672	0.1756	0.5006
t16	0.2651	0.2738	0.4983	0.1273	0.0014	0.3012	0.2519	0.5032	0.5314	0.2148	0.2595	0.4436
t17	0.0632	0.0014	0.5547	0.0681	0.4080	0.3798	0.2336	0.0988	0.6119	0.1216	0.1694	0.5155
t18	0.1269	0.0000	0.4644	0.3436	0.0902	0.3478	0.1313	0.0000	0.5519	0.2006	0.0301	0.4547
t19	0.2053	0.5559	0.6342	0.3724	0.2683	0.7113	0.1073	0.3345	0.8222	0.2283	0.3862	0.7225
t20	0.0000	0.0000	0.6209	0.0284	0.1218	0.4484	0.1355	0.1023	0.6126	0.0546	0.0747	0.5606
Mean	0.1140	0.1899	0.6152	0.2274	0.3010	0.4651	0.2216	0.2897	0.6521	0.1877	0.2602	0.5774

(D = desired values, M1 = actual value (simulation result) by Method 1, M2 = actual value by Method 2, M3 = actual value by Method 3).

The same methodology is applied when the workload of critical machine is set to both 4,800 and 4,600 minutes. The desired objectives for each experiment are listed as follows: (1) when WR is equal to 4,800 minutes; the mean of flow time is less than 1554 minutes; the mean of slack time is equal to 725 minutes; and the mean of remaining processing time is equal to 150 minutes; and (2) when WR is equal to 4,600 minutes; the mean of flow time is less than 1,514 minutes; the mean of slack time is equal to 740 minutes, and the mean of remaining processing time is equal to 145 minutes. Both Tables 8 and 9 show the final normalized results of these experiments. To compare the overall performance of Method 1 with that of Methods 2 and 3 for each experiment, statistical tests were performed for each experiment and the results of the tests are shown in Table 10.

From Table 10, we conclude that Method 1 is more effective than both Method 2 and Method 3 for the overall performance in all three experiments when the level of significance α is equal to 0.05.

5. Related Studies

Dispatching rules are very effective for shop floor control and most of the shop floor control approaches in fact adopt dispatching rules to decide what job should be chosen next when a machine becomes available. This section reviews other studies not directly related to semiconductor wafer production and not mentioned in Section 2.

Park *et al.*(1997) used an induction learning methodology to choose an appropriate dispatching rule at each dispatching point, based on the observed pattern of six system parameters, and showed the superiority of their proposed approach over the repeated applications of single rules. Note that the approach of Park *et al.* might be inappropriate for real time dispatching because their rules were induced based on the long term performance of dispatching rules.

Table 8. Normalized differences between actual and performance measures (WR = 4,800).

	Mean of flow time			Mean of slack time			Mean of total remaining processing time			Overall		
	|M1-D|	|M2-D|	|M3-D|	|M1-D|	|M2-D|	|M3-D|	|M1-D|	|M2-D|	|M3-D|	|M1-D|	|M2-D|	|M3-D|
t1	0.2327	0.3535	0.5555	0.3870	0.3081	0.0845	0.2240	0.0961	0.1101	0.2813	0.2526	0.2500
t2	0.0000	0.0000	0.5523	0.0225	0.0431	0.9542	0.0597	0.1853	0.6488	0.0274	0.0761	0.7185
t3	0.0000	0.0465	0.7338	0.1274	0.2944	0.7726	0.3713	0.0302	0.6031	0.1662	0.1237	0.7032
t4	0.0000	0.0000	0.4125	0.2346	0.1420	0.6413	0.5380	0.3287	0.5279	0.2575	0.1569	0.5272
t5	0.0000	0.0000	0.3613	0.0889	0.1843	0.1393	0.2636	0.1085	0.1798	0.1175	0.0976	0.2268
t6	0.0000	0.4569	0.3570	0.1139	0.9234	0.4139	0.0690	0.5264	0.4256	0.0610	0.6356	0.3988
t7	0.0241	0.0000	0.3213	0.4083	1.0000	0.4070	0.2884	0.6388	0.3550	0.2402	0.5463	0.3611
t8	0.0000	0.5836	0.3879	0.2344	0.3523	0.1385	0.3705	0.3271	0.2302	0.2017	0.4210	0.2522
t9	0.0000	0.0000	0.2716	0.3375	0.4145	0.4762	0.1822	0.3271	0.5364	0.1732	0.2472	0.4281
t10	0.0000	0.0000	0.3435	0.3571	0.4564	0.4370	0.2186	0.1078	0.4961	0.1919	0.1880	0.4256
t11	0.3210	0.9009	0.0000	0.1745	0.8291	0.0035	0.0000	0.8101	0.0372	0.1652	0.8467	0.0136
t12	0.0000	0.0539	1.0000	0.0200	0.0535	0.6742	0.4295	0.2039	0.6558	0.1498	0.1038	0.7767
t13	0.0000	0.0765	0.3668	0.0169	0.0162	0.4984	0.0023	0.1287	0.4496	0.0064	0.0738	0.4383
t14	0.6526	0.0000	0.3638	0.2465	0.0375	0.2144	0.8271	0.1612	0.2729	0.5754	0.0662	0.2837
t15	0.2244	0.3510	0.4269	0.3194	0.4545	0.7880	0.5008	0.2178	0.7434	0.3482	0.3411	0.6528
t16	0.0000	0.0059	0.4467	0.0000	0.7075	0.4658	0.1426	0.5310	0.4155	0.0475	0.4148	0.4426
t17	0.0573	0.0463	0.5488	0.1674	0.5515	0.3346	0.3380	1.0000	0.3597	0.1876	0.5326	0.4144
t18	0.2617	0.0000	0.2738	0.2956	0.5717	0.6352	0.7581	0.7109	0.6093	0.4385	0.4275	0.5061
t19	0.0000	0.0000	0.2647	0.1524	0.4589	0.7445	0.1419	0.0426	0.6977	0.0981	0.1672	0.5690
t20	0.0000	0.0000	0.5221	0.0154	0.3460	0.3641	0.0674	0.3814	0.3450	0.0276	0.2425	0.4104
Mean	0.0887	0.1438	0.4255	0.1860	0.4072	0.4594	0.2897	0.3432	0.4350	0.1881	0.2981	0.4399

(D = desired values, M1 = actual value (simulation output) by Method 1, M2 = actual value by Method 2, M3 = actual value by Method 3).

Table 9. Normalized differences between actual and performance measures (WR = 4,600).

	Mean of flow time			Mean of slack time			Mean of total remaining processing time			Overall		
	|M1-D|	|M2-D|	|M3-D|	|M1-D|	|M2-D|	|M3-D|	|M1-D|	|M2-D|	|M3-D|	|M1-D|	|M2-D|	|M3-D|
t1	0.3587	0.5071	0.1642	0.0795	0.0369	0.2428	0.0126	0.0073	0.1470	0.1503	0.1837	0.1847
t2	0.0000	0.1579	0.0476	0.0948	0.0592	0.0246	0.1053	0.0252	0.1009	0.0667	0.0808	0.0577
t3	0.0000	0.1691	0.3252	0.0779	0.0300	0.0696	0.0771	0.0039	0.0509	0.0517	0.0676	0.1486
t4	0.0000	0.0000	0.2269	0.0442	0.2518	0.0589	0.0442	0.1499	0.0859	0.0295	0.1339	0.1239
t5	0.0000	0.0000	0.1731	0.0672	0.0938	0.3237	0.1140	0.0684	0.1228	0.0604	0.0541	0.2065
t6	0.0119	0.1691	0.9073	0.0001	0.0604	0.6940	0.0150	0.0733	0.2838	0.0090	0.1009	0.6284
t7	0.0000	0.0000	1.0000	0.2247	0.1794	0.3273	0.2072	0.2246	0.1101	0.1440	0.1347	0.4792
t8	0.1803	0.3703	0.8454	0.0369	0.1115	0.2684	0.0039	0.1776	0.2115	0.0737	0.2198	0.4418
t9	0.3517	0.3451	0.5239	0.0308	0.0774	0.0710	0.0888	0.0359	0.1019	0.1571	0.1528	0.2322
t10	0.0000	0.3858	0.1736	0.0882	0.0068	0.1158	0.0437	0.0403	0.1116	0.0440	0.1443	0.1337
t11	0.0858	0.0649	0.3272	0.0313	0.0433	0.2239	0.1752	0.0378	0.2115	0.0974	0.0487	0.2542
t12	0.0000	0.0000	0.4688	0.1218	1.0000	0.0130	0.0985	1.0000	0.0000	0.0734	0.6667	0.1606
t13	0.1902	0.0000	0.2380	0.0246	0.5038	0.0048	0.0228	0.5080	0.0082	0.0792	0.3373	0.0837
t14	0.0000	0.0000	0.0184	0.1259	0.0185	0.0373	0.1548	0.0650	0.0213	0.0936	0.0278	0.0257
t15	0.4169	0.1719	0.2325	0.0104	0.2785	0.0723	0.1994	0.3857	0.1218	0.2089	0.2787	0.1422
t16	0.2207	0.0000	0.2128	0.0673	0.1649	0.0293	0.0296	0.1844	0.0602	0.1059	0.1164	0.1007
t17	0.0613	0.0000	0.0819	0.0218	0.1070	0.0452	0.0296	0.0427	0.1004	0.0376	0.0499	0.0759
t18	0.1337	0.6261	0.1047	0.0346	0.2042	0.1001	0.0577	0.1557	0.0257	0.0753	0.3287	0.0769
t19	0.0368	0.0000	0.2991	0.0583	0.0000	0.1406	0.0393	0.0243	0.1334	0.0448	0.0081	0.1910
t20	0.0000	0.0368	0.2645	0.0299	0.0712	0.1494	0.0689	0.0781	0.0539	0.0329	0.0620	0.1559
Mean	0.1024	0.1502	0.3317	0.0635	0.1649	0.1506	0.0794	0.1644	0.1032	0.0818	0.1598	0.1952

(D = desired values, M1 = actual value (simulation output) by Method 1, M2 = actual value by Method 2, M3 = actual value by Method 3)

Table 10. Statistical comparisons.

|M2-D| and |M1-D|	|M3-D| and |M1-D|
1. Null hypothesis: $\mu_1 - \mu_2 = 0$ (where μ_1 is the mean of |M2-D| and μ_2 is the mean of |M1-D|. Alternative hypothesis: $\mu_1 - \mu_2 > 0$. 2. Level of significance: $\alpha = 0.05$. 3. Criterion: Reject the null hypothesis if $z > 1.645$, where $$\mathbf{z} = \frac{\bar{\mathbf{x}}_1 - \bar{\mathbf{x}}_2}{\sqrt{\left(\frac{\sigma_1^2}{\mathbf{n}_1} + \frac{\sigma_2^2}{\mathbf{n}_2}\right)}}$$ and $\bar{\mathbf{x}}_1$ and $\bar{\mathbf{x}}_2$ are the mean values of |M2-D| and |M1-D|, and σ_1^2 and σ_2^2 are variances of |M2-D| and |M1-D| respectively, and n_1 and n_2 are the numbers of observations. 3. Result: *(1) $z = 1.89$, when WR = 5000* *(2) $z = 5.66$, when WR = 4800* *(3) $z = 2.17$, when WR = 4600* $z > 1.645$ for all three scenario, therefore performance of Method 1 is superior to that of Method 2 at level $\alpha = 0.05$.	1. Null hypothesis: $\mu_1 - \mu_2 = 0$ (where μ_1 is the mean of |M3-D| and μ_2 is the mean of |M1-D|. Alternative hypothesis: $\mu_1 - \mu_2 > 0$. 2. Level of significance: $\alpha = 0.05$. 3. Criterion: Reject the null hypothesis if $z > 1.645$, where $$\mathbf{z} = \frac{\bar{\mathbf{x}}_1 - \bar{\mathbf{x}}_2}{\sqrt{\left(\frac{\sigma_1^2}{\mathbf{n}_1} + \frac{\sigma_2^2}{\mathbf{n}_2}\right)}}$$ and $\bar{\mathbf{x}}_1$ and $\bar{\mathbf{x}}_2$ are the mean values of |M3-D| and |M1-D|, and σ_1^2 and σ_2^2 are variances of |M3-D| and |M1-D| respectively, and n_1 and n_2 are the numbers of observations. 4. Result: *(4) $z = 12.81$, when WR = 5000* *(5) $z = 10.49$, when WR = 4800* *(6) $z = 3.14$, when WR = 4600* $z > 1.645$ for all three scenario, therefore performance of Method 1 is superior to that of Method 3 at level $\alpha = 0.05$.

On the other hand, Sun and Yih (1996) proposed a neural network-based control system to choose appropriate dispatching rules for machines and a robot based on the real time system status. However, their neural network approach suffers from the incomprehensibility of the learned model. Kwak and Yih (2004) presented a data-mining-based production control approach for the testing and rework cell in a dynamic computer-integrated manufacturing system. They developed a competitive decision selector (CDS), which is equipped with two algorithms for combining two different knowledge sources, the long-run performance and the short-term performance of each rule on the various status of the system. The short-term performance information was mined by a decision tree-based approach from large-scale training data generated by simulation with data partition. They showed that the CDS dynamic control outperformed other common control rules with respect to the number of tardy jobs.

Geiger *et al.* (2006) presented a data mining system that is capable of automatically discovering new dispatching rules for a given environment. The proposed system called SCRUPLES (for **SC**heduling **RU**le Discovery and **P**arallel **LE**arning **S**ystem) combines an evolutionary learning mechanism, specifically genetic programming, with a simulation model of the industrial facility of interest, which automates the process of examining different rules and using the simulation to evaluate their performance. They evaluated the performance of their system in a variety of single machine environments.

6. Conclusions

Semiconductor wafer fabrication involves perhaps the most complex and capital-intensive manufacturing process ever used. This creates a number of decision problems. A successful system control strategy would assign appropriate decision rules for the decision variables. This chapter describes how data mining can be use to assist in developing a real time scheduler for the selection of dispatching rules for both machines and automated material handling systems in order to obtain desired performance measures at the end of a short production interval. In this proposed data mining methodology, a simulation experiment was conducted to collect the data containing the relationship between changes of the decision rule set and the current system status and performance measures in the dynamic nature of a semiconductor manufacturing fab. Next, a competitive neural network was applied to obtain the scheduling knowledge from the collected data.

The results of this study indicate that applying this methodology to obtain a dispatching strategy is an effective method considering the complexity of semiconductor wafer fabrication systems. Especially in a real time control system, it is useful to use pre-defined control knowledge as a time-saving way to achieve prompt response in a dynamically changing environment.

Considering the high investment in a semiconductor manufacturing system, it is important to select the appropriate decision rules for the decision variables by use of the proposed approach. So far the results of the study are promising based on the results of the experiments. However, our study has some limitations and further investigations are required to improve the proposed methodology.

In this study, we collected the training data for the neural network by randomly changing decision rules for decision variables at each production interval. Some data may have poor performance measures that never would be selected for the desired objectives by a user. Those data should be eliminated from the training data set of the neural network. However, the decision to eliminate the bad data must be made by a user. We may include an option in the scheduler to delete the bad data that a user is not interested in, before training the neural network. Having selected data during the training phase will improve the quality of the knowledge within the scheduler and reduce the effort of training the neural network.

A user's prior knowledge about the system behavior and the correlation between the desired performance measures could increase the accuracy of matching the desired objectives by the scheduler. If a user does not have any prior knowledge about the system behavior or the correlation between performance measures, he/she may set the desired performance measures that are infeasible for the scheduler to match. A better way would be to provide a user with the option to view the expected performance likely to result from the selection of desired objective values.

Our scheduler can be applied at any point of time, but it only finds the decision rules for the next certain time period, which is predefined in the scheduler. Practically, a user wants to have the flexibility to control the system for various time periods such as an hour, a day or a week. Therefore, it would be advantageous for the scheduler to be used for any time period (duration) as well as at any point of time.

The parameters required for a competitive neural network, such as number of output nodes and number of training epochs, were determined based on trial and error and might not be the optimal values for this study. Therefore, we should consider the methodology for obtaining appropriate parameters for the development of a neural network in future work in order to gain more precise control knowledge.

The determination of the length of each production period is also an issue in a semiconductor wafer fab system. Different lengths of production periods in a planning horizon may impact the system performance and system status in the long term.

Acknowledgements

The core of this paper was originally published in the *International Journal of Production Research* (http://www.tandf.co.uk) in 2003 (Vol. 41, No. 16, 3921-3941). The research work was supported by the National Science Foundation under an NSF Young Investigator Award (Grant No. 9358158-DMI).

References

Baek, D. H., Yoon, W. C. and Park, S. C. (1998). A spatial rule adaptation procedure for reliable production control in a wafer fabrication system, *Int. J. of Production Research*, **36**(6), 1475-1491.

Cardarelli, G. and Pelagage, P. J. (1995). Simulation tool for design and management optimization of automated material handling and storage systems for large wafer fab, *IEEE Trans. Semiconductor Manufacturing*, **8**(1), 44-49.

Demuth, D. R. and Beale, M. (1998). *Neural Network Toolbox*, The Math works, Natick, MA, U.S.A

Egbelu, P. J., and Tanchoco, M. A. (1984). Characterization of automatic-guided vehicle dispatching rules, *Int. J. of Production Research*, **22**, 359 - 374.

Geiger, C., Uzsoy, R., and Aytuğ, H. (2006). Rapid modeling and discovery of priority dispatching rules: an autonomous learning approach, *J. of Scheduling*, **9**, 7-34.

Hung, Y. F. and Chen, I. R. (1998). A simulation study of dispatch rules for reducing flow times in semiconductor wafer fabrication, *Production Planning & Control*, **9**(7), 714-722.

Kumar, P. R. (1994). Scheduling Semiconductor Manufacturing Plants, *IEEE Control Systems*, December, 33–40.

Kim, Y. D., Kim, J. U., Lim, S. K. and Jun, H. B. (1998b). Due-date based scheduling and control policies in a multiproduct semiconductor wafer fabrication facility, *IEEE Trans. Semiconductor Manufacturing*, **11**(1), 155 – 164.

Kohonen, T. (1988) An introduction to neural computing, *Neural Networks*, **1**, 3 - 16.

Kwak, C. and Yih, Y. (2004). Data-mining approach to production control in the computer-integrated testing cell, *IEEE Trans. Robotics and Automation*, **20**(1), 107-116.

Li, S., Tang, T., and Collins, D. W. (1996). Minimum inventory variability schedule with application in semiconductor fabrication, *IEEE Trans. Semiconductor Manufacturing*, **9**(1), 145–149.

Lin, J. T., Wang, F., and Yen, P. (2001). Simulation analysis of dispatching rules for an automated interbay material handling system in wafer fab, *Int. J. of Production Research*, **39**(6), 1221-1238.

Lu, S. C. H, Kumar, P. R. (1991). Distributed scheduling based on due dates and buffer priorities, *IEEE Trans. Automatic Controls*, **36**, 1406-1416.

Lu, S. C. H., Ramaswamy, D., Kumar, P. R. (1994). Efficient scheduling policies to reduce mean and variance of cycle-time in semiconductor manufacturing plants, *IEEE Trans. Semiconductor Manufacturing*, **7**(3), 374-388.

Min, H. S. Yih, Y. and Kim, C. O. (1998). A competitive neural network approach to multi-objective FMS scheduling, *Int. J. of Production Research*, **36**(7), 1749-1765.

Nakata, T., Matsui, K, Miyake, Y. and Nishioka, K. (1999). Dynamic bottleneck control in wide variety production factory, *IEEE Trans. Semiconductor Manufacturing*, **12**(3), 273-280.

Park, S. C., Raman, N., and Shaw, M. J. (1997). Adaptive scheduling in dynamic flexible manufacturing systems: a dynamic rule selection approach, *IEEE Trans. Robotics and Automation*, **13**, 486-502.

Peters, B. A. and Yang T. (1997). Integrated facility layout and material handling system design in semiconductor fabrication facilities, *IEEE Trans. Semiconductor Manufacturing*, **10**(3), 360 - 369.

Sun, Y.-L. and Yih, Y. (1996). An intelligent controller for manufacturing cells, *Int. J. Production Research*, **34**(8), 2353-2373.

Wein, Lawrence M. (1988). Scheduling semiconductor wafer fabrication, *IEEE Trans. Semiconductor Manufacturing*, **1**(3), 115 – 130.

Authors' Biographical Statements

Hyeung-Sik Jason Min is a Senior Member of Technical Staff in Critical Infrastructure Modeling and Simulation at Sandia National Laboratories. Dr. Min received his Ph.D. in Industrial Engineering from Purdue University. Prior to joining Sandia National Laboratories, he worked as a NRC post-doctoral research associate at the National Institute of Science and Technology (NIST). His current research interests include multi-paradigm modeling and simulation, hybrid and distributed simulation for applications with various scales and complexities in areas of manufacturing and homeland security. He is currently a member of INFORMS and IIE.

Yuehwern Yih is a Professor and Director of Smart Systems and Operations Laboratory at the School of Industrial Engineering, Purdue University. She received her Ph.D. from University of Wisconsin – Madison in 1998. Her research interests include design, monitor, and control of complex systems, behavior-based dynamic control, process/system modeling, analysis, and improvement, machine learning and artificial intelligence, and healthcare system reengineering. Her research publications appear in *IIE Transactions, IEEE Transactions on Robotics and Automation, International Journal of Production Research,* etc.

Chapter 7[1]

Predicting Wine Quality from Agricultural Data with Single-Objective and Multi-Objective Data Mining Algorithms

Mark Last[1], Sigal Elnekave[1], Amos Naor[2], and Victor Schoenfeld[3]

[1]Dept. of Information Systems Engineering, Ben-Gurion University of the Negev, Beer-Sheva 84105, Israel. E-mail: {mlast, elnekave}@bgu.ac.il

[2]Golan Research Institute, University of Haifa, P.O. Box 97, Kazrin 12900, Israel E-mail: amosnaor@research.haifa.ac.il

[3]Yarden - Golan Heights Winery, Katzrin, Israel, E-mail: victor@golanwines.co.il

Abstract: Wine quality is determined by a series of complex chemical processes. Factors affecting grape and wine performance range from climate conditions during the growing period to harvesting decisions controlled by humans. In this chapter, we apply single-objective and multi-objective classification algorithms for prediction of grape and wine quality in a multi-year agricultural database maintained by Yarden - Golan Heights Winery in Katzrin, Israel. The goal of the study is to discover relationships between 138 agricultural and meteorological attributes collected or derived during a single season and 27 dependent parameters measuring grapevine and wine quality. We have induced ordered (oblivious) decision-tree models from the target dataset using information-theoretic classification algorithms. The induced models, called *single-objective* and *multi-objective information networks*, have been combined into multi-level *information graphs*, each level standing for a different stage of the wine production process. The results clearly demonstrate the hitherto unexploited potential of the KDD technology for knowledge discovery in agricultural data.

***Key Words*:** Winemaking, Agricultural data, Multi-objective classification, Information theory, Information graphs.

---

[1] Liao, T.W. and E. Triantaphyllou, (Eds.), **Recent Advances in Data Mining of Enterprise Data: Algorithms and Applications**, *World Scientific*, Singapore, pp. 323-365, 2007.

1. Introduction

According to a UN official website (http://apps.fao.org) grapes are the most planted fruit crop on earth (7.7 million HA in 2004) and they also lead in tonnage produced (65.5 Metric tons in 2004). About 270 million hectoliters of wine are produced worldwide every year according to (http://www.wineinstitute.org/communications/statistics/). The Merriam-Webster Online Dictionary defines wine as "a beverage made of the fermented juice of any of various kinds of grapes" (http://www.webster.com/). This simple definition belies the vast complexity of the liquid itself and of the myriad factors that affect its quality. So far, approximately 1,000 compounds have been found in wine, and nearly half of these in the last 20 years (Peynaud, 1984; Robinson, 1994).

Premium wine production represents a combination of *viticulture* (cultivation of grapes) and *enology* (study of wine). With the technological advances in winemaking over the last few decades, attention has now been focused on the vineyard as "the remaining frontier" of wine quality (Gladstones, 1992). In the high end of the industry, there is much discussion of "terroir." This French term describes the natural environment of the vines which, ultimately, affects wine quality, and generally includes the soil (physical and chemical) composition, topography and climate. Even though there is general agreement as to the importance of these factors, research has not yielded a "best" terroir and it seems that many possible successful combinations exist (Robinson, 1994).

Yarden - Golan Heights Winery of Katzrin, Israel (for more information one can visit http://www.golanwines.co.il) has invested significant resources over the years in studying the terroir of the Golan Heights, such as establishing a network of meteorological stations throughout its vineyards. In addition, the winery has collected a huge amount of historical data relating to vine phenology and juice and wine quality. The winery, along with the project sponsor - Netafim Irrigation Company (http://www.netafim.co.il), is interested in exploring data mining as a tool for several reasons. Most importantly, the winery seeks to investigate the existence of as-yet unrecognized correlations in order to advance the progress to increased quality. The same problem is faced by growers of any agricultural crop. In addition, if significant factors could be isolated, the amount of data recorded could possibly be reduced, thereby increasing efficiency.

In this chapter, we apply predictive data mining techniques to a multi-year agricultural database maintained by the Yarden - Golan Heights Winery. The winery is processing grapes of 20 varieties from 15 vineyards on the Golan Heights and one in the Upper Galilee. One common variety of the red wine, Cabernet Sauvignon, which is grown on about 20% of the Winery fields, was chosen for this study. The target dataset was spread over the period of 17 seasons (1987 – 2003). Due to the large number of dependent attributes representing various aspects of grape and wine quality, single-objective classification models have been compared to multi-objective models induced with a multi-objective classification algorithm.

The rest of the chapter is organized as follows. Section 2 defines the problem of knowledge discovery in a winery database. Section 3 presents the concepts of information networks and information graphs. In Section 4 we describe the stages of the knowledge discovery process and evaluate the obtained results. Related work is discussed in Section 5. Section 6 concludes the chapter.

2. Problem Description

The goal of this case study, sponsored by the Netafim Irrigation Company (www.netafim.co.il), is defined as examining the feasibility of applying data mining technology for discovering useful knowledge in agricultural data. The wine domain was chosen due to the availability of a multi-year database at Yarden - Golan Heights Winery. The following specific objectives are pursued:

(1) Identification of raw and derived variables having a significant impact on grape and wine quality (feature selection);

(2) Induction of probabilistic models that can predict the quality scores as a function of identified predictive features (prediction / classification);
(3) Extraction of *if... then...* rules explaining the relationships between predictive features and target attributes (rule induction);
(4) Estimating the predictive accuracy of induced models on future seasons (accuracy estimation);

As indicated above, grape and wine quality is measured by multiple interdependent parameters, mostly determined by human experts. Since all quality parameters are measured on a continuous scale, we have discretized the measured values to three equal-frequency intervals, generally corresponding to low, medium, and high quality levels. According to the wine experts, this granularity is sufficient for prediction purposes. The discretization of continuous values has converted the original *prediction* problem of estimating continuous values (Han and Kamber, 2001) into the problem of *classification*.

For each grape field in every season, the Winery keeps three scores of wine quality and 24 parameters measuring vine quality and yield. This implies that Objective 2 above (induction of classification models) is a task of *multi-objective classification* (Last, 2004)(Suzuki *et al*., 2001). We have used the M-IN algorithm (Last, 2004) to induce multi-objective classification models. Furthermore, quality parameters ("dependent variables") are associated with the following five groups (levels) based on the source and timing of their measurement:

- Level 1: Overall Wine Score (the top level);
- Level 2: Aroma and Flavor Scores of produced wine;
- Level 3: 13 parameters measuring grape quality and yield at the harvest;
- Level 4: Canopy and Grape Scores of the field measured just before the harvest;
- Level 5: Nine additional parameters measuring grape quality in the field just before the harvest.

The complete list of target (dependent) attributes is shown in Table 1.

Table 1. List of the target attributes.

Ser No	Table Name	Field Name	Level (1 - Top)	Measured by
1	Grape Score	Wine Score	1	Human
2	Grape Score	Aroma Score	2	Human
3	Grape Score	Flavor Score	2	Human
4	Harvest Data	Grape Qty to Pay	3	Human
5	Harvest Data	Price Per Ton	3	Human
6	Harvest Data	BX	3	Machine
7	Harvest Data	Cluster Count	3	Machine
8	Harvest Data	Cluster Weight	3	Machine
9	Harvest Data	Grape Qty	3	Machine
10	Harvest Data	K+	3	Machine
11	Harvest Data	MA	3	Machine
12	Harvest Data	NH4+	3	Machine
13	Harvest Data	PH	3	Machine
14	Harvest Data	Pruning Weight	3	Machine
15	Harvest Data	TA	3	Machine
16	Harvest Data	Yield	3	Machine
17	Grape Score	Canopy Score	4	Human
18	Grape Score	Grape Score	4	Human
19	Grape Score	Canopy Density	5	Human
20	Grape Score	Fruit Appearance	5	Human
21	Grape Score	Fruit Exposure	5	Human
22	Grape Score	Grape Color	5	Human
23	Grape Score	Lateral Growth	5	Human
24	Grape Score	Leaf Color	5	Human
25	Grape Score	Rot	5	Human
26	Grape Score	Shoot Length	5	Human
27	Grape Score	Growing Tips	5	Machine

The Winery Database also contains the following groups of candidate input attributes that can be used as predictive features ("independent variables") in their raw or calculated form:

(1) Record ID information: a combination of field code and year (season);
(2) Field geographical data: longitude, latitude, and height over sea level;
(3) Fertilization data: three chemical parameters (K, N, and P) measured once in a season;
(4) Leaf analysis data: seven chemical parameters measured once in a season;
(5) Phenology[2] data: the dates of the following important events are recorded in the database for every season – budburst, bloom, veraison, and harvest;
(6) Ripening monitoring data: three time-dependent chemical parameters (BX[3], TA[4], and pH[5]) measured several times during a season (between veraison and harvest);
(7) Meteorology data: the Winery Database has been joined with meteorological measurements obtained from the Israeli Meteorological Service (www.ims.gov.il). The data is recorded by 14 meteorological stations in Northern Israel and it includes three types of measurements: daily, hourly, and every 10 minutes. The number of measured parameters (wind, temperature, radiation, etc.) is 22, 14 and 13 for each measurement type, respectively. Each grape field was associated with its nearest meteorological station;

Figure 1 shows the relationships between various levels of dependent and independent variables that the winemakers are interested to explore. To represent these relationships, we have developed an information-theoretic model called *multi-level information graph*, which is introduced in the next section.

---

[2] *Phenology* is defined as a branch of science dealing with the relations between climate and periodic biological phenomena (www.sws-wis.com/lifecycles/).
[3] BX, or Brix – approximate sugar percentage.
[4] TA - Titratable acidity.
[5] pH – A different measure of acidity. The pH values range from 0 to 14 (the lower the number, the higher the acidity).

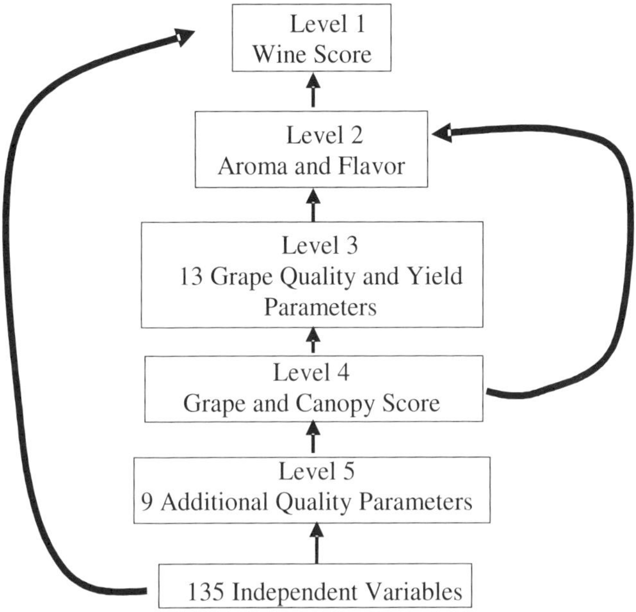

Figure 1. Problem description - target relationships.

3. Information Networks and the Information Graphs

3.1 An Extended Classification Task

In order to be able to provide a unified framework for single-target and multi-target classification, we have defined in (Last, 2004) an *extended classification task* using the following notation:

- $R = (A_1,..., A_k)$ - a set of k attributes ($k \geq 2$);
- C - a non-empty subset of n candidate input features ($C \subset R$, $|C| = n \geq 1$). The values of these features are usually known and they can be used to predict the values of target attributes (see next);

- O - a non-empty subset of m target ("output") attributes ($O \subset R$, $|O| = m \geq 1$). This is a subset of attributes representing the variables to predict. The extended classification task is to build an accurate model (or models) for predicting the values of all target attributes, based on the corresponding dependency subset (or subsets) $I \subseteq C$ of input features;

In our framework, we impose the following constraints on the partition of the attribute set:

- $C \cap O = \emptyset$, i.e. the same attribute cannot be both a candidate input and a target at the same time.
- $C \cup O \subseteq R$, i.e. some dataset attributes are allowed to be neither candidate inputs nor targets. Usually, these attributes are used for identification purposes, but their values are meaningless from the classification viewpoint (e.g., SSN).

Information-theoretic algorithms aimed at inducing compact and accurate models for the extended classification task are described in the sub-sections below.

3.2 *Single-Objective Information Networks*

Information theory (for example, see (Cover and Thomas, 1991)) suggests a general modeling of conditional dependency between random variables. If nothing is known on the causes of a variable X, its degree of uncertainty can be measured by the *unconditional entropy* $H(X) = -\Sigma\, p(x) \log p(x)$ (i.e., the expected value of $\log [1/p(x)]$). When $\log_2$ (also denoted as *log*) is used, entropy is measured in *bits* and is called *binary entropy*. The entropy of a random variable Y given another random variable X, (the *conditional entropy*) is given by $H(Y/X) = -\Sigma\, p(x,y) \log p(y/x)$ (expected value of $\log [1/p(y/x)]$). A decrease in uncertainty (entropy) of Y as a result of knowing X and vice versa is measured by the *mutual information* between X and Y:

$$I(X;Y) = H(Y) - H(Y/X) = H(X) - H(X/Y)$$
$$= \sum_{x,y} p(x,y) \times \log \frac{p(y/x)}{p(y)}$$

where *p (x)* is the unconditional probability of *x, p (y/x)* is the conditional probability of *y* given *x*, and *p(x, y)* is the joint probability of *x* and *y*. Mutual information is a non-negative quantity, which reaches a maximum value of $I(X; Y) = H(Y) = H(X)$ when $Y = f(X)$ and a minimal value of zero when *X* and *Y* are independent variables.

When more than one input variable affect certain target (dependent) variable(s), the contributions of several input variables to an overall decrease in a target's (or targets') uncertainty can be added up using the so-called *chain rule* (Cover and Thomas, 1991): $I(X_1,..., X_n; Y) = \Sigma I(X_i;Y / X_{i-1},..., X_1)$, where $I(X; Y / Z)$ is a *conditional mutual information* between *X* and *Y* given variable(s) *Z*. This is the underlying principle of the single-objective information-theoretic algorithm presented in (Last and Maimon, 2002). This algorithm chooses a subset of input variables that maximize a decrease in the target(s) entropy and ranks the selected variables by their contribution to the mutual information of the induced predictive model called *IN - Information Network*[6] (see Figure 2).

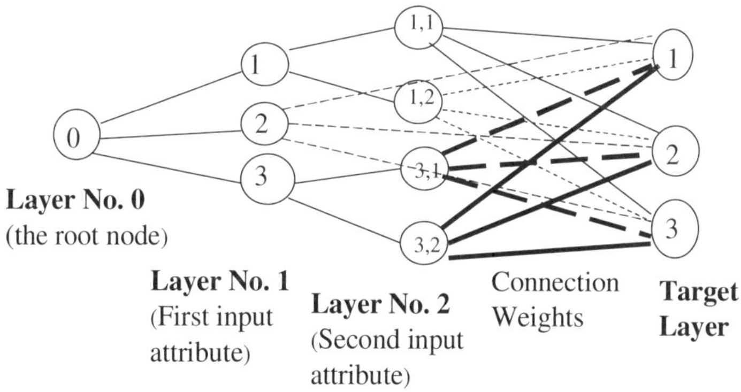

Figure 2. A single-objective information network.

[6] In (Maimon and Last, 2000), this model is called *Info-Fuzzy Network* (IFN) due to its fuzzy-based ability to evaluate the reliability of target attribute values in a dataset.

An information network is an oblivious read-once decision graph (Kohavi and Li, 1995), where each node represents a value or a conjunction of values of random variables. In (Last and Maimon, 2004) the information-theoretic algorithms are shown empirically to produce much more compact models than other methods of decision-tree learning, while preserving nearly the same level of classification accuracy. According to (Last *et al.*, 2001), the information-theoretic algorithms can also be used as effective *feature selection* tools, which is the most important objective of the wine-makers in this project (see Section 2 above).

The main components of a single-target information network are as follows (based on Maimon and Last, 2000):

(1) *I* - a subset of *input* features used by the model to predict the values of a target attribute. The input features are selected from a set *C* of *candidate input features* (see above). Like in oblivious read-once decision trees (Kohavi and Li, 1995), each hidden layer of an information network is uniquely associated with a single input feature by representing the interaction of that feature and the input features of the previous layers. The first layer (Layer 0) includes only the root node and is not associated with any input feature.

(2) L_l - a subset of *branching* (internal) nodes *z* in a hidden layer *l*. Like in any decision-tree model, each node represents a conjunction of values of the first *l* input features in the network.

(3) *K* - a subset of *target* (category) nodes in the network. Each target node is associated with a distinct category or a class of the target attribute. In case of a continuous target attribute, the target nodes represent a set of disjoint intervals in the attribute range.

(4) *(z, j)* - a connection between a terminal (leaf) node *z* and a target node *j*. Each connection represents a probabilistic rule of the form "*if node is z then the class of the target attribute is j with probability* $P(V_j/z)$," and it has an information-theoretic weight associated with it, which is calculated as follows (based on Maimon and Last, 2000):

$$w_z^j = P(V_j, z) \times \log \frac{P(V_j / z)}{P(V_j)},$$

where

$P(V_j, z)$ - an estimated joint probability of the target value j and the node z.

$P(V_j / z)$ - an estimated conditional (*a posteriori*) probability of the target value j given the node z.

$P(V_j)$ - an estimated unconditional (*a priori*) probability of the target value j.

A connection weight is positive if the conditional probability of a target attribute value given the node is higher than its unconditional probability and is negative otherwise. A weight close to zero means that the target attribute value is nearly independent of the node value. This means that each positive connection weight can be interpreted as an *information content* of an appropriate rule of the form *if node, then target value*. Accordingly, a negative weight refers to a rule of the form *if node, then **not** target value*. Thus, in addition to the classification task, an IN can be used as a kind of a *Probability Estimation Tree*, or *PET* (for a comprehensive overview of PETs, see (Provost and Domingos, 2003). To simplify the network representation, one can omit zero-weight connections from IN charts.

The construction algorithm of a single-objective information network has been described in (Maimon and Last, 2000) and (Last and Maimon, 2004). Its main characteristics include conditional mutual information as a splitting criterion, multi-way splits of continuous attributes, and pre-pruning based on the likelihood-ratio statistical test. The main flow of the network construction algorithm is outlined below:

Procedure: Generate_Information_Network

Input: the set D of training instances; the set C of n candidate input attributes (discrete and continuous); the target (classification) attribute T; the minimum significance level *sign* for splitting a network node (default: *sign* = 0.1%).

Output: a set *I* of selected input attributes and an information-theoretic network *IN*. Each input attribute has a corresponding hidden layer in the network.

Step 1 – Initialize_Network. Initialize the information-theoretic network.

Step 2 – Add_Layers. Expand the network by introducing new hidden layers. Each layer represents a single input attribute.

Step 3 – Return the set *I* of selected input attributes and the network structure.

The *Initialize_Network* procedure includes the following steps:

Procedure: Initialize_Network

Step 1 – Generate the single root node representing all training instances.

Step 2 – Generate the target layer with a node for each value of the target attribute.

Step 3 – Connect the root node to each target node.

An example of an initialized Information Network having three target nodes is shown in Figure 3.

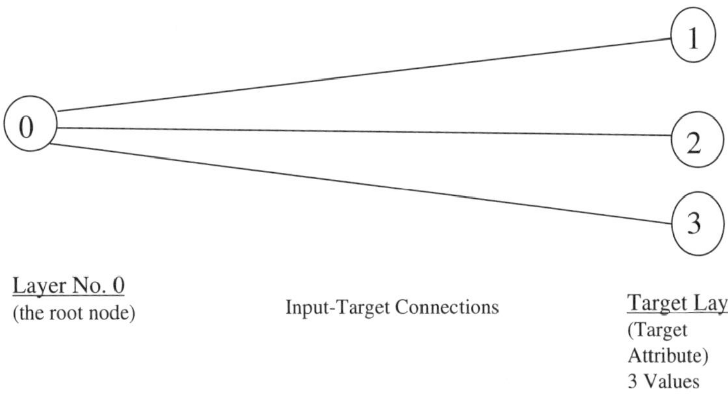

Figure 3. An initial information network.

The *Add_Layers* procedure includes the following steps:

Procedure: *Add_Layers*

Step 1 – While the number of layers $l < n$ (number of candidate input attributes) **do**

Step 1.1 – *Find_Best_Attribute.* Find the candidate input attribute A_{i*} maximizing conditional mutual information $cond\_MI_i$ between A_i and T

Step 1.2 – **If** $cond\_MI_{i*} = 0$, **then End do.**

Else

Step 1.2.1 – Expand the network by introducing a new hidden layer associated with the attribute A_{i*} and increment the number of layers l.

Step 1.2.2 – Update the set I of selected input attributes: $I = I \cup A_{i*}$

End do.

The *Find_Best_Attribute* procedure includes the following steps:

Procedure: *Find_Best_Attribute*

Step 1 – **For each** candidate input attribute $A_i \notin I$ **do**

If A_i is discrete **then**

Return the statistically significant conditional mutual information $cond\_MI_i$ between A_i and T.

Else

Return the best threshold splits of A_i and the statistically significant conditional mutual information $cond\_MI_i$ between A_i and the target attribute T.

End do

Step 2 – Find the candidate input attribute A_{i*} maximizing $cond\_MI_i$

Step 3 – Return $i*$ and $cond\_MI_{i*}$

Figure 4 shows the network initialized in Figure 3 after the first iteration, where a 3-valued attribute was selected as the attribute having the maximum conditional mutual information.

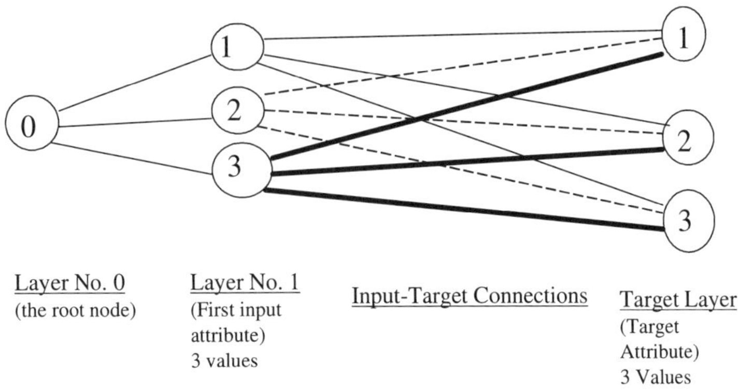

Figure 4. The information network after iteration 1.

In Figure 4 each node in the final (first) hidden layer is connected to all three target nodes implying that each target value has a non-zero probability given every node in the final hidden layer.

Figure 2 shows the structure of the same network after adding the second layer related to a 2-valued attribute. In the previous layer (No. 1), only nodes having a statistically significant contribution to the conditional mutual information (Nodes 1 and 3) are split on the values of the second input attribute. The unsplit Node 2 is connected directly to the target nodes.

3.3 *Multi-Objective Information Networks*

As shown in (Last, 2004), an m-target classification function can be represented by a *multi-objective information network* (M-IN), where the nodes of the target layer represent the values of all output attributes. In other words, a set of *target* (category) nodes in M-IN is a union of the domains of all target attributes:

$$K = \bigcup_{i=1}^{m} D_i$$

We further assume that a multi-target information network has a single *root node* and its internal "read-once" structure is identical for all target variables. This means that every hidden node is shared among *all* outputs and each terminal (leaf) node is connected to at least one target node associated with every output. Figure 5 shows an example of a *multi-target* information network, which corresponds to two Boolean functions $F_1 = X_2 \ AND \ \overline{X_1}$ and $F_2 = X_2 \ XOR \ X_1$. Since both functions are Boolean, this M-IFN has four nodes in its target layer: nodes 0-1 corresponding to the first target variable (F_1) and nodes 2-3 corresponding to the second target variable (F_2). Due to the deterministic nature of both Boolean functions, each terminal node has only two outgoing edges leading to the values of the two output variables. Thus, the terminal node 3 is connected to the second value of F_1 (represented by target node 1) and to the second value of F_2 (represented by target node 3). It is easy to verify that this network has an "oblivious read-once" structure: hidden nodes 1 and 2 of the first layer correspond to the values of the first input feature (X_2), while hidden nodes 3 – 6 of the second layer represent the values of the second input feature (X_1).

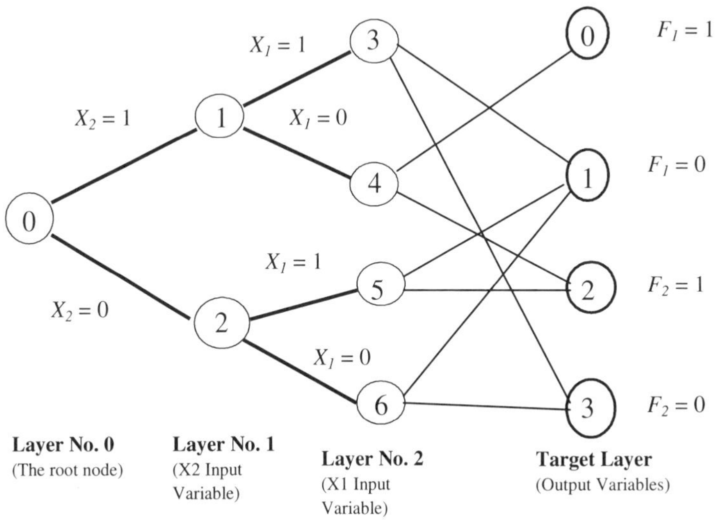

Figure 5. A multi-objective information network.

A multi-objective information network is constructed from a set of candidate input features using the *Generate_Information_Network* algorithm described in sub-section 3.2 above. However, the multi-objective algorithm is calling a different version of the *Find_Best_Attribute* procedure (called *Find_Best_Attribute_MO*), which is summarized below:

Procedure: *Find_Best_Attribute_MO*
Step 1 – **For each** candidate input attribute $A_i \notin I$ **do**
If X_j is continuous **then**
Find the best threshold splits of A_i over all output attributes O
Calculate the total conditional mutual information between A_i and the subset of output attributes O:

$$cond\_MI_i = \sum_{Y_j \in O} MI(A_i;Y_j / I)$$

End do
Step 2 – Find the candidate input attribute A_{i*} maximizing $cond\_MI_i$
Step 3 – Return $i*$ and $cond\_MI_{i*}$

3.4 *Information Graphs*

In our study of wine quality data, we combine the information networks induced at multiple levels of dependent variables into a multi-level *information graph*, where variables are represented by nodes and variable relationships by directed arcs. Two types of information graphs are used: a *single-objective information graph*, which shows the impact of input variables at each target variable (see Figure 6) and a *multi-objective information graph*, which shows the impact of input variables at *all* target variables of a given level (see Figure 7).

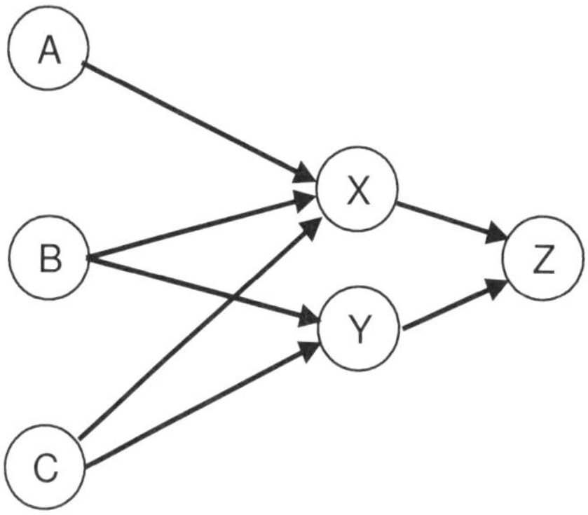

Figure 6. A multi-level single-objective information graph.

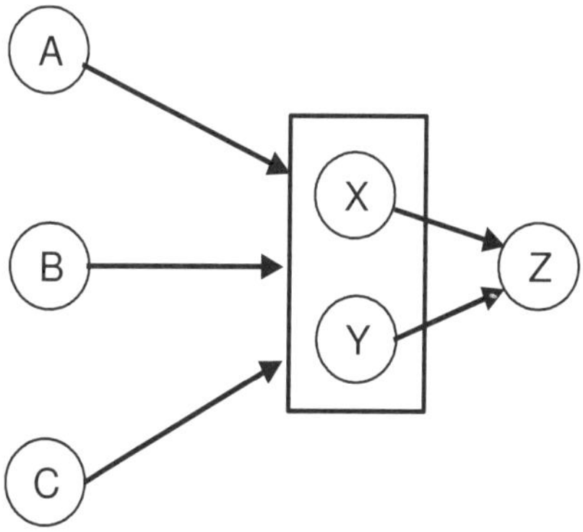

Figure 7. A multi-level multi-objective information graph.

In addition to the top-level target variables (e.g., the Wine Score), both graph types retain only variables that affect at least one target variable (or a set of target variables) at an upper level. In contrast to *Bayesian Belief Networks*, which describe *probabilistic relationships* between random variables (represented by conditional probability tables), information networks and information graphs represent *information-theoretic relationships*, which use mutual information to measure the relative influence of each predictive feature.

The main steps for constructing a multi-level information graph from a hierarchy of candidate input and target attributes (like the one shown in Figure 1) are presented below:

Procedure: Generate_Information_Graph
Input: The set D of training examples; the set C of candidate input features (denoted as level 0); the set O of candidate target (output) attributes partitioned into L levels (l = 1 to L); the set of inter-level relationships: $i \rightarrow j$ means that the attributes at level i affect directly the attributes at level j; the network induction algorithm (single-objective or multi-objective); the minimum significance level *sign* for splitting an information network node (default: *sign* = 0.1%).

Output: A subset $O' \subseteq O$ of target (output) attributes affecting target attributes at upper levels and a dependency subset $I \subseteq C$ of input features affecting target attributes in the O' subset.
Step 1 – Initialize_Graph. Initialize the information graph.
Step 2 – Add_Attributes. Select input / target attributes in each graph layer.
Step 3 – Return the information graph structure, where each attribute belonging to either the O' subset or the I subset is represented by a node and the directed links stand for dependency relationships between the corresponding attributes. In case of a multi-objective information graph, the links connect an input attribute to a *set* of target attributes at the affected level (Figure 7). Otherwise, the two attributes are connected directly as in Figure 6.

The *Initialize_Graph* procedure includes the following steps:

Procedure: Initialize_ Graph
Step 1 – Initialize the O' subset as a set of all target attributes in the top-most level (L).
Step 2 – Initialize the set I of selected inputs as an empty set: I = ∅.

The initialized Information Graphs in Figures 6 and 7 will include only one node denoted by Z.

The *Add_Attributes* procedure includes the following steps:

Procedure: Add_Attributes
Step 1 – **For** $l = L$ to 1 **do**

> *Step 1.1* – Apply the *Generate_Information_Network* algorithm to each target attribute in the l-th level (to induce single-objective information networks) or to the set of all target attributes in the l-th level (to induce a multi-objective information network). Use as candidate inputs all attributes in the levels affecting the l-th level.
>
> *Step 1.2* – Remove from the $(l\text{-}1)$-th level all attributes that were not included in any information network.
>
> *Step 1.3* – **If** $l > 1$ **then**
>
> > Extend the O' subset by all attributes that were included in at least one information network.
> >
> > **Else**
> >
> > Extend the I subset of selected features by all attributes that were included in at least one information network.
>
> **End do**

Step 2 – Return O' and I

In Figures 6 and 7, the nodes X and Y in the second layer represent selected target attributes that affect the Z attribute in the top-most (third) layer and the nodes A, B, and C represent selected features (input attributes) that affect at least one target attribute in the second layer.

4. A Case Study: the Cabernet Sauvignon Problem

4.1 Data Selection

The Yarden - Golan Heights Winery grows ten red grape varieties and ten white grape varieties. The majority of grape fields (about 65%) grow red varieties, with *Cabernet Sauvignon (CS)* being the leading variety of red wine for many years. Thus, Cabernet Sauvignon has been chosen for this data mining case study. Available data refers to 61 CS grape fields located in 15 vineyards. The 451 records of the resulting dataset cover a period of 17 seasons (1987- 2003). The database also includes daily meteorological measurements of 14 meteorological stations during the period of 8 years only (1996 – 2004).

Figure 8 shows the schema of the original Winery Database implemented in MS-Access™. Each record in the Fields table is identified by the *fCode* attribute and uniquely related to a vineyard and a meteorological station. Each record in an agronomical data table (Fertilization, Grape Score, Harvest Data, Leaf Analysis, Ripening, and Phenology) is uniquely identified by a combination of two fields: *fCode + Year* or *fCode + Date*. The Grape Score, Ripening, and Harvest Data tables store the grape and wine quality parameters (target attributes) for a specific field in a specific year. We have extracted all raw data and calculated data related to a grape field in a year (season) to a flat table called Full_Table, which consists of 135 independent (candidate input) variables (including the composite key *fCode + Year)* and 27 dependent (target) variables. On average, the records in the Full_Table have about 20% of missing values. The pre-processing of the raw data values is described in the next sub-section.

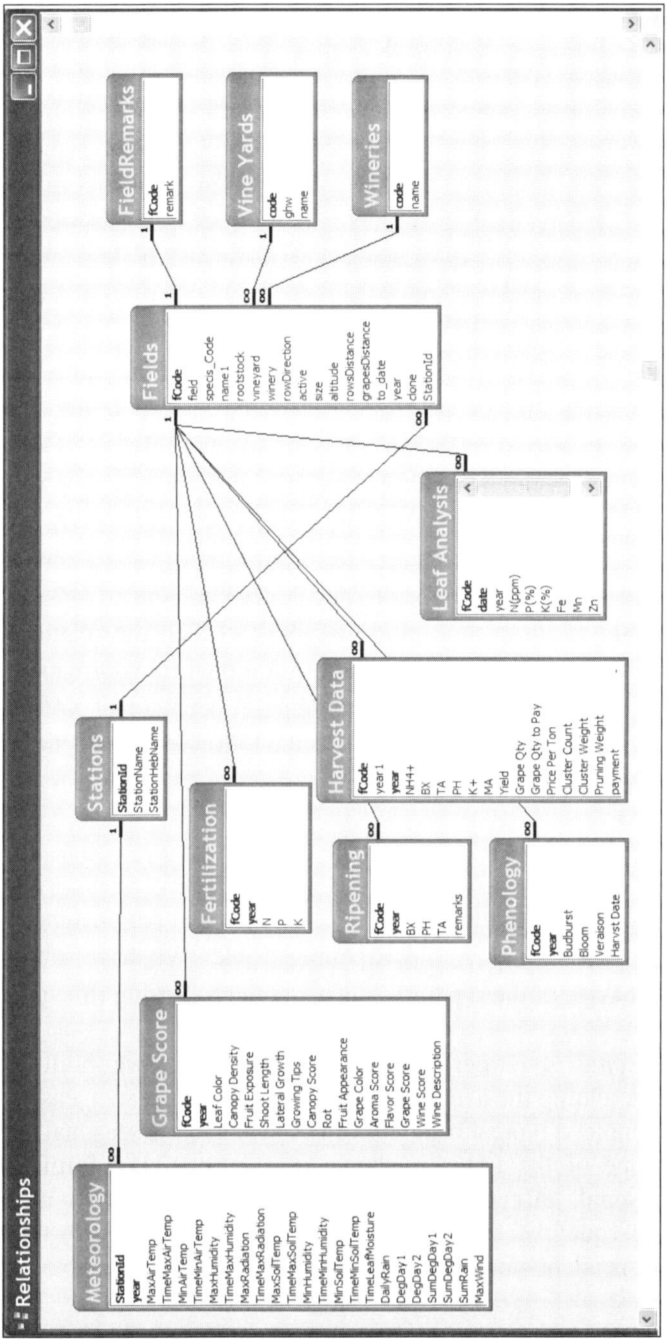

Figure 8. The winery database schema.

4.2 Data Pre-Processing

The MS-Access™ Winery Database contains two types of time-dependent data that is measured several times during a season: ripening data, stored in the Ripening Table, and meteorology data, where daily measurements are stored in the Meteorology Table and more frequent measurements are available from separate text files (see sub-section 4.2.2 below). Each season in the database is identified by the year of its harvest date (around September-October), which is recorded in the Phenology Table for every grape field. A new season starts after the harvest date of a previous season. Thus, the timestamp of each measurement relates it to a specific season at the corresponding field.

According to the *classical decomposition* (Provost and Domingos, 2003), a time series can be described by four separate components: trend, seasonality, cycle, and noise. For all time-dependent parameters, we have built time plots of measurements taken during various seasons at each field to evaluate the importance of each series component. Based on the visual analysis of these time plots, we have chosen the features to be extracted from the raw time series data. Additional transformations have been defined by domain experts. The temporal behavior of ripening and meteorology data is studied separately in the following sub-sections.

4.2.1 Ripening Data

The ripening process is monitored by three chemical parameters BX, TA and pH that are stored in the Ripening Table. We have studied the temporal behavior of these parameters using the following time plots:

- *Seasonal Averages.* For each grape field, we built a chart representing the average value of the data by years (seasons). For example, a typical behavior of BX, TA and pH seasonal averages at one of the fields is shown in Figure 9. **We found minor seasonal effects on averages, mainly in BX and TA.** Consequently, seasonal averages have been added to the set of independent variables.

- *Seasonal Standard Deviations.* For each field, we built a chart representing the standard deviation of the data by seasons. A typical behavior of BX, TA and pH seasonal standard deviations is demonstrated in Figure 10. **We found significant fluctuations in seasonal standard deviations of BX and TA.** Thus, seasonal standard deviations have also been added to the set of the independent variables.
- *Individual Values.* For all grape fields, we built charts representing series of individual measurements in every season. For example, behavior of BX time series at one of the fields is shown in Figure 11. As expected by domain experts, **we found a clear increasing trend in the values of pH and BX along the season, while TA is always decreasing.** In practical terms, this means that as grapes develop along the season, their sugar level, measured by BX, goes up, while their acidity, measured by pH[7] and TA, goes down. Since the BX parameter is known to be nonlinear in time (Bates, 2001), the experts have suggested partitioning the BX measurements into three segments: under 21, between 21 and 23 and over 23. The slope of each segment in every season has been computed separately and then added to the set of independent variables.

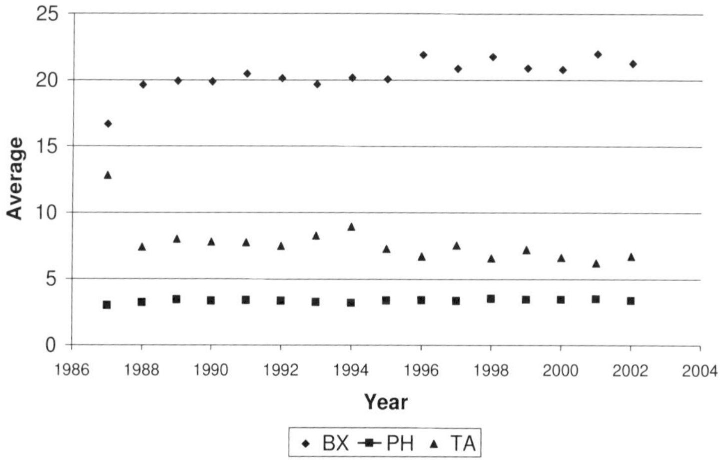

Figure 9. Ripening average values.

[7] Please note that pH, like BX, is an *inverse* function of acidity.

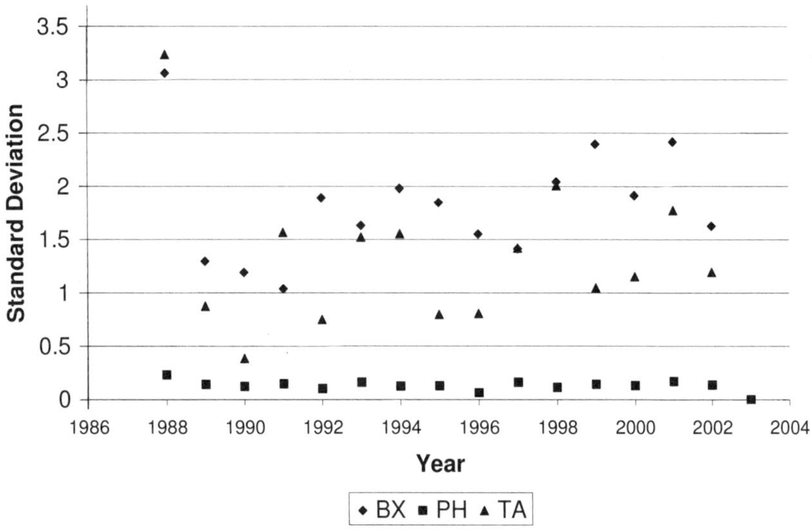

Figure 10. Ripening standard deviation values.

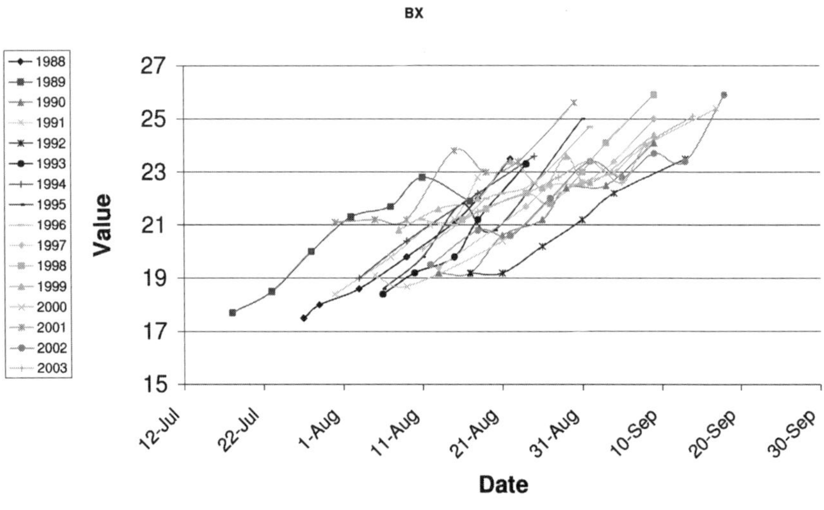

Figure 11. The BX time series.

For all three parameters (including BX) we have also calculated an overall slope of all seasonal measurements, except for the last one taken at the harvest time, using a linear regression model. All regression models were found statistically significant at either the 0.05 or 0.01 level.

4.2.2 Meteorological Measurements

The raw measurements recorded by each meteorological station are stored in a flat text file. Each data row in the file starts with an indicator of the measurement type stored in that row (daily, hourly, or every 10 minutes) followed by a timestamp and a list of measured values, which depend on the measurement type.

Since daily measurements are already available in the Meteorology Table of the Winery Database, we have extracted only hourly and 10-minutes measurements from the file of each station. We have removed illegal values from these tables by using validation rules defining the minimum and the maximum possible values of each parameter.

The one-to-many relationship between stations and fields in the Winery Database has enabled us to associate each grape field with its respective measurements. The exposure of crops to cold (during the dormancy period) and heat (during the growing period) can be calculated in several ways depending on the start and the end dates of each period (see Table 2). These dates result in four possible definitions of the dormancy period and two possible definitions of the growing period. The seasonal exposure to low / high temperatures has been accumulated as the total amount of *degree hours* or *degree days* during the period of dormancy / growing, respectively. The degree hour / day is calculated as the hourly / daily average temperature (max + min / 2) below (during dormancy) or above (during growing) the base temperature, which is 7°C for dormancy and 5°C or 10°C for growing. All temperature thresholds have been defined by the domain experts.

The following calculated attributes have been added to the flat table:

- *Seasonal degree hours.* Eight attributes representing degree hours during four possible definitions of the dormancy period and two possible definitions of the growing period relative to two possible base temperatures (5°C and 10°C).
- *Seasonal degree days.* Four attributes representing degree days during two definitions of the growing period relative to two base temperatures and eight attributes representing degree days relative to two possible base temperatures during the following four sub-periods of the growing period: budburst to bloom, bloom to veraison, veraison to harvest, and the two last weeks before the harvest.

Table 2. Possible defintions of dormancy and growing periods.

Period	Start Date	End Date
Dormancy	October 1 / November 1 of the previous year	The budburst date / one month before the budburst date
Growing	The budburst date / one month before the budburst date	The harvest date

In addition to cold and heat exposure, we have also calculated seasonal averages and standard deviations of all the 22 daily meteorological measurements during the dormancy and the growing period of each season. More calculated attributes, suggested by the domain experts, include maximum air temperature and maximum VPD (Vapor Pressure Deficit) during the last two weeks prior to the harvest and the number of days between the budburst and the dates of bloom, veraison and harvest in each season.

4.3 Design of Data Mining Runs

We have explored the multi-level relationships defined in Section 2 above by using two approaches. Under the *single-objective classification* approach, a separate classification model is induced for each dependent variable in every level. Under the *multi-objective classification* approach, a shared classification model is built for each level of dependent variables. The resulting classification models are combined in a single *information graph* (see Section 3 above). In our study, we have also induced shared classification models for increasing aggregations of dependent levels: Levels 1 and 2; Levels 1, 2, and 3, etc. up to a shared model for predicting all 27 quality-related variables (Levels 1-5).

The output of each run of an information-theoretic algorithm includes the following information:

- **List of predictive factors** included by the algorithm in the classification model.
- **Percentage of uncertainty** (entropy) explained by the whole model and by each separate predictive factor. In the ideal case of a model with prediction accuracy of 100%, the percentage of explained entropy will also reach 100%.
- **The error rate** of the model calculated over 160 testing records covering the last three years of the collected data (2001-2003). The 291 records related to the years 1987-2000 have been used for training.
- **Prediction rules** describing the influence of predictive factors on the dependent variable. Beyond information-theoretic weights (see sub-section 3.2 above), we have represented the importance of each induced rule by the following two parameters:
    - *Support* - percentage of the observations satisfying both sides of the rule (antecedent + consequent).
    - *Gain* - calculated as a positive or a negative difference between the conditional probability of the predicted interval given the conditions of the rule and the unconditional (a-priory) probability of the same interval in the entire training set. This is an indicator of a change in the frequency of a certain interval when the rule condition is true vs. the frequency of the same interval in the entire population.

4.4 Single-Objective Models

As indicated in Section 2, the dependent (target) variables in the Winery Database include 27 quality-related parameters divided into 5 levels. To examine possible relationships between dependent and independent variables, we have performed 47 runs of a single-objective algorithm following the top-down order defined by Figure 1: impact of Level 2 on Level 1 (Wine Score), impact of Level 3 on Level 2, etc. As explained in sub-section 3.4, dependent variables having no effect on the upper level variables (such as *Cluster Weight* at Level 3, which was not included in any Level 2 model) have been skipped in the process.

The number of predictive attributes in a single-objective model varied between one and five, except for one run, where no predictive attributes were found and, consequently, no model was built. The values of the top-most dependent variable (Wine Score) have been discretized to three equal-frequency intervals, while the number and boundaries of discretization intervals of dependent variables at lower levels have been determined from the best (most accurate) run at an upper level, where that variable has been selected as a predictive feature and discretized automatically by the information-theoretic algorithm. The induced relationships are summarized graphically in a multi-level, single-objective information graph (Figure 12), where dependent variables are denoted as rectangles and independent variables as hexagons.

The width of an arrow connecting two variables indicates the percentage of decrease in uncertainty (entropy) of a target variable resulting from the corresponding input variable. The most significant predictive factors in the single-objective information graph are the following:

- **Grape Score** explains about 32% of the uncertainty in the Aroma Score implying that there is a strong relationship between grape and wine quality.
- **Canopy Density** explains about 53% of the uncertainty in the Canopy Score, since both variables are related to the same quality parameter (canopy).

- **Standard Deviation of Total Rain during Hibernation** explains about 31% of the uncertainty in the Lateral Growth. This means that the precipitation variance affects the lateral growth.
- **Field Code** explains about 30% of the uncertainty in the Grape Color. In other words, there is some unexplained variance across grape fields with respect to this quality parameter

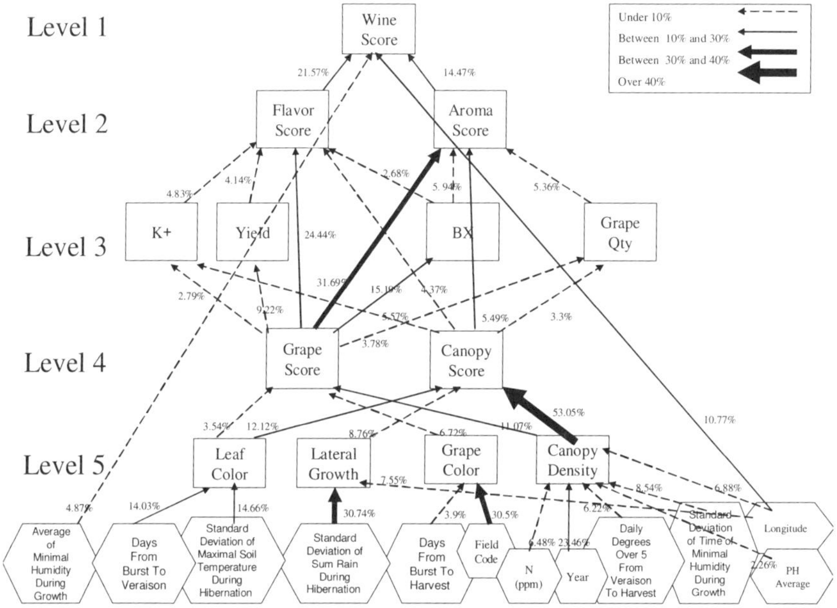

Figure 12. A five-level single-objective information graph.

The 24 rules extracted from the model of Aroma Score as a function of Level 4 variables are shown in Table 3. Next are the detailed explanations of two sample rules:

Table 3. The effect of Level 4 variables on Aroma Score.

Rule No.	Rule Text	Gain	Support
1	If Grape Score is between 0 and 17 then Aroma Score is between 5 and 12	61%	13%
2	If Grape Score is between 17 and 61.5385 then Aroma Score is between 5 and 12	11%	4%
3	If Grape Score is between 17 and 61.5385 then Aroma Score is between 12 and 15	9%	3%
4	If Grape Score is between 17 and 61.5385 then Aroma Score is not more than 15	-20%	1%
5	If Grape Score is between 61.5385 and 86.1538 then Aroma Score is not between 5 and 12	-34%	0%
6	If Grape Score is between 61.5385 and 86.1538 then Aroma Score is between 12 and 15	69%	6%
7	If Grape Score is between 86.1538 and 91.9 then Aroma Score is not between 5 and 12	-33%	1%
8	If Grape Score is between 86.1538 and 91.9 then Aroma Score is between 12 and 15	18%	5%
9	If Grape Score is between 86.1538 and 91.9 then Aroma Score is more than 15	16%	6%
10	If Grape Score is between 91.9 and 108.3 then Aroma Score is between 5 and 12	61%	3%
11	If Grape Score is between 108.3 and 135.385 and Canopy Score is between 0 and 51.7 then Aroma Score is not between 5 and 12	0%	4%
12	If Grape Score is between 108.3 and 135.385 and Canopy Score is between 0 and 51.7 then Aroma Score is not between 12 and 15	-17%	1%
13	If Grape Score is between 108.3 and 135.385 and Canopy Score is between 0 and 51.7 then Aroma Score is more than 15	17%	6%
14	If Grape Score is between 108.3 and 135.385 and Canopy Score is between 51.7 and 59.4 then Aroma Score is between 5 and 12	4%	11%
15	If Grape Score is between 108.3 and 135.385 and Canopy Score is between 51.7 and 59.4 then Aroma Score is between 12 and 15	13%	10%
16	If Grape Score is between 108.3 and 135.385 and Canopy Score is between 51.7 and 59.4 then Aroma Score is not more than 15	-17%	5%
17	If Grape Score is between 108.3 and 135.385 and Canopy Score is more than 59.4 then Aroma Score is not between 5 and 12	-8%	1%
18	If Grape Score is between 108.3 and 135.385 and Canopy Score is more than 59.4 then Aroma Score is between 12 and 15	36%	2%
19	If Grape Score is between 108.3 and 135.385 and Canopy Score is more than 59.4 then Aroma Score is not more than 15	-28%	0%
20	If Grape Score is more than 135.385 and Canopy Score is between 51.7 and 59.4 then Aroma Score is not between 5 and 12	-36%	0%
21	If Grape Score is more than 135.385 and Canopy Score is between 51.7 and 59.4 then Aroma Score is more than 15	62%	12%
22	If Grape Score is more than 135.385 and Canopy Score is more than 59.4 then Aroma Score is not between 5 and 12	-3%	2%
23	If Grape Score is more than 135.385 and Canopy Score is more than 59.4 then Aroma Score is not between 12 and 15	-4%	1%
24	If Grape Score is more than 135.385 and Canopy Score is more than 59.4 then Aroma Score is more than 15	7%	2%

- Rule 1 - *If Grape Score is between 0 and 17 then Aroma Score is between 5 and 12* (Gain = 61%, Support = 13%). This "positive" rule occurs in 13% of the observations and its condition (Grape Score is between 0 and 17) increases the probability of the Aroma Score to fall between 5 and 12 by 61%.
- Rule 16 - *If Grape Score is between 108.3 and 135.385 and Canopy Score is between 51.7 and 59.4 then Aroma Score is not more than 15* (Gain = -17%, Support = 5%). This "negative" rule occurs in 5% of the observations and its condition (Grape Score is between 108.3 and 135.385) decreases the probability of the Aroma Score to exceed the value of 15 by 17%.

4.5 Multi-Objective Models

As shown in Table 4, we have used the multi-objective information-theoretic algorithm, presented in sub-section 3.2, to induce eight shared (multi-objective) classification models. The ranges of all target attributes have been discretized to three equal-frequency intervals.

Table 4. List of multi-objective classification runs.

Run No.	Level of Target Variables	Number of Target Variables	Level of Candidate Input Variables	Number of Candidate Input Attributes	Number of Predictive Attributes
1	2	2	3	13	2
2	2	2	4	2	2
3	1 – 2	3	Independent	135	2
4	3	13	4	2	2
5	1 – 3	16	Independent	135	4
6	1 – 4	18	Independent	135	3
7	4	2	5	9	3
8	1 – 5	25	Independent	135	2

The number of predictive attributes in the multi-objective models varies between two and four, implying that a relatively small number of features can be shared among most target variables in this dataset. This result can be partially explained by the associations between the target variables revealed with single-objective classification models in sub-section 4.4.

The induced multi-objective relationships are summarized graphically in a multi-level, multi-objective information graph (Figure 13), where all the dependent variables of the same level are contained in a frame. Only selected predictive features are shown on the chart, though multi-objective models have been induced with respect to *all* target variables of the corresponding level. The arrows starting at each input variable point to an upper level of the dependent variables rather than to a specific dependent variable. The arrow width is related this time to the percentage of decrease in uncertainty (entropy) of *all* target variables at a given level.

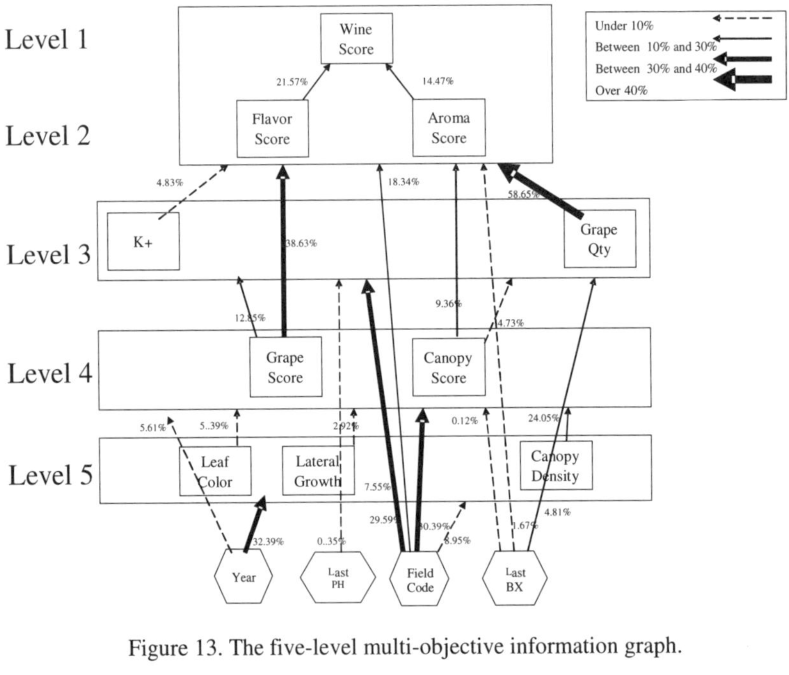

Figure 13. The five-level multi-objective information graph.

Table 5. The effect of Level 3 variables on Aroma Score and Flavor Score.

Rule No.	Rule Text	Gain	Support
1	If Grape Qty is between 0 and 5 then Aroma Score is between 0 and 5	10%	23%
2	If Grape Qty is between 0 and 5 then Flavor Score is between 0 and 8.57143	40%	36%
3	If Grape Qty is between 5 and 8 then Aroma Score is between 0 and 5	10%	9%
4	If Grape Qty is between 5 and 8 then Flavor Score is not between 0 and 8.57143	-32%	1%
5	If Grape Qty is between 5 and 8 then Flavor Score is more than 8.57143	32%	3%
6	If Grape Qty is between 13.8667 and 24 then Aroma Score is between 0 and 5	10%	10%
7	If Grape Qty is between 13.8667 and 24 then Flavor Score is not between 0 and 8.57143	-40%	3%
8	If Grape Qty is between 13.8667 and 24 then Flavor Score is more than 8.57143	40%	10%
9	If Grape Qty is more than 24 then Aroma Score is not between 0 and 5	-83%	0%
10	If Grape Qty is more than 24 then Aroma Score is more than 5	83%	6%
11	If Grape Qty is more than 24 then Flavor Score is not between 0 and 8.57143	-48%	1%
12	If Grape Qty is more than 24 then Flavor Score is more than 8.57143	48%	8%
13	If Grape Qty is between 8 and 8.08333 and K+ is between 0 and 13.8667 then Aroma Score is between 0 and 5	10%	5%
14	If Grape Qty is between 8 and 8.08333 and K+ is between 0 and 13.8667 then Flavor Score is more than 8.57143	60%	8%
15	If Grape Qty is between 8 and 8.08333 and K+ is between 13.8667 and 23.3 then Aroma Score is between 0 and 5	10%	0%
16	If Grape Qty is between 8 and 8.08333 and K+ is between 13.8667 and 23.3 then Flavor Score is between 0 and 8.57143	40%	1%
17	If Grape Qty is between 8.08333 and 13.8667 and K+ is between 0 and 13.8667 then Aroma Score is between 0 and 5	10%	2%
18	If Grape Qty is between 8.08333 and 13.8667 and K+ is between 0 and 13.8667 then Flavor Score is between 0 and 8.57143	40%	4%
19	If Grape Qty is between 8.08333 and 13.8667 and K+ is between 13.8667 and 23.3 then Aroma Score is between 0 and 5	10%	7%
20	If Grape Qty is between 8.08333 and 13.8667 and K+ is between 13.8667 and 23.3 then Flavor Score is between 0 and 8.57143	40%	10%
21	If Grape Qty is between 8.08333 and 13.8667 and K+ is more than 23.3 then Aroma Score is between 0 and 5	10%	2%
22	If Grape Qty is between 8.08333 and 13.8667 and K+ is more than 23.3 then Flavor Score is not between 0 and 8.57143	-35%	1%
23	If Grape Qty is between 8.08333 and 13.8667 and K+ is more than 23.3 then Flavor Score is more than 8.57143	35%	2%

One can see from Figure 13 that the most significant predictive factors in multi-objective models are the following:

- **Grape Quantity** explains about 59% of uncertainty in Levels 1 and 2, which represent the three wine quality parameters (Wine, Flavor, and Aroma scores).
- **Grape Score** explains about 39% of uncertainty in Levels 1 and 2.
- **Field Code** explains about 32% of uncertainty in grape quality parameters at Level 3 and about 30% of uncertainty in grape quality parameters at Level 4.
- **Year** explains about 32% of uncertainty in grape quality parameters at Level 5.

The rules extracted from the shared Level 2 model (Aroma Score + Flavor Score) as a function of Level 3 variables are shown in Table 5.

Here is an example of a multi-objective rule obtained as a combination of Rules 6 and 8: *If Grape Qty is between 13.87 and 24 then Aroma Score is between 0 and 5* (Gain = 10%, Support = 10%) *and Flavor Score is more than 8.57* (Gain = 40%, Support = 10%). The condition of this "positive" rule (Grape Qty is between 13.87 and 24) increases the probability of Aroma Score to fall into the 0-5 range by 10% in 10% of the observations. The same condition increases the probability of Flavor Score to exceed the value of 8.57 by as much as 40% in 10% of the observations. Accordingly, the probability of Flavor Score to fall below the value of 8.57 is decreased by 40%, as indicated by the "negative" Rule No. 7.

4.6 Comparative Evaluation

To evaluate the multi-objective and the single-objective approaches to inducing classification models from this dataset, we have chosen Levels 1 and 2 of dependent variables, which include the following three quality parameters: Aroma Score, Flavor Score, and Wine Score.

In Table 6 we compare the average performance of the single-objective models for predicting these parameters (C4.5 and single-objective information network - IN) to a shared multi-objective information network (M-IN) induced from the same set of independent variables. The first row shows that, on average, IN is more accurate on this data than C4.5 and the M-IN model is even more accurate than the single-objective IN models. Both differences are statistically significant at the confidence level of 95%.

Table 6. Comparative evaluation: Levels 1 + 2.

	C4.5	IN	M-IN
Average Error Rate (test set 2001-2003)	0.464	0.421	0.350
Total Internal Nodes	57	59	65
Total Prediction Rules	30	52	62

The difference between IN and M-IN agrees with our previous information-theoretic result that the average accuracy of a multi-objective model in predicting the categories of m dependent variables is not expected to be worse than the average accuracy of m single-objective models using the same set of input features (Last, 2004). In terms of interpretability, the M-IN model is slightly more complex than the C4.5 and the IN models as it uses more nodes and prediction rules.

4.7 The Knowledge Discovered and its Potential Use

This pilot study was the first attempt by the project sponsor (Netafim Irrigation Company) and the data provider (Yarden - Golan Heights Winery) to use state-of-the-art data mining techniques for knowledge discovery in an agricultural database.

As expected, some of the discovered relationships (such as Canopy Density affecting Canopy Score) have confirmed the early knowledge of the domain experts. Weather-related independent variables included in the single-objective models (see Figure 12) such as Standard Deviation of Total Rain during the Hibernation (Dormancy) period, can assist the winery to predict the grape and wine quality in future seasons based on the winter time precipitation data, which becomes available about six months before the harvest. The significant impact of the Field Code and the Year in the multi-objective models (see Figure 13) indicates that there is a considerable amount of unexplained variance in grape and wine quality across different grape fields and seasons. The wine-makers should search for additional field and season characteristics that, if recorded over years, may explain this variance.

5. Related Work

5.1 Mining of Agricultural Data

Corsi and Ashenfelter (2000, 2001) used regression models to estimate how a variety of subjective measures of wine quality are determined by the weather conditions during the relevant season. They have examined three different ratings of Italian wines defined on an ordinal scale of 4 to 12 levels. The determinants of the ordinal quality ratings have been found using an *ordered probit* model based on a latent continuous dependent variable that is assumed to represent the vintage quality. Each interval of this unobserved variable is associated with a specific experts' rating. The four explanatory variables represent total rainfalls (in millimeters) and the average monthly temperature during certain months of the season. The total summer rainfall was found as the only significant quality predictor (having a negative impact on the vintage quality). The predictive accuracy of the probit models varied between 48% and 69% *on the training data.*

Tarara *et al.* (2004) used linear regression models to estimate relationships between the tension in the support wire of the trellis and grapevine yield as a function of temperature, wind speed, time of season, and other factors. The data was collected from a controlled experiment performed in a single vineyard during one season, which was divided into five consecutive periods separated by agricultural events (bloom, veraison, etc.). For each period, a separate regression equation was calculated. A strong linear relationship between final yield and change in wire tension throughout the season has enabled to reach the average predictive accuracy within 10% to 14.5% of the mean yield.

A previous attempt to apply the data mining methodology to agricultural data is made by Wang *et al.* (2002). In their work, a time-based algorithm for mining sequential patterns is applied to a pest density database. The goal is to find relationships between three input attributes (temperature, humidity, and rainfall) and the target attribute (pest density). The algorithm of (Wang *et al.*, 2001) has found 22 sequential patterns in a pest database of 2,400 records covering a period of 19 years.

5.2 *Multi-Objective Classification Models and Algorithms*

Multi-Objective Classification is defined in (Last, 2004) as the task of simultaneously predicting the values of several class dimensions (dependent variables) for a given instance. The Multi-Objective Classification task is different from *Multitask Learning* described by Caruana in (Caruana, 1997). The explicit goal of Multitask Learning is to improve the accuracy of predicting the values of a *single-dimensional class* (defined as the *main* learning task) by training the classification model, such as a neural network or a decision tree, on several *related* tasks. This is called *inductive transfer* between learning tasks. As emphasized by Caruana, the only concern of Multitask Learning is the generalization accuracy of the model rather than its compactness and interpretability. In contrast to (Caruana, 1997), this case study was aimed at inducing multi-objective classification models for simultaneous prediction of *equally important* dependent variables associated with the same level of an information graph.

A multi-objective classifier called a *bloomy decision tree* is presented in (Suzuki *et al.*, 2001). Like ID3 and C4.5, it employs a "divide and conquer" strategy by recursively partitioning the training set. However, its leaf nodes (called *flower nodes*) may predict only a subset of class dimensions. Recursive partitioning along a given path continues as long as there are unpredicted class dimensions left. Consequently, the same path may include a "sandwich" of several flowers and split nodes, which need to be traversed in order to predict the values of all class dimensions. This approach increases the total number of internal nodes in a tree while reducing the number of dimensions predicted by smaller partitions of the training set.

Binary Decision Diagrams (Bryant, 1986) are commonly used in VLSI design, system testing, and other areas of computer science for representing single-output and multiple-output Boolean functions. A Binary Decision Diagram is a rooted acyclic graph containing two types of vertices: *non-terminal* vertices related to input variables and *terminal* vertices representing the possible output values of a Boolean function. A *Function Graph* (Bryant, 1986) is an *ordered* Binary Decision Diagram, where the input variables appear in the same order on every path of the graph.

As shown by Bryant in (Bryant, 1986), each Boolean function has a unique (up to isomorphism) reduced function graph representation, while any other function graph denoting the same function contains more vertices. Function graphs can be easily enhanced for representation of multi-input multi-output functions by constructing a *Shared Binary Decision Diagram* with multiple roots (one for each output variable). In data mining, the idea of inducing single-objective function graphs from real-world data has been introduced by Kohavi and Li (1995) in the form of *Oblivious Read-Once Decision Graphs (OODG)*. A similar model, called *Info-Fuzzy Networks (IFN)* (Maimon and Last, 2000), has been extended in (Last, 2004) for dealing with multi-objective functions.

6. Conclusions

Wine quality is measured in terms of several inter-related parameters that depend on multiple factors. In this study, we apply single-objective and multi-objective classification algorithms to a historical database collected by Yarden - Golan Heights Winery, where the number of recorded variables considerably exceeds the size of the datasets used in previous studies of wine quality (Corsi and Ashenfelter, 2000, 2001)(Tarara *et al.*, 2004). The induced models, represented as information graphs, reveal complex relationships between multiple levels of quality-related parameters. Each model is associated with a set of significant input attributes and represented as a set of probabilistic *if...then...* rules characterizing the most favorable / unfavorable conditions for certain quality levels. A comparative evaluation demonstrates the advantage of multi-objective models in terms of predictive accuracy at the possible expense of a minor increase in the model complexity. The obtained results have been characterized as novel and interesting by the domain experts at Yarden - Golan Heights Winery who are currently studying the detailed models to determine their practical implications for improving grape and wine quality in the forthcoming seasons.

Future studies may lead to more accurate and compact prediction models as a result of applying data mining techniques to larger and more diverse agricultural datasets. Specific directions for future research in knowledge discovery from agricultural datasets may include the following:

- *Feature Extraction.* Developing more sophisticated techniques for extracting useful features from time-dependent agricultural data.
- *Utility-Based Data Mining.* Incorporating utility factors, such as feature costs and product quality, in the knowledge discovery process.
- *Design of Experiments.* Utilizing data mining models for the design of agricultural experiments.

Acknowledgments

This work was partially supported by the Netafim Irrigation Company, Israel, and by the National Institute for Systems Test and Productivity at the University of South Florida under the USA Space and Naval Warfare Systems Command Grant No. N00039-01-1-2248. We thank the Yarden - Golan Heights Winery and the Israeli Meteorological Service for providing data for this study.

References

Bates, T. Fruit Development after Veraison. [http://lenewa.netsync.net/public/bates/BatesVER2001.htm] (last accessed February 2005).

Bisson, L. F.. *VEN 124 - Wine Production.* University of California at Davis, University Extension. [http://wineserver.ucdavis.edu/lfbisson/lecture.htm] (last accessed February 2005).

Bryant, R. E. (1986). Graph-based algorithms for Boolean function Manipulation. *IEEE Transactions on Computers*, C-**35**-8, pp. 677-691.

Caruana, R. (1997). Multitask Learning. *Machine Learning*, 28, pp. 41–75.

Corsi, A. and Ashenfelter, O. (2001). Wine quality: experts' ratings and weather determinants, in *71st EAAE Seminar "The Food Consumer in the Early 21st Century"*, Zaragoza, 19-20/4/2001, (CD ROM) pp. 135-154.

Corsi, A. and Ashenfelter, O. (2001). Predicting Italian wines quality from weather data and experts' ratings, *Oenometrics VII Conference*, Reims, May 11-13.

Cover, T.M. and Thomas, J.A. (1991). *Elements of Information Theory*. Wiley.

FAOSTAT data. (2004). [http://apps.fao.org/] (last accessed February 2005).

Gladstones, J. (1992). *Viticulture and Environment.* Winetitles, Adelaide.

Han, J. & Kamber, M. (2001). *Data Mining: Concepts and Techniques*. Morgan Kaufmann: San Francisco, CA, U. S. A.

Israel Meteorological Service [http://www.ims.gov.il/].

Kohavi, R. and Li, C.-H. (1995). Oblivious decision trees, graphs, and top-down pruning. in *Proc. of International Joint Conference on Artificial Intelligence (IJCAI)*, pp. 1071-1077.

Last, M. (2002). Online classification of nonstationary data streams. *Intelligent Data Analysis*, **6**(2), pp. 129-147.

Last, M. (2004). Multi-objective classification with Info-Fuzzy networks, in *Proceedings of the 15th European Conference on Machine Learning (ECML*

2004), Springer-Verlag, *Lecture Notes in Artificial Intelligence 3201*, pp. 239-249.

Last, M. Kandel, A. and Maimon, O. (2001). Information-theoretic algorithm for feature selection. *Pattern Recognition Letters*, **22**(6-7), pp. 799-811.

Last, M. and Maimon, O. (2004). A compact and accurate model for classification. *IEEE Transactions on Knowledge and Data Engineering*, **16**(2), pp. 203-215.

Last, M., Maimon, O. and Minkov, E. (2002). Improving stability of decision trees. *International Journal of Pattern Recognition and Artificial Intelligence*, **16**(2), pp. 145-159.

Maimon, O. and Last, M. (2000). *Knowledge Discovery and Data Mining – The Info-Fuzzy Network (IFN) Methodology*. Kluwer Academic Publishers.

Merriam-Webster Online Dictionary [http://www.webster.com/].

Netafim Irrigation Company [http://www.netafim.co.il/].

Peynaud, E. (1984). *Knowing and Making Wine*. Wiley-Interscience, New York, NY, U.S.A.

Phenology, The Study of Nature's Cycles of Life [http://www.sws-wis.com/lifecycles/].

Provost, F. & Domingos, P. (2003). Tree induction for probability-based ranking. *Machine Learning*, **52**, pp. 199–215.

Pyle, D. (1999). *Data Preparation for Data Mining*. Morgan Kaufmann, San Francisco, CA, U.S.A.

Quinlan, J. R. (1993). *C4.5: Programs for Machine Learning*. Morgan Kaufmann: San Francisco, CA, U.S.A.

Robinson, J. (1994). *The Oxford Companion to Wine*. Oxford University Press, Oxford, U. K.

Suzuki, E. Gotoh, M., and Choki, Y. (2001). Bloomy decision tree for multi-objective classification. L. De Raedt and A. Siebes (Eds.): *PKDD 2001*, LNAI 2168, pp. 436 –447.

Tarara, J. M., Ferguson, J. C., Blom, P. E., Pitts, M. J., and Pierce, F. J. (2004). Estimation of Grapevine Crop Mass and Yield via Automated Measurements of Trellis Tension. *Transactions of the ASAE*, **47**(2), 647–657.

Wine Institute, the Voice for California Wine. [http://www.wineinstitute.org/communications/statistics/] (last accessed February 2005).

Wang, Z. Xiong, F., and Hang, X. (2002). A New Algorithm for Mining Sequential Patterns and the Application in Agriculture. In *Proceedings of the World Congress of Computers in Agriculture and Natural Resources*, ASAE, pp. 622-628.

Yarden - Golan Heights Winery [http://www.golanwines.co.il].

Authors' Biographical Statements

Mark Last is currently a Senior Lecturer at the Department of Information Systems Engineering, Ben-Gurion University of the Negev, Israel and the Head of the Data Mining and Software Quality Lab. Prior to that, he was a Visiting Research Scholar at the National Institute for Systems Test and Productivity, University of South Florida, USA (Summer 2001, 2002, and 2003), Visiting Assistant Professor at the Department of Computer Science and Engineering, University of South Florida, USA (1999 – 2001), a Senior Consultant in Industrial Engineering and Computing (1994-1998), and the Head of Production Control Department at AVX Israel (1989-1994). He obtained his Ph.D. degree from Tel Aviv University, Israel. His main research interests are focused on data mining, multi-lingual text mining, cyber intelligence, and software assurance. He has developed a unified approach to knowledge discovery in databases called IFN (Info-Fuzzy Network), which has been applied by him to the real-world problems of classification, feature selection, anytime model induction, data quality assurance, and data stream mining.

Dr. Last is a Senior Member of the IEEE Computer Society and a Professional Member of the Association for Computing Machinery (ACM). He currently serves as an Associate Editor of IEEE Transactions on Systems, Man, and Cybernetics - Part C. Dr. Last has published over 120 papers and chapters in scientific journals, books, and refereed conferences. He is a co-author of two monographs and a co-editor of six edited volumes. He has also been a consultant to government institutions and industry.

Sigal Elnekave is currently a M.Sc. student in Information Systems Engineering at Ben-Gurion University of the Negev, Israel. She has obtained her B.Sc. degree from the same department in 2006. Her main research field is mining spatio-temporal data.

Amos Naor received his M.Sc. (1981) and Ph.D. (1988) degrees in soil science from the Hebrew University of Jerusalem, Israel. He is a research fellow in the Golan Research Institute of the University of Haifa, Israel since 1985, and serves as the scientific coordinator of research activities in deciduous orchards and winegrapes in the Northern R&D of Israel since 1995. Amos Naor has published over 40 papers and chapters in scientific journals, books, and refereed conferences. Amos Naor is an applied environmental physiologist and he is focused on: 1) Irrigation and crop load interactions in perennial trees; 2) Trees water relations; 3) Soil and plant water status indicators. His current research activities are: 1) Water stress indicators for irrigation scheduling, mainly concentrating on midday stem water potential; 2) Optimizing irrigation at different phenological stages in apple, pear, nectarine, prune, and cherry; almond 3) Modeling the effects of temperature and light intensity on apple sunscald.

Victor Schoenfeld received his degree in Fermentation Science (Enology) in 1988 from the University of California at Davis. After working at several prestigious wineries in California and France, Mr. Schoenfeld was appointed (1992) Chief Winemaker of Yarden- Golan Heights Winery, considered to be Israel's leading quality wine producer. Yarden- Golan Heights Winery is the leader in wine and vineyard research and development in Israel. Under Victor Schoenfeld's stewardship, the winery has established its own vine material propagation block (one of two in Israel), has carried out a joint research project on Botrytis cinerea growth with Baruch Sneh, Department of Plant Sciences and the Institute of Nature Conservation Research, Tel Aviv University, has established a network of meteorological stations, has partnered in a project resulting in the ability to correlate diurnal trunk diameter measurements to pressure bomb data, has been the pioneer in Israel in the use of NDVI and ECS technologies in wine vineyards and has established a complete small scale experimental winery. Yarden- Golan Heights winery has the largest agricultural database in Israel and has developed a unique system for data collection, storage and analysis. Victor Schoenfeld is a Professional Member of the American Society for Enology and Viticulture.

Chapter 8[1]

Enhancing Competitive Advantages and Operational Excellence for High-Tech Industry through Data Mining and Digital Management

Chen-Fu Chien, Shao-Chung Hsu, and Chia-Yu Hsu
Department of Industrial Engineering and Engineering Management, National Tsing Hua University, Hsin Chu, Taiwan. Email: cfchien@mx.nthu.edu.tw

Abstract: As global competition continues to intensity in high-tech industry such as the semiconductor industry, wafer fabs have been placing more importance on the increase of die yield and the reduction of costs. Because of automatic manufacturing and information integration technologies, a large amount of raw data has been increasingly accumulated from various sources. Mining potentially useful information from such large databases becomes very important for high-tech industry to enhance operational excellence and thus maintain competitive advantages. However, little research has been done on manufacturing data of high-tech industry. Due to the complex fabrication processes, the data integration, system design, and requirement for cooperation among domain experts, IT specialists, and statisticians, the development and deployment of data mining applications is difficult. This chapter aims to describe characteristics of various data mining empirical studies in semiconductor manufacturing, particularly defect diagnosis and yield enhancement. We analyze engineering data and manufacturing data in different cases and discuss specific needs for data preparation in light of different characteristics of these data. This study concludes with several critical success factors for the development of data mining applications in high-tech industry.

***Key Words*:** Data mining, Semiconductor manufacturing, Failure diagnosis, Decision analysis, Decision trees, Artificial neural network, Wafer acceptance test, Wafer bin map.

---

1 Liao, T.W. and E. Triantaphyllou, (Eds.), **Recent Advances in Data Mining of Enterprise Data: Algorithms and Applications**, *World Scientific*, Singapore, pp. 367-412, 2007.

1. Introduction

In high-tech industry like semiconductor manufacturing, reducing cycle time, producing high quality products, on-time delivery, continual reduction of costs and improving service capability are all direct and effective ways to create value for customers. The wafer fabrication process for producing integrated circuits (ICs) is very complex and typically has a long cycle time (Chien and Wu, 2003). Semiconductor fabrication facilities (fabs) can only maintain competitive advantages by effective control of process variation, fast yield ramp up, and quick response to yield excursion, especially when the complexity of the process and product increase rapidly (Chien & Shi, 2004; Chien et al., 2004; Cunningham et al., 1995; Leachman & Hodges, 1996).

Semiconductor fabrication consists of a lengthy sequence of complex physical-chemical processes on the surface of single crystal silicon wafers. The fabrication steps generally involve the cycling processes of thin-film deposition, oxidation, photolithography, thin-film etching, and ion implantation. The total number of process steps for wafer fabrication is generally more than 400. During fabrication, massive amounts of process data including lot history and tool history are collected. At the end of fabrication processes wafer acceptance test (WAT), which consists of a number of electrical tests, is performed on test keys distributed across the wafer to monitor the characteristics of fabricated ICs. The total test items may be more than 100 including the threshold voltage, channel length, channel width, and contact resistance. Once the wafers pass the wafer acceptance test, the functionality test is conducted on each die on the wafers in the wafer sort area. Finally, the wafers which pass all the tests are sent to assembly for packaging and the final test. Figure 1 illustrates the whole process.

Owing to the rise of e-commerce and information technology (IT), a large amount of data has been automatically or semi-automatically collected in modern industry. Information technology allows structuring of information-intensive cooperation and work distribution in a more flexible way (Liu et al., 1998). Over the last decade, most semiconductor manufacturers have developed their own solutions for data analysis because of the lack of appropriate commercial solutions to meet

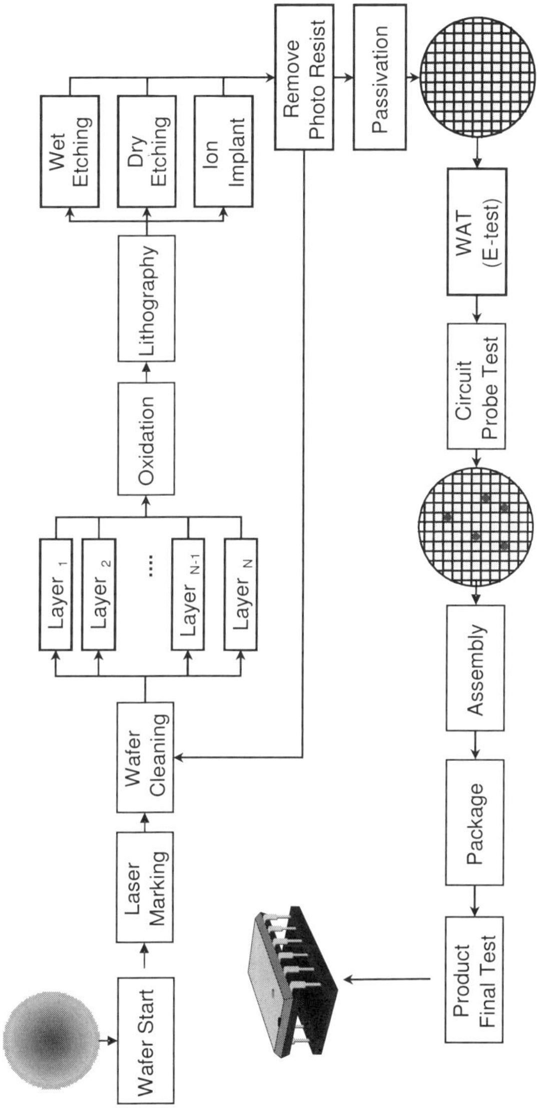

Figure 1. The semiconductor manufacturing process.

industrial needs in real setting. This kind of solutions has been called Engineering Data Analysis (EDA) systems for many years. An EDA system is an off-line analysis-oriented information system that is integrated with databases, data analysis methodologies, and user interface (Peng & Chien, 2003). For a semiconductor company with multiple products and multiple processes, the volume of the collected data from wafer fabrication to the final test daily is very huge.

The challenge today is not only to integrate all these data into a single data repository but also to use statistical methods and data analysis techniques to transform these collected data into useful information to support engineers (Chien et al., 2007). Mining potentially useful information from such a large database becomes very important in both research and application. Decision makers may potentially use the information buried in large databases to support their decisions through data mining possibly by identifying specific patterns in the data. For example, any defect problems in semiconductor manufacturing should be quickly detected and the root causes should then be resolved in order to reduce the loss of hundreds of thousands of dollars in scraped wafers as soon as possible. However, engineers need to analyze large amounts of data collected from the Computer Integrated Manufacturing (CIM) system, metrology tools and testers to identify the root causes. Effective data mining methodologies and related applications are needed here to assist engineers to solve the problems in a timely manner.

2. Knowledge Discovery in Databases and Data Mining

In the age of digital information, knowledge management becomes more and more important to industry. How to retrieve the knowledge is critical in knowledge management. Taking advantage of the progress in information technology (IT), large amounts of data are recorded in a data warehouse or data mart. Such data can provide a rich resource for knowledge discovery from databases and decision support. To discover hidden knowledge, unexpected patterns, and new rules from a large database, special techniques different from conventional tools are needed.

Data mining has been proposed to understand, analyze, and effectively use such data (Peng & Chien, 2003). Data mining is the process of discovering interesting knowledge from large amounts of data stored either in databases, data warehouses, or other information repositories using a multidisciplinary approach (Fu, 1997). Other researchers use another term "Knowledge Discovery in Database" (KDD) to define the nontrivial process of identifying valid, novel, potentially useful, and ultimately understandable patterns in data (Fayyad et al., 1996). Figure 2 illustrates the major steps of the data mining process that include problem definition, selection of the data, preprocessing of the data, building the model, and using the model.

Each of the following steps is indispensable in order to ensure the effectiveness and the quality of data mining.

(1) Problem definition is to define the problem to be solved by understanding the background knowledge and to make a clear statement of the data mining objectives. Depending upon the problem definition and domain knowledge, the problem will be turned into a data mining application, which calls for some specific analysis skills.
(2) Data selection is to identify all internal or external available sources of information, and to select subsets of identified data needed for analysis. These data may be relevant to solve the problem identified in the previous step. Data selection usually depends on the defined problem, which was determined by the type of targeted application.
(3) Data pre-processing is performed prior to building the model, and it can substantially improve the overall quality and reduce the processing time of data mining. There are several data pre-processing techniques. Data integration merges data from multiple sources into a coherent data store. Data cleaning is applied to remove noisy data, identify outliers, fill in missing data, and correct inconsistencies. Data transformation is to transform or consolidate the data in a form appropriate for mining. For instance, many decision trees used for classification require grouping of continuous data into a finite number of bins. Data reduction can reduce the data size by aggregation, by eliminating redundant feature, or by selecting instances (Han & Kamber, 2001).

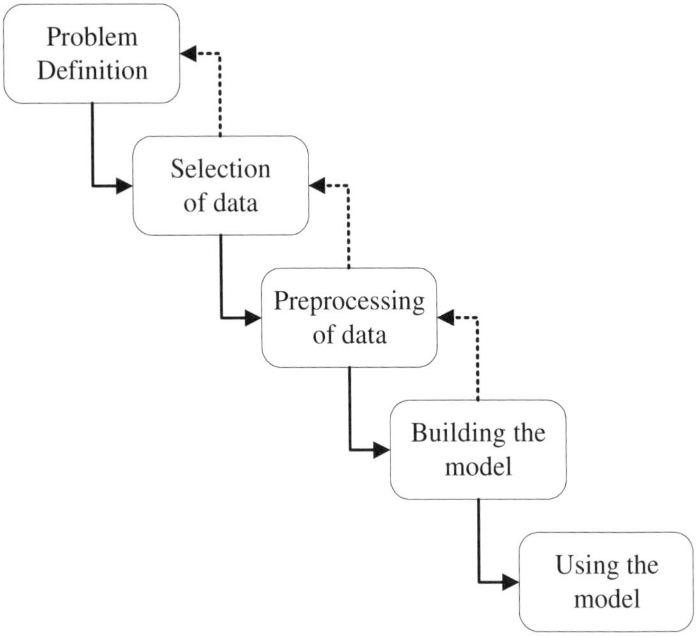

Figure 2. The major data mining steps.

(4) Building the model is the most important step in the data mining process and it is often accomplished through an iterative process. In this step, we need to explore several alternative models to find the best one to solve the given problem. When trying to build a model, we must choose a modelling technique; the technique may be a decision tree, a logistic regression, or a neural network, and this chosen technique will affect the data preparation. After building the model we evaluate the result and try to interpret it, and identify those which should be further explored.

(5) Finally, the data mining results may range from their simple use as part of the input to a decision process, to its full integration into an end-user application. The results can also be used in a knowledge-based system or decision support system.

Data mining has been shown to be useful in several application areas, including finance, health-care, marketing, law, science, and education.

The typical applications involve market basket analysis, target customer identification, and fraud detection of credit card usage. For example, a supermarket can carry out market basket analysis by going through the transactions of customers to find out consumer behaviours such as the famous beer-and-diaper purchasing pattern. Furthermore, data mining also plays a critical role in e-manufacturing for semiconductor fabrication, including advanced process control and advanced equipment control (APC/AEC) (Chien & Hsu, 2006). For example, Hsu et al. (2005) developed a multi-scale Principal Component Analysis (PCA) for fault detection and classification in semiconductor manufacturing.

2.1 Problem Types for Data Mining in the High-Tech Industry

The model functions of data mining are very diverse because many types of patterns may exist in a large database. Different methods and techniques are needed to find different kinds of patterns. Based on the patterns we are looking for, the type of problems in data mining can be categorized into association, clustering, classification, and prediction (Han & Kamber, 2001; Fu, 1997; Fayyad et al., 1996).

Association is the discovery of association rules showing attribute-value conditions that occur frequently together in a given dataset (Peng et al., 2004). A popular application of association is market basket analysis, which finds the buying habits of customers by searching for sets of items that are frequently purchased together.

Clustering is the process of dividing a dataset into several different groups called clusters. The objects within a cluster are very similar to each other and dissimilar to the objects in the other clusters.

Classification derives a function or model that identifies the categorical class of an object based on its attributes. A classification model usually is constructed by analysing the relationship between the attributes and the classes of the objects in the training dataset.

Prediction is a model that predicts a continuous value or future data trends. For example, linear regression including one response variable Y and some predictor variable X_i can be applied. A bivariate linear regression model is as follows:

$$Y=a+bX,$$

where a represents the intercept and b is the slope of this line. Other prediction models such as polynomial regression, logistic regression and Poisson regression can also be used to forecast some other continuous value data. For example, Chien et al. (2005) employed data mining to predict the lengthy cycle time for wafer fabrication to improve the accuracy of the committed due date and to enhance the customer satisfaction.

2.2 Data Mining Methodologies

Through the data mining process, hidden information can be explored to support decisions. Indeed, a number of data mining tools can be implemented for different problems. Two general methods that have been widely applied in semiconductor manufacturing are briefly explained next:

2.2.1 Decision Trees

A decision tree is a flow-chart-like tree structure where the root is at the top and the leaves at the bottom (e.g., see Figure 3). The root node contains the entire dataset and the tree grows through several tests on the attributes; each branch represents the outcomes of the test, and the leaves indicate classes or class distributions. Each path from the root node to a leaf can be interpreted as a rule. For example, a decision rule can be derived as follows: If "Size" is "medium" and "Transmission" is "auto", then the "Price" of the car is "medium", from the decision tree that represents the knowledge for car prices as shown in Figure 3. A decision tree can represent a classification system or a predictive model.

Decision tree methods are a good choice when the data mining model is used for either classification or prediction. A decision tree can be used to extract models to describe important data classes or to predict future data trends. Decision trees have been applied in various areas including medicine, business, and fault detection. They are the basis of several commercial rule induction systems. Many challenges in using the decision tree method include performance in terms of accuracy, scalability, evolving datasets, and unexplored new applications.

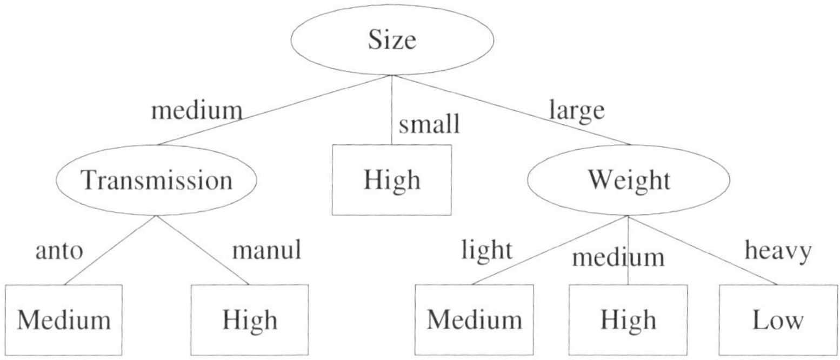

Figure 3. A decision tree for car prices.

2.2.1.1 Decision tree construction

A dataset must be prepared to construct a decision tree model. Each instance in this dataset has several predictor attributes and one target variable. If the target variable is categorical, the tree is called a classification tree. On the other hand, if the target variable is continuous, the tree is called a regression tree. There are two general strategies for decision tree construction, one is called exploring and the other is called forecasting. If we want to explain the dataset by means of a decision tree, we can choose the exploring strategy. We can set the original dataset as training dataset without partition. On the other hand, we choose the forecasting strategy if we intend to use the decision tree to predict future data. In this case, we partition the original dataset into the training dataset for growing a full decision tree and the testing dataset for estimating the real accuracy and for pruning the tree in order to improve the prediction accuracy. The testing dataset is not for growing a tree.

Several algorithms have been developed to construct a decision tree. CHAID (Chi-squared Automatic Interaction Detection) is a non-binary decision tree that determines the best multi-way partitions of the data on the basis of some significance tests (Kass, 1980). CHAID is designed specifically to deal with categorical variables. CART (classification and regression tree) is a binary decision tree with the Gini-index of diversity as the splitting criterion, and it is pruned by minimizing the true misclassification error estimate (Breiman et al., 1984). CART can deal with both categorical and continuous variables. C4.5 is a variant and extension of the well-known decision tree algorithm ID3 (Quinlan, 1993). The splitting criterion of the C4.5 algorithm is the gain ratio that expresses the proportion of information generated by a split. The error-based criterion is used in C4.5 for pruning. Lim et al. (2000) compared the prediction accuracy, complexity, and training time of thirty-three classification algorithms, and indicated that decision trees produce good accuracy and are easily interpretable.

The entire decision tree construction process can be divided into three basic elements: growing the tree, pruning the tree, and extracting rules from the tree. Those elements are illustrated in Figure 4.

The key operation in growing a decision tree is to select a split such that the descendent nodes are purer than the data in the parent node. When a training dataset enters the root node of a decision tree, a test is performed to search for all possible splits for all attributes using a splitting criterion, which measures the quality of a possible split. By calculating the value of the splitting criterion of each possible split, the best discriminating attribute is chosen and the child node to be split next is determined. Various splitting criteria have been used in many different decision tree algorithms. They include entropy reduction, Gini-index of diversity, Chi-square test, F-test, variance reduction, and so on. The entropy reduction, Gini-index of diversity and Chi-square test are for a categorical target, and the F-test and variance reduction are for a continuous target. Splitting will be stopped if the splitting criterion fails to be satisfied. For example, if the F-test is insignificant for all attributes, then the splitting will be stopped.

The purpose of pruning is to improve the predictive accuracy of a tree model by removing some tree branches. The size of an over-fitted tree might be too big with some branches inducing anomalies in the training data due to noise or outliers. It is well known that the size of the overall tree strongly influences the tree performance (Breiman et al., 1984).

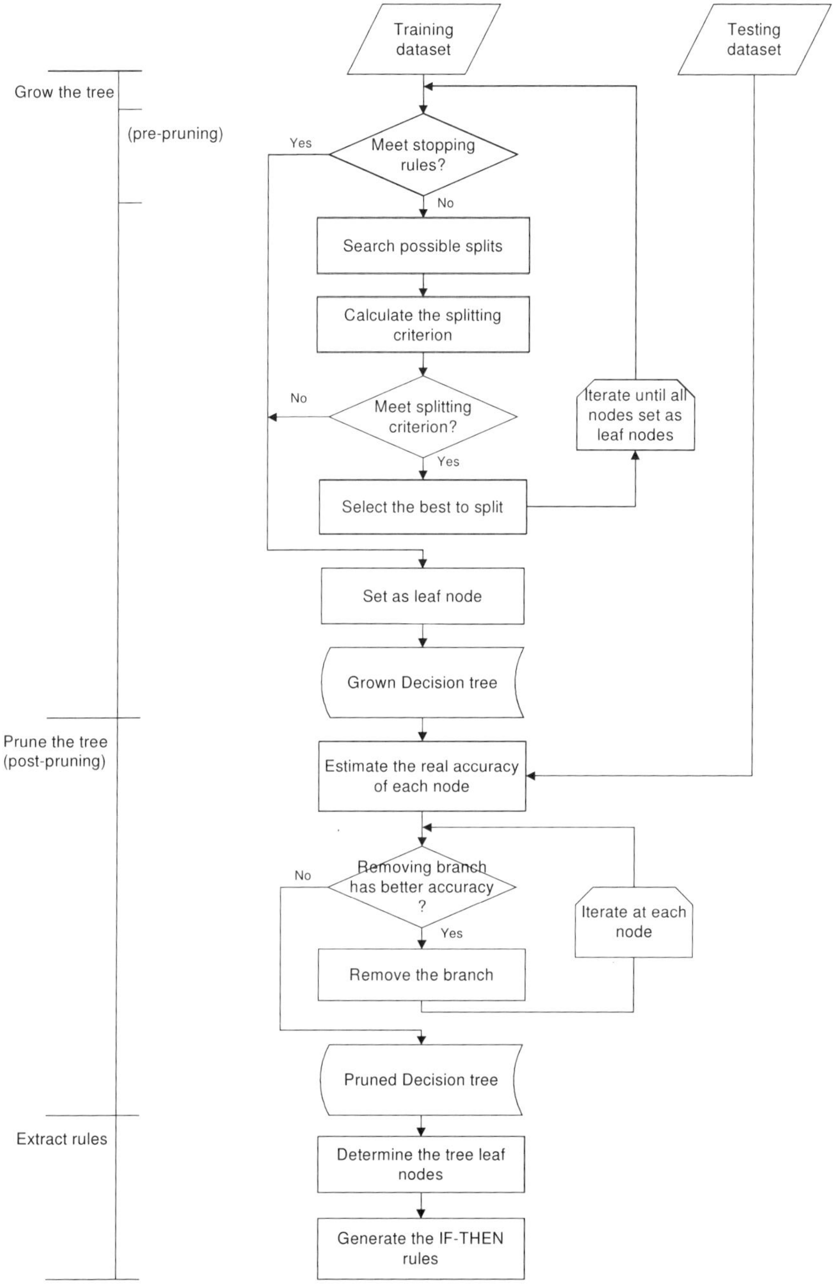

Figure 4. Decision tree construction step.

There are two different approaches to decision tree pruning; one is pre-pruning and the other is post-pruning. In the pre-pruning approach, a tree is pruned by preventing further splitting based on some stopping rules such as follows:

- All instances reaching a node belong to the same class.
- All instances reaching a node have the same attribute vector but not necessarily belong to the same class.
- The number of instances in a node is less than a certain threshold. For example, the number of instances in a leaf node must be no less than 5.

The post-pruning approach removes some branches after the tree has been grown. Some methods use a statistical measure to estimate the accuracy of each node and remove the least reliable branches. Several post-pruning approaches such as cost-complexity pruning (Breiman et al., 1984) and error-based pruning (Quinlan, 1993) have been implemented as an extension of a decision tree method.

To better understand the tree model, the knowledge in the decision tree should be extracted (Han & Kamber, 2001). One rule can be created for each path from the root node to a leaf node in the form of an If-Then rule. All attribute values along a path form a conjunction in the rule antecedent (the If part) whereas the leaf node determines the predicted class or value with the plurality rule, forming the rule consequent (the Then part). For example, if attribute "X" is less than "5", then the target belongs to class "A". The If-Then rules extracted from a decision tree are easier for humans to understand.

If the tree size is large, there may be some redundant rules. One can remove any condition in its antecedent that does not improve the performance of the rule. For example, consider the following rule "If attribute X is less than 30, and attribute Y equals U or C, and attribute Y equals C, and attribute X is less than 20, then the target belongs to class A". This rule can be reduced to "If attribute Y equals C, and attribute X is less than 20, then the target belongs to class A". In addition, one can merge some rules that are similar to each other. For example, consider one rule such as "If attribute X is A then target belongs to class C", and the other rule such as "If attribute X is B, then target belongs to class C".

Then these two rules can be merged as a new rule: "If attribute X is A or B, then the target belongs to class C".

2.2.1.2 CART

CART (classification and regression tree) builds binary decision trees with the Gini-index of diversity as the splitting criterion (Breiman et al., 1984). For a given node t, the node impurity defined by Gini-index is as follows:

$$i(t) = 1 - \sum_i p_i^2 , \quad (1)$$

where p_i is the proportion of class i in node t. For all possible splits in the values for all attributes, the goodness of a split s is calculated as follows:

$$\Delta i(s,t) = i(t) - p_L i(t_L) - p_R i(t_R) , \quad (2)$$

where t_L and t_R are the left and right child nodes of t and p_L and p_R are the probabilities of instances in those child nodes. If $\Delta i(s,t) > 0$, it means that the descendent nodes are purer than the data in the parent node. If $\Delta i(s,t) \leq 0$, it means that the descendent nodes are not purer than the data in the parent node. By exhaustive searching all possible splits, CART chooses the split $s*$ that causes the maximum reduction in impurity such that $\Delta i(s^*,t) = \max_{s \in S} \Delta i(s,t)$.

A grown decision tree will have an apparent error rate of zero or close to zero on the training dataset from which the tree was built. However, the error rate of the decision tree may not be true due to noise or outliers in the training dataset. The purpose of pruning is to improve the prediction accuracy by removing some branches that produce the least true error. A simple pruning approach is as follows: Start from the bottom of the tree and examine each node and subtree. If replacement of this subtree with a leaf or with its most frequently used branch would lead to a lower true error rate, then prune the tree accordingly.

CART utilizes the cost-complexity function to prune the decision tree. Cost complexity is a function which is the weighted sum of its complexity (i.e., the number of leaf nodes) and its error on the training dataset. The testing dataset can be used primarily to determine an appropriate weighting. Given a critical value of α and a tree T, the cost-complexity function is defined as follows:

$$R_\alpha(T) = R(T) + \alpha|\tilde{T}|, \tag{3}$$

where $|\tilde{T}|$ is the number of leaf nodes in T. $R_\alpha(T)$ is a linear combination of the cost of the tree and its complexity. For each α, there is a tree T that minimizes the cost-complexity. As α increases, the tree gets shorter. As α is equal to zero, the pruned tree and the original tree are the same. There will be a sequence of decreasing cost-complexity subtrees in the pruning process. Their corresponding true error rates can be determined by a testing dataset or cross-validation datasets. As the cost-complexity decreases, the true error rate will also decrease until it reaches a minimum and then it increases again. Obviously, the final pruned tree is determined as the one with the minimum true error rate.

2.2.1.3 C4.5

C4.5 is a variant and extension of a well-known decision tree algorithm, the ID3 (Quinlan, 1993). ID3 utilizes an entropy criterion for splitting nodes. Given a node t, the splitting criterion of ID3 defined by the entropy criterion is:

$$\text{Entropy}(t) = -\sum_i p_i \log p_i\,, \tag{4}$$

where p_i is the proportion of class i in node t. An attribute and split are selected in a way that maximizes entropy reduction. Each split in the decision tree can produce two or more direct descendants. In C4.5, the splitting criterion is the gain ratio that expresses the proportion of the information generated by a split. An attribute and a split are selected that maximize the gain ratio. The calculation of the gain ratio is as follows:

1) Define the "info" at node t as the entropy

$$\text{info}(t) = -\sum_i p_i \log p_i \tag{5}$$

2) Suppose t is split into child nodes $t_1, \ldots, t_n$, by attribute X. Define

$$\text{info}_X = \sum_i \text{info}(t_i)N(t_i)/N(t) \tag{6}$$

$$\text{gain}(X) = \text{info}(t) - \text{info}_X(t) \tag{7}$$

$$\text{split\_info}(t) = -\sum_i N(t_i)/N(t)\log_2\{N(t_i)/N(t)\} \tag{8}$$

$$\text{gain\_ratio}(X) = \frac{\text{gain}(X)}{\text{split\_info}(X)} \tag{9}$$

C4.5 also selects the best split by exhaustive search. If $\text{gain\_ratio}(X) > 0$, it means that the descendent nodes are purer than the data in the parent node. If $\text{gain\_ratio}(X) \leq 0$, it means that the descendent nodes are not purer than the data in the parent node.

C4.5 uses a significance test that compares a parent node to its descendants. This pruning method is called error-based pruning. A leaf t can be considered as a statistical sample and it is possible to estimate a confidence interval for the probability of misclassification of t. Under the assumption that errors in the training dataset are binomially distributed with probability p, the pruning process can be implemented as follows:

(1) Suppose $NE(t)$ learning instances are misclassified in node t
(2) C4.5 estimates the true misclassification probability with the upper 75% confidence bound p where

$$\sum_{i=0}^{N_E(t)} \frac{N(t)!}{i!(N(t)-i)!} p^i (1-p)^{N_E(t)-i} = 0.25 \tag{10}$$

(3) Let $v1 = 2(N(t) - N_E(t) + 1)$, $v2 = 2N_E(t)$ and $F_{v1,v2;0.75}$ be the 75% percentile of the $F_{v1,v2}$ distribution. Then

$$p = 1 - \frac{N_E(t)}{N_E(t) + (N(t) - N_E(t) + 1)F_{v1,v2;.075}} \tag{11}$$

(4) The misclassification cost at t is estimated by $N(t)p$. A branch is pruned if its estimated cost is larger than the cost at its root node.

2.2.1.4 CHAID

CHAID (Chi-squared Automatic Interaction Detector) (Kass, 1980) builds non-binary decision trees which determine the best multi-way partitions of the data. The split at each node is based on a Chi-square analysis of the attributes and target variable. CHAID sorts categorical attribute levels based on the target variable and uses the Chi-square test as the splitting criterion for each attribute. If neighboring levels do not have significant differences, these levels will be merged together. CHAID considers all possible merges and determines the best attribute to split on. There is no pruning in CHAID.

CHAID also uses the Bonferroni method to calculate the significance for multiple testing. The CHAID Bonferroni multipliers depend on the type of attributes. There are three attribute types: monotonic, free and floating.

- Monotonic: categories lie on an ordinal scale.
- Free: categories are purely nominal.
- Floating: ordinal categorical with exception of a single category that either does not belong to the rest or whose position on the ordinal scale is unknown, e.g., it is the "missing" category.

Suppose an attribute with the original categories is merged into a new one. Then the Bonferroni multiplier is defined as follows:

$$\text{Monotonic:} \quad B = \binom{c-1}{r-1}$$

$$\text{Free:} \quad B = \sum_{i=0}^{r-1} (-1)^i \frac{(r-i)^c}{i!(r-i)!}$$

$$\text{Floating:} \quad B = \binom{c-2}{r-2} + r\binom{c-2}{r-1}$$

Let α_1, α_2 ($\alpha_1 > \alpha_2$) and α_3 be the given significance levels. Then the CHAID algorithm is summarized as follows:

(1) For each attribute X, cross-tabulate categories of X with categories of Y.

(2) Find the allowable (according to the type of attribute) pair of categories of X whose 2 × J sub-table is least significant. If the p-

value > α_1, merge the two categories, consider the merger a single category and repeat this step.

(3) For each compound category containing three or more of the original categories, find the most significant binary split (constrained by the type of attribute). If the p-value < α_2, split the compound category and return to Step 2.

(4) Compute the Bonferroni-corrected p-value of the χ^2 statistic for each merged attribute.

(5) If the smallest corrected p-value < α_3, split the node according to the merged categories of the chosen attribute. Otherwise, we set the node as a leaf node.

CHAID is designed to deal with categorical variables. Continuous variables must be grouped into a finite number of bins to create categories. Continuous variables are typically sorted and then are divided into equally populated bins. The "equally populated bins" are groups, each with the same number of samples. For example, if there are 1,000 instances, creating 10 equally populated bins will result in 10 bins, each containing 100 instances.

The KS algorithm, a modification of the CHAID algorithm, uses the F-test as the splitting criterion when the target variable is continuous. The KS algorithm selects the pair of categories of the attribute which is most similar on the basis of an F-test considering only pairs which can be merged, and it calculates the significance of each of the sets of groupings of categories using the F-test. Table 1 provides a summary of all decision tree algorithms described above.

2.2.2 Artificial Neural Networks

Artificial Neural Networks (ANNs) is a popular methodology for data modelling and analysis since 1980. The ANN idea was introduced to simulate the training mechanism of a biological neural network, which is consisted of many simple units, called neurons, and connections with each other.

The neurons operate only on their local data and on the inputs they receive via a connection. Comparing with the operation of a biological neuron, the neurons of an ANN adjust the weights of inputs, then summarize and transform them to outputs by a specified mathematical function.

Table 1. Summary of decision tree algorithms.

	CART	C4.5	CHAID
Splitting criterion for categorical target	Gini-index	Gain ratio	Chi-square test
Splitting criterion for continuous target	Variance reduction	Variance reduction	F-test
Number of branches for categorical target	2	2 or more	2 or more
Number of branches for continuous target	2	2	2 or more
Pruning method	Cost-complexity pruning	Error-based pruning	None

The architecture of a neural network can be divided into three levels:

- The processing element (PE) or neuron: the basic unit to compose the network. The functions of a PE include the summation function, the activity function, and the transfer function. The summation function is to sum the input (X) from other units and the network connections (W). The purpose of the activity function is to integrate the summation function and the current status of the PE. The transfer function is to transfer the activity function into the output of the PE. Figure 5 illustrates the function of the process element. Two mathematical functions frequently used as the summation function are as follows:

$$\text{Weighted summation: } I_j = \sum_i W_{ij} X_i$$

$$\text{Euclidian distance: } I_j = \sum_i (X_i - W_{ij})^2$$

The frequently used activity functions include directly using the summation function as the activity function, adding to the prior summation function, and adding to the prior activity function. Three mathematical functions usually applied as the transform function are as follows:

The Step function: $f(x)=\begin{cases}1 & if\ x\geq\theta\\ 0 & if\ x<\theta\end{cases}$

The Sigmoid function: $f(x)=\dfrac{1}{1+e^{(-a(x-\theta))}}\quad(0<f(x)<1)$

The Hyperbolic tangent function:

$$f(x)=\frac{1-e^{(-a(x-\theta))}}{1+e^{(-a(x-\theta))}}\quad(-1<f(x)<1)$$

- Layer: A layer is formulated by several similar processing elements. There are three types of layers used in neural networks, which include normalized output, competitive output and competitive learning. The purpose of the normalized output is to normalize the original output vector of the same layer into a unit length vector; the competitive output is to choose the best neuron from the original output in the same layer and set its value to 1 (winner), others to 0; the competitive learning is to adjust the weights of the connection to the winner neuron.
- Network: The network operation can be divided into two major processes: the learning process to adjust the connection weights by learning from the training set, and the recalling process to generate the output for a given input.

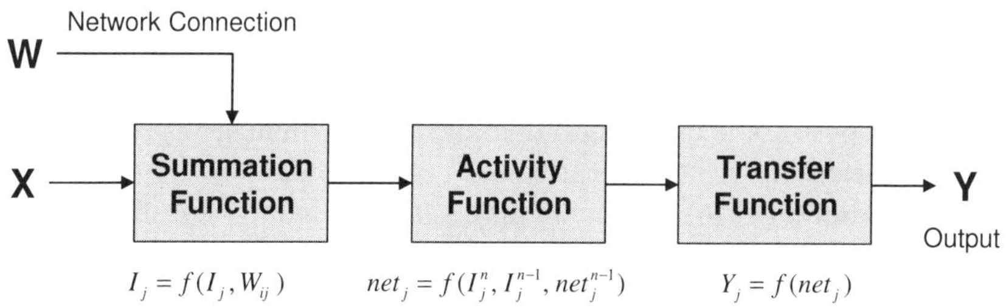

Figure 5. Function of the processing element.

There are several characteristics of ANNs that are different from other analytical tools like statistical methods:

a) Experience knowledge is acquired, stored, and utilized by the ANNs through a learning process which is independent from prior assumptions.
b) ANNs normally have great potential for parallelism.
c) ANNs are useful for classification/prediction and function approximation/mapping problems.
d) For linear and non-linear data types, ANNs are effective.

According to the learning strategy, we can divide them into three major categories: associate leaning networks, supervised learning networks, and unsupervised learning networks.

2.2.2.1 Associate learning network

An associate learning network is learning from the status variables, keeps rules in the network and applies a new case with incomplete status to estimate the complete status. The typical applications include pattern extraction and noise filtering. The Hopfield neural networks and the annealed neural networks are two frequently used algorithms for Associate Learning Networks.

<u>Hopfield Neural Networks (HNNs)</u>

A Hopfield neural network (Hopfield, 1982) is an auto-associative learning network, which is provided with many training patterns in advance to memorize their characteristics in the network, then input an incomplete vector to associate it to the nearest training pattern. It can also be applied to an optimization application, which is subject to certain constraints in order to find the optimal conditions for some specific objectives (energy functions).

The steps to solve the general optimization problem are as follows:

(1) Determine the status variables.
(2) Determine the status requirements including constraints and objectives.

(3) Choose an energy function to evaluate the solution. This is usually done by selecting the Liapunov function as the energy function:

$$E = (-\frac{1}{2})\sum_i \sum_j X_i W_{ij} X_j + \sum_j \theta_j X_j$$

(4) Set up the network parameters (W_{ij} and θ_j).

(5) Network associated learning: Input initial status variables and update the network literately until converging to the lowest value of the energy function:

$$X_j^{n+1} = f(\sum_i W_{ij} X_i^n - \theta_i) = \begin{cases} 1 & if \ \sum_i W_{ij} X_i^n - \theta_i > 0 \\ X_j^n & if \ \sum_i W_{ij} X_i^n - \theta_i = 0 \\ 0 & if \ \sum_i W_{ij} X_i^n - \theta_i = 0 \end{cases}$$

Annealed Neural Networks (AnNNs)

The annealed neural network (Van den Bout & Miller, 1989) approach was developed from the simulated annealing algorithm, which was applied to probabilistic hill-climbing search to avoid the local optimal problem often seen in other algorithms. The applications of AnNNs are focused on solving the optimization problems, which include the travelling salesman problem and the graph partitioning problem. The advantages of applying AnNNs include near-optimal results and quick convergence like HNN.

The AnNN algorithm can be described as follows:

(1) Set up the initial status variable *X*.
(2) Set up the initial temperature of the simulated annealing, *T*.
(3) Calculate the initial energy function *E*.
(4) Repeat the following steps until the energy function converges to a small value.
(5) For *i* = 1 to *n* Do

Calculate the energy gap of the ith neuron ΔE_i

Calculate the new status variable of the ith neuron X_i, where

$$X_i \propto \exp(-\Delta E_i / T)$$

Continue

(6) Calculate the new energy function E.

(7) Reduce the temperature T and go to step (4).

2.2.2.2 Supervised learning networks

A supervised learning network uses an existing training set with input and output variables, and constructs the internal mapping rules for the inputs and outputs by training. A new case with only input variable values is fed into the learned network to forecast its output value. The applications of supervised learning networks include classification and prediction. There are two main steps to construct such a model:

(1) The training phase: The correct results (target values or desired outputs) are known and are given to the ANN model during training so that the model can adjust its weights to try to match its outputs to the target values.

(2) The validation phase: The model is tested for a set of unseen input values to check how close the generated outputs are to the correct target values.

There are two major kinds of supervised learning ANN: Back-Propagation Networks (BPNs) and Radial Basis Function Neural Networks (RBFs).

Back-Propagation Networks (BPNs)

The most widely used ANN is the back-propagation networks. It is the first model to include a hidden layer to determine the connection weights by iterative learning (Werbos, 1974; Parker, 1985). A BPN learns by cases with some input examples and the known correct output for each case. The BPN applies the gradient steepest descent method to minimize the error between the neuron output and the estimated output.

The architecture of a BPN includes an input layer, one or more hidden layer and an output layer. The input layer is to process the input variables. The number of neurons is dependent on the problem. The hidden layer is to map the interactions between the input variables. A non-linear function such as the sigmoid function is usually employed in the hidden layer. It is possible to have more than one hidden layer in the network. The output layer is to produce the network output. The number of neurons is dependent on the problem, and the output neurons also make use of non-linear functions.

The BPN learning process can be described as follows:

(1) Set up the weight of each neuron randomly.
(2) One training example is fed to the network and the network produces some output based on the current weights of the neurons.
(3) The model output is compared to the known correct output, and a mean squared error is calculated. The error value is then propagated backward through the network, and small changes are made to the weights in each layer.
(4) If the error value drops below a pre-determined threshold, then stop; otherwise, the learning process is repeated for each of the remaining training examples, then go back again to the first example.

Radial Basis Function Neural Networks (RBF)

The idea of the Radial Basis Function Neural Networks (RBF) was proposed in (Duda & Hart, 1973) to avoid the long training process of BPNs, i.e., to improve the network learning efficiency. RBF networks are feed-forward, but have only one hidden layer. An RBF network can learn an arbitrary mapping, while the primary difference is in the hidden layer. The hidden layer neurons represent a series of centres in the input data space. Each of these centres has an activation function based on the Gaussian distribution. The activation depends on the distance between the presented input vector and the centre. One advantage of RBF networks over BPNs is that, if the input signal is non-stationary, the localized nature of the hidden layer response makes the networks less susceptible to "memory loss". Till now, RBF networks have been successfully applied to many areas like stock price forecasting, voice recognition, quality control and fraud detection.

The RBF learning process can be described as follows:

(1) Decide the number of neurons in the hidden layer.
(2) For each neuron, decide the centre (mean) and sharpness (standard deviation) of their Gaussian distribution.
(3) Train the output layer.

2.2.2.3 Unsupervised learning networks

The method of learning by using an unsupervised neural network is unique in that the network is given a set of inputs without any indication of what the output should be. We can divide unsupervised learning networks into two categories: (1) the input variable is binary taking 0 or 1 as its value; (2) the input variable is continuous. There are two major kinds of unsupervised learning ANNs: Self-Organizing Maps (SOMs) and the Adaptive Resonance Theory (ART).

Self-Organizing Maps (SOMs)

Self-Organization map (Kohonen, 1995) was inspired from the particular characteristic of the human brain structure that gathers similar functions in a specific area. After the learning process, the neighbourhood weights will be adjusted. The learning process is competitive and unsupervised. This means that only one output map node is activated at a time corresponding to each input. A SOM constructs a topology which preserves mapping from the high dimension space onto output neurons in such a way that relative distances between data points are preserved. The neurons of the output map usually form a two dimensional shape such as a square, a circle or a rectangle. Since the data points with similar attributes are gathered in a neighbourhood, the SOM can thus serve as a clustering tool of high-dimensional data. The advantages of SOMs include easy visualization, and the capability to interpolate between previously encountered inputs. The SOM structure includes an input layer, an output layer and the connections between the input layer and the output layer.

The SOM algorithm is described as follows:

(1) Calculate the distance between the training example and each output neuron. The Euclidian distance is usually applied here.
(2) Find out the winning neuron (winner): The winner is the output neuron having the shortest distance with the training example, among all output neurons.
(3) Adjust the weights of the input and the output layer. The weights are adjusted by adding:
$\Delta W_{ij} = \eta \cdot (X - W_{ij}) \cdot f(R, r_j)$,

where η is the learning rate of the network, R is the neighbourhood radius, r_j is the neighbourhood distance between the input data and the neighbourhood centre in the topological coordinates. The expression $f(R, r_j)$ is the neighbourhood function to express the relationship between the neighbourhood radius and the neighbourhood distance. Frequently-used neighbourhood functions include the exponential, the power, or the step function.

(4) The training cycle is defined as all the training examples are executed from Steps 1-3. The neighbourhood radius and the learning rate are reduced when completing a training cycle.

Adaptive Resonance Theory (ART)

The Adaptive Resonance Theory (ART) has been applied in many areas including pattern recognition and spatial analysis. ART is derived from the adaptive resonant feedback between two layers of neurons (Carpenter & Grossberg, 1988). To manage the variety of input, ART has the following characteristics: (1) balance on stability and plasticity, (2) match and reset, and (3) balance on search and direct access. ART solves the stability-plasticity dilemma that is caused by learning new data, which in turn leads to unstable conditions and loss of data. Several algorithms have been derived from the original ART, which include ART1, ART2, ART3, ARTMAP, and Fuzzy ART. The ART1 algorithm is described next to illustrate the operation of an ART network.

(1) Assume that the status vector and the input signal in the short-term memory (STM) at the comparison level, *F1*, are given by *X* and *S*, respectively; the status vector and the input signal at the recognition level, *F2*, are given by *Y* and *T*, respectively. The output vector from top to down is given by *U*. The pattern vector of feed forward (from *F1* to *F2*) is given by *V*.

(2) Set up the initial values: The neurons of the recognition level *F2* are in the steady status. The initial status at the comparison level *F1* is set to $x_i = c_1$. The initial values of the weights from *F1* to *F2* are given by $Wb_{ij} = \lambda_j$,

where $0 < \lambda_N < \lambda_{N-1} < \cdots < \lambda_1 < L$. The initial values of the weights from *F2* to *F1* are given by $Wt_{ji} = 1$.

(3) Change the status of the short-term memory (STM) and the output signal in *F1*: After the input vector, *I*, enters *F1*, the status vector of STM in *F1* is adjusted to $x_i = c_2 * I_i$ The output of *F1* is given by

$$S_i = \begin{cases} 1, & if\ x_i > 0 \\ 0, & otherwise. \end{cases}$$

(4) Competition in *F2*: When the pattern vector is sent to *F2*, the input signal to *F2* is changed. After competition in *F2*, only one neuron, the jth neuron, wins in *F2* and the output signal is changed.

(5) Pattern Comparison and Matching: When the output signal of *F2* is fed back to *F1*, the pattern signal is obtained, and the weights are updated. Then, the status of STM in *F1* is updated after matching of the input and pattern vectors. The vigilance statistic for the vigilance test can be calculated as $\frac{|S|}{|I|} = \frac{\sum_i S_i}{\sum_i I_i}$.

(6) Search and Resonance: If $\frac{|S|}{|I|} < \rho$, then the winning neuron (the jth neuron) is reset to the initial value and the algorithm returns to Step 3 to search for the next possible target. Conversely, if $\frac{|S|}{|I|} \geq \rho$, then the STM is in resonant status and the long term memory (LTM) starts to learn and update.

(7) Long-term memory (LTM) learning: After searching and matching, only the weights of the winning neuron (the jth neuron) are changed.

(8) Input a new vector and return to Step 2.

3. Application of Data Mining in Semiconductor Manufacturing

3.1 Problem Definition

Data mining techniques have a variety of applications in semiconductor manufacturing. Several studies have applied data mining techniques to solve manufacturing yield problems. During the fabrication process, large amounts of process data are automatically or semi-automatically recorded and are accumulated in the engineering database. Engineers will conduct several tests to monitor and control the stability of manufacturing and the quality of the products. In general, six types of data are recorded during the fabrication processes.

(1) WIP (wafers in process) data: This includes basic information of every wafer during the manufacturing process such as the lot id, product name, process station, operation machine of the process station, operation time, and date.
(2) Metrology data: This includes measurement data collected for a specific lot (for example: critical dimension, oxide thickness) such as the lot id, measured parameter name of the product, measured parameter value of the product, and specification of upper and lower limits of the product.
(3) Non-Lot data: This includes measurement data collected for a specific machine (for example: the number of particles, the etching rate). Such data are usually collected for preventive maintenance including the operation machine, the measurement parameter of the machine, measured value, measurement time and date, and the specifications of upper and lower limits of the machine.
(4) Defect data: The data that describe the defects of a product, usually collected from the inspection equipment, failure analysis, SEM, and signature analysis including the lot id, product name, defect layer, number of defects in a layer, defect density, and the number of defects in a wafer.
(5) Wafer acceptance test (WAT) data: These data include the electrical measurements of test structures on the wafer. There are hundreds of parameters of WAT in a specific process procedure. In general, the test parameters may be divided into key parts and non-key parts,

which are depended on the correlation to the manufacturing process. The present protocol adopted by most semiconductor factories is to choose five wafers from each lot for testing and then to test five points in each wafer. Because all electric parameters have their standards, the measured data points will be compared with the corresponding standard to monitor the quality of the device.

(6) CP data: The results of the CP (Circuit Probe) test include the lot id, product name, and the location of the wafer. The CP test is an electrical test that involves various functional tests for all the dies on each wafer

In the following, we list some data issues of the data mining process in semiconductor manufacturing since they may impact subsequent processes such as the choice of data mining methods for modeling:

(1) Imbalanced data: In automated manufacturing systems, the number of defective products that comes off an assembly line tends to be much smaller than the number of non-defective products. Usually, this type of data is called "imbalanced data". This situation may cause the performance of classifications methods to drop significantly. The standard classifiers like decision trees, Bayesian networks and instance-based classifiers are often biased towards the majority class and unable to classify correctly new unseen cases from the minority class. That is because these classifiers attempt to achieve global optimization by reducing the error rate, not taking the data distribution into consideration. Thus, false-positive predictions are (implicitly) given more weight in error-rate based assessments. Several independent studies have proposed to improve the performance of classification for the "imbalanced data" problem. These improvement methods can be divided into three categories: re-sampling, down-sizing and learning by recognition (Japkowicz & Shaju, 2002). Re-sampling methods involve over-sampling the class represented by a small data set so as to match the size of the other cases while down-sampling methods remove some examples from the class represented by the larger class so as to match the size of the class with the fewer examples. The learning by recognition method mostly ignores one of the two classes altogether by using a recognition-based instead of a discrimination-based inductive scheme.

(2) Disjunct data or outliers: The performance of clustering methods such as *k*-means or hierarchy clustering methods may be impacted by small disjunct data or outliers. This happens because small disjunct

data may form a cluster by itself instead of be grouped with other data. The computation slows down with a large number of outliers or small disjunct data existing in the model and the result may not be easily interpreted. A simple non-parametric rule can be applied to detect outlier data. The upper and lower outlier limits are defined as the value of Median+2×IQR and Median-2×IQR, respectively, where IQR = 75th Quartile – 25th Quartile.

(3) Missing data: Most of the missing data are caused during the sampling. For example, high portions of missing data might exist in WAT and metrology data. WAT is a sampling test and inspection, which usually samples 5 or 9 sites to test a wafer and 2 to 3 wafers from a lot. On the other hand, the CP test is to probe all of the dies in every wafer of a lot. This may cause the information to be incomplete within a lot, which in turn increases the analysis difficulty when it is correlated with other data like process information, in-line measurement and CP data. In general, these data are excluded in modeling.

(4) Temporal data: Most of the on-line manufacturing data have the temporal property. The data mining process must be extended to handle temporal data during the data preparation step, or to perform data mining by using some incremental algorithms that use a sliding window of time to find suspicious events.

(5) Constant value: The data may be constant in semiconductor manufacturing. For example some WAT parameters, such as the current leakage, mostly stay the same with a constant value.

3.2 Types of Data Mining Applications

Based on the collected data, the engineers can analyze the relationship between the testing results and the paths of different lots in the manufacturing process for trouble shooting and low yield analysis. In general, the applications can be classified into four main groups: extracting characteristics from WAT data, process failures diagnosis of CP and engineering data, process failures diagnosis of WAT and engineering data, and extracting characteristics from semiconductor manufacturing data.

3.2.1 Extracting Characteristics from WAT Data

WAT data have the characteristics of high dimensionality and high correlation among the test results. A product usually possesses hundreds of parameters to be tested. Since WAT data include measurements of voltage, current and other electrical characteristics of different devices, there are some physical relationships among these parameters. The devices of different sizes also have high correlation in similar parameters. Figure 6 shows the correlation of some WAT parameters of a single product.

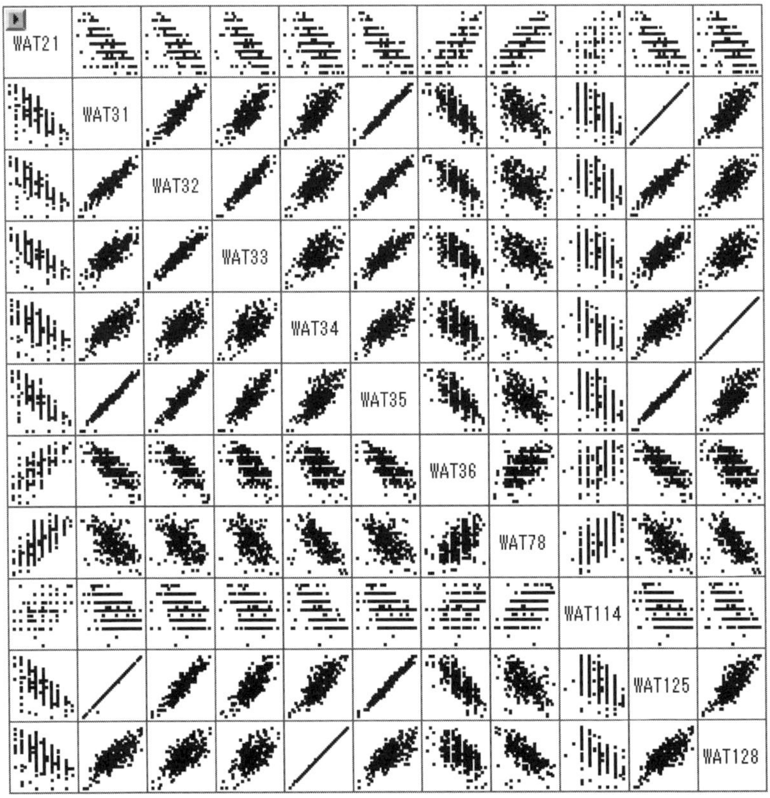

Figure 6. Scatter plot matrix of the high correlation WAT parameters.

The characteristics of WAT data call for the need of multivariate methods and dimension reduction methods to effectively monitor these parameters. Principal component analysis (PCA) and factor analysis (FA) can be applied to reduce the dimensionality of WAT data. A case in point, Chien et al. (2007) applied data mining methods for WAT and on-line data fault diagnosis.

3.2.2 Process Failures Diagnosis of CP and Engineering Data

The CP data are collected from functional tests after completing wafer manufacturing. There are two kinds of data, which can be used as the input for analysis: one is the CP bin summary data, which is the sum of the dies of a specific failing bin in a wafer. The failing bin represents some functional failure of the product, which could be correlated with a specific layer of the wafer manufacturing process; another is the CP's wafer bin map (WBM). WBM spatial patterns contain useful information about potential manufacturing problems. For example, mask misalignment in the lithographic process generates a checker board pattern; the abnormal temperature control in the rapid thermal annealing process (RTP) can generate a ring of failing chips around the edge of the wafer. Figure 7 shows 9 types of frequently seen CP failure patterns during wafer manufacturing. The failure patterns of WBM can be classified into three major categories: (1) random defects, (2) systematic defects, and (3) mixed defects. Most of the wafer bin maps belong to the mixed defect type. It is up to the engineers to separate random defects from systematic defects in a WBM because a systematic defect can reveal the process problem by its special signature (Friedman et al., 1997; Hansen & Nair, 1995; Staper, 2000; Hsu & Chien, 2007).

There are many applications and studies of failure diagnosis of CP and engineering data that apply the decision trees method to identify faulty equipment and their corresponding failure dates (Bergert & Gall, 2003; Chien et al., 2001; Wang et al., 2002; Peng et al., 2003). While most existing studies for WBM analysis focus on diagnosing systematic defects or patterns in wafer maps (Friedman et al., 1997; Hansen & Nair, 1995), Chien et al. (2002) applied ART and spatial randomness tests for

WBM clustering to recognize specific spatial failure patterns, and thus identify the underlying assignable causes.

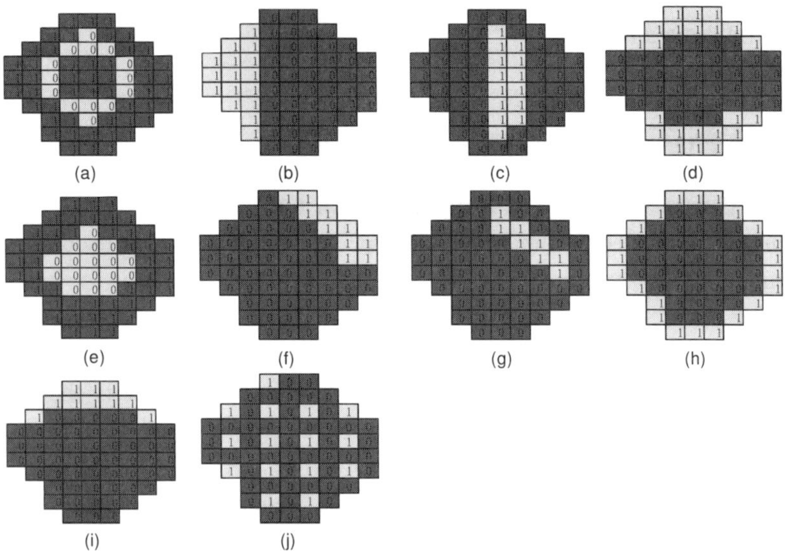

Figure 7. Frequently seen systematic defects in semiconductor manufacturing.

3.2.3 Process Failures Diagnosis of WAT and Engineering Data

Since WAT parameters are used to monitor the characteristics of the devices, such as N-MOS, P-MOS with different sizes, which are related to single layer or multilayer properties, WAT data can provide an assessment of the overall process performance and impact on product yield (Chien et al., 2001). For example, if the threshold voltage (Vt) is too high, this often implies that the dopant of the ion-implantation is too high for fabrication.

Engineers can diagnose the cause of the abnormal wafer by monitoring some specific WAT parameters. However, in a single layer different electrical characteristics are measured for different purposes, such as resistance, voltage, current and inductance. When the technology gets more complicated, it is difficult for engineers to use their domain knowledge directly to diagnosis process failure. Such a situation needs analysis of the application to assist the engineer in making the right decision.

Some functions in the EDA system have applied statistical methods, such as ANOVA or the nonparametric Kruskal-Wallis (K-W) test to identify the problem tools used in specific process steps. There are many studies which have applied data mining methods to diagnose process failures through WAT data. For example, SOM has been applied to cluster WAT data, CP failure bins and metrology data to detect failure patterns (Chien et al., 2003). Other studies include the application of decision trees to correlate the WAT failure with process tool and date (Chien et al., 2007), and also the application of key node screening to the diagnosis of WAT and in-line data faults.

3.2.4 Extracting Characteristics from Semiconductor Manufacturing Data

Besides the WAT and CP data, other types of data can also be analyzed to reveal on-line process problems. For example, metrology data and defect data are collected during wafer manufacturing to control process quality and to detect faults; thus tool operation data are recorded during processing.

Several data mining methods such as clustering algorithms, decision trees, principal component analysis, and neural networks have been applied for the purpose of classification, prediction and multivariate process control. For example, Wang and Spanos (2002) use classification methods to check recipes and temporal data collected from process conditions in a furnace tool. Koç and Lee (2002) proposed an Intelligent Maintenance System (IMS) for tool maintenance in semiconductor manufacturing, which consists of an intelligent machine degradation assessment, prognostics, and e-diagnostics to enable manufacturers and customers to have products and production machines with near-zero-breakdown conditions. Braha and Shmilovici (2002) applied three classification-based data mining tools including decision tree induction, neural networks, and composite classifiers to refine dry-cleaning technology for process improvement. Braha and Shmilovici (2003) also applied a decision tree approach to discover the interactions in the photolithographic process.

3.3 A Hybrid Decision Tree Approach for CP Low Yield Diagnosis

The fabrication of a semiconductor circuit is a multi-step process which includes up to hundreds of individual steps. The low yield problem may be caused by one single process station or operation machine in a certain time period, and there may also be some local interaction effects between different stations. We integrated the CP data and WIP data to diagnose defects if there are causal relationships between the machines of a specific process and the yield rate. In this study, we construct a data mining conceptual framework for analyzing semiconductor manufacturing data, and propose a hybrid decision tree approach, including the K-W test and CART to explore the huge engineering data, and to infer the possible causes of manufacturing process variation and fault. Such information can be helpful to engineers as the basis of trouble shooting and defect diagnosis. Figure 8 shows the framework of our hybrid decision tree approach.

The collected data often include noise, and/or missing and inconsistent data. Data preprocessing can improve the quality of the data and work efficiency in the following steps. Preprocessing techniques include data integration, data cleaning, and data transformation. Data integration merges data from multiple sources into a coherent data store. Data cleaning is applied to remove noisy data, identify outliers, fill in missing data, and correct inconsistencies. Data transformation aims at transforming or consolidating the data in a form appropriate for mining.

All of the data can be accessed and managed from the engineering data warehouse, which was built by the company. Next, we used some data cleaning methods to handle the missing values and remove some rows and columns that are not representative of the problem. If there are too few wafer lots passed through a process station, that process station could be neglected. After eliminating the lots with missing data, and also with spelling errors, 71 lots were revised for further analysis. The CP yields of these lots are plotted in Figure 9. Finally, we transformed the cleaned data into a format necessary for decision tree construction.

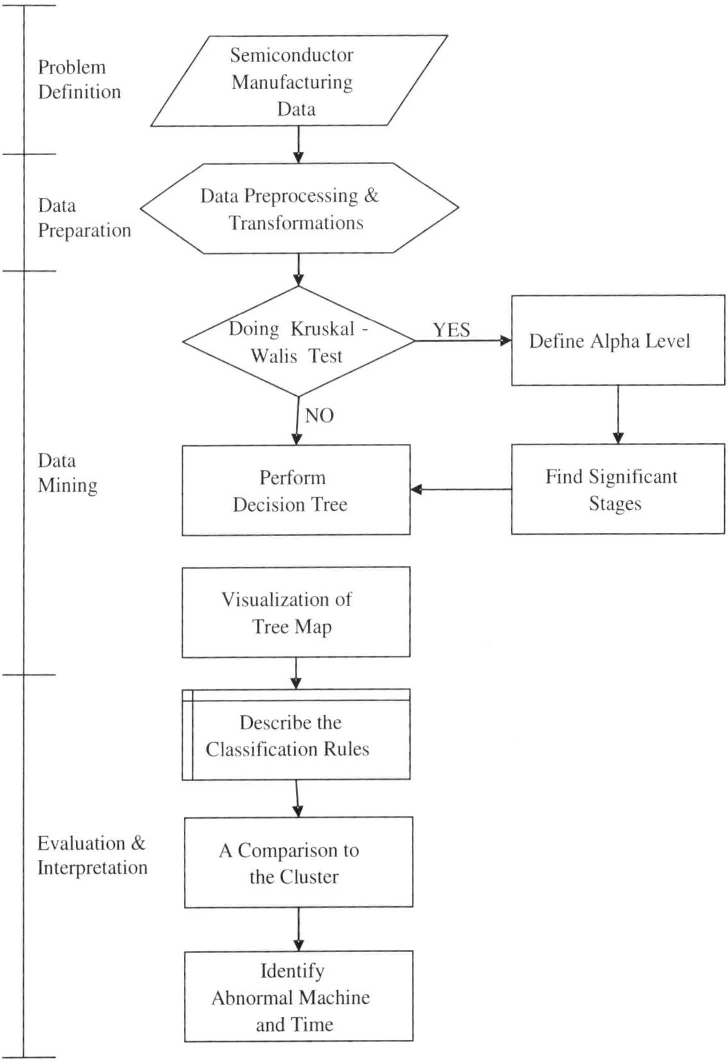

Figure 8. Framework of the hybrid decision tree analysis for CP low yield diagnosis.

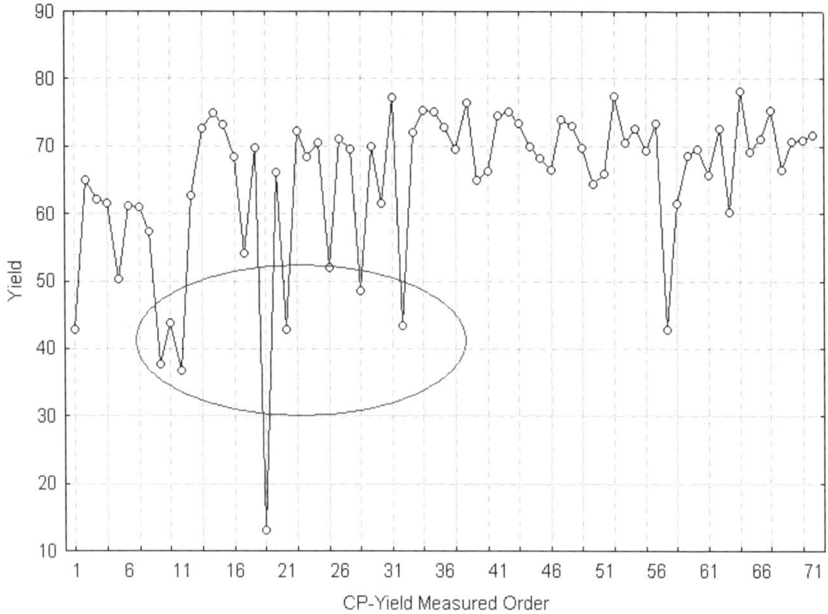

Figure 9. Plot of the CP yield.

3.4 Key Stage Screening

This step was carried out to explore the large database of process stages to choose a number of factors that may have significant effects on yield performance. To achieve that, we applied a statistical test to screen out non-significant process steps to improve the efficiency of the analysis. Because the distributions of the semiconductor fabrication data are not all normally distributed, the K-W test was applied at each process stage to examine whether there are significant differences among the outputs of the machines at the same process stage.

The K-W test is a nonparametric method for evaluating the equality of treatment means and is an alternative to the usual ANOVA, which tests the null hypothesis that the k treatments are identical against the alternative hypothesis that some of the treatments generate observations that are larger than others. Therefore, the procedure is designed to be sensitive to testing the difference in means.

The variation caused by the difference in process stages and machines may be identified for possible root causes. According to the test results, engineers could distinguish the problematic process stages by their domain knowledge from those stages with a significant difference among machines. The P-values of 455 process stages were sorted in ascending order and are listed in Table 2. We selected the process stages with P-value less than 0.3 (the threshold of P-value could be defined by the user) and discussed with the domain engineers to select possible process issues for further investigation.

Excluding the process stages with only one machine, there were 168 process stages having P-value less than 0.3 and the results were confirmed with the engineers. Indeed, after the key stage screening phase, the identified process stages may be the root cause of variation in the problem. Thus, the 168 process stages were considered as critical factors and thus they were used as the inputs for subsequent decision tree analysis.

Table 2. The K-W test table.

Stage	P_Value	Stage	P_Value	Stage	P_Value
Var.182	.000324	Var.95	.009871	Var.115	.0245
Var.2	.001028	Var.119	.011304	Var.7	.025607
Var.41	.001121	Var.54	.011588	Var.359	.025646
Var.192	.004364	Var.436	.012371	Var.397	.028328
Var.93	.004464	Var.163	.01531	Var.172	.030467
Var.210	.006226	Var.225	.016786	Var.75	.031922
Var.94	.007372	Var.52	.017417	Var.183	.031922
Var.103	.008567	Var.20	.017668	Var.208	.031922
Var.124	.008942	Var.64	.022412	Var.230	.031922
Var.170	.009526	Var.42	.024365	Var.252	.031922

*1: Due to space restriction, only thirty process stages are listed.

3.5 Construction of the Decision Tree

The training data used in the construction of the decision tree include one continuous target variable and 168 attribute variables, which are all of the categorical data type. The target variable is the CP yield rate and the attribute variables include the manufacturing key stages and their corresponding values, as well as the machine number and its processing time. The splitting criterion used in the construction of the decision tree is ANOVA's F test and the constructed decision trees were not pruned. The final decision tree constructed is shown in Figure 10.

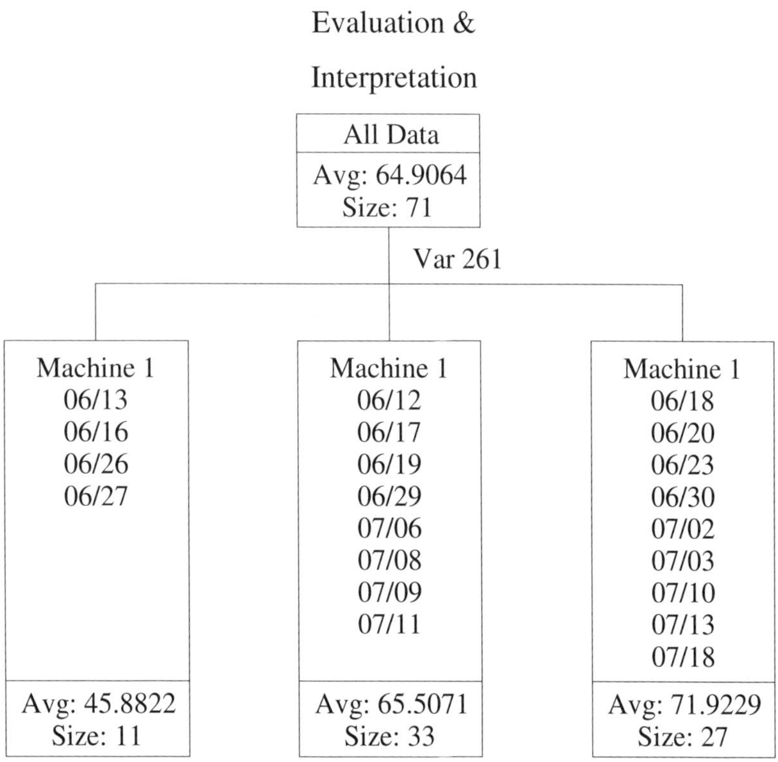

Figure 10. Result of the hybrid decision tree.

According to the decision tree shown in Figure 10, the mean of all the training data was equal to 64.0964. After the first split, the low yield group could be identified as the left tree leaf with the mean of the yield equals to 45.8822, which is apparently lower than the overall mean. In addition, the tree indicates that Machine 1 of stage "Var. 261"in 06/13, 06/16, 06/26 and 06/27 leads to this tree leaf. This means that Machine 1 of stage "Var. 261" had produced 11 low yield lots in 06/13, 06/16, 06/26 and 06/27. This information could be provided to the domain engineers for trouble shooting and fault diagnosis.

Based on the analysis results and our discussion with the domain engineers, we could uncover the knowledge that the yield rates of 11 lots were decreasing rapidly in Machine 1 of Var. 261 process stage as shown in Figure 11. This information should be highlighted and noted, because it may be the root cause of the low yield problem.

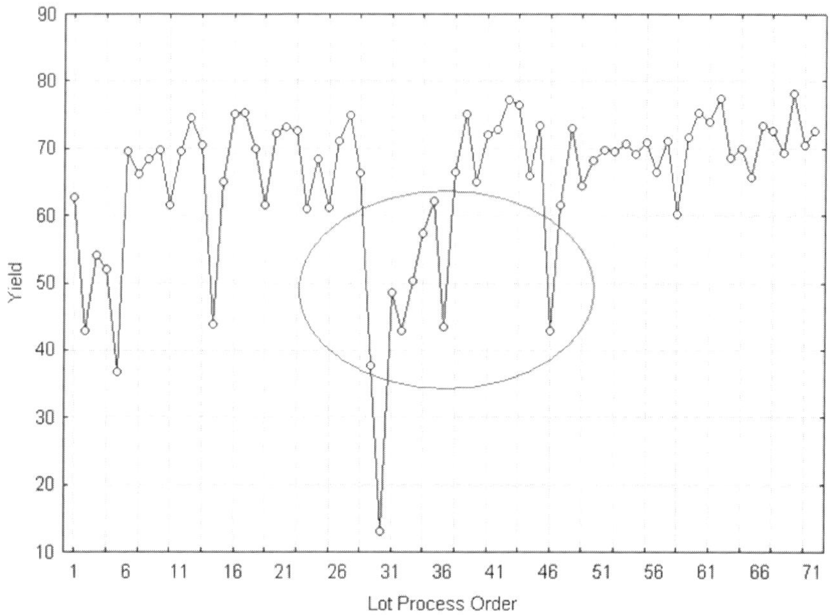

Figure 11. The scatter plot of Var. 261 on Machine 1.

After consulting with the engineers, this machine had some problems after 6/13. Indeed, we could derive some information about manufacturing issues to be used as the reference for trouble shooting and defect diagnosis for the engineers. The target variable used in this study is the yield rate that is like a synthetic index of the performance of hundreds of processes. Thus, it may be inconvenient for diagnosing defects because the fault causes may be obscure. Therefore, additional studies should be done for fault detection and classification.

4. Conclusions

This chapter discussed some empirical studies of semiconductor manufacturing to validate the practical viability of data mining approaches in this application field. The proposed framework combines traditional statistical methods and data mining techniques to explore huge semiconductor manufacturing data often available to engineers. Engineering data are fully utilized and developed effectively. Following the conceptual framework, hybrid decision tree approaches are proposed to solve different problems including the low yield diagnosis.

The results can help domain engineers identify root causes when certain issues occur and provide information for decision makers to understand how to overcome the problem by using the analysis framework. Indeed, data mining and knowledge discovery from database may range from its use as input for a decision process to its full integration into an end-user application. The results can also be used in an IT-enabled knowledge-based system for supporting manufacturing and business decisions in the high-tech industry.

New electronic ways of cooperation, manufacturing, and doing business are emerging because of the innovations in information technologies. Meanwhile, an increasingly large amount of raw data are automatically or semi-automatically been accumulated from various sources from suppliers to end customers. However, most of the data collected tend to be archived rather than be used due to the difficulty of data analysis and information extraction. Therefore, mining potentially useful information from a large database has become very important in maintaining the competitive advantage and enhancing the service quality for high-tech companies facing global competition.

References

Bergert, F. & Gall, C.L. (2003). Yield improvement using statistical analysis of process dates. *IEEE Transactions on Semiconductor Manufacturing*, **16**(3), 535-542.

Braha, D. & Shmilovici, A. (2002). Data mining for improving a cleaning process in the semiconductor industry. *IEEE Transactions on Semiconductor Manufacturing*, **15**(1), 91-101.

Braha, D. & Shmilovici, A. (2003). On the use of decision tree induction for discovery of interactions in a photolithographic process. *IEEE Transactions on Semiconductor Manufacturing*, **16**(4), 644-652.

Breiman, L., Friedman, J. H., Olshen, R. J., & Stone, C. J. (1984). *Classification and Regression Trees*, Wadsworth: Belmont, CA, U.S.A.

Carpenter, G. A. & Grossberg, S. (1988). The ART of adaptive pattern recognition by a self-organization neural network. *Computer*, **21**(3):77-88.

Chien, C. (2005). Modifying the inconsistency of Bayesian network and a comparison study for fault location on electricity distribution feeder. *International Journal of Operational Research*, **1**(1-2), 188-203.

Chien, C., & Hsu, C. (2006). A novel method for determining machine subgroups and backups with an empirical study for semiconductor manufacturing. *Journal of Intelligent Manufacturing*, **17**, 429-440.

Chien, C. & Shi, Y. (2004). Global manufacturing network and supply chain management for the electronics industry. *International Journal of Business*, **9**(4), 327-28.

Chien, C. & Wu, J. (2003). Analyzing repair decisions in the site imbalance problem of semiconductor test machines. *IEEE Transactions on Semiconductor Manufacturing*, **16**(4), 704-711.

Chien, C., Chen, S. & Lin, Y. (2002). Using Bayesian network for fault location on distribution feeder of electrical power delivery systems. *IEEE Transactions on Power Delivery*, **17**(13), 785-793.

Chien, C., Chang, K. & Chen, C. (2003). Design of sampling strategy for measuring and compensating overlay errors in semiconductor manufacturing. *International Journal of Production Research*, **41** (11), 2547-2561.

Chien, C., Hsiao, A., & Wang, I. (2004). Constructing semiconductor manufacturing performance indexes and applying data mining for manufacturing data analysis. *Journal of the Chinese Institute of Industrial Engineers*, 21(4), 313-27.

Chien, C., C. Hsiao, C. Meng, K. Hong, & S. Wang. (2005). Cycle time prediction and control based on production line status and manufacturing data mining." *Proceedings of International Symposium on Semiconductor Manufacturing Conference*, 13-15 September, San Jose, California, USA, 327-330.

Chien, C., Lee, P. & Peng, C. (2003). Semiconductor manufacturing data mining for clustering and feature extraction. *Journal of Information Management*, **10**(1), 63-84.

Chien, C., Lin, D., Peng, C., & Hsu, S. (2001). Developing data mining framework and methods for diagnosing semiconductor manufacturing defects and an empirical study of wafer acceptance test data in a wafer fab. *Journal of the Chinese Institute of Industrial Engineers,* **18**(4), 37-48.

Chien, C., Lin, D., Liu, Q., Peng, C., Hsu, C., & Huang, C. (2002). Developing a data mining method for wafer binmap clustering and an empirical study in a semiconductor manufacturing fab. *Journal of the Chinese Institute of Industrial Engineers*, **19**(2), 23-38.

Chien, C., Wang, W., & Cheng, J. (2007). Data mining for yield enhancement in semiconductor manufacturing and an empirical study. *Expert Systems with Applications*, **33**(1), 192-198.

Cunningham, S.P., Spanos, C.J. & Voros, K. (1995). Semiconductor yield improvement: results and best practices. *IEEE Transactions on Semiconductor Manufacturing,* **8**(2), 103-109.

Duda, R. O. & Hart, P. E. (1973). *Pattern Classification and Scene Analysis.* Wiley: New York, NY, U.S.A.

Fayyad, U., Piatesky-Shapiro, G. & Smyth, P. (1996). From data mining to knowledge discovery: an overview. In *Advances in Knowledge and Data Mining*, AAAI Press: Menlo Park, CA, U.S.A.

Feeldersa, A., Danielsa, H. & Holsheimer M. (2000). Methodological and practical aspects of data mining. *Information & Management*, **37**, 271-281.

Friedman D.J., Hansen, M.H., Nair, V.N., & James D.A. (1997). Model-free estimation of defect clustering in integrated circuit fabrication. *IEEE Transactions on Semiconductor Manufacturing,* **10**(3), 344-359.

Fu, Y. (1997). Data mining. *IEEE Potentials*, **164**, 18-20.

Han. J. & Kamber, M. (2001). *Data Mining: Concepts and Techniques.* Morgan Kaufmann Publishers: San Francisco, CA, U.S.A.

Hansen, M.H. & Nair, V.N. (1995). Monitoring wafer map from integrated circuit fabrication processes for spatially clustered defects. *Technometrics*, **39**(3), 241-253.

Hopfield, J.J. (1982). Neural networks and physical systems with emergent collective computational abilities. *Proceedings of the National Academy of Sciences*, **79**, 2554-2558.

Hsu, S. & Chien, C. (2007). Hybrid Data Mining Approach for Pattern Extraction from Wafer Bin Map to Improve Yield in Semiconductor Manufacturing. *International Journal of Production Economics*, **107**, 88-103.

Hsu, C., C. Chien, P. Chen, H. Luo, S. Wang, C. Chen, & H. Dai. (2005). Applying multiscale PCA to fault detection and classification in semiconductor manufacturing. *Proceedings of the 3rd AEC/APC Asia Symposium*, 1-2 December, 2005, Hsinchu, Taiwan (CD-ROM a48).

Japkowicz, N. & Shaju, S. (2002). The class imbalance problem: a Systematic study. *Intelligent Data Analysis*, **6**(5), 429-450.

Kass, G. V. (1980). An exploratory technique for investigating large quantities of categorical data. *Applied Statistics*, **29**(2), 119-127.

Koç, M. & Lee, J. (2002). E-Manufacturing and e-Maintenance -Applications and Benefits. *International Conference on Responsive Manufacturing (ICRM)*, 26–29.

Kohonen, T. (1995). *Self-Organizing Maps*. Springer: Berlin, Heidelberg, Germany.

Leachman, R.C. & Hodges, D.A (1996). Benchmarking semiconductor manufacturing. *IEEE Transactions on Semiconductor Manufacturing*, **9**(2), 158-169.

Lim, T., Loh, W., & Shih, Y. A. (2000). Comparison of Prediction Accuracy, Complexity, and Training Time of Thirty-Three Old and New Classification Algorithms. *Machine Learning*, **40**(3), 203-228.

Liu, C., Chien, C., & Ho. I. (1998). An object-oriented analysis and design method for shop floor control systems. *International Journal of Computer Integrated Manufacturing*, **11**, 379-400.

Parker, D. B. (1985). Learning-Logic. *Technical Report TR-47*. Center for Computational Research in Economics and Management Science. MIT. Cambridge, MA, U.S.A.

Peng, C. & Chien, C. (2003). Data value development to enhance yield and maintain competitive advantage for semiconductor manufacturing. *International Journal of Service Technology and Management*, **4**(4-6), 365-83.

Peng, J., Chien, C., & Tseng, B. (2004). Rough set theory for data mining for fault diagnosis on distribution feeder. *IEE Proceedings-Generation, Transmission, and Distributions,* **151**(6), 689-97.

Peng, J., Chang, Chang, S., Chien, C., & Yang, J. (2005). Constructing a data mining framework of association rule and an empirical study for fault location. *Journal of Information Management*, **12** (4), 121-141.

Quinlan, J. R. (1993). *C4.5: Programs for Machine Learning*. Morgan Kaufmann: San Francisco, California, U.S.A.

Stapper, C.H. (2000). LSI Yield Modeling and Process Monitoring. *IBM Journal of Research and Development*, **44**(2), 112-118.

Van den Bout, D. E. & Miller III, T. K. (1989). Improving the performance of the Hopfield-Tank neural network through normalization and annealing. *Biological Cybernetics*, **62**, 129-139.

Wang, J. & Spanos, C. J. (2002). Real-Time Furnace Modeling and Diagnostics. *IEEE Transactions on Semiconductor Manufacturing*, **15**(4), 393-403.

Wang, H., Chien, C., Hsu, S., & Lee, P. (2002). A data mining framework and an empirical study of decision tree analysis in semiconductor manufacturing, *Journal of Technology Management*, 7(1), 137-60.

Werbos, P. J. (1974). Beyond Regression: New Tools for Prediction and Analysis in the Behavioral Sciences, *Ph.D. Thesis*, Harvard University, Cambridge, MA, U.S.A.

Authors' Biographical Statements

Chen-Fu Chien received B.S. with double majors in Industrial Engineering and Electrical Engineering from the National Tsing Hua University, Taiwan in 1990. He received M.S. and Ph.D. degrees in Industrial Engineering, with two minors in Statistics and Business, from the University of Wisconsin-Madison in 1994 and 1996, respectively. He was a Fulbright Scholar in UC Berkeley from 2002 to 2003. Dr. Chien is a Professor of Industrial Engineering and Engineering Management at the National Tsing Hua University. Since 2005, he has been on-leave to serve as Deputy Director of Industrial Engineering Division at Taiwan Semiconductor manufacturing Company (TSMC). Before joining TSMC, he has served as a Senior Consultant in Manufacturing Technology Center, TSMC and Industrial Technology Research Institute (ITRI), Taiwan. He is also a member of the Phi Tao Phi Honor Society, INFORMS, IIE, CIIE, and CIDS.

His research and development efforts center on modeling and analysis for semiconductor manufacturing, decision analysis, data mining, and manufacturing strategy. His research works appear in *Computers & I.E.*, *Decision Support Systems*, *Expert Systems with Applications*, *IEEE Trans. on Power Delivery*, *IEEE Trans. on Power Systems*, *IEEE Trans. on Semiconductor Manufacturing*, *Int. J. Production Economics*, *Int. J. of Production Research*, *J. of MCDA*, *J. of Intelligent Manufacturing*, *OR Spectrum*, and *R&D Management*. He is associate editor for *IEEE Transactions on Automation Science and Engineering* and also on the editorial board of several journals. He has served in the Steering Committee of Industrial Engineering and Management Division in National Science Council, Taiwan, since 2002. He received the Distinguished University-Industry Collaboration Award from the Ministry of Education, Best Research Awards and Tier 1 Principal Investigator (2005-2008) from National Science Council, Distinguished Young Faculty Research Award and Distinguished University-Industry Collaboration Award from the National Tsing Hua University, Best Engineering Paper Award by the Chinese Institute of Engineers,

Distinguished Young Industrial Engineer and Best Paper Award from the Chinese Institute of Industrial Engineers, Taiwan.

Shao-Chung Hsu received the B.S. in Industry Engineering and M.S. in Statistics from the National Tsing Hua University, Taiwan in 1989 and 1992, respectively. He is now a PhD candidate in Industrial Engineering at the National Tsing Hua University. Mr. Hsu is Manager of Strategy Program in the Industrial Engineering Division at the Taiwan Semiconductor manufacturing Company (TSMC). Before joining TSMC, Mr. Hsu has worked for Macronix International Co., Ltd. for more than 10 years, where he led a team that integrates the statistics, data mining, and information technology to support the activities of SPC, DOE and Engineering/Production Data Analysis System, and to provide company-wide consulting service on data analysis.

Chapter 9[1]

Multivariate Control Charts from a Data Mining Perspective

Giovanni C. Porzio
Department of Economics, University of Cassino,
Via S.Angelo I-03043 Cassino (FR) - Italy, porzio@eco.unicas.it
Giancarlo Ragozini
Department of Sociology, Federico II University of Naples
Vico Monte di Pietà 1, I-80132 Naples - Italy, giragoz@unina.it

Abstract: This chapter aims at presenting our data mining vision on Statistical Process Control (SPC) analysis, specifically on the design of multivariate control charts for individual observations in the case of independent data and continuous variables. We first argue why the classic multivariate SPC tool, namely the Hotelling T^2 chart, might not be appropriate for large data sets, and then we provide an up-to-date critical review of the methods suitable for dealing with data mining issues in control chart design. In order to address new SPC issues such as the presence of multiple outliers and incorrect model assumptions in the context of large data sets, we suggest exploitation of some multivariate nonparametric statistical methods. In a model-free environment, we present the way we handle large data sets: a multivariate control scheme based on the data depth approach. We first present the general framework, and then our specific idea on how to design a proper control chart. There follows an example, a simulation study, and some remarks on the choice of the depth function from a data mining perspective. A brief discussion of some open issues in data mining SPC closes the chapter.

***Key Words*:** Data depth, Convex hull peeling, Hotelling's T^2, Nonparametric Control Charts, Outliers, Robustness, Skewness.

[1] Liao, T.W. and E. Triantaphyllou, (Eds.), **Recent Advances in Data Mining of Enterprise Data: Algorithms and Applications**, *World Scientific*, Singapore, pp. 413-462, 2007.

1. Introduction

Data mining, as a process of knowledge discovery in databases, has found applications in a wide range of fields, especially in the world of business and industry. However, in such a world there are still areas where data mining has been under-exploited, in spite of large amounts of available data. One such area, at the very core of industry, is production process quality control.

We believe that this is mainly due to the fact that the statistical tools adopted for production process quality control rely on very specific models for the data generating process. However, a new data mining perspective is also required in this field. As discussed in Montgomery (2001), records on many process variables and product characteristics open a new environment within process quality performance analysis where there is a significant need to be able to both detect and diagnose patterns, changes, and problems. Such an environment is ideal for data mining, where the main aim is to seek interesting or valuable information within large datasets (Hand *et al.*, 2000).

The aim of this chapter is to discuss how a data mining vision can effectively improve statistical process control, and to assess which methods are most appropriate to deal with large process datasets. We note that classic statistical process control (SPC) techniques may fail in such a context. On the other hand, classic data mining methods cannot be directly applied to production process monitoring. Hence, we believe that standard SPC tools should be revised from a data mining perspective, and that specific new methods have to be developed.

Consequently, we first discuss why standard SPC tools may be inappropriate for large datasets, and then how to adapt some data mining methods to SPC goals. In addition, we also introduce some new SPC techniques mainly based on multivariate nonparametric statistical methods that appear particularly appropriate from a data mining perspective.

We focus specifically on tools for multivariate process control in the case of independent data and product features modeled through continuous variables. We discuss the design of a multivariate control chart for individual observations, critically reviewing some contributions aimed at addressing issues related to management of the production process when much information regarding products and process variables is available.

This chapter is organized as follows. First, we illustrate the classic methods for on-line SPC, and then we deal with our data mining perspective on production process analysis. In Section 2 we present SPC aims, distinguishing between Phase I and Phase II of a quality control procedure, and we outline how a production process may be monitored through the use of control charts. Section 3 illustrates classic multivariate SPC, offering first the statistical setting, and then how the Hotelling T^2 chart works. In Section 4 we provide our viewpoint on how multivariate process control may be affected by some data mining issues.

We first discuss problems related to the presence of multiple outliers, and then what may happen when the distribution assumptions do not hold. Section 5 presents our perspective on dealing with large datasets: a multivariate control scheme based on the data depth approach. We first present the general framework, then our specific idea on how to design a proper control chart. There follows an example, a simulation study, and a discussion on the choice of the depth function from a data mining perspective. Section 6 offers some final remarks, including a list of some open data mining issues in SPC.

2. Control Charts and Statistical Process Control Phases

A large set of techniques for monitoring production processes is available, and for a review we refer the interested reader to the textbook by Montgomery (2004). Among the techniques, control charts play a key role. Generally speaking, they are graphical devices that carry information on the process behavior, and several kinds of charts have been proposed to deal with different possible deviations from the in-control production process.

The main kinds of charts are the Shewhart chart (Shewhart, 1931) that allows detection of large shifts in the process, the cumulative sum (CUSUM) control chart (Page, 1954) and the exponential weighted moving average (EWMA) chart (Roberts, 1959) that are effective at detecting a small persistent shift in the process level and variability. First charts dealt with single variable monitoring, and were developed under the assumption that data come from a normal distribution. Subsequently, many extensions were proposed to manage different distributional hypotheses for the process data, including autocorrelation, non-normal distributions, and skewness (see, for example, (Castagliola and Tsung, 2005), (Marcellus, 2005), (Cheng and Thaga, 2006), to quote some of the most recent developments).

Control charts share the same structure. They display the value of a statistic computed for each produced item (or batch of them). As long as the observed value of the statistic belongs to some control region, the process is considered to be *in-control*. Conversely, as the statistic exceeds some control limits, the process is declared *out-of-control*. Statistically speaking, such graphical analysis corresponds to sequentially testing if the new incoming observation is sampled from a defined null in-control distribution.

Hence, to design a control chart the following have to be defined:

i) the null in-control distribution
ii) the appropriate test-statistic
iii) the related control region.

Such a designing step is usually called Phase I of a statistical process control procedure. The use of the control chart to monitor the production process is then referred to as Phase II. To better illustrate the two steps, we display a scheme (Figure 1) of the two phases.

In Phase I, the production process has just started and measures on the item's quality begin to be collected. It is assumed that the process is in control, and hence that these first data come from an in-control distribution. This dataset, which is used to set up a control chart, is usually called the reference sample or the historical dataset (HDS).

A statistician can define a reference distribution for the in-control process data. If the data support some distribution family (usually the normal distribution), then the HDS is used to estimate the unknown parameters, and the null in-control distribution is completely specified. With the null distribution at hand, a statistical hypothesis system on the parameters is defined and an appropriate test statistic is derived.

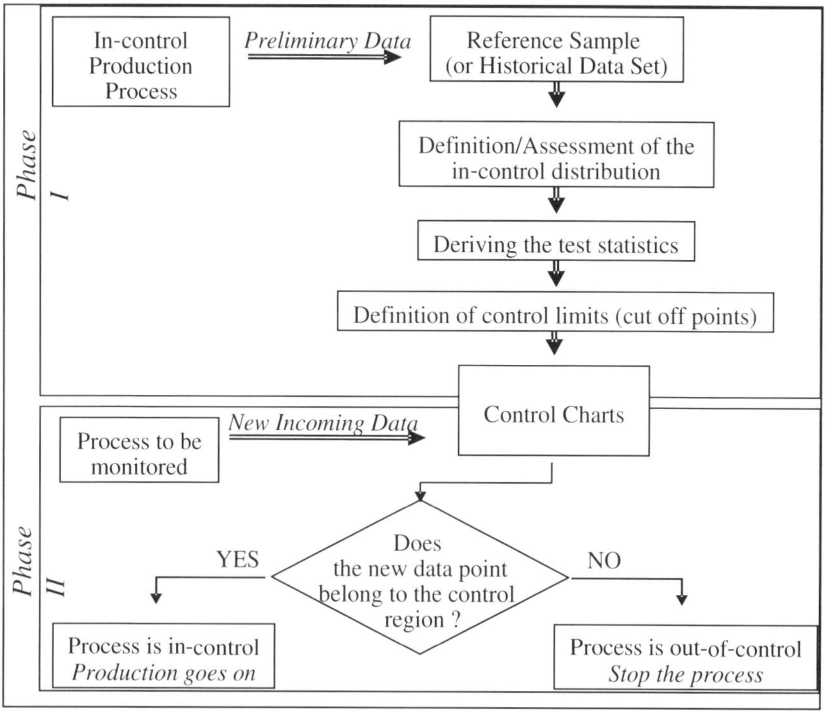

Figure 1. Summary scheme of Phases I and II of a statistical process control procedure.

The null distribution of the test statistic is eventually used to compute cut-off values defining in-control and out-of-control regions. The control chart graphically represents this information. As an example, in Figure 2 we display how a simple Shewhart chart for monitoring a process mean under normality is defined. A null distribution from the HDS data (some specified normal density with $\mu=\mu_0$) is depicted, which in turn defines a null distribution for a test statistic (in the figure the sample value itself) to evaluate the hypothesis H_0: $\mu=\mu_0$. In the chart, a central line is displayed which represents μ_0 (the null expected value of the statistic). In addition, two parallel lines are drawn, corresponding to the test cut-off values that embed the in-control region (the Upper Control Limit, *UCL*, and the Lower Control Limit, *LCL*).

Once the chart has been designed, Phase II starts and the actual process monitoring may be performed. For each new item, or batch of them, the related quality measure is collected and a new observed value of the test statistic is depicted on the chart. If it lies within the control region the process is considered in-control, while if it lies outside the control limits, the process is declared out-of-control. Figure 2 also shows how the simple Shewhart control chart works. Each dot in the chart corresponds to the value of the statistic for each new incoming item. In the graph, the last dot lies outside the in-control region, signaling that the process has gone out-of-control.

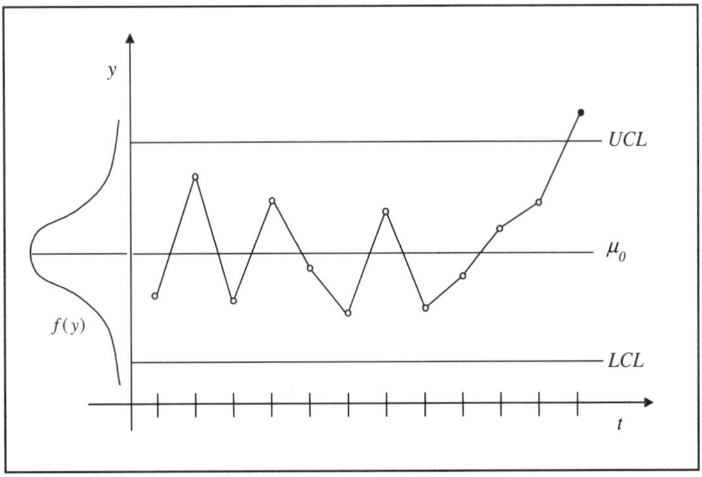

Figure 2. A typical control chart at work.

Finally, each chart is characterized by its Average Run Length (*ARL*) function, which provides the expected number of items that should be collected before declaring the process out-of-control. The *ARL* functions are used to evaluate the performance of a chart under both the null and the alternative hypothesis, and to decide upon the batch size if the quality measure is itself computed on a group of items.

3. Multivariate Statistical Process Control

Data mining Statistical Process Control (SPC) implies that a large process dataset is available and hence many variables have to be monitored at the same time (Testik and Runger, 2003). A simple approach to dealing with this problem is to control each feature separately. That is, k univariate control charts, one for each characteristic to be monitored, are used to control k multivariate quality features. However, relying on single variables to study multivariate features is known to mislead analysis. In particular, the relationship structure of the multivariate underlying distribution makes the univariate control tools less effective in term of sensitivity to out-of-control detection (see e.g. (Alt, 1985), (Alt and Smith, 1988)). However, it should be noted that this is in some respects a well-worn issue, as the first (and probably still the main) tool for multivariate SPC is the well known T^2 statistic and the related chart introduced by Hotelling in 1947.

3.1 The Sequential Quality Control Setting

In order to better illustrate the process control procedure, we introduce a general setting along with the notation we will use throughout this chapter. From a data mining perspective we will focus merely on the multivariate case, for which many quality measurements for each item are recorded (the univariate case can be treated as a special case).

First, let us denote with $\mathbf{Y} \in \Re^k$, $\mathbf{Y} = (Y_1, \ldots, Y_k)$, the k component random variable vector describing the process: the observed value of this random variable is the vector of quality measures of a produced item. In Phase I, a crucial step is the specification of an appropriate statistical hypothesis system. In a sequential quality control setting (Antoch and Jaruskova, 2002), the problem is to test if (and when) a change in the process occurred. To do that, a sequence of items

$\mathbf{Y}_1,\ldots,\mathbf{Y}_{r-1},\mathbf{Y}_r,\mathbf{Y}_{r+1},\ldots,$ is considered, for which the observed values will be collected in Phase II. In addition, two alternative distributions, one for the in-control process $\left(F^0\right)$ and one for the out-of-control process $\left(F^1\right)$ are specified. Then, the more general hypothesis system is defined as:

$$H_0 : \mathbf{Y}_1,\ldots,\mathbf{Y}_{r-1},\mathbf{Y}_r,\mathbf{Y}_{r+1},\ldots \sim F^0$$

$$H_1 : \mathbf{Y}_1,\ldots,\mathbf{Y}_{r-1}, \sim F^0 \quad \mathbf{Y}_r,\mathbf{Y}_{r+1},\ldots \sim F^1, \tag{1}$$

with r unknown. The time of detection, say t ($t \geq r$), is called the stopping time; if H_0 is rejected then some action, like stopping the process, has to be taken.

In this general framework, a very special case is the parametric setting. In such a case, the F distribution is assumed to be completely known up to some parameters $\boldsymbol{\theta}$ belonging to the parameter space $\boldsymbol{\Theta}$. In this case, $F^0 = F(\boldsymbol{\theta}_0)$ and $F^1 = F(\boldsymbol{\theta}_1)$, with $\boldsymbol{\theta}_0 \cup \boldsymbol{\theta}_1 = \boldsymbol{\Theta}$ and $\boldsymbol{\theta}_0 \cap \boldsymbol{\theta}_1 = \varnothing$. Such a parametric assumption simplifies the test scheme and the hypothesis system (1), which becomes:

$$H_0 : \mathbf{Y}_1,\ldots,\mathbf{Y}_{r-1},\mathbf{Y}_r,\mathbf{Y}_{r+1},\ldots \sim F(\boldsymbol{\theta}_0)$$

$$H_1 : \mathbf{Y}_1,\ldots,\mathbf{Y}_{r-1}, \sim F(\boldsymbol{\theta}_0) \qquad \mathbf{Y}_r,\mathbf{Y}_{r+1},\ldots \sim F(\boldsymbol{\theta}_1) \tag{2}$$

where F is some known distribution function.

For the hypotheses in (2) a likelihood ratio test (*LRT*) can be defined, assuming that the corresponding density function f exists and is known. The stopping time t will be the first time the log-likelihood ratio is greater than a given threshold h:

$$t = \inf\left\{ n \middle| \log \prod_{i=1}^{n} \frac{f(\mathbf{Y}_i, \boldsymbol{\theta}_1)}{f(\mathbf{Y}_i, \boldsymbol{\theta}_0)} > h \right\}.$$

The *LRT* setting allows the control procedure properties to be studied in terms of *ARL* functions. In other words, it is possible to investigate the average run length under H_0 (ARL_0), i.e. the expected time for a false alarm to occur $E(t|H_0)$, and the average run length under H_1 (ARL_1), i.e. the expected time to decide correctly that the process is out-of-control $E(t|H_1)$. Knowledge of these quantities is important for comparing control procedures and implementing them correctly.

The Shewhart control scheme is a special simple case of this setting. The parametric hypothesis system in (2) is reduced to a test on the last new incoming items $\mathbf{Y}_n$ with $H_0 : \mathbf{Y}_n \sim F(\boldsymbol{\theta}_0)$ and $H_1 : \mathbf{Y}_n \sim F(\boldsymbol{\theta}_1)$. That is, only the last observation $\mathbf{Y}_n$ is used to decide upon the process, the likelihood ratio is reduced to the comparison between the $\mathbf{Y}_n$ densities, and hence the stopping time will be the first time the log-likelihood ratio for the last observed item turns out to be greater than a threshold:

$$t = \inf\left\{ n \middle| \log \frac{f(\mathbf{Y}_n, \boldsymbol{\theta}_1)}{f(\mathbf{Y}_n, \boldsymbol{\theta}_0)} > h \right\}. \tag{3}$$

Phase I requires specification of the distribution family *F*. The test statistic and the corresponding cut-off values yield a partition of the sample space into the acceptance and rejection regions that correspond to the in-control and out-of-control regions on the chart, respectively. With this information the chart can be drawn, and Phase II can start.

3.2 *The Hotelling T^2 Control Chart*

Hotelling's T^2 control chart is a chart that assumes the Shewhart scheme in the case of multivariate process control. The in-control distribution is assumed to be a multivariate normal and the historical dataset is used.

The historical data is used both to assess such an assumption and to estimate the mean vector and/or the covariance matrix, if they are unknown. For the sake of illustration, let us assume that both the mean and the covariance matrix of the process are known. Then, under the null hypothesis (in-control process) we have

$$\mathbf{Y}_i \sim N(\boldsymbol{\mu}_0;\boldsymbol{\Sigma}_0), i=1,\ldots,r,r+1,\ldots,$$

with $\boldsymbol{\mu}_0$ and $\boldsymbol{\Sigma}_0$ as the null mean vector and the covariance matrix, respectively. Considering that the out-of-control process suffers a shift in level, the hypothesis system in (1) will be:

$$\begin{aligned}
&H_0:\mathbf{Y}_1,\ldots,\mathbf{Y}_{r-1},\mathbf{Y}_r,\mathbf{Y}_{r+1},\ldots \sim N(\boldsymbol{\mu}_0;\boldsymbol{\Sigma}_0)\\
&H_1:\mathbf{Y}_1,\ldots,\mathbf{Y}_{r-1},\sim N(\boldsymbol{\mu}_0;\boldsymbol{\Sigma}_0) \qquad \mathbf{Y}_r,\mathbf{Y}_{r+1},\ldots \sim N(\boldsymbol{\mu}_1;\boldsymbol{\Sigma}_0),
\end{aligned}$$

which, in light of the previous discussion, can be reduced to a simple test on the means of the new incoming item $\mathbf{Y}_n$ with the hypothesis system:

$$\begin{aligned}
&H_0:\boldsymbol{\mu}=\boldsymbol{\mu}_0\\
&H_1:\boldsymbol{\mu}\neq\boldsymbol{\mu}_0.
\end{aligned} \tag{4}$$

The *LRT* derived test statistic, which follows a χ^2 distribution with k degrees of freedom, is the Hotelling T^2 statistic:

$$T^2=(\mathbf{Y}_n-\boldsymbol{\mu}_0)'\boldsymbol{\Sigma}_o^{-1}(\mathbf{Y}_n-\boldsymbol{\mu}_0).$$

Given a significance level α, the corresponding cut-off value is $\chi^2_{(1-\alpha),k}$, the (1-α)-*th* percentile of the χ^2 distribution (the upper control limit - *UCL*- in the chart). In Figure 3 (*b*) the Hotelling T^2 control chart is represented. For each new item, a dot appears in the chart with a value equal to the corresponding T^2 observed value. If this dot lies under the *UCL*, then the process is considered in-control, while as soon as the dot lies over the *UCL*, the process is declared out-of-control. In this figure we also draw some dots to illustrate a typical pattern in the chart that leads from an in-control to an out-of-control process. From a geometrical point of view, note that the T^2 statistic is a quadratic form that defines ellipsoids in the k-dimensional sample space (ellipses on the plane), and measures in the Mahalanobis metric the distance of the new item point from the center of the ellipsoid (the $\boldsymbol{\mu}_0$ vector). The *UCL* (the (1-α)-*th* percentile of the χ^2 distribution) determines an elliptical boundary enclosing the in-control (acceptance) region in the k-dimensional space.

In Figure 3 (a) we show the elliptical boundary in the k-dimensional sample space (k=2), that corresponds to the *UCL* of Figure 3 (b). We also depict the point pattern that leads the process out of control. Points lying at the core of the ellipsoid are mapped into points in the lower part of the control chart, while points lying either at the boundary or out of the ellipsoid correspond to points lying close or above the *UCL*.

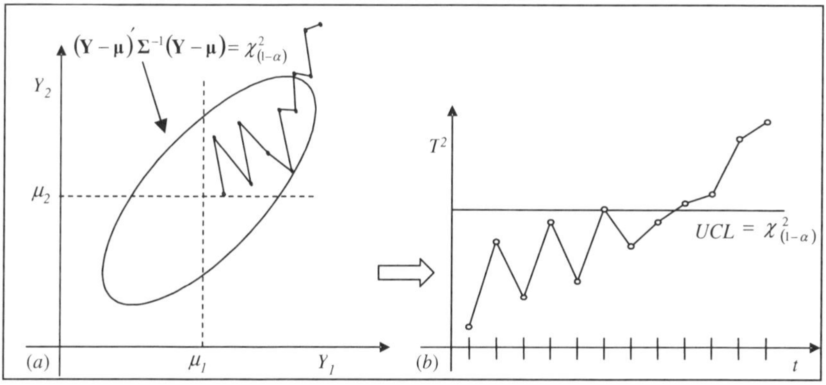

Figure 3. The Hotelling T^2 control scheme: *(a)* the sample space, the elliptical in-control region, and some points describing a path towards an out-of-control status; *(b)* the corresponding T^2 chart.

If either the process mean or covariance of the in-control distribution is unknown, then they are estimated in Phase I using the HDS. In this case, the test statistic is still the Hotelling T^2, but with a different sample distribution. In particular, if the HDS is used only to estimate the parameters, and $\mathbf{Y}_n$ is not included in the estimation, then the T^2 distribution is proportional to a Snedecor-Fisher F distribution. On the other hand, if $\mathbf{Y}_n$ belongs to the HDS, and hence it is included in the estimation process, the T^2 is distributed like a *Beta* random variable, up to some constant. For details on the issues concerning the T^2 approach and related methods we suggest the reader to refer to the book length review by Mason and Young (2002).

4. Is the T^2 Statistic Really Able to Tackle Data Mining Issues?

When many observations and many variables are available, not only can a large amount of information be exploited to improve our knowledge of processes, but also new challenges arise, both in terms of methodology and computation. Focusing on the former without neglecting the latter, we point out some relevant issues that affect Phase I of an SPC process below.

In a T^2 data mining SPC framework, during Phase I large numbers of observations are rapidly collected. As a consequence, the HDS is quite large and hence the parameters of the null distribution may be estimated accurately. However, such large amounts of data may cause some trouble. Firstly, there may be many outliers. Secondly, the multivariate normality assumption underlying the T^2 chart may not be appropriate.

In the following sections, we address these two quality control data mining issues from our perspective. We discuss both of them, providing an up-to-date review of the available methods along with some new possibilities. For the second issue in Section 5 we detail a recent Phase I SPC methodology based on data depth.

4.1 Many Data, Many Outliers

As is well known in the data mining community, when many data are available the probability of observing outliers is high. For this reason, data mining textbooks devote some pages to describing methods that address this problem (see e.g. (Kantardzic, 2002), (Dasu and Johnson, 2003), (Larose, 2006)).

When a large HDS is used to estimate the null distribution, this problem may strongly affect Phase I of the SPC procedures. In the case of the T^2 chart, the presence of even a small percentage of outliers may yield a biased estimate of the parameters of the null distribution (the mean vector and the covariance matrix). Biased estimates make the Phase II control procedure ineffective: many in-control items will be declared out-of-control, and some actual out-of-control items will go undetected.

As discussed earlier in Section 3.2, from a geometrical point of view the T^2 statistic measures the distance of the observed item from the center of the process in the Mahalanobis metric (the statistic is precisely the square of the Mahalanobis distance under the null distribution). In the k-dimensional sample space the in-control region is an ellipsoid centered in $\boldsymbol{\mu}_0'$ and with shape determined by $\boldsymbol{\Sigma}_0$. Under independence and homoscedasticity, that is if $\boldsymbol{\Sigma}_0 = \sigma_0^2\mathbf{I}$ with σ_0^2 the common variance, the in-control region will be a hypersphere (circle on the plane). The presence of outliers modifies the in-control ellipsoid both in location and shape. Few observations lying far from the others make the center of the null distribution different from its actual value $\boldsymbol{\mu}_0'$. This also yields a bias in the variance and covariance estimates, inflating the variability and changing the estimated relationship structure.

A biased estimate of the center of the null distribution shifts the in-control region, while a biased estimate of the covariance structure modifies its shape. As a consequence, the in-control region will include some parts of the sample space that would have belonged to the unbiased out-of-control region, and vice versa. We represent this idea in Figure 4. An HDS of 1,000 observations drawn from a mixture of bivariate normal distributions:

$$(1-\lambda)\ \Phi(x \mid \boldsymbol{\mu}_0;\boldsymbol{\Sigma}_0)+\lambda\ \Phi(x \mid \boldsymbol{\mu}_1;\boldsymbol{\Sigma}_0)$$

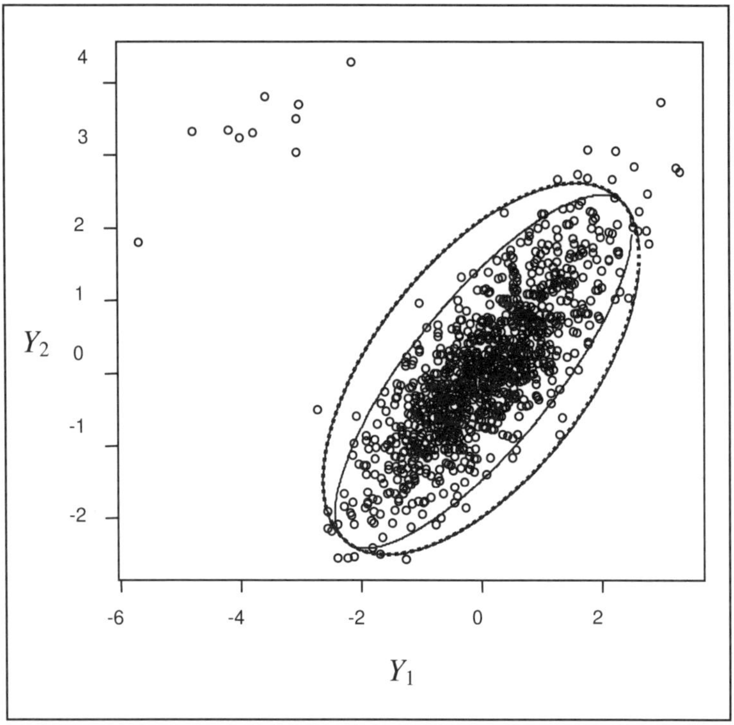

Figure 4. The Hotelling T^2 control scheme: effect of outlier contamination on the in-control region.

with $\boldsymbol{\mu}_0' = [0 \quad 0]$, $\boldsymbol{\mu}_1' = [-4 \quad 3]$, $\sigma_{11}^2 = \sigma_{22}^2 = 1$, $\sigma_{12} = \sigma_{21} = 0.8$, and $\lambda = 0.01$ is depicted. Two in-control regions based on the T^2 statistic for the test in equation (3.4) with significance level α=0.05 are superimposed in the plot. The inner solid ellipsis represents the region computed on the estimated parameters of the uncontaminated distribution, while the outer dotted one has been computed using the means and covariance matrix estimated on the whole HDS. Note that even if the mixture coefficient λ has been set at a low value (1% of outlier contamination) a major change in the in-control region appears: the means are slightly shifted, while the estimated variances increase from 1.03 and 0.99 to 1.17 and 1.09, respectively, and the correlation decreases from 0.806 to 0.680. This modified covariance structure makes the "biased" in-control region larger than the "unbiased". A point that in Phase II lies within the outer ellipsis but not within the inner one will be an undetected out-of-control item.

To tackle the outlier contamination of the HDS two possible strategies can be pursued: robust estimation and outlier detection. The first uses estimating methods resistant to the presence of outliers to assign values to means and covariances of the null distribution. In such a case, the T^2 statistic is computed in Phase II using these robust estimates of the parameters. Although many methods are available ((Maronna, 1976), (Huber, 1981) (Rousseeuw, 1984), (Hampel *et al.*, 1986), see also (Maronna *et al.*, 2006) for an extensive review), they do not fit well with the SPC aims. Even under normality, the null distribution of the robust T^2 statistic is generally unknown, and hence the UCL in the chart cannot be exactly determined. Vargas (2003) computed the T^2 control limits for several robust methods through simulations. Jensen *et al.* (2005), after an in-depth discussion of the use of a high breakdown estimator for T^2 charts, provide asymptotic results and also compare the performance of some robust charts. They found that as HDS size increases, the Minimum Covariance Determinant estimator should be preferred.

From a data mining perspective, we note that this method may also rely on a faster algorithm (Rousseeuw and van Driessen, 1999). Furthermore, we point out that these robust control limits may also be computed by exploiting the approximated distribution for the T^2 statistic derived by Willems *et al.* (2002). They proposed a robust Hotelling test with the covariance structure evaluated through the Minimum Covariance Determinant estimator.

Moreover, we notice that robust methods particularly suitable for high-dimensional datasets have recently been proposed for location and covariance estimations (Maronna and Zamar, 2002; Wang and Raftery, 2002). Such methods, which pay special attention to computational issues, are data mining oriented and have not yet been introduced in the SPC framework.

When the outliers have a time-dependent structure that induces a shift or a trend in the HDS mean vector, Sullivan and Woodall (1996) suggest using the differences of successive observations to robustly evaluate the

HDS covariance structure. In such a case, an approximated distribution for the T^2 statistic has been provided (Williams *et al.*, 2004).

Instead of relying on some robust version of the T^2 chart, one may alternatively aim first to find outliers, and then remove them from the HDS before estimating the process parameters. Very few single outliers may be easily identified, but the detection of multiple outliers is a difficult task, and the literature on this topic is extensive. A first approach consists either in sequentially deleting from the dataset the most outlying point at each step (see for a review (Barnett and Lewis, 1994)), or deleting blocks of observations at a time (Wilks, 1963). The sequential approach may easily fail due to masking (some outliers go unnoticed) and swamping (spurious outliers are detected) in the case of multiple outliers, while the block omission approach has to face some computational problems.

Alternatively, one may consider distances from the center of a "clean set" as a starting point for an outlier search ((Rousseeuw and van Zomeren, 1990), (Hadi, 1992, 1994), (Atkinson, 1994), (Atkinson and Riani, 2004)). This approach is essentially based on a robust estimate of the location parameter and the covariance matrix in some Mahalanobis-like distance: observations are ordered with respect to their distance from the "robust" center, and the most extreme points are taken as candidate outliers. Through an extensive simulation study Wisnowski *et al.* (2002) compared some detection outlier methods in terms of their ability not to signal false alarms for clean data and detect outliers. Their findings indicate that, although several methods display a consistently solid performance, the method of Rocke and Woodruff (1996) performs best overall.

We also note that all these outlier detection methods, relying on Mahalanobis-like distances, assign the same degree of outlyingness to points symmetrically far away from the distribution center. These ideas fit well with the assumption that the null distribution is normal or at most with elliptical probability contours. However, if this assumption is not verified, Mahalanobis-like distances can fail as outlier detection tools. In the case of severe multivariate skewness, an outlier may be at the same distance from the center as other non-discordant observations (Porzio and Ragozini, 2000).

As a toy example, consider the artificial dataset in Figure 5 that amounts to 300 observations, with three outliers sticking out on the left of the data cloud (represented as crossed points). The superimposed ellipsis corresponds to the largest Mahalanobis distance. The sample scatter has an asymmetrical shape with the means in the axis origins: the outliers are closer to this center than other observations. However, they are isolated and discordant with respect to the main data structure, even if they lie inside the ellipsis.

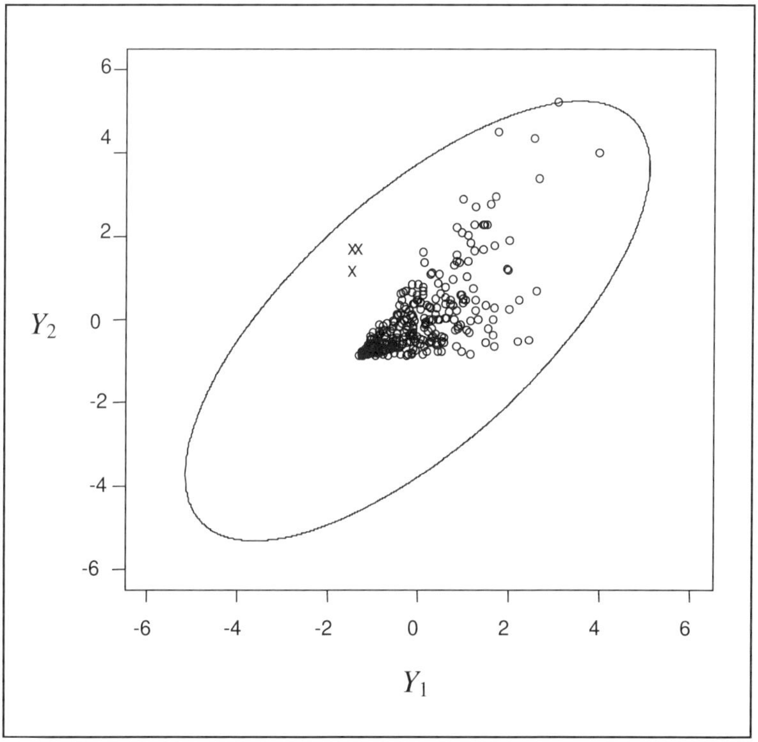

Figure 5. Effect of skewness on the detection of outliers through Mahalanobis-like distances.

In order to detect this kind of outlier, different approaches are required, based on other outlyingness measures and/or exploratory tools (Maronna *et al*, 1992; Zani *et al.* 1998; D'Esposito and Ragozini, 1999; Porzio and Ragozini, 2000). A more data mining oriented approach is in Castejón Limas *et al.* (2004).

To summarize, if the null process distribution belongs to the multivariate normal family, or to some of its close neighborhoods, it is possible to handle the presence of outliers in the HDS, ending up with a proper T^2 chart. However, if the process distribution is highly skewed, the T^2 statistic is not adequate, even if it is possible to perform some outlier detection. We will address this latter issue in the following section.

4.2 Questioning the Assumptions on Shape and Distribution

Multivariate normality is commonly assumed as a model for real process data in order to easily monitor the process through the T^2 chart, exploiting the well-known statistical properties of such distribution. However, when large datasets involving many item features are treated, two different problems arise concerning this assumption.

First, we note that it is no easy task to assess multivariate normality, even if the multivariate normality assumption plays a central role in many statistical methods. It is not surprising that the literature on this issue is extensive, and different approaches have been pursued. Some rely on evaluating the marginal normality of each variable, while others seek to evaluate the joint normality of a set of random variables through a single statistic summarizing the whole distribution. It is no coincidence that two of the most commonly used tools, Mardia's measures of multivariate skewness and kurtosis (Mardia, 1970) and the chi-square Q-Q plot proposed by Andrews *et al.* (1973), are highly related to the T^2 statistic.

We note in addition that not only it is hard to evaluate the joint normality assumption for an HDS, but also that it is crucial to know what kind of departure from the assumption most likely holds if the hypothesis of joint normality for the HDS is rejected. For example, multivariate kurtosis does not modify the elliptical structure of the distribution, and therefore the T^2 statistic proves still adequate, albeit with appropriate modification of the control limit value. According to Mason and Young (2002, Sec. 3.2), the T^2 statistic may also be used in the case of a truncated multivariate normal distribution. They state that if the T^2 empirical distribution evaluated on some HDS resembles the theoretical behavior under the multivariate normality assumption, then it can be used in Phase II.

However, we wish to stress that focusing only on the univariate T^2 statistic empirical distribution hides the real data structure in the multivariate space, and this is particularly true when many variables are involved. In other words, although the idea of using the empirical T^2 distribution quantiles to define an appropriate control limit might appeal due to its practical use, it may be misleading. Indeed, it can be shown that this method would not fail if the null process distribution, even if not normal, had elliptical contours. However, some non-elliptical (and hence non-normal) multivariate distribution may greatly disturb the production control process in Phase II.

As a simple example, let us consider the case of multivariate skewness in the HDS scatter. In such a case, even if the T^2 empirical distribution appears to work well with modified control limits, major errors in Phase II may occur: items that belong to the core of the null distribution will be declared out-of-control, while out-of-control items may go undetected.

We illustrate the latter point in Figures 6 and 7 using bivariate simulated data. Figure 6 represents an HDS drawn according to a bivariate normal model, with zero means and identity covariance matrix. On the scatter, a circle centered in the axis origin has been superimposed. Its area is the in-control region at level $\alpha = 0.95$: sample points that in Phase II will lie within the circle will be declared in-control, while points outside it will signal some process deficiencies. The two large grey dots in this figure represent possible item measures gathered in Phase II. As the underlying random variable is an elliptically contoured distribution, these two dots correctly lie within/out of the circle.

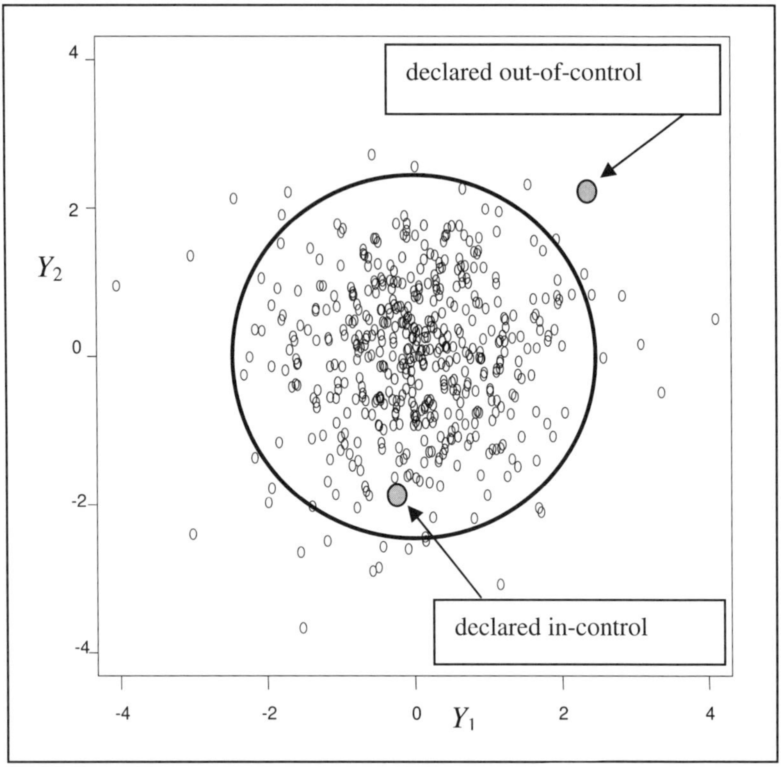

Figure 6. The Hotelling T^2 control scheme applied to a bivariate normal sample.

In Figure 7 we represent instead a bivariate skewed scatter, drawn from a shifted *Gamma* distribution with independent component, unit variances and zero mean values for the sake of comparison. The circle superimposed is the in-control region at level $\alpha = 0.95$ defined through the T^2 Hotelling statistic. The effect on Phase II is quite weird-looking. The large dot outside the circle will be declared out-of-control in Phase II although it belongs to the HDS null distribution area, while the one that will be declared fully in-control actually does not even belong to the null distribution support. This corresponds to the fact that a larger value of the T^2 statistic will be yielded by the first dot rather than by the second.

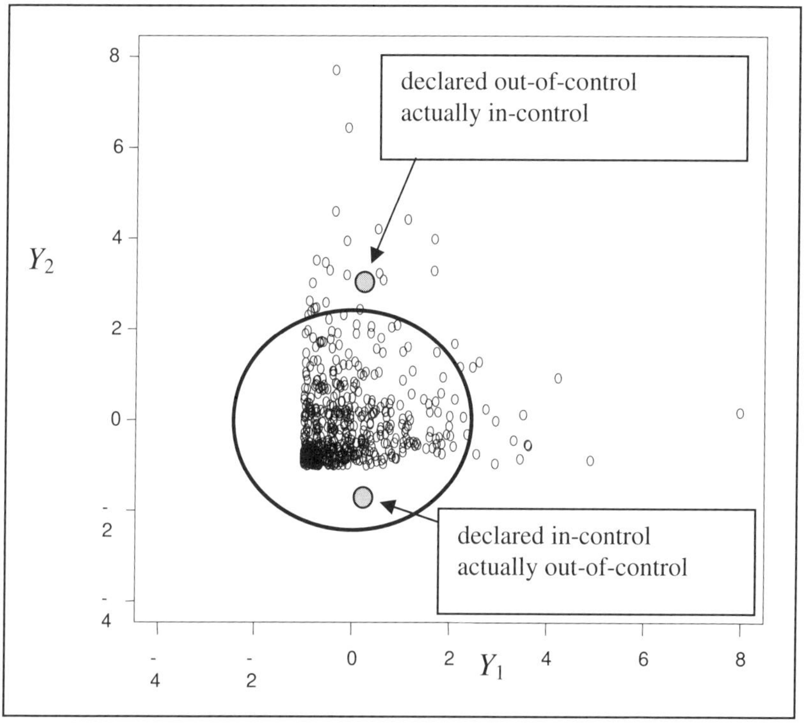

Figure 7. The Hotelling T^2 control scheme applied to a bivariate *Gamma* sample.

Obviously, in such a simple example a scatter plot of the HDS highlights this structure, and the analyst will be induced to implement some corrective action. However, in a data mining framework, with more variables involved, such a plot is inadequate, and even a pairwise scatter plot matrix (if feasible) may hide this anomalous data structure (see e.g. Hand *et al.*, 2000). In addition, the more variables are involved, the farther from normal the multivariate empirical distribution is likely to be.

As a remedy, one may exploit a variable transformation procedure, such as the widely used Box-Cox transformation class (Box and Cox, 1964) and its multivariate extension (Andrews *et al.*, 1971). However, it should first be noted that there is no guarantee that there is a normalizing transformation for the empirical distribution under analysis, even if it is possible to find some normalizing transformations for the marginal distributions. In addition, even if such a transformation exists, algorithms may fail to find such a solution, typically due to the presence of too many local minima when dealing with many variables. We conclude that multivariate joint transformations are not suitable within a data mining framework.

Other methods to manage departures from normality have been designed. Aiming to hold the parametric setting (2), one may wish to assume other multivariate family distributions. This strategy has been developed for some special cases, such as that of a multiple *Gamma* correlated distribution (Jearkpaporn *et al.*, 2003).

However, it is quite difficult to guess what kind of family fits a multivariate data scatter without previous knowledge of the process distribution, a common situation in data mining. In addition, even if some non-normal parametric null distribution can be reasonably assumed for the process, evaluating and assessing such a hypothesis may be infeasible. In the end, if this strategy is successfully pursued, what remains is to find an appropriate test statistic with a known distribution.

5. Designing Nonparametric Charts When Large HDS Are Available: the Data Depth Approach

When large HDS are available, data mining is called into action: previous knowledge of the process is usually not available or cannot yield a unique model for all the features. Hence, any specific parametric model proves inappropriate and some alternative solutions should be adopted.

In this framework, Polansky (2005) suggested ignoring the multivariate distribution generating the process and focusing on the empirical distribution of some appropriate estimators of the parameters concerned. In this case one can exploit the nonparametric kernel density estimation along with some bootstrap techniques to construct a distribution-free control chart. However, if the aim is to monitor the multivariate location of a process, and hence a vector of estimators has to be considered, this method will share all the drawbacks of kernel density estimation in high dimensions.

Without any knowledge of the process distribution, Chang and Bai (2004) recently suggested deviations from normality be managed through a T^2 chart that includes some additional parameters. They developed a model that provides approximated non-elliptical contours for asymmetric distributions through the use of some weighted standard deviations, obtained by decomposing the standard deviation into upper and lower deviations according to the direction and degree of skewness. This idea seems appealing, especially if few observations are available. However, the chart is explicitly designed only for non-normality due to asymmetry and, in addition, the degree of the approximation does not appear easy to evaluate. Furthermore, as they themselves admit, if enough data are at hand, control charts based on the empirical multivariate distribution may be preferred.

Thus the idea of exploiting nonparametric methods to build a control chart seems a natural solution within a data mining framework. First, this approach is able to deal with any kind of distribution, as it does not rely on any distribution assumption. Secondly, the large number of observations which can be collected swiftly in Phase I allows nonparametric charts to match the performance of their parametric counterparts.

Among possible nonparametric techniques, we suggest using data depth, which has found growing interest in multivariate quality control, starting from the first work of Liu based on Simplicial Depth (Liu and Singh, 1993; Liu, 1995; Liu *et al.*, 2004).

However, in such a complete nonparametric setting the chart cannot be evaluated in terms of the *ARL* functions. This is why Porzio and Ragozini (2004) more recently proposed a data depth sequential control scheme that turns the nonparametric hypothesis system into an equivalent parametric setting. Within this scheme, they developed a Shewhart-type chart based on the convex hull peeling depth and a nonparametric test based on the empirical center-outward quantiles (Porzio and Ragozini, 2001; 2002).

We will discuss the latter approaches below. After a brief description of data depth control charts, we will define an appropriate framework to analyze their properties. The key idea is that depth quantile properties allow us to approach SPC issues nonparametrically, ending up with a parametric setting. That is, while the process multivariate distribution is unknown, the charts are based on a parametric distribution family.

Specifically, we will define a Shewhart sequential quality control procedure based on the univariate *Beta* density, with the *Beta* describing the sample distribution of a data depth based statistic. A likelihood ratio test is then defined to derive appropriate control limits and to study some Average Run Length functions for several alternative hypotheses. The correspondence among each of these hypotheses and different out-of-control cases is also examined.

5.1 Data Depth and Control Charts

Data depth is a function $D(y \mid F)$ that measures the centrality of a point $y \in \Re^k$ with respect to a given multivariate distribution *F*. The deepest points lie at the core of the distribution, while points with lower depths are located in the distribution tails. Initial applications of data depth consisted of multivariate center-outward ordering of data scatters. It has been used to obtain a robust estimate of location and dispersion, for multiple outlier detection, and as a multivariate exploratory tool (Tukey, 1975; Barnett, 1976; Liu *et al.*, 1999). In a data mining framework it has been introduced as a tool for data cleaning (Dasu and Johnson, 2003).

Within multivariate statistical process control, data depth was first introduced by Liu (1995). In detail, let $Y \in \Re^k$ be the vector of the quality measures to be monitored, F^0 a given in-control multivariate distribution for *Y*, and $D(\cdot \mid F^0)$ a depth function defined on F^0. Hence the depth function contours of the in-control distribution are the sets:

$$C(d) = \{y \in \Re^k : D(y \mid F^0) = d\}.$$

If the region $R(d)=\left\{y\in\Re^k : D\left(y\mid F^0\right)=d\right\}$ enclosed by contour $C(d)$ of depth d has a probability content equal to p under F^0, and F^0 is absolutely continuous and its density function is nonzero everywhere, then depth contours are coincident with the p-th center-outward quantile Q_p of F^0:

$$Q_p=\left\{y\in\Re^k : D\left(y\mid F^0\right)=d_p\right\},$$

where d_p is such that $P\left(y\in R\left(d_p\right)\right)=p$. Center-outward ($CO$) quantiles define a sequence of nested convex regions of increasing depth. In the special case of F^0 belonging to the class of the elliptically symmetric distributions, Q_p's are surfaces of ellipsoids.

Note that the center-outward quantiles do not correspond to the usual quantile notion. To illustrate the difference, let us consider the simplest case of a univariate random variable. When k=1, the usual p-th quantile is the single point $Q_p^*=\left\{y:F(y)=p\right\}, y\in\Re^1$, while the p-th center-outward quantile is the set:

$$Q_p=\left\{(y_1,y_2):F(y_1)=p/2, F(y_2)=1-p/2\right\}.$$

That is, the CO-quantiles are the two points y_1 and y_2 symmetric in terms of the probability with respect to the median of the distribution $Q_{0.5}^*=\left\{y:F(y)=0.5\right\}=Q_1$.

In the multivariate SPC setting, the deepest points will correspond to items of higher quality, under the assumption that the center of the in-control distribution is the quality target to be achieved. Therefore, with respect to the process, the outer-inward sequence of these CO-quantiles defines a sequence of increasing quality levels.

Consider now the function $p\left(\cdot\mid F^0\right):\Re^k\rightarrow\Re^1$:

$$p\left(\cdot\mid F^0\right)=P\left(Y\in R\left(d_p\right)\right)=p$$

that maps a point y, having $D(y \mid F^0) = d_p$, with the probability content p of the center-outward quantile Q_p to which it belongs.

For each produced item y, if $p(y \mid F^0)$ is close to zero (i.e., y belongs to one of the deepest center-outward quantiles of F^0), the process will be considered in-control. Similarly, if $p(y \mid F^0)$ is close to one, the point y will be in the distribution tails, and the process is out-of-control.

Consequently, data depth control charts can be defined through the values of $p(y \mid F^0)$ that can be associated to each item. Liu (1995) defined some Shewhart and CUSUM charts based on a quality index that is equivalent to 1- $p(y \mid F^0)$. In analogy with the T^2 control scheme, Porzio and Ragozini (2002) proposed a nonparametric procedure based on the center-outward quantiles to design a chart where the $p(y \mid F^0)$ values are directly plotted.

For simplicity, in the following $p(y)$ will stand for $p(y \mid F^0)$, as in our setting such a probability is always evaluated through the F^0 center-outward quantiles. However, while the $p(y)$ values always depend on F^0, it is not necessary that $\mathbf{Y} \sim F^0$.

5.2 *Towards a Parametric Setting for Data Depth Control Charts*

As discussed earlier in Section 3, in standard SPC the parametric hypothesis system (2) is defined as a specification of system (1). This allows the derivation of an appropriate test statistic with known distribution.

In nonparametric SPC, the sequential quality control scheme (1) still holds, but with F^0 and F^1 completely unknown. In this case, the *LRT* approach is infeasible and nonparametric procedures have to be adopted. As a consequence, *ARL* functions for nonparametric schemes can generally only be studied through simulations for specific cases (see e.g. (Stoumbos *et al.*, 2001)). Notwithstanding, we are able to introduce a mapping among the undefined hypothesis system (1) and a well-defined parametric hypothesis system in the case of data depth control charts. It thus becomes possible to study *ARL* functions for some specific alternative hypotheses even for data depth based control procedures.

In order to define our setting, consider first the following result: if $D(\mathbf{Y} \mid F^0)$ has a continuous distribution, then $p(\mathbf{Y} \mid F^0)$ is uniformly distributed on [0, 1]. Consequently, it holds that

$$\mathbf{Y} \sim F^0 \Rightarrow p(\mathbf{Y} \mid F^0) \sim \mathrm{U}(0,1).$$

That is, as long as the process is in-control, the $p(y \mid F^0)$ values will come from a *Uniform* distribution with support in [0, 1]. When the process goes out-of-control the $p(y \mid F^0)$'s will be generated from a different distribution, obviously still supported in [0, 1].

Among the univariate distributions with support in [0, 1], which includes the *Uniform* distribution as a special case, we propose to consider the *Beta(a, b)* distribution as a reasonable model to rewrite the hypotheses in (1) as:

$$H_0 : p(\mathbf{Y}_1),\ldots, p(\mathbf{Y}_{r-1}), p(\mathbf{Y}_r), p(\mathbf{Y}_{r+1}),\ldots \sim Beta(1,1)$$

$$H_1 : p(\mathbf{Y}_1),\ldots, p(\mathbf{Y}_{r-1}), \sim Beta\ (1,1) \qquad p(\mathbf{Y}_r), p(\mathbf{Y}_{r+1}),\ldots \sim Beta\ (a,b) \quad (5)$$

Rejecting the null hypothesis in (5) implies rejecting the null in (1). On the other hand, parameters a and b (a and/or $b \neq 1$) describe out-of-control distributions. As the a and b values change, the unknown F^0 changes to some F^1. For the sake of illustration, and to provide further arguments for our proposed setting, let us consider the case of shift in location: F^1 differs from F^0 just in its position in the multivariate space. Let $F^1_{\Delta L}$ be such a distribution, and let us evaluate the similarity between F^0 and $F^1_{\Delta L}$ in terms of coverage probability. That is, in terms of the probability with which $\mathbf{Y}$ occurs under $F^1_{\Delta L}$ in the inner region $R(d_p)$ of F^0.

We have $P(Y \in R(d_p) \mid F^0) = p$ by definition, and obviously $P(Y \in R(d_p) \mid F^1_{\Delta L}) < p$. In particular, as long as $F^1_{\Delta L}$ goes further from

F^0, the probability decreases, and hence $P(Y \in R(d_p) | F^1_{\Delta L})$ is a measure of the difference between locations. This probability can be parameterized in terms of the width of the shift *s*, *s*≥0, through any continuous function $g_p(s)$ decreasing in *s*. Specifically, among the possible $g_p(s)$, if it is assumed that $P(Y \in R(d_p) | F^1_{\Delta L}) = p^{s+1}$, then it can be proved that $P(Y \in R(d_p) | F^1_{\Delta L}) \sim Beta(s+1,1)$. Hence, the *Beta* parameter $a = s+1$ (when *b*=1) can be interpreted as a measure of the shift width as well. In particular, we note that for *a*=1 (*s*=0), we have $P(Y \in R(d_p) | F^1_{\Delta L}) = p$, and $F^1_{\Delta L} = F^0$. Following the same arguments, it can be shown that the *Beta*(*a*,1) density also describes increases in spread.

A worsening in process quality given by both shifts in location and/or increased variances will be then detected by this kind of chart. This feature is shared more or less by all the other multivariate charts, and is well known in the literature. Some consider this as an additional advantage, as one is able to discover any change in the process through just one chart. In any case, following some out-of-control signals, further analyses should be performed in order to investigate the out-of-control cause. We provide a short discussion on this issue in the final remarks at the end of this chapter.

To empirically verify the proposed hypothesis system (5), we designed a small simulation study. We generated an HDS of 10,000 observations from a bivariate standard normal distribution (our F^0) to evaluate the empirical center outward quantiles of the null distribution (Phase I). Then, as if Phase II were running, we generated 1,000 more data from the same distribution, and 1,000 more data from an alternative distribution, computing the $p(y | F^0)$ for all of them.

According to the above results, for the first 1,000 data we expect that their $p(y | F^0)$ are generated from a *Uniform* distribution supported in [0, 1]. In Figure 8 we depict their empirical distribution through a histogram scaled as a probability density. The *Uniform* scheme implies that all the histogram bars should have the same average height. The figure seems to confirm this expected behavior.

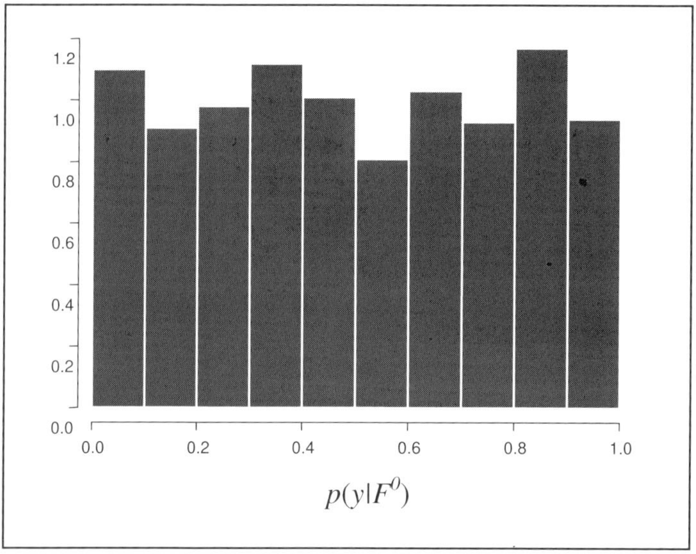

Figure 8. Empirical distribution of the test statistic under the null hypothesis.

The second 1,000 data were generated from a bivariate normal distribution shifted in mean ($+1\sigma$) with respect to F^0, and with the same variances. Under our setting, these latter $p(y \mid F^0)$ should be generated according to a *Beta*(a,1) density, with $a > 1$. In Figure 9 their empirical distribution is drawn. The histogram behavior seems to support our discussion.

In this example, and throughout the rest of the chapter, we choose to evaluate the null distribution center-outward quantiles and the $p(y \mid F^0)$'s by means of a modified version of the convex hull peeling depth, which we will describe in Section 5.6.

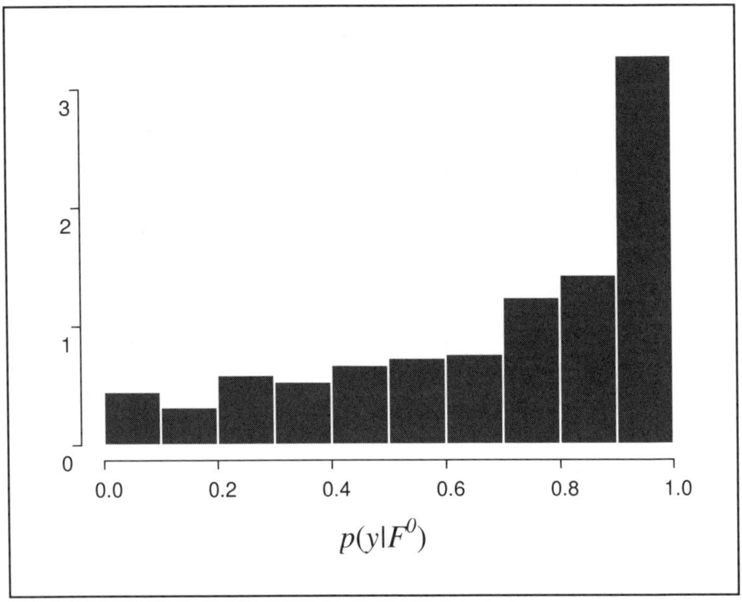

Figure 9. Empirical distribution of the test statistic under an alternative hypothesis.

5.3 A Shewhart Chart for Changes in Location and Increases in Scale

The hypothesis in (5) allows derivation of an *LRT* according to the parametric sequential quality control setting (3). In particular, we derive an *LRT* for a strictly increasing *Beta* density $(a > 1, b = 1)$ for the $p(\mathbf{Y}_r), p(\mathbf{Y}_{r+1}),\ldots$, as such a density characterizes a shift in location and/or an increase in scale of F^1 with respect to F^0. We then test:

$$H_0 : p(\mathbf{Y}_1),\ldots, p(\mathbf{Y}_{r-1}), p(\mathbf{Y}_r), p(\mathbf{Y}_{r+1}),\ldots \sim Beta(1,1)$$

$$H_1 : p(\mathbf{Y}_1),\ldots, p(\mathbf{Y}_{r-1}), \sim Beta(1,1) \qquad p(\mathbf{Y}_r), p(\mathbf{Y}_{r+1}),\ldots \sim Beta(a,1),$$

where $a > 1$.

In such a case, under the out-of-control distribution, the $\mathbf{Y}_r, \mathbf{Y}_{r+1}, \ldots$ belong to the outer F^0 center-outward quantiles with higher probability and the $p(\mathbf{Y})$ will thus assume values close to 1 with higher probability. Hence, adopting the Shewhart scheme (3), the stopping time t is given by:

$$t = \inf\left\{ n \left| \log \frac{f_1(p(\mathbf{Y}_n))}{f_0(p(\mathbf{Y}_n))} \geq h \right. \right\} = \inf\left\{ n \left| \log a\left[p(\mathbf{Y}_n)\right]^{a-1} \geq h \right. \right\}$$
$$= \inf\left\{ n \left| p(\mathbf{Y}_n) \geq \exp\{[h - \log a]/(a-1)\} = \tilde{h} \right. \right\}. \tag{6}$$

An *LRT* can then be performed through the test statistic $p(\mathbf{Y}_n)$, with the rejection region given by $p(y_n) > \tilde{h}$. Therefore, a Shewhart chart for detecting changes in location and scale could be designed by plotting the $p(y_n)$ values against time, with the Upper Control Limit (*UCL*) defined by the cut-off value $\tilde{h}$. The process will be declared out-of-control as soon as $p(y_n)$ lies above the *UCL*. The threshold value $\tilde{h}$ depends on the $p(\mathbf{Y}_n)$ null distribution, and is fixed by the user considering either the amount of false-positive or the desired ARL_0. In the first case, as the distribution of $p(\mathbf{Y}_n)$ under F^0 is *Uniform*(0,1), given a significance level α, then $\tilde{h} = 1 - \alpha$, as by definition $\left\{\tilde{h} : P\left(p(\mathbf{Y}_n) \geq \tilde{h}\right) = \alpha\right\}$.

5.4 *An Illustrative Example*

In order to illustrate how the proposed chart works, we present a simulated data example, and we consider a process null bivariate *Gamma* distribution to present its behavior under some asymmetries.

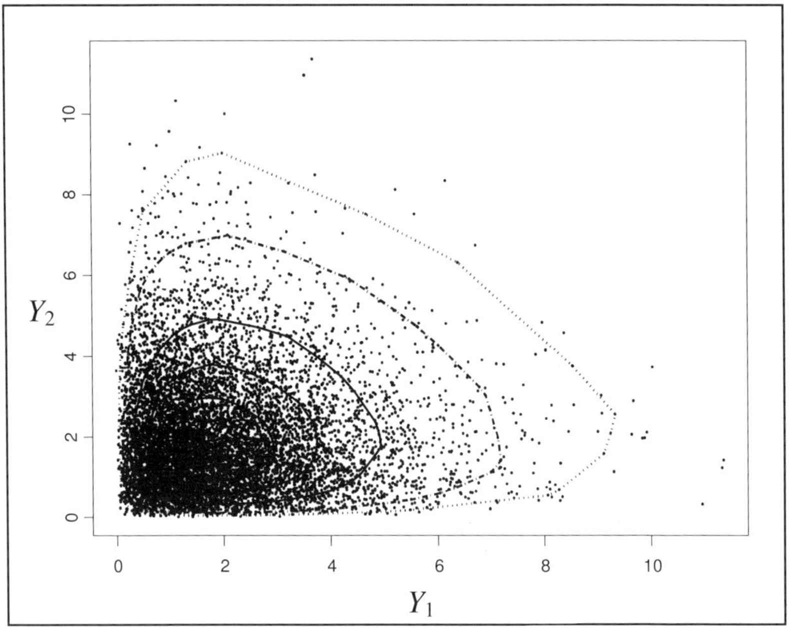

Figure 10. Simulated *Gamma*(2,1) HDS with some center outward quantiles superimposed (from the outer to the inner: $Q_{0.99}$, $Q_{0.95}$, $Q_{0.75}$, $Q_{0.50}$, and $Q_{0.25}$).

In Figure 10, an HDS of 10,000 observations is displayed. It has been drawn from a bivariate independent $Gamma(\alpha,\beta)$ distribution with shape parameter α=2 and scale parameter β=1. In this figure, we superimpose some of the center outward quantiles ($Q_{0.99}$, $Q_{0.95}$, $Q_{0.75}$, $Q_{0.50}$, and $Q_{0.25}$ from the outer to the inner) to show how they are able to catch the distribution shape.

Then, as if in Phase II, we generated 20 more observations from a $Gamma(\alpha,\beta)$ distribution with α=2 and β=1,2,3,4 for 5 new observations, each in sequence. In other words, the first 5 new observations come from the null process distribution, while the others are drawn from some shifted in scale *Gamma* distributions, with the process going slowly out-of-control from the 6th item on.

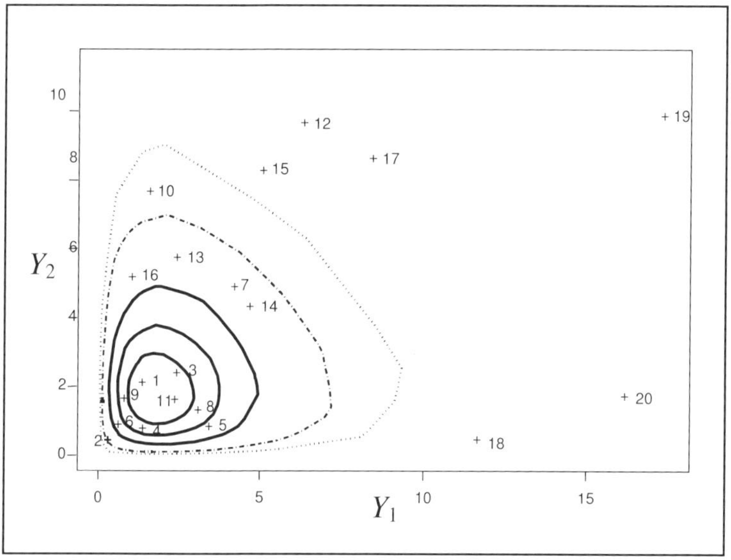

Figure 11. Center-outward quantiles estimated on the HDS along with a sequence of 20 observations drawn from some shifted in scale *Gamma*(2,β) distributions (β=1,2,3,4).

In Figure 11 we plot these 20 observations in their sample space, identified with their indices. We also plot the center-outward quantiles described above so that the pattern from the in-control process towards a shifted in scale out of control distribution is highlighted.

Finally, Figure 12 represents the corresponding control chart. The solid line is the center line (the expected value of the statistic under the null), while the dashed line is the *UCL* at a significance level α=0.05, and the dotted line is the *UCL* at α=0.01. We note that the first 5 in-control points lie under the control limits, while the data move towards the out-of-control region as the shift in scale increases.

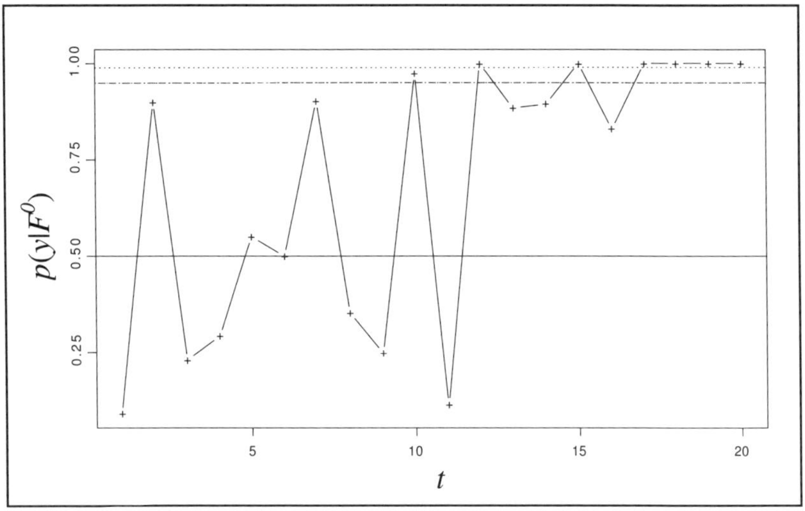

Figure 12. Data depth Shewhart control chart, with center line (the solid line), α=0.05 *UCL* (dashed line), and α=0.01 *UCL* (dotted line). The points correspond to the 20 observations displayed in Figure 11. The first 5 points come from the in-control distribution, while the others move towards some out-of-control distribution.

5.5 Average Run Length Functions for Data Depth Control Charts

The *Beta* setting we introduced permits proper *ARL* functions to be derived for the data depth Shewhart chart. Specifically, we study the *ARL* as a function of the *Beta* parameter a to evaluate the performance of the chart under different alternatives. We cannot consider the usual ARL_0 function used in SPC in order to decide upon the batch size, as we are focusing on single observation charts (i.e., with the batch size set at one). In our case, the ARL_0 is by definition the value of the *ARL* function evaluated under the null hypothesis.

To derive the function, note first that the *ARL* is the expected values of t, $E_a(t)$. Then, as t is the waiting time for the first alarm, it can be described by a *Geometric* distribution with parameter $\pi_a = P_a\left(p(\mathbf{Y}_n) \geq \tilde{h}\right)$, with $p(\mathbf{Y}_n) \sim Beta(a,1), a \geq 1$, and we have:

$$
\begin{aligned}
E_a(t) &= (1/\pi_a) = \left[P_a\left(p(\mathbf{Y}_n) \geq \tilde{h}\right)\right]^{-1} \\
&= \left[1 - F_{p(\mathbf{Y}_n)}\left(\tilde{h}\right)\right]^{-1} = \left[1 - \int_0^{\tilde{h}} a x^{a-1} dx\right]^{-1} \\
&= \left[1 - \tilde{h}^a\right]^{-1} = \left[1 - (1-\alpha)^a\right]^{-1}. \qquad (7)
\end{aligned}
$$

The *ARL* are then decreasing functions of a $(a \geq 1)$, and for a = 1 we have $ARL_o = 1/\alpha$. For the sake of illustration, we draw such *ARL* functions in Figure 13 for three different significance levels.

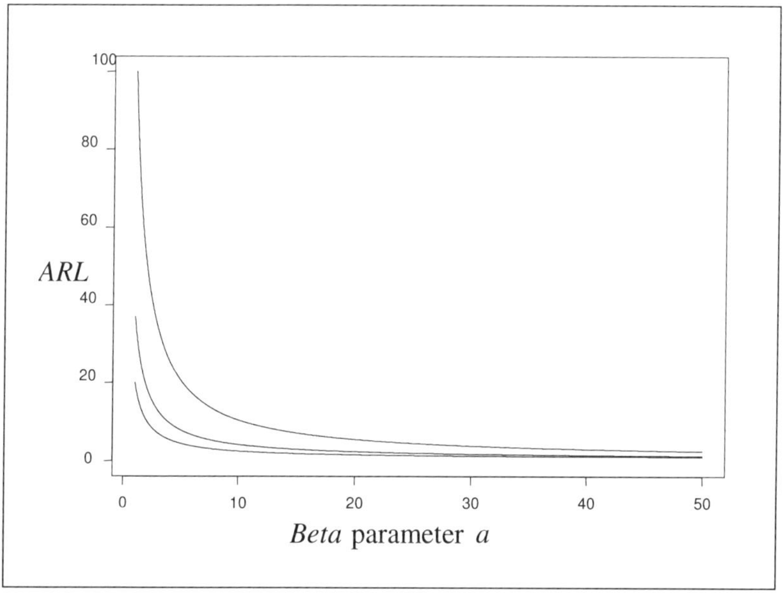

Figure 13. Average Run Length (*ARL*) as a function of the *Beta* parameter a for different significance levels α= 0.05, 0.027, 0.01 (from bottom up).

Finally, we recall that parameter a measures differences in location and/or spread between F^0 and F^1. However, while in the parametric SPC such differences can be described through differences among the family distribution parameters, in nonparametric SPC such an interpretation is lacking. Hence, for better interpretation and use of the chart, we express how far F^1 is from F^0 in terms of parameter a for the case of changes in location and/or increase in scale through the coverage probability $P(\mathbf{Y} \in R(d_p) \mid F^1)$. In particular, for a given significance level α, we have:

$$a = \frac{\log(P(\mathbf{Y} \in R(d_{(1-\alpha)}) \mid F^1))}{\log(P(\mathbf{Y} \in R(d_{(1-\alpha)}) \mid F^0))} = \frac{\log(P(\mathbf{Y} \in R(d_{(1-\alpha)}) \mid F^1))}{\log(1-\alpha)} \tag{8}$$

As an example, for α = 0.01, if $P(\mathbf{Y} \in R(d_{0.99}) \mid F^1) = 0.95$, i.e. F^1 is close to F^0, then a=5.1 and the ARL = 20. On the other hand, if F^1 and F^0 are quite different (say $P(\mathbf{Y} \in R(d_{0.99}) \mid F^1) = 0.20$), then a = 160 and the ARL = 1.25.

5.6 A Simulation Study of Chart Performance

In order to evaluate our proposed framework, we performed a simulation study. For the sake of comparison, we made simulations under normality, because under such a model the exact value for the *Beta* parameter a may be derived both under the null hypothesis and under mean-shift alternative distributions.

Specifically, let us measure the shifts in means through the parameter $\lambda = \mu_1^2 + \mu_2^2 + \ldots + \mu_k^2$. As under normality depth contours are surfaces of ellipsoids (Zuo and Serfling, 2000b), then, if $\mathbf{Y} \sim \mathrm{N}(\boldsymbol{\mu}; \boldsymbol{\Sigma})$, $P(\mathbf{Y} \in R(d_{(1-\alpha)})) = P(T^2 \leq \chi^2_{k,(1-\alpha)})$, with $\chi^2_{k,(1-\alpha)}$ the $(1-\alpha)$ quantile of the χ^2 distribution with k degrees of freedom. Hence $P(\mathbf{Y} \in R(d_{(1-\alpha)}) \mid F^0)$ = $P(\chi^2_k \leq \chi^2_{k,(1-\alpha)})$ = 1-α.

In the case of a shift in location, the T^2 statistic is distributed as $\chi_k^2(\lambda)$, a non-central χ^2 random variable with k degrees of freedom and noncentrality parameter $\lambda = \mu_1^2 + \mu_2^2 + \ldots + \mu_k^2$. Consequently, $P\left(\mathbf{Y} \in R\left(d_{(1-\alpha)}\right) \mid F^1\right) = P\left(\chi_k^2(\lambda) \le \chi_{k,(1-\alpha)}^2\right)$.

From Equation (8) we eventually get an one-to-one correspondence between the non-central parameter λ and the *Beta* parameter a:

$$a = \frac{\log\left(P\left(\chi_k^2(\lambda) \le \chi_{k,(1-\alpha)}^2\right)\right)}{\log(1-\alpha)} \tag{9}$$

This relationship provides a benchmark to compare the performance of data depth charts under normality, a case when it is expected that the classic T^2 chart performs better than any nonparametric methodology. Notwithstanding, we expect also that in a data mining SPC framework a large HDS will render the performance of the T^2 chart and of nonparametric methodologies substantially equivalent.

We then generated 10,000 HDS's observations from k-variate standard normal distributions with independent components. These datasets are used to estimate the center-outward quantiles of the null distributions. As if Phase II were running, we then generated new incoming observations from k-variate normal distributions with an identity covariance matrix, both under the null hypothesis ($\boldsymbol{\mu} = \mathbf{0}$) and under some alternatives (radial shifts given by the mean vectors $\boldsymbol{\mu} = \mathbf{0.5, 1.0, 1.5, \ldots, 3}$). For each case we drew an 1,000-observation random sample, and we replicated such a simulation scheme for k=2, 3, 4. To evaluate the $p(y_n)$ values we used the modified version of the convex hull peeling depth as described in the example in Section 5.2 above.

For a significance level $\alpha = 0.05$, in Table 1 *(a), (b), (c)*, for k=2, 3, 4, respectively, we reported the $\hat{ARL}$ values (i.e., the estimated *ARL* through the simulated data) as a function of the shift in mean $\boldsymbol{\mu}$, the corresponding non-centrality parameter λ, the *Beta* parameter a as given by Equation (9), and the theoretical *ARL* values given by Equation (7) as a function of a.

Table 1. *(a)* Estimated *ARL* values for the data depth control chart under *k*-variate normality for various radial shifts, *k*=2.

k=3				
μ	λ	a	*ARL(a)*	$\hat{ARL}(a)$
0	0	1	20	22.22
0.5	0.5	1.82	11.16	9.01
1	2	4.98	4.43	5.21
1.5	4.5	12.03	2.17	2.11
2	8	24.65	1.39	1.39
2.5	12.5	44.17	1.11	1.11
3	18	71.50	1.03	1.02

Table 1. *(b)* Estimated *ARL* values for the data depth control chart under *k*-variate normality for various radial shifts, *k*=3.

k=3				
μ	λ	a	*ARL(a)*	$\hat{ARL}(a)$
0	0	1.00	20.00	19.23
0.5	0.75	2.01	10.20	10.00
1	3	6.25	3.64	3.64
1.5	6.75	16.56	1.74	1.74
2	12	35.76	1.19	1.18
2.5	18.75	65.89	1.04	1.04
3	27	108.24	1.00	1.01

Table 1. *(c)* Estimated *ARL* values for the data depth control chart under *k*-variate normality for various radial shifts, *k*=4.

k=4				
μ	λ	a	*ARL(a)*	$\hat{ARL}(a)$
0	0	1.00	20.00	20.00
0.5	1	2.17	9.48	10.75
1	4	7.52	3.12	3.31
1.5	9	21.23	1.51	1.62
2	16	47.35	1.10	1.14
2.5	25	88.57	1.01	1.01
3	36	146.50	1.00	1.00

In addition, in Figures 14, 15, and 16 we visually compare these empirical values $A\hat{R}L(a)$ with the theoretical *ARL* functions superimposing them as large dots. These figures respectively show results for k=2, 3, 4.

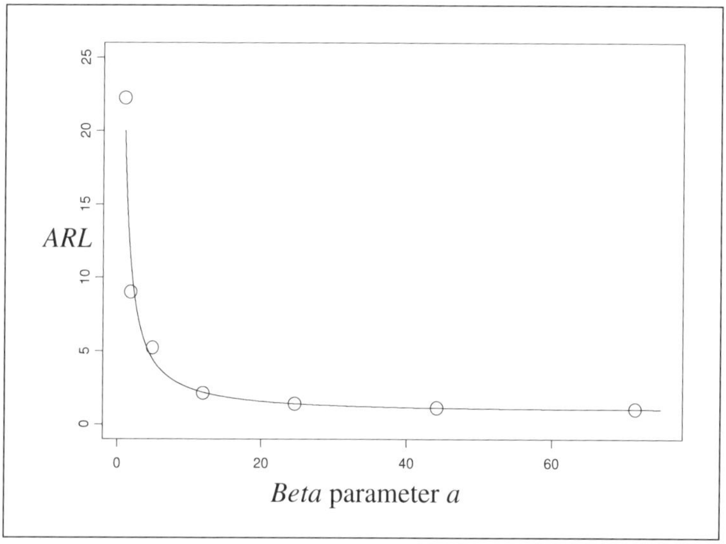

Figure 14. *ARL* function and estimated *ARL* for some *Beta* parameter a values (dots) under k-variate normality, k=2.

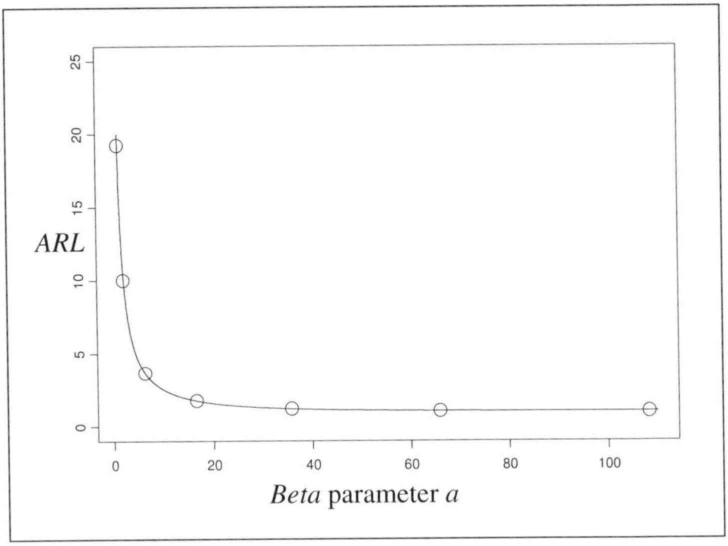

Figure 15. *ARL* function and estimated *ARL* for some *Beta* parameter *a* values (dots) under *k*-variate normality, *k*=3.

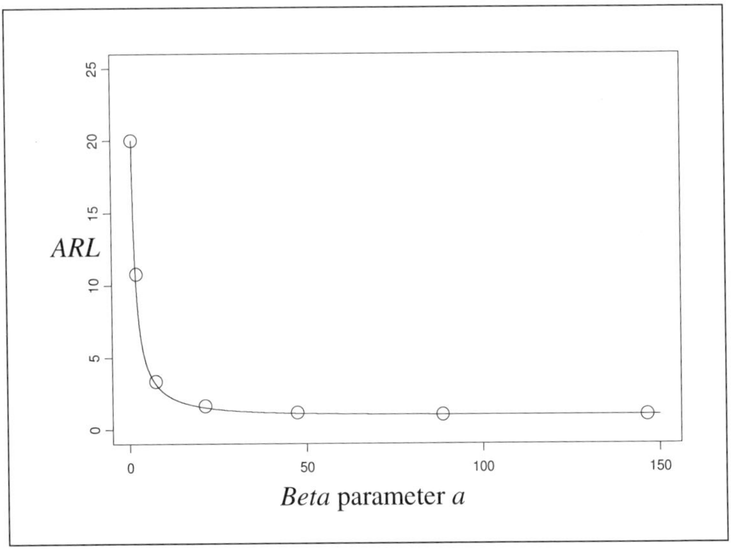

Figure 16. *ARL* function and estimated *ARL* for some *Beta* parameter *a* values (dots) under *k*-variate normality, *k*=4.

We note that the correspondence between the theoretical *ARL* functions derived from our *Beta* framework and the observed *ARL* values obtained from our simulation is strong, and this aspect is maintained while the space dimension increases.

5.7 Choosing an Empirical Depth Function

Although many notions of depth are available in the literature (e.g., (Liu *et al.*, 1999), (Zuo and Serfling, 2000a), (Mosler, 2002), (Mizera and Müller, 2004)), it is not necessary to adopt any specific depth function in order to define a depth based control chart. However, in practice one particular empirical data depth $\hat{D}(y \mid F)$ has to be chosen, and among a wide range of possibilities, we suggest considering a notion of depth arising from the convex hull peeling depth (Barnett, 1976).

The convex hull peeling depth for a sample point $\mathbf{X}_i$ with respect to the sample $\mathbf{X}$ is its layer in the sequence of the nested convex hull of $\mathbf{X}$. We propose modification of this notion in order to obtain a depth function that works properly in our setting. In brief, the idea is to associate to each convex hull layer its probability content, so that the depth of a point $\mathbf{X}_i$ will be the probability of lying inside the convex hull layer to which it belongs. Other details on this depth notion and related computational aspects go beyond the scope of this chapter, and we refer the interested reader to Porzio and Ragozini (2001, 2007).

This kind of depth is mostly appropriate for nonparametric data depth control charts from a data mining perspective, as it is computationally affordable in high dimensions, unlike the most common depth functions available in the literature (we recall that for the most popular half-space and simplicial depths exact algorithms are unavailable if $k>3$ (Rousseeuw and Struyf, 1998)). In addition, a further computational saving is gained with respect to other depth functions, as for this depth the sequence of all the center-outward quantiles is computed only once on the HDS, while points incoming in Phase II are located in the layer sequence through a fast algorithm reproducing the quick sort algorithm. In other words, only the HDS layer equations are needed in Phase II, and the $p(y_n)$ computation consists in locating a point y_n in a hyperplane arrangement. Other depth-based charts, including the most commonly used simplicial depth, generally require greater computational effort. All the HDS points must be stored, and the depth algorithm has to be run all over again for each new incoming point.

6. Final Remarks

We have presented the main issues to be tackled when large datasets are available for monitoring a production process. We briefly reviewed classic methodology for multivariate control charts, and then we discussed how the presence of many recorded quality measures and product features may affect such a technique. In particular, we provided first an up-to-date critical review of suitable methods for dealing with the presence of multiple outliers in the dataset used to define the chart. Then we offered ideas for addressing the drawbacks arising from the assumption of multivariate normality that underlies the use of the Hotelling T^2 chart and related methods. Specifically, we presented a nonparametric approach based on the data depth notion.

Few other nonparametric approaches for multivariate production process control have been proposed in the literature. Martin and Morris (1996) proposed relying directly on a nonparametric estimation of the null density distribution using some multivariate kernel density estimators. However, this approach runs up against the "curse of dimensionality", and leaves the selection of the multivariate bandwidth parameter wide open. Alternatively, Chen *et al.* (2000) used univariate kernel density estimates to define an appropriate control limit on some first PCA components: their independence enabled the analyst to avoid managing multivariate kernel density estimators. Qiu and Hawkins (2001) suggested monitoring a process through a CUSUM scheme based on the anti-rank of the quality measure vector. D'Esposito and La Rocca (2002) discussed a control chart based on an empirical likelihood ratio test derived from the empirical likelihood function (Owen, 1990), which requires neither any assumption on the process null distribution, nor the computation of the variance/covariance matrix.

When a large set of variables are jointly monitored, both classic T^2 statistic and nonparametric methods may fail. Substantially, mean shifts become indistinguishable or undetectable because the large number of variables offset the shift. In a parametric context, this corresponds to the fact that the power of the Hotelling test decreases as a function of the number of variables for a given non-centrality parameter under the alternative hypothesis (see the tables in (Haynam *et al.*, 1970), which provide for some non-centrality parameters the power values up to the case of 100 variables).

In such a case, it may be preferred to first carry out some dimension reduction. Instead of monitoring a process through the analysis of all the measured characteristics, a few summary variables may in some way be extracted for actually controlling the behavior of the process. The SPC methodology (either classic or nonparametric) will exploit the summary variables to control the process. Whilst many methods for dimension reduction exist, in a quality control setting the most frequently used is principal component analysis (Jackson, 1991; further investigated by Runger and Montgomery, 1997, among others); the T^2 chart is then defined on the subspace of the first k components.

From our data mining perspective, outliers and/or non-elliptical structure may affect classic PCA analysis. Hence, in the first case some robust dimension reduction technique should be preferred (see e.g. (Hubert *et al.*, 2005)), while some nonlinear PCA should be adopted when normality does not hold at all, as discussed in a quality control setting by Martin and Morris (1998). An interesting treatment of nonlinearities and data reduction in data mining is via the optimal scaling approach, first introduced by Gifi (1990). This approach has not yet been investigated in SPC.

Last but not least, a crucial point in multivariate process control is to follow up an out-of-control signal with analysis aimed at discovering what causes (i.e., which variables) mainly led the process out of control. This knowledge extraction process is called retrospective analysis, as it extracts past quality measures from the databases with the goal of discovering clusters, outliers, and unusual patterns. In a data mining framework, neural networks were used by Chen and Wang (2004), while Porzio and Ragozini (2003) and Albazzaz *et al.* (2005) preferred to exploit the power of some visual data mining techniques with the same aim.

Acknowledgements

The authors are indebted to Jaromir Antoch for useful discussions on the sequential quality control setting. They also wish to thank Domenico Vistocco for his contribution to the simulation study, and the two referees for their suggestions that helped to improve the final version of this chapter.

References

Albazzaz H., Wang X.Z. and Marhoon F. (2005). Multidimensional visualisation for process historical data analysis: a comparative study with multivariate statistical process control, *Journal of Process Control*, **15**, 285–294.

Alt F.B. (1985). Multivariate quality control, in: *Encyclopedia of Statistical Sciences*, vol. 6, Johnson N.L., Kotz S. (eds.), Wiley, New York, NY, U.S.A., 111–122.

Alt F.B. and Smith N.D. (1988). Multivariate process control, in: *Handbook of Statistics*, vol. 7, Krishnaiah P.R., Rao C.R. (eds.), Elsevier, Amsterdam, The Netherlands, 333–351.

Andrews D.F. Gnanadesikan R. and Warner J.L. (1971). Transformation of Multivariate Data, *Biometrics*, **27**, 825–840.

Andrews D.F. Gnanadesikan R. and Warner J.L. (1973). Methods for assessing multivariate normality, in: *Multivariate Analysis III*, Krishnaiah P.R. (ed.), Academic Press, New York, NY, U. S. A.

Antoch J. and Jaruskova D. (2002). On-line statistical process control, in: *Multivariate Total Quality Control*, Lauro C., Antoch J., Esposito Vinzi V., Saporta G. (eds.), Physica-Verlag, Heidelberg, Germany, 87–124.

Atkinson A.C. (1994). Fast Very Robust Methods for the Detection of Multiple Outliers, *Journal of the American Statistical Association,* **89**, 1329–1339.

Atkinson A.C. and Riani M. (2004). Forward Search and Data Visualization, *Computational Statistics*, **19**, 29–54.

Barnett V. (1976). The ordering of multivariate data (with discussion), *Journal of Royal Statistical Society, Ser. A*, **139**, 318–354.

Barnett V. and Lewis T. (1994), *Outliers in Statistical Data* (3rd ed.), Wiley, New York, NY, U. S. A.

Box G.E.P. and Cox D.R. (1964). An Analysis of Transformations, *Journal of the Royal Statistical Society, Series B*, **26**, 211–252.

Castagliola P. and Tsung F. (2005). Autocorrelated SPC for Non-Normal Situations, *Quality and Reliability Engineering International*, **21**, 131–161.

Castejón Limas M., Ordieres Merél J.B., Martínez de Pisón Ascacibar F.J. and Vergara González E.P. (2004). Outlier Detection and Data Cleaning in Multivariate Non-Normal Samples: The PAELLA Algorithm, *Data Mining and Knowledge Discovery*, **9**, 171–187.

Chang Y.S. and Bai D.S. (2004). A Multivariate T^2 Control Chart for Skewed Populations Using Weighted Standard Deviations, *Quality and Reliability Engineering International*, **20**, 31–46.

Chen L.H. and Wang T.Y. (2004). Artificial neural networks to classify mean shifts from multivariate χ^2 chart signals, *Computers & Industrial Engineering*, **47**, 195–205.

Chen Q., Wynne R.J., Goulding P. and Sandoz D. (2000). The application of principal component analysis and kernel density estimation to enhance process monitoring, *Control Engineering Practice*, **8**, 531–543.

Cheng S.W. and Thaga K. (2006). Single Variables Control Charts: an Overview, *Quality and Reliability Engineering International*, Published Online: 28 Feb 2006.

Dasu T. and Johnson T. (2003). *Exploratory Data Mining and Data Cleaning*, Wiley, New York, NY, U. S. A.

D'Esposito M.R. and La Rocca M. (2002). Nonparametric control charts for multivariate processes based on the empirical likelihood (*in Italian*), In: *Analisi Multivariata per la Qualità totale*, Lauro N.C., Scepi G. (eds.), Franco Angeli, Milan, Italy, 200–210.

D'Esposito M.R. and Ragozini G. (1999). Detection of Multivariate Outliers by Convex Hulls, in *Classification and Data Analysis. Theory and Application*, Vichi M., Opitz O. (eds.), Springer-Verlag, Heidelberg, Germany, 279–286.

Gifi A. (1990). *Nonlinear Multivariate Analysis*, Wiley, Chichester, NJ, U.S.A.

Hadi A.S. (1992). Identifying multiple outliers in multivariate data, *Journal of the Royal Statistical Society, Series B*, **54**, 761–777.

Hadi A.S. (1994). A modification of a method for the detection of outliers in multivariate samples, *Journal of the Royal Statistical Society, Series B*, **56**, 393–396.

Hampel F.R., Ronchetti E.M., Rousseeuw P.J. and Stahel W.A. (1986). *Robust Statistics: The Approach Based on Influence Functions*, Wiley, New York, NY, U.S.A.

Hand D.J., Blunt G., Kelly M.G. and Adams N.M. (2000). Data Mining for Fun and Profit, *Statistical Science*, **15**, 111–131.

Hastie T., Tibshirani R. and Friedman J. (2001). *The Elements of Statistical Learning: Data Mining, Inference, and Prediction*, Springer, New York, NY, U.S.A.

Haynam G.E., Govindarajulu Z. and Leone F.C. (1970). Tables of the cumulative non-central chi-square distribution, in *Selected Tables in Mathematical Statistics*, Harter H.L., Owen D.B. (eds.), Markham, Chicago, IL, U. S. A.

Hotelling H. (1947). Multivariate Quality Control, in: *Techniques of Statistical Analysis*, Eisenhart C., Hastay M.W., Wallis W.A. (eds.), McGraw-Hill, New York, 111–184.

Huber P.J. (1981). *Robust Statistics*, Wiley, New York, NY, U.S.A.

Hubert M., Rousseeuw P.J. and Vanden Branden K. (2005). ROBPCA: a New Approach to Robust Principal Component Analysis, *Technometrics*, **47**, 64–79.

Jackson J.E. (1991). *A User's Guide to Principal Components*, Wiley, New York, NY, U.S.A.

Jearkpaporn D., Montgomery D.C., Runger G.C. and Borror C.M. (2003). Process monitoring for correlated gamma-distributed data using generalized-linear-model-based control chart, *Quality and Reliability Engineering International*, **19**, 477–491.

Jensen W.A., Birch J.B. and Woodall W.H. (2005). *High Breakdown Estimation Methods for Phase I Multivariate Control Charts*, Technical Report N°. 05-6, Dept. of Statistics, Virginia Tech University, Blacksburg, VA, U.S.A.

Kantardzic M. (2002). Data Mining: Concepts, Models, Methods, and Algorithms, Wiley, New York, NY, U.S.A.

Larose D.T. (2006). *Data Mining Methods and Models*, Wiley, New York, NY, U.S.A.

Liu R.Y. (1995). Control Charts for Multivariate Process, *Journal of the American Statistical Association*, **90**, 1380–1387.

Liu R.Y., Parelius J.M. and Singh K. (1999). Multivariate Analysis by Data Depth: Descriptive Statistics, Graphics and Inference, *The Annals of Statistics*, **27**, 783–858.

Liu R.Y. and Singh K. (1993). A Quality Index Based on Data Depth and Multivariate Rank Tests, *Journal of the American Statistical Association*, **88**, 257–260.

Liu R.Y., Singh K. and Teng J.H. (2004). DDMA-charts: Nonparametric multivariate moving average control charts based on data depth, *Allgemeines Statisches Archiv*, **88**, 235–258.

Marcellus R.L. (2005). Performance Measures for $\overline{X}$ Charts with Asymmetric Control Limits, *Quality and Reliability Engineering International*, Published Online: 28 Dec.

Mardia K.V. (1970). Measures of multivariate skewness and kurtosis with applications, *Biometrika*, **57**, 519–530.

Maronna R.A. (1976). Robust M-estimators of multivariate location and scatter, *Annals of Statistics*, **4**, 51–67.

Maronna R.A., Martin D.R. and Yohai V.J. (2006). *Robust statistics: Theory and Methods*, Wiley, New York, NY, U.S.A.

Maronna R.A., Stahel W.A. and Yohai V.J. (1992). Bias-robust estimates of multivariate scatter based on projections, *Journal of Multivariate Analysis*, **42**, 141–161.

Maronna R.A. and Zamar R. (2002). Robust estimation of location and dispersion for high-dimensional datasets, *Technometrics*, **44**, 307–317.

Martin E.B. and Morris A.J. (1996). Non-parametric confidence bounds for process performance monitoring charts, *Journal of Process Control*, **6**, 349–358.

Martin E.B. and Morris A.J. (1998). Non-linear Principal Components Analysis for Process Fault Detection, *Computers and Chem. Engng.*, **22**, Suppl, S851–S854.

Mason R.L. and Young J.C. (2002). *Multivariate Statistical Process Control with Industrial Applications*, ASA-SIAM Series on Statistics and Applied Probability, Philadelphia, PA, U.S.A.

Mizera, I. and Müller, C. H. (2004). Location-Scale Depth (with discussion), *Journal of the American Statistical Association*, **99**, 949–966.

Montgomery D.C. (2001). Research in industrial statistics – part I. *Quality and Reliability Engineering International*, **17** (6), iii–iv.

Montgomery D.C. (2004). *Introduction to Statistical Quality Control* (5th ed.), Wiley, New York, NY, U.S.A.

Mosler K. (2002). *Multivariate Dispersion, Central Regions and Depth*, Springer-Verlag, New York, NY, U.S.A.

Owen A.B. (1990). Empirical likelihood ratio confidence regions, *Annals of Statistics*, **18**, 90–120.

Page E.S. (1954). Continuous inspection schemes, *Biometrika*, **41**, 100–115.

Polansky A.M. (2005). A General Framework for Constructing Control Charts, *Quality and Reliability Engineering International*, **21**, 633–653.

Porzio G.C. and Ragozini G. (2000). Exploring the Periphery of Data Scatters: Are There Outliers?, in *Data Analysis, Classification, and Related Methods*, Kiers H.A.L., Rasson J.P., Groenen P.J.F., Schader M. (eds.), Springer, Heidelberg, Germany, 235–240.

Porzio G.C. and Ragozini G. (2001). Testing through Empirical Center-Outward Quantiles, in *Modelli Complessi e Metodi Computazionali Intensivi per la Stima e la Previsione*, Provasi C. (ed.), CLEUP, Padova, Italy, 409–414.

Porzio G.C. and Ragozini G. (2002). A nonparametric approach to monitor multivariate processes (*in Italian*), in: *Analisi Multivariata per la Qualità Totale*, Lauro N.C., Scepi G. (eds.), Franco Angeli, Milan, Italy, 211–223.

Porzio G.C. and Ragozini G. (2003). Visually Mining Off-line Data for Quality Improvement, *Quality and Reliability Engineering International*, **19**, 273–283.

Porzio G.C. and Ragozini G. (2004). A parametric framework for data depth control charts, in: *Compstat2004*, Antoch J.(ed.), Physica-Verlag, Heidelberg, Germany, 1661–1668.

Porzio G.C. and Ragozini G. (2007). Convex Hull Probability Depth, International Workshop on Robust and Nonparametric Statistical Inference, poster presentation, Hejnice, Czech Republic.

Qiu P. and Hawkins D.M. (2001). A rank-based multivariate CUSUM procedure, *Technometrics*, **43**, 120–132.

Roberts S.W. (1959). Control charts tests based on geometric moving averages, *Technometrics,* **1**, 239–250.

Rocke D.M. and Woodruff D.L. (1996). Identification of outliers in multivariate data. *Journal of the American Statistical Association*, **91**, 1047–1061.

Rousseeuw P.J. (1984). Least Median of Squares Regression, *Journal of the American Statistical Association*, **79**, 871–880.

Rousseeuw P.J. and Struyf A. (1998). Computing location depth and regression depth in higher dimensions, *Statistics and Computing*, **8**, 193–203.

Rousseeuw P.J. and Van Driessen K. (1999). Algorithm for the minimum covariance determinant estimator, *Technometrics*, **41**, 212–223.

Rousseeuw P.J. and van Zomeren B.C. (1990). Unmasking multivariate outliers and leverage points, *Journal of the American Statistical Association,* **85**, 633–639.

Runger G.C. and Montgomery D.C. (1997). Multivariate and Univariate Process Control: Geometry and Shift Directions, *Quality and Reliability Engineering International*, **13**, 153–158.

Shewhart W.A. (1931), *Economic Control of Quality of Manufactured Product*, Van Nostrand, New York, NY, U.S.A.

Soukup T. and Davidson I. (2002). Visual Data Mining: Techniques and Tools for Data Visualization and Mining, Wiley, New York, NY, U.S.A.

Stoumbos Z.G., Jones L.A., Woodall W.H. and Reynolds M.R.J. (2001). On Nonparametric Multivariate Control Charts Based on Data Depth, in: *Frontiers in Statistical Quality Control 6*, Lenz H.J., Wilrich P.T. (eds.), Physica-Verlag, Heidelberg, Germany, 207–227.

Sullivan J.H. and Woodall W.H. (1996). A comparison of multivariate control charts for individual observations, *Journal of Quality Technology*, **28**, 398–408.

Testik M.C. and Runger G.C. (2003). Mining Manufacturing Quality Data, in: *The Handbook of Data Mining*, Ye N. (ed.), Lawrence Erlbaum Associates Publishers, New Jersey, U.S.A., 657–668.

Tukey J.W. (1975). Mathematics and the picturing of data, *Proceedings of the International Congress of Mathematicians* 2, Montreal, Canada, 523–531.

Vargas J.A. (2003). Robust Estimation in Multivariate Control Charts for Individual Observations, *Journal of Quality Technology*, **35**, 367–376.

Wang N. and Raftery A.E. (2002). Nearest neighbor variance estimation (NNVE): robust covariance estimation via nearest neighbor cleaning (with discussion), *Journal of the American Statistical Association*, **97**, 994–1019.

Wilks S.S. (1963). Multivariate Statistical Outliers, *Sankhya Ser. A*, **25**, 407–426.

Willems G., Pison G., Rousseeuw P.J. and Van Aelst S. (2002). A Robust Hotelling Test, *Metrika*, **55**, 125–138.

Williams J.D., Woodall W. H., Birch J.B. and Sullivan J.H. (2004). *On the Distribution of Hotelling's T^2 Statistic Based on the Successive Differences Covariance Matrix Estimator*, Technical Report No. 04-5, Dept. of Statistics, Virginia Tech University, Blacksburg, VA, U.S.A.

Wisnowski J.W., Simpson J.R. and Montgomery D.C. (2002). A Performance Study for Multivariate Location and Shape Estimators, *Quality and Reliability Engineering International*, **18**, 117–129.

Zani S., Riani M. and Corbellini A. (1998). Robust Bivariate Boxplot and Multiple Outlier Detection, *Computational Statistics and Data Analysis*, **28**, 257–270.

Zuo Y. and Serfling R. (2000a). General notions of statistical depth function, *Annals of Statistics*, **28**, 461–482.

Zuo Y. and Serfling R. (2000b). Structural properties and convergence results for contours of sample statistical depth functions, *Annals of Statistics*, **28**, 483–499.

Authors' Biographical Statements

Giovanni C. Porzio is a Professor in the Department of Economics at Cassino University in Italy. He is also Director of the Graduate School in Economics at the same University. He received an MSc in Statistics from the University of Minnesota, and a PhD in Computational Statistics from the Federico II University of Naples, Italy. His research interests include data mining, statistical process control, graphical methods and data visualization, model building and diagnostics, nonparametric multivariate analysis and data depth. He has published in many technical journals, including Quality and Reliability Engineering International, Quality and Quantity, Applied Stochastic Models in Business and Industry, Statistics in Medicine, Metron.

Giancarlo Ragozini is a Professor in the Department of Sociology at Federico II University of Naples, Italy. He received a PhD in Computational Statistics from the Federico II University of Naples, Italy. He was research assistant at Center for Computational Statistics of Department of Applied and Engineering Statistics of George Mason University, Fairfax in Virginia. His research interests include computational geometry, outlier detection, data mining, statistical process control, graphical methods and data visualization, and data depth. He participated also to several evaluation programs of public policies for poverty and unemployment reduction. He has published in many technical journals, including Quality and Reliability Engineering International, Computational Statistics, and Italian Journal of Applied Statistics.

Chapter 10[1]

Data Mining of Multi-Dimensional Functional Data for Manufacturing Fault Diagnosis

Myong K. Jeong[1], Seong G. Kong[2], and Olufemi A. Omitaomu[3]

[1] Department of Industrial & Information Engineering
University of Tennessee, Knoxville, TN 37996-0700, USA. Email: mjeong@utk.edu

[2] Temple University, Department of Electrical and Computer Engineering
Philadelphia, PA 19122, USA

[3] Oak Ridge National Laboratory, Computational Sciences and Engineering Division
Oak Ridge, TN 37831-6017, USA

Abstract: Multi-dimensional functional data, such as time series data and images from manufacturing processes, have been used for fault detection and quality improvement in many engineering applications such as automobile manufacturing, semiconductor manufacturing, and nano-machining systems. Extracting interesting and useful features from multi-dimensional functional data for manufacturing fault diagnosis is more difficult than extracting the corresponding patterns from traditional numeric and categorical data due to the complexity of functional data types, high correlation, and nonstationary nature of the data. This chapter discusses accomplishments and research issues of multi-dimensional functional data mining in the following areas: dimensionality reduction for functional data, multi-scale fault diagnosis, misalignment prediction of rotating machinery, and agricultural product inspection based on hyperspectral image analysis.

***Key Words*:** Band selection, Data mining, Dimensionality Reduction, Functional data, Hyperspectral image, Shaft alignment, Wavelets.

---

[1] Liao, T.W. and E. Triantaphyllou, (Eds.), **Recent Advances in Data Mining of Enterprise Data: Algorithms and Applications**, *World Scientific*, Singapore, pp. 463-504, 2007.

1. Introduction

The recent advances in information technology, such as the various automatic data acquisition and sensor systems, have created tremendous opportunities for collecting valuable process and operational data for several enterprises including manufacturing. The timely processing of such data for meaningful information remains a challenge. In this chapter, we address such a challenge in a manufacturing enterprise. On-line measurements of large volume of multi-dimensional functional data such as time series data and images are available in many current manufacturing processes. Time series data (or functional data) and images have been used for fault detection and quality improvement in many engineering applications such as automobile manufacturing (Jin & Shi, 2001), semiconductor manufacturing (Lada, Lu, & Wilson, 2002), and nano-machining systems (Ganesan, Das, Sikdar, & Kumar, 2003). Multidimensional functional data from various sources of sensors characterize the quality or reliability performance of many manufacturing processes, and are informative in process monitoring and fault diagnosis.

Multi-dimensional functional data mining is the process of discovering interesting and previously unknown, but potentially useful patterns from functional or image databases (Jeong, Lu, Huo, Vidakovic, & Chen, 2006). The complexity of functional and image data of intrinsic high-correlation limits the applicability of conventional data mining techniques for extracting useful patterns. Efficient tools for extracting information from multi-dimensional function data are crucial to the on-line fault diagnosis based on large volume of multi-dimensional functional datasets. General-purpose data mining tools such as *Enterprise Miner* are designed for the purpose of analyzing large commercial databases. However, extracting interesting and useful patterns from functional or image data for manufacturing fault diagnosis is more difficult than extracting the corresponding patterns from traditional numeric and categorical data. The characteristics of functional data are: high correlation, high level of noise, high-dimensionality, and nonstationarity. Due to such characteristics, conventional data mining algorithms may not perform satisfactorily on functional data.

This chapter presents some major accomplishments in the emerging field of multi-dimensional data mining and applications, especially in the areas of dimensionality reduction for functional data, misalignment prediction of rotating machinery, and hyperspectral image analysis. The organization of this chapter is as follows. Section 2 presents data mining issues in one-dimensional functional data such as dimensionality reduction techniques for high-dimensional functional data, multi-scale diagnosis procedures, and misalignment prediction of rotating machinery. In Section 3, the data mining issues in image and on-line machine vision for poultry skin tumor detection using hyperspectral fluorescence images are discussed. Section 4 concludes this chapter with a discussion of research needs in multi-dimensional functional data mining.

2. Data Mining of Functional Data

Timely synthesized information is often times needed for product design validation, process trouble shooting and production quality improvement in manufacturing systems (Jeong *et al.* 2006). However, a large volume of data makes the real-time process monitoring difficult. Also, it is recognized that multi-functional data with nonstationary, correlated or dynamically changing patterns contributed from potential process faults are difficult to handle. In this Section, we introduce three data mining topics in relation to functional data: wavelet-based dimensionality reduction (Section 2.1), multi-scale fault diagnosis procedures (Section 2.2), and regression modeling based on functional data (Section 2.3).

2.1 Dimensionality Reduction Techniques for Functional Data

The wavelet transform models irregular patterns of multi-dimensional functional data in a way which is better than the Fourier transform and standard statistical procedures (e.g., splines and polynomial regressions).

Applications of wavelet-based procedures for solving manufacturing problems have been reported in the literature (Jeong *et al.* 2003; Jin &

Shi 1999; Kong *et al.* 2004; Lada *et al.* 2002). Consider a sequence of data $\mathbf{y} = \left(y(t_1),\ldots,y(t_N)\right)^T$ taken from $f(t)$ or obtained as a realization of

$$y(t) = f(t) + \varepsilon_t, \tag{1}$$

at equally spaced discrete time points $t_i, i = 0,1,2,\ldots$, where ε_{t_i} is Gaussian random noise $N\left(0,\sigma^2\right)$ with zero mean and variance σ^2. In practice, the following orthonormal basis of a wavelet transform is used to represent a signal function $f(t) \in L^2(\mathbb{R})$:

$$\tilde{f}(t) = \sum_{k\in\mathbb{R}} c_{L,k}\phi_{L,k}(t) + \sum_{j=L}^{J}\sum_{k\in\mathbb{R}} d_{j,k}\psi_{j,k}(t), \tag{2}$$

where $\mathbb{R}$ denotes the set of integers, and the coefficients $c_{L,k}$'s are considered to be the coarser-level coefficients characterizing smoother data patterns, $d_{j,k}$'s are viewed as the finer-level coefficients describing (local) details of data patterns, $J > L$ and L corresponds to the coarsest resolution-level.

The discrete wavelet transform (DWT) of $\mathbf{y}$ is defined as $\mathbf{d} = \boldsymbol{W}\,\mathbf{y}$, where $\boldsymbol{W}$ is the orthonormal $N \times N$ DWT-matrix. In the wavelet domain, we obtain $\mathbf{d} = \boldsymbol{\theta} + \boldsymbol{\eta}$, where $\mathbf{d}$, $\boldsymbol{\theta}$, and $\boldsymbol{\eta}$ represent the collections of all coefficients, parameters and errors, transformed from the data $y(t_i)$, the true function $f(t_i)$ and the error $\varepsilon(t_i)$ in the time-domain, respectively. Donoho and Johnstone (1995) have developed several wavelet-based "shrinkage" techniques to find a smooth estimate $\left(\hat{f}\right)$ of f from the "noisy" data $\boldsymbol{y}$. Because smaller coefficients are usually contributed from data noise, thresholding out these coefficients has an effect of "removing data noise." The *VisuShrink* (Donoho & Johnstone, 1994), *RiskShrink* (Donoho & Johnstone, 1995), and *SURE* (Donoho & Johnstone, 1995) are three popular thresholding methods commonly used in practice.

Data-denoising procedures such as *VisuShrink* (Donoho & Johnstone, 1994) and *RiskShrink* (Donoho & Johnstone, 1995) are used as dimensionality-reduction tools in a wide range of applications (e.g., Jin & Shi, 2001; Ganesan *et al.* 2003). However, dimensionality-reduction and denoising methods are distinct for different purposes. Data-denoising procedures aim to find the estimate $\hat{\theta}$ (and $\hat{f}$) for reducing the "modeling error" of θ (and f). The data-denoising methods are therefore more aggressive in reducing the modeling errors. Conversely, dimensionality-reduction methods select the "reduced-size" data with a more aggressive data-reduction ratio. However, the selected reduced-size data should be representative enough in capturing key data characteristics for subsequent planned or unplanned decision analyses. In general, data-denoising and nonlinear signal approximation methods retain more coefficients based on some derivations of the threshold λ.

Jeong *et al.* (2006) proposed the following data-reduction criterion developed for balancing two ratios: (1) the relative data-energy in the approximation model and (2) the relative number of coefficients used (that is, the data-reduction ratio).

$$RRE_h(\lambda) = \frac{E\left\|d - \hat{d}_h(\lambda)\right\|^2}{E\left\|d\right\|^2} + \omega\frac{E\left\|\hat{d}_h(\lambda)\right\|_0}{N}, \tag{3}$$

where $\left\|\hat{d}_h(\lambda)\right\|_0 = \sum_{i=1}^{N}\left|\hat{d}_{h,i}(\lambda)\right|_0$ is the number of coefficients selected, E is the expectation of random variables, and

$\left|\hat{d}_{h,i}(\lambda)\right|_0 = 1$ if $|d_{h,i}| > \lambda$; $\left|\hat{d}_{h,i}(\lambda)\right|_0 = 0$, otherwise.

The weighting parameter ω is user-selected or can be provided by methods such as the generalized cross-validation (GCV) method (Weyrich & Warhola, 1998).

The following theorem presents some analytical properties of the proposed data-reduction method (see Jeong *et al.* (2006) for the proof). The closed-form solution of the optimal threshold becomes handy in practical implementations.

Theorem: Consider the model stated as $\mathbf{d} = \boldsymbol{\theta} + \boldsymbol{\eta}$, *where* $\mathbf{d}, \boldsymbol{\theta}$, *and* $\boldsymbol{\eta}$ represent the collections of all coefficients, parameters, and errors. Then, we have:

(i) the objective function $RRE_h(\lambda)$ is minimized uniquely at $\lambda = \lambda_{N,h}$ where

$$\lambda_{N,h} = \left(\frac{1}{N} E \|d\|^2 \right)^{1/2};$$

The moment estimate of $\lambda_{N,h}$,

$$\hat{\lambda}_{N,h} = \left(\frac{1}{N} \sum_{i=1}^{N} d_i^2 \right)^{1/2} = \left(\frac{\hat{\xi}}{N} \right)^{1/2}$$

(ii) $\left(\hat{\lambda}_{N,h} - \lambda_{N,b} \right)$ *converges to* 0 *with probability* 1.

(iii) $\sqrt{N} \left(\hat{\lambda}_{N,h} - \lambda_{N,h} \right) / \sigma^*_{N,h} \xrightarrow{d} N(0,1)$, *where*

$$\left(\sigma^*_{N,h} \right)^2 = \frac{1}{4N} \left(\frac{4\sigma^2 \sum_{i=1}^{N} \theta_i^2 + 2N\sigma^4}{\sum_{i=1}^{N} \theta_i^2 + \sigma^2} \right).$$

From our simulation study, the denoising methods that use a larger number of wavelet coefficients were less effective in data-reduction and for the signals with larger signal-to-noise ratio (SNR). With noisy data, the difference in modeling errors from denoising methods was smaller (Jeong *et al.* 2006).

2.2 *Multi-Scale Fault Diagnosis*

Wavelet transforms of a signal are multi-resolutional and allow decision-makers to use the information contained in each resolution for fault diagnosis. For example, the coarser-scale coefficients represent the global shape of the signal in the lower (coarser) resolution level, while the fine-scale coefficients represent the details of the signal in the higher (finer) resolution level. However, one deficiency in the procedures developed from the wavelet coefficients provided from the DWT is the lack of shift-invariance. Therefore, direct assessment of the wavelet coefficients can lead to inaccurate decisions. Thus, a scale-wise energy representation such as a scalogram provides a more robust signal feature for fault detection against time-shift than the DWT coefficients do directly (Jeong, Lu, & Chen 2003). Scalogram is a technique for representing signal energy at various frequency bands for easy decision making. The problem with the implementation of this technique is how to generate the representation for each distinct signal.

Therefore, Jeong *et al.* (2003) proposed the following thresholded scalogram for the detection of time-shifted fault patterns:

$$S_{d_j}^{*}\left(\hat{\lambda}\right)=\sum_{k=0}^{m_j-1} I\left(\left|d_{jk}\right|>\hat{\lambda}\right) d_{jk}^{2}, \tag{4}$$

where m_j is the number of wavelet coefficients in the j-th resolution level, and $\hat{\lambda}$ is the threshold value decided from data in various methods. We use the notation $S_{c_L}^{*}$ for the thresholded energy at the coarser level. The screening of smaller wavelet coefficients makes the detection of process fault more robust in a noisy environment.

2.2.1 A Case Study: Data Mining of Functional Data

Quadruple mass spectrometry (QMS) is commonly used in semiconductor manufacturing processes for monitoring the quality of thin-film deposition. The multi-resolution fault diagnosis idea is applied to a rapid thermal chemical vapor deposition (RTCVD) process that deposits thin films on semiconductor wafers using a temperature-driven surface chemical reaction. As the feature size decreases, the functional operation of devices (e.g., transistors) becomes increasingly susceptible to failure because of variations in deposition processes. Therefore, detecting a process condition different from the nominal is critical (Rying 1997).

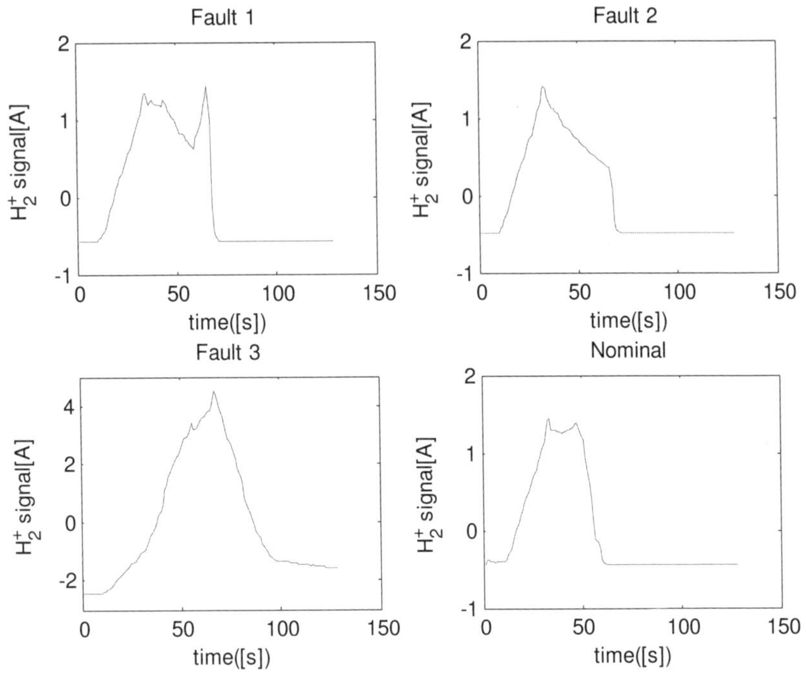

Figure 1. Plot of the H_2^+ intensity signals acquired from the QMS sensor during the deposition process.

Figure 1 presents the normalized H_2^+ intensities for different fault classes acquired from the QMS sensor during the deposition process in a research project to develop an in-situ measurement technique for online process monitoring (Rying, 1997). The subfigures represent one of the 21 nominal RTCVD process runs and three sets of data from different faulty processes.

Let S_j^* represent the thresholded scalogram, S_{dj}^* and S_{cL}^*; where S_{dj}^* is the energy at scale *j* and S_{cL}^* is the energy at the coarsest level. The approximated distribution was derived for constructing a set of "lower and upper bounds" of values of the thresholded scalograms in process monitoring. Based on the approximated normal distribution, the $(1 - \alpha)100\%$ confidence interval for the log_2- scale thresholded scalogram is obtained as $\log_2 S_j^* \pm z_{\alpha/2}\hat{\sigma}_{mj} / \left[\hat{u}_j^*(\ln 2)\right]$, where z_α is the usual upper $\alpha \times 100\%$th percentile value of the standard normal distribution (see Jeong, Lu, & Chen (2003) for the detailed Theorem of this asymptotic distribution). The values of this confidence interval will serve as the "monitoring bounds" for our scalogram plots

Figure 2 presents a thresholded scalogram plot (in a log_2-scale) of the RTCVD experimental data from three fault classes. Comparably, the scalogram values for the data in the Fault 3 class are very different from the nominal one at all resolution levels. Because of the similarity of the data curves in the original time domain, Fault classes 1 and 2 have similar scalogram values at the finer resolution levels, but not at the coarsest resolution level.

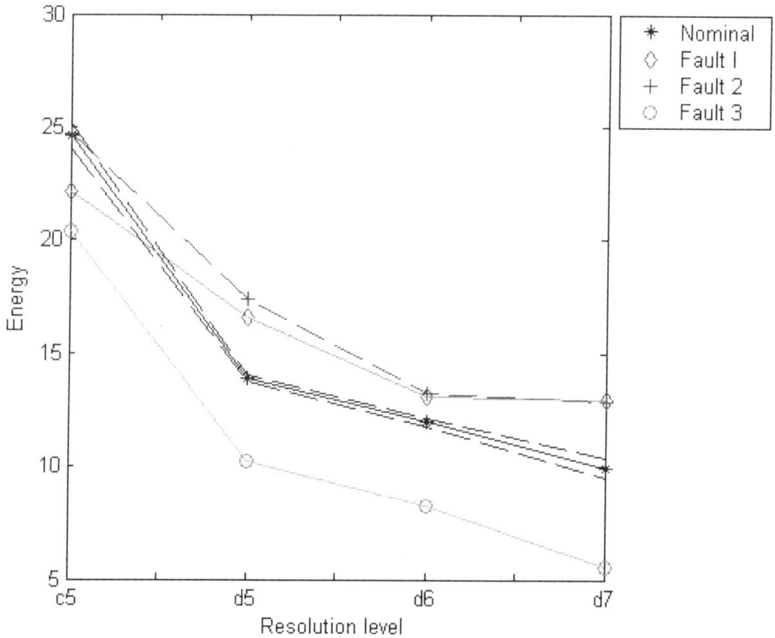

Figure 2. Thresholded scalograms with pointwise confidence intervals (adopted from Jeong *et al.* 2003).

The sharp drop in the curve in the Fault Class 1 may partly explain why the value of its coarsest level scalogram is so different from its nominal value as compared with the value obtained from the Fault Class 2. Fault Class 2 and the nominal curves have similar finer and coarsest level scalogram values, but this is not seen at the middle level of the scalograms. Results plotted in Figure 2 show that these three classes of curves are clearly out of bounds at almost all resolution levels except at the coarsest level for the Fault 2 class.

2.3 *Motor Shaft Misalignment Prediction Based on Functional Data*

A typical mechanical system consists of a driver machine, a driven machine, and a coupling, which could be a rotating shaft, rigid or elastic joints, belt and gear trains as depicted in Figure 3 (Omitaomu *et al.*, 2006, 2007). A shaft transmission system is one of the most fundamental and important parts of rotary machinery; therefore, the ability to estimate and predict shaft alignment or misalignment accurately can significantly enhance the predictive maintenance task of a production system.

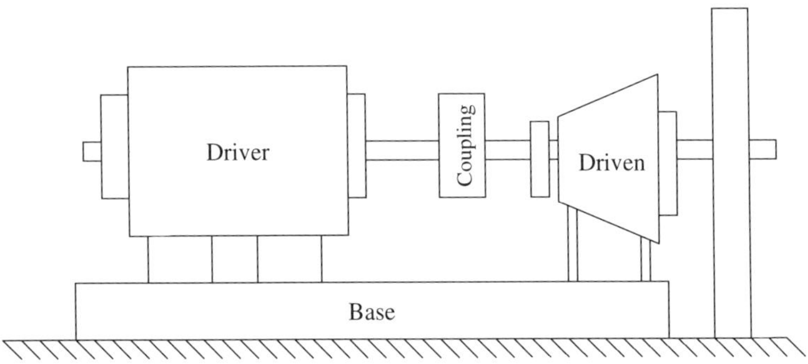

Figure 3. A schematic diagram of a driver-coupling-driven system (from (Omitaomu, Jeong, Badiru, & Hines, 2006 and 2007)).

A proper shaft alignment is inevitable because it reduces excessive axial and radial forces on the most vulnerable parts of a machine system such as the bearings, seals, and couplings (Wowk, 2000). It also minimizes the amount of shaft bending thereby permitting full transmission of power from the driver machine to the driven machine and eliminates the possibility of shaft failure from cyclic fatigue.

In addition, it minimizes the amount of wear in the coupling components, reduces mechanical seal failure, and lowers vibration levels in machine casings, bearing housings, and rotor. Therefore, monitoring and predicting the shaft alignment condition is important in order to make intelligent decisions on when to perform alignment maintenance, which plays an essential role in increasing maintenance effectiveness and reducing maintenance costs.

Shaft misalignment is one of the prevalent faults associated with rotating machines and it occurs when the shaft of the driven machine and the shaft of its driver machine do not rotate on a common axis; that is, the shafts are not coaxial. Shaft misalignment is a measure of how far apart the two centerlines are away from each other (Wowk, 2000; Kuropatwinski, Jesse, Hines, Edmondson, & Carley, 1997). Such shift in the centers can be in parallel position (when the centerlines of the two shafts are parallel with each other, but at a constant distance apart), in angular position (when the centerlines are at an angle to each other), or a combination of these positions (Piotrowski, 1995) as shown in Figure 4, where σ is the vertical displacement in parallel alignment and θ is the angular displacement in angular alignment.

Several linear and nonlinear techniques including principal components regression (PCR), partial least squares (PLS), and artificial neural networks (ANN) have been proposed for condition monitoring. A comprehensive review of these models and their applications to condition monitoring is presented by Venkatasubramanian, Rengaswamy, Kavuri, and Yin (2003).

In addition, an overview of PCR and PLS in condition monitoring was given in (Geladi & Kowalski, 1986; Joliffe, 2002). All these techniques vary in their accuracy, prediction efficiency, robustness, and transparency. PLS is widely used because it is fast, easy, simple, and has good approximation.

This section uses two of these advanced data mining techniques to determine if high-dimensional motor power spectrum frequency can be used to detect and predict the alignment and misalignment conditions of rotating machinery. The desired application of this technique will be an *online system* that gives real time alignment data to an operator so that corrective actions could be taken before any damage occurs to the motor system. Such notification would allow the maintenance of the rotating machine to be performed at scheduled shutdowns rather than creating an unnecessary loss of revenue due to unexpected downtime (Omitaomu *et al.*, 2006 and 2007).

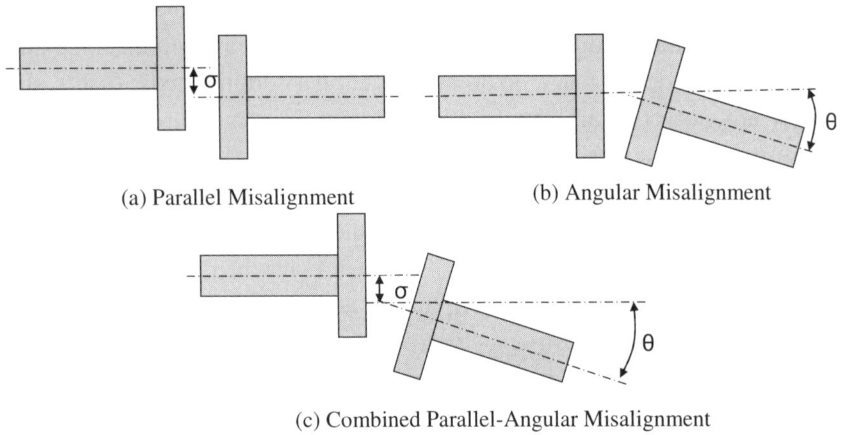

Figure 4. An illustration of parallel, angular, and combined misalignment conditions (Omitaomu *et al.* 2006 and 2007).

2.3.1 Techniques for Predicting with Higher Number of Predictors

When the number of predictors is much greater than the number of samples, some of the predictors may constitute noise and others may be correlated. Models developed with correlated and noisy variables will not generalize very well on new test sets.

Therefore, the first step is to reduce the number of predictors in order to avoid the use of correlated variables and possibly reduce the inclusion of noise in the final model. Two of the most popular techniques used for condition monitoring when the number of predictors is high when compared to the number of observations are partial least squares (PLS) regression and principal components regression (PCR). However, principal components regression and partial least squares regression differ in the methods used in extracting significant variables to use for developing the final model. Basically, principal components regression produces the weight matrix ***W*** reflecting the covariance structure between the predictor variables, whereas partial least squares regression produces the weight matrix ***W*** reflecting the covariance structure between the predictor and response variables.

Partial least squares (PLS) regression is based on the nonlinear iterative partial least squares (NIPALS) algorithm introduced by Wold (1966). PLS is a supervised technique that transforms inputs and outputs into uncorrelated latent factors thus removing the collinearity. It focuses on the correlation between the inputs and the outputs. The decompositions are given by:

$$\begin{aligned} \mathbf{X} &= \mathbf{T}_i \mathbf{P}_i + e_i \\ \mathbf{Y} &= \mathbf{U}_i \mathbf{Q}_i + \mathbf{f}_i \end{aligned} \tag{5}$$

where ***e*** and ***f*** are the residual matrices. ***U*** is related to ***T*** by the inner relation given by:

$$\mathbf{U} = \mathbf{bT} + \mathbf{H} \tag{6}$$

where ***b*** is a diagonal matrix and ***H*** is a residual matrix. The predictive formulation for ***Y*** is given by:

$$\mathbf{Y} = \mathbf{T}^{\mathrm{T}} \mathbf{C} + \hat{\mathbf{f}} \tag{7}$$

Therefore, four parameters are needed to define a PLS prediction model: ***P***, ***Q***, ***w***, and ***b***; where ***P*** is ***X*** principal factor loadings, ***Q*** is ***Y*** principal factor loadings, ***w*** is the matrix of weights, and ***b*** is the vector containing the inner relationships.

The PLS method is an iterative technique where first principal components are used to approximate the input and output data. Next, an inner mapping is performed relating the orthogonal spaces to determine the approximate output factor space. Next, the approximate values are returned to their original spaces and are subtracted from the actual values to determine the errors of the approximations. The new input and output matrices are then set to the errors and the process is repeated until the maximum rank of the matrices is reached. When used for prediction, not all of the PLS factors are usually used (Geladi & Kowalski, 1986). An optimal number of PLS factors are chosen in a qualitative fashion with a technique similar to cross validation.

This method reduces the inputs and the outputs to orthogonal spaces to remove the collinearity of the data. It uses the most correlated input data to the output for the prediction so it converges quickly giving rotated X and Y factors. There are as many factors available to use as the rank of the matrix. Once the model has been developed, the optimal number of PLS factors must be determined to allow the model to perform the best prediction. The easiest way to determine the number of factors is by determining the errors for the training and testing data and then choosing a qualitative number based on them similar to the cross validation training method for ANNs. It is desirable to have the best prediction with the least number of factors while learning the training data to a minimum error.

The optimal PLS model generally performs better on test data than simple MLR because overfitting in the model can be controlled by removing factors. The non-linear PLS (NLPLS) model usually performs better than the PLS model if there is a nonlinear relationship between the inputs and outputs because it allows the model to learn the non-linearities that might be present in the data. The NLPLS model should perform better than any of the other models because it uses all of the input data and reduces it in a supervised manner to retain the most useful information and then trains on this data with a method that allows any non-linearities to be mapped. This method uses information from all of the data in the ANN instead of picking features to use in the mapping.

The principal component regression is used in this chapter as the second approach for reducing a larger number of variables. In this case, the unsupervised principal component analysis is used to perform multiple linear regression. Principal component analysis (PCA) is used to reduce the dimensionality of the data without loss of significant amount of information. PCA is based on an orthogonal decomposition of the covariance matrix of the given variables in directions that explain the maximum variation of the data. That is, the PCA technique selects variables that contain most of the information of the entire dataset. Therefore, other variables that are "fillers" are eliminated without any significant impact in the final model. The uncorrelated principal components are then used in regression; this process is called principal components regression and was proposed by Massy (1965). One problem in implementing this technique is the determination of which principal components to use in the regression model. There are four methods in the literature: the selection of principal components that contain most of the information, selection of the principal components that are correlated with the output, use of all principal components, and a trial and error method.

2.3.2 A Case Study: Motor Shaft Misalignment Prediction

The experiment set-up at the Oak Ridge National Laboratory (ORNL) Advanced Motor Testing Facility consisted of the motor dynamometer system with current and voltage sensors attached to it and connected to a recorder. Data were recorded for three different types of couplings. Once the data were collected, they were digitized to computer media for analysis. The alignment measurements were made using a Computational Systems Incorporated (CSI) UltraSpec® laser alignment system with the motor off line. The thermal growth measurements were made using permanently installed CSI lasers and were verified by using Essinger bars. Current and voltage sensors were placed on each of the three phase inputs to the motor. The sensors were attached to an eight-channel TEAC digital tape recorder.

The data used were collected using a three-phase 50 hp AC motor attached through a gear type flexible coupling to a 150 hp dynamometer at controlled parallel and angular offset conditions. For this analysis the input data is the power frequency spectrum and the output data is the misalignment condition. Figure 5 shows a plot of input data (the power spectrum profile) for one of the misalignment conditions.

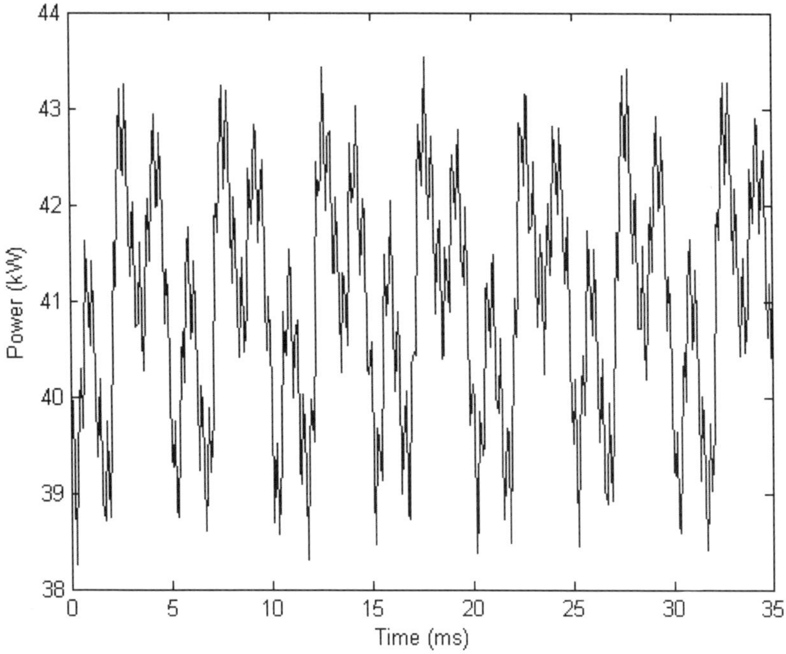

Figure 5. Time signal for a shaft misalignment condition.

The dataset consists of five sub sets. The size of each input sub set is 10×3,000 while the size of each output sub set is 10×2; therefore, the size of the entire input set and output set was duplicated to 50×3,000 and 50×2, respectively. That is, there are five sets of each misalignment condition. The essence of the data duplication was to increase the number of samples without necessarily performing additional experiments. This is a cost effective technique in cases where it is very expensive to perform additional experiments. The output (misalignment condition) data ranges from 0 to 50 mils for the parallel offset and from 0 to 15mils/inch for the angular offset. The objective then is to use the power frequency spectrum (input) data to predict the misalignment condition (output) data using the PLS and PCR techniques.

The PLS and PCR models were developed by using the MATLAB software. The models were developed by using a lesser number of variables and by using all available variables. The model that uses a lesser number of variables is called a Reduced Model; while the model developed by using all available variables is called a Full Model. The methodology used is depicted in Figure 6.

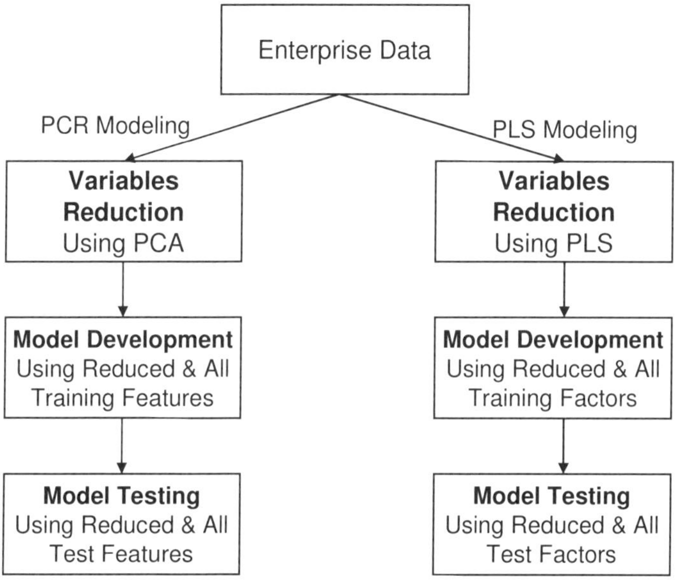

Figure 6. A data prediction methodology using PLS and PCR for enterprise data.

The reduced models for PCR use 50 principal components each for parallel and angular offset and the full models use 3,000 principal components for each offset case. For the PLS technique, the reduced models use 2,900 and 2,000 variables for parallel and angular offset predictions, respectively, and the full models use 3,000 variables for each offset case. Since the dataset consists of five sets of each misalignment condition, the models were developed using the leave-five-out cross validation technique. This means that for each model, one misalignment condition is used for testing while the remaining misalignment conditions are used for training. This approach will guarantee that the developed models are tested using never-seen data (misalignment conditions). Therefore, 50 different models were developed for each technique. The developed models are evaluated using the Average Mean Square Error

(AMSE) defined as $AMSE = \sum_{i=1}^{m} \left[(y_i - \hat{y}_i)^T (y_i - \hat{y}_i) \right]$, where $\hat{y}_i$ is the predicted value of the dependent variable y_i and m is the number of the developed models.

The results generated using PLS and PCR are summarized in Tables 1 and 2, respectively. From Table 1, we see that the full model performs better than the reduced model, which indicates that all the variables have predictive value in the final model. However, we note that the MSE for parallel offset are much smaller than the MSE for angular offset; which implies that modeling the angular offset is slightly more difficult, at least for the given training data. It should also be noted that the original dataset was expanded in order to use this technique.

Table 1. Prediction results for 50 PLS models based on AMSE.

Misalignment	**Reduced PLS Models**		**Full PLS Models**	
	AMSE	**# of factors**	**AMSE**	**# of factors**
Parallel	25.67	2,900	17.22	3,000
Angular	67.99	2,000	58.11	3,000

From the PCR results in Table 2, the reduced models with 50 principal components performed better than the full models with 3,000 principal components (PCs). However, these results also support the conclusion from PLS results that it is more difficult to predict angular offset than parallel offset for the given training data.

Table 2. Prediction results for 50 PCR models based on AMSE.

Misalignment	**Reduced PCR Models**		**Full PCR Models**	
	MSE	**# of PCs**	**MSE**	**# of PCs**
Parallel	13.88	50	11.98	3,000
Angular	59.23	50	43.21	3,000

These results indicate that both PLS and PCR generalized very well on the new test sets. However, as expected, we notice that using all the variables does not give significant test errors when compared to using some of the variables. This supports our initial observation that some of the variables are "fillers."

3. Data Mining in Hyperspectral Imaging

Vision-based inspection techniques have been widely applied for inspection and quality control in automated production processes. Manufacturers in many industries depend on machine vision inspection systems in order to produce high-quality products. For this application, poultry carcasses with pathological problems must be identified and removed from food processing lines to meet the requirement of high standards of food safety. Traditionally, trained human inspectors carry out the inspection processes and examine a small number of representative samples from a large production run. Manual inspection and classification of agricultural products can be a highly repetitive and tedious task. Human inspectors are often required to examine 30-35 poultry samples per minute in the course of an eight-hour day. Such working conditions can lead to repetitive motion injuries, distracted attention and fatigue problems, and result in inconsistent quality. Rapid, non-invasive machine vision inspection methods for assessing hazardous conditions in food production would provide a substantial benefit in the quest to ensure the highest quality of poultry inspection.

Poultry skin tumors are ulcerous lesions that are surrounded by a rim of thickened skin and dermis (Clanek, Barnes, Beard, Reid, & Yoder, 1991). Skin cancer causes skin cells to lose the ability to divide and grow normally, and induce abnormal cells to grow out of control to form tumors. Tumorous carcasses often demonstrate swollen or enlarged tissue caused by the uncontrolled growth of new tissue. A tumor may not be as visually obvious as other pathological diseases such as septicemia, air sacculitis, and bruise since its spatial signature appears as shape distortion rather than a discoloration. Therefore, conventional vision-based inspection systems operating in the visual spectrum may reveal limitations in detecting skin tumors on poultry carcasses.

Hyperspectral imaging combines photonic technologies of conventional imaging and spectroscopy to produce images for which each picture element (pixel) is associated with a spectral signature (spectrum). The spectral information provided by each pixel is valuable in the discrimination, detection, and classification of elements and structures within the image. Each hyperspectral image pixel is typically composed of hundreds of contiguous narrow bands from the electromagnetic spectrum. The data produced by hyperspectral imaging sensors constitute a three-dimensional (3-D) cube in two spatial dimensions and one spectral dimension. Spectral components to be measured often involve quantities such as reflectance and fluorescence ranging from the visible to short-wave infrared spectra.

This spectral imaging has the ability to exploit multiple regions of the electromagnetic spectrum to probe and analyze the composition of a material. The materials comprising various objects in a scene reflect, absorb, and emit electromagnetic radiation in amounts that vary with the wavelength. If the radiation arriving at the sensor is measured over a sufficiently broad spectral range, the resulting spectral signature can be used to uniquely characterize and identify any given material. Hyperspectral imaging systems have been utilized in a wide variety of scientific disciplines that include airborne-satellite remote sensing of earth resources, environmental monitoring, mapping the Earth, management of water or agricultural resources, forestry, microscopic studies, agricultural product inspection, and the detection and classification of hidden targets in military applications.

This section presents an analysis of hyperspectral fluorescence images for detecting skin tumors on poultry carcasses. A number of compounds emit fluorescence in the visible region of the spectrum when excited with ultraviolet (UV) radiation. Fluorescence imaging has demonstrated higher contrast of poultry skin tumor than reflectance. An important pre-processing step in hyperspectral image processing is to eliminate the redundancy in the spectral and spatial sample data while preserving the essential features needed for discrimination. Compression of the huge amount of hyperspectral data leads to significant reductions in computational complexity. Extraction of features indicative of spectral behaviors is preferable to a straightforward classification because it also leads to the reduction of computational complexity. This study utilizes the spectral bands that correspond to those spectral features that provide meaningful information for the detection of skin tumors. The hyperspectral imaging system is used as a research tool to determine the several spectral bands that can be implemented in a multispectral imaging system for the online inspection of poultry carcasses. Features are obtained from the spectral peaks of relative fluorescence intensity (RFI) of hyperspectral image samples.

3.1 A Hyperspectral Fluorescence Imaging System

The Instrumentation and Sensing Laboratory (ISL) at Beltsville Agricultural Research Center, Maryland, has developed a laboratory-based line-by-line hyperspectral imaging system capable of reflectance and fluorescence imaging for uses in food safety and quality research (Kim, Chen, & Mehl, 2001). The system employs a pushbroom method in which a line of spatial information with a full spectral range per spatial pixel is captured sequentially to cover a volume of spatial and spectral data. Figure 7 shows the ISL hyperspectral imaging system equipped with a CCD camera, a spectrograph, a sample transport mechanism, and two lighting sources for reflectance and fluorescence sensing.

Two fluorescent lamp assemblies are used to provide a near uniform UV-A (365 *nm*) excitation to the sample area for fluorescence measurement. A short-pass filter placed in front of the lamp housing is used to prevent transmittance of radiations greater than approximately 400 *nm* and thus eliminate the potential spectral contamination by pseudo-fluorescence.

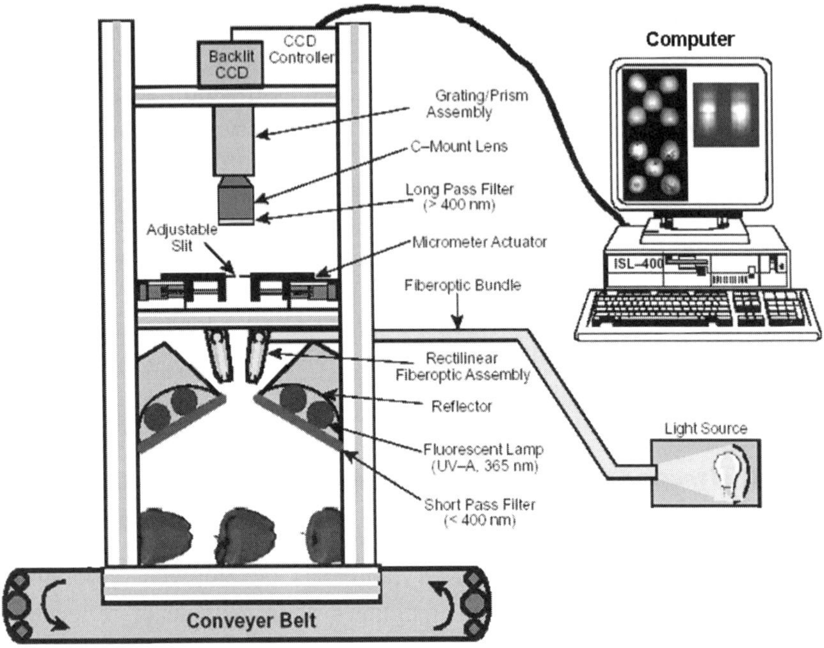

Figure 7. Hardware components of the ISL hyperspectral imaging system (Kong, Chen, Kim, & Kim, 2004).

The system acquires the data via line-by-line scans while transporting sample materials via a precision positioning table. Data produced by hyperspectral imaging systems can be represented by a 3-D cube of images $I(m, n, \lambda_i)$, where (m, n) denotes the spatial coordinate of a pixel in the image of the size $M \times N$ ($m = 0,1,\ldots,M-1$, $n = 0,1,\ldots,N-1$) and λ_i denotes the wavelength of the i-th spectral band ($i = 1,2,\ldots,L$). The value $I(m, n, \lambda_i)$ indicates the fluorescence response of the pixel (m, n) at a wavelength λ_i of the i-th spectral band. The ISL hyperspectral image system captures 65 spectral bands ($L = 65$) at the wavelengths from λ_1 (425.4 *nm*) to λ_{65} (710.7 *nm*) in visible light spectrum. A hyperspectral image of a poultry sample consists of a spatial dimension of 400×460 pixels where each pixel denotes 1 *mm* × 1 *mm* of spatial resolution. Each pixel has a 16-bit gray-scale resolution. The data size of a hyperspectral image sample is approximately 24 mega-bytes (= 460 pixels × 400 pixels × 65 bands × 2 bytes). The speed of the conveyer belt was adjusted based on the predetermined CCD exposure time and data transfer rate.

3.2 Hyperspectral Image Dimensionality Reduction

Hyperspectral data analysis requires efficient processing of the massive amounts of data that result from the combination of spatial and spectral information acquired by the sensors. The high-dimensional data space generated by the hyperspectral sensors creates a new challenge for conventional spectral data analysis techniques. Dimensionality reduction can be achieved without significantly degrading detection performance or decreasing the separability among the different classes. Hyperspectral images contain a large amount of data. The hyperspectral database will grow rapidly in size. The efficient distribution and use of this amount of information will be challenging.

The spatial content of hyperspectral images of poultry carcass samples are compressed by use of Discrete Wavelet Transform (DWT). The PCA provides an efficient means for the compression of the spectral signatures without losing relevant information. The DWT can be effectively used to reduce a high volume of hyperspectral data (Luigi-Gragotti, Poggi, & Ragozini, 2000). For images, the wavelet decomposition is executed along the row- and columnwise directions. The 2-D wavelet decomposition transforms an image of $N \times M$ size to approximation (cA), horizontal (cH), vertical (cV), and diagonal (cD) details of approximately $N/2 \times M/2$ size each. The approximation is the high-scale, low-frequency components of the signal. The details correspond to the low-scale, high-frequency components. Figure 8(a) shows a level-1 discrete wavelet decomposition procedure of a 2-D image. Different choice of wavelets produces different sets of decomposed signals. Only the approximation component cA is used in the analysis to reduce the amount of data. The components of the details cH, cV, and cD show relatively low energy content, and therefore are not considered. Figure 8(b) shows the components of the approximation and the details of a level-1 2-D discrete wavelet decomposition of the band-5 poultry image sample. The components of details are shown in reverse gray levels. The Daubechies wavelets of order 5 are used to decompose the hyperspectral images (Daubechies, 1992) into components. Visual characteristics are well preserved in the approximation component at smaller image sizes.

PCA finds the best approximation that minimizes the sum of the squares of the errors introduced by the dimensionality reduction (Bishop, 1995). The goal of dimensionality reduction is to map data vectors $\boldsymbol{y}$ in an L-dimensional space (y_1 , …, y_L) onto the feature vectors $\boldsymbol{a}$ in an M-dimensional space (a_1 , …, a_M) with $M < L$. Let $\boldsymbol{e}_1,\cdots,\boldsymbol{e}_L$ be a set of eigenvectors of the covariance matrix of the n vectors $\boldsymbol{y}_1,\cdots,\boldsymbol{y}_n$ for training. Then a vector $\boldsymbol{y}$ can be represented as a linear combination of orthogonal eigenvectors as:

$$\mathbf{y} = \sum_{i=1}^{L} a_i \mathbf{e}_i \tag{8}$$

where $a_i = \boldsymbol{e}_i^t \boldsymbol{y},\ i = 1,\cdots,L$. One can achieve dimensionality reduction by retaining only a subset M of the basis vectors $\boldsymbol{e}_i$.

Choosing eigenvectors corresponding to M largest eigenvalues minimizes the square error of the approximation. The M coefficients a_i that represent the original data are referred to as principal components. The spectral dimension can be transformed into a vector space with M dimension spanned by M principal components or factors. The first M factors account for most of the variance, with the first factor corresponding to the largest possible variance. The minimum error equals the sum of the L-M smallest eigenvalues. Each spectrum can be adequately represented by a few factors in the factor space instead of the original spectral vectors. Figure 9 shows the energy content of the principal components obtained from the hyperspectral image data. Most energy is concentrated on the first few components. The first three principal components retain almost all the energy of the spectral signature of each hyperspectral image pixel.

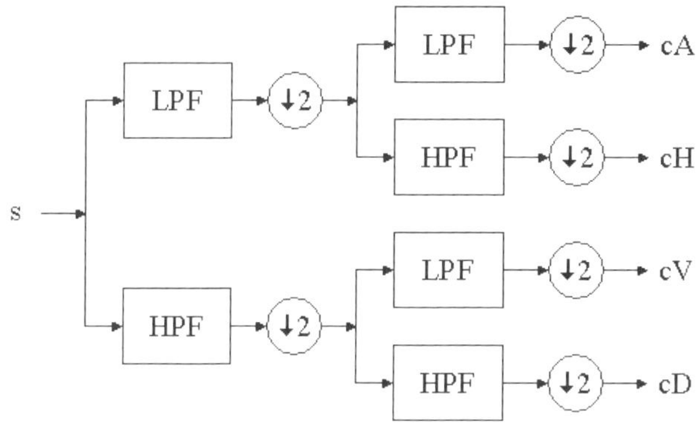

(a)

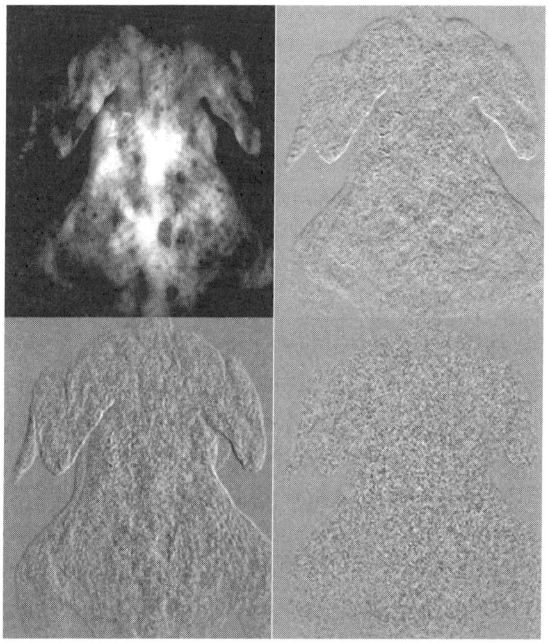

(b)

Figure 8. 2-D discrete wavelet decomposition. (a) Recursive filter tree implementation of DWT filter banks for discrete wavelet transforms, (b) Level-1 wavelet decomposition of a single-band image. The components of details (cH, cV, and cD) are shown in reversed gray levels.

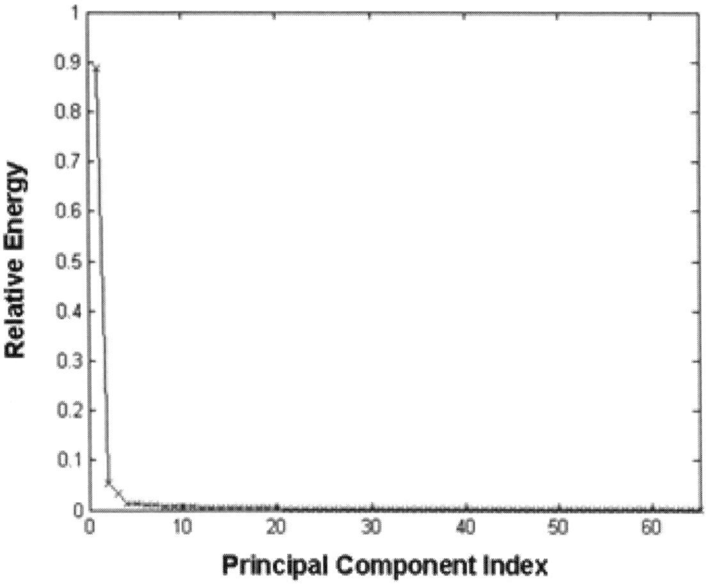

Figure 9. Energy content of the principal components of spectral signatures.

A spectral characterization is crucial in hyperspectral image analysis. Figure 10 demonstrates that spectral signals of the hyperspectral images are represented with a small number of principal components. PCA(n) indicates spectral representation by use of the first n principal components. Owing to a relatively large number of normal pixels, the first PCA component closely represents the spectral characteristics of normal tissue. Five PCA components were enough to represent the spectral signals of both the normal and tumor pixels.

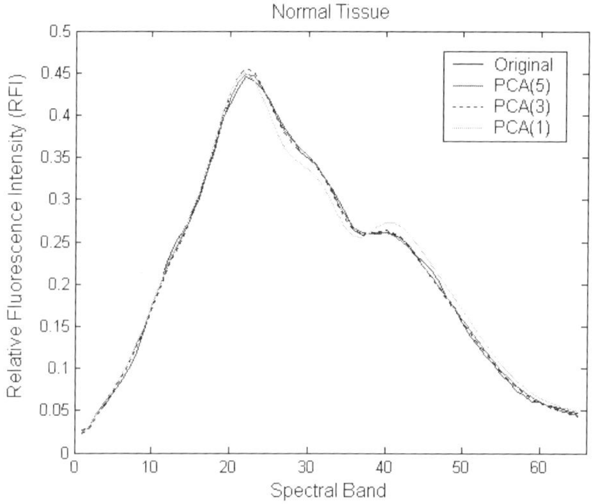

(a) Normal tissue

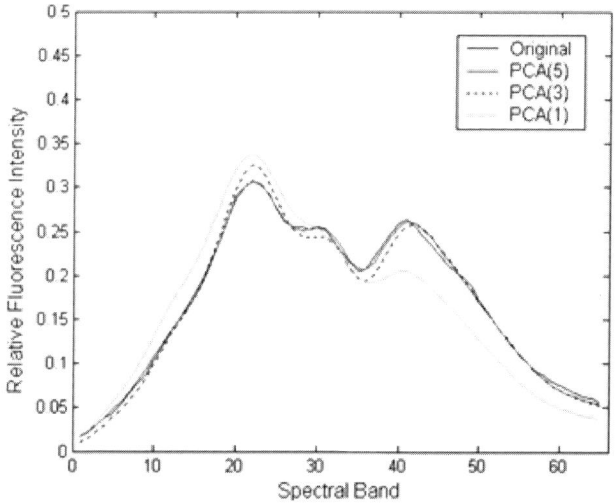

(b) Tumor

Figure 10. Representation of spectral signals of (a) normal tissue and (b) tumor tissue with a small number of principal components.

3.3 *Spectral Band Selection*

Spectral signature reveals the characteristics of the different types of tissues. Figure 11 shows the relative fluorescence intensity of hyperspectral image data at each spectral band for normal tissue and tumors. Normal tissues have a large peak response at approximately band 22 and a smaller peak at approximately band 45. On the average, tumors show lower fluorescence intensities than normal tissue, but have a strong response between the bands 40 to 45 relative to the peak near the band 22. Background pixels show low fluorescence intensity and an almost flat response over the entire spectral range since the carrying tray is covered with a non-fluorescent flat black paint.

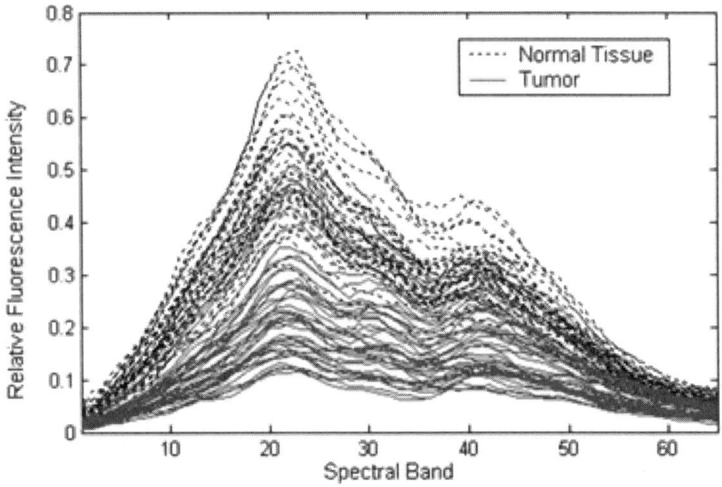

Figure 11. Spectral signature of the tumor and normal tissue.

Band ranking prioritizes all the spectral bands in terms of the information content for classification. Linear discriminant analysis finds a direction of projection that provides the best discrimination among the classes. This can be achieved by computing a transformation that maximizes the between-class distance while minimizing the within-class scatter. The ratio of between-class distance and within-class scatter defines the class separability at a spectral band. The between-class distance represents the dissimilarity between the classes, while the within-class scatter shows how much the data of each class are clustered. The spectral band with larger values of class separability indicates that the classes are more separable in that band.

The class separability is used as a criterion for spectral band ranking. For a two-class case, the class separability of the i-th band λ_i can be defined as

$$J_i^{\mathrm{MCS}} = \frac{1}{2}\frac{|\mu_{1i} - \mu_{2i}|^2}{\sigma_{1i}^2 + \sigma_{2i}^2} \tag{9}$$

where μ_{ki} and σ_{ki}^2 are the mean and the variance of the normalized fluorescence intensity $I(m,n,\lambda_i)$ of the class k in the i-th spectral band. Spectral bands are ranked in the descending order from the band with the largest value of class separability to the smallest. Figure 12 shows a spectral band ranking method in terms of maximum class separability (MCS) in 65 spectral bands. The spectral bands from 3 to 20 demonstrate relatively large class separability values.

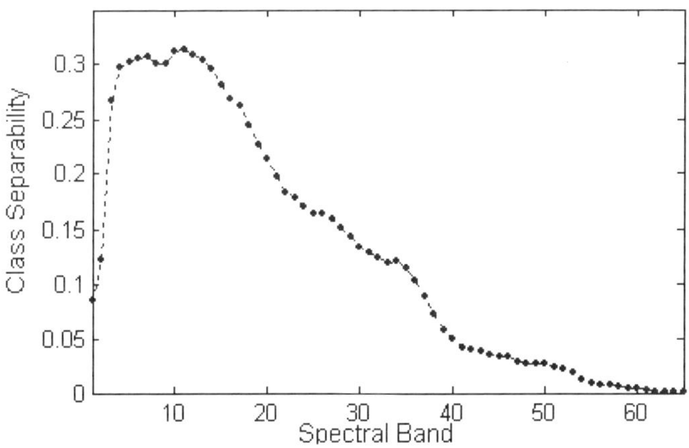

Figure 12. Band ranking with maximum class separability.

A band selection algorithm based on canonical analysis (CA) for dimensionality reduction is proposed (Tu, Chen, Wu, & Chang, 1998). Canonical analysis computes a transformation that maximizes the between-class scatter and minimizes the within-class scatter. Let $\boldsymbol{x}_{ki}$ be the i-th sample and μ_k be the mean of class k ($k = 1, 2, \ldots, K$). Let N_k be the number of samples in class k. Then the within-class scatter matrix is defined as

$$S_w = \sum_{k=1}^{K} \sum_{l=1}^{N_k} (x_{kl} - \mu_k)(x_{kl} - \mu_k)^T \tag{10}$$

The between-class scatter matrix is defined as the sum of outer products of the centered means of each class.

$$S_b = \sum_{k=1}^{K} (\mu_k - \mu)(\mu_k - \mu)^T \tag{11}$$

where μ indicates the mean of all the data. A linear transformation is given by a matrix whose columns are the eigenvectors of the matrix $S_w^{-1} S_b$:

$$S_w^{-1} S_b \boldsymbol{e}_j = \boldsymbol{e}_j d_j \tag{12}$$

where d_j are eigenvalues arranged in descending order ($d_1 \geq d_2 \geq \ldots \geq d_L$). The eigenvector $\boldsymbol{e}_j$ corresponds to the eigenvalue d_j. The term $r_{ji} = \sqrt{d_j}\,(e_{ji} / \|\boldsymbol{e}_j\|)$ denotes the loading factor of canonical component j at the i-th band. The discriminating power of the i-th band can be measured by the CA score as

$$J_i^{\mathrm{CA}} = \sum_{j=1}^{K-1} r_{ji}^2 = \sum_{j=1}^{K-1} \frac{d_j e_{ji}^2}{\|\boldsymbol{e}_j\|^2} \tag{13}$$

The bands are ranked in terms of the CA score. The CA selects the spectral bands corresponding to the first P largest CA scores.

A band ranking method based on the PCA was proposed by Campbell (1996). Chang, Du, Sun, & Althouse (2001) proposed two eigenanalysis-based criteria, the PCA-based criterion and the classification based criterion, to prioritize individual spectral bands. A divergence-based band decorrelation removes the spectral correlation. Spectral angle mapper is used as the metrics to quantify the distance between two spectra (Keshava, 2001). An independent component analysis (ICA) based band selection method calculates the weight matrix to obtain the weight coefficients of individual bands as the criteria for band selection. Bands are ranked based on the information content and redundancy (Groves & Bajcsy, 2003).

Adjacent spectral bands of most hyperspectral images are highly correlated. Ranked bands also contain a large amount of spectral redundancy. Band decorrelation removes the redundancy between the bands. If the correlation exceeds a threshold, the two band images are determined as highly correlated. The band images with low separability can be removed in the band-selection process. The complete spectral range is divided into P sub-spectral regions $S_1, S_2, \ldots, S_P$, where P is the number of desired spectral bands. Assume that all the bands are arranged in the descending order of class separability. Let $\{x_1, x_2, \ldots, x_L\}$ be a set of ranked bands based on the class separability, where x_1 denotes the band with maximum class separability. The correlation of x_1 with all the other bands $C(x_1, x_j)$, $j = 2, 3, \ldots, L$, defines the relative degree of redundancy of the bands with respect to the band of maximum class separability. The threshold ε for each subset is defined as

$$\varepsilon = \frac{1 - C_{\min}}{P} \qquad (14)$$

where $C_{\min}$ denotes the minimum correlation of $C(x_1, x_j)$. The first sub-spectral region S_1 contains the bands corresponding to the correlation coefficient values in $[1, 1-\varepsilon]$. The second region S_2 includes the bands with the correlation coefficients within $[1-\varepsilon, 1-2\varepsilon]$. The bands with the correlation values in $[1-(P\text{-}1)\varepsilon, 1-P\varepsilon]$ are contained in the sub-spectral region S_P. Only one spectral band is selected from each sub-spectral region. The spectral band with the maximum class separability is selected from each sub-spectral region to form a set of selected spectral bands $\{u_1, u_2, \ldots, u_P\}$. Table 3 lists sub-spectral regions and the selected spectral bands for a given number of desired bands from 1 to 6.

Table 3. Sub-spectral regions and the selected bands.

P	Sub-Spectral Regions	Maximum Class Separability	Canonical Analysis
1	[1,65]	11	17
2	[5,39], [40,65]	11, 40	17, 12
3	[5,23], [24,46], [47,65]	11, 24, 47	17, 12, 32
4	[7,21], [5,6] [22, 39], [40, 51], [52,65]	11, 6, 40, 52	17, 12, 32, 9
5	[8,19], [5,7] [20, 30], [31, 43], [44,55], [56, 65]	11, 7, 31, 44, 56	17, 12, 32, 9, 22
6	[7,17], [5,7] [18, 23], [24, 39], [40,46], [47, 57], [58, 65]	11, 7, 24, 40, 47, 58	17, 12, 32, 9, 22, 37

3.4 A Case Study: Data Mining in Hyperspectral Imaging

This section describes the data mining method used and the results of an experimental analysis using this method. Support vector machines (SVM) (Vapnik, 1998; Cristianini & Shawe-Taylor, 2000) can find the optimal separating hyperplane that maximizes the margin between the classes. Consider the case of classifying a set of linear separating data. Assume a set of training vectors $\boldsymbol{x}_j$ that belong to two classes with the class label $y_j = \{+1, -1\}$. A linear decision function is represented by the equation $f(\boldsymbol{x}) = \boldsymbol{w}^t \boldsymbol{x} + b$, where w denotes the weight vector and b indicates the bias. The problem reduces to determining the weight vector w and bias b that maximizes the margin.

$$y_j \left[\left(\boldsymbol{w}^t \boldsymbol{x}_j + b \right) - 1 \right] \geq 0 \tag{15}$$

The discriminant function can be represented as

$$f(\boldsymbol{x}) = \operatorname{sgn}\left(\sum_j y_j \alpha_j \left(\boldsymbol{x} \cdot \boldsymbol{x}_j \right) + b \right) \tag{16}$$

For a nonlinearly separable case, the input vectors are mapped to a higher dimensional feature space to make them linearly separable. Suppose the data are mapped to a space using a mapping Φ. Then the training algorithm depends on $\Phi(\boldsymbol{x}_i) \cdot \Phi(\boldsymbol{x}_j)$. Now if a "kernel function" exists such that $K(\boldsymbol{x}_i, \boldsymbol{x}_j) = \Phi(\boldsymbol{x}_i) \cdot \Phi(\boldsymbol{x}_j)$, then the discriminant function for a nonlinearly separable problem can be written as

$$f(\boldsymbol{x}) = \operatorname{sgn}\left(\sum_j y_j \alpha_j K(\boldsymbol{x}, \boldsymbol{x}_j) + b \right) \tag{17}$$

Radial basis function kernels are a popular choice of kernels (Vapnik, 1998). A radial basis function (RBF) kernel defined as $K(\boldsymbol{x}, \boldsymbol{x}_j) = \exp\left(-\left\| \boldsymbol{x} - \boldsymbol{x}_j \right\|^2 / 2p^2 \right)$ with the width parameter $p = 1$ was used in the experiments. A SVM implementation (Gunn, 1997) is used to perform the SVM training and classification.

The selected bands are classified with the SVM classifier with RBF kernel for skin tumor detection. Figure 13 shows the original images with tumors detected by the CA and MCS methods. White spots indicate tumors which were correctly detected and the white areas enclosed by a rectangle indicate false positives. Circled areas are the tumors not detected by the algorithms. The MCS criterion significantly reduced the number of false positives while maintaining the same classification accuracy.

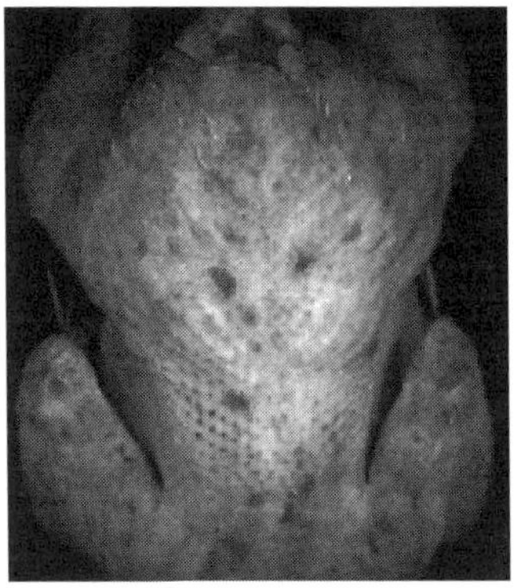

(a) Original image

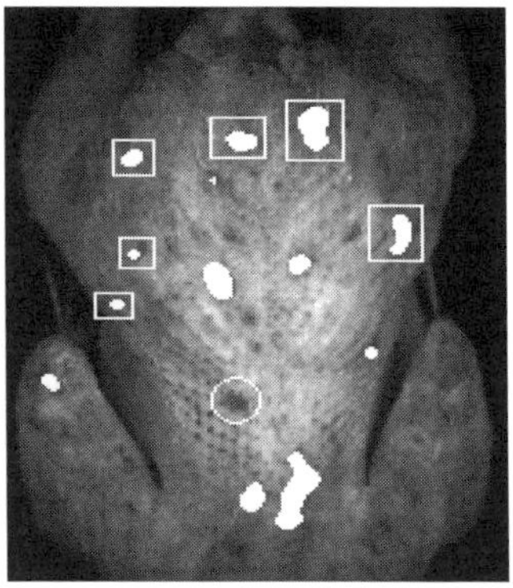

(b) CA

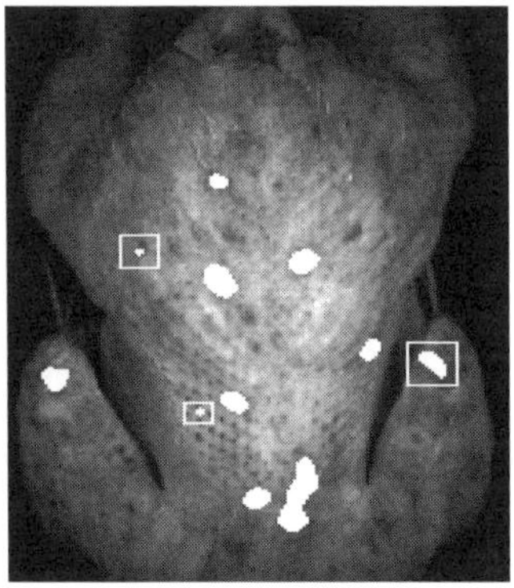

(c) MCS

Figure 13. Tumor detection results with the six spectral bands selected. (a) Original image at the wavelength of 508.92 *nm*, (b) Tumor detection result with CA, and (c) Tumor classification result with MCS.

4. Conclusions

This chapter presents some major research achievements and techniques that have emerged from multi-dimensional functional data mining. First, we presented a wavelet-based dimensionality reduction procedure in order to handle high-dimensional functional data in data analysis and decision-making.

The proposed procedures are more effective for both signals having larger signal to noise ratio and transient signals (or signals with smaller energy), while denoising procedures have good performance for noisy or smooth signals. In addition, some data mining techniques were presented for the prediction of shaft misalignment. Since both parallel and angular offset have the same level of prediction difficulty, the same set of data can be used to predict misalignment in each case within a reasonable prediction error. Second, a hyperspectral image analysis technique was introduced to find a small number of spectral bands to reduce the computational complexity for real-time processing of hyperspectral images. A support vector machine classifier with a radial basis function kernel finds an optimal decision boundary in a reduced feature space for detecting skin tumors. The tumor detection accuracies with six spectral bands selected from the maximum class separability and the canonical analysis were tested for different hyperspectral image samples. The maximum class separability criterion obtained higher accuracies with smaller number of false positives than the canonical analysis method.

Future work is needed to extend the multi-dimensional functional data mining techniques to traditional quality improvement and SPC areas (for example, analysis of variance of functional data or spatial data based on thresholded wavelet coefficients). Also, one of the distinguishing properties of hyperspectral image data is the high dimensional spectral information coupled with a two-dimensional pictorial representation amenable to image interpretation. In future work, one also needs to develop the band selection procedures that incorporate the spatial and spectral information of the data.

Acknowledgement

This work was supported in part by NSF Career Award CMMI-0644830. The views expressed in this article are those of the authors and do not reflect the official policy or position of the Oak Ridge National Laboratory, UT-Battelle, Department of Energy, or the United States Government.

References

Antoniadis, A., Gijbels, I., Gr´egoire, G. (1997). Model Selection Using Wavelet Decomposition and Applications, *Biometrika*, **84**(4), 751–763.

Bishop, C.M. (1995). *Neural Networks for Pattern Recognition*. Oxford University Press: New York, NY, U.S.A.

Burrus, B., Gopinath, R., Guo, H. (1998). *Introduction to Wavelets and Wavelet Transforms: A Primer*, 1st ed., Prentice-Hall: Englewood Cliffs, NJ, U.S.A.

Calnek, B.W., Barnes, H.J., Beard, C.W., Reid, W.M., Yoder, H.W. (1991). *Diseases of Poultry*. Iowa State University Press: Iowa City, Iowa, U.S.A.

Campbell, J. (!996). *Introduction to Remote Sensing*. Guilford Press: New York, NY, U.S.A.

Chang, C., Du, Q., Sun, T., Althouse, M. (2001). A joint band prioritization and band-decorrelation approach to band selection for hyperspectral image classification. *IEEE Transactions on Geoscience and Remote Sensing*, **37** (6), 2631–2641.

Cherkassky, V., Shao, X. (2001). Signal estimation and denoising using VC-theory, *Neural Networks*, **14**, 37–52.

Cristianini, N. Shawe-Taylor, J. (2000). *An Introduction to Support Vector Machines and Other Kernel-based Learning Methods*. Cambridge University Press: New York, NY, U.S.A.

Daubechies, I. (1992). *Ten Lectures on Wavelets*, Volume 61 of CBMS-NSF Regional Conference Series in Applied Mathematics, SIAM Press: Philadelphia, PA, U.S.A.

Donoho, D. L., Johnstone, I. M. (1994). Ideal spatial adaptation by wavelet shrinkage, *Biometrika*, **81**(4), 425–455.

Donoho, D. L., Johnstone, I. M. (1995). Adapting to unknown smoothness via wavelet shrinkage, *Journal of the American Statistical Association*, **90**(432), 1200–1224.

Du, Z., Jeong, M. K., Kong, S. G. (2007). Hyperspectral band selection for automatic detection of poultry skin tumors, in press.

Fletcher, J.T., Kong, S.G. (2003). Principal Component Analysis for Poultry Tumor Inspection using Hyperspectral Fluorescence Imaging, *Proceedings of International Joint Conference Neural Networks (IJCNN-2003),* July, Portland, OR, U.S.A.

Ganesan, R., Das, T. K., Sikdar, A., Kumar, A. (2003). Wavelet based detection of delamination defect in CMP using nonstationary acoustic emission signal, *IEEE Transactions on Semiconductor Manufacturing*, **16**(4), 677–685.

Geladi, P., Kowalski, B. (1986). Partial least squares regression: A tutorial. *Analytica Chemica Acta*, **185**, 1–7.

Giordana, Attilio, Saitta, L., Bergadano, F., Brancadori, F., and De Marchi, D. (1993). ENIGMA: A system that learns diagnostic knowledge. *IEEE Transactions on Knowledge and Data Engineering,* **50**(1), 15–28.

Groves, P. Bajcsy, P. (2003). Methodology for hyperspectral band and classification model selection. *Proceedings of 2003 IEEE Workshop on Advances in Techniques for Analysis of Remotely Sensed Data*. 120–128.

Gunn, S. R. (1997). Support vector machines for classification and regression, Technical Report, Image Speech and Intelligent Systems Research Group, University of Southampton, UK. (Online Version: http://www.isis.ecs.soton.ac.uk/isystems/kernel/.

Ihara, I. (1993). *Information Theory for Continuous System*, World Scientific: Singapore.

Jeong, M. K., Chen, D., Lu, J. C. (2003). Fault detection using thresholded scalogram, *Applied Stochastic Models in Business and Industry*, **19**(3), 231–244.

Jeong, M. K., Lu, J. C., Huo, X., Vidakovic, B., Chen, D. (2006). Wavelet-based dimensionality reduction techniques for process fault detection, *Technometrics*, **48**(1), 26–40.

Jin, J., Shi, J. (1999). Feature-preserving data compression of stamping tonnage information using wavelets, *Technometrics*, **41**(4), 327–339.

Jin, J., Shi, J. (2001). Automatic feature extraction of waveform signals for in-process diagnostic performance improvement, *Journal of Intelligent Manufacturing*, **12**, 257–268.

Joliffe, I.T. (2002). *Principal Component Analysis* (2nd ed.). Springer-Verlag: Berlin, Germany.

Jung, U., Jeong, M. K., Lu, J. C. (2006). A Vertical-Energy-Thresholding Procedure for Data Reduction with Multiple Complex Curves, *IEEE Transactions on Systems, Man, Cybernetics, Part B*, **36**(5), 1128–1138.

Keshava, N. (2001). Best bands selection for detection in hyperspectral processing. *Proceedings of IEEE Int'l Conf. on Acoustics, Speech, and Signal Processing*. 5, 3149–3152.

Kim, I. Chen, Y. R., Kim, M S., and Kong, S. G. (2004). Detection of skin tumors on chicken carcasses using hyperspectral fluorescence imaging, *Transactions of the American Society of Agricultural Engineers*, **47**(5), 1785–1792.

Kim, M., Chen, Y. R., Mehl, P. (2001). Hyperspectral reflectance and fluorescence imaging system for food quality and safety. *Trans. of the American Society of Agricultural Engineers*, **44** (3), 721–729.

Koh, C. K. H., Shi, J., Williams, W. J., Ni, J. (1999). Multiple fault detection and isolation using the Haar transform, Part 2: Application to the Stamping Process, *Transactions of the ASME*, **121**(2), 295–299.

Kong, S. G., (2003). Cutting edge applications of hyperspectral image processing, *Proceedings of Annual Conference on Science, Technology, and Entrepreneurship*, August, Pasadena, CA, U.S.A.

Kong, S. G. (2003). Inspection of poultry skin tumor using hyperspectral fluorescence imaging, *Proceedings of the 6th International Conference on Quality Control by Artificial Vision (QCAV-2003),* May, Gatlinburg, TN, U.S.A.

Kong, S. G., Chen, Y. R., Kim, I., Kim, M. S. (2004). Analysis of hyperspectral fluorescence images for poultry skin tumor inspection, *Applied Optics*, **43**(4), 824–833.

Kuropatwinski, J. J., Jesse, S., Hines, J. W., Edmondson, A., Carley, J. (1997). Prediction of motor misalignment using neural networks, *Proceedings of Maintenance and Reliability Conference (MARCON 97),* Knoxville, TN, U.S.A., May 20–22.

Lada, E. K., Lu, J.-C., Wilson, J. R. (2002). A wavelet based procedure for process fault detection, *IEEE Trans. on Semiconductor Manufacturing*, **15**(1), 79–90.

Liu, B., and Ling, S. F. (1999). On the selection of informative wavelets for machinery diagnosis, *Mechanical Systems and Signal Processing*, **13**(1), 145–162.

Lu, J.-C. (2001). Methodology of mining massive data Set for improving manufacturing quality/efficiency, In *Data Mining for Design and Manufacturing: Methods and Applications,* D. Braha (Ed.), Kluwer Academic Publishers, Boston, MA, U.S.A.

Luigi-Dragotti, P., Poggi, G., Ragozini, A.R.P. (2000). Compression of multispectral images by three-dimensional SPIHT algorithm, *IEEE Transactions Geosci. Remote Sensing*, **38**, 416–428.

Mallat, S.G. (1989). A theory for multiresolution signal decomposition: the wavelet representation, *IEEE Transactions on Pattern Analysis and Machine Intelligence*, **11**(7), 674–693.

Mallat, S. G. (1998). *A Wavelet Tour of Signal Processing*, Academic Press: San Diego, CA, U.S.A.

Massy, W. F. (1965). Principal components regression in exploratory statistical research. *Journal of the American Statistical Association*, **60**, 234–246.

Olufemi A. Omitaomu, Myong K. Jeong, Adedeji B. Badiru, and J. Wesley Hines (2006). On-line Prediction of Motor Shaft Misalignment Using Fourier-Transformed Power Spectrum Data and Support Vector Regression. *Journal of Manufacturing Science and Engineering*, **128**(4): 1019–1024.

Olufemi A. Omitaomu, Myong K. Jeong, Adedeji B. Badiru, and J. Wesley Hines (2007). On-Line Support Vector Regression for Machine Condition Monitoring with Applications to Motor Shaft Misalignment Prediction. *IEEE Transactions on Systems, Man, and Cybernetics: Part C*, **37**(5).

Piotrowski, J. (1995). *Shaft Alignment Handbook*. Marcel Dekker, Inc.: New York, NY, U.S.A.

Portilla, J., Simoncelli, E. P. (2000). Image denoising via adjustment of wavelet coefficient maginitude correlation, Center for Neural Science, and *Proceedings of the 7th International Conference on Image Processing*, Vancouver, BC, Canada, 10-13. September 2000, 277–280.

Rioul, O., Vetterli, M. (1991). Wavelets and signal processing, *IEEE Signal Processing Magazine*, October, 14–38.

Rying, E. A., Gyurcsik, R. S., Lu, J. C., Bilbro, G., Parsons, G., Sorrell, F. Y. (1997). Wavelet analysis of mass spectrometry signals for transient event detection and run-to-run process control, In *Proceedings of the Second International Symposium on Process Control, Diagnostics, and Modeling in Semiconductor Manufacturing*, Meyyappan, M., Economou D., J., Bulter, S. W. (Eds.), 37–44.

Saito, N. (1994). Simultaneous noise suppression and signal compression using a library of orthonormal bases and the minimum description length criterion," In *Wavelets in Geophysics*, E. Foufoula-Georgiou and P. Kumar (Eds.). Academic Press: New York, NY, U.S.A.

Scargle, J.D. (1997). Wavelet methods in astronomical time series analysis, In *Application of Time Series Analysis in Astronomy and Meteorology*, T. S. Rao, M. B. Priestly, and O. Lessi (Eds.), Chapman and Hall: New York, NY, U.S.A., 226–248.

Tu, T.-M., Chen, C.-H., Wu, J.-L., Chang, C.-I. (1998). A fast two-stage classification method for high-dimensional remote sensing data. *IEEE Transactions on Geoscience and Remote Sensing*, **36** (1), 182–191.

Vapnik, V. (1998*). Statistical Learning Theory*. John Wiley & Sons: New York, NY, U.S.A.

Venkatasubramanian, V., Rengaswamy, R., Kavuri, S. N., Yin, K. (2003). A review of process fault detection and diagnosis. Part III: Process history based methods. *Computers and Chemical Engineering*, **27**, 327–346.

Vidakovic, B. (1999). *Statistical Modeling by Wavelets*, John Wiley & Sons: New York, NY, U.S.A.

Wang, X. Z., Chen, B. H., Yang, S. H., McGreavy, C. (1999). Application of wavelets and neural networks to diagnostic system development, 2, An integrated Framework and its Application, *Computers and Chemical Engineering*, **23**, 945–954.

Weyrich, N., Warhola, G. T. (1998). Wavelet shrinkage and generalized cross validation for image denoising, *IEEE Trans. on Image Processing*, **7**(1), 82–90.

Wold, H. Estimation of principal components and related models by iterative least squares. In *Multivariate Analysis*, Krishnaiah P.R. (Ed.), Academic Press: New York, NY, U.S.A.

Wowk, V. (2000). *Machine Vibration: Alignment*. McGraw Hill: New York, NY, U.S.A.

Authors' Biographical Statements

Myong K. Jeong (M) received BS in industrial engineering from Han Yang University, Seoul, Korea, in 1991, MS in industrial engineering from Korea Advanced Institute of Science and Technology, Taejon, Korea, in 1993, MS in statistics from Georgia Institute of Technology, Atlanta, Georgia, in 2002, and Ph.D. in industrial and systems engineering from Georgia Institute of Technology, Atlanta, Georgia, in 2004. He is an Assistant Professor in the Department of Industrial and Information Engineering, the University of Tennessee, Knoxville. His research interests include statistical data mining, machine health monitoring, spectral data analysis, and sensor data analysis. Dr. Jeong is a member of INFORMS, IIE, and SME. He won the Freund International Scholarship and NSF CAREER Award, in 2002 and 2006, respectively.

Seong G. Kong received the B.S. and the M.S. degrees in electrical engineering from Seoul National University, Seoul, Korea in 1982 and 1987. He received the Ph.D. degree in electrical engineering from the University of Southern California, Los Angeles in 1991. He was an Assistant Professor from 1992 to 1995, and an Associate Professor from 1996 to 2000 in Department of Electrical Engineering at Soongsil University, Seoul. He served as chair of the department from 1998 to 2000. During the years 2000-2001, he was with School of Electrical and Computer Engineering at Purdue University, West Lafayette, Indiana, as a visiting scholar. Dr. Kong joined the University of Tennessee, Knoxville as an Associate Professor in Electrical and Computer Engineering Department from 2002 to 2007. He is an Associate Professor of Electrical and Computer Engineering Department at Temple University, Philadelphia from 2007. His research interests include pattern recognition, image processing, and intelligent systems.

Dr. Kong was awarded Best Paper Award from International Conference on Pattern Recognition in 2004, Honorable Mention Paper Award from American Society of Agricultural and Biological Engineers and Professional Development Award from the University of Tennessee in 2005. In 2007, he received Most Cited Paper Award. His professional services include Associate Editor of IEEE Transactions on Neural Networks, Standards Committee of IEEE Computational Intelligence Society, Program Committee members of various international conferences including IEEE International Joint Conference on Neural Networks (IJCNN), International Conference on Computational Intelligence for Homeland Security and Personal Security (CIHSPS), and publication chair of IEEE International Conference on Fuzzy Systems (FUZZ-IEEE). Dr. Kong is a senior member of IEEE and a member of SPIE.

Olufemi A. Omitaomu received the B.S. degree in mechanical engineering from Lagos State University, Lagos State, Nigeria, the M.S. degree in mechanical engineering from University of Lagos, Lagos, Nigeria, and the Ph.D. degree in industrial and information engineering from the University of Tennessee, Knoxville, in 1995, 1999, and 2006 respectively. Currently, he is with the Computational Sciences & Engineering Division at the Oak Ridge National Laboratory, Oak Ridge, Tennessee. Earlier, he was a postdoctoral fellow at McMaster University, Hamilton, ON, Canada. Prior to his Ph.D. program, he was a Project Engineer at Exxon-Mobil facilities in Nigeria from 1995 to 2001. His research interests include signal processing and machine learning applications in enterprise data mining, quality and reliability engineering, and computational economic analysis. Dr. Omitaomu is a member of the Institute of Industrial Engineers (IIE), the Institute for Operations Research and the Management Sciences (INFORMS), and the Institute for Electrical and Electronic Engineers (IEEE). His work has appeared in *ASME Journal of Manufacturing Science and Engineering*, *IEEE Transactions on Systems, Man, and Cybernetics*, *Journal of Information Science and Technology*, *Journal of Machine Tools and Manufacture*, *The Engineering Economist*, and *Journal of Computers and Industrial Engineering*.

Chapter 11[1]

Maintenance Planning Using Enterprise Data Mining

L. P. Khoo, Z. W. Zhong and H. Y. Lim†
School of Mechanical and Aerospace Engineering, Nanyang Technological University
North Spine (N3) Level 2, 50 Nanyang Avenue, Singapore 639798
†Fabristeel Pte Ltd, 9, Tuas Avenue 10, Singapore 639133
Emails: mlpkhoo@ntu.edu.sg, mzwzhong@ntu.edu.sg
Web pages : http://www.ntu.edu.sg/home/mlpkhoo/,
http://www.ntu.edu.sg/home/mzwzhong/

Abstract: In recent years, extracting useful information from enterprise data and subsequently making sense of the extracted knowledge are IT (information technology) activities of utmost importance to many organizations. Frequently, the extracted knowledge is represented in the form of rules. This chapter describes a hybrid approach that integrates rough sets, tabu search, and genetic algorithms (GAs) for extracting rules from enterprise data for maintenance. The intensification and diversification strategies of tabu search are embedded in a GA search engine, in a bid to facilitate rule extraction. A case study on the maintenance of bridge cranes in an organization was used to illustrate the effectiveness of the proposed hybrid approach. The extracted rules appear to be reasonable. The details of the hybrid approach, the results of a comparative study between a traditional GA search engine and a tabu-enhanced GA search engine, and the details of the case study are presented.

Key Words: Rule extraction, Rough sets, Tabu search, Genetic algorithms, Enterprise data mining.

---

[1] Liao, T.W. and E. Triantaphyllou, (Eds.), **Recent Advances in Data Mining of Enterprise Data: Algorithms and Applications**, *World Scientific*, Singapore, pp. 505-544, 2007.

1. Introduction

Extracting useful information from enterprise data and making sense of the extracted knowledge are important goals for many organizations. The process for achieving the previous goals is frequently referred to as knowledge discovery from databases. Over the years, the process of extracting useful knowledge from enterprise data has evolved into an important technique known as data mining (Westphal, 1995) for engineering as well as for non-engineering applications. Data mining employs detailed analytical approaches and presents them in such a way that organizations can easily discover the characteristics of the analyzed data and make sense of the newly derived knowledge. It can be used to predict future trends and behaviors, and enables organizations to make proactive, knowledge-driven decisions. Indeed, the effective use of data mining to facilitate knowledge driven decision-making is one of the key competitive thrusts for many organizations while performing critical tasks such as maintenance.

Some popular data mining techniques include neural networks (Khanna, 1990) and rule induction (Khoo & Zhai, 2001; Triantaphyllou & Felici, 2006). These techniques provide solutions to problems that in the past were too time-consuming to solve. They also allow engineers to infer patterns from data stored in enterprise databases. Basically, neural networks are able to produce good predictions but are not capable of discovering the specific nature of any interrelations among the variables on which the predictions are based. In contrast, rule induction offers a simpler approach. It generates rules, which describe the characteristics of the data being analyzed. Rule induction techniques have a major advantage over neural networks in the interpretability of the knowledge eventually discovered.

Other techniques are fairly diverse and can be differentiated depending on the nature of the problems to be solved. As an example, exploratory data analysis employs visualization to discover data patterns. The major drawback of such a technique is that it is not able to reduce the amount of data stored in a dataset. If the dataset is huge, it may not be easy to visualize its patterns. The reason is that when all the data items are portrayed separately, they may be incomprehensible. Furthermore, it may be difficult to decide which information is more valuable or important.

Khoo and Zhai (2002) proposed a rule induction approach, which employed a genetic algorithm (GA) (Goldberg, 1995) as the engine to search through the space of potential solutions. In that work, randomness was used as a major strategy for the extraction of decision rules. These decision rules were encoded into data-strings known as chromosomes. Essentially, a GA applies Darwin's theory of survival of the fittest by means of genetic operators such as crossover and mutation to produce a new population of offspring chromosomes from the current population. It uses a probabilistic rule to direct the search and a performance evaluation scheme to assess the fitness of each chromosome in order to narrow down the search. After a number of evolutions, fitter chromosomes can be obtained and are used as optimal or semi-optimal solutions to a problem.

In practice, most engineering applications, such as maintenance planning, require treatment of uncertainty. By embedding the theory of rough sets (Pawlak, 1992) into rule induction approaches (Khoo & Zhai, 2002), uncertainty can be dealt with effectively. However, as the search space for possible solutions can be enormous, it is difficult to obtain reasonable and sufficient rules in just a few GA runs. Thus, some ways to improve the search process become necessary. Tabu search (Glover, 1997), which is a meta-heuristic approach, provides search strategies to solve optimization problems.

This chapter describes a hybrid approach that integrates rough sets, GAs, and tabu search to maintenance planning. The basic concepts of rough sets, GAs and tabu search are described in Section 2. Section 3 gives an account on the proposed hybrid approach. A case study on the planning of a maintenance schedule for large bridge cranes, which is used to illustrate the capability of the proposed approach, is provided in Section 4. Section 5 concludes this chapter.

2. Rough Sets, Genetic Algorithms, and Tabu Search

2.1 Rough Sets

2.1.1 Overview

The theory of rough sets was proposed by Pawlak (1992) as a novel mathematical tool for reasoning about imprecision, vagueness and uncertainty. It overlaps, to some extent, with many other theories for uncertainty and vagueness, especially with the Dempster-Shafer theory of belief functions (Slowinski & Stefanowski, 1992) and fuzzy set theory (Wygralak 1989; Dubois & Prade, 1990; Dubois & Prade, 1992). Nevertheless, it can be viewed as an independent, complementary, and non-competing technique (Pawlak, 1992). The major difference between the theory of rough sets and the Dempster-Shafer theory is that the former makes use of a set of lower and upper approximations, whereas the latter uses belief functions as the main tool. On the other hand, the relationship between rough sets and fuzzy sets is rather complicated (Pawlak & Slowinski, 1994; Yao, 1998) and is discussed later.

The notion of the theory of rough sets is based on the concept of classification. The ability to classify is a fundamental feature of any living organism, robot, intelligent system or agent, which, in order to behave rationally in the external world, needs to constantly classify concrete or abstract objects such as processes and signals. As a result, minor differences between objects are ignored, thus forming classes of objects that are not noticeably different, i.e. indiscernible. These indiscernible classes can be viewed as *elementary concepts* used by an intelligent system or an agent to build up its knowledge about reality.

Consider, for example, the task of monitoring and diagnosing a group of bridge cranes in a typical container port. Normally, the maintenance engineers will check a set of data points such as the conditions of mounting brackets, the sea inner or outer guide rollers and the land inner or outer guide rollers. All the bridge cranes having the same characteristics are *discernible (similar)*. In view of this, the available information can be classified into blocks, which can be understood as *elementary granules (atoms)* of knowledge about the conditions of the bridge cranes. These granules are known as *elementary sets* or *concepts*, which constitute the elementary building blocks of knowledge about these bridge cranes. Elementary concepts can be combined into compound concepts that are uniquely defined in terms of elementary concepts. Any union of elementary sets is called a *crisp set*. However, the granularity of knowledge results in situations in which some concepts cannot be expressed precisely within the available knowledge. These notions can only be defined approximately, and such concepts are referred to *as rough (vague, imprecise)*.

In the theory of rough sets, for every set, X, it is possible to associate it with two crisp sets known as *the lower* and *the upper approximations* of X. Thus, each vague concept can be replaced by a pair of precise concepts. The lower approximation of a concept consists of all the objects that *surely* belong to the concept, whereas the upper approximation of a concept consists of all the objects that *possibly* belong to the concept. For example, the concept of scheduling of maintenance is precise, because for every machine it can be decided whether it is 'to schedule for maintenance' or 'not to schedule for maintenance'. However, based on visual inspection, the concept of "good working condition of a bridge crane" is vague unless it is thoroughly examined.

Between the two approximations of a concept is a *boundary region* of the concept. The boundary region consists of all the objects that cannot be classified with certainty under the concept or its complement by employing available knowledge. The greater the boundary region, the vaguer is the concept. As a special case, if the boundary region of a concept is empty, the concept becomes precise. In other words, approximation is the basic and most important tool (operator) in the philosophy of rough sets to deal with uncertainty and vagueness.

2.1.2 Rough Sets and Fuzzy Sets

The similarity of the terms 'rough sets' and 'fuzzy sets' tends to create some confusion. A fuzzy set is a class with blurred boundary whereas a rough set is a crisp set that is *coarsely* defined. There is a close connection between the concept of a rough set and that of a fuzzy graph (Pawlak, 1985).

A fuzzy graph is a disjunction of granules that collectively approximate a function or relation. A granule is basically a collection of points that are drawn together by the indiscernibility, similarity or functionality. In rough sets, these granules are equivalence classes, which are the elements of a partition. The theories of rough sets and fuzzy sets evolved in different directions and are largely complementary rather than competitive. They are two independent approaches to handle imperfect knowledge. Their relationships have been studied extensively and many proposals have been made for the combination of rough sets and fuzzy sets (Pawlak, 1985; Wygralak 1989). The results of these studies led to the introduction of the notions of fuzzy rough sets and rough fuzzy sets (Dubois & Prade 1990; Dubois & Prade, 1992; Nanda & Majumdar 1992).

2.1.3 Applications

Since its inception in the early 80's and within two decades, the theory of rough sets has turned out to be a technique that is of substantial importance to artificial intelligence and cognitive sciences. It has many applications, which include in medicine, pharmacology, industry, engineering, control, and social sciences. The theory of rough sets is mainly used for vague data analysis, which includes:

- Characterisation of a set of objects in terms of attribute values;
- Determination of dependencies (total or partial) between attributes;
- Reduction of superfluous attributes (data);
- Identification of the most significant attributes; and
- Decision rule generation.

It offers simple algorithms to handle the above domains and allows straightforward interpretation of the results.

2.1.4 The Strengths of the Theory of Rough Sets

Over the years, the theory of rough sets has been used extensively in the analysis of imprecise information. Compared with other techniques dealing with uncertainty and vagueness, it possesses some unique advantages in solving such problems (Pawlak, 1996; Pawlak, 1997). The most outstanding advantage of the theory of rough sets is that it does not require:

- Any preliminary or additional information about the data such as probability distributions in statistics; and
- The basic probability assignment in the Dempster-Shafer theory of belief functions, or the grade of membership or the value of possibility in the fuzzy set theory (Pawlak, Grzymala-Busse, Slowinski & Ziarko, 1995).

Basically, the theory of rough sets is more suitable when the dataset is too small to employ statistical methods. There are two other advantages of using it as a tool for information analysis. First, it provides a collection of mathematical techniques to handle, with full mathematical rigor, data classification problems, particularly when the data are noisy, incomplete or imprecise. Second, it includes a formal model of knowledge defined as a family of indiscernibility relations. As a result, the knowledge has a clearly defined mathematical sense, and can be analysed and manipulated using mathematical techniques (Ziarko, 1994).

Inductive learning often involves the interpretation of uncertainty. Uncertainty, in general, can be due to incomplete or inconsistent information or knowledge. This imprecise nature of information (knowledge) is the greatest obstacle to the classification of objects and rule induction. The theory of rough sets provides a natural way to solve uncertainty problems. It has experienced some modifications since its introduction, whereas, the basic notions remain unchanged. The approximation space and the lower and upper approximations of a set form two important notions. Essentially, the approximation space of a rough set classifies the domain of interest into disjoint categories (Pawlak, 1991). In doing so, all the classes in a domain can be characterised. The upper and lower approximations represent the classes of indiscernible objects that possess sharp descriptions on concepts but with no sharp boundary.

2.1.5 Enterprise Information and the Information System

Oftentimes the enterprise data used in data mining may be imperfect and imprecise. They may also contain unknown or missing values. Rough sets provide a means to handle vagueness and uncertain information that is inherent in decision-making. The theory of rough sets basically simplifies the search for dominating attributes leading to specific properties, or just rules describing the data. It does not correct the vagueness in the representation. Instead, the theory of rough sets provides an effective tool, which can be used to produce rules that are classified as certain or uncertain. This set of rules can justify a decision making policy and may be employed for decision support.

Generally speaking, rule induction based on rough sets begins with a set of raw data known as an *information system*. An information system consists of a set of observations, which is required for data analysis. It can be viewed as an information table with its rows and columns corresponding to observations (objects) and attributes, respectively. Each observation or object can be characterized by a set of conditions and decision attributes. Through the application of lower and upper approximations and the indiscernibility properties provided by the theory of rough sets, it is possible to discover a type of regularity in a dataset, where data are clustered into positive, negative and boundary regions (Figure 1). While analyzing a dataset, some data may be clearly labeled as being in a set, say X, (i.e., the "positive region") and some data may be clearly classified as not being in set X (i.e., the "negative region").

However, there might be instances where limited information prevents clearly labeling some of the data. When the remaining data cannot be distinguished, they are said to be in the so-called "boundary region". In rough sets, a positive region is also known as the lower approximation of set X that yields no false positives. Whereas, the positive and boundary regions form the upper approximation of the set X that yields no false negatives.

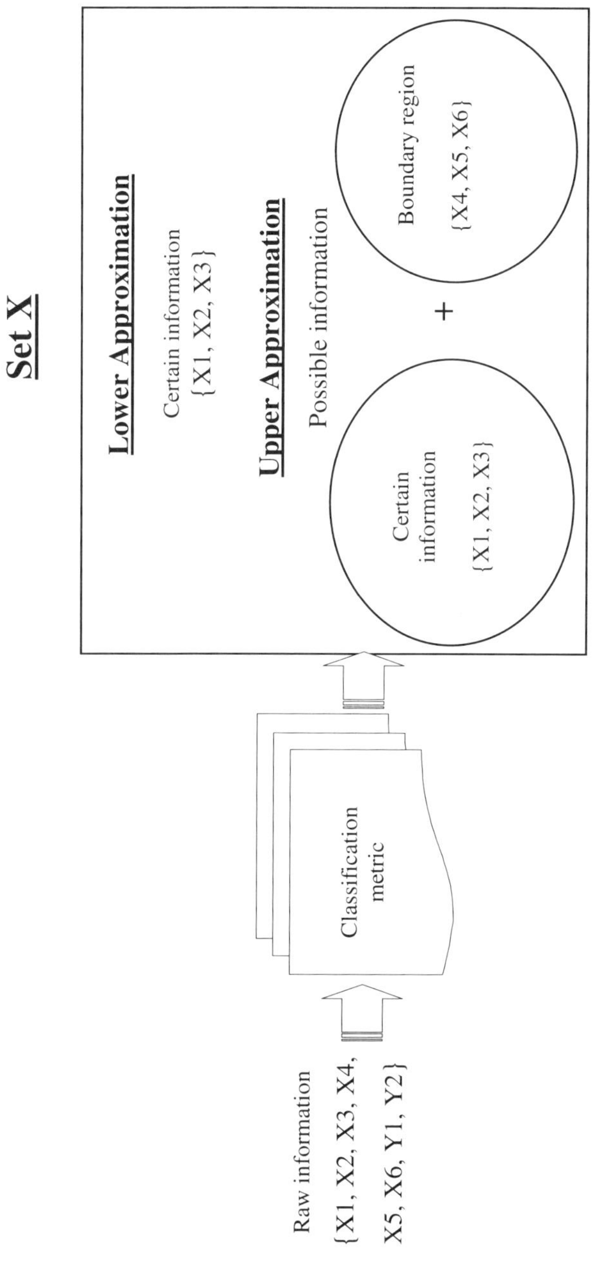

Figure 1. Upper and lower approximation in rough sets.

The following example is used to provide a detailed explanation on how to find the lower approximation and the upper approximation, which are fundamental issues to the concept of the theory of rough sets.

Let an information system, U, consisting of 10 observations (O_1, O_2, ..., O_{10}) be described by 4 attributes A_1, A_2, A_3 and A_4. The decision attribute, D, may attain a value of either '0' or '1'. Thus, the data in the information system can be grouped in accordance to Concept 1 (i.e., C_1, where the decision attribute is '0') or Concept 2 (i.e., C_2, where the decision attribute is '1'). A summary of such a classification is shown as follows:

U = [O, A, D]

where O = $\{O_1, O_2, O_3, O_4, O_5, O_6, O_7, O_8, O_9, O_{10}\}$,

A = $\{A_1, A_2, A_3, A_4\}$ and D = {1, 0}.

Thus,

Concept 1, $C_1 = \{O_3, O_4, O_6, O_8, O_9, O_{10}\}$ → Decision = 0

Concept 2, $C_2 = \{O_1, O_2, O_5, O_7\}$ → Decision = 1

Table 1 shows the condition and decision attributes for these 10 observations.

The lower approximation can be determined by selecting those observations that surely belong to a certain concept. In this case, it is given by $\{O_4, O_6, O_9$, and $O_{10}\}$, which contain decisions with no ambiguity regarding Concept 1. As for the upper approximation for Concept 1, it is given by $\{O_3, O_4, O_6, O_8, O_9$, and $O_{10}\}$. Notice that observations 3 and 8 have been appended to $\{O_4, O_6, O_9$, and $O_{10}\}$. Using the notations "$\underline{L}$" and "$\overline{L}$" for the lower approximation and the upper approximation respectively, "$\underline{L}$" and "$\overline{L}$" for Concept 1 can be expressed mathematically as follows:

$$\underline{L}(C_1) = \{O_4, O_6, O_9, O_{10}\}, \text{ and}$$

$$\overline{L}(C_1) = \{O_3, O_4, O_6, O_8, O_9, O_{10}\}.$$

Hence, the boundary region for Concept 1 is:

$$BR(C_1) = \overline{L}(C_1) - \underline{L}(C_1) = \{O_3, O_8\}.$$

By performing the same analysis for Concept 2, the lower approximation can be found to be as follows:

$$\underline{L}(C_2) = \{O_5, O_7\}.$$

Similarly, the upper approximation is as follows:

$$\overline{L}(C_2) = \{O_1, O_2, O_5, O_7\}.$$

Hence, the boundary region for Concept 2 is given by

$$BR(C_2) = \overline{L}(C_2) - \underline{L}(C_2) = \{O_1, O_2\}.$$

Thus, from Table 1, the regions can be deduced accordingly as follows:

Table 1. Sample observations with condition and decision attributes.

Observations O_j	**Attributes A_i**				**Decision D_j**
	A_1	A_2	A_3	A_4	
O_1	1	0	1	0	1
O_2	0	1	1	0	1
O_3	1	0	1	0	0
O_4	0	0	0	1	0
O_5	1	1	1	0	1
O_6	0	1	0	1	0
O_7	1	0	0	1	1
O_8	0	1	1	0	0
O_9	1	0	0	0	0
O_{10}	0	1	0	0	0

Certain information for Decision '1' (which corresponds to Concept 2) : $\{O_5, O_7\}$ = {1110, 1001}

Boundary region: $\{o_1, o_2\}$ = {1010, 0110}

Possible information for Decision '1': $\{o_1, o_2, o_5, o_7\}$ =

{1010, 0110, 1110, 1001}

Upon completion, the various regions have been determined and can be analyzed separately. It is important to note that the boundary regions of Concepts 1 and 2 always overlap, as observations O1 and O3, and O2 and O8 have the same attribute values but are associated with different decisions.

2.2 Genetic Algorithms

Inspired by Darwin's theory of survival of the fittest, Holland (1975) developed the concept of genetic algorithms (GAs) and published the book *Adaptation in Natural and Artificial Systems* in 1975. Since then, GAs have evolved and become one of the most widely used techniques for solving problems which lack a precise description of the search domain. The successful applications of GAs can be seen in various optimization problems such as PCB assembly (Khoo & Loh, 2000), assembly planning (Khoo, Lee & Yin, 2003), manufacturing scheduling (Khoo, Lee & Yin, 1999), and manufacturing diagnosis (Khoo & Zhai, 2001). The central themes of GA related research have been on the robustness of the technique, and the balance between efficiency and efficacy necessary for survival under many different environments (Pawlak, 1992).

As mentioned previously, in GAs the pertinent information can be encoded into strings called *chromosomes*, and genetic operators such as selection, crossover, and mutation are performed to produce the next generation of chromosomes. GAs also require a probabilistic rule to direct the search and a performance evaluation function to estimate the fitness of each chromosome so as to narrow down the search. In summary, a GA for a particular problem must be equipped with the following capabilities (Zbigniew, 1994):

i. A genetic representation for potential solutions to the problem;
ii. A way to generate a key population of potential solutions;
iii. A fitness function also known as an "evaluation" function that plays the role of the 'environment' in natural evolution to assess the fitness of potential solutions;
iv. Genetic operators that derive the composition of offspring chromosomes; and
v. Values for the various parameters such as the population size and the probabilities of applying the various genetic operators.

More specifically, using GAs an initial population of chromosomes is generated randomly. Upon completion, each member in the population is evaluated by a fitness function which is unique to the problem at hand. The role played by the fitness function in GAs is similar to that played by the environment in natural evolution, where the interaction and the response of an individual with its environment provide a measure of its fitness. Subsequently, based on Darwin's theory of survival of the fittest, chromosomes with higher fitness values are selected to undergo genetic operations such as crossover and mutation (Westphal, 1995).

Crossover is the predominant operation in GAs and is performed with a higher probability such as 0.80. It is regarded as a critical accelerator of a GA search process (Davis, 1991). In natural evolution, crossover occurs when two parent chromosomes exchange parts of their corresponding genes. The crossover operation in GAs recombines genetic materials in the two parent chromosomes to produce two offspring chromosomes (Figure 2). As for mutation, it is normally fixed at a fairly low probability such as 0.01 so as to avoid degenerating into random search. Mutation has the effect of fine-tuning the optimization results. Figure 3 shows that one of the genes of a chromosome has been randomly selected to undergo mutation.

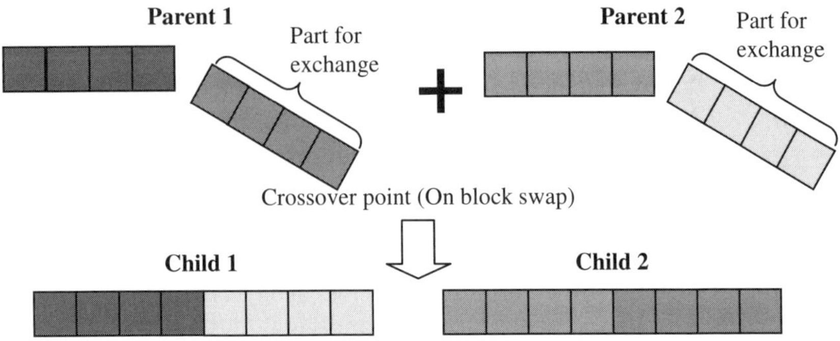

Figure 2. The crossover operation.

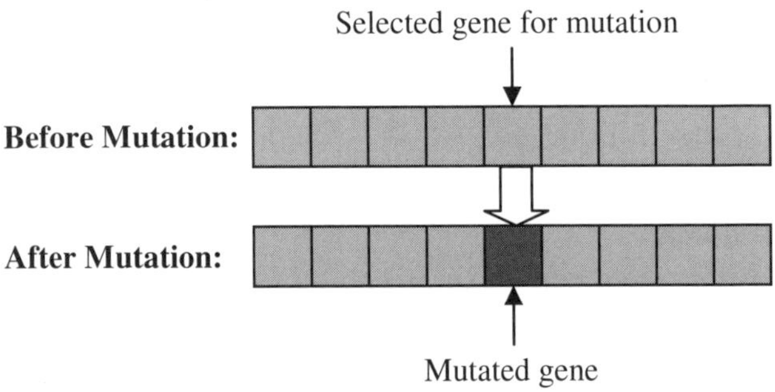

Figure 3. The mutation operation.

A typical GA process is depicted in Figure 4. Briefly, a random population is first created. The fitness of each of the chromosomes in the population is then evaluated using a fitness function. Upon completion, chromosomes with fitness values above average are randomly paired up and undergo the above mentioned genetic operations, crossover and mutation, to produce a new population of chromosomes. The process repeats itself until the termination criterion is met.

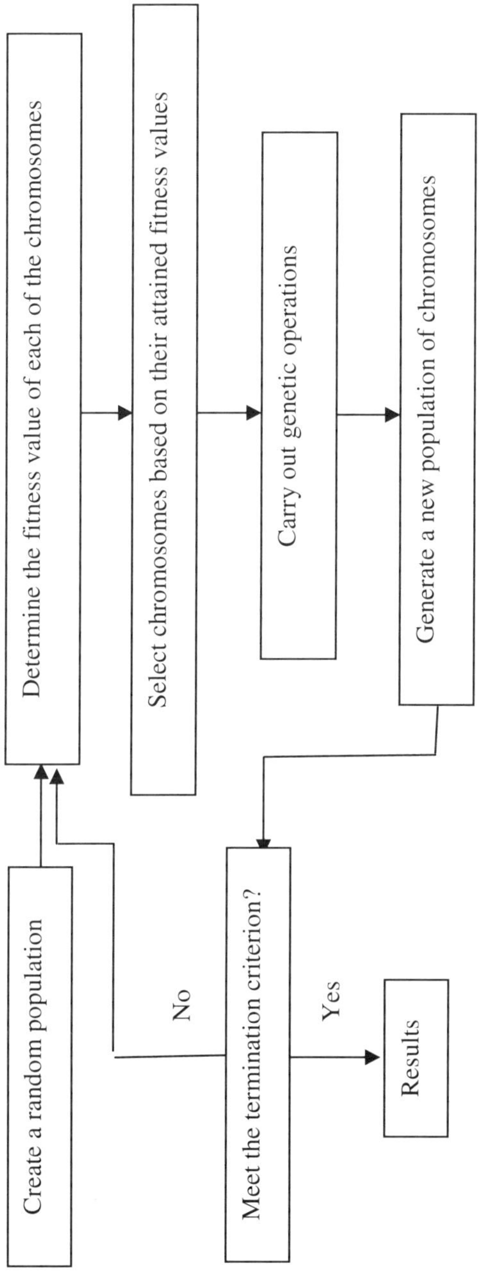

Figure 4. A typical GA process.

The weaknesses of GAs can be summarized as follows.

- There is no theoretical framework associated with them, unlike statistical algorithms which have their assumptions;
- Premature convergence may prevent an optimal solution to be found; and
- GAs basically implement a blind search. Hence, at times, their results are difficult to predict.

Holland (1975) suggested that GAs could be used as a preprocessor to perform the key search, before turning the search process over to a domain-knowledge guided local search system. This implies the necessity to incorporate other techniques to complement GAs.

2.3 Tabu Search

As previously mentioned, tabu search (TS) is a meta-heuristic that can be used to solve complex combinatorial optimization problems. Glover (1997) likened tabu search as a mountaineer having to selectively remember the routes taken when making his way up a mountain. In order to do that, the mountaineer has to take notes along the way and avoid taking the same route again as illustrated in Figure 5. He/she needs to compare the many routes taken using the routes registered in his notebook and explore potentially good ones.

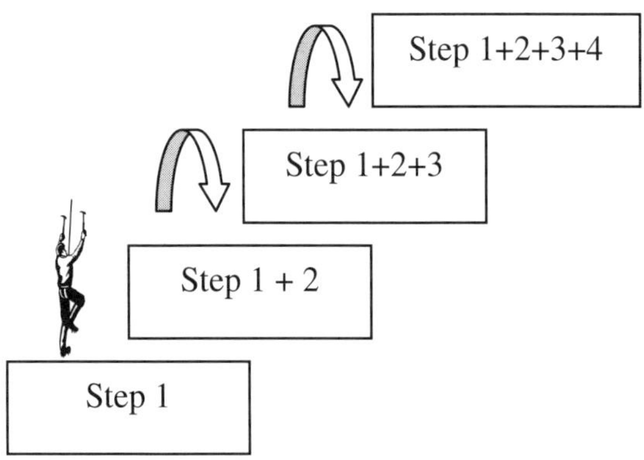

Figure 5. A mountaineer taking notes of the routes taken.

As for TS, it helps in preventing recurrence of previous solutions during the process of performing optimization. It can be employed to further explore all the feasible solutions within the search space by introducing a series of moves, i.e. feasible moves, in the neighborhood. To escape from local optimal solutions and circumvent premature convergence, those feasible moves that have already been made are classified as forbidden or tabu, and are stored in one or more tabu lists during the search. In other words, tabu lists contain the history of successful moves and constitute a so-called TS short-term memory. Typically, the length of a tabu list is capped at 10. The use of TS short-term memory can make the search process more effective. As previously mentioned, GAs employ a blind search and hence are memoryless. The TS short-term memory can therefore be used to facilitate the GA search for optimal solutions when it is integrated with it.

3. The Proposed Hybrid Approach

3.1 Background

As it was mentioned earlier this chapter describes a hybrid approach that integrates rough sets with TS and GAs for rule induction. The proposed approach comprises three processing engines, namely a rough set engine to deal with uncertainty, a tabu enhanced GA engine for rule induction and a rules organizer to organize and rationalize the extracted rules (Figure 6).

3.2 The Rough Set Engine

The rough set engine applies the above-mentioned upper and lower approximations of rough sets (Section 2.1) to classify input information, observations or enterprise data into different concepts. It carries out three sub-tasks namely consistency check, concept forming, and approximation. It begins with checking the consistency of the training dataset or available enterprise data.

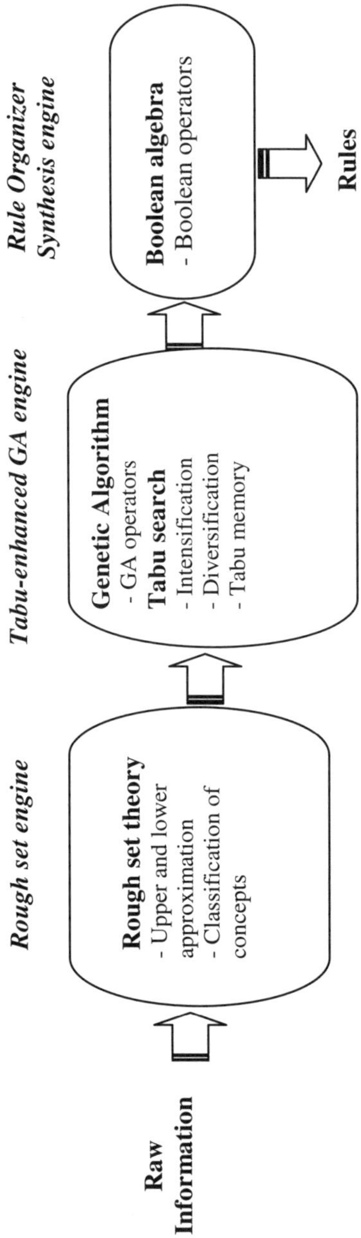

Figure 6. The proposed hybrid approach.

Once an inconsistency such as two observations with identical condition attributes but with different decision attributes is spotted, the dataset is treated using the theory of rough sets. Upon completion of the treatment, the resulting groups of enterprise data are forwarded to the tabu-enhanced GA engine for rule extraction. More specifically, as described in Section 3.3, the upper and lower approximations derived by the rough set engine are used by the tabu-enhanced GA engine to generate possible rules and certain rules, respectively.

3.3 The Tabu-Enhanced GA Engine

The GA engine: The tabu enhanced GA engine for rule induction is realized by embedding TS into a GA. The power of GAs lies in their use of random choice as a means to guide the search towards regions of the search space having a probable improvement (Li et al., 2002). This random nature is difficult to control as it may result in situations where the solutions obtained are few, i.e. to have premature convergence. As a consequence, more GA runs may fail to produce solutions that are significantly better. The incorporation of TS short-term memory into a GA may help in directing the search towards the neighborhood of near optimal solutions. This may result in a more thorough search and increases the chances of deriving more and better near optimal solutions.

The OX (order crossover) path representation method of GAs and the function proposed by Khoo and Zhai (2001) are employed for chromosome representation and fitness evaluation, respectively. The aforementioned chromosome representation requires different attributes to be located at different positions along the chromosome string, for example, Attribute 1 at Position 1, Attribute 2 at Position 2 and so on. Each of these attributes may have different numbers of states, 1, 2, 3, …, n. For example, Chromosome 121436 indicates that it has six attributes, and Attribute 5 has attained State 3. Basically, the objective of using GAs in this work is to extract rules that can maximise the probability of classifying objects correctly. Thus, the fitness of a chromosome can be calculated by testing the rules using an existing training dataset. Mathematically speaking, it is given by

Fitness of chromosome =

$$\left(\frac{\text{number of examples classified correctly by the rule}}{\text{number of example related to the rule}}\right)^2 \tag{1}$$

Using Equation (1), the ability of a rule to classify these observations can be easily quantified. It is apparent that rules with higher fitness value can be used to describe the observations more accurately. The above quadratic fitness function favours rules that are able to classify the observations correctly. It satisfies both the completeness and the consistency criteria. A rule is said to be consistent if it contains no negative samples and is complete if it covers all the positive samples (De Jong, Spears & Gordon, 1993). Please note that by "samples" we mean training data points (e.g., examples). In GA operations, chromosomes with fitness values above the average are selected for reproduction.

As a GA makes use of randomness in its search for optimal solutions, at times, it may experience difficulties in converging to a feasible solution. By incorporating the tabu search, its intensification and diversification strategies can be used to facilitate the search for optimal solutions. Intensification means retaining certain traits of "good" solutions and continuing to search for solutions that exhibit these traits. Diversification attempts to avoid solutions that have already been solicited and continues to search for new solutions in unexplored (or virgin) regions. In this way, better solutions can possibly be obtained.

TS engine: It adopts two strategies, namely intensification and diversification, to guide the search for near optimal solutions. As previously mentioned, the intensification strategy looks for elite solutions, i.e. solutions that have been found to be good. These elite solutions are recorded on a tabu list so that their immediate neighborhood can be explored. The length of the tabu list is problem dependent (Khoo & Loi, 2002). It is longer for regions which are rich in solutions. It can be shortened significantly when the region is barren. As for the intensification strategy, it generates neighborhood solutions by either grafting together components of good solutions or by using modified evaluations that favor the introduction of such components to the current solution (Glover, 1997).

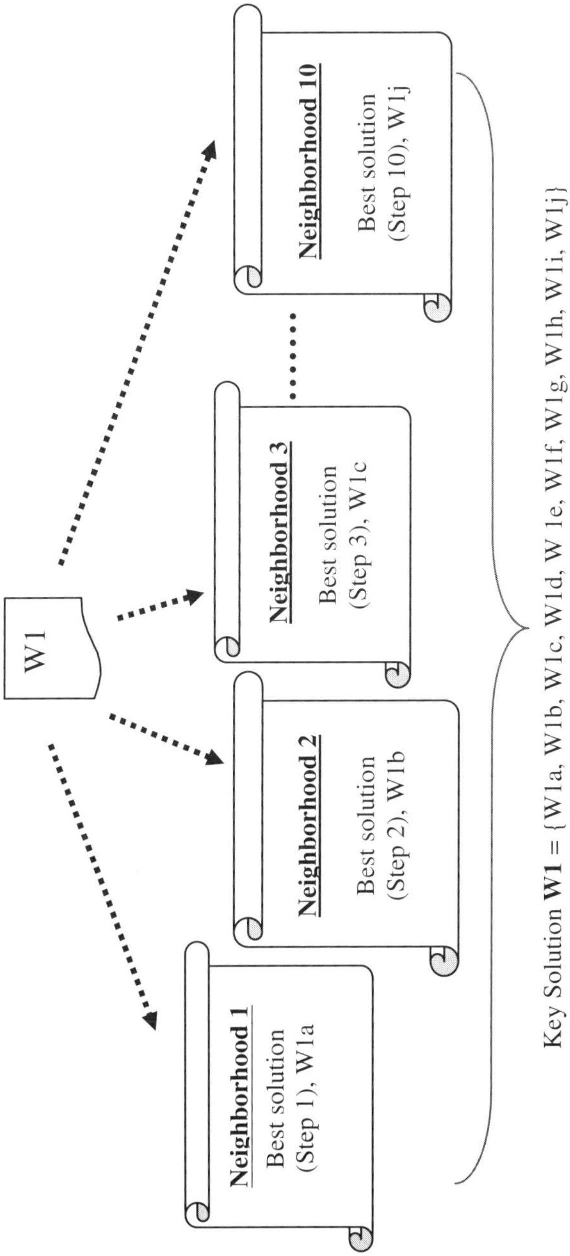

Figure 7. The intensification strategy.

The best neighborhood solutions obtained may normally contain some desirable attributes of key solutions. For example, as shown in Figure 7, given a key solution, W1, TS uses the intensification strategy to look for improved solutions in the neighborhood surrounding it. The best solution is eventually chosen from these neighborhood solutions. On the other hand, the diversification strategy (Figure 8) is the direct opposite of the intensification strategy. Instead of searching the regions using the good attributes of elite key solutions, it searches virgin regions, i.e. unexplored regions, which do not possess any of the attributes present in the elite key solutions.

It is postulated that sometimes, the best solution might not contain any of the good attributes found initially. By exploring other regions, TS widens the scope of search and increases the possibility of reaching an optimal solution. Hence, the solutions obtained using the diversification strategy might totally differ from the original ones, as they enable TS to achieve better performance. Aspiration criteria have also been introduced in TS to decide when to lift the tabu restriction so as to allow new and entirely different searches to be conducted. When it is effectively employed, the process of TS is able to break away from local optimality, to cross over barriers and reach other regions, and hopefully to move towards a global optimum solution.

The algorithm: The proposed hybrid approach begins with the application of the intensification strategy. A set of key initial solutions is first obtained from a GA. The intensification strategy next proceeds to search the neighborhood of each key solution. If a neighborhood solution with better fitness value than that of the key solution has been identified, the key solution is replaced by the neighborhood solution. At the same time, the neighborhood solution is registered on the tabu list. This process is repeated until the tabu list has been filled up.

Upon completion, the set of key solutions undergoes genetic operations to produce the next generation of key solutions. When the search for near optimal solutions has been exhausted, the diversification strategy, which attempts to guide the search to virgin regions in order to break away from local optima, is invoked. Similar to the intensification

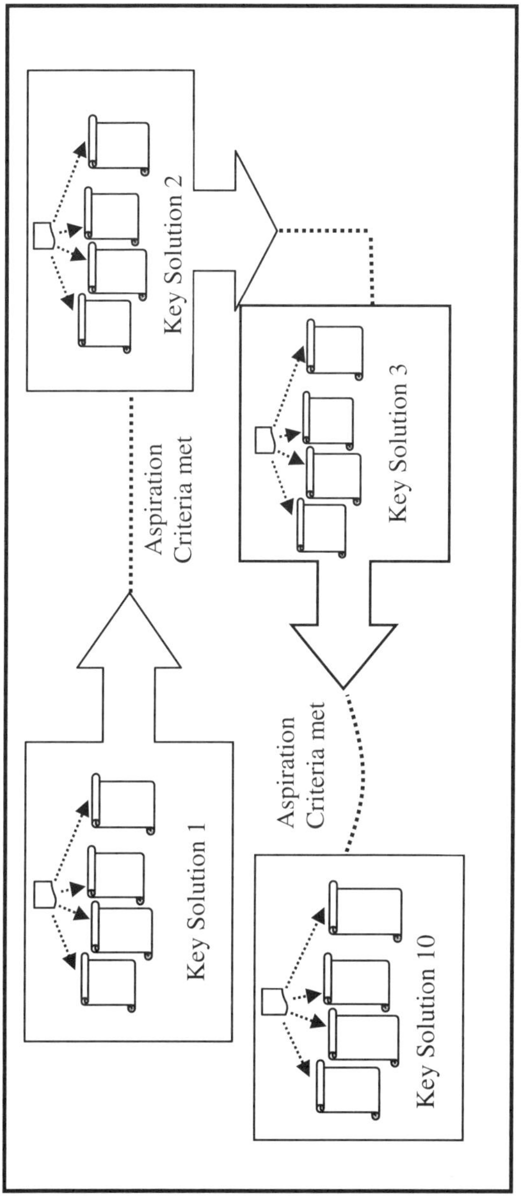

Figure 8. The diversification strategy.

strategy, promising solutions extracted from these virgin regions are used to replace some of the key solutions. Subsequently, the resulting key solutions undergo genetic operations to produce the next generation of key solutions. The above-mentioned search process is repeated until near optimal solutions are obtained. These near optimal solutions are then decoded into rules. A summary of the enhanced searching process is shown in Figure 9.

3.4 Rule Organizer

The rule organizer checks the rules induced by the tabu-enhanced GA engine. It attempts to look for redundancy or duplication of rules. Those rules that can be combined are identified. Some Boolean operations are next carried out to amalgamate them and form composite rules.

4. A Case Study

4.1 Background

Bridge cranes are typical hoisting machines that are widely used in many industrial sites such as steel mills and container ports. In a container port, for example, bridge cranes play an important role in the handling of containers from container ships to trucks or vice versa (Figure 10). It was found that one of the common mechanical problems with bridge cranes is the skewing of the trolley house. Such a problem tends to produce uneven side forces on the guide rollers and causes them to shear off eventually. If the defect is not rectified, it may pose a hazard to the personnel working under the cranes.

Preventive maintenance is frequently adopted to ensure that bridge cranes are in good working condition. It includes devising maintenance schedules so as to carry out maintenance work at planned intervals. At the same time, engineers are required to closely monitor the conditions of the bridge cranes and store the information obtained as part of the enterprise data.

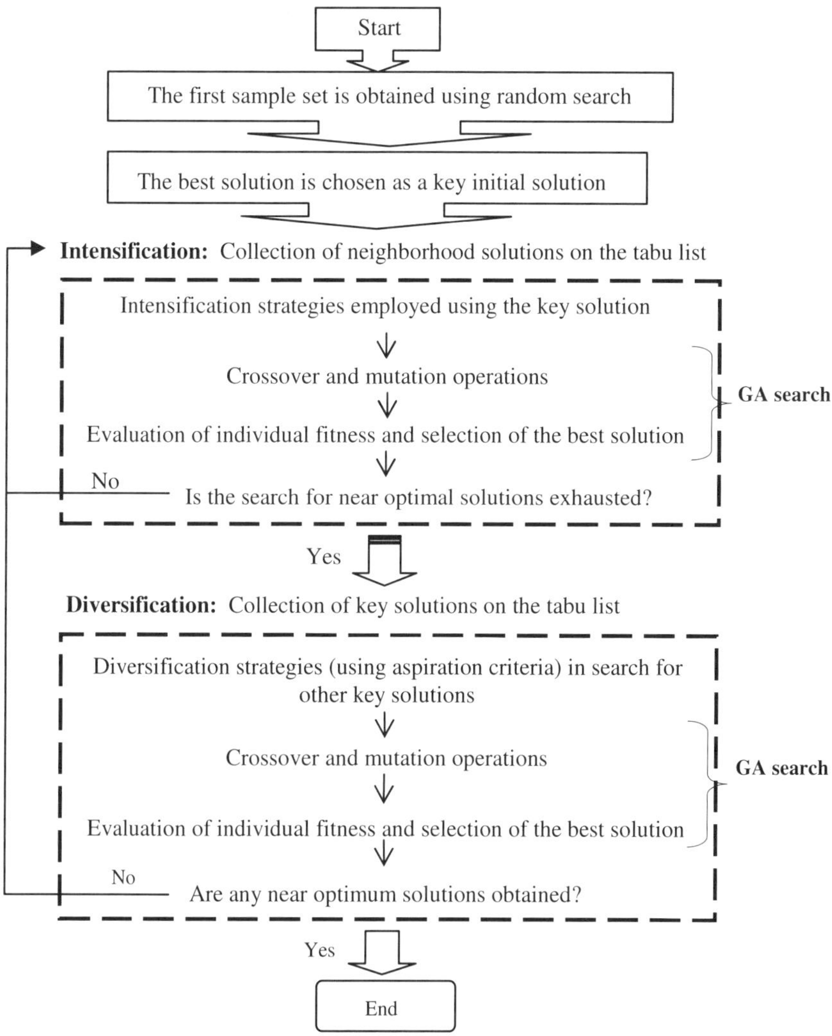

Figure 9. Flowchart of the enhanced search engine during the search stage.

Using preventive maintenance, these bridge cranes are scheduled for maintenance every six months of operation. In reality, not all bridge cranes have the same amount of usage in an industrial site. As a result, there are some bridge cranes, which are frequently called up for checking due to failing conditions or frequent usage. This disrupts the servicing priority of bridge cranes, and eventually, the planned maintenance schedule. Thus, at times, the planned maintenance schedule might be inadequate in determining which bridge cranes are in need of servicing and which are not. Accordingly, the maintenance of some of the bridge cranes, which have been scheduled, needs to be postponed to a later date and allow maintenance work to be carried out on those bridge cranes that are in urgent need of servicing.

In this case study, a series of interviews with maintenance engineers was conducted. From the interviews, it had been established that the maintenance schedule was largely decided based on past experience. As such, human judgment and some degrees of uncertainty were expected. Furthermore, the maintenance schedule appeared to be somewhat disorganized. The maintenance data of 44 bridge cranes at the sea port were extracted from the enterprise database. These maintenance data were recorded with the help of 30 technicians over a period of 3 years.

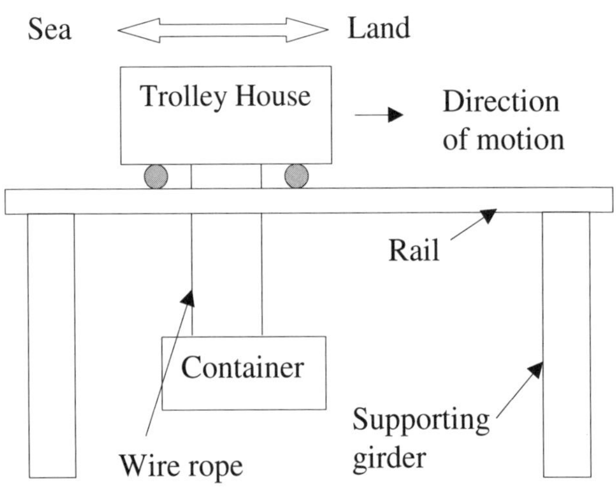

Figure 10. Front view of a bridge crane.

The four main causes for the skewing of the trolley house, as observed from the data, are:

(1) Mounting bracket failure;
(2) Alignment problem/Insufficient grease;
(3) Sea inner/outer guide roller failure; and
(4) Land inner/outer guide roller failure.

The above issues are further described below.

4.1.1 Mounting Bracket Failure

Figure 11 shows an exploded view of the wheel of a trolley house. Basically, the mounting bracket connects the guide roller to the trolley house assembly. When one or more of the connecting bolts are sheared off, the bracket becomes unstable and the trolley house starts to skew.

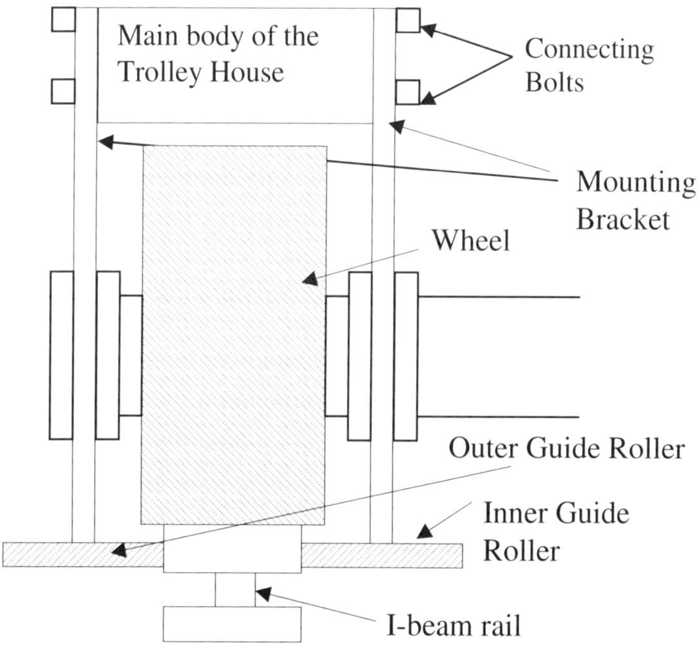

Figure 11. Exploded side-view of the trolley wheel.

4.1.2 The Alignment Problem

The alignment problem refers to the misalignment of the rail and the girder of a bridge crane. As a result of thermal expansion during the day and contraction in the night, the straightness of the rail as well as the girder are often difficult to maintain. Thus, a small misalignment in any of the two is sufficient to cause the trolley house to steer off-track. Such a problem is more evident in situations where the trolley house has traveled a long distance.

4.1.3 Sea/Land Inner/Outer Guide Roller Failures

Insufficient grease on critical moving parts of the trolley house travel mechanism could cause large frictional forces and to shorten their life-span. This might eventually lead to trolley skewing problems. However, the main contributor to the trolley skewing problem is the failure of guide rollers. The guide rollers can be categorized into landward and seaward guide rollers (Figure 10). The rotary bearings inside the guide rollers often time give way either under extreme pressure (when the trolley house is initially skewed) or after prolonged usage. The immediate consequence is the malfunction of the guide rollers that leads to them being sheared off and ultimately, the trolley house skews dangerously to one side.

4.2 Analysis Using the Proposed Hybrid Approach

From the background information presented in Section 4.1, it is apparent that a timely assessment of the status of bridge cranes and prediction of the urgency of maintenance are of utmost importance to ensure smooth operation. The proposed hybrid approach can be used to analyze the pattern of maintenance decisions for bridge cranes.

As mentioned in Section 3.1, relevant maintenance data of forty-four (44) bridge cranes were extracted from the enterprise database. These raw data are first treated and partitioned into different concepts using the rough sets engine. Each of these concepts, which can be associated with a number of condition attributes, corresponds to a decision attribute, i.e., level of maintenance urgency, namely Concept 1 (low priority), Concept 2 (medium priority), and Concept 3 (high priority). Details of the condition and the decision attributes are shown in Table 2.

Table 2. Condition and decision attributes for analyzing the bridge cranes.

<table>
<tr><td><u>Attribute 1 (Sea Inner/Outer Guide Roller)</u>
Nothing happens → Code '0'
Sea Inner Guide Roller is broken (SIGR)
→ Code '1'
Sea Outer Guide Roller is broken (SOGR)
→ Code '2'
Both Sea Guide Rollers are broken (BSGR)
→ Code '3'</td><td><u>Attribute 2 (Land Inner/Outer Guide Roller)</u>
Nothing happens → Code '0'
Land Inner Guide Roller broken (LIGR)
→ Code '1'
Land Outer Guide Roller broken (LOGR)
→ Code '2'
Both Land Guide Rollers broken (BLGR)
→ Code '3'</td></tr>
<tr><td><u>Attribute 3 (Mounting Bracket)</u>
Nothing happens → Code '0'
Land Mounting Bracket has failed (LMB)
→ Code '1'
Sea Mounting Bracket has failed (SMB)
→ Code '2'
Both Mounting Brackets have failed (BMB)
→ Code '3'</td><td><u>Attribute 4 (Others)</u>
Nothing happens → Code '0'
Alignment Problem (AP) → Code '1'
Insufficient Grease (IG) → Code '2'
Alignment Problem and Insufficient Grease
(AP, IG) → Code '3'</td></tr>
<tr><td colspan="2"><u>Concept (Decision level)</u>
Not required for servicing in the next 2 months → Code '1' (low priority)
Requires servicing in the next 2 months → Code '2' (medium priority)
Requires servicing in the next 1 month → Code '3' (high priority)</td></tr>
</table>

Upon completion, the tabu-enhanced GA engine is invoked to extract the pattern of decision-making or decision rules. In this case study, the probabilities of crossover and mutation were set at 0.80 and 0.01, respectively. As mentioned in Section 2.2, such a parameter setting would help in accelerating the search and suppressing the process to degenerate into a random search. The population size and the length of the tabu list were fixed at 300 and 10, respectively. A large population size of 300 would allow for a more comprehensive rule set to be gleaned from the enterprise data, while a longer tabu list would enable more 'virgin areas' to be explored. The tabu-enhanced GA engine was executed until no new rule could be discovered, i.e., convergence was reached. The rule organizer was then activated to amalgamate related rules into composite rules (Tables 3a and 3b). The numerical codes of each of the states are summarized in Table 2.

Basically, the extracted rules describe the patterns about how past maintenance decisions are made. Using these rules, it is possible to identify those bridge cranes that require urgent maintenance and attend to them before breakdown occurs. As shown in Table 2, three decision levels on maintenance urgency, namely "Not required for servicing in the next 2 months", "Requires servicing in the next 2 months" and "Requires servicing in the next 1 month" are available. These three decision levels are based on the inputs from the service engineers. They help the engineers in prioritizing the servicing of bridge cranes, thus making the decision-making process simpler.

The confidence levels depicted in Tables 3a and 3b can be viewed as the probability of inducing the decision rules correctly from the inconsistent training dataset, i.e., the training data describing the status of the 44 bridge cranes. Certain rules have a confidence level of 100%, and possible rules have confidence levels lower than 100%. There are three concepts (Concepts 1, 2, and 3) in relation to the maintenance decision. For each of these concepts, certain rules and possible rules can be derived. In this case study, to qualify as a certain rule (Table 3a), the confidence level of the rule has to be 100%. As for a possible rule (Table 3b), the confidence level is set at 60% or more. This is to avoid the inclusion of rules that are less reliable. The views of maintenance engineers about the correctness of the extracted rules were sought. The rules were found to be reasonable.

Table 3a. A sample of certain rules.

	Rules	***Confidence level***
Certain rules for Concept 1 (Concept 1a)		
1.	If (SIGR is/are broken) and (LOGR is/are broken), then decision level is 1	1/1 = 100%
:	....	
4.	If (LOGR is/are broken) and (AP is/are present), then decision level is 1	1/1 = 100%
Certain rules for Concept 2 (Concept 2a)		
1.	If (LIGR is/are broken) and (SMB fails), then decision level is 2	3/3 = 100%
:	....	
3.	If (SIGR is/are broken) and (LIGR is/are broken), then decision level is 2	1/1 = 100%
Certain rules for Concept 3 (Concept 3a)		
1.	If (BSGR is/are broken) and (AP & IG is/are present), then decision level is 3	5/5 = 100%
2.	If (BSGR is/are broken) and (LIGR is/are broken), then decision level is 3	4/4 = 100%
:	....	
8.	If (BLGR is/are broken) and (LMB fails), then decision level is 3	1/1 = 100%
:	....	
14.	If (BSGR is/are broken) and (LOGR is/are broken), then decision level is 3	1/1 = 100%

Note: See Table 2 for the abbreviations used.

Table 3b. A sample of possible rules.

	Rules	**Confidence level**
Possible rules for Concept 1 (Concept 1b)		
1.	If (LIGR is/are broken), (AP is/are present), then decision level is 1	5/6 = 83.3%
:	....	
4.	If (LOGR is/are broken), then decision level is 1	2/3= 66.7%
Possible rules for Concept 2 (Concept 2b)		
1.	If (SMB fails), then decision level is 2	4/6 = 70%
Possible rules for Concept 3 (Concept 3b)		
1.	If (AP and IG is/are present), then decision level is 3	13/14 = 92.9%
:	....	
4.	If (SIGR is/are broken), (BLGR is/are broken), then decision level is 3	3/5 = 60%

Note: See Table 2 for the abbreviations used.

The higher the confidence level of a possible rule, the more accurate is its prediction. Interestingly, Rule 1 of Concept 3a, "If (BSGR is/are broken) and (AP and IG is/are present), then decision level is 3", and Rule 1 of Concept 3b, "If (AP and IG is/are present), then decision level is 3", seem fairly similar. It is important to note that Rule 1 of Concept 3a is a certain rule while Rule 1 of Concept 3b is a possible rule with high confidence level (92.9%). Based on the high confidence level attained by Rule 1 of Concept 3b, the maintenance engineer is likely to proceed with the decision to service the crane when this rule is triggered. As for Rule 1 of Concept 3a, it can be viewed as a sub-set of Rule 1 of Concept 3b. The reason is that it further specifies the condition of both sea guided rollers (BSGR). Based on the description of the rule (Rule 1 of Concept 3a), the maintenance engineer will certainly need to service the crane in the following month. Such an action is reasonable for safety. This case study presents an example demonstrating the capability of the hybrid engine. It is anticipated that with a larger set of training data, more reliable rule sets can be extracted to handle even more complex real-world problems.

4.3 Discussion

4.3.1 Validity of the Extracted Rules

The extracted rules provide a means for maintenance engineers to perform effective decision-making. They enable engineers to decide which bridge crane needs to undergo maintenance in the upcoming months. In this manner, the decision-making process can possibly be made simpler. Essentially, the certain and the possible rules obtained embody the knowledge and past experience of engineers in maintaining the bridge cranes. Based on a set of condition attributes such as the condition of the rollers and the mounting brackets, the extracted rules can be used to suggest an appropriate maintenance decision. As an example, if the sea inner and land outer guide rollers of a bridge crane are broken, Rule 1 of Concept 1a in Table 3a is triggered. Hence, there is no need to service it in the next 2 months (Decision level = 1). However, if both the sea guide rollers and the land inner guide roller of a bridge crane are broken, then immediate maintenance needs to be carried out in the following month (Concept 3a, Rule 14).

As for the possible rules (Table 3b), if the land outer guide roller of the bridge crane is broken (Concept 1b, Rule 4), then there is a *high chance* (66.7%) that servicing it in the next 2 months is not required. In general, a bridge crane with a higher decision level will have a higher priority for scheduling its maintenance. In addition, the decision level derived from the certain rules will be ranked higher than that of the possible rules. In the situations where two bridge cranes have the same decision level derived by the same set of rules, i.e. certain rules or possible rules, a detailed evaluation is needed before a final decision is reached.

After extracting the rules, more data (for Cranes 15, 23, 24, 39 and 42) were gathered over a period of six months. These were used as test data (Table 4) to ascertain the validity of the obtained rules. From this test, it was found that the rules (Rule 1 of Concept 3a and Rule 1 of Concept 1a) could only predict two of the decision levels (Cranes 24 and 39) correctly. As for Cranes 15, 23 and 42, no prediction could be made, as no rule was triggered.

Further analysis shows that the inability of the rules to carry out the prediction is essentially due to insufficient maintenance data collected over the past three years. As a result, the rules, which were extracted based on the maintenance data, were not comprehensive enough to cover all the possible scenarios. As more maintenance data are being collected and used for rule generation, it is anticipated that the performance of the proposed hybrid approach will improve over time.

Table 4. Test data collected over a period of six months.

Observations	Condition Attributes				Decision level*
	Sea Inner/ Outer Guide Roller	Land Inner/ Outer Guide Roller	Mounting Bracket	Others	
Crane 15	1	1	0	0	3
Crane 23	1	0	3	0	3
Crane 24	3	0	0	3	3
Crane 39	0	0	1	0	1
Crane 42	0	3	1	0	2

Note: * The decision level indicates the actual maintenance decision made by the engineers.

4.3.2 A Comparative Analysis of the Results

The performance of the tabu-enhanced GA engine was compared with that of the traditional GA engine, using the same hardware configuration. Based on the enterprise maintenance data gathered thus far, it appears that there is no significant difference on the number of extracted rules by both engines. In fact, the extracted rules were identical. From the study, it was apparent that using the tabu-enhanced GA engine, the rules could be extracted within a few generations of the search, which was faster than that of the traditional GA engine (Table 5).

Table 5. Performance of traditional GA engine and tabu-enhanced GA engine.

Concepts (Total no of rules)	**GA**	**GA + TABU**
Concept 1a (4 rules)	3 program runs Average of 1 rule per run	1 program run Average of 4 rules per run.
Concept 1b (4 rules)	3 program runs Average of 1 rule per run.	2 program runs Average of 2 rules per run.
Concept 2a (3 rules)	3 program runs Average of 1 rules per run	2 program runs Average of 1.5 rules per run
Concept 2b (1 rule)	1 program run Average of 1 rule per run	1 program run Average of 1 rule per run
Concept 3a (14 rules)	5 program runs Average of 3 rules per run	3 program runs Average of 5 rules per run
Concept 3b (4 rules)	4 program runs Average of 1 rule per run.	2 program runs Average of 2 rules per run.

This could be attributed to the fact that the tabu-enhanced GA engine provided a more thorough search strategy. More specifically, for each initial solution, the tabu-enhanced GA engine was able to search out many other alternatives during the local search, i.e. the straight-forward tabu search. In addition, using the diversification strategy, the search for possible solutions was steered towards unexplored regions. Those near optimal solutions might require the combination of less fit members, which in the first place, would have been ignored by the traditional GA search. As such, more rules could possibly be extracted.

The rules extracted by the two search engines are generally identical because both use rough sets to discern data and genetic algorithms to search for possible solutions. However, this (having identical rule sets) is not always the case, as the only enhancement is the application of tabu search to moderate the 'speed' at which solutions are being converged. It is apparent from Table 5 that with tabu-search capabilities, the inclusion of intensification and diversification strategies helps in accelerating the search process with more rules being churned out at each program run. As a result, convergence can be reached in fewer generations of GA runs.

5. Conclusions

This chapter describes the work that led to the integration of rough sets, genetic algorithms (GAs) and tabu search to realize a so-called rough set based tabu-enhanced GA approach for rule extraction. The proposed approach uses the theory of rough sets to handle uncertainty, which is inherent in many engineering problems. The approach adopts GAs for rule induction from a set of enterprise data gathered from the field, and the tabu search's intensification and diversification strategies to further exploit the search space for possible solutions, i.e. rules. The capability of the tabu-enhanced GA approach was illustrated by using a case study on the maintenance of bridge cranes. Using the maintenance data of 44 bridge cranes retrieved from the enterprise database, the proposed approach was able to extract rules that described the relationship between the level of maintenance decision and the various parameters such as the sea inner/outer guide rollers, the land inner/outer guide rollers and the mounting bracket that were being monitored.

An analysis shows that the extracted rules are reasonable and they are able to provide the information pattern of the maintenance data. Five additional sets of maintenance data were collected over a period of six months. The data were used to ascertain the validity of the extracted rules. It was found that the extracted rules were able to correctly suggest two of the decision levels for maintenance. As for the remaining three sets of maintenance data, no prediction could be made, as no rule was triggered. This could be attributed to the maintenance data collected over the past three years were not comprehensive enough to cover all the cases. With more maintenance data, which are currently being gathered, it is anticipated that the performance of the proposed hybrid approach will improve over time, and more accurate rules can be derived. A comparative analysis of the performance of a traditional GA engine and the tabu-enhanced GA engine was also performed. It was established that the extracted rules were identical. The tabu-enhanced GA engine, however, required fewer generations to extract the rules.

Although the applications of the rough set based tabu-enhanced GA approach for rule extraction are wide and diverse, the proposed approach can be further enhanced. Future enhancements may include handling of missing attribute values (Triantaphyllou and Felici, 2006), which are frequent in real-life applications and treating attributes with non-discrete values (Khoo and Zhai, 2002). These enhancements would enable the proposed approach to extract useful knowledge from the raw data obtained from different engineering applications.

References

Davis L. (1991). *Handbook of Genetic Algorithm.* Van Nostrand Reinhold: New York, NY, U.S.A.

De Jong K.A., Spears W.M., and Gordon D.F. (1993). Using genetic algorithms for concept learning. *Machine Learning*, 13, 161-188.

Dubois D., and Prade H. (1990). Rough fuzzy sets and fuzzy rough sets. *Int. J. of General Systems*, 17, 191-209.

Dubois D., and Prade H. (1992). Putting rough sets and fuzzy sets together. In *Intelligent Decision Support - Handbook of Applications and Advances of the Rough Sets Theory*, R. Slowinski (Ed.), Kluwer Academic Publishers: Dordrecht, The Netherlands, 203-231.

Glover F. (1997). *Tabu Search.* Kluwer Academic Publishers: Boston, MA, U.S.A.

Goldberg D. (1995). *Genetic Algorithms in Search, Optimization, and Machine Learning.* Addison-Wesley Publishing Company: New York, NY, U.S.A.

Holland J.H. (1975). *Adaptation in Natural and Artificial Systems.* Ann Arbor: University of Michigan Press: Ann Arbor, MI, U.S.A.

Khanna T. (1990). *Foundations of Neural Networks.* Addison-Wesley Publishing Company: New York, NY, U.S.A.

Khoo L.P., Lee S.G., and Yin X.F A. (1999). Prototype genetic algorithm enhanced multi-objective scheduler for manufacturing systems. *International Journal of Advanced Manufacturing Technology,* **16**(2), 131-138.

Khoo L.P., Lee S.G., and Yin X.F. (2003). Multiple-objective optimization of machine cell layout using genetic algorithms. *International Journal of Computer Integrated Manufacturing*, **16**(2), 140-155.

Khoo L.P., and Loh K.M. (2000). A genetic algorithms enhanced planning system for surface mount PCB assembly. *International Journal of Advanced Manufacturing Technology,* **16**(4), 289-296.

Khoo L.P., and Loi M.Y. (2002). A tabu-enhanced genetic algorithm approach to agile manufacturing. *International Journal of Advanced Manufacturing Technology,* **20**(9), 692-700.

Khoo L.P., and Zhai L.Y. (2001). "RClass*: a prototype rough-set and Genetic Algorithm enhanced multi-concept classification system for manufacturing diagnosis." In *Computational intelligence in Manufacturing Handbook,* J.Wang, A.Kusiak (Eds.), CRC Press: Boca Raton, FL, U.S.A., 19-1—19-16.

Khoo L.P., and Zhai L.Y. (2002). A rough set approach to the treatment of continuous-valued attributes in multi-concept classification for machine diagnosis, *Artificial Intelligence for Engineering Design, Analysis and Manufacturing*, **15**, 211-221.

Li J.R. Khoo L.P., and Tor S.B. (2003). A tabu-enhanced genetic algorithm approach for assembly process planning. *International Journal of Advanced Manufacturing Technology*, **14**(2), 197-208.

Nanda S., and Majumdar S. (1992). Fuzzy rough sets. *Fuzzy Sets and Systems*, **45**, 157-60.

Pawlak Z. (1985). Rough sets and fuzzy sets. *Fuzzy Sets and Systems*, **17**, 99-102.

Pawlak Z. (1991). *Rough Sets - Theoretical Aspects of Reasoning about Data.* Kluwer Academic Publishers: Dordrecht.

Pawlak Z. (1992). Rough Sets: A new approach to vagueness, in *Fuzzy Logic for the Management of Uncertainty.* John Wiley and Sons: New York, NY, U.S.A., pp 105-108.

Pawlak Z. (1996). Why rough sets? In *Proceedings of IEEE Int. Conf. on Fuzzy Systems*, Piscataway, NJ, 2, 738-743.

Pawlak Z. (1997). Rough sets, In *Rough Sets and Data Mining - Analysis for Imprecise Data*, T.Y. Lin, N. Gercone (Eds.), Kluwer Academic Publishers: Boston, MA, U.S.A, 3-7.

Pawlak Z., Grzymala-Busse J., Slowinski R., and Ziarko W. (1995). Rough sets. *Communications of the ACM*, 38(11), 89-95.

Pawlak Z., and Slowinski R. (1994). Rough set approach to multi-attribute decision analysis. *European Journal of Operational Research*, **72**(3), 443-459.

Slowinski R., and Stefanowski J. (1992). ROUGHDAS and ROUGH-CLASS software implementation of the rough sets approach. In *Intelligent Decision Support - Handbook of Applications and Advances of the Rough Sets Theory,* R. Slowinski (Ed.), Kluwer Academic Publishers: Dordrecht, 445-456.

Triantaphyllou E., and Felici G. (Eds.), (2006). Data Mining and Knowledge Discovery Approaches Based on Rule Induction Techniques. Springer: New York, NY, U.S.A.

Westphal C. (1995). Data Mining Solutions, Methods and Tools for Solving Real-World Problems. John Wiley & Sons, Inc.: New York, NY, U.S.A.

Wygralak W. (1989). Rough sets and fuzzy sets - some remarks on interrelations. *Fuzzy Sets and Systems*, **29**, 241-243

Yao Y.Y. (1998). A comparative study of fuzzy sets and rough sets. *Information Sciences*, 109(1-4), 227-242

Zbigniew M. (1994). *Genetic Algorithm + Data Structures = Evolution Programs*. Springer-Verlag: Berlin Heidelberg, Germany.

Ziarko W. (1994). Rough sets, fuzzy sets and knowledge discovery. In *Proceedings of the Int. Workshop on Rough Sets and Knowledge Discovery*, Spring –Verlag: Berlin Heidelberg, Germany, 11-11.

Authors' Biographic Statements

Dr. L P Khoo is a Professor at the School of Mechanical and Aerospace Engineering, Nanyang Technological University, Singapore. His current research interests include artificial intelligence and its applications, systems diagnosis, design for X, kansei engineering and precision engineering.

Dr. Z W Zhong received the Doctor of Engineering degree in precision engineering from Japan. He worked at the Engineering Division of RIKEN (The Institute of Physical and Chemical Research), Saitama, Japan. He is currently an Associate Professor at the School of Mechanical and Aerospace Engineering of the Nanyang Technological University, Singapore. His research interests include mechatronics and design, precision engineering and nanotechnology, microelectronics packaging, finite element modeling and analysis.

H Y Lim received a Bachelor of Engineering degree (Mechanical, 1st Class Honors) and a Minor in Business degree from the Nanyang Technological University in 2004. Upon graduation, he worked in China and led cross functional regional teams in cities such as Shanghai, Xiamen, Chengdu. He is currently with Fabristeel Pte Ltd, Singapore leading a contract manufacturing department.

Chapter 12[1]

Data Mining Techniques for Improving Workflow Models

Dimitrios Gunopulos
Department of Computer Science and Engineering
University of California at Riverside, Riverside, CA, USA. Email: dg@cs.ucr.edu
Sharmila Subramaniam
Google Inc., Mountain View, CA, USA; Email: sharmi@cs.ucr.edu

Abstract: Workflow management systems are widely used by business enterprises as tools for administrating, automating and scheduling the business process activities with the available resources. Workflow models are the fundamental components of workflow management systems, and are used for defining, scheduling, and ordering of workflow tasks. Since the control flow specifications of workflows are manually designed, they entail assumptions and errors, leading to inaccurate workflow models. Moreover, companies increasingly follow flexible workflow models in order to adapt to changes in business logic, making it more challenging to understand or forecast process behavior. In this chapter we describe recently proposed techniques for optimizing business processes by analyzing the execution details of previously executed processes, stored as a workflow log. The applications of workflow mining that we describe include the (re)discovery of process models, the optimization of process models, and the development of mechanisms to predict the future behavior of a currently running invocation of a process.

Key Words: Workflow, Workflow model, Flexible workflow, Workflow log mining, Business process, Business process optimization, Workflow model evolution.

---

[1] Liao, T.W. and E. Triantaphyllou, (Eds.), **Recent Advances in Data Mining of Enterprise Data: Algorithms and Applications**, *World Scientific*, Singapore, pp. 545-576, 2007.

1. Introduction

Over the recent years, there has been a tremendous growth in the field of business process integration and automation. Workflow Management Systems (WfMS) have been used by business enterprises as tools for administrating, automating and scheduling their processes. A good and accurate design and efficient enactment of workflow systems improve the competency of business enterprises and enhance the service provided to their customers.

Workflow models are the primary components in WfMS that define the ordering and scheduling of workflow tasks and represent the process constraints and components. Workflow models are thus the tools that represent the function, ordering, scheduling and resource requirements of the constituent tasks of a business process. Since the efficiency of WfMS depends on the quality and accuracy of the workflow models used, a completely specified correct workflow model becomes essential to accomplish a workflow process. In addition of WfMS, other systems like ERP(Enterprise Resource Planning systems), B2B (Business to Business applications), SCM (Supply Chain Management systems) also employ workflow models for their systems.

Workflow modeling has been a challenging task due to the difficulty in capturing complex business logics. Typically, workflow models are designed by a modeler, with contributions from domain experts (Figure 1). Even with knowledge input from domain experts, some of the rules followed by the businesses are not captured during the modeling phase. Moreover, today's business processes are very dynamic, requiring their definition to change over time. This rapid change in the goals and requirements of the processes make it difficult for modelers to have an updated workflow model at any time. Due to the above reasons, obtaining a model that defines the processes in a correct and updated manner has become far from trivial. In some scenarios, the enterprises lack an initial description of the workflows followed by their processes, making it more difficult to comprehend the process behavior.

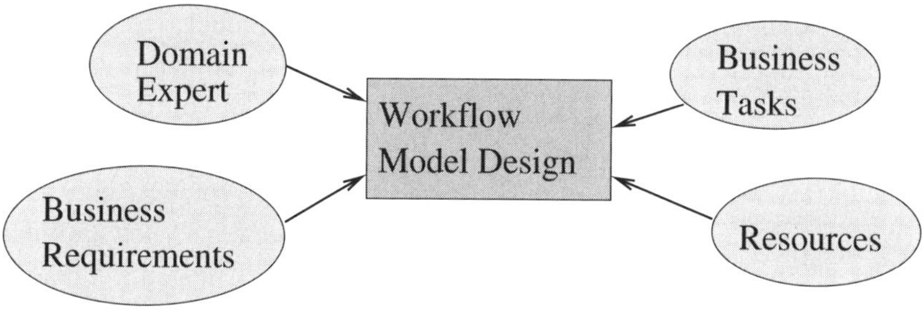

Figure 1. Workflow model design.

Workflow mining has emerged as a new technique in the last decade to assist industries in the above issues. Workflow mining is the field of study where the workflow log, i.e. the process execution details such as the ordered set of activities and their output, are used in understanding and fine-tuning the process (see Figure 2).

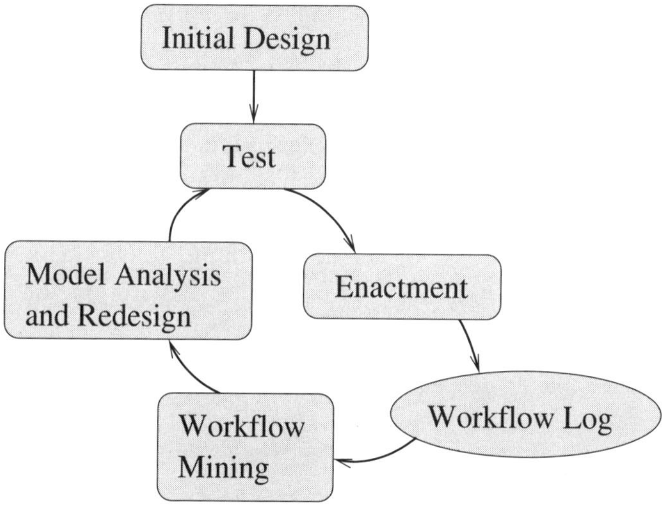

Figure 2. Role played by Workflow Mining in the life cycle of a workflow.

An example of its application is process model (re)discovery (Agrawal *et al.*, 1998; Weijters and van der Aalst, 2002; Silva *et al.*, 2005; Greco *et al.*, 2004). This is a process by which workflow models are rediscovered from the ordered set of events. For enterprises that had no workflow to start with, process model discovery provides the means to obtain a model that describes the executions in the log. When an initial model is present, model discovery assists the industries in estimating how far the process executions adhere to the original process definition. This step is widely known as delta analysis in the life-cycle of a workflow system (van der Aalst *et al.*, 2003; van der Aalst and Weijters, 2003; Guth and Oberweis, 1997).

In addition to process discovery, the characteristics of the warehoused process invocations can be analyzed to provide insight into the process behaviors such as execution delays and exceptions. Due to the complex nature of the business processes, the complete set of exceptions and failures is not always available initially, making it difficult for the user to develop an efficient failure/exception handling mechanism. Workflow mining has proven to be efficient in discovering reasons for exceptions (Grigori *et al.*, 2001) and providing models for failure handling (Gaaloul and Godar, 2005).

While WfMS has been in focus for more than a decade, applying data mining techniques in the domain of workflow systems is a fairly recent development with prospects for ample future research work. A first survey of process mining related research is presented by van der Aalst *et al.* (2003) and by van der Aalst & Weijters (2003). In this chapter, we discuss the contributions of process mining to business process management in general, and provide the description of various techniques evolved recently.

2. Workflow Models

Various classes of models have been proposed in the literature toward formalizing workflow models. In the process algebra based model (Singh, 1995), the authors propose a set of model-theoretic semantics to define events and their dependencies. Kappel *et al.* (1995) describes an active object oriented model where the activities are considered as objects and the relationship between activities are specified in terms of ECA (Event Condition Action) rules. Following a different approach, Wodtke and Weikum (1997) propose a state chart model that given a set of semantics of state and activity charts to specify workflows. CTR (Concurrent Transaction Logic) is studied as the workflow modeling language in (Davulcu *et al.*, 1998). In addition to specifying the model and scheduling the workflow, CTR also allows reasoning about their properties. The Petri Net based model proposed in (van der Aalst, 1998; van der Aalst and van Hee, 1996) has gained significance as a graph-based model in recent years due to its expressiveness and its firm mathematical foundations.

An important aspect of workflow modeling is to ensure that they are sound and free from structural conflicts, i.e. to make sure that processes following the proposed models do not end in any unacceptable state. In addition it is necessary to analyze the workflows, before putting them into production, to ensure that they are error free and provide services of acceptable level. By mapping workflow task structures to workflow nets (based on petri-nets), the authors of (van der Aslst and Hofstede, 2000) and (van der Aslst, 2000) develop tools for analysis of validation, verification and performance analysis of workflows (staffware, in particular). The above soundness property of WF-nets is investigated extensively along with liveness and boundedness. In (Sadiq and Orlowska, 1996, 2000), the authors study deadlocks and lack of synchronization in workflow models and propose techniques to verify if a graph based model is free of the above conflicts. A given model is reduced by applying certain graph reduction rules and the graphs that are reducible to null are shown to be free of conflicts.

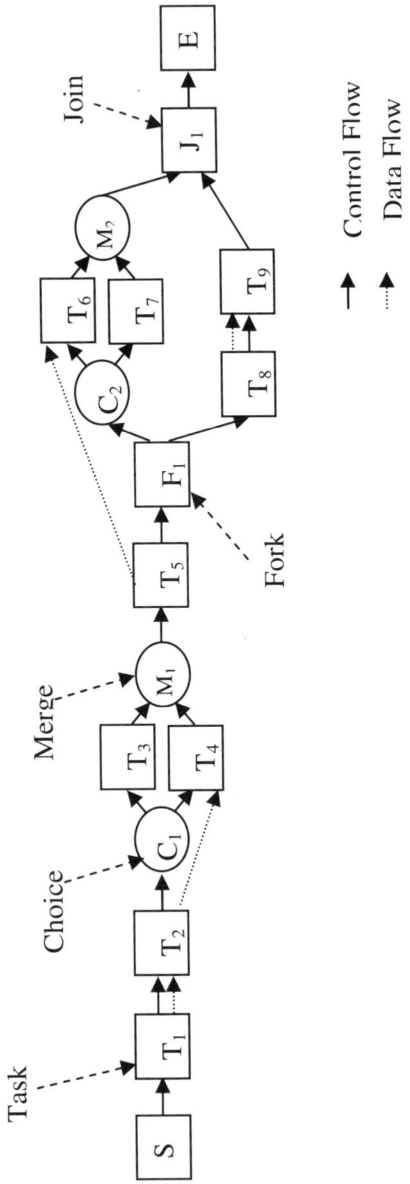

Figure 3. Example of a workflow graph model (S: start node, E: end node).

The stored sets of execution details of the workflow processes are referred to as the ***Workflow log***. The workflow log can include different sets of information, at different granularities of detail. As an example, the tuples shown in Figure 4 are the ordered set of events corresponding to the workflow process in Figure 3. The log can also consist of the output data of variables, as shown in Figure 5.

S, T_1, T_2, T_3, T_5, T_8, T_6, T_9, E
S, T_1, T_2, T_4, T_5, T_6, T_8, T_9, E
S, T_1, T_2, T_3, T_5, T_7, T_8, T_9, E
S, T_1, T_2, T_4, T_5, T_8, T_9, T_7, E
S, T_1, T_2, T_3, T_5, T_8, T_9, T_6, E

Figure 4. Workflow Log: Ordered set of activities.

S(10:25, ID=134), T_1(10:33, v_1=*yes* ; v_2=*100*), T_2(11:45, v_1=*good*), T_3(12:35, v_1=*good*), T_5(13:15, v_1=1500), T_8(13:26, v_1=*635*), T_6(14:23, v_1=*fair*), T_9(14:53, v_1=*15*), E(14:53)
S(11 :23, ID=135), T_1(11:44, v_1=*no* ; v_2=*35*), T_2(12 :13, v_1=*poor*), T_4(13:14, v_1=*896*), T_5(14:11, v_1=1500), T_6(14:33, v_1=*poor*), T_8(15:33, v_1=*456*), T_9(16:21, v_1=*09*), E(16 :21)

Figure 5. Workflow Log: Ordered set of activities with timestamps and values of variables associated with the activities.

As illustrated, the log in Figure 5 consists of the activity completion timestamps and the values of the corresponding variables. In addition to workflow mining, we can also perform intelligent analysis on the workflow log to compute values for *business metrics*, understand their causes and optimize operations to improve them (Costellanos *et al.*, 2005).

3. Discovery of Models from Workflow Logs

Workflow models of processes describe the flow control among the activities that make up the processes. Figure 6 shows some commonly used components for the construction of workflow models. Designing workflow models for business processes is a non trivial task due to the complexity of the processes.

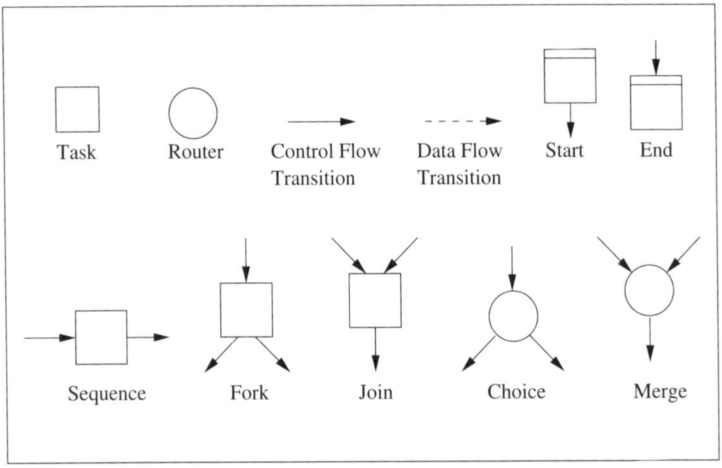

Figure 6. Workflow graph constructs.

Typically, the modeler gets input from domain experts to understand the process logic. Following this, he/she comes up with a model that best describes the process, maximizes throughput and minimizes resource utilization. However, discovery of workflow models from a log of events (as shown in Figure 7) becomes essential in the following two scenarios:

- In some business organizations, no workflow model is available to define their processes. In such cases, the organization may want to infer workflow models from the log of instantiations to gain a better understanding of the processes and to set business policies.
- In cases where there exists an initial workflow model for the processes, the user may still want to learn the model from the log,

for the following reasons: Business process requirements change over time and the models need to be re-designed to include the new changes. In addition, if the initial model was designed manually, it may not incorporate the complete set of business logics that drive the process. For this reason, the user can use a learned model to study the difference between the process described by the initial model and that defined by the executions. The user may analyze the discrepancies to update the model accordingly.

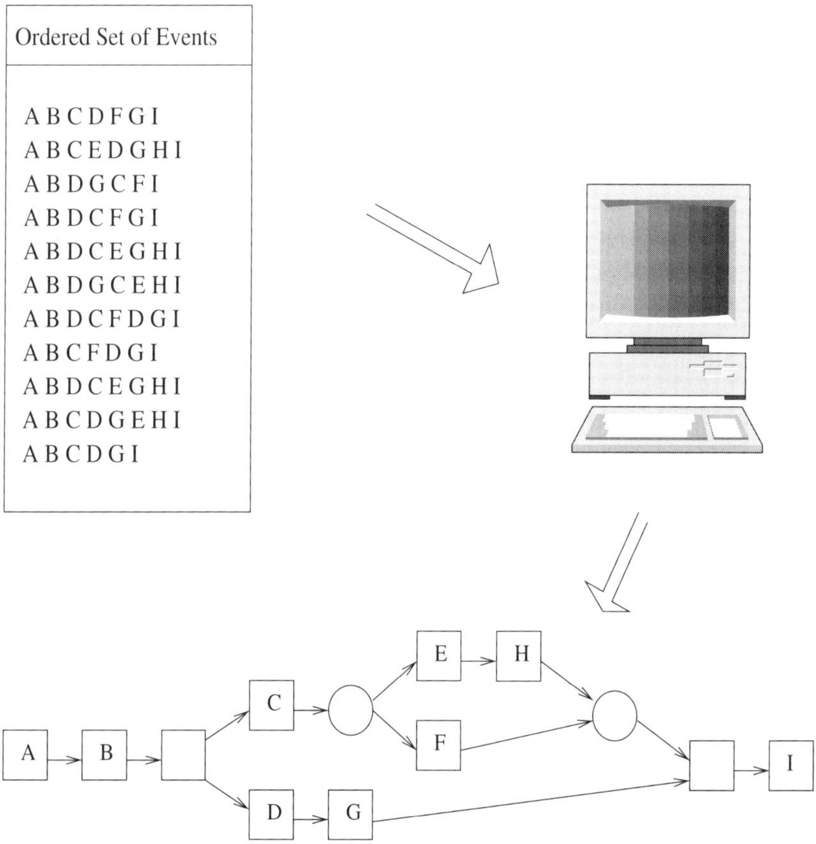

Figure 7. Model Discovery: The model shown corresponds to the log of ordered sets of events (each such sequence represents one process execution).

Both of the above scenarios have a common goal: to learn the workflow model from the log of past executions. A closely related research topic is process discovery in software engineering (Cook and Wolf, 1995; Scacchi, 1995; Jensen and Scacchi, 2004). Cook and Wolfe propose three approaches in (Cook and Wolf, 1998a) for process discovery in software engineering: Neural network based, algorithmic, and Markovian approaches. Extending the approaches for concurrent processes (Cook and Wolf, 1998b), the authors propose various metrics such as entropy, event type counts etc. for discovering models from streams of events. Following this, the authors propose metrics to quantify the divergence between a process model and the process enactment (as given by the event log) in (Cook and Wolf, 1999).

Process discovery in the context of business processes is first studied by (Agrawal *et al.*, 1998). In their approach, a directed graph representing the control flow of the model is generated from the given log. The authors generate a graph that permits all the executions in the log, preserves all the dependencies between the activities and introduces no spurious dependencies (Figures 7 and 8). A different approach for workflow process mining is proposed by Herbst and Karagiannis (1998) based on inductive approaches. The authors describe workflow models in the ADONIS modeling language and propose techniques involving merging of models starting with a most specific model encoding the observations, or splitting of models starting with a most general model encoding the observations. Extending the sequential models in (Herbst and Karagiannis, 1998), the authors propose methods for concurrent model discovery in (Herbst, 2000a, 2000b; Herst and Karagiannis, 1999).

In (Weijters and van der Aalst, 2002), the problem of discovering workflow models as WorkFlow Nets (WF-nets) is studied. The approach involves construction of a dependency/frequency (D/F) table that captures the frequency of the precedence ordering between the tasks, and subsequently constructing a WF-net from the D/F table. Recently, Silva *et al.* (2005) discussed mining of probabilistic workflow models where nodes are incrementally added to the graph with an Ordering Oracle and Independence Oracle based on Markov conditions. The oracles determine the set of activities and edges are added in every step of the learning process.

A problem related to model discovery is to learn frequently occurring instances or patterns (i.e., a block of activities scheduled together) from a collection of workflow instances. This can assist the process administrator to extract valuable knowledge about the process and subsequently in decisions about future instances. The problem of mining frequent patterns, i.e., the sub-graphs, of a process model has been studied by (Greco *et al.*, 2003). The proposed technique finds all frequent connected patterns of the workflow model and compares favorably with (modifications of) the existing algorithms for mining frequent item sets, such as *Apriori* (Agrawal and Srikant, 1994).

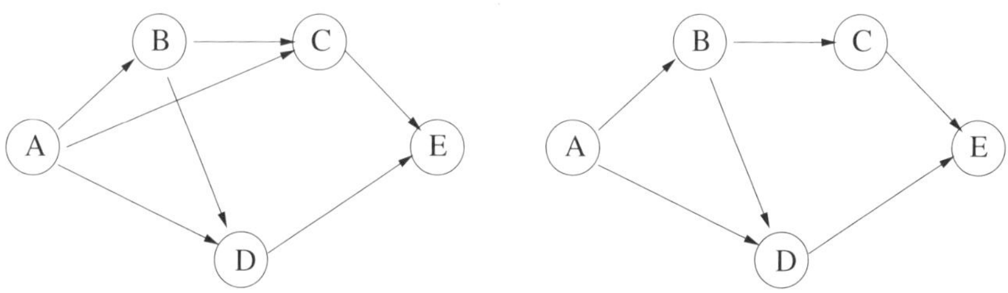

Figure 8. Finding the minimal graph that encodes all the dependencies.

4. Managing Flexible Workflow Systems

In this section we discuss the problem of identifying the invocations that deviate from the definition provided by the workflow model, and discover reasons for such evolutions in workflows. In current business enterprises, processes follow "flexible" workflows, where the workflow graph models serve as only a guidance for the process execution (Reichert and Dadam, 1998; Sadiq *et al.*, 2005; Weski, 2000; Wargitsch *et al.*, 1998).

This flexibility in workflow systems is necessary to allow process refinement and accommodate process logics that were missed in the design phase. For example, an instance resulting in an exception may follow an ad-hoc change in the process flow to complete the instance gracefully. In addition, the instance may deviate from the definition to capture an evolutionary change in the business logic. In such scenarios, traces can deviate from the process definition provided by the graph model. Such deviations could belong to one of the following types:

- Exceptions, i.e., a rare occurrences, or
- Evolutions, i.e., the traces adapting to a change in the process logic.

When a resource serving a business task fails, the invocations consisting of the task deviate from the usual flow and may execute different tasks toward completion. Such cases are grouped as exceptions and the modeler is required to device efficient strategies to handle the exceptions. On the contrary when the business logic changes, new activities are added to the workflow or the order of existing activities are modified, resulting in workflow evolution. In such cases, it becomes necessary to periodically identify the corresponding traces and restructure the graph model accordingly. This process is very significant in workflow systems in order to keep a check on the discrepancies between the workflow process definition and process enactment.

Rinderle *et al.* (2005) study a case-based reasoning approach, where the knowledge about previous process changes is applied to make changes in the process at both the *process instance level* (e.g., ad-hoc changes) and the *process type level* (e.g., evolutionary changes). This is a semi-automated way in which the users are required to enter the information when an instance deviates from its workflow definition. The authors use CCBR (Conversational Case Based Reasoning) where with the help of the knowledge of previous cases, questions are fired at the user, thus matching the current case with similar earlier cases. The authors also propose techniques for process schema evolution and process instance migration.

Another challenging problem in process management is to recover from failures and exceptional cases. Similar to database transactions, handling failures in workflow transactions involves rollback of certain activities and re-execution of certain other, to take the workflow execution to an acceptable state. The knowledge of transactional behavior during past cases of failures has been identified as a potential source to guide future failures. Gaaloul & Godart (2005) employ mining of event-based logs to generate a set of rules to guide workflow failure handling. A related problem is to predict if there exists a successful extension of a *partially executed execution* (i.e., an execution that has arrived at a given point). Here, a successful extension represents an extension that results in successful termination. Greco *et al.* (2005) propose to predict successful termination by mining frequent *patterns*, and checking if there exist frequent patterns containing all the activities in the partially executed execution.

5. Workflow Optimization through Mining of Workflow Logs

5.1 Repositioning Decision Points

A business process, represented by a workflow model, executes alternate sets of tasks on a case-by-case basis. A **Decision Point** is a node in the workflow graph model, where one among the alternate paths is chosen, based on the data corresponding to the current execution. Typically, each decision point is associated with a rule that maps the current state of the workflow to a decision about the succeeding path chosen to complete the process. Recent work on workflow mining (Subramaniam *et al.*, 2007) is motivated by the observation that the efficient placement of the decision points in a workflow model improves service efficiency of the business by

- enabling identification and removal of redundant tasks and
- reducing uncertainty of a running invocation.

The term "**redundant tasks**" is used to refer to those tasks whose execution is not necessary for the successful completion of the process. When the decision points are placed at their earliest point, some business tasks are identified as redundant and can be removed from the workflow. When no redundant tasks are identified, taking the decisions at the earliest point reduces uncertainty in the process execution, and assists in making intelligent decisions about resource allocation.

Subramaniam *et al.* (2007) propose a technique to discover the earliest positions for decision points through process mining. Specifically, they present techniques to analyze the dependencies between the data processed by the tasks of a process. The information about the earliest positions is used to guide the user (which can be a workflow modeler or a domain expert who is evaluating the quality of a specific workflow model) to redesign the process model.

As a simple example, consider a student admission process as in Figure 9(top). The decision node "Incomplete Student File?" is triggered after executing the task "Admission Decision Process". The label "*y*" indicates the path taken when a student's file is incomplete with information and "*n*" represents the path taken otherwise. If the user knew that the decision at "Incomplete Student File?" requires only the output of the task "Get Application" and does not take the output of the tasks "Admission Decision Process" and "Contact SIS (Student Information System)", then the user could make this decision earlier, right after the "Get Application" step.

Figure 9(bottom) shows the restructured model where the decision point Get Application is placed at its earliest position. For those invocations having incomplete student information files, the tasks "Admission Decision Process" and "Contact SIS" do not yield any useful output because the application is incomplete. Thus, the tasks are identified as redundant and are removed from the *y*-path of the decision point. By removing the redundant tasks, the goal is to reduce the average execution time of the process and thus improve efficiency. Though in this example the dependency relation between "Get Application" and "Incomplete Student File?" is somewhat obvious, such dependencies are not easily perceived or understood in complex processes, and have to be discovered from the execution data.

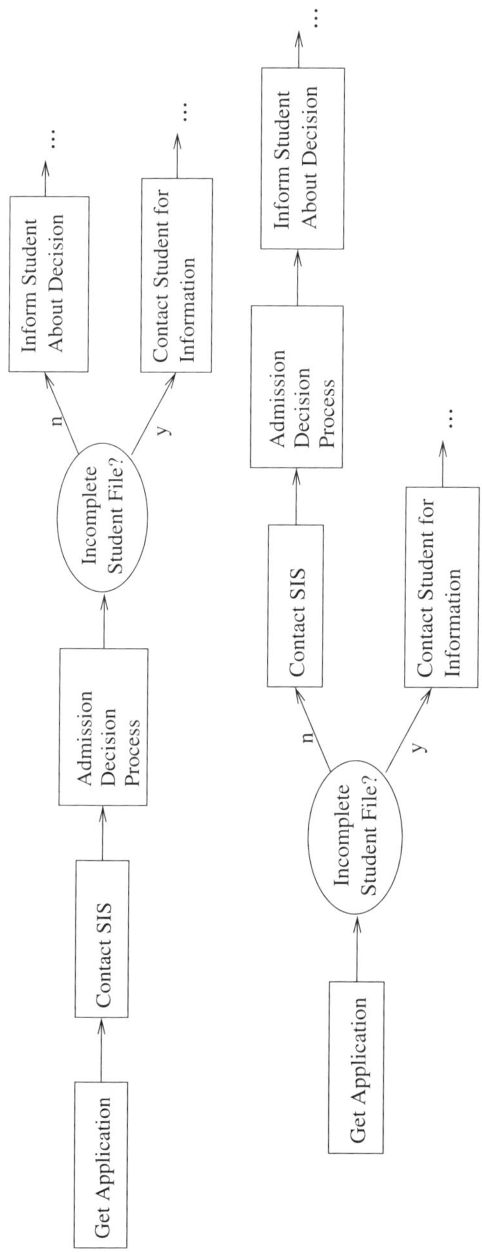

Figure 9. (top) Graph model for a student admission process; (bottom) Restructured graph model for a student admission process.

An important consideration is maintaining the correctness of the workflow graph while a change is performed to improve its efficiency. To achieve that, a formal definition of the workflow graph equivalency is needed, and is used as a tool to show which operations can be taken while the resulting graph remains equivalent to the original. It is important to note that in many cases, improving a workflow may result in changes that create workflow graphs that are no longer equivalent.

The formalism presented in the above work allows the system to identify such cases and to ask for user input before making any such changes (Subramaniam *et al.*, 2007). A similar problem is discussed by Marjanovic and Orlowska (1999). In addition, related work appears in (Lin *et al.*, 2002; Sadiq and Orlowska, 2000) where the authors discuss methods for transforming a given graph to an equivalent graph by applying reduction rules. However, these techniques describe how to reduce a graph with the goal of proving its correctness and do not reposition any nodes in the graph.

5.2 Prediction of Execution Paths

In this section we consider the problem of predicting the behavior (i.e., determine the future tasks) of a long running process invocation, by analyzing the data stored in the workflow log of the corresponding process. Predicting the future of running invocations helps in assessing their future resource requirements and in scheduling their execution efficiently. Latency in resource allocation often results in suboptimal service performance (Du *et al.*, 1997; Du and Shan, 1999). In order to avoid this, enterprises are forced to assume worst case scenarios and allocate more resources than what is required. We observe that with an efficient method to predict the future behavior of running invocations, the number of invocations likely to be served by a particular resource can be estimated, resulting in optimum resource allocation.

Even in cases when the invocations follow the graph model, the complexity of the workflows makes it very difficult to predict the future state of a running invocation accurately. In flexible workflows, the problem is even more complicated due to deviations. An interesting observation about the invocations that deviate from the initial definition is that when we discover the reasons for such deviations, we get good insight about the missed business logics (as in the case of fixed workflow) or about the new changes in the business requirements (as in the case of flexible workflow). Therefore, for the invocations that do not follow the graph model, we identify the likely conditions for the deviations that happen. We use these conditions to change the workflow models, where appropriate.

As a motivating example, consider the graph model shown in Figure 10. Let us assume that the administrator is required to schedule the upcoming tasks at the stage of execution. Let R1 and R2 be the resource requirement on resource *R* (e.g., CPU, memory, disk) for the sub-process marked as S1 and S2, respectively, with R1 > R2; where the load on resource *R* is constrained by its maximum value R_{max}. Suppose there are *m* invocations waiting at stage ST and the administrator has to verify if all these invocations can be scheduled to proceed, without overloading *R*. Such a scenario is very frequent in any resource constrained business environment.

A pessimistic approach would be to assume the worst case scenario and ensure that the sum of the maximum resource requirements of all the *m* invocations is less than *m*R1 at any point of time. This could be achieved by doing offline analysis of all the processes and their corresponding resource requirements. However, as stated above, this is a pessimistic approach, and may end up under-utilizing the resources, because it does not take into account the possibility that S2 could be chosen at ST. A better approach is to predict how many of the *m* invocations are likely to follow each path. Predicting the path will enable us to schedule the execution of the invocations accordingly and, thus, achieve better resource management.

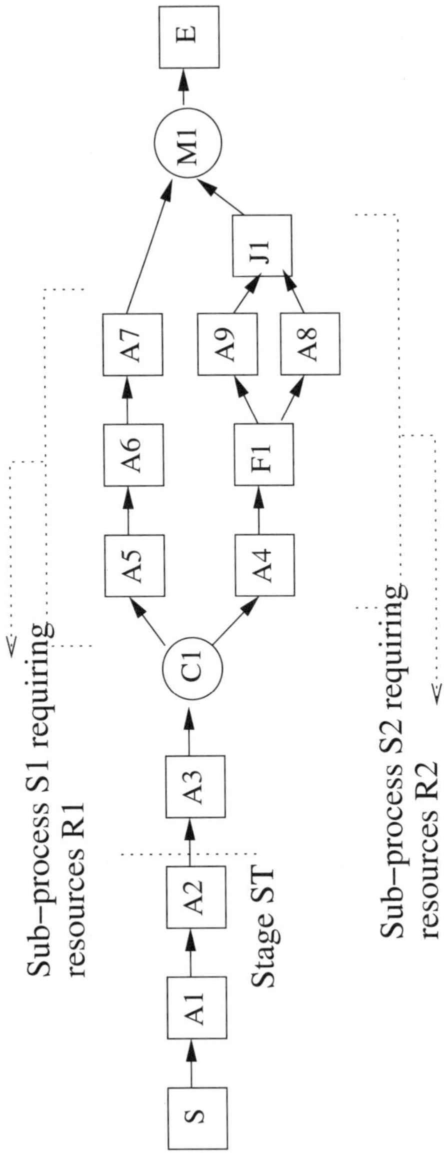

Figure 10. Resource management example.

Another problem that arises in a flexible workflow environment, where the invocations in the workflow log or the predicted path of the current invocations need not adhere to the workflow model graph, is that how to appropriately modify the workflow graph model so that it predicts at least the mojority of the executions. For example, some invocations in the workflow log corresponding to the process shown in Figure (11) may have the following task execution order: T1, T2, T10, T11, and T12. If the frequency of occurrence for such invocations is found to be high, then the initial graph model should be modified to reflect this change. Characteristics of such instances, (for example, they occur if a certain condition holds), are identified and the model graph is modified accordingly, as shown in Figure 11.

In the remainder of this section we look at various problems studied and solutions proposed in the recent literature. In one of the earliest studies, Grigori *et al.* (2001) discuss a technique to predict reasons for exceptions in business processes. This work focuses on analyzing the characteristics of the values of the input and output variables attributed to the activities. The correlations between these values and the exceptional cases present in the historical data are used to predict and prevent future exceptions. Based on the above work, Subramaniam *et al.* (2005) propose a method to find the optimal placement of decision points in workflow models. Decision points are the XOR nodes in the workflow graph models where the values of workflow data are analyzed to select one of the successive paths for completion of the process. The solution is based on mapping the problem to a classification problem where the outcomes of the decision points were considered as *classes*. The authors show that the earliest placement of decision points can result in the removal of activities that are *redundant,* i.e., whose output does not contribute to the successful completion of the process. The resulting workflow model was shown to be efficient in terms of the average execution time of the process.

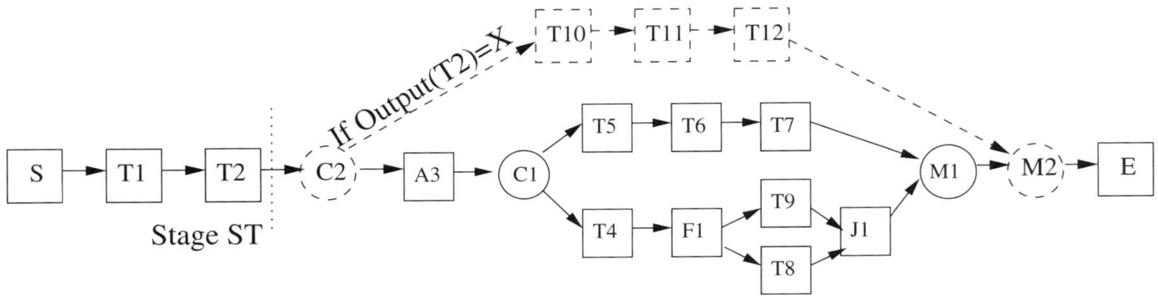

Figure 11. Tasks T10, T11, and T12 are added to the process model when the frequency of instances where such a path is taken is sufficiently high in the workflow log. The characteristic of this instance is determined as M2 and a choice node is added to capture it.

Similar to other process environments, efficient and in-time allocation of resources to the forthcoming activities of a business process plays an important part in determining its service competency. Due to the presence of conditional activities in a workflow model, the process invocations may execute different sets of activities, making it complex to predict the resource requirements. Subramaniam *et al.* (2006) propose a method to predict the set of tasks that are likely to be executed, by grouping all possible instances as *instance types*. For given ongoing executions, their future behaviors are predicted in terms of *instance types*, thus making it possible for the agents of the activities (whether human or machine) to predict their future load. This enables the process administrator to make informed decisions on resource allocations.

6. Capturing the Evolution of Workflow Models

Workflow modeling continues to be a challenging task because it needs to cope with the dynamics of today's business environment, where business demands and goals undergo rapid changes. Flexible workflows have been proposed in the literature to accommodate such varying business requirements (van der Aalst *et al.*, 2003; Sadiq *et al.,* 2005). In a system following flexible workflow models, the workflow processes are adaptive and the definition of the process given by the workflow is considered only as guidance and is therefore not strictly followed by the process invocations. Thus, the process invocations do not always follow the workflow graph model. We observe the following as the reasons why the invocations deviate from the definition given by the workflow.

- As discussed earlier, workflow models are designed manually and might not incorporate the complete set of business logics that drive the processes. Thus in a flexible workflow environment, the invocations might follow different patterns of executions to capture business logics that were missed during the design phase.
- Business requirements and goals of the current enterprises change very frequently in order to enhance their competency. Such frequent changes trigger corresponding changes in the definition of the

process workflow (Casati *et al.*, 1998; van der Aalst *et al.*, 2003; Subramaniam *et al.*, 2006). When the process executions adapt to such changes, the invocations inevitably deviate from the initial definition of the workflow.

Workflow evolution has been discussed extensively (Ellis *et al.*, 1995; Casati *et al.*, 1998; Weske, 2001; van der Aalst and Basten, 2002; Reichert *et al.*, 2003; Rinderle *et al.*, 2004a, 2004c). The deviations occurring in traces are identified as either instance level changes or process type level changes, and the process type level changes lead to workflow evolution. The above studies discuss and propose frameworks for workflow schema modifications and how workflow instances can (dynamically) adapt a newly evolved workflow schema. The issues here involve updating data- and flow-dependent tasks while updating or deleting a business task as part of the schema change. In addition, problems related to correctness arise while migrating the running invocations to a modified model. While many approaches exist for guiding the modification process, all of them assume a prior knowledge of the structural changes due in the evolving workflow.

In a new approach, Subramaniam *et al.* (2006) propose to capture the reasons for evolutionary changes by identifying instances whose *instance types* are not defined by the workflow model. For such new instance types, the rules associated with the instance types describe the conditions under which the deviations occurred. When the support for such a rule is high, i.e., when there are many occurrences of such deviations, the workflow model is modified to include the new instance type.

7. Applications in Software Engineering

Software process models are networks of activities and objects, connected by transitions that indicate their transformations. In addition, they may include events that embody strategies for accomplishing software evolution (Scacchi, 2001). In addition to providing insights about the software process enactment patterns, software process models also assist in deducing the resource requirements of the process.

Moreover, they play a significant role in precisely formalizing the software life cycle model. In the literature, software models have been designed as interconnected task chains (Scacchi, 2001). Task chains in turn are comprised of interconnected task actions. The task actions transform the computational objects into intermediate or finished products, and are represented in turn as networks of more primitive actions such as a value or a menu entry by the user.

As we see from the definition, workflow process models and software process models share much in common with respect to their design and usage. Software process discovery has been studied extensively in the literature where the ordered sets of actions (or events) recorded during executions are analyzed to produce models of the software processes (Cook and Wolf, 1995, 1998a; Jensen and Scacchi, 2004). In this work, we provide an initial study of various ways in which the output data of the variables of interest, recorded during the execution of software processes, can be analyzed to enhance the software systems. In particular, we focus on the following:

7.1 Discovering Reasons for Bugs in Software Processes

Software testing is a process that is aimed at determining if the software systems meet specific requirements. In addition, certain metrics are evaluated on the systems during software testing to asses their quality. Despite its significance in maintaining the quality of software programs, software testing still remains a difficult process due to the complexity of software systems. Software debugging is a part of the testing process in which various tests are performed on the system to find out any design defects in it. In particular, it is aimed at assuring that the system will perform satisfactorily under the expected deployment environment.

The current methodologies proposed for software debugging include visualization approaches (Baecker *et al.*, 1997; Pauw and Sevitsky, 2000) and automated debugging through program sliding (Horwitz *et al.*, 1990). We propose an interesting alternative approach wherein the system test run details are recorded and analyzed using data mining techniques. The execution detail recorded as software system log can be studied to find reasons for bugs in terms of the values of the variables associated with the system. In addition, the technique can also be used for checking the possibility of execution of certain error (or exception) conditions in the code.

7.2 Predicting the Control Flow of a Software Process for Efficient Resource Management

In distributed software systems resource usage prediction is essential for efficient resource allocation and load balancing. Dynamic load sharing based on predictive analysis of the resource usage has been studied in (Devarakonda and Iyer, 1989; Goswami *et al.*, 1993). Software programs use various resources like CPU-time, file I/O and memory for successful completion of their instances.

Predictive analysis of the run-time resource consumption of software systems has been studied in (Jonge *et al.*, 2003; Devarakonda and Iyer, 1989, Goswami *et al.*, 1993). In (Devarakonda and Iyer, 1989, Goswami *et al.*, 1993), the authors present a statistical based approach that uses the knowledge of the program's resource usage in its last execution along with a state-transition model to predict the resource usage on its next execution. The state transition diagram is constructed by clustering the executions based on their historical resource usage.

Thus, the resource usage (CPU, memory etc.) of running program instances can be predicted by analyzing the values of their variables so far. In contrast to the approach in (Devarakonda and Iyer, 1989, Goswami *et al.*, 1993), this approach takes advantage of the state of the current instance in addition to the resource-usage history. Here, the state of a running instance is given by the control flow traced by the instance so far, and the values recorded by the executed task actions.

8. Conclusions

Workflow process models form the backbone of business enterprises. However, workflow modeling has been a challenging problem due to the complex nature of the enterprises. Workflow models very often fail to capture the complete set of the business logics driving the enterprises, thus leading to discrepancies between the process definition given by the workflow models and the process enactment. In addition, the business logics themselves undergo frequent changes to adapt to updated requirements and goals.

Workflow mining has emerged as the field of study where past process execution data, recorded as the workflow log, is analyzed to understand the process behavior. A widely known example of the main contributions of workflow mining to workflow management system is process discovery. This discovery process aims at constructing workflow models that are representatives of the executions in the workflow log, and the discovered models can help the user in detecting the discrepancies between the initial model and the process enactment. Workflow logs are proving to be valuable sources of data that can be analyzed to understand the process enactment behavior and analyze the goodness-of-fit of the proposed models.

References

van der Aalst, W. M. P. (1998). The application of petri nets to workflow management. *Journal of Circuits, Systems and Computers*, **8**(1), 21-66.

van der Aalst, W. M. P. (2000). Workflow verification: Finding control-flow errors using petri-net-based techniques. *Business Process Management*, 161-183.

van der Aalst, W. M. P. and Basten, T. (2002). Inheritance of workflows: An approach to tackling problems related to change. *Theoretical Computer Science*, **270**(1-2), 125-203.

van der Aalst, W. M. P., van Dongena, B. F., Herbst, J., Marustera, L., Schimm, G., and Weijters, A. J. M. M. (2003). Workflow mining: A survey of issues and approaches. *Data and Knowledge Engineering*, **47**(2), 237--267.

van der Aalst, W. M. P, and van Hee, K. M. (1996). Business process redesign: A petri-net-based approach. *Computers in Industry*, **29**(1-2), 15--26.

van der Aalst, W. M. P. and Hofstede, A. H. M.. (2000). Verification of workflow task structures: A Petri-net-based approach, *Information Systems,* **25**(1), 43--69.

van der Aalst, W. M. P., Hirnschall, A., and Verbeek, H. M. W. (2002). An alternative way to analyze workflow graphs. In Banks-Pidduck, A., Mylopoulos, J., Woo, C., and Ozsu, M., editors, *Lecture Notes in Computer Science: Proceedings of the 14th International Conference on Advanced Information Systems Engineering (CAiSE'02)*, Volume 2348, 535--552. Springer Verlag, Berlin, Germany.

van der Aalst, W. M. P. and Weijters, A. (2003). Process mining: a research agenda, *Computers in Industry,* **53**(3), 233-241.

Agrawal, R., Gunopulos, D., and Leymann, F. (1998). Mining process models from workflow logs. *EDBT '98: Proceedings of the 6th International Conference on Extending Database Technology*, pages 469--483, Springer-Verlag: London, UK.

Agrawal, R. and Srikant, R. (1994). Fast algorithms for mining association rules in large databases. *Proceedings VLDB*, 487-499.

Baecker, R., DiGiano, C., and Marcus, A. (1997). Software visualization for debugging. *Communications of the ACM*, **40**, 44-54.

Casati, F. Ceri, S. Pernici, B. and Pozzi, G. (1998). Workflow evolution. *Data and Knowledge Engineering*, **24**(3), 211--238.

Castellanos, M., Casati, F., Shan, M.-C., and Dayal, U. (2005). ibom: A platform for intelligent business operation management. *International Conference on Data Engineering* (ICDE), 1084-1095.

Cook, J. E. and Wolf, A. L. (1995). Automating process discovery through event-data analysis. *International Conference on Software Engineering*, 73-82.

Cook, J. E. and Wolf, A. L. (1998a). Discovering models of software processes from event-based data. *TOSEM '98: ACM Transactions on Software Engineering and Methodology*, **7**(3), 215-249.

Cook, J. E. and Wolf, A. L. (1998b). Event-based detection of concurrency. *Proceedings of the Sixth International Symposium on the Foundation of Software Engineering (FSE-6)*, 35-45.

Cook, J. E. and Wolf, A. L. (1999). Software process validation: quantitatively measuring the correspondence of a process to a model. *ACM Transactions on Software Engineering and Methodology*, **8**(2), 147--176.

Davulcu, H., Kifer, M., Ramakrishnan, C. R., and Ramakrishnan, I. V. (1998). Logic based modeling and analysis of workflows. *Proceedings of the 17th ACM Symposium on Principles of Database Systems*, 25-33.

Devarakonda, M. V. and Iyer, R. K. (1989). Predictability of process resource usage: A measurement-based study on Unix. *IEEE Trans. Software Eng.* **15**(12), 1579-1586.

Du, W., Eddy, G., and Shan, M.-C.. (1997). Distributed resource management in workflow environments. *Proceedings of the Fifth International Conference on Database Systems for Advanced Applications (DASFAA),* Melbourne, Australia, volume 6, pp. 521--530, April 1997.

Du, W. and Shan, M.-C. (1999). Enterprise workflow resource management. *Proc. RIDE,* 108--115.

Ellis, C. Keddara, K., and Rozenberg, G. (1995). Dynamic change within workflow systems. *COCS '95: Proceedings of conference on Organizational computing systems*, ACM Press: New York, NY, USA, 10-21.

Gaaloul, W. and Godart, C. (2005). Mining workflow recovery from event based logs. *Proceedings of the 3rd International Conference on Business Process Management (BPM).*

Georgakopoulos, D., Hornick, M. F., and Sheth, A. P. (1995). An overview of workflow management: From process modeling to workflow automation infrastructure, *Distributed and Parallel Databases*, **3**(2), 119--153.

Goswami, K. K., Devarakonda, M. V., and Iyer, R. K. (1993). Prediction-based dynamic load-sharing heuristics. *IEEE Trans. Parallel Distrib. Syst.*, **4**(6), 638--648.

Greco, G., Guzzo, A. and Manco, G. (2005). Mining and reasoning on workflows. *IEEE Transactions on Knowledge and Data Engineering*, **17**(4), 519-534.

Greco, G., Guzzo, A., Manco, G., and Sacca, D. (2003). Mining frequent instances on workflows. *PAKDD*, 209--221.

Greco, G. Guzzo, A., Pontieri, L., and Sacca, D. (2004). Mining expressive process models by clustering workflow traces. *Pacific-Asia Conference on Knowledge Discovery and Data Mining (PAKDD),* 52-62.

Grigori, D., Casati, F., Dayal, U., and Shan, M.-C. (2001). Improving business process quality through exception understanding, prediction, and prevention. *VLDB '01: Proceedings of the 27th International Conference on Very Large Data Bases*, Morgan Kaufmann Publishers: San Francisco, CA, USA, 159-168.

Guth, V. and Oberweis, A. (1997). Delta-analysis of Petri net based models for business processes. *Proceedings of the 3rd International Conference on Applied Informatics*, 23-32.

Herbst, J. (2000). Dealing with concurrency in workflow induction. *Proceedings of European Concurrent Engineering Conference (SCS).*

Herbst, J. (2000). A machine learning approach to workflow management. *ECML 2000, 11th European Conference on Machine Learning,* Barcelona, Catalonia, Spain, May 31 - June 2, 2000, Springer: Berlin, Germany, 183-194.

Herbst, J. and Karagiannis, D. (1998). Integrating machine learning and workflow management to support acquisition and adaptation of workflow models. *DEXA '98: Proc. of the 9th Intl. Workshop on Database and Expert Systems Appln.,* IEEE Computer Society: Washington, DC, USA, 745.

Herbst, J. and Karagiannis, D. (1999). An inductive approach to the acquisition and adaptation of workflow models. *Proceedings of the IJCAI'99 Workshop on Intelligent Workflow and Process Management: The New Frontier for AI in Business*, Stockholm, Sweden, August 1999, 52-57.

Horwitz, S., Reps, T., and Binkley, D. (1990). Interprocedural slicing using dependence graphs. *ACM Trans. Program. Lang. Syst.*, **12**(1), 26--60.

Jensen, C. and Scacchi, W. (2004). Data mining for software process discovery in open source software development communities. *Proc. Workshop on Mining Software Repositories*, Edinburgh, Scotland, May 2004.

de Jonge, M., Muskens, J., and Chaudron, M. (2003). Scenario-based prediction of run-time resource consumption in component-based software systems. *Proceedings: 6th ICSE Workshop on Component-Based Software Engineering: Automated Reasoning and Prediction*, April 2003.

Kappel, G., Lang, P., Rausch-Schott, S., and Retschitzegger, W. (1995). Workflow management based on objects, rules, and roles. *IEEE Data Engineering Bulletin*, **18**(1), 11--18.

Lin, H., Zhao, Z., Li, H., and Chen, Z. (2002). A novel graph reduction algorithm to identify structural conflicts. *HICSS '02: Proceedings of the 35th Annual Hawaii International Conference on System Sciences (HICSS'02)-Volume 9*, IEEE Computer Society: Washington, DC, USA, 289.

Marjanovic, O. and Orlowska, M. E. (1999). On modeling and verification of temporal constraints in production workflows. *Knowledge and Information Systems*, **1**(2), 157-192.

Pauw, W. D. and Sevitsky, G. (2000). Visualizing reference patterns for solving memory leaks in Java. *Concurrency: Practice and Experience*, **12**(14), 1431-1454.

Reichert, M. and Dadam, P. (1998). ADEPT flex -supporting dynamic changes of workflows without losing control. *Journal of Intelligent Information Systems*, **10**(2), 93-129.

Reichert, M., Rinderle, S. and Dadam1, P. (2003). On the common support of workflow type and instance changes under correctness constraints. *CoopIS*.

Rinderle, S., Reichert, M., and Dadam, P. (2004a). Correctness criteria for dynamic changes in workflow systems: a survey. *Data and Knowledge Engineering,* **50**(1), 9-34.

Rinderle, S. Reichert, M., and Dadam, P. (2004b). Flexible support of team processes by adaptive workflow systems. *Distrib. Parallel Databases*, **16**(1), 91-116.

Rinderle, S., Reichert, M., and Dadam, P. (2004c). On dealing with structural conflicts between process type and instance changes. *2nd Inter. Conf. On Business Process Management,* Postdam, Germany, LNCS 3080, 274-289.

Rinderle, S., Weber, B., Reichert, M., and Wild, W. (2005). Integrating process learning and process evolution - a semantics based approach. *Business Process Management*, LNCS 3649, 252-267.

Sadiq, W. and Orlowska, M.E. (1996). Modeling and verification of workflow graphs. Computer Science Technical Report, Department of Computer Science, The University of Queensland.

Sadiq, W. and Orlowska, M. E. (2000). Analyzing process models using graph reduction techniques. *Information Systems*, **25**(2), 117--134.

Sadiq, S. W., Orlowska, M.E., Lin, J. Y.-C., and Sadiq, W. (2005). Quality of service in flexible workflows through process constraints. 3rd *International Conference on Enterprise Information Systems (ICEIS)*, 29-37.

Sadiq, S. W., Orlowska, M. E., and Sadiq, W. (2005). Specification and validation of process constraints for flexible workflows. *Information Systems*, **30**(5), 349-378.

Sadiq, S. W., Orlowska, M. E., Sadiq, W., and Foulger, C. (2004). Data flow and validation in workflow modelling. *CRPIT '04: Proceedings of the fifteenth conference on Australasian database*, Australian Computer Society: Darlinghurst, Australia, Australia, 207-214.

Scacchi, W. (2001). Process models in software engineering. *Encyclopedia of Software Engineering*, 2nd Edition.

Silva, R., Zhang, J., and Shanahan, J. G. (2005). Probabilistic workflow mining. *KDD '05: Proceeding of the eleventh ACM SIGKDD international conference on Knowledge discovery in data mining*, ACM Press: New York, NY, USA, 275-284.

Singh, M. P. (1995). Semantical considerations on workflows: An algebra for intertask dependencies. *Workshop on Database Programming Languages,* page 5.

Subramaniam, S., Kalogeraki, V., Gunopulos, D., Casati, F., Dayal, U., Sayal, M., and Castellanos, M. (2005). Workflow process models: Discovering decision point locations by analyzing data dependencies. *ICDM Intl. Conf. on Data Mining - Temporal Data Mining (TDM'05)*, November 2005.

Subramaniam, S., Kalogeraki, V., Gunopulos, D., Casati, F., Dayal, U., Sayal, M., and Castellanos, M. (2007). Improving Business Process Models by Discovering Decision Points, *Information Systems Journal, Elsevier*, to appear.

Subramaniam, S., Kalogeraki, V., and Gunopulos, D. (2006). Business processes: Behavior prediction and capturing reasons for evolution. *International Conference on Enterprise Information Systems (ICEIS)*, May 2006.

Wargitsch, C., Wewers, T., and Theisinger, F. (1998). An organizational-memory-based approach for an evolutionary workflow management system -- concepts and implementation. *Proceedings of the 31st Annual Hawaii Int. Conf. on System Sciences,* January 1998, 174-183.

Weijters, A. J. M. M., and van der Aalst, W. M. P. (2002). Rediscovering workflow models from event-based data. *Proceedings of the Third International NAISO Symposium on Engineering of Intelligent Systems (EIS 2002),* NAISO Academic Press, Sliedrecht, The Netherlands, 65-65.

Weske, M. (2001). Formal foundation and conceptual design of dynamic adaptations in a workflow management system. *Proceedings of the 34th Hawaii International Conference on System Sciences.*

[WFM] http://www.wfmc.org/

Wodtke, D. and Weikum, G. (1997). A formal foundation for distributed workflow execution based on state charts. *Proceedings of the Sixth International Conference of Database Theory (ICDT),* 230--246.

Authors' Biographical Statements

Dimitrios Gunopulos is a Professor at the Dept. of Computer Science and Engineering, in the University of California Riverside. His research is in the areas of Data Mining and Knowledge Discovery in Databases, Databases, and Algorithms. He has co-authored over a hundred journals, conference papers, and book chapters, and a book. Dr. Gunopulos has held positions at the IBM Almaden Research Center and at the Max-Planck-Institut for Informatics. He completed his undergraduate studies at the University of Patras, Greece (1990) and graduated with M.A. and Ph.D. degrees from Princeton University (1992 and 1995 respectively). His research has been supported by NSF (including an NSF CAREER award and an ITR award), the DoD, the Institute of Museum and Library Services, the Tobacco Related Disease Research Program, and AT&T. Dr. Gunopulos has served as a PC co-Chair in ACM SIGKDD 2006 and in SSDBM 2003, as a Vice PC-Chair in IEEE ICDE 2004 and in IEEE ICDM 2005, and he is currently an associate Editor at IEEE TKDE and at ACM TKDD.

Sarmila Subramaniam has been working in Google sicne graduating with M.S. and Ph.D. degrees from the University of California, Riverside in 2006. She completed her Bachelor of Engineering in Computer Science at the Regional Engineering College (REC) Trichy. Her research interests research interests include data mining and workflow management systems, focusing on process mining and data analysis as well as compression in wireless sensor systems.

Chapter 13[1]

Mining Images of Cell-Based Assays

Petra Perner
Institute of Computer Vision and Applied Computer Sciences, IBaI
Leipzig, Germany
Email: www.ibai-institut.de

Abstract: In the rapidly expanding fields of cellular and molecular biology, fluorescence illumination and observation is becoming one of the techniques of choice to study the localization and dynamics of proteins, organelles, and other cellular compartments, as well as a tracer of intracellular protein trafficking. The automatic analysis of these images and signals in medicine, biotechnology, and chemistry is a challenging and demanding field. Signal-producing procedures by microscopes, spectrometers and other sensors have found their way into wide fields of medicine, biotechnology, economy and environmental analysis. With this arises the problem of the automatic mass analysis of signal information. Signal-interpreting systems which automatically generate the desired target statements from the signals are therefore of compelling necessity. The continuation of mass analyses on the basis of the classical procedures leads to investments of proportions that are not feasible. New procedures and system architectures are therefore required. We will present, based on our flexible image analysis and interpretation system *Cell_Interpret*, new intelligent and automatic image analysis and interpretation procedures. We will demonstrate it in the application of the HEp-2 cell pattern analysis.

Key Words: Image analysis and interpretation, High-content analysis of images, Automation and standardization of visual inspection tasks, Image-mining, Systems for knowledge discovery and interpretation, Microscopic cell image analysis.

---

[1] Liao, T.W. and E. Triantaphyllou, (Eds.), **Recent Advances in Data Mining of Enterprise Data: Algorithms and Applications**, *World Scientific*, Singapore, pp. 577-641, 2007.

1. Introduction

In the rapidly expanding fields of cellular and molecular biology, fluorescence illumination and observation is becoming one of the techniques of choice to study the localization and dynamics of proteins, organelles, and other cellular compartments, as well as a tracer of intracellular protein trafficking.

Quantitative imaging of fluorescent proteins and patterns is accomplished with a variety of techniques, including wide-field, confocal and multiphoton microscopy, ultra fast low light level digital cameras and multitracking laser control systems. These microscopic images can be of 2-dimensional or 3-dimensional nature, or even videos recording the life cycle of a cell.

The interpretation of the resulting pattern in these digital images to date is usually done manually. However, the huge amount of data created and the growing use of these techniques in industry for pharmacological aspects or diagnostic purposes in medicine require automatic image interpretation procedures. These image interpretation procedures should allow to interpret these images automatically, and also to detect automatically new knowledge to study the cellular and molecular processes.

The continuation of mass image analyses on the basis of the classical procedures leads to investments of proportions that are not feasible. New procedures based on image mining and case-based reasoning are therefore required.

We are developing methods that allow the automatic analysis of these images for the discovery of patterns, new knowledge and relations. The present work is done for 2-dimensional microscopic fluorescent images, but will be continued with 3-dimensional image and video analysis. We will demonstrate the usage of our system in the application of HEp-2 cell pattern analysis. The aim of our work is to provide the system with image analysis, feature extraction and knowledge discovery functions that are suited for mining a set of microscopic cell images for the automatic detection of image interpretation knowledge and then applying this knowledge within the same system for automatic image interpretation of the HEp-2 cell images. At the end the system can work on-line in a medical diagnostic laboratory to process and automatically interpret the patterns on the cells in the image and to calculate quantitative information about the cell patterns.

The developed processing functions should make the system flexible enough to deal with different kinds of cell images and different image qualities and require a minimal number of interactions with the user for knowledge mining. The image interpretation process is running fully automatically, based on the image analysis and feature extraction procedures developed for this kind of image analysis and the learned interpretation knowledge by the developed knowledge mining procedures.

Although we are focusing on the analysis of cell-based assays for drug design in the pharmacological industry in this chapter, the described methods and the methodologies are highly suitable for other enterprise data. Other areas which use imaging technologies in modern enterprises are numerous including in quality and production environment control, food processing, robotics, just to name a few. More and more robots are equipped with digital cameras. At the same time, many screening operations for quality control are based on the skills and capabilities of human operators. Thus, current methods may be susceptible to fatigue problems by human operators, and also problems due to limited capabilities / skills of individual human operators. The automation of image analysis and interpretation leads to objective results, make the results reproducible and often more accurate.

Digital image analysis techniques are the only way to alleviate such problems and catapult such operations into the digital age 100%. We have used our methods and methodology for the continuous monitoring of airborne biological agents in food processing (Perner *et al.*, 2003), for controlling the quality of grains in mills (Perner *et al.*, 2005), and for defect recognition and diagnosis in offset printing (Perner, 1994). Further work on other applications is in progress. Thus, the methods described in this chapter have a great potential in the field of enterprise data mining.

In Section 2 we describe a sample application. Next we describe the requirements for the system in Section 3. The system architecture developed so far is described in Section 4. The individual components of the architecture and the underlying methods of these components are described in Section 5 for image segmentation, in Section 6 for feature extraction, in Section 7 for decision tree induction, in Section 8 for case-based reasoning, and in Section 9 for conceptual clustering. A case study based on the application of HEp-2 cells is given in Section 10. Finally, we summarize our work in Section 11.

2. The Application used for the Demonstration of the System Capability

The kinds of cells that are considered in this application are HEp-2 cells, which are used for the identification of antinuclear autoantibodies (ANA). ANA testing for the assessment of systemic and organ-specific autoimmune diseases has increased progressively since immunofluorescence techniques were first used to demonstrate antinuclear antibodies in 1957. HEp-2 cells allow for the recognition of over 30 different nuclear and cytoplasmic patterns, which are given by upwards of 100 different autoantibodies.

The identification of the patterns has up to now been done manually by a human inspecting the slides with the help of a microscope. The lacking automation of this technique has resulted in the development of alternative techniques based on chemical reactions, which do not have the discrimination power of the ANA testing. An automatic system would pave the way for a wider use of ANA testing. Prototypical images of HEp-2 cell patterns for six different classes are shown in Figure 1. These images were taken by an image acquisition unit consisting of an AXIOSKOP microscope from Carl Zeiss Jena, coupled with a video camera.

In the knowledge acquisition process (Perner, 1994) with a human operator, using an interview technique and a repertory grid method, we acquired the knowledge of this operator, while classifying the different cell types. Some of this knowledge is shown in Table 1. The symbolic terms show that a mixture of different image information is necessary for classification. The operator uses the intensity as well as some texture information. In addition, the appearances of the cell parts within the cells are of importance, like "dark nuclei", which also requires spatial information.

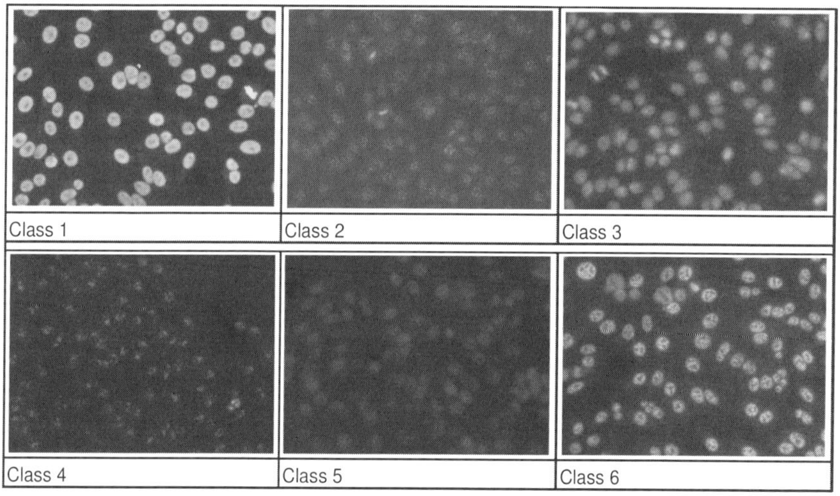

Figure 1. Prototypical images of six classes.

Table 1. Some knowledge about the class description given by a human operator.

Class	Class Name	Description
Homogeneous nuclei fluorescence	Class_1	Smooth and uniform fluorescence of the nuclei. Nuclei appear sometimes dark. The chromosome fluorescence is from weak to very intense.
Fine speckled nuclei fluorescence	Class_2	Dense fine speckled fluorescence
...	...	...
Nuclei fluorescence	Class_9	Nuclei are weakly homogenous or fine-grained and can hardly be discerned from the background.

3. Challenges and Requirements for the Systems

Application oriented systems that can only solve one specific task are very costly and it takes time to develop them. The success of automatic image interpretation systems can only be guaranteed when the development effort is as low as possible and when they can be adapted quickly to different needs and tasks. That requires developing systems that can run on a class of applications such as microscopic fluorescent images. Such systems should have functions that are able to:

- automatically detect single cells in the image regardless of the image quality with high accuracy, robustness and flexibility,
- automatically describe the properties of the cell nucleus and the cytoplasm by image features (numerical and symbolical),
- automatically interpret the images into cell patterns or other decisions (prediction),
- automatically detect new knowledge from image data and apply it to automatic interpretation.

The challenges are:

- New strategies are necessary which should be able to adapt the system to changing environmental conditions, user needs and process requirements.
- Introduction of case-based reasoning (CBR) strategies and data mining strategies into image interpretation systems on the low level and high level unit satisfy these requirements.

4. The Cell-Interpret's Architecture

Figure 2 shows a scheme of the tool *Cell Interpret* (Perner, 2005). There are two main parts in the tool:

- The on-line part that is comprised of the image analysis and an image interpretation part.
- The off-line part that is comprised of the database and the data mining and knowledge discovery part.

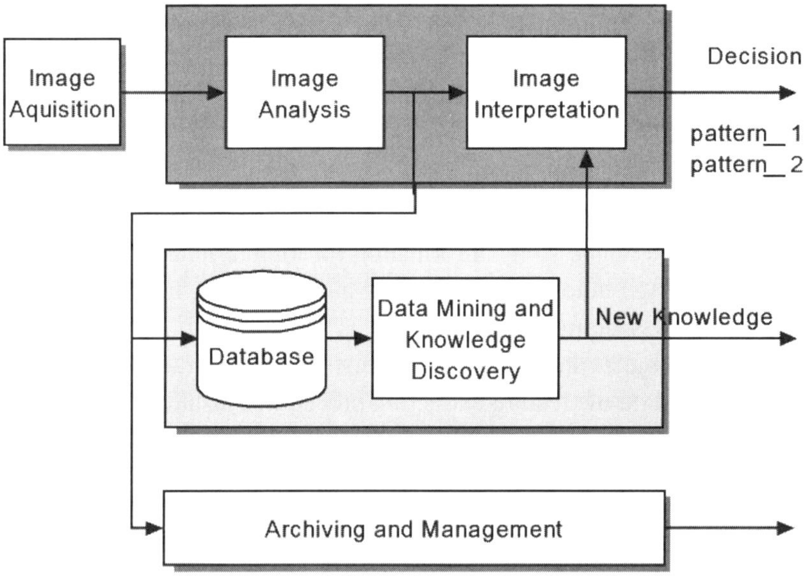

Figure 2. The architecture of *Cell_Interpret.*

The tool is written in C++ and runs under Windows NT. These two units communicate over a database of image descriptions, which is created in the frame of the image processing unit. This database is the basis for the image mining unit.

The on-line part can automatically detect the objects, extract image features from the objects and classify the recognized objects into the respective classes based on the previously stored decision rules. It is comprised of an image segmentation unit, a feature extraction unit and the interpretation unit.

The interface between the off-line and the on-line part is the database where images and calculated image features are stored.

The off-line part can mine the images for a prediction model or discover new groups of objects, features or relations. The discovered similar groups can be used for learning the classification model or just for understanding the domain. In the latter case the discovered information is displayed to the user on the terminal of the system.

Once a new prediction model has been learned, the rules are inserted into the image interpretation unit after approval by the user. Then the system can run automatically based on the learned knowledge. The data mining and knowledge discovery unit is comprised of a decision tree induction unit, a case-based reasoning unit and a conceptual clustering unit.

Besides that there is an archiving and management part that controls the whole system and stores information for long term archiving. Images can be processed automatically or semi-automatically. In the first case a set of images specified by the expert is automatically segmented into background objects and objects of interest. For all the recognized objects features based on the feature extracting procedures installed in the system are automatically calculated. In this way as many as possible features are calculated, regardless of whether they make sense for a specific application or not. This requires feature subset selection methods later on. In the second case, an image from the image archive is selected by the expert and then it is displayed on the monitor. In order to perform image processing an expert communicates with a computer. In this mode he/she has the option to calculate features based on the feature extracting procedures and/or insert symbolic features based on his/her expert knowledge. In both modes the features are stored into the database.

5. Case-Based Image Segmentation

Image Segmentation is a crucial step in extracting information from a digital image. It is not easy to set up the segmentation parameter so that it fits best over the entire set of images. Most segmentation techniques contain numerous control parameters, which must be adjusted to obtain optimal segmentation performance.

The parameter selection is usually done on a large enough test dataset, which should represent the entire domain well enough in order to be able to build up a general model for the segmentation. However, it is not often possible to obtain a large enough dataset and therefore the segmentation model may not fit well to the entire data and needs to be adjusted to new data. Note that a general model does not guarantee the best segmentation for each image, it rather guarantees an average best fit over the entire set of images.

Another aspect goes along with changes in image quality caused by variations in environmental conditions, image devices, etc. Thus the segmentation performance needs to be adapted to these changes in image quality. All these suggest using CBR for image segmentation.

CBR is used to select the segmentation parameters according to the current image characteristics. By taking into account the non-image and the image information, we break down our complex solution space to a subspace of relevant cases where the variation in image quality between the cases is limited. It is assumed that images having similar image characteristics will show similar good segmentation results when the same segmentation parameters are applied to these images.

The overall architecture of our CBR image segmentation unit is divided into the image segmentation unit based on case-based reasoning (see Figure 3) and the unit for the case base management part (see Figure 4).

5.1 The Case-Based Reasoning Unit

The case-based reasoning unit for image segmentation consists of a case base in which formerly processed cases are stored. A case is comprised of image information, non-image information (e.g. image acquisition parameters, object characteristics and so on), and image segmentation parameters. The task is now to find the best segmentation for the current image by looking up the case base for similar cases.

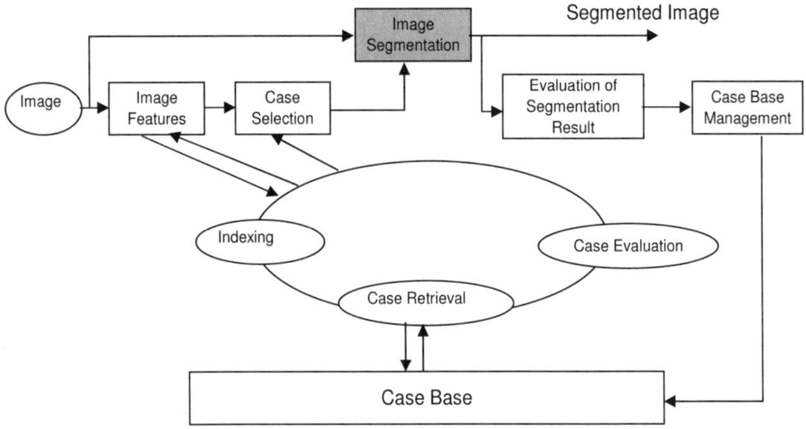

Figure 3. The CBR image segmentation unit.

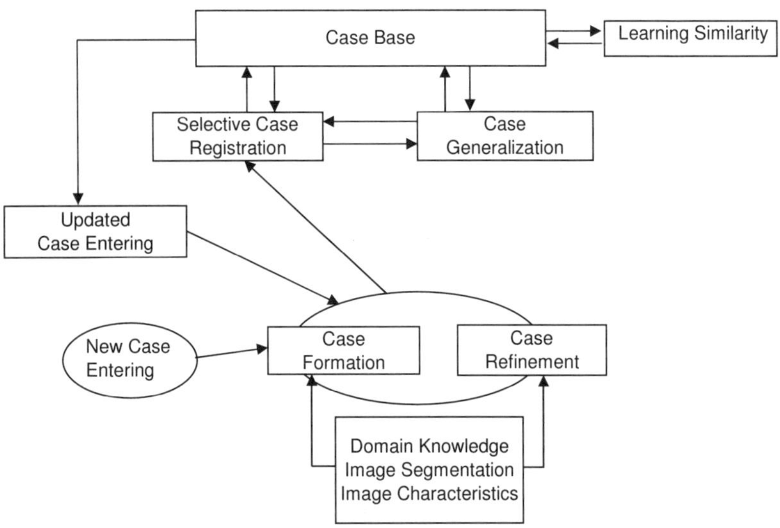

Figure 4. The CBR maintenance unit.

Similarity determination is done based on non-image information and image information. The evaluation unit will take the case with the highest similarity score for further processing.

In case there are two or more cases with the same similarity score, the case appearing first will be taken. After the closest case has been chosen, the image segmentation parameters associated with the selected case will be given to the image segmentation unit and the current image will be segmented (see Figure 3). It is assumed that images having similar image characteristics will show similar good segmentation results when the same segmentation parameters are applied to these images. The image segmentation algorithm is in our case a histogram-based image-segmentation algorithm (Perner, 1999) and a watershed-based image-segmentation algorithm (Frucci *et al*., 2007).

5.2 Management of Case Bases

The result of the segmentation process is observed by a user. He/she compares the original image with the labeled image on display. If he/she detects deviations of the marked areas in the segmented image from the object area in the original image, which should be labeled, then he/she will evaluate the result as incorrect and the management of case base will start. This will also be done if no similar case is available in the case base. The proposed method is close to the critique modify framework described by Grimnes et al. (1996).

The evaluation procedure can also be done automatically (Zhang, 1997). However, the drawback is that there is no general procedure available. It can only be done in a domain dependent fashion. Therefore, an automatic evaluation procedure would constrain the usage of the system. Once the user observes a bad result, he/she will tag the case as a bad case. The tag describes the user's critique in more detail.

In an off-line phase, the best segmentation parameters for the image are determined and the attributes, which are necessary for similarity determination, are calculated from the image. Both, the segmentation parameters and the attributes calculated from the image, are stored into the case base as a new case. In addition to that the non-image information is extracted from the file header and stored together with the other information in the case base. During storage, case generalization will be done to ensure that the case base will not become too large. The unit for modifying the segmentation is shown in Figure 4.

6. Feature Extraction

The unit for feature extraction is shown in Figure 5. The expert can calculate image features for the labeled objects. These features are composed of statistical gray level features, the object contour, square, diameter, shape (Zamperoni, 1996), and a novel texture feature that is flexible enough to describe different textures on objects (Perner *et al.*, 2002). The architecture allows adding a new feature extraction procedure. Consequently, we are developing a new feature extraction procedure suitable for the description of cell properties.

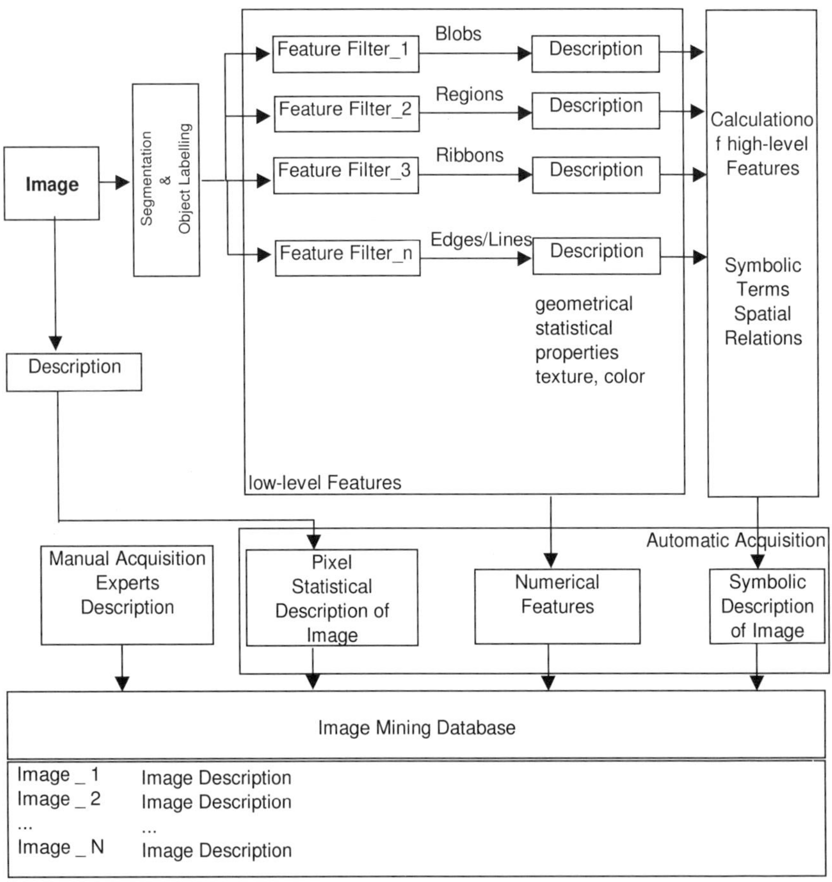

Figure 5. The feature extraction unit.

The expert evaluates or calculates image features and stores their values in a database of image features. Each entry in the database presents features of the object of interest. These features can be numerical (calculated on the image) and symbolical (determined by the expert as a result of image reading by the expert). In the latter case the expert evaluates object features according to the attribute list, which has to be specified in advance for object description, or is based on a visual ontology available for visual content description. Then he/she feeds these values into the database. When the expert has evaluated a sufficient number of images, the resulting database can be used for the mining process.

6.1 *Our Flexible Texture Descriptor*

The method for the texture description is based on random sets (Matheron, 1975). The texture model X is obtained by taking various realizations of compact random sets, implanting them in Poisson points in R^n, and taking the supremum. The functional moment $Q(B)$ of X, after Booleanization, is calculated as:

$$P(B \subset X^c) = Q(B) = \exp(-\theta \overline{Mes}(X' \oplus \check{B})) \qquad \forall B \in \kappa \tag{1}$$

where κ is the set of the compact random set of R^n, θ is the density of the process, and $\overline{Mes}(X' \oplus \check{B})$ is an average measure that characterizes the geometric properties of the remaining set of objects after dilation $\oplus$. Relation (1) is the fundamental formula of the model. It completely characterizes the texture model. $Q(B)$ does not depend on the location of B, thus it is stationary. One can also prove that it is ergodic, thus we can calculate the measure for a specific portion of the space without referring to the particular portion of the space.

Formula 1 tells us that the texture model depends on two parameters:

1. On the density θ of the process and

2. A measure $\overline{Mes}(X^{`} \oplus \check{B})$ that characterizes the objects. In the 1-dimensional space it is the average length of the lines and in the 2-dimensional space $\overline{Mes}(X^{`} \oplus \check{B})$ is the average measure of the area and the perimeter of the objects under the assumption of convex shapes.

We considered the 2-dimensional case and developed a proper texture descriptor. Suppose now that we have a texture image with 8-bit gray levels. Then we can consider the texture image as the superposition of various Boolean models, each of them taking a different gray level value on the scale from 0 to 255 for the objects within the bit plane.

To reduce the dimensionality of the resulting feature vector, the gray levels ranging from 0 to 255 are now quantized into 12 intervals t. Each image $f(x,y)$ containing only a cell gets classified according to the gray level into t classes, with $t = \{0,1,2,..,11\}$. For each class a binary image is calculated containing the value "1" for pixels with a gray level value falling into the gray level interval of class t and value "0" for all other pixels. The resulting bit plane $f(x,y,t)$ can now be considered as a realization of the Boolean model. The quantization of the gray level into 12 intervals was done with equal distance. We call the image $f(x,y,t)$ in the following class image. Object labeling is done in the class images with the contour following method (Zamerponi, 1996). Afterwards, features from the bit-plane and from these objects are calculated.

The first one is the density of the class image t which is the number of pixels in the class image labeled by "1", divided by the area of the cell. If all pixels of a cell are labeled by "1", then the density is one. If no pixel in a cell is labeled, then the density is zero. From the objects in the class image t the area, a simple shape factor, and the length of the contour are calculated. According to the model, not a single feature of each object is taken for classification, but the mean and the variance of each feature is calculated over all the objects in the class image t. We also calculate the frequency of the object size in each class image t. An in-depth study of the behavior of the Boolean model for texture classification as well as for the features describing the objects in the bit planes can be found in Perner (2002).

7. The Decision Tree Induction Unit

7.1 The Basic Principle

With decision tree induction we can automatically derive from a set of individual observations a set of rules that generalize these data (see Figure 6). The set of rules is represented as a decision tree. Decision trees recursively partition the solution space based on the attribute splits into subspaces until the final solution is reached. The resulting hierarchical representation is very natural to the human problem solving process. During the construction of the decision tree selected from the whole set of attributes are only those attributes that are most relevant to the classification problem. Once the decision tree has been learned and the developer is satisfied with the quality of the learned model, this model can be used in order to predict the outcome of new samples.

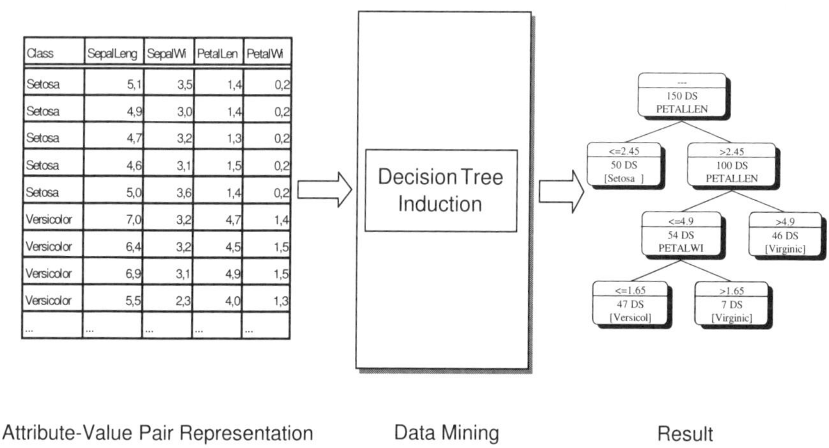

Figure 6. The basic principle of decision tree induction.

This learning method is also called supervised learning, since samples in the data collection have to be labeled by the class. Most decision tree induction algorithms allow using numerical attributes as well as categorical attributes. Therefore, the resulting classifier can make the decision based on both types of attributes.

7.2 *Terminology of the Decision Tree*

Since the reading of a decision tree is not easy to understand for many users, we will explain here the basic properties of a diagnostic decision tree. A decision tree is a directed acyclic graph consisting of edges and nodes (Figure 7). The node with no entering edges is called the root node. The root node contains all class labels. Every node except the root node has exactly one entering edge. A node having no successor is called a leaf or terminal node. All other nodes are called internal nodes. The nodes of the tree contain decision rules such as

IF attribute $A \leq$ some value THEN D.

The decision rule is a function f that maps the attribute A to D. The sample set in each node is split into two subsets based on the constant *some value* for the attribute. This constant is called the cut point.

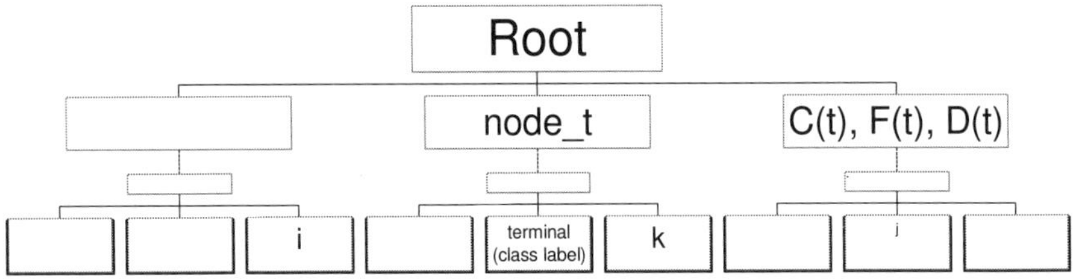

Figure 7. Representation of a decision tree.

In case of a binary tree, the decision is either true or false. Geometrically, the test describes a partition that is orthogonal to one of the coordinates of the decision space. A terminal node should contain only samples of one class. If there is more than one class in the sample set, we say there is class overlap. An internal node contains always more than one class in the assigned sample set.

A path in the tree is a sequence of edges, (v_1,v_2), (v_2,v_3), ... , (v_{n-1},v_n). We say the path is from v_1 to v_n and is of length n. There is a unique path from the root to each node. The depth of a node v in a tree is the length of the path from the root to v. The height of node v in a tree is the length of the largest path from v to a leaf. The height of a tree is the height of its root. The level of a node v in a tree is the height of the tree minus the depth of v.

A binary tree is a tree ordered such that each successor of a node is distinguished either as a left or a right child; no node has more than one left child or more than one right child. Otherwise it is a multivariate tree.

Let us now consider the decision tree learned from Fisher's iris dataset. This dataset has three classes (1-Setosa, 2-Vericolor, 3-Virginica) with 50 observations for each class and four predictor variables (petal length, petal width, sepal length and sepal width). The learned tree is shown in Figure 8.

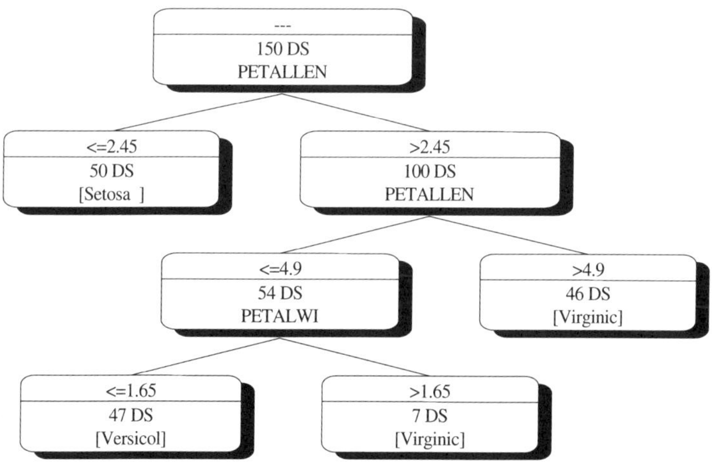

Figure 8. Decision tree learned from the iris dataset.

It is a binary tree. The average depth of the tree is 1+3+2=6/3=2. The root node contains the attribute petal length. Along a path the rules are combined by the AND operator. Following the two paths from the root node we obtain two rules such as:

Rule1: IF petal_lenght $\leq$ 2.45 THEN Setosa

Rule 2: IF petal_lenght > 2.45 AND petal_lenght > 4.9 THEN Virginic.

In the latter rule we can see that the attribute petal length will be used twice during the problem-solving process. Each time a different cut-point is used on this attribute. This representation results from the binary tree building process, since only axis-parallel decision surfaces (see Section 7.3) based on single cut-points are created. However, it only means that the values for an attribute should fall into the interval [2.45, 4.9] for the desired decision rule.

7.3 Subtasks and Design Criteria for Decision Tree Induction

The overall procedure of the decision tree building process is summarized in Figure 9. Decision trees recursively split the decision space into subspaces based on the decision rules in the nodes, until the final stopping criteria are reached or the remaining sample set does not suggest further splitting. For this recursive splitting the tree building process must always pick among all attributes the one that shows the best result on the attribute selection criteria for the remaining sample set. Whereas for categorical attributes the partition of the attributes values is given a-priori, the partition (also called attribute discretization) of the attribute values for numerical attributes must be determined.

Attribute discretization can be done before or during the tree building process. We will consider the case where the attribute discretization will be done during the tree building process. The discretization must be carried out before the attribute selection process, since the selected partition on the attribute values of a numerical attribute highly influences the prediction power of that attribute.

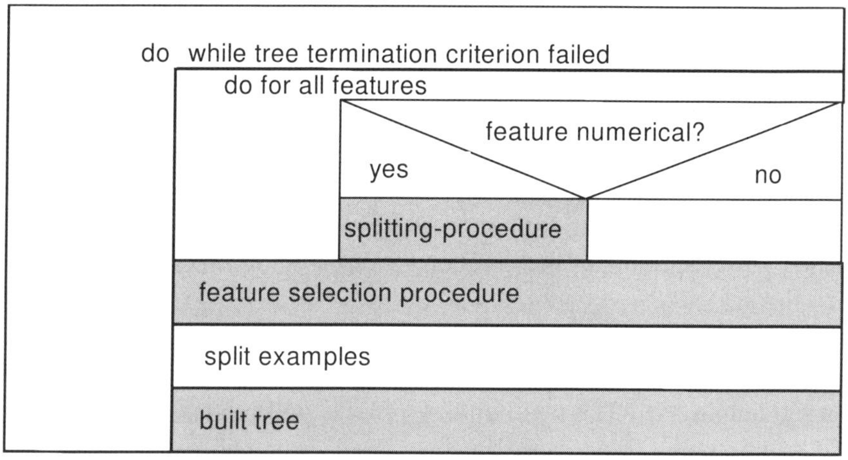

Figure 9. Overall tree induction procedure.

After the attribute selection criteria are calculated for all attributes based on the remaining sample set, the resulting values are evaluated and the attribute with the best value for the attribute selection criteria is selected for further splitting of the sample set. Then the tree is extended to two or more new nodes. Each node is assigned the subset of samples obtained when splitting on the attribute value in the node and afterwards the tree building process is repeated.

Attribute splits can be done several different ways as follows:

- univariate on numerically or ordinal ordered attributes X such as $X \leq a$,
- multivariate on categorical or discretized numerical attributes such as $X \in A$, or
- as a linear combination split on numerical attributes $\sum_i a_i X_i \leq c$.

The influence of the kind of attribute splits on the resulting decision surface for two attributes is shown in Figure 10. The axis-parallel to the decision surface results in a rule such as

IF F3 ≥4.9 THEN CLASS Virginic

while the linear decision surface results in a rule such as

IF -3.272+0.3254∗F3+F4 ≥ 0 THEN CLASS Virginic

The latter decision surface discriminates better between the two classes than the axis-parallel to one (see Figure 10). However, by looking at the rules we can see that the explanation capability of the tree will decrease in the case of the linear decision surface. Figure 11 shows the recursive axis-parallel splitting of the decision space based on two attributes of the iris dataset.

The induced decision tree tends to over-fit the data. This is typically caused due to noise in the attribute values and class information present in the training set. The tree building process will produce sub-trees that fit to this noise. This causes an increased error rate when classifying unseen cases. Pruning the tree, which means replacing the sub-trees with leaves, will help to avoid this problem.

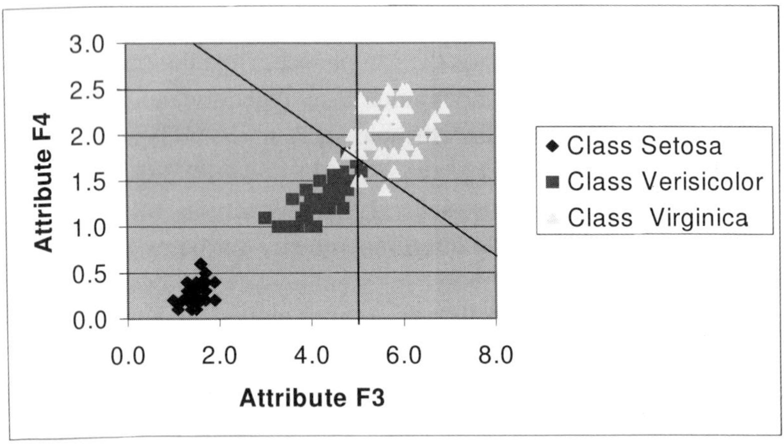

Figure 10. Axis-parallel and linear attribute splits graphically viewed in decision space.

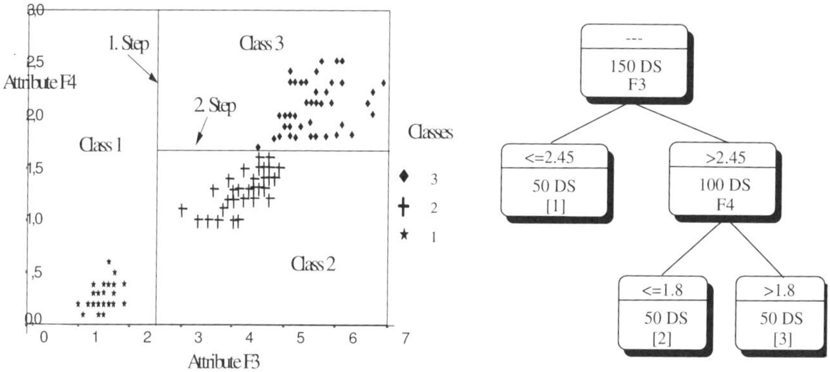

Figure 11. Demonstration of recursive splitting of decision space based on two attributes of the iris dataset.

Now, we can summarize the main subtasks of decision tree induction as follows:

- attribute selection (Information Gain (Quinlan, 1986), χ^2-Statistic (Kerber, 1992), Gini-Index (Breiman et al., 1984), Gain Ratio (Quinlan, 1988), Distance measure-based selection criteria (de Mantaras, 1991)),
- attribute discretization (Cut-Point (Quinlan, 1986), Chi-Merge (Kerber, 1992), MLDP (Fayyad *et al.*, 1993) , LVQ-based discretization, Histogram-based discretization, and Hybrid Methods (Perner *et al.*, 1998), and
- pruning (Cost-Complexity (Breiman *et al.*, 1984), Reduced Error Reduction Pruning (Quinlan, 1986), Confidence Interval Method (Quinlan, 1987), Minimal Error Pruning (Niblett *et al.*, 1987)).

7.4 Attribute Selection Criteria

Formally, we can describe the attribute selection problem as follows. Let Y be the full set of features, with cardinality k, and let n_i be the number of samples in the remaining sample set i. Let the feature selection criterion function for the attribute be represented by $S(A,n_i)$.

Without any loss of generality, let us consider a higher value of S to indicate a good attribute A. Formally, the problem of attribute selection is to find an attribute A based on our sample subset n_i that maximizes our criteria S so that

$$S(A, n_i) = \max_{Z \subseteq Y, |Z|=1} S(Z, n_i) \tag{2}$$

The attribute selection criteria used in our tool *Cell_Interpret* will be described next.

7.4.1 Information Gain Criteria and the Gain Ratio

Following the theory of the Shannon channel (Philipow, 1987), we consider the dataset as the source and measure the impurity of the received data when transmitted via the channel. The transmission over the channel results in the partition of the dataset into subsets based on splits on the attribute values J of the attribute A. The aim should be to transmit the signal with the least loss of information. This can be described by the following criterion:

IF $I(A) = I(C) - I(C/J) = Max$ THEN *Select Attribute A*

where $I(A)$ is the entropy of the source, $I(C)$ is the entropy of the receiver or the expected entropy to generate the message $C_1, C_2, \ldots, C_m$ and $I(C/J)$ is the losing entropy when branching on the attribute values J of attribute A.

For the calculation of this criterion we first consider the contingency table as shown in Table 2 with m the number of classes, n the number of attribute values J, N the number of examples, L_i being the number of examples with the attribute value J_i, R_j the number of examples belonging to class C_j, and x_{ij} the number of examples belonging to class C_j and having attribute value J_i.

Now, we can define the entropy of class C by:

$$I(C) = -\sum_{j=1}^{m} \frac{R_j}{N} \times \log_2 \frac{R_j}{N} \tag{3}$$

The entropy of the class given the feature values is:

$$I(C/J) = \sum_{i=1}^{n} \frac{L_i}{N} \cdot \sum_{j=1}^{m} -\frac{x_{ij}}{L_i} \log_2 \frac{x_{ij}}{L_i} = \frac{1}{N} \sum_{i=1}^{n} L_i \log_2 L_i - \sum_{i=1}^{n} \sum_{j=1}^{m} x_{ij} \log_2 x_{ij} \tag{4}$$

Table 2. Contingency table for an attribute.

Class / **Attribute values**	C_1	C_2	...	C_j	...	C_m	SUM
J_1	x_{11}	x_{12}	...	x_{1j}	...	x_{1m}	L_1
J_2	x_{21}	x_{22}	...	x_{2j}	...	x_{2m}	L_2
.	.	.	...	.	...	.	.
.	.	.	...	.	...	.	.
.	.	.	...	.	...	.	.
J_i	x_{i1}	x_{i2}	...	x_{ij}	...	x_{im}	L_i
.	.	.	...	.	...	.	.
.	.	.	...	.	...	.	.
.	.	.	...	.	...	.	.
J_n	x_{n1}	x_{n2}	...	x_{nj}	...	x_{nm}	L_n
SUM	R_1	R_2	...	R_j	...	R_m	N

The best feature is the one that achieves the lowest value of (2) or, equivalently, the highest value of the "mutual information" $I(C) - I(C/J)$. The main drawback of this measure is its sensitivity to the number of attribute values. In the extreme case, a feature that takes N distinct values for the N examples achieves complete discrimination between different classes, giving $I(C/J)=0$, even though the features may consist of random noise and be useless for predicting the classes of future examples.

Therefore, Quinlan (1988) introduced normalization by the entropy of the attribute itself:

$$G(A)=\frac{I(A)}{I(J)} \text{ with } I(J)=-\sum_{i=1}^{n}\frac{L_i}{N}\log_2\frac{L_i}{N} \tag{5}$$

Other normalizations have been proposed by Coppersmith *et. al.* (1999) and Mantaras (1991). Comparative studies have been done by White and Lui (1994).

7.4.2 The Gini Function

This measure takes into account the impurity of the class distribution. The Gini function is defined as:

$$G=1-\sum_{i=1}^{m}p_i^2 \tag{6}$$

The selection criterion is defined as:

IF $Gini\,(A)=G(C)-G(C/A)=Max$ THEN *Select Attribute A*

The Gini function for class C is:

$$G(C)=1-\sum_{j=1}^{m}\left(\frac{R_j}{N}\right)^2 \tag{7}$$

The Gini function of the class given the feature values is defined as:

$$G(C/J)=\sum_{i=1}^{n}\frac{L_i}{N}G(J_i) \tag{8}$$

with

$$G(J_i) = 1 - \sum_{j=1}^{m} \left(\frac{x_{ij}}{L_i} \right)^2 \tag{9}$$

7.5 *Discretization of Attribute Values*

A numerical attribute may take on any value on a continuous scale between its minimal value x_1 and its maximal value x_2. Branching on all these distinct attribute values does not lead to any generalization and would make the tree very sensitive to noise. Rather, we should find meaningful partitions of the numerical values into intervals. The intervals should abstract the data in such a way that they cover the range of attribute values belonging to one class and that they separate them from those belonging to other classes. Then we can treat the attribute as a discrete variable with $k+1$ intervals. This process is called discretization of attributes.

The points that split our attribute values into intervals are called cut-points. The k cut-points are always on the border between the distributions of two classes. Discretization can be done before the decision tree building process or during decision tree learning (Dougherty *et al.*, 1995). We just consider discretization during the tree building process. We call them dynamic and local discretization methods. They are dynamic since they work during the tree building process on the created subsample sets and they are local since they work on the recursively created subspaces.

In Figure 12, we see the conditional histogram of the values of the attribute petal length of the iris dataset. In the binary case (k=1), the attribute values would be split at the cut-point 2.35 into an interval from 0 to 2.35 and a second interval from 2.36 to 7. If we do multi-interval discretization, we will find another cut-point at 4.8. That groups the values into 3 intervals (k=2): intervall_1 from 0 to 2.35, interval_2 from 2.36 to 4.8, and interval_3 from 4.9 to 7.

We will also consider attribute discretization on categorical attributes. Many attribute values of a categorical attribute will lead to a partition of the sample set into many small sub-sample sets. This again will result into a quick stop of the tree building process. To avoid this problem, it might be wise to combine attribute values into a more abstract attribute value. We will call this process attribute aggregation. It is also possible to allow the user to combine attributes interactively during the tree building process. We call this process manual abstraction of attribute values, see Figure 13. If we use the class label of each example, we consider the method as supervised discretization method. If we do not use the class label of the samples, we call them unsupervised discretization methods. We can partition the attribute values into two (k=1) or more intervals (k>1). Therefore, we distinguish between binary and multi-interval discretization methods, see Figure 13.

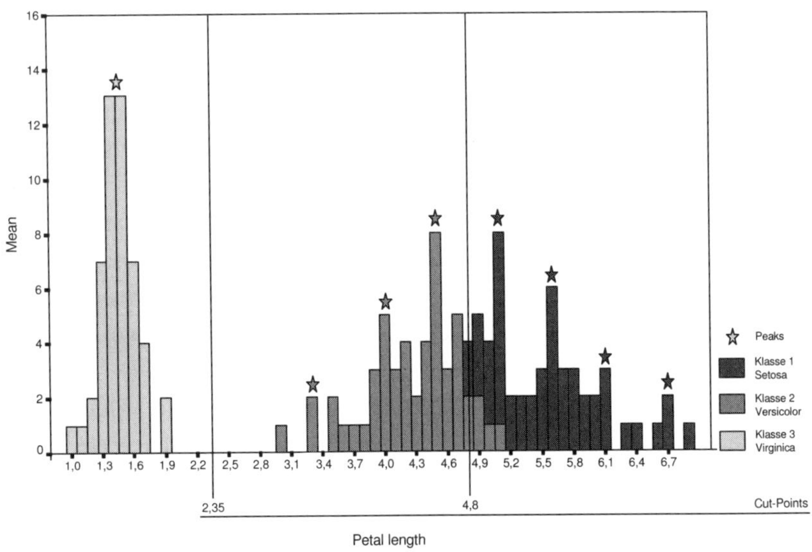

Figure 12. Histogram of attribute petal length and cut-points.

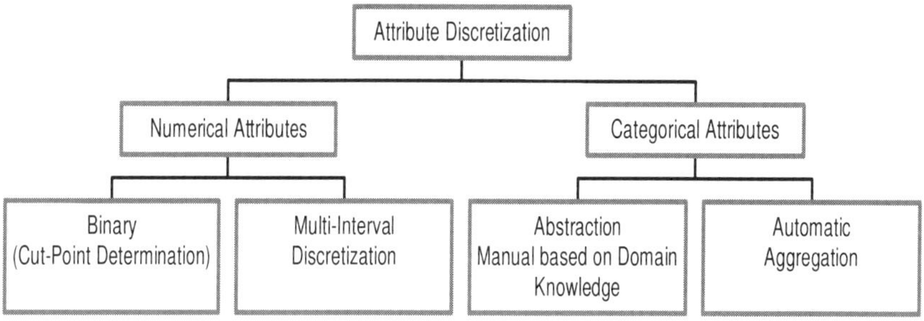

Figure 13. Overview of attribute discretization.

7.5.1 Binary Discretization

7.5.1.1 Binary discretization based on entropy

Decision tree induction algorithms like ID3 and C4.5 use the entropy criterion for the separation of attribute values into two intervals. On the attribute range between x_{min} and x_{max} each possible cut-point T is tested and the one that fullfils the following condition is chosen as cut-point T_A:

$$\text{IF} \quad I(A,T_A,S)=MIN \quad \text{THEN} \quad Select \quad T_A \quad for \quad T$$

with S the subsample set, A the attribute, and T the cut-point that separates the samples into subset S_1 and S_2. $I(A, T_A, S)$ is the entropy for the separation of the sample set into the subset S_1 and S_2:

$$I(A,T,S)=\frac{S_1}{S}I(S_1)+\frac{S_2}{S}I(S_2) \tag{10}$$

$$I(S)=-\sum_{j=1}^{m} p(C_i,S)\log_2 p(C_j,S) \tag{11}$$

The calculation of the cut-point is usually a time consuming process, since each possible cut-point is tested against the selection criteria. Therefore, some algorithms have been proposed that speed up the calculation of the right cut-point (Seidelmann, 1993).

7.5.1.2 Discretization based on inter- and intra-class variance

To find the threshold we can also do unsupervised discretization. Therefore, we consider the problem as a clustering problem in a one-dimensional space. The ratio between the inter-class variance s_B^2 of the two subsets S_1 and S_2 and the intra-class variance s_w^2 in S_1 and S_2 is used as criteria for finding the threshold:

$$s_B^2 = P_0(m_o - m)^2 + P_1(m_1 - m)^2 \; and \quad s_W^2 = P_0 s_0^2 + P_1 s_1^2 \tag{12}$$

The variances of the two groups are defined as:

$$s_0^2 = \sum_{i=x1}^{T} (x_i - m_0)^2 \frac{h(x_i)}{N} \; and \quad s_1^2 = \sum_{i=T}^{x2} (x_i - m_1)^2 \frac{h(x_i)}{N} \tag{13}$$

Where N is the number of all samples and $h(x_i)$ is the frequency of attribute value x_i. T is the threshold that will be tentatively moved over all attribute values. The values m_0 and m_1 are the mean values of the two groups that give us:

$$m = m_0 P_0 + m_1 P_1 \tag{14}$$

where P_0 and P_1 are the probabilities for the values of the subset 1 and 2, respectively:

$$P_0 = \sum_{i=x1}^{T} \frac{h(x_i)}{N} \; and \quad P_1 = \sum_{i=T}^{x2} \frac{h(x_i)}{N} \tag{15}$$

The selection criterion is:

$$\text{IF } \frac{s_B^2}{s_w^2} = MAX \text{ THEN } Select\ T_A\ for\ T$$

7.5.2 Multi-Interval Discretization

Binary interval discretization will result in binary decision trees. This might not always be the best way to model the problem. The resulting decision tree can be very bushy and its explanation capability might not be good. The error rate might increase, since the approximation of the decision space based on the binary decisions might not be advantageous and, therefore, leads to a higher approximation error. Depending on the data it might be better to create decision trees having more than two intervals for numerical attributes. For multi-interval discretization we have to solve two problems:

1. Find multi intervals and
2. Decide about the sufficient number of intervals.

The determination of the number of the intervals can be done statically or dynamically. In the latter case the number of intervals will be calculated automatically during the learning process, whereas in the static case the number of intervals will be given prior to the learning process by the user. Then the discretization process will calculate as many intervals as possible until it reaches the predefined number, regardless of whether the class distribution in the intervals is sufficient or not. This always results in trees having the same number of attribute partitions in each node. All algorithms described above can be used for this discretization process. The difference to binary interval discretization is that this process does not stop after the first cut-point has been determined, the process is repeated until the given number of intervals is reached (Perner *et al.*, 1998).

During a dynamic discretization process the sufficient number of intervals is automatically calculated. The resulting decision tree will have different attribute partitions in each node, depending on the class distribution of the attribute. For this process we need a criterion that allows us to determine the optimal number of intervals.

7.5.2.1 The basic (Search strategies) algorithm

In general, we have to test all possible combinations of k cut-points, in order to find the best cut-points. This would be computationally expensive. Since we assume that cut-points are always on the border of two distributions of x given class c, we have a heuristic method for our search strategy.

Discretization can be done bottom-up or top-down. In the bottom-up case, we will start with a finite number of intervals. In the worst case, these intervals are equivalent to the original attribute values. They can also be selected by the user or be estimated based on the maximum of the second-order probability distribution that will give us a hint where the class borders are located. Starting from that the algorithm merges intervals that do meet the merging criteria, until a stopping criterion is reached. In the top-down case, the algorithm first selects two intervals and recursively refines these intervals until the stopping criterion is reached.

7.5.2.2 Determination of the number of intervals

In the simplest case the user will specify how many intervals should be calculated for a numerical attribute. This procedure might become worse when there is no evidence of the required number of intervals in the remaining dataset. This will result in bushy decision trees, or will stop the tree building process sooner than what is needed. A better approach might be to calculate the number of intervals directly from the data.

Fayyad and Irani (1993) developed a stopping criterion based on the minimum description length principle. Based on this criterion the number of intervals is calculated for the remaining dataset during the decision tree induction process. This discretization procedure is called MLD-based discretization. Another criterion uses a cluster utility measure to determine the best suitable number of intervals (Perner, 2000).

7.5.2.3 Cluster utility criteria

Based on the inter-class variance and the intra-class variance we can create a cluster-utility measure that allows us to determine the optimal number of intervals. We assume that inter-class variance and intra-class variance are the inter-interval variance and intra-interval variance, respectively.

Let s_w^2 be the intra-class variance and s_B^2 be the inter-class variance. Then we can define our utility criterion as follow:

$$U = \frac{\sum_{k=1}^{n} s_{wk}^2 - s_{bk}^2}{n} \tag{16}$$

The number of intervals n is chosen for minimal U.

7.5.2.4 MLD-based criteria

The MLD-based criteria were introduced by Fayyad and Irani (1993). Discretization is done based on the gain ratio. The gain ratio $I(A, T, S)$ is tested after each new interval against the MLD-criteria:

$$I(A,T,S) > \frac{\log_2(N-1)}{N} + \frac{\nabla(A,T,S)}{N} \tag{17}$$

where N is the number of instances in the set S and

$$\nabla(A,T,S) = \log_2\left(3^k - 2\right) - \left[k \cdot I(S) - k_1 \cdot I(S_1) - k_2 I(S_2)\right] \tag{18}$$

One of the main problems with this discretization criterion is that it is relatively expensive. It must be evaluated n-1 times for each attribute (with n being the number of attribute values). Typically n is very large. Therefore, it would be good to have an algorithm which uses a reasonable assumption in order to reduce the computation time.

7.5.2.5 LVQ-based discretization

Vector quantization is also related to the notion of discretization (Perner *et al.*, 1998) for our experiment. LVQ (Kohonen, 1995) is a supervised learning algorithm. This method attempts to define class regions in the input data space. Firstly, a number of codebook vectors W_i labeled by a class are placed into the input space. Usually several codebook vectors are assigned to each class.

The learning algorithm is realized as follows. After an initialization of the neural net, each learning sample is presented one or several times to the net. The input vector X will be compared to all codebook vectors W in order to find the closest codebook vector W_c. The learning algorithm will try to optimize the similarity between the codebook vectors and the learning samples by shifting the codebook vectors in the direction of the input vector if the sample represents the same class as the closest codebook vector. In case of the codebook vector and the input vector having different classes, the codebook vector gets shifted away from the input vector, so that the similarity between these two decreases. All other codebook vectors remain unchanged. The following equations represent this idea:

$$\text{For equal classes: } W_C(t+1) = W_C(t) + \alpha(t) \cdot [X(t) - W_C(t)] \tag{19}$$

$$\text{For different classes: } W_C(t+1) = W_C(t) - \alpha(t) \cdot [X(t) - W_C(t)] \tag{20}$$

$$\text{For all other: } W_j(t+1) = W_j(t) \tag{21}$$

This behavior of the algorithms can be employed for discretization. A potential cut-point might be in the middle of the learned codebook vectors of two different classes. Figure 14 shows this method based on one attribute of the IRIS domain. Since this algorithm tries to optimize the misclassification probability, we expect to get good results. However, the proper initialization of the codebook vectors and the choice of learning rate $\alpha(t)$ is a crucial problem.

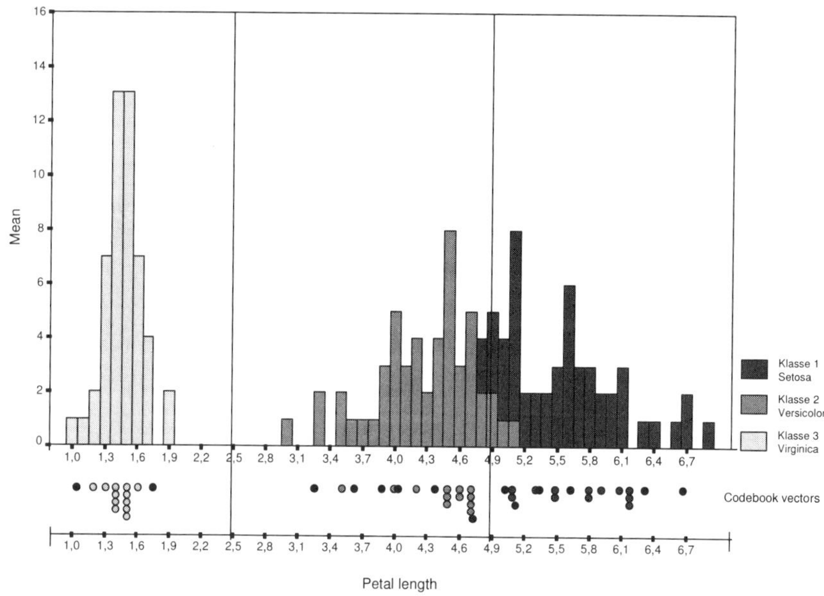

Figure 14. Class distribution of an attribute and codebook vectors.

7.5.2.6 Histogram-based discretization

A histogram-based method has been suggested first by Wu et al. (1975). They used this method in an interactive way during top-down decision tree building. By observing the histogram, the user selects the threshold which partitions the sample set in groups containing only samples of one class. In Perner et al. (1998) an automatic histogram-based method for feature discretization is described.

The class conditional distribution of one attribute a is calculated. The curve of the distribution is approximated by a first-order polynomial and the minimum square error method is used for calculating the coefficients:

$$E = \sum_{i=1}^{n} (a_1 x_i + a_0 - y_i)^2 \tag{22}$$

$$a_1 = \frac{\sum_{i=1}^{n} x_i \cdot i}{\sum_{i=1}^{n} i^2} \tag{23}$$

The cut-points are selected by finding two maxima of different classes situated next to each other.

We used this method in two ways. First, we used the histogram-based discretization method as described before. Second, we used a combined discretization method based on the distribution $p(a\,|\,a\ S_k)P(S_k)$ and the entropy-based minimization criteria. We followed the corollary derived by Fayyad and Irani (1993), which says that the entropy-based discretization criteria for finding a binary partition for a continuous attribute will always partition the data on a boundary point in the sequence of the examples ordered by the value of that attribute. A boundary point partitions the examples into two sets, having different classes. Taking into account this fact, we determine potential boundary points by finding the peaks of the distribution. If we found two peaks belonging to different classes, we used the entropy-based minimization criteria in order to find the exact cut-point between these two classes by evaluating each boundary point K with $P_i \leq K \leq P_{i+1}$ between these two peaks. An example is shown in Figure 15.

This method is not as time consuming as the other ones. We want to see if this method can be an alternative to the methods described before and if we can find a hybrid version which combines the advantages of the low computation time of the histogram-based method with the entropy minimization heuristic method in the context of discretization.

7.5.2.7 Chi-Merge discretization

The Chi-Merge algorithm introduced by Kerber (1992) consists of an initialization step and a bottom-up merging process, where intervals are continuously merged until a termination condition is met. Kerber used the Chi-Merge method statically. In our study we apply Chi-Merge dynamically to discretization.

The potential cut-points are investigated by testing two adjacent intervals by the χ^2 independence test. The statistical test value is:

$$\chi^2 = \sum_{i=1}^{m} \sum_{j=1}^{k} \frac{(A_{ij} - E_{ij})^2}{E_{ij}} \quad (24)$$

where $m=2$ (the intervals being compared), k - number of classes, A_{ij} - number of examples in the *i-th* interval and the *j-th* class, R_i - number of examples in the *i-th* interval $R_i = \sum_{j=1}^{k} A_{ij}$; C_j - number of examples in the *j-th* class $C_j = \sum_{i=1}^{m} A_{ij}$; N – the total number of examples $N = \sum_{j=1}^{k} C_j$; E_{ij} – the expected frequency $E_{ij} = \frac{R_i \cdot C_j}{N}$.

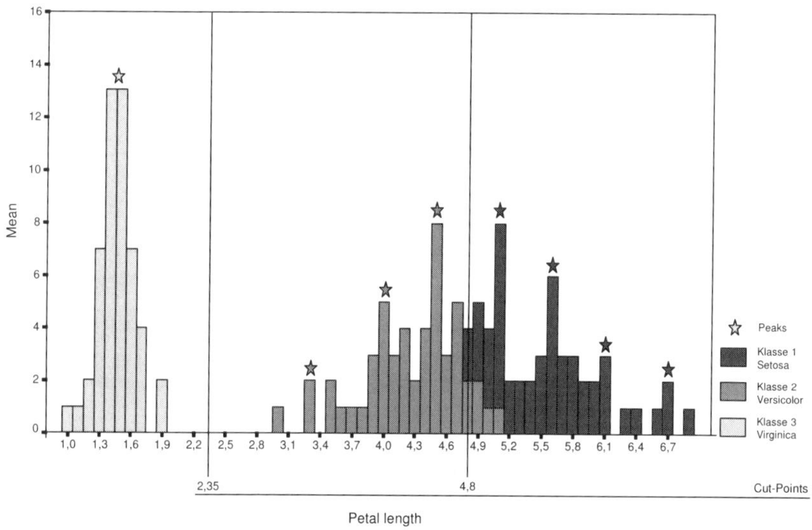

Figure 15. Examples sorted by attribute values for attribute A and labeled peaks.

Firstly, all boundary points will be used for cut-points. In the second step one can compute the χ^2-value for each pair of adjacent intervals. The two adjacent intervals with the lowest χ^2-value will merge together. This step is repeated continuously until all χ^2-values exceed a given threshold. The value for the threshold is determined by selecting a desired significance level and then using a table or formula to obtain the χ^2.

7.5.3 The Influence of Discretization Methods on the Resulting Decision Tree

Figures 16 to 19 show the learned decision trees based on different discretization methods. They show that the chosen kind of discretization method influences the attribute selection. The attribute in the root node is the same for the decision tree based on Chi-Merge discretization (see Figure 16) and LVQ-based discretization (see Figure 18). The calculated intervals are rarely the same. Since the tree generation based on histogram discretization requires always two cut-points and since in the remaining sample set there is no evidence for two cut-points, the learning process stops after the first level.

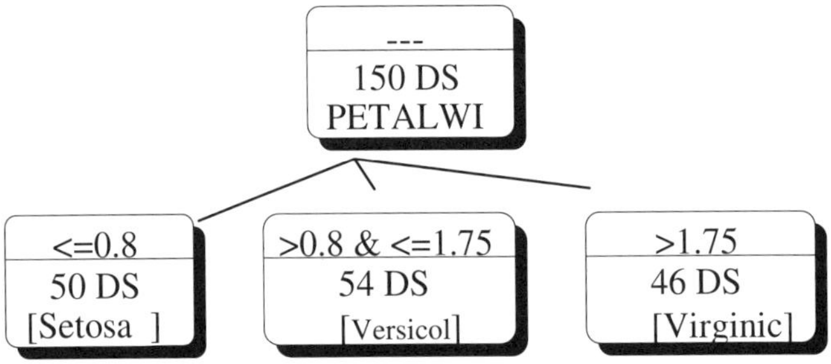

Figure 16. Decision tree based on Chi-Merge discretization (k=3).

The two trees generated based on histogram-based discretization and MLD principle-based discretization have also the same attribute in the root. The intervals are also selected slightly differently by the two methods. The tree in Figure 18 is the bushiest tree. However, the error rate (see Table 3) of this tree that was calculated based on leave-one out is not better than the error rate of the tree shown in Figure 17. Since the decision is based on more attributes (see Figure 18), the experts might not like this tree much more than the tree shown in Figure 19.

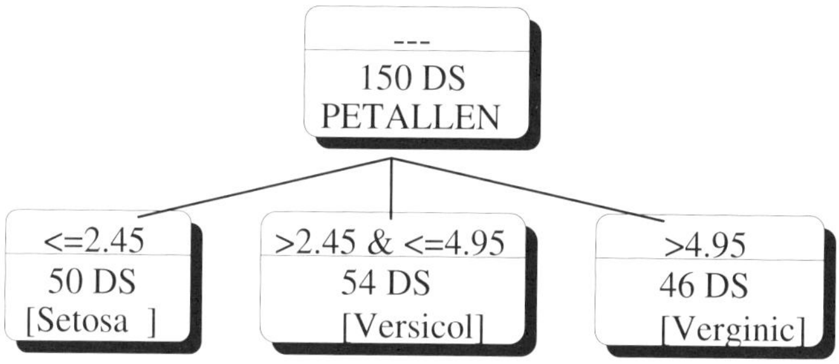

Figure 17. Decision tree based on histogram-based discretization (k=3).

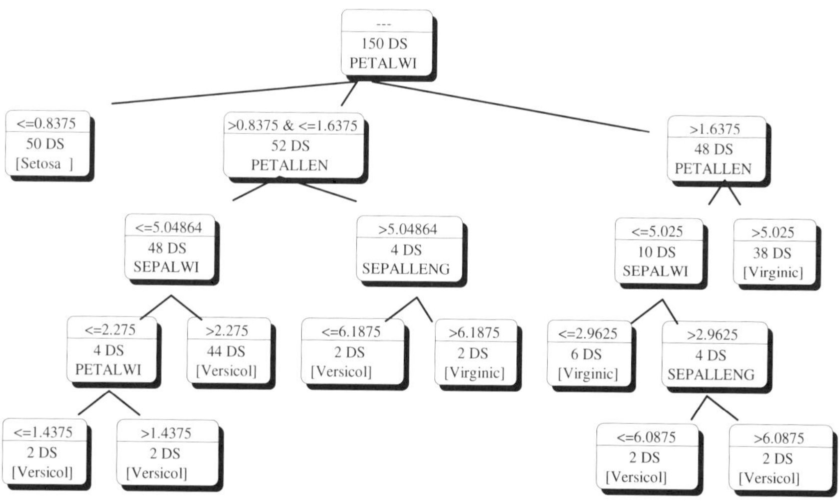

Figure 18. Decision tree based on LVQ-based discretization.

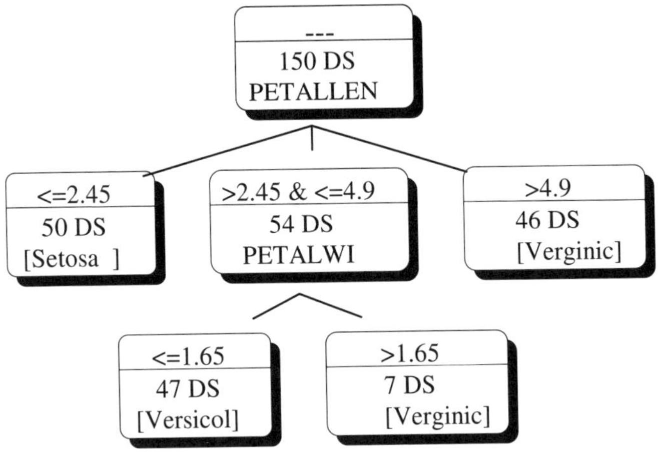

Figure 19. Decision tree based on MLD-principle discretization.

Table 3. Error rate for decision trees based on different discretization methods.

Descretization Method	Error Rate	
	Unpruned Tree	Pruned Tree
Chi-Merge	4.67	4.67
Histogram-based Discr.	6	6
LVQ-based Discr.	4.67	5.33
MLD-based Discr.	4.67	4.67

7.5.4 Discretization of Categorical or Symbolic Attributes

7.5.4.1 Manual abstraction of attribute values

In opposition to numerical attributes, symbolic attributes may have a large number of attribute values. Branching on such an attribute causes a partition into small sub sample sets that will often lead to a quick stop of the tree building process or even to trees with low explanation capabilities. One way to avoid this problem is the construction of meaningful abstractions on the attribute level at hand, based on a careful analysis of the attribute list (Perner *et al.*, 1996). This has to be done in the preparation phase. The abstraction can only be done on the semantic level. Advantageous is that the resulting interval can be named with a symbol that a human can understand.

7.5.4.2 Automatic aggregation

However, it is also possible to do abstraction automatically on symbolic attribute values during the tree building process, based on the class-attribute interdependence. In that case the discretization process is done bottom-up, starting from the initial attribute intervals. The process stops when the criterion is satisfied.

7.6 Pruning

If the tree is allowed to grow up to its maximum size, it is likely that it over-fits the training data. Noise in the attribute values and class information will amplify this problem. The tree building process will produce sub-trees that fit to noise. This unwarranted complexity may cause an increased error rate when classifying unseen cases. This problem can be avoided by pruning the tree, i.e., replacing sub-trees by leaves based on some statistical criteria. This idea is illustrated in Figures 20 and 21 on the iris dataset. The unpruned tree is large and bushy with an estimated error rate of 6.67%. Up to the second level of the tree subtrees get replaced by leaves. The resulting pruned tree is smaller and the error rate becomes 4.67%, calculated with cross-validation.

Pruning methods can be categorized either in pre-pruning or post-pruning methods. In pre-pruning, the tree growing process is stopped according to a stopping criterion before the tree reaches its maximal size. In contrast to that, in post-pruning, the tree is first developed to its maximum size and afterwards it is pruned back according to a pruning procedure.

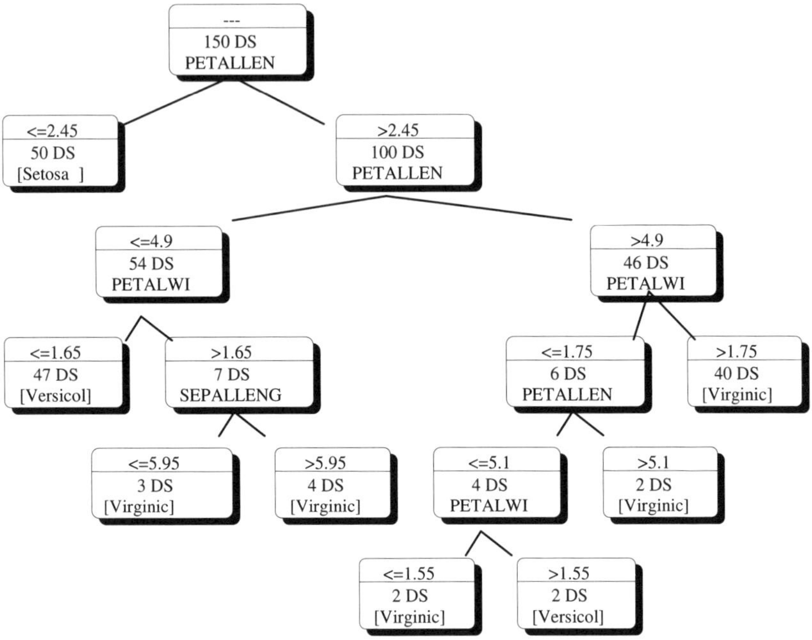

Figure 20. Unpruned decision free for the iris dataset.

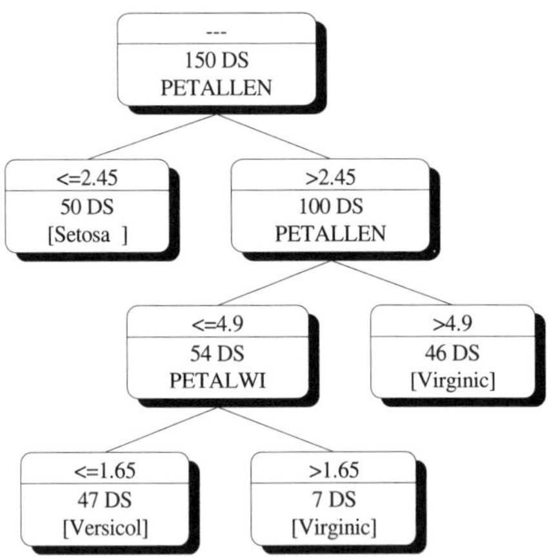

Figure 21. Pruned tree for the iris dataset based on minimal error pruning.

7.6.1 Overview of Pruning Methods

Post-pruning methods can mainly be categorized into methods that use an independent pruning set and methods that do not use a separate pruning set (see Figure 22). The latter one can be distinguished further into methods that use traditional statistical measures, re-sampling methods like cross-validation and bootstrapping, and code-length motivated methods. Here we only want to consider cost-complexity pruning and confidence-interval pruning that belong to the methods with separate pruning sets. An overview of all the methods can be found in Kuusisto (1998).

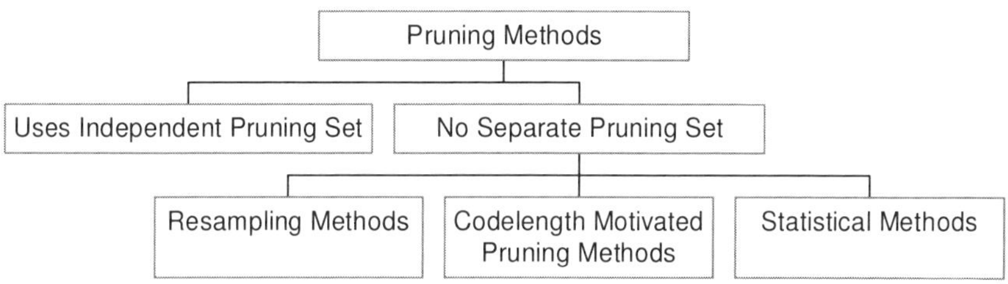

Figure 22. General overview of pruning methods.

7.6.2 Cost-Complexity Pruning

The cost-complexity pruning method was introduced by Breiman et al. (1984). The main idea is to keep the balance between the misclassification costs and the complexity of the subtree (T) described by the number of leaves. Therefore, Breiman created a cost-complexity criterion as follows:

$$CP(T) = \frac{E(T)}{N(T)} + \alpha \times Leaves(T) \tag{25}$$

with $E(T)$ being the number of misclassified samples of the subtree T, $N(T)$ – the number of samples belonging to the subtree T, $Leaves(T)$ -the number of leaves of the subtree T, and α, a free defined parameter, often called complexity parameter. The subtree whose replacement causes the least costs is replaced by a leaf:

$$\text{IF} \quad \alpha = \frac{M}{N(T)(Leaves(T)-1)} \Rightarrow MIN \quad \text{THEN} \quad Substitute\_Subtree$$

The algorithm tentatively replaces all subtrees by leaves, if the calculated value for α is minimal compared to the values α of the other replacements. This results in a sequence of trees $T_0 < T_2 < \ldots < T_i < \ldots < T_n$ where T_0 is the original tree and T_n is the root. The trees are evaluated on an independent dataset. Among this set of tentative trees the smallest tree is selected as the final tree that minimizes the misclassifications on the independent dataset. This is called the 0-SE (0-standard error) selection method. Other approaches use a relaxed version, called 1-SE method, in which the smallest tree does not exceed $E_{min}+SE(E_{min})$. E_{min} is the minimal number of errors that a decision tree T_i yields and $SE(E_{min})$ is the standard deviation of an empirical error estimated from the independent dataset. $SE(E_{min})$ is calculated as follows:

$$SE(E_{\min}) = \sqrt{\frac{E_{\min} \cdot (N - E_{\min})}{N}}$$ with N being the number of test samples.

7.7 Some General Remarks

Decision tree induction is a powerful method for learning classification knowledge from examples. In contrast to rule induction, decision trees present the resulting knowledge in a hierarchical manner that suits the human reasoning behavior. Nonetheless, decision trees can be converted into a set of rules.

We have given a sound description of decision tree induction methods that can learn binary and *n*-ary decision trees. We introduced the basic steps of decision tree learning and described the methods on which our tool *Cell_Interpret* is based.

Some general remarks should help the reader to better understand the results and the behavior of decision tree induction. One main problem is the dependence of the attribute selection on the order of the attributes.

Always the attribute that appears first in the data table will be chosen in the case where two attributes show both the best possible values for the selection criteria. Whereas this may not influence the accuracy of the resulting model, the explanation capability might become worse. A trained expert might not find the attribute he/she is usually using. Therefore, his/her trust in the model may be affected. One way to get around this problem would be to let the user select which one of the attributes the tree should use. However, in that case the method would act in an interactive way and not automatically. In the case of large data bases it might be preferable to neglect this problem.

Like other learning techniques, decision tree induction strongly depends on the sample distribution. If the class samples are not equally distributed, the induction process might rely on the distribution of the largest class. Usually, users ignore this problem. They run the experiment, even if one class dominates in the sample set, while others are only represented by a few examples. We have demonstrated the influence of the class distribution in the sample set on the IRIS dataset (see Figures 23, 24, and 25, and also Table 4).

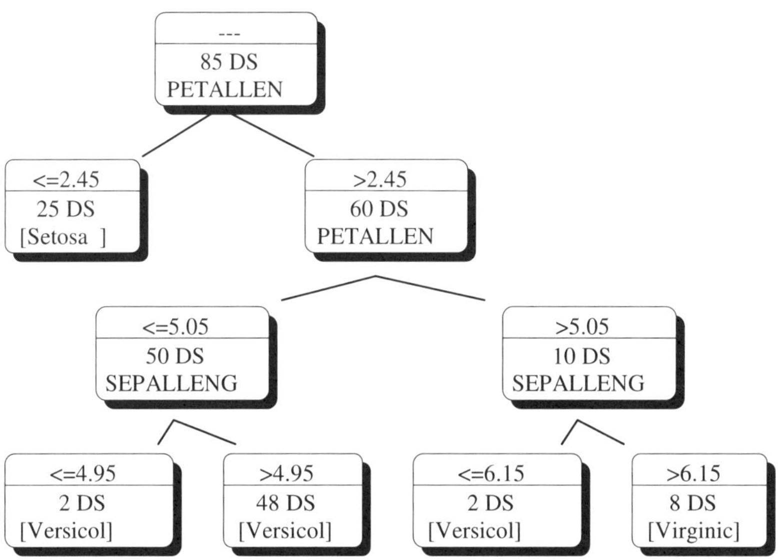

Figure 23. Decision tree for the iris dataset distribution_1.

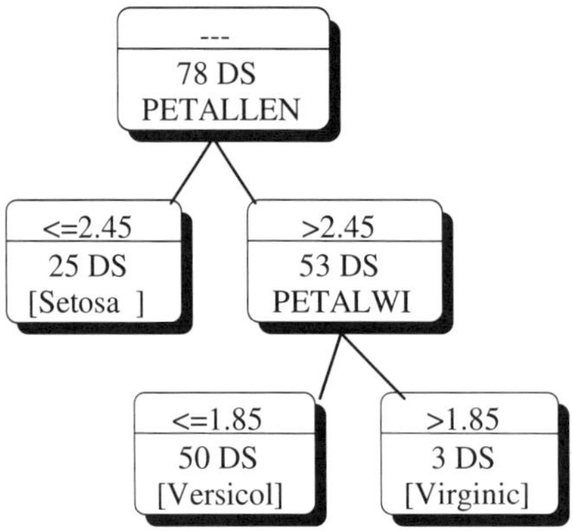

Figure 24. DT iris dataset distribution_2.

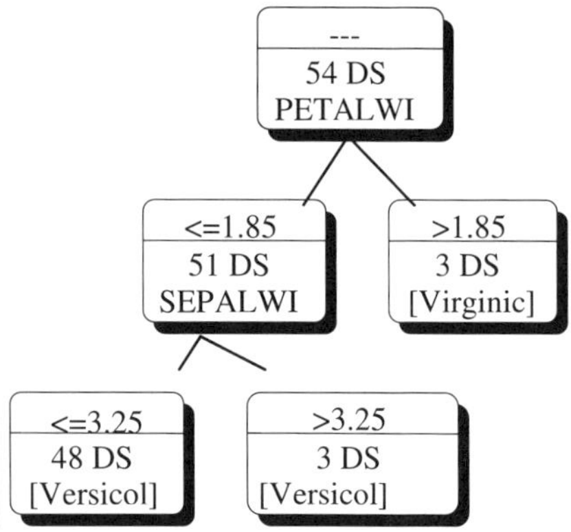

Figure 25. DT iris dataset distribution_3.

Table 4. Error rate for different sample sizes.

Class Distribution				Error Rate	
No.	Setosa	Versicolor	Virginic	Unpruned	Pruned
	50	50	50	6.66	4.66
1	25	50	9	5.88	5.88
2	25	50	3	2.56	2.56
3	1	50	3	7.407	5.55

It can be seen that for the first two examples the resulting decision tree is more or less the same for the top level of the trees as the original tree, but the upper levels have changed. As the class distribution gets even worse, the tree changes totally. However, the error rate calculated with the "leave one out method" stays in the range of the original tree.

A categorical attribute with n attribute values branches into n subsets when the attribute is used for splitting in a node. If the distribution of data is equal in the dataset, the entry dataset m will result in n subsets of size $k=m/n$. It is clear that the larger n is, the smaller is the size of the k

subsets. As a result of using categorical attributes with many attribute values the decision tree building process will stop very soon, since the remaining subsets will meet the stopping criteria very soon.

8. The Case-Based Reasoning Unit

It is difficult to apply decision trees in domains where generalized knowledge is lacking. However, often there is a need for a prediction system, even though there is not enough generalized knowledge. Such a system should (a) solve problems using the already stored knowledge and (b) capture new knowledge, making it immediately available to solve the next problem. To accomplish these tasks case-based reasoning is useful. Case-based reasoning explicitly uses past cases from the domain expert's successful or failing experience.

Therefore, case-based reasoning can be seen as a method for problem-solving as well as a method to capture new experience in an incremental fashion and make it immediately available for problem-solving. It can be seen as a learning and knowledge discovery approach, since it can capture from new experience some general knowledge such as case classes, prototypes and some higher level concepts. We find these methods especially applicable to inspection and diagnosis tasks. In the case of these applications people would rather store prototypical images than a large set of different images into a digital image catalogue.

We have developed a unit for *Cell_Interpret* that can perform similarity determination between cases, as well as prototype selection (Chang, 1974) and feature weighting (Wetterscherek *et al.*, 1995). We call $x_n' \in \{x_1, x_2, \ldots, x_n\}$ a nearest neighbor to x if $\min d(x_i, x) = d(x_n', x)$, where $i = 1,2,\ldots,n$. The instance x is classified into category C_n, if x_n is the nearest neighbor to x and x_n belongs to class C_n.

In the case of the k-nearest neighbors we require k-samples of the same class to fulfill the decision rule. As a distance measure we use the

Euclidean distance. Prototype selection from a set of samples is done by Chang's Algorithm (Chang, 1974). Suppose a training set T is given as $T = \{t^1,\ldots,t^m\}$. The idea of the algorithm is as follows. We start with every point in T as a prototype. We then successively merge any two closest prototypes p^1 and p^2 of the same class by a new prototype p, if the merging will not downgrade the classification of its patterns in T. The new prototype p may simply be the average vector of p^1 and p^2. We continue the merging process until the number of incorrect classifications of the patterns in T starts to increase.

The wrapper approach is used for selecting a feature subset from the whole set of features. This approach conducts a search for a good feature subset by using the k-NN classifier itself as an evaluation function. The 1-fold cross-validation method is used for estimating the classification accuracy and the best-first search strategy is used for the search over the state space of possible feature combinations. The algorithm terminates if we have not found an improved accuracy over the last k search states. The feature combination that gave the best classification accuracy is the remaining feature subset. After we have found the best feature subset for our problem, we try to further improve our classifier by applying a feature weighting technique.

The weights of each feature w_i are changed by a constant value δ: $w_i = w_i \pm\delta$. If the new weight causes an improvement of the classification accuracy, the weight will be updated accordingly; if not, the weight will remain as it is. After the last weight has been tested the constant δ will be divided into half and the procedure is repeated. The procedure terminates if the difference between the classification accuracy of two iterations is less than a predefined threshold.

9. Conceptual Clustering as Knowledge Discovery

The intention of clustering is to find groups of similar cases among the data according to the new observations to be classified. This can be done based on one feature or a combination of features (Liao, 2005). The resulting groups give an idea how the data may fit together and how they can be classified into interesting categories.

Classical clustering methods only create clusters, but do not explain why a cluster has been established. Conceptual clustering methods build clusters and explain why a set of objects forms a cluster. Thus, conceptual clustering is a type of learning by observations and it is a way of summarizing data in an understandable manner (Fisher, 1987). In contrast to hierarchical clustering methods, conceptual clustering methods build the classification hierarchy not only based on merging two groups but the algorithmic properties are flexible enough to dynamically fit the hierarchy to the data. This allows incremental incorporation of new instances into the existing hierarchy and updating this hierarchy according to the new instance.

A concept hierarchy is a directed graph in which the root node represents the set of all input instances and the terminal nodes represent individual instances. Internal nodes stand for sets of instances attached to the nodes and represent a super-concept. The super-concept can be represented by a generalized representation of this set of instances, such as the prototype, the medoid or a user-selected instance. Therefore a concept C, called a class, in the concept hierarchy is represented by an abstract concept description and a list of pointers to each child concept $M(C)=\{C_1, C_2, ..., C_i, ..., C_n\}$, where C_i is the child concept, called a subclass of concept C.

Our conceptual clustering algorithm presented here is based on similarities (Jänichen *et al.*, 2006). Due to its concept description, it explicitly supplies for each cluster a generalized shape case which represents this group and a measure for the degree of its generalization. The result will be a sequence of partitions (concept hierarchy), where the root node contains the complete set of input cases and hence it follows that this node is represented by the most generalized case. The nodes in lower hierarchy levels are comprised of fewer cases (at least one) and are more specific.

In addition to *create* and *add*, we also introduced the operators *split* and *merge* into the algorithm. We prefer to apply these local operators because they preserve the incremental fashion of the algorithm. Order dependency also decreases sufficiently, even if it is not guaranteed that the local changes have a sufficiently strong effect on the global data.

The algorithm (see Figure 26) implements a top-down method. Initially the concept hierarchy only consists of an empty root node. A new case is placed into the actual concept hierarchy level by level, beginning with the root node until a terminal node is reached. In each hierarchy level, one of these four different kinds of operations is performed:

- The new case is incorporated into an existing child node,
- a new empty child node is created where the new case is incorporated,
- two existing nodes are merged to form a single node where the new case is incorporated, and
- an existing node is split into its child nodes.

The new case is tentatively placed into the next hierarchy level by applying all of these operations. Finally that operation is performed which gives the best score to the partition according to the evaluation criteria. A proper utility function prefers compact and well-separated clusters. These are clusters with small inner-cluster variances and large inter-class variances. Thus we calculate the score of a partition comprised of the clusters $\{X_1, X_2, \ldots X_m\}$ by:

$$SCORE = \frac{1}{m} \sum_{i=1}^{m} p_i \left(SB_i - SW_i \right),$$

where m is the number of clusters in this partition, p_i is the relative frequency of the i-th cluster, SB_i is the inter-cluster variance and SW_i is the intra-cluster variance of the i-th cluster. The normalization according to m is necessary to compare partitions of different sizes.

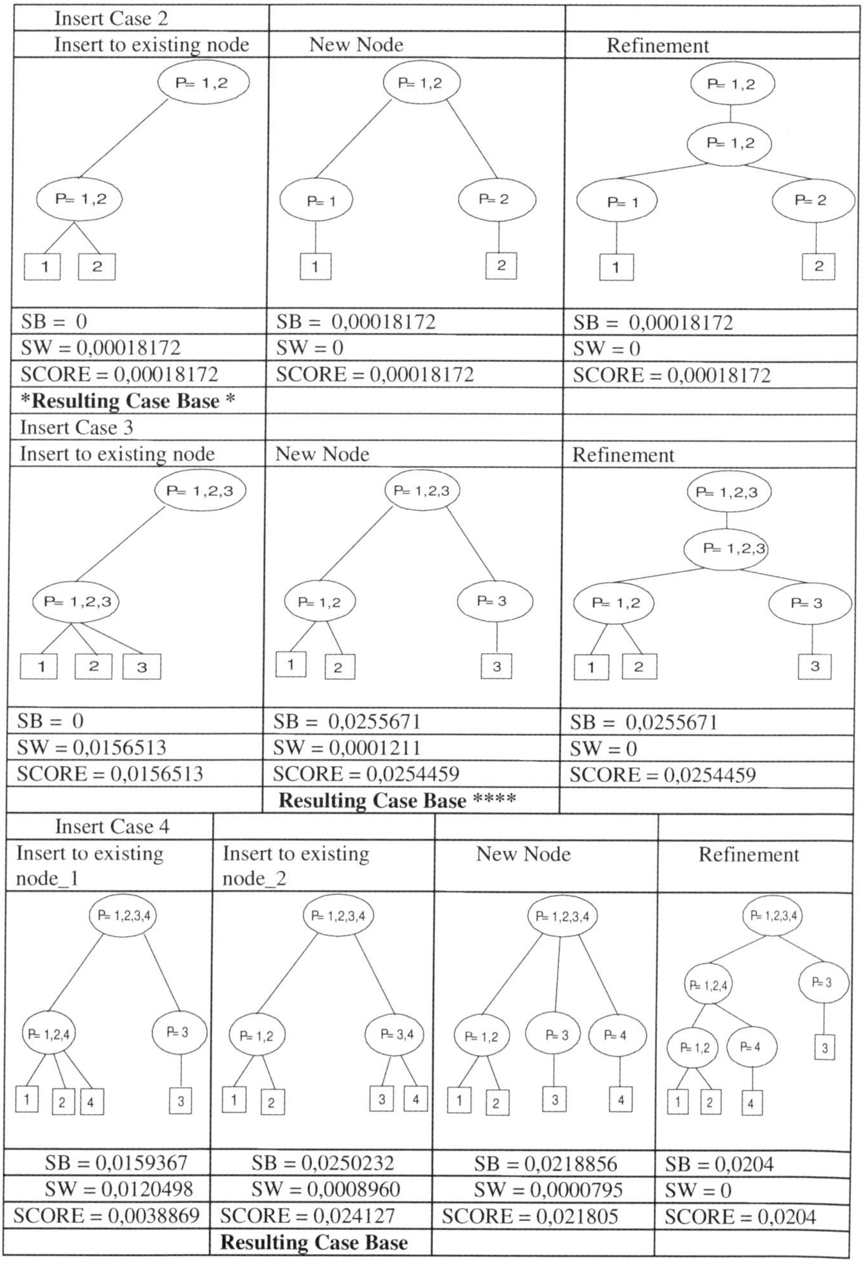

Figure 26. Demonstration of the concept clustering algorithm.

The relative frequency p_i of the i -th cluster is: $p_i = n_i / n$, where n_i is the number of cases in the i -th cluster and n is the number of cases in the parent node. The inter-cluster variance of a cluster X is calculated by: $SB_X = \frac{1}{n_x} \sum_{i=1}^{n_x} d(x_i, \bar{\mu}_P)^2$, where $\bar{\mu}_P$ is the cluster centre of the parent node and x_i are the instances in all child nodes.

The output of our algorithm for applying eight exemplary shape cases of fungal strain *Ulocladium Botrytis* is shown in Figure 27. On the top level the root node is shown which is comprised of all input cases. The tree is successively partitioned into nodes until each input case forms its own cluster.

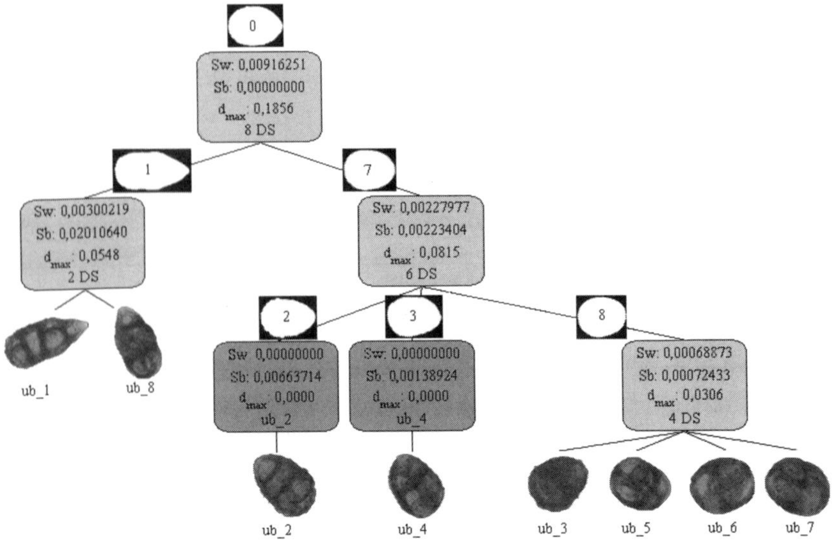

Figure 27. Output of the conceptual clustering algorithm for 2-D shapes obtained from fungal spores.

The main advantage of our conceptual clustering algorithm is that it brings along a concept description. Thus, in comparison to agglomerative clustering methods, it is easy to understand why a set of cases forms a cluster. During the clustering process the representative case, and also the variances and maximum distances in relation to this representative case are calculated, since they are part of the concept description. The algorithm is of incremental fashion, because it is possible to incorporate new cases into the existing learned hierarchy.

10. The Overall Image Mining Procedure

The whole procedure for image mining is summarized in Figure 28. It is partially based on our developed methodology for image knowledge engineering (Perner, 1994). The process can be divided into five major steps as follows:

1. Brainstorming
2. Interviewing process
3. Collection of image descriptions into the database
4. Mining experiment, and
5. Review.

Brainstorming is the process of understanding the problem domain and identifying the important knowledge pieces on which the knowledge engineering process will focus.

For the interviewing process we used our developed methodology for image knowledge engineering described in Perner (1994) in order to elicit the basic attributes as well as their attribute values. Then the proper image processing and feature extraction algorithms are identified for the automatic extraction of the features and their values.

Based on these results we then collected into the data base image readings done by the expert and done by the automatic image analysis and feature extraction tool. The resulting database is the basis for our mining experiment. The error rate of the mining result was then determined, based on sound statistical methods such as cross-validation. The error rate and the rules were then reviewed together by the experts. Depending on the quality of the results the mining process stops or goes into a second trail, starting either at the top with the elicitation of new attributes or at a deeper level, e.g. with reading new images or incorporating new image analysis and feature extraction procedures.

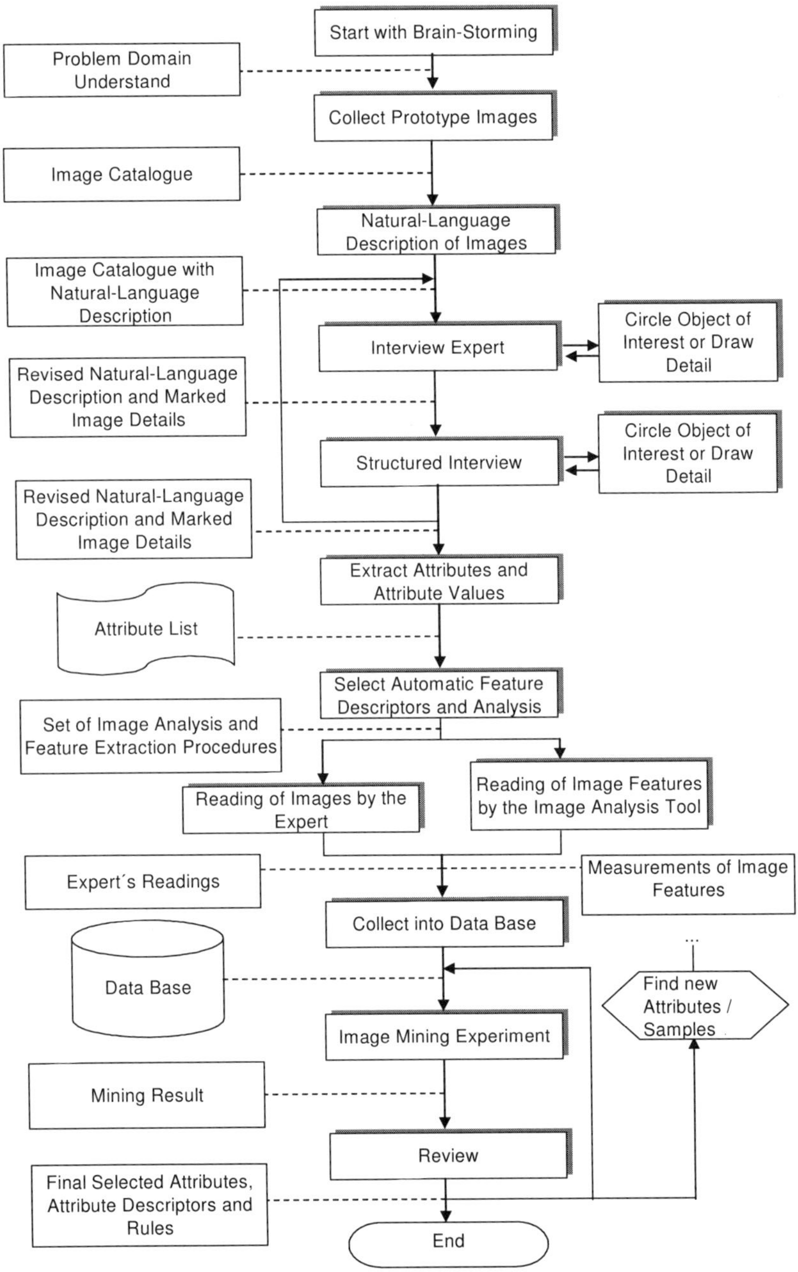

Figure 28. The overall image mining procedure.

The incorporation of new image analysis and feature extraction procedures seems to be an interactive and iterative process at the moment, since it is not possible to provide ad-hoc sufficient image analysis procedures for all image features and details appearing in the real world. The mining procedure stops as soon as the expert is satisfied with the results.

10.1 A Case Study

The scope of our work was to mine the images for proper classification knowledge, so that it can be used in medical practice for diagnosis or for teaching novices. Besides that it should give us the basis for the development of an automatic image diagnosis system. Our experiment was supported by an immunologist who is an expert in the field and acts as a specialist to other laboratories in case of diagnostically complex cases.

10.2 Brainstorming and Image Catalogue

First, we started with a brainstorming process that helped us to understand the expert's domain and to identify the basic sources of knowledge. We could mainly identify four sources of knowledge: The HEp-2 cell atlas, the expert, slide preparation and a book describing the basic parts of a cell and their appearance.

Next the expert collected prototype images for each of the six classes appearing most frequently in his daily practice. The expert wrote down a natural language description for each of these images. As a result we obtained an image catalogue having a prototype image for each class (see Figure 1) and associated to each image is a natural language description of the expert (see Table 1).

10.3 The Interviewing Process

Based on these image descriptions we started our interviewing process. First, we only tried to understand the meaning of the expert description in terms of the image features. We let him circle the interesting object in the image to understand the meaning of the description. After having done this we went into a structured interviewing process asking for specific details, such as: "Why do you think this object is *fine-speckled* and the other one is not? Please describe the difference between these two." This helped us to verify the expert description and to make the object features more distinct.

Finally, we could extract from the natural language description the basic vocabulary (attributes and attribute values, see Table 1) and associate a meaning to each attribute.

In a last step we reviewed the chosen attributes and the attribute values with the expert and found a common agreement on the chosen terms. The result was an attribute list which is the basis for the description of object details in the images. Furthermore, we identified from the whole set of the feature descriptors the set of a feature descriptor which might be useful for the objective measurement of image features. In our case we found that describing the cells by their boundary and calculating the size and the contour of the cell might be appropriate. The different descriptors of the nuclei of the cells might be sufficiently described by the texture descriptor of our image analysis tool.

10.4 Collection of Image Descriptions into the Database

At this point we could start to collect a data base of image descriptions based on these attributes and attribute values as well as on feature measurements calculated with the help of the image analysis tool. For our experiment we used a dataset of 120 images. The dataset contained 6 classes, each equally distributed. For each class we had 20 images.

The expert used the image analysis tool and displayed one after another each image from our database. He watched the images on display and described the image content on the basis of our attribute list and fed the attribute values into the database. Besides that he marked the objects of interest in the image on display and used the necessary feature descriptors selected during the interviewing process and provided by the image analysis unit to measure the image features such as size, contour, and texture. The resulting values for these features are automatically fed into the database and stored together with the expert's image description into the database (see Figure 29).

Class	Contour	Area	Shape Factor	Mean	...	NUCLEOLI	CHROMO	Cytoplasma	Background
100000	14,3734	14,3189	144,2812	87,1507	...	1	1	0	1
100320	10,3675	7,2986	147,2687	144,6974	...	1	0	0	0
320200	11,9142	9,4348	150,4512	132,5286	...	2	0	0	1
200000	9,0332	5,2114	156,5795	94,5199	...	2	0	0	1
...	...	...	...	...	...	...	...	...	...

Figure 29. Excerpt from the database.

10.5 The Image Mining Experiment

The collected dataset was then given to the tool *ImageMiner*. The decision tree induction algorithm that showed the best results on this dataset is based on the entropy criterion for the attribute selection, cut-point strategy for the attribute discretization and minimal error reduction pruning. We performed three experiments. First, we learned a decision tree only based on the image reading by the expert; then we learned a decision tree only based on the automatically calculated image features; and finally, we learned a decision tree based on a database containing both feature descriptions. The resulting decision tree for the expert's reading is shown in Figure 30 and the resulting decision tree for the expert's reading together with the measured image features is shown in Figure 31. We do not show the tree for the measured image features, since the tree is too complex. The error rate was evaluated by leave-one-out cross-validation.

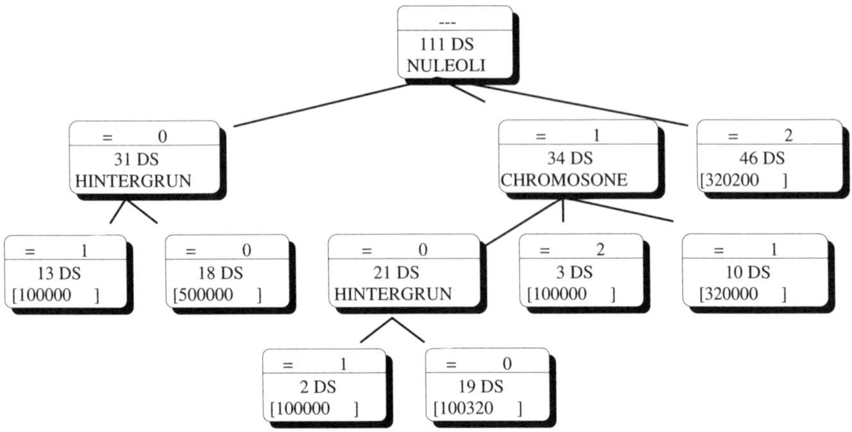

Figure 30. Decision tree obtained from expert's readings.

The error rate of the decision trees from the first two experiments is higher than the error rate made by the expert (see Table 5). None of the trees, whether based on the expert's reading or based on the measured image features, give a sufficiently low error rate. Only the combined database from the expert's reading and measured image features gives us an error rate that comes close to an expert's error rate.

Table 5. Error rate for decision trees obtained from the different data bases.

	Error Rate		
Dataset	Expert	Unpruned Tree	Pruned Tree
Original Dataset	25 %		
Expert Readings		27.9 %	27.9 %
Automatic Feature Analysis		27.9 %	27.9 %
Combined Dataset		6.9 %	6.9 %

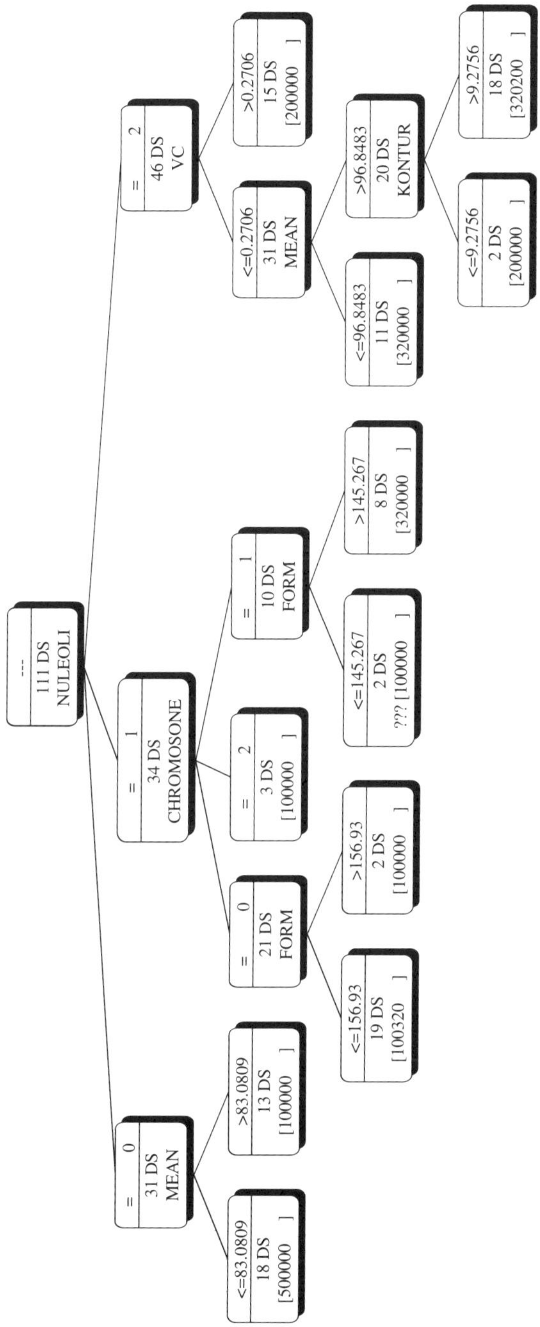

Figure 31. Decision tree obtained from both expert's readings and image readings.

10.6 Review

The tree created based on the image readings from the expert has an error rate of 27.9% (see Table 5). Under the assumption that the class labels represent the true class (gold standard), we can only conclude that there is a knowledge gap. There must be some hidden knowledge which the expert is using during decision making, but he could not make this knowledge explicit during the interviewing process. Here we have an example for the problem "difference between showing and naming". However, the expert's error rate is also high.

Our first objection was: Is the assumption that the class label is the true class label true or not? As far as we know the chemical investigation of the serum which was used to determine the gold standard does not accurately discriminate between the different classes. The experiment based on the features automatically measured in the images gives us no better results. The resulting tree is very bushy and deep and uses almost all attributes.

Only the combination between the expert's readings and the readings by the image analysis unit shows us reasonable results. The feature "nucleoli" is the most important feature and the correct description of the nucleoli will improve the results dramatically. During the image analysis phase we did not describe this object separately. The hope was that the texture descriptor for the whole cell is sensitive enough to model the different visual appearances of the different cells. The experiment shows that only the combination of basic image descriptors from the image analysis with expert reading gave sufficient good results. Therefore, we believe that our first objection concerning the true class label does not hold any more. We think that in order to improve the accuracy of the classifier, we must find a good feature descriptor for the different appearances of the object nucleoli.

10.7 Lessons learned

We have found out that our methodology of data mining allows a user to learn the decision model and the relevant diagnostic features. A user can independently use such a methodology of data mining in practice. He/She can easily perform different experiments until he/she is satisfied with the result. By doing so, he/she can explore his/her application and find out the connection between different knowledge sources. However, some problems should be taken into account for future system design.

As we have already pointed out in a previous experiment (Perner *et al.*, 1996), an expert tends to specify symbolic attributes by means of a large number of attribute values. For instance in this experiment the expert specified for the attribute "margin" fifteen attribute values such as "non-sharp", "sharp", "non-smooth", "smooth", and so on. A large number of attribute values will result in small sub-sample sets soon after the tree building process started. This may result in a fast termination of the tree building process. This is also true for small sample sets that are usual in medicine. Therefore, a careful analysis of the attribute list should be done after the physician has specified it.

During the process of building the tree, the algorithm picks the attribute with the best attribute selection value. If two attributes have the same value, the one that appears first in the attribute list will be chosen. That might not always be the attribute the expert himself/herself would have chosen. In order to avoid this problem, we think that in this case we should allow the expert to choose manually the attribute that he/she prefers. We expect that this procedure will bring the resulting decision model closer to the expert's one.

The developed image analysis tool allows extracting image features (see Sections 3 and 4). It supported the analysis and exploration of other image diagnosis tasks, such as the analysis of heep follicle and lymph nodule analysis. It proved to be very useful for the analysis of microscopic images of different cell-based assays. New applications might require further feature descriptors. Therefore, the image analysis tool must have an open architecture that allows incorporating new feature descriptors into the tool.

Compared to our first version of the image-mining tool, the new features of case-based image segmentation, case-based reasoning and clustering gave a new flexibility to the image mining process depending on the characteristics of the data of the particular application. The clustering method allowed discovering new groups according to the considered observation(s) that could be used further for the construction of the prediction model. Case-based image segmentation gave the flexibility needed to discover objects of interest in different image modalities and qualities. In the case of rare data or image catalogues case-based reasoning was the right method to construct a decision model and to acquire new images in incremental fashion.

11. Conclusions and Further Work

In this chapter we have presented our methods and the methodology for image mining. Based on this we built our system called *Cell_Interpret*. This tool has shown excellent performance for a wide range of image mining tasks for microscopic cell images. The tool is comprised of a wide range of functions, such as functions for image analysis, feature extraction, image interpretation, and data mining and knowledge discovery. We have explained the methods underlying *Cell_Interpret's* processing functions and how to apply them in practice. For the image segmentation we have developed a case-based image segmentation technique that is flexible and robust enough to deal with different image qualities and the limited dataset problem. We have also described the feature extraction methods recently that were implemented in the feature extraction unit. Our developed texture descriptor is flexible enough to describe the different pattern appearances on cells.

The data mining and knowledge discovery unit is based on a unit for decision tree induction, case-based reasoning, and conceptual clustering. The most flexible unit right now is the decision tree induction unit. We have explained the methods underlying this unit and explained it in a methodological way, so that an interested user understands the behavior of the methods and the results he/she can obtain with them. The recent case-based reasoning and the conceptual clustering method have been explained. Finally we gave a case study on the HEp-2 cell image interpretation and explained the results.

We were able to learn the important attributes needed for image interpretation and to understand the way in which these attributes were used for decision-making by applying data mining methods to the database of image descriptions. We showed how the domain vocabulary should be set up to get good results and which techniques should be used in order to check the reliability of the chosen features.

Although we are focusing on the analysis of cell-based assays for drug design in the pharmacological industry in this chapter, the described methods and the methodologies are highly suitable for other enterprise data. We have used our methods and methodology for the continuous monitoring of airborne biological agents in food processing, for controlling the quality of grains in mills, and for defect recognition and diagnosis in offset printing. Further work on other applications is in progress. Thus, the methods described in this chapter have a great potential in the field of enterprise data mining.

Acknowledgement

The author wishes to thank the two referees for their suggestions that helped to improve the final version of this chapter.

References

Breiman L., Friedman J.H., and Olhen R.A. (1984). *Classification and Regression Trees*, The Wadsworth Statistics/Probability Series, Belmont, CA, U.S.A.

Chang C.L. (1974), Finding prototypes for nearest neighbor classifiers. *IEEE Transactions on Computers*, C-**23**(11), 1179--1184.

Copersmith D., Hong S.J., and Hosking J. (1999). Partitioning nominal attributes in decision trees, *Journal of data mining and knowledge discovery*, **3**(2), 100-200.

Dougherty J., Kohavi R., and Sahamin M. (1995). Supervised and unsupervised discretization of continuous features, *Machine Learning*, *14th IJCAI*, 194-202.

Fayyad U.M., and Irani K.B. (1993). Multi-interval discretization of continuous valued attributes for classification learning, *Machine Learning, 13th IJCAI*, vol. 2.,Chambery, France, Morgan Kaufmann, 1022-1027.

Fisher D.H. (1987), Knowledge acquisition via incremental conceptual clustering. *Machine Learning*, Kluwer Academic Publishers: Hingham, MA, USA. **2**(2). 139-172.

Frucci M., Sanniti di Baja G., and Perner, P. (2007). CBR-based Image Segmentation, In: *Case-Based Reasoning for Images and Signals*, P. Perner (Ed.), Series on Computational Intelligence, Springer-Verlag: Berlin Heidelberg, Germany (to appear).

Grimnes M., and Amondt A. (1996). A two layer case-based reasoning architecture for medical image understanding, In: I. Smith and B. Faltings (Eds.), *Advances in Case-Based Reasoning*, Springer-Verlag, Berlin Heidelberg, Germany, LNAI 1168, 164-178.

Gennari J.H., Langley P., and Fisher D.H. (1989). Models of incremental concept formation. *Artificial Intelligence*, Elsevier Science Publishers Ltd.: Essex, UK, **40**(1-3), 11-61.

Jänichen S., and Perner, P. (2006). Conceptual clustering and case generalization of 2-dimensional forms, *Computational Intelligence,* **22**(3/4), 178-193.

Kerber R. (1992), ChiMerge: discretization of numeric attributes, *Learning: Inductive, AAAI 92*, 123-128.

Kohonen T. (1995), *Self-Organizing Maps*, Springer Verlag: Berlin, Germany

Kuusisto S. (1998), Application of the PMDL Principle to the Induction of Classification Trees, *PhD-Thesis*, Tampere Finland.

Liao, T. W. (2005). Clustering of time series data - A survey, *Pattern Recognition*, **38** (11), 1857-1874

Matheron G. (1975), *Random Sets and Integral Geometry*, J. Wiley & Sons Inc., New York London.

de Mantaras R.L. (1991). A distance-based attribute selection measure for decision tree induction, *Machine Learning*, **6**, 81-92.

Niblett T., and Bratko I. (1987), Construction decision trees in noisy domains, In *Progress in Machine Learning*, Bratko I and Lavrac N. (eds.), Sigma Press, England, 67-78.

Quinlan J.R. (1986). Induction of Decision Trees, *Machine Learning,* **1**, 81-106.

Quinlan J.R. (1987). Simplifying decision trees, *Machine Learning*, **27**, 221-234.

Quinlan J.R. (1988). Decision trees and multivalued attributes, In: *Machine Intelligence 11*, Hayes JE, Michie D, and Richards J (eds.), Oxford University Press.

Perner P. (1994). A knowledge-based image inspection system for automatic defect recognition, classification, and process diagnosis. *International Journal on Machine Vision and Applications*, **7**, 135-147.

Perner P. (1999), An architecture for a CBR image segmentation system, *Engineering Applications of Artificial Intelligence*, **12** (6), 749-759.

Perner P. (2000), *Feature Discretization*, IBaI Report.

Perner P. (2005). Utility model, computer system for the automatic data analysis, classification, interpretation and data mining of cells, cell structures, microorganism, biotic particle, parts and products in digital images, DE 20206003294 U1.

Perner P. (2002), The Boolean model and its application to texture classification, *IBaI Report.*

Perner P. (2006). A comparative study of catalogue-based classification, In: Roth-Berghofer Th., Göker M.H., Altay Güvenir H. (Eds.), *Advances in Case-Based Reasoning*, lncs 4106, Springer-Verlag, Berlin Heidelberg, Germany, 301-308.

Perner P., Belikova T.B., and Yashunskaya N.I. (1996). Knowledge acquisition by decision tree induction for interpretation of digital images in radiology, In: P. Perner, P. Wang, and A. Rosenfeld (Eds.), *Advances in Structural and Syntactical Pattern Recognition*, Springer-Verlag, Berlin Heidelberg, Germany, LNCS 1121, 301-311.

Perner P., Günther T., Perner H., Fiss G., and Ernst R. (2003). Health Monitoring by an Image Interpretation System - A System for Airborne Fungi Identification, In: *Medical Data Analysis*, Perner P., Brause R., Holzhütter H.-G. (Eds.),Springer-Verlag, Berlin Heidelberg, Germany, LNCS 2868, 64-77.

Perner P., and Günther Th. (2005). Detection of hygiene-relevant parameters from cereal grains based on intelligent image interpretation and data mining, , In: *Lernen, Wissensentdeckung und Adaptivität (LWA) 2005*, Bauer M., Brandherm B., Fürnkranz J., Grieser G., Hotho A., Jedlitschka A., Kröner A. (Eds.), GI Workshops, Saarbrücken DFKI 2005, 216-219.

Perner P., Perner H., and Müller B. (2002). Mining knowledge for HEp-2 cell image classification, *Journal Artificial Intelligence in Medicine*, **26**, 161-173.

Perner P., and Trautzsch S. (1998). Multinterval discretization for decision tree learning, In: *Advances in Pattern Recognition*, Amin A., Dori D., Pudil P., Freeman H. (Eds.), LNCS 1451, Springer, Heidelberg, Germany, 475-482.

Philipow E. (1987). *Handbuch der Elektrotechnik*, Bd 2 Grundlagen der Informations-technik, Technik Verlag, Berlin, Germany, 158-171.

Seidelmann G. (1993). Using Heuristics to Speed Up Induction on Continuous-Valued Attributes, In: P. B. Brazdil (Ed.), *Machine Learning: ECML-93*, Springer, Berlin, Heidelberg, Germany, 390- 395.

Wettschereck D., and Aha D.W. (1995). Weighting features, In: Veloso M.M., Aamodt A. (Eds.), *Case-Based Reasoning Research and Development*, Springer-Verlag: Berlin Heidelberg, Germany, LNCS 1010, 347-358.

White A.P., and Lui W.Z. (1994). Bias in information-based measures in decision tree induction, *Machine Learning*, **15**, 321-329.

Wu C., Landgrebe D., and Swain P. (1975), *The decision tree approach to classification*, School Elec. Eng., Purdue Univ., W. Lafayette, IN, U.S.A. Report RE-EE 75-17.

Zamperoni P. (1996), Feature Extraction, In *Progress in Picture Processing*, H. Maitre, J. Zinn-Justin (Eds.), Elsevier Science, 121-184.

Zhang S. (1997), Evaluation and comparison of different segmentation algorithm, *Pattern Recognition Letters*, **18**(10), 963-968.

Author's Biographical Statement

Petra Perner is the director of the Institute of Computer Vision and Applied Computer Sciences IBaI. She received her Diploma degree in electrical engineering in 1981 and her PhD degree in computer science in 1985. She has been the principal investigator of various national and international research projects. She received several research awards for her research work and has been recently awarded with 3 business awards for her work on bringing intelligent image interpretation methods into business. Her research interest is image analysis and interpretation, machine learning, data mining, machine learning, image mining and case-based reasoning. Recently, she is working on various medical, chemical and biomedical applications, information management applications, technical diagnosis and e-commerce applications. Most of the developments are protected by legal patent rights and can be licensed to qualified industrial companies. She has published numerous scientific publications and patents and is often invited as a plenary speaker in distinct research fields as well as across disciplines. Her vision is to build intelligent flexible and robust data-interpreting systems that are inspired by the human case-based reasoning process.

Chapter 14[1]

Support Vector Machines and Applications

Theodore B. Trafalis[1] and Olutayo O. Oladunni[2]
[1]School of Industrial Engineering
University of Oklahoma, Norman, OK, U.S.A., Email: ttrafalis@ok.edu
[2]Department of Engineering Education
Purdue University, West Lafayette, Indiana, U.S.A.

Abstract: Support Vector Machines (SVMs) methods have become a popular tool for predictive data mining problems and novelty detection. They show good generalization performance on many real-life datasets and they are motivated theoretically through convex programming formulations. There are relatively few free parameters to adjust using cross validation and the architecture of the SVM learning machine does not need to be found by experimentation as in the case of Artificial Neural Networks (ANNs). We discuss the fundamentals of SVMs with emphasis to multiclass classification problems and applications in science, business and engineering.

Key Words: Support vector machines, Kernel, Least squares, Multi–classification, Enterprise, Data mining, Machine learning, Classification, Classifiers.

---

[1] Liao, T.W. and E. Triantaphyllou, (Eds.), **Recent Advances in Data Mining of Enterprise Data: Algorithms and Applications**, *World Scientific*, Singapore, pp. 643-690, 2007.

1. Introduction

In this chapter we introduce the subject of SVMs, describing the application of SVMs to multiclass classification, regression, novelty detection, as well as different optimization formulations used for SVM training. This chapter is not exhaustive and many approaches (e.g., Kernel Principal Component Analysis (KPCA) (Schőlkopf et al., 1999), density estimation (Weston et al., 1999) have not been considered. More detailed treatments are contained in the books by Cristianini and Shawe-Taylor (2000), Vapnik's classic textbook on statistical learning theory (1998), Schőlkopf & Smola (2002) and edited volumes (Schőlkopf et al., 1998; Smola et al., 2001).

An ability of intelligent learning is that we can apply what we have learned to new situations. In the mathematical theory of learning, this is called generalization (Vapnik, 1995 & 1998). SVMs have been applied to a wide range of problems such as finance (Trafalis & Ince, 2000), science (Ding & Dubchak, 2001; Santosa et al., 2002; Lee et al., 2003), political science (Malyscheff & Trafalis, 2003), and engineering (Trafalis & Oladunni, 2004; Trafalis et al., 2005). The prime advantage for classification problems is the ability to perform a mapping of the in a high (possibly infinite) feature space, thus, providing an avenue for exploring nonlinear kernel-based classifiers (Burges, 1998; Cristianini & Shawe-Taylor, 2000). Hence, SVMs are equipped to discriminate between classes that are linearly separable, linearly inseparable, and nonlinearly separable. SVMs avoid overfitting by maximizing the margin between two classes of training data; i.e., maximizing the distance between the separating hyperplane and the training data on either side of it (see Figure 1). A learning algorithm observes many training examples and computes a function that maps inputs to outputs.

The learned function has good generalization behavior if it does as well on new inputs as on the old ones. A classical result in learning theory shows that the function learned through the empirical risk minimization (ERM) principle generalizes well if the "hypothesis space" from which they are chosen is simple (Vapnik, 1998). The classical definition of a "simple" hypothesis space (low complexity) is technically involved. An example of a "simple" hypothesis space is the set of linear functions defined on the plane. The complexity of the set of functions or VC dimension (Vapnik, 1998) is three since this is the greatest number of points in the plane that can be arranged so that suitable linear functions assume any desired combination of signs when evaluated at the points. This approach has generated effective learning algorithms (Vapnik, 1998) such as SVMs. However the complexity of the hypothesis space (VC dimension) becomes too hard to measure.

More recent work by Poggio et al. (2004) shifts attention from the hypothesis space and concentrating on the concept of stability of learning algorithms. In simple words, a learning algorithm is stable if the removal of a training sample from a large set of samples results in a small change in the learned function. SVMs enjoy this stability property. Moreover they are stable with respect to data perturbations.

The application of data mining methods to problems involving the discovery or prediction of rare events and patterns has shown promising and surprising results in areas as diverse as predicting tornadoes, electrical power consumption, customer retention, loan default and bank failure (Brierley and Batty 1999, Piramuthu 1999, Wai-Ho et al. 2003, Trafalis et al. 2005). The need for reform and understanding of various enterprise systems will provide an opportunity in the area of supply chain and inventory management to explore the application of data mining methods such as SVMs to help determine how much inventory exists in a warehouse, when to order items, how much to order, and how to measure and forecast demand for an item (Beardslee & Trafalis, 2005).

Through experimentation, it was determined that information gain is a good indicator of important features when improving the prediction of mid and long-term weather forecasts (Howard and Rayward-Smith 1999). Another analysis of the impact of feature selection was conducted on two "rare event" discovery problems, identifying loan default-prone customers and predicting bank failures. That analysis presents and evaluates the feature selection method through the application of the Hausdorff distance measure. It was found that the classification accuracy of the decision tree algorithm, after pre-processing through the Hausdorff distance measure filter, was the same as that obtained without the pre-processing. However, the same accuracy was obtained with fewer features (Piramuthu 1999).

Dhond et al. (2000) exclusively targeted mining transaction data in a supply chain or inventory management environment, and they provided good results revealing that, through the analysis of thousands of transactions by a neural network, a data mining implementation could result in a significant reduction of the inventory cost held by a pharmaceutical company.

This chapter is organized as follows. In Section 2, the fundamentals of SVMs are described along with numerical testing on a simple problem. In Section 3, an overview of the least square support vector machines is presented. In Section 4, a review of multi-classification SVMs is presented along with a short description on central representations of version space. In Section 5, modeling for enterprise related (novelty detection) and not enterprise related applications are presented. Finally Section 6 concludes this chapter.

2. Fundamentals of Support Vector Machines

2.1 Linear Separability

In this section, we consider the two-class classification problem. Specifically, l data points $(x_i, y_i)_{i=1}^{l}$ are given where $x_i \in \Re^n$ are the input training vectors, and $y_i \in \{+1,-1\}$ are the corresponding labels.

Making the assumption that the classification problem is linearly separable, the issue becomes finding a (w,γ) that defines a separating hyperplane, such that, the following separation constraints hold (see Figure 1):

$$\begin{aligned} w \cdot x_i - \gamma &\geq 1, \quad y_i = 1 \\ w \cdot x_i - \gamma &\leq -1, \quad y_i = -1, \quad i = 1,\dots,l \end{aligned} \tag{1}$$

where w is the normal vector perpendicular to the separating hyperplane, and γ is the bias—the position of the hyperplane analyzed in input space. Combining constraints (1) into one set of inequalities gives:

$$y_i\left(w \cdot x_i - \gamma\right) \geq 1, \quad i = 1, \ldots, l \tag{2}$$

The decision function is:

$$f(x) = sign\left(w \cdot x_i - \gamma\right) \tag{3}$$

There are infinite many hyperplanes that separate the two classes of Figure 1. However, our objective is to compute the optimal hyperplane corresponding to the SVM solution.

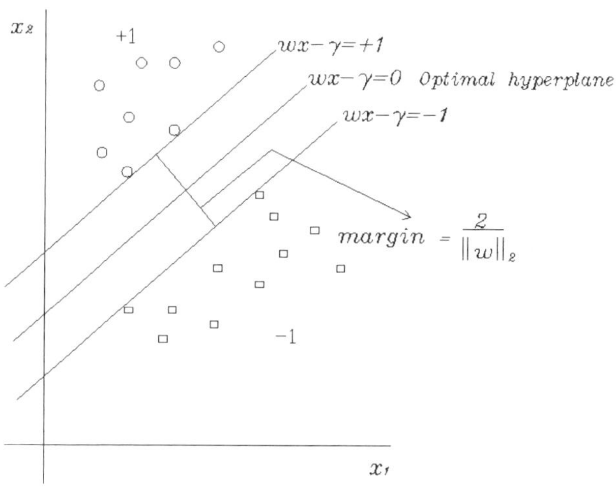

Figure 1. Linearly separable problem. The optimal hyperplane is orthogonal to the shortest line connecting the two classes, and intersects it halfway; circles in +1 class and squares in -1 class.

The motivation for considering SVMs from the statistical learning point of view comes from theoretical bounds on the generalization error (Burges, 1998; Vapnik, 1998). The upper bound on the generalization error does not depend on the dimension of the input data space and it is minimized by maximizing the margin ℓ (the minimal distance between the hyperplane separating the two classes and the closest data points to this hyperplane, see Figure 1).

For the separating hyperplane $w \cdot x - \gamma = 0$, the normal vector is $\frac{w}{\|w\|_2}$, where $\|w\|_2$ is the Euclidean norm of *w*. Hence, the margin ℓ is computed by the projection of $x_2 - x_1$ onto this vector. Since $w \cdot x_1 - \gamma = 1$ and $w \cdot x_2 - \gamma = -1$ then, $\ell = \frac{1}{\|w\|_2}$. Therefore, in order to maximize ℓ, we need to minimize $\frac{1}{2}\|w\|_2^2$.

The formulation of a linearly separable problem written in its primal form (Burges, 1998; Cristianini & Shawe-Taylor, 2000; Chang & Lin, 2001; Hsu et al., 2003) is as follows:

$$\begin{aligned} &\min_{w,\gamma} \frac{1}{2}\|w\|^2 \\ &s.t.\ \ y_i\left(w \cdot x_i - \gamma\right) \geq 1, \quad i = 1,\dots,l \end{aligned} \tag{4}$$

$\|w\|^2 = w^T w$ is the square of the 2-norm of the normal vector defining the separating hyperplane and it is a convex function. For the SVM model its Lagrangian function is given by:

$$L(w,\gamma,\alpha) = \frac{1}{2}\|w\|^2 - \sum_{i=1}^{l} \alpha_i \left(y_i (w \cdot x_i - \gamma) - 1 \right) \tag{5}$$

At the global saddle point, *L* should be minimized with respect to *w*, *γ* and maximized with respect to $\alpha_i \geq 0$, where α_i are positive Lagrange multipliers.

The Karush Kuhn Tucker conditions (KKT) (Reklaitis et al., 1983; Bazaraa et al., 1993) for the primal problem are given below:

$$\frac{\partial L}{\partial \gamma} = 0 \Rightarrow \sum_{i=1}^{l} \alpha_i y_i = 0 \tag{6}$$

$$\frac{\partial L}{\partial w} = 0 \Rightarrow w - \sum_{i=1}^{l} \alpha_i y_i x_i = 0 \Rightarrow w = \sum_{i=1}^{l} \alpha_i y_i x_i \tag{7}$$

$$\alpha_i \left[y_i \left(w \cdot x_i - \gamma \right) - 1 \right] = 0 \tag{8}$$

Substituting equations (6) and (7) into (5), provides the Wolfe dual problem in the following form:

$$\max_{\alpha} w(\alpha) = \max_{\alpha} \sum_{i=1}^{l} \alpha_i - \frac{1}{2} \sum_{i=1}^{l} \sum_{j=1}^{l} \alpha_i \alpha_j y_i y_j \langle x_i, x_j \rangle$$

$$s.t. \quad \sum_{i=1}^{l} \alpha_i y_i = 0 \tag{9}$$

$$\alpha_i \geq 0, \quad i = 1, \ldots, l$$

The *optimal point* solution is given by:

$$w^* = \sum_{i=1}^{l} \alpha_i^* y_i x_i \, , \tag{10}$$

where a training vector for which $\alpha_i^* > 0$ is called a support vector. The decision function is:

$$f(x) = sign\left(\sum_{i=1}^{l} \alpha_i y_i \langle x_i, x_j \rangle - \gamma \right) \tag{11}$$

The KKT complementary condition (8) can be used to determine the threshold value, γ, for any i such that α_i is not zero.

2.2 Linear Inseparability

The problem is to find a (w, γ) that defines a separating hyperplane, such that, the following separation constraints hold:

$$\begin{aligned} w \cdot x_i - \gamma &\geq 1 - \xi_i, \quad y_i = 1 \\ w \cdot x_i - \gamma &\leq -1 + \xi_i, \quad y_i = -1, \quad i = 1, \ldots, l \end{aligned} \tag{12}$$

where ξ_i is a non-negative slack. Condition (12) is a linearly inseparable separation constraint analyzed in input space, and can be expressed as a single set of inequalities:

$$y_i \left(w \cdot x_i - \gamma \right) \geq 1 - \xi_i, \quad i = 1, \ldots, l \tag{13}$$

The formulation of a linearly inseparable problem can be written in its primal form (Burges, 1998; Cristianini & Shawe-Taylor, 2000; Chang & Lin, 2001; Hsu et al., 2003) as follows:

$$\begin{aligned}&\min_{w,\gamma,\xi}\frac{1}{2}\|w\|^2+\lambda\sum_{i=1}^{l}\xi_i\\&s.t.\ \ y_i\left(w\cdot x_i-\gamma\right)+\xi_i\geq 1\\&\qquad \xi_i\geq 0\ \ i=1,\ldots,l\end{aligned}\tag{14}$$

The linearly inseparable case has an error term, $\lambda\sum_{i=1}^{l}\xi_i$, included in the objective function of model (14) and it is minimized together with the square of the 2-norm. It is evident that if two disjoint sets are linearly separable, then the error slacks will be zero (see Figure 1).

The non-negative slack variable, ξ_i, measures the degree of violation of the constraints (see Figure 2). The parameter λ is a constant called the regularization parameter. It controls the tradeoff between minimizing the training errors and minimizing the 2-norm of the normal vector (generalization ability). This parameter is chosen by the modeler, keeping in mind that a larger λ corresponds to a higher penalty of errors with less generalization ability resulting in a more complex model. A smaller λ corresponds to fewer penalties with higher generalization ability resulting in a less complex model. Thus, there is a need to obtain a suitable tolerance level for errors. For the quadratic programming solution, λ is usually determined by employing cross validation techniques (Hsu et al., 2003).

To apply the KKT (Reklaitis et al., 1983; Bazaraa et al., 1993), the Lagrangian of problem (14) is defined as:

$$L(w,\gamma,\xi,\alpha,\beta)=\frac{1}{2}\|w\|^2+\lambda\sum_{i=1}^{l}\xi_i-\sum_{i=1}^{l}\alpha_i\left(y_i(w\cdot x_i-\gamma)-1+\xi_i\right)-\sum_{i=1}^{l}\beta_i\xi_i\tag{15}$$

At the global saddle point, L should be minimized with respect to w, γ, ξ, and maximized with respect to $\alpha_i,\beta_i\geq 0$; where α_i,β_i are positive Lagrange multipliers.

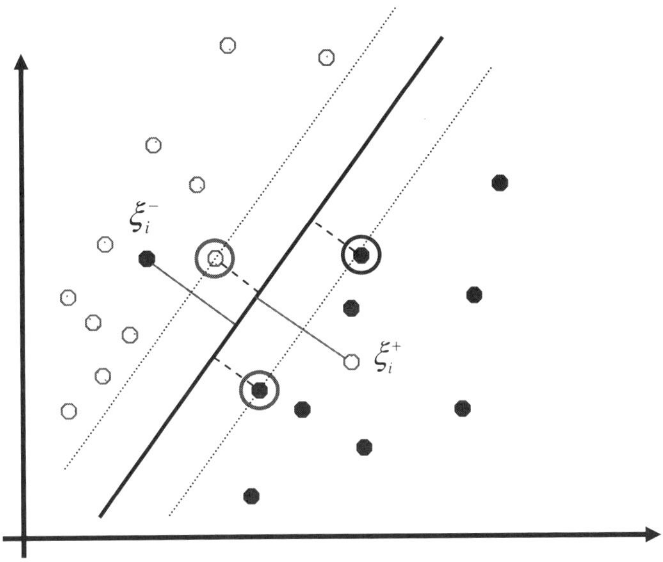

Figure 2. A Support Vector Machine classification schematic, with violation of separation constraints (linearly inseparable problem).

The Karush Kuhn Tucker conditions (KKT) for the primal problem are given below:

$$\frac{\partial L}{\partial \gamma} = 0 \Rightarrow \sum_{i=1}^{l} \alpha_i y_i = 0 \tag{16}$$

$$\frac{\partial L}{\partial w} = 0 \Rightarrow w - \sum_{i=1}^{l} \alpha_i y_i x_i = 0 \Rightarrow w = \sum_{i=1}^{l} \alpha_i y_i x_i \tag{17}$$

$$\frac{\partial L}{\partial \xi_i} = 0 \Rightarrow \lambda - \alpha_i - \beta_i = 0 \Rightarrow \alpha_i + \beta_i = \lambda \tag{18}$$

$$y_i(wx_i - \gamma) - 1 + \xi_i \geq 0 \tag{19}$$

$$\xi_i \geq 0 \tag{20}$$

$$\alpha_i \geq 0 \tag{21}$$

$$\beta_i \geq 0 \tag{22}$$

$$\beta_i \xi_i = 0 \tag{23}$$

$$\alpha_i\left[y_i\left(w\cdot x_i-\gamma\right)-1+\xi_i\right]=0 \tag{24}$$

Equation (18) combined with Equation (23) indicates that $\xi_i=0$ if $\alpha_i<\lambda$; therefore substituting the necessary KKT (16) and (17) in the Lagrangian (15) provides the Wolfe dual problem below:

$$\max_{\alpha} w(\alpha)=\max_{\alpha}\sum_{i=1}^{l}\alpha_i-\frac{1}{2}\sum_{i=1}^{l}\sum_{j=1}^{l}\alpha_i\alpha_j y_i y_j\left\langle x_i,x_j\right\rangle$$

$$s.t\ \sum_{i=1}^{l}\alpha_i y_i=0 \tag{25}$$

$$0\le\alpha_i\le\lambda,\quad i=1,\ldots,l$$

We can use the KKT complementary conditions (23) and (24) to determine the threshold value, γ, for any i such that α_i is not zero.

2.3 *Nonlinear Separability*

In the case of nonlinear separation, the input vector x, of the SVM, can be transformed into a higher dimensional space called the feature space F, using a function $\phi: x\in X\rightarrow\phi(x)\in F$.

This transformation allows the solution of the classification problem to be solved in feature space utilizing linear techniques. Note that the function $\phi(x)$ might not be available or cannot be computed. However, while $\phi(x)$ might not be available, one can still compute the inner product $\phi(x_1)\cdot\phi(x_2)$ in feature space implicitly through a kernel function. This function can be viewed as determining the similarity or distance between the input vectors. The inner product in feature space can be expressed by the kernel function (Cristianini & Shawe-Taylor, 2000):

$$k:\Re^n\times\Re^n\rightarrow\Re:k(x_1,x_2)=\phi(x_1)\cdot\phi(x_2) \tag{26}$$

Figure 3 illustrates the transformation process from input space to feature space.

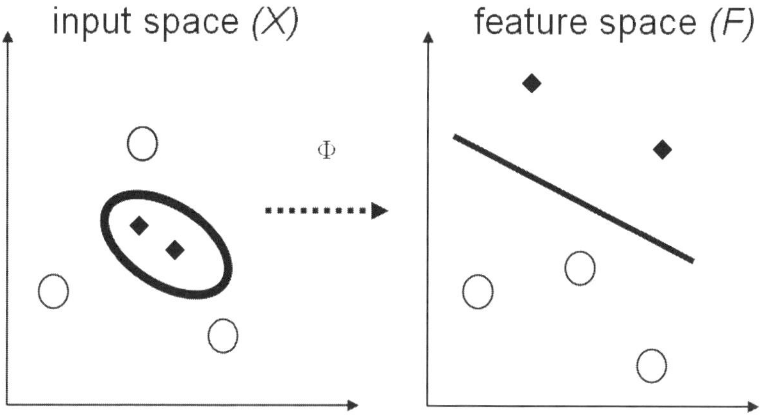

Figure 3. Feature space schematic.

Therefore, in the case of nonlinear separability, we can replace $\langle x_i, x\rangle$ in the dual problem (25) by the kernel function $k(x_i, x)$. Then, problem (25) becomes:

$$\begin{aligned} &\max_{\alpha} w(\alpha) = \max_{\alpha} \sum_{i=1}^{l} \alpha_i - \frac{1}{2}\sum_{i=1}^{l}\sum_{j=1}^{l} \alpha_i \alpha_j y_i y_j k(x_i, x_j) \\ &s.t \;\; 0 \le \alpha_i \le \lambda, \quad i = 1,\dots,l \\ &\quad \sum_{i=1}^{l} \alpha_i y_i = 0 \end{aligned} \tag{27}$$

and the decision function becomes:

$$f(x) = sign\left(\sum_{i=1}^{l} \alpha_i y_i k(x_i, x) - \gamma\right) \tag{28}$$

Below are examples of two widely used kernel functions:

- The polynomial kernel.

$$k(x_i, x) = (x_i^T x + 1)^P, \tag{29}$$

where p is the degree of the polynomial for the polynomial kernel function.

- The Gaussian radial basis function (RBF) kernel

$$k(x_i, x) = \exp(-\frac{\|x_i - x\|^2}{2\sigma^2}), \tag{30}$$

where σ is the spread for the Gaussian RBF kernel. There are several other kernel functions that can be used (see Cristianini & Shawe-Taylor, 2000).

Depending on the structure of the problem, the SVM model performs training on a given dataset. The fundamental idea of the SVM model is to maximize the margin between two disjoint sets and minimize the training error. The SVM model can be expressed as a convex quadratic optimization problem, which solves for the classification weights in primal or dual space, and the bias, an offset constant. The primal weight variables reflect the degree of importance for each attribute, while the dual variables α_i reflect the degree of importance for each training point. The dual variables can also be used to compute the classification weights in primal space. After all parameters have been solved for or identified, the decision function or surface as defined in (3) or (28) will be used to aid our decision making.

2.4 *Numerical Testing*

To illustrate the workings of the SVM method, two small problems are considered, the AND problem and the XOR problem. The computations for the two small problems were conducted using MATLAB.

2.4.1 The AND Problem

Given sets:

$$X^{(1)} = \begin{pmatrix} 1 & 1 \end{pmatrix},\ X^{(2)} = \begin{pmatrix} -1 & -1 \\ -1 & 1 \\ 1 & -1 \end{pmatrix} \tag{31}$$

where $X^{(1)}$ is an $m_1 \times n$ matrix whose rows are points in class 1, and m_1 (= 1) is the number of data in class 1. Let $X^{(2)}$ be an $m_2 \times n$ matrix whose rows are points in class 2, m_2 (= 3) is the number of data in class

2, and $y_i = +1$ for class 1 and $y_i = -1$ for class 2, where $i = 1, \ldots\ldots, l,\ \ l = m_1 + m_2$. Table 1 illustrates the relationship between the inputs and outputs for the AND problem.

Table 1. Relationship between input and output of the AND problem.

x_1	x_2	**AND (output)**
1	1	1
-1	-1	-1
1	-1	-1
-1	1	-1

Problem (14) is solved with the given sets in (31) and parameter $\lambda = 1$. We obtain a solution to the SVM formulation problem (14):

$$w = \begin{bmatrix} 1 \\ 1 \end{bmatrix}, \quad \lambda = [1] \tag{32}$$

Optimal separating hyperplane for $\lambda = 1$ (the middle line in Figure 4):

$$w^T x - \gamma = 0 \ \Rightarrow \ \begin{pmatrix} w_1 & w_2 \end{pmatrix} \begin{pmatrix} x_1 \\ x_2 \end{pmatrix} - \gamma = (1 \ \ 1) \begin{pmatrix} x_1 \\ x_2 \end{pmatrix} - 1 \Rightarrow x_1 + x_2 = 1 \tag{33}$$

Supporting hyperplanes for $\lambda = 1$ (the top and bottom lines in Figure 4):

$$w^T x - \gamma = 1 \ \Rightarrow \ \begin{pmatrix} w_1 & w_2 \end{pmatrix} \begin{pmatrix} x_1 \\ x_2 \end{pmatrix} - \gamma - 1 = (1 \ \ 1) \begin{pmatrix} x_1 \\ x_2 \end{pmatrix} - 1 - 1 \Rightarrow x_1 + x_2 = 2 \tag{34}$$

$$w^T x - \gamma = -1 \ \Rightarrow \ \begin{pmatrix} w_1 & w_2 \end{pmatrix} \begin{pmatrix} x_1 \\ x_2 \end{pmatrix} - \gamma + 1 = (1 \ \ 1) \begin{pmatrix} x_1 \\ x_2 \end{pmatrix} - 1 + 1 \Rightarrow x_1 + x_2 = 0 \tag{35}$$

Decision function:

$$f(x) = sign\left(x_1 + x_2 - 1\right) \tag{36}$$

The points touching the separating hyperplanes are called support vectors (Figure 4).

2.4.2 The XOR Problem

Given sets:

$$X^{(1)} = \begin{pmatrix} 1 & 1 \\ -1 & -1 \end{pmatrix}, \; X^{(2)} = \begin{pmatrix} -1 & 1 \\ 1 & -1 \end{pmatrix} \tag{37}$$

where $X^{(1)}$ is an $m_1 \times n$ matrix whose rows are points in class 1, and m_1 (= 2) is the number of data in class 1. Let $X^{(2)}$ be an $m_2 \times n$ matrix whose rows are points in class 2, m_2 (= 2) is the number of data in class 2, and $y_i = +1$ for class 1 and $y_i = -1$ for class 2, where $i = 1,...,l$, and $l = m_1 + m_2$.

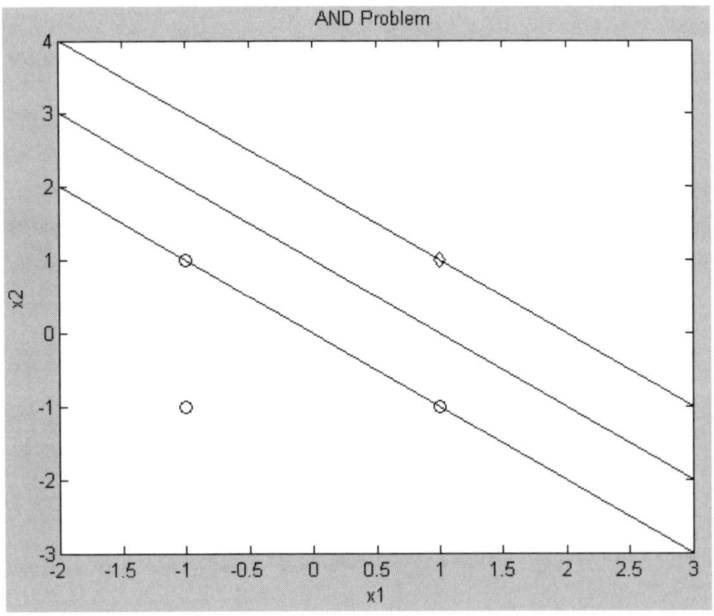

Figure 4. Illustration of SVM for the AND problem decision function $f(x) = sign[x_1 + x_2 - 1]$. Diamonds for point(s) belonging to class A[1], Circles for point(s) belonging to class A[2].

The XOR problem was trained with a polynomial kernel (29) with degree 2 and the computations were conducted using MATLAB. Table 2 illustrates the relationship between the inputs and outputs for the XOR problem.

Table 2. Relationship between input and output of the XOR problem.

x_1	x_2	**XOR (output)**
1	1	1
-1	-1	1
1	-1	-1
-1	1	-1

Problem (27) is solved with the given sets in (37) and parameter $\lambda = 1$. We obtain a solution to the SVM kernel formulation problem (27):

$$\alpha = \begin{bmatrix} 0.125 \\ 0.125 \\ 0.125 \\ 0.125 \end{bmatrix}, \quad \lambda = [0] \tag{38}$$

Optimal hyperplane for $\lambda = 1$ (Figure 5):

$$\sum_{i=1}^{l} \alpha_i y_i k(x_i, x) - \gamma = 0 \quad \Rightarrow \quad x_1 x_2 = 0 \tag{39}$$

Decision function:

$$f(x) = sign\left(x_1 x_2\right) \tag{40}$$

3. Least Squares Support Vector Machines

Suykens & Vandewalle (1999b) proposed a modified version of the SVM called the least squares SVMs (LS-SVMs). In their formulation, equality separation constraints were used and the square norm of the error term is minimized. This idea is similar to the ridge regression concept (Saunders et al., 1998) and the Tikhonov scheme (Tikhonov, 1977), but with binary targets {-1, 1} as outputs. As a result, the classification problem becomes a linear system of equations solved using the method of least squares.

In the classical QP formulation, many support vector values are zero, while in the least square case the support vector values are proportional to the errors at the data points. Hence, sparsity of the solution is lost. In the case of large scale classification problems, Suykens et al. (1999) suggested an iterative training algorithm for LS-SVM that is based on a conjugate gradient method. The iterative procedure is considered in order to avoid storage of the input matrix.

To demonstrate the performance of the LS-SVM, Baesens et al. (2000) and Van Gestel et al. (2004) performed an empirical study of the LS-SVM on several benchmark datasets using some kernel functions. The linear kernel was used for linear separability. In order to attain further insight into the degree of nonlinearity of the problem, a polynomial and a Gaussian RBF kernel was used for nonlinear separability. Based on standard cross validation techniques for hyperparameter selection, both studies confirm that the SVM and LS-SVM with the Gaussian RBF kernel achieve comparable performances and consistently yield the best results for each dataset.

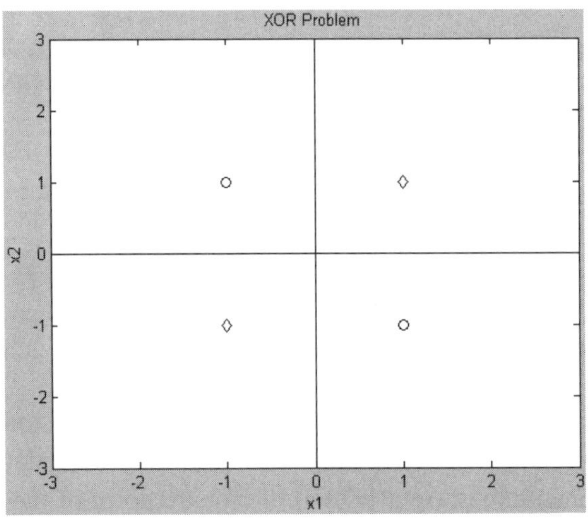

Figure 5. Illustration of SVM for the XOR problem decision function $f(x) = sign[x_1 x_2]$. Circles for point(s) belonging to class A^1, Diamonds for point(s) belonging to class A^2.

A drawback of the LS-SVM is that sparsity of solution is lost, i.e., the dual variables are mostly nonzero values and are unrestricted in sign. This becomes important in finding equivalence between sparse approximation and SVMs (Girosi, 1998). To obtain a sparse solution, Suykens et al. (2000) proposed a heuristic method for pruning the support value continuum. This is done by gradually removing the least important data from the training set and re-estimating the LS-SVM. A small number of points—e.g. 5% of the training set—with smallest values in the sorted support value continuum is removed. The procedure is performed as a second stage operation for obtaining a solution to the LS-SVM classification problem.

Fung & Mangasarian (2001) developed a linear and nonlinear classification algorithm called proximal support vector machine (PSVM). The idea is to classify new points by assigning them to the closer of the two parallel planes that are as far apart as possible. Their formulation has similar interpretation to the regularized LS-SVM (Pelckmans et al., 2004) because it depends on the strong convexity of the objective function. However, it does differ slightly from the broad perspective of regularized networks (Evgeniou et al, 2000), which is not always convex. The solution to the PSVM models is based on a linear system of equations, as opposed to the traditional SVM, that solves a quadratic programming problem requiring a considerably longer computation time.

A survey of recent developments in the context of SVMs was described in Mangasarian (2001). Four SVM algorithms were investigated; generalized SVMs (a very general mathematical programming framework for SVMs), smooth SVMs (a smooth nonlinear equation representation of SVMs solvable by a fast Newton method), Lagrangian SVMs (an unconstrained Lagrangian representation of SVMs leading to an extremely simple iterative scheme capable of solving classification problems with millions of points), and reduced SVMs (a rectangular kernel classifier that utilizes as little as 1% of the data).

Similar to the PSVM formulation, Pelckmans et al. (2004) compared three related regularization schemes for kernel machines using a *least square criterion*. The regularization schemes considered are as follows: Tikhonov & Ivanov regularization (1977 & 1976), and Morozov's (1984) discrepancy principle. Below are the cost functions of the three regularization schemes.

- Tikhonov, similar to the LS-SVMs (Suykens & Vandewalle, 1999b), where λ expresses the tradeoff between data fitting and smoothness in the trust region of parameters and noise level respectively:

$$\min_{w,b,\xi} f_T(w,\xi) = \frac{1}{2} w^T w + \frac{\lambda}{2} \sum_{i=1}^{l} \xi_i^2 \quad s.t.\ w \cdot \phi(x_i) - \gamma + \xi_i = y_i, \quad i = 1,\ldots,l \tag{41}$$

- Morozov's discrepancy principle (Morozov, 1984), where the minimal 2-norm of w realizing a fixed noise level σ^2 is to be found:

$$\min_{w,b,\xi} f_M(w) = \frac{1}{2} w^T w \quad s.t \begin{cases} w \cdot \phi(x_i) - \gamma + \xi_i = y_i, & i = 1,\ldots,l \\ l\sigma^2 = \sum_{i=1}^{l} \xi_i^2 \end{cases} \tag{42}$$

- Ivanov's regularization (Ivanov, 1976) amounts to solving for the best fit with a 2-norm on w smaller than π^2:

$$\min_{w,b,\xi} f_I(\xi) = \frac{1}{2} \xi^T \xi \quad s.t \begin{cases} w \cdot \phi(x_i) - \gamma + \xi_i = y_i, & i = 1,\ldots,l \\ \pi^2 = w^T w \end{cases} \tag{43}$$

The derivative of the cost functions (41) to (43) results in a linear system which after some simple manipulation, can be solved using linear techniques. The three regularization schemes allow incorporation of prior or model-free estimates of the noise variance for tuning the regularization constant in LS-SVMs.

Consider the two-class classification problem. Specifically, l data points $(x_i, y_i)_{i=1}^{l}$ are given, $x_i \in \Re^n$ are the input training vectors, and $y_i \in \{+1,-1\}$ are the corresponding labels. The least square version to the SVM classifier is given by the following optimization problem (Suykens &Vandewalle, 1999b):

$$\begin{aligned} &\min_{w,b,\xi} \frac{1}{2}\|w\|^2 + \lambda \frac{1}{2} \sum_{i=1}^{l} \xi_i^2 \\ &s.t.\ y_i\left(w \cdot \phi(x_i) - \gamma\right) = 1 - \xi_i, \quad i = 1,\ldots,l \end{aligned} \tag{44}$$

The mapping function, $\phi: x \in X \rightarrow \phi(x) \in F$, maps the input space to a high dimensional feature space. This formulation has equality constraints rather than inequality constraints, and takes into account a penalized sum of square errors term.

Similar to Vapnik's SVM, its Lagrangian function is defined below:

$$L(w,\gamma,\xi,\alpha)=\frac{1}{2}\|w\|^2+\lambda\sum_{i=1}^{l}\xi_i-\sum_{i=1}^{l}\alpha_i\left(y_i(w\cdot\phi(x_i)-\gamma)-1+\xi_i\right) \quad (45)$$

where α_i are the Lagrange multipliers that can either be positive or negative due to the equality constraints of problem (44). From the conditions for optimality, the KKT system is obtained as follows:

$$\frac{\partial L}{\partial \gamma}=0 \Rightarrow \sum_{i=1}^{l}\alpha_i y_i=0 \quad (46)$$

$$\frac{\partial L}{\partial w}=0 \Rightarrow w-\sum_{i=1}^{l}\alpha_i y_i\phi(x_i)=0 \Rightarrow w=\sum_{i=1}^{l}\alpha_i y_i\phi(x_i) \quad (47)$$

$$\frac{\partial L}{\partial \xi_i}=0 \Rightarrow \lambda\xi_i-\alpha_i=0 \Rightarrow \alpha_i=\lambda\xi_i \quad (48)$$

$$\frac{\partial L}{\partial \alpha_i}=0 \Rightarrow y_i(w\cdot\phi(x_i)-\gamma)-1+\xi_i=0 \quad (49)$$

Eliminating variables w and ξ, the following linear system is obtained,

$$\begin{pmatrix}0 & y^T\\ y & ZZ^T+\lambda^{-1}I\end{pmatrix}\begin{pmatrix}\gamma\\ \alpha\end{pmatrix}=\begin{pmatrix}0\\ 1\end{pmatrix} \quad (50)$$

where $y=[y_1,\ldots\ldots,y_l]$, $\xi=[\xi_1,\ldots\ldots,\xi_l]$, $\alpha=[\alpha_1,\ldots\ldots,\alpha_l]$ and 1 is the vector of ones with appropriate dimension. To guarantee a solution, Mercer's condition (Burges, 1998; Cristianini & Shawe-Taylor, 2000) can be applied to the matrix $\Omega = ZZ^T$, where

$$\Omega_{ij}=y_i y_j\phi(x_i)\cdot\phi(x_j)=y_i y_j K(x_i,x_j) \quad (51)$$

The decision function becomes

$$f(x)=sign\left(\sum_{i=1}^{l}\alpha_i y_i K(x_i,x)-\gamma\right) \quad (52)$$

The solution to system (50) provides the classification weights in dual space, and when used as parameters in the decision function, a new point can be classified.

4. Multi-Classification Support Vector Machines

In this section, the most general formulations that address the discrimination of two or more classes ($k \geq 2$) are presented. Most developed classification models are for discriminating between two classes. To address the problem of multi-classification, researchers have in the past adopted methods which involve solving k SVM models (OAA method) to produce k classifiers, or solving $k(k-1)/2$ SVM models (OAO method) to produce $k(k-1)/2$ classifiers, where k is the number of classes.

Hsu & Lin (2002) developed a decomposition strategy and made a comparison of the above methods. Methods include the OAA, OAO, and Direct Acyclic Graph SVM (Platt et al., 2000). It was reported that the OAO method and DAGSVM are more suitable for practical use, and that for large scale problems methods that consider all data at once, in general, use fewer support vectors.

In expressing and solving a multi-class problem as a single optimization problem the following models were suggested (Bredensteiner & Bennet, 1999; Weston & Watkins, 1999; Szedmak & Shawe-Taylor, 2004; Trafalis & Oladunni, 2005; Oladunni & Trafalis, 2005). These models were developed as a generalization of the binary classification model.

4.1 The One-Against-All (OAA) Method

In the OAA method, k SVM classifiers are constructed where k is the number of classes. Each model is trained on data for one class versus the rest of the classes. For example, if we have a three-class classification problem, we have to construct k =3 classifiers, $P^{1v(2,3)}$, $P^{2v(1,3)}$, $P^{3v(1,2)}$. To obtain classifier $P^{1v(2,3)}$, data points from class 1 are labeled with +1 and all the points from classes 2 and 3 are labeled with -1, then training is performed for the separation of the +1 labels (class 1 data points) and the -1 labels (classes 2 and 3 data points). Similarly for classifier $P^{2v(1,3)}$, data points belonging to class 2 are labeled with +1, classes 1 and 3 are labeled with -1 and then training is performed, and for classifier $P^{3v(1,2)}$, class 3 is label +1, and classes 1 and 2 are labeled -1. Given l data points $(x_i, y_i)_{i=1}^{l}$, where $x_i \in \Re^n$ are the input training vectors, and

$y_i \in \{1,\dots,k\}$ is the class of x_i. The i-th SVM model solves the following problem of the form:

$$\begin{aligned}
&\min_{w^i,\gamma^i,\xi^i_t} \ \frac{1}{2}\left\|w^i\right\|^2 + \lambda\sum_{t=1}^{l}\xi^i_t \\
&s.t. \\
&(w^i)^T\phi(x_t) - \gamma^i \ge 1 - \xi^i_t, \quad if\ y_t = i \\
&(w^i)^T\phi(x_t) - \gamma^i \le -1 + \xi^i_t, \quad if\ y_t \ne i \\
&\xi^i_t \ge 0, \qquad t = 1,\dots,l
\end{aligned} \tag{53}$$

Solving (53) produces k SVM classifiers defined by the following functions:

$$\begin{aligned}
&(w^1)^T\phi(x) - \gamma^1, \\
&\qquad\vdots \\
&(w^k)^T\phi(x) - \gamma^k,
\end{aligned} \tag{54}$$

Then, we predict x as being in the class with the largest value of the decision function:

$$\text{class of } x \equiv \arg\max_{i=1,\dots,k}[(w^i)^T\phi(x) - \gamma^i] \tag{55}$$

Basically, we solve the dual of (53), whose number of variables is the same as the number of data points of the problem. Hence, if we are to solve a problem with l data points, we then have to solve k quadratic programming problems where each of them has l data points (Hsu & Lin, 2002).

4.2 The One-Against-One (OAO) Method

In the OAO method, one constructs $k(k\text{-}1)/2$ SVM classifiers, each one of which is trained on data for two classes. For example, if we have a three-class classification problem, we have to construct 3 classifiers P^{12}, P^{13}, P^{23}. When we train P^{12} all points from class 1 are labeled with +1 and all the points from class 2 are labeled with -1. Similarly, for P^{13}, class 1 is labeled with +1, class 3 with -1, and for P^{23}, class 2 has label +1, and class 3 label -1. For training data from the *i*-th and the *j*-th classes, we solve the following binary classification problem (Hsu & Lin, 2002; Santosa et al., 2002):

$$
\begin{aligned}
&\min_{w^{ij},\gamma^{ij},\xi_t^{ij}} \ \frac{1}{2}\left\|w^{ij}\right\|^2 + \lambda\sum_{t=1}^{l}\xi_t^{ij} \\
&s.t. \\
&(w^{ij})^T\phi(x_t) - \gamma^{ij} \geq 1-\xi_t^{ij}, \quad if\ y_t = i \\
&(w^{ij})^T\phi(x_t) - \gamma^{ij} \leq -1+\xi_t^{ij}, \quad if\ y_t = j \\
&\xi_t^{ij} \geq 0
\end{aligned}
\tag{56}
$$

There are different strategies for performing the testing for points not in the training set after all $k(k\text{-}1)/2$ classifiers have been constructed. The strategy employed is called the "Max Wins" strategy. This strategy is a voting approach (Hsu & Lin, 2002; Santosa et al., 2002). For example, if sign $[\,(w^{ij})^T\phi(x)+\gamma^{ij}\,]$ indicates that x is in the *i*-th class, then the vote for the *i*-th class is increased by one. Otherwise, the vote for the *j*-th class is increased by one. Then we predict x as being in the class with the highest vote. In the case that those two classes have identical votes, select the one with the smallest index. Basically we solve the dual of (56), of which the number of variables is the same as the number of data points in the two classes. Hence, if each class has *l/k* data points, we have to solve $k(k\text{-}1)/2$ quadratic programming problems where each of them has *2l/k* data points (Hsu & Lin, 2002).

4.3 Pairwise Multi-classification Support Vector Machines

In trying to solve the classification problem as a single optimization problem, problem (56) can be generalized with the introduction of indices provided that the size of each class is of moderate size and/or its designs are balanced (equal sizes) (Trafalis & Oladunni, 2005) (see Figure 6).

Given that the datasets in R^n are represented by a matrix $A^i \in R^{m_i \times n}$, where $i = 1,..,k$ (for k classes). Let A^i be an $m_i \times n$ matrix whose rows are points in the i-th class, and let A^j be an $m_j \times n$ matrix whose rows are points in the j-th class. If $x \in R^n$ can be classified as follows

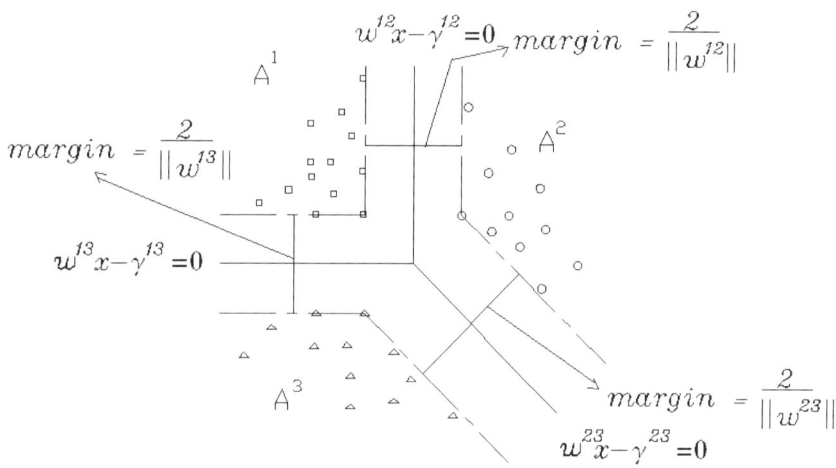

Figure 6. A Multi-Classification diagram. Three classes, class 1, 2 and 3 are represented by small squares, circles and triangles respectively; the broken fainted lines touching the class objects are the supporting hyperplanes for each pairwise comparison; the optimal hyperplane is orthogonal to the shortest line connecting each pairwise comparison, and intersects it halfway.

$$x^T w^{ij} - \gamma^{ij} \geq 1, \quad x \in A^i$$
$$x^T w^{ij} - \gamma^{ij} \leq -1, \quad x \in A^j, \quad i < j \tag{57}$$

Then, below is a general proposition for obtaining *k*(*k*-1)/2 classifiers from a single optimization model in primal form that solves problems of multi-class discrimination (Trafalis & Oladunni, 2005):

$$\begin{aligned} &\min_{w,\gamma} \frac{1}{2}\sum_{i<j}^{k}\left\|w^{ij}\right\|^2 + \lambda\sum_{i<j}^{k}\sum_{t=1}^{l_{ij}}\xi_t^{ij} \\ &s.t.\ y^{ij}(A^{ij}w^{ij} - \gamma^{ij}) + \xi_t^{ij} \geq 1, \quad i<j \\ &\xi_t^{ij} \geq 0 \end{aligned} \tag{58}$$

with $A^{ij} = \begin{bmatrix} A^i \\ A^j \end{bmatrix}$ ($m_{ij} \times n$ matrix) and $y^{ij} = \pm 1$ for i-th class and j-th class, respectively. The parameter λ is a constant called the regularization parameter which controls the tradeoff between minimizing training errors ξ^{ij} and minimizing the norm of the normal vector (generalization ability). The dual of problem (58) is given below:

$$\begin{aligned} &\max_{\alpha} \sum_{i<j}^{k}\sum_{c=1}^{m_{ij}}\alpha_c^{ij} - \frac{1}{2}\sum_{i<j}^{k}\sum_{c,d=1}^{m_{ij}}\alpha_c^{ij}\alpha_d^{ij}y_c^{ij}y_d^{ij}A_c^{ij}, A_d^{ij^T} \\ &s.t.\ \sum_{c=1}^{m_{ij}}\alpha_c^{ij}y_c^{ij} = 0 \\ &\qquad 0 \leq \alpha_c^{ij} \leq \lambda, \quad i<j \end{aligned} \tag{59}$$

where $\alpha^{ij} \geq 0$ are Lagrangian multipliers, and $\alpha^{ij} > 0$ are support vectors.

Bredensteiner & Bennet (1999) developed a piecewise quadratic programming multi-classification model. A set of points $A^i, i = 1, \cdots, k$ represented by matrices $A^i \in R^{m_i \times n}$ are piecewise-linearly separable if there exist $w^i \in R^n$ and $\gamma^i \in R$ such that:

$$A^i w^i - \gamma^i e > A^i w^j - \gamma^j e, \ i, j = 1, ..., k, \ i \neq j \tag{60}$$

In canonical form

$$x^T(w^i - w^j) - e(\gamma^i - \gamma^j) > 1, \ i, j = 1, ..., k, \ i \neq j \tag{61}$$

The bounding plane separating classes i and j is defined as $x^T(w^i - w^j) = e(\gamma^i - \gamma^j)$.

The piecewise M-SVM problem is to minimize the following:

$$\begin{aligned}
&\min_{w,\gamma,\xi} \ \frac{1}{2}\sum_{i<j}^{k}\left\|w^i - w^j\right\|_2^2 + \frac{1}{2}\sum_{i=1}^{k}\left\|w^i\right\|_2^2 + \lambda\sum_{i<j}^{k}\sum_{m=1}^{l}\xi_m^{ij} \\
&s.t. \ \ A^i(w^i - w^j) - e(\gamma^i - \gamma^j) \geq e - \xi_m^{ij}, \\
&\qquad \xi_m^{ij} \geq 0 \\
&\qquad i, j = 1,\cdots,k \quad i \neq j
\end{aligned} \tag{62}$$

Weston & Watkins (1999) also developed a quadratic programming model that satisfies condition (60). This model is similar to problem (62), with the notable difference being the objective function. The model minimizes the following problem.

$$\begin{aligned}
&\min_{w,\gamma,\xi} \ \frac{1}{2}\sum_{m=1}^{k} w_m{}^T w_m + \lambda\sum_{i=1}^{l}\sum_{m\neq y_i}\xi_i^m \\
&s.t. \ \ w_{y_i}^T x_i - \gamma_{y_i} \geq w_m^T x_i - \gamma_m + 2 - \xi_i^m, \\
&\qquad \xi_i^m \geq 0, \ \ i = 1,\cdots,k \ \ m \in \{1,....,k\} \setminus y_i
\end{aligned} \tag{63}$$

Both model problems (62 & 63) use the same decision function of the form:

$$f(x) = \arg\max_k [w_i^T x - \gamma_i], \ \ i = 1,...,k \tag{64}$$

They do not generalize better than the OAA and OAO methods. However, they do report fewer support vectors. Hence, there is no theoretical justification of the better generalization of OAA and OAO methods, which happens to be the two most widely used multi-classification SVMs techniques.

Szedmak et al. (2004) proposed a multi-class model for large sample sizes and number of features. In their formulation, the OAA framework is used, and the L_1 norm of the normal vector w of the separating hyperplanes is minimized. Their formulation solves k SVM optimization problems simultaneously, and since there are no interactions between the variables of the k SVM problems, their method, which essentially is the OAA considering all data at once, produces the same solution as that of the separated k SVM problems using the L_1 norm. The formulation is a generalization of problem (58) with additional L_1 norms in the objective function, and the constraints containing all data points. Considering all data at once transforms the problem into a large scale problem. Hence, the size of the problem can be a drawback of the method, if it gets too large.

Trafalis & Oladunni (2005), also proposed a multi-classification model, by using the OAO framework. The formulation is given in problem (58). It solves *k(k-1)/2* SVM problems simultaneously, and since there are no interactions between the variables of the *k(k-1)/2* SVM problems the method can be considered a pairwise multi-classification method considering all data at once. The formulation produces the same solution as that of the separated *k(k-1)/2* SVM problems. The method works well but has a drawback related to the size of the multi-class problem. Large scale problems become very expensive to compute the solution especially when considering a quadratic programming solution. Solving a quadratic programming problem involves the number of the data points. So an increase in data points increases the dimensionality of the problem, requiring more time to obtain a solution.

Linear programming formulations have also been considered. Bennett & Mangasarian (1994), proposed minimizing the sum of errors violating condition (60) i.e., finding a feasible solution. Weston & Watkins, (1999) also developed a linear machine for multi-class classification by considering a dual representation for problem (63). They represented the normal vector w in its dual representation form and minimized the dual variable α_i in the objective function. The dual representation of w is as follows:

$$w = \sum_{i=1}^{l} \alpha_i x_i \tag{65}$$

Recently, multi-classification problems have been investigated in the context of the least square approximations (Suykens & Vandewalle, 1999c; Oladunni & Trafalis, 2005) and the broad perspective of regularized networks (Evgeniou et al., 2000).

Suykens & Vandewalle, (1999c) extended their LS-SVMs methodology to accommodate multi-classification LS-SVM problems. The cost function and constraints (with equality constraint) of the multi-class LS-SVM is given as:

$$
\begin{aligned}
&\min_{w_i,\gamma_i,\xi_{k,i}} f_{LS}^{L}(w_i,\gamma_i,\xi_{k,i}) = \frac{1}{2}\sum_{i=1}^{l} w_i^T w_i + \frac{\lambda}{2}\sum_{k=1}^{N}\sum_{i=1}^{L}\xi_{k,i}^2 \\
&s.t.\ y^{(1)}_k[w_1^T\phi_1(x_k)-\gamma_1] = 1-\xi_{k,1}, \quad k=1,\ldots,N \\
&\quad y^{(2)}_k[w_2^T\phi_2(x_k)-\gamma_2] = 1-\xi_{k,2}, \quad k=1,\ldots,N \\
&\ldots \\
&\quad y^{(L)}_k[w_L^T\phi_L(x_k)-\gamma_L] = 1-\xi_{k,L}, \quad k=1,\ldots,N
\end{aligned} \tag{66}
$$

The linear system that is obtained from the formulation above after writing its Lagrangian function and taking its derivatives, becomes the classification problem to solve and is given as:

$$
\begin{pmatrix} 0 & Y_L^T \\ Y_L^T & \Omega_L \end{pmatrix}\begin{pmatrix} \gamma_L \\ \alpha_L \end{pmatrix} = \begin{pmatrix} 0 \\ 1 \end{pmatrix} \tag{67}
$$

$$
Y_L = \text{blockdiag}\{\begin{bmatrix} y_1^{(1)} \\ \vdots \\ y_N^{(1)} \end{bmatrix},\ldots,\begin{bmatrix} y_1^{(L)} \\ \vdots \\ y_N^{(L)} \end{bmatrix}\} \tag{68}
$$

$$
\Omega_L = \text{blockdiag}\{\Omega^{(1)},\ldots,\Omega^{(L)}\} \tag{69}
$$

$$
\Omega_{kj}^{(i)} = y_k^{(i)} y_j^{(i)} \psi_i(x_k, x_j) + \lambda^{-1} I \tag{70}
$$

The solution vectors are

$$
\gamma_L = [\gamma_1;\ldots..;\gamma_l] \tag{71}
$$

$$
\alpha_L = [\alpha_{1,1};\ldots.;\alpha_{N,1};\ldots.;\alpha_{1,l};\ldots.;\alpha_{N,l}] \tag{72}
$$

This formulation is different from Oladunni & Trafalis (2005), which includes inequality constraints in its formulation, but also minimizes the L_2 norm of the error slack variable. In their study two formulations where provided, one for pairwise multi-class classification and the other for piecewise multi-class classification. For the pairwise multi-class classification the linear system is derived from the following formulation (Oladunni & Trafalis, 2005):

$$\begin{aligned}
&\min_{w,\gamma,\xi} \frac{1}{2}\sum_{i<j}^{k}\left\|w^{ij}\right\|_2^2 + \lambda\sum_{i<j}^{k}\sum_{m=1}^{l}(\xi_m^{ij})^2 \\
&s.t.\ \ y^{ij}(A^{ij}w - e\gamma^{ij}) + \xi_m^{ij} \geq e, \\
&\quad\ \ \xi_m^{ij} \geq 0 \\
&\quad\ \ i,j = 1,\cdots,k \quad i \neq j
\end{aligned} \tag{73}$$

The resulting linear system is as follows:

$$\begin{pmatrix} 0 & E^TY & 0 \\ YE & YAA^TY + \lambda^{-1}I & \lambda^{-1}I \\ 0 & \lambda^{-1}I & \lambda^{-1}I \end{pmatrix}\begin{pmatrix} \gamma \\ \alpha \\ \beta \end{pmatrix} = \begin{pmatrix} 0 \\ e \\ 0 \end{pmatrix} \Rightarrow A_{ls}x_{ls} = b_{ls} \tag{74}$$

dropping the last contraint $\xi_m^{ij} \geq 0$ in (73) reduces $A_{ls}x_{ls} = b_{ls}$ to

$$\begin{pmatrix} 0 & E^TY \\ YE & YAA^TY + \lambda^{-1}I \end{pmatrix}\begin{pmatrix} \gamma \\ \alpha \end{pmatrix} = \begin{pmatrix} 0 \\ e \end{pmatrix} \Rightarrow A_{ls}x_{ls} = b_{ls}$$

Here is a three class problem in matrix form:

$$A = \begin{pmatrix} A^1 & 0 & 0 \\ A^2 & 0 & 0 \\ 0 & A^1 & 0 \\ 0 & A^3 & 0 \\ 0 & 0 & A^2 \\ 0 & 0 & A^3 \end{pmatrix},\ E = \begin{pmatrix} e^1 & 0 & 0 \\ e^2 & 0 & 0 \\ 0 & e^1 & 0 \\ 0 & e^3 & 0 \\ 0 & 0 & e^2 \\ 0 & 0 & e^3 \end{pmatrix},\ Y = \begin{pmatrix} Y^{(12)} & 0 & 0 \\ 0 & Y^{(13)} & 0 \\ 0 & 0 & Y^{(23)} \end{pmatrix} \tag{75}$$

where $A^i \in R^{m_i \times n}$, $A^j \in R^{m_j \times n}$, $i < j$ are matrices whose row vector belong to the ith and j^{th} class; $e^i \in R^{m_i \times 1}$ and $e^j \in R^{m_j \times 1}$, $i < j$ are vectors of ones; $Y^{(ij)}$ are diagonal matrices whose diagonals are ± 1 for classes i and j respectively.

The solution vectors are

$$\gamma = \left[\gamma^{12}, \gamma^{13}, \ldots, \gamma^{(k-1)k}\right]^T, \alpha = \left[\alpha^{12}, \alpha^{13}, \ldots, \alpha^{(k-1)k}\right]^T \tag{76}$$

The piecewise multi-class classification linear system is derived from formulation (62) and the resulting linear system is given below (Oladunni & Trafalis, 2005):

$$\begin{pmatrix} 0 & \hat{E}^T & 0 \\ \hat{E} & \frac{1}{k+1}\hat{A}\hat{A}^T + \lambda^{-1}I & \lambda^{-1}I \\ 0 & \lambda^{-1}I & \lambda^{-1}I \end{pmatrix} \begin{pmatrix} \gamma \\ \alpha \\ \beta \end{pmatrix} = \begin{pmatrix} 0 \\ e \\ 0 \end{pmatrix} \Rightarrow \hat{A}_{ls}\hat{x}_{ls} = \hat{b}_{ls} \tag{77}$$

dropping the last contraint $\xi_m^{ij} \geq 0$ in (62) reduces $\hat{A}_{ls}\hat{x}_{ls} = \hat{b}_{ls}$ to

$$\begin{pmatrix} 0 & \hat{E}^T \\ \hat{E} & \frac{1}{k+1}\hat{A}\hat{A}^T + \lambda^{-1}I \end{pmatrix} \begin{pmatrix} \gamma \\ \alpha \end{pmatrix} = \begin{pmatrix} 0 \\ e \end{pmatrix} \Rightarrow \hat{A}_{ls}\hat{x}_{ls} = \hat{b}_{ls}$$

Here is a three class problem in matrix form:

$$\hat{A} = \begin{pmatrix} A^1 & -A^1 & 0 \\ A^1 & 0 & -A^1 \\ -A^2 & A^2 & 0 \\ 0 & A^2 & -A^2 \\ -A^3 & 0 & A^3 \\ 0 & -A^3 & A^3 \end{pmatrix}, \quad \hat{E} = \begin{pmatrix} -e^1 & e^1 & 0 \\ -e^1 & 0 & e^1 \\ e^2 & -e^2 & 0 \\ 0 & -e^2 & e^2 \\ e^3 & 0 & -e^3 \\ 0 & e^3 & -e^3 \end{pmatrix} \tag{78}$$

with solution vectors

$$\gamma = \left[\gamma^1, \gamma^2, \ldots, \gamma^k\right]^T, \alpha = \left[\alpha^{ij^T}, \alpha^{ji^T}, \ldots\ldots, \alpha^{(k-1)k}, \alpha^{k(k-1)}\right]^T \tag{79}$$

Problems (62) and (73) have nonnegative error constraints. However, if the error variable is negative, then the first constraint of both problems can still be satisfied if the error variable is set to zero. Setting the error variable to zero also decreases the objective function value; hence, the error constraint can be removed. In classification, the main concentration is the ability to generalize with weights obtained from a model, i.e., the solution to the decision variables. The functional value of the objective function is not so much of a problem. However, if one is overly concerned about the objective function, then the nonnegative constraints can be dropped from both models (62) and (73). Hence, the last row and column of block matrices (74) and (77) will not be necessary.

Fung & Mangasarian (2005) extended the PSVM idea to the multi-classification case. This SVM formulation is called multi-category proximal support vector machine (MPSVM)—similar to the binary case—which classifies new points by assigning them to the closer of the two parallel planes that are as far apart as possible. The idea is closely aligned with the OAA method where the i-th class is separated from the rest.

The Linear Proximal Support Vector Machine (LPSVM) is described through the following optimization problem.

$$\min_{(w,\gamma)\in R^{n+1}} \frac{\nu}{2}\left\|D(Aw-e\gamma)-e\right\|^2+\frac{1}{2}\left\|\begin{bmatrix} w \\ \gamma \end{bmatrix}\right\|^2 \tag{80}$$

The membership of each point in A is specified by an $m\times m$ matrix, D, whose diagonals are labels $D_{ii}\in\{+1,-1\}$. To obtain the nonlinear classifying weights, problem (80) is modified using a dual representation of $w = A'D\alpha$, where α is a dual variable.

The Nonlinear Proximal Support Vector Machine is described through the following optimization problem:

$$\min_{(\alpha,\gamma)\in R^{m+1}} \frac{\nu}{2}\left\|D(K(A,A')D\alpha-e\gamma)-e\right\|^2+\frac{1}{2}\left\|\begin{bmatrix} \alpha \\ \gamma \end{bmatrix}\right\|^2 \tag{81}$$

In order to obtain the classification weights, we need to solve the optimality conditions of problems (80) and (81).

4.4 Further Techniques Based on Central Representations of the Version Space

So far we have considered methods based on linear and quadratic programming. Next, we consider additional approaches which use the concept of the center of a convex set, and general nonlinear programming techniques. We will consider recent approaches to improve generalization performance over standard SVMs and to create hypotheses which are sparse. Our interpretation is based on the observation that the dual of input space data points become hyperplanes and separating hyperplane becomes points. Version space is defined as the space of all hypotheses (points) consistent with the data and this space is bounded by the set of hyperplanes representing the data.

An SVM solution can be viewed as the centre of the largest inscribable hypersphere in version space; the support vectors correspond to those examples with hyper-planes tangentially touching this hyperphere (Figure 7). If a version space is elongated, then the centre of the largest inscribed hypersphere does not appear to be the best choice (Figure 7). A better choice would be the Bayes point which is approximately the centre of mass of the version space. Bayes Point Machines (BPMs) construct a hypothesis based on this centre of version space and this choice can be justified by theoretical arguments (Opper & Haussler, 1991; Watkin & Rau, 1993) in addition to having a geometric appeal.

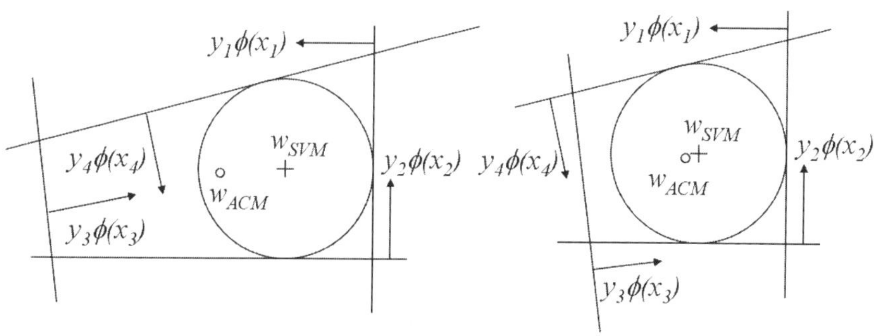

Figure 7. The analytic centre of version space (W_{ACM}) and the centre of the largest inscribed sphere (W_{SVM}) in an elongated version space (Trafalis & Malyscheff, 2002.)

In one approach the centre of mass is determined using a kernelized billiard algorithm in which the version space is traversed uniformly and an estimate of the centre of mass is repeatedly updated. For a large majority of datasets the version space diverges from sphericality and the BPM outperforms an SVM at statistically significant levels. For artificial examples with very elongated version spaces the generalization error of a BPM can be half that of an SVM (Herbrich, et al., 2001; Herbrich, et al., 2000). However, current implementations of BPMs have a number of drawbacks: the algorithm can be slow in execution and better mechanisms for a soft boundary (imitating a soft margin) need to be found. Rather than using the centre of mass of version space an alternative might be to use a hypothesis that lies towards the centre of this space but which is easier to compute. Such an example is the Analytic Center Machine (Trafalis & Malyscheff, 2002). The Bayes Point Machine may exhibit good generalization but it has the disadvantage that the hypothesis is dense, i.e., nearly all data points appear in the final hypothesis. Ideally, we would also like to derive kernel classifiers which give sparse hypotheses using a minimal number of data points. The most effective means of obtaining sparse hypotheses remains the object of research but an excellent approach is the Relevance Vector Machine of Tipping (Tipping, 2000).

5. Some Applications

The application of SVMs in the field of tornado forecasting has been investigated by Trafalis et al. (2003; 2004; 2005). Trafalis et al. (2003) compared SVMs with other classification methods such as neural networks and radial basis function networks and showed that SVMs are more effective in tornado classification. Trafalis et al. (2004; 2005) also investigated the Bayesian approach in SVMs and neural networks and suggested that Bayesian SVMs and Bayesian neural networks provide significantly higher skills compared to traditional neural networks. In the breast cancer research, Lee et al. (1999) suggested that SVMs can be used to classify breast cancer patients into three prognostic groups (good, intermediate, and poor) with well separated Kaplan-Meier survival curves and select variables that are important for prognosis.

5.1 Enterprise Modeling (Novelty Detection)

For many real-world problems the task is not to classify but to detect novel or abnormal instances. Novelty or abnormality detection has potential applications in many problem domains such as condition monitoring or medical diagnosis.

One approach is to model the support of a data distribution (rather than having to find a real-valued function for estimating the density of the data itself). Thus, at its simplest level, the objective is to create a binary valued function which is positive in those regions of input space where the data predominantly lies and negative elsewhere. One approach (Tax & Duin, 1999) is to find a hypersphere with a minimal radius which contains most of the data with the novel test points lying outside the boundary of this hypersphere. This technique was originally suggested by Vapnik (1995), see also Burges (1998). Then it was interpreted as a novelty detector by Tax and Duin (1999) and was also used for real life applications (Tax, et al., 1999). The effect of outliers is reduced by using slack variables to allow for data points outside the sphere and the task is to minimize the volume of the sphere and number of data points outside the sphere (Burges, 1998).

Using a combination of feature selection and input engineering approaches, (Guyon & Elisseeff, 2003; Witten & Frank, 2005; Liu & Yu, 2005) a number of attribute sets and their effectiveness toward improving the predictive performance of the data mining algorithms examined were analyzed. This set of attributes was drawn from the transaction stream gathered by an enterprise supply-chain software system during the normal management of the bench stock inventory. These transactions include the date, time and often quantity related to the specific event or action, such as orders, receipts, stock shortage notices, stock outages, and inventory location reviews.

Though, the inventory under examination, and the processes that support its management do not allow for the typical inventory metric collection. Important features such as time of demand and quantity issued were not recorded; maintenance workers remove items from the inventory locations for immediate use in the maintenance task. This fact complicates the problem of predicting these rare events. In the preliminary analysis, researchers established, through a series of experiments, that several data mining algorithms could provide a prediction capability with a minimum degree of confidence (Beardslee and Trafalis 2005). However, a limitation of that work is the lack of a methodical feature selection approach and the analysis of the impact of the various attributes on the performance of the data mining algorithms examined.

Detection of credit card fraud behavior is of great importance for financial institutions. One of the biggest problems associated with credit card fraud detection is the lack of both literatures that provides experimental results and real world data for academic researchers to perform experiments on. Fraud detection is often associated with sensitive and confidential financial data for reasons of client privacy, and as a result such information is hard to come by. In credit card fraud detection, the key idea is to apply some learning algorithm to a set of training data which consists of some feature values (credit card transaction data) that is inherent to the credit card transaction system. After learning is performed (training of the input data), the objective is to correctly classify the transaction it has never seen before (new features of the credit card transaction data) as fraudulent or not fraudulent.

Maes et al. (2002) acquired real world data provided by Serge Waterschoot at Europay International (EPI). The data consists of a set of features that contain useful information about credit card transactions. Two machine learning techniques were applied to the transaction data, artificial neural networks (ANN) and Bayesian belief networks (BBN). They contend that the BBN performs better that the ANN when applied to the transaction data, with the BBN detecting 8% more of the fraudulent transactions. Other observations were noted such as learning times for the ANN taking several hours, while it takes about 20 minutes for the BBN, and evaluation of new examples (feature values) are typically much faster for ANN than for BBN.

Yohda et al. (2002) proposed a new methodology using neural networks and Fourier transforms for new product demand forecasting in supply chain management. The time series data of sales results used are transformed into a combination of frequency data by discrete Fourier transform (DFT) and identified from objective indexes, which consist of product properties or economic indicators (input attributes). The accuracy of the demand forecasting is expected to improve using frequency data instead of time series data because the frequency data has feature information, which is extracted from the time series data. Based on the analysis, the forecast of the Fourier transform based network is superior to the forecast only by neural networks.

In the study conducted by Chinnam (2002), it was described how a SVM model can be used for recognizing shifts in correlated and non-correlated manufacturing processes. Traditionally, shifts in processes have been detected by using statistical process control (SPC) techniques of control charting. However, its suitability and applicability in process industries (chemical industries) that generate autocorrelated data makes it a difficult task of identifying the presence of assignable causes. Using the papermaking and viscosity datasets (available in the literature), the application of SVMs was shown to be effective in minimizing both Type-I errors (probability that the method would wrongly declare the process to be out of control or generate a false alarm) and Type-II errors (probability that the method will be unable to detect a true shift or trend present in the process) in these autocorrelated processes when compared with other machine learning methods. SVMs were also found to be effective at minimizing both Type-I and Type-II errors when monitoring non-correlated processes, and once again performed as well or better than the classical Shewhart control charts and other machine learning methods. These observations show how powerful and useful SVMs can be in the analysis of process industry data, and more importantly it presents the invaluable use of SVMs as an alternative to SPC techniques in the area of quality engineering.

In an attempt to develop an automated procedure for the selection of partners for the successful operation and management of virtual enterprises (VEs), Wang et al. (2004) proposed an SVM solution. The increasing competitiveness in the global market, dynamic alliances and virtual enterprises are becoming essential components of the economy in order to meet the market requirements for quality, responsiveness, and customer satisfaction. Partner selection is a key stage in the formation of a successful VE. The partners are selected based on their skill and resources to fulfill the requirements of the VEs which include variables such as organizational fit, technological capabilities, relationship development, quality, price and speed. Partner selection is an unstructured and multi-criterion decision problem, which can be considered as multi-class classification problem. As a result, the SVM model in a multi-class framework (model problem 56) was used to select the partners of VEs. In comparison with other methods in the literatures, the SVM-based method is advantageous in terms of generalization performance and the fitness accuracy with a limited number of training datasets.

Recently, Ahn et al. (2006) proposed a hybrid genetic algorithm and case-based reasoning (CBR) system for customer classification. An important issue in customer relationship management is customer classification, by which a company classifies its customers into predefined groups with similar behavior patterns. This is done so that companies build a customer classification model to find the prospects for a specific product. In their study, they classify prospects into either purchasing or non-purchasing groups, a simple two-class classification problem. Benefits of this kind of knowledge may create a variety of marketing opportunities for the company such as one-to-one marketing, direct mailing, and sales promotion via telephone or e-mail.

A CBR is a problem-solving technique that reuses past experiences to find a solution. It often improves the effectiveness of complex and unstructured decision making, and so it has been applied to various problem-solving areas including manufacturing, finance and marketing. However, it has a critical limitation as a classification technique because its prediction accuracy is generally much lower than the accuracy of other artificial intelligence techniques such as artificial neural networks and SVMs. As a result, simultaneous optimization of several components in CBR using a genetic algorithm (GA) was employed, and was found to improve the classification accuracy. The hybrid system of GA and CBR outperforms the other machine learning methods, but with a much longer computational time due to the optimization of the optimal parameters. The SVM model also performed well for customer classification, outperforming the LOGIT (logistic regression), MDA (multiple discriminant analysis), and ANNs (artificial neural networks).

More recently SVMs have been applied to short term portfolio management (Ince and Trafalis, 2006a), exchange rate prediction (Ince and Trafalis, 2006b) and stock price prediction (Ince and Trafalis, 2003, Ince and Trafalis, 2006c). Other interesting applications are in the area of production (Alenezi et al., 2005), inventory transactions (Beardslee and Trafalis, 2005), bioinformatics and gene analysis (Santosa et al., 2002, Santosa et al., 2006) and web mining (Chung et al., 2002). SVMs have also been applied in manufacturing (Malyscheff et al., 2002, Prakasvudhisarn et al., 2003). Some interesting applications are also described in the special issue on Support Vector Machines and Applications, *Computational Management Science* (Trafalis, 2006).

5.2 Non-Enterprise Modeling Application (Multiphase Flow)

Multiphase flow is the simultaneous flow of two or more phases in a conduit. The simultaneous flow causes certain flow patterns to evolve depending on the pipe size, the flow rates, the fluid properties, and the pipe inclination angle (when appropriate). Accurate determination of the flow regime is critical in the design of multiphase flow systems, which are used in various industrial processes including boiling and condensation, oil and gas pipelines, and the design of cooling systems for nuclear reactors.

The problem of identifying flow regimes is the result of lack of universal delineation criteria for the transition zones from one pattern to the other. Considerable progress has been made in defining flow patterns (Trafalis et al., 2005); however there is no exact theory for the characterization of these patterns. Furthermore, the subjective character of the flow pattern identification often causes disagreements between researchers. While there is agreement on the existence of several flow patterns, there is often disagreement about the delineation point/transition boundaries for each flow pattern. Such disagreements make the selection of an appropriate flow correlation a complicated issue.

The multiphase flow phenomenon was investigated using a multi-classification SVM (MSVM) (Trafalis et al., 2005). In that study, the MSVM model was trained using the vertical and horizontal two-phase flow patterns data. The attributes of interest were the size of pipe, and the superficial gas and liquid velocities. In comparison with the theoretical correlations developed by multiphase flow researchers, the MSVM model reported the best accuracy.

The MSVM based two-phase flow regime maps were qualitatively similar to the theoretical maps available in the literature (i.e., the flow regimes appeared at the same region of the map), but differed in the exact position of the transition boundaries (see Figure 8). The transition zones of the MSVM maps were based strictly on the support vectors of the training data. These support vectors are the most critical points of each flow pattern, and they were used to define the transition boundaries from one flow pattern to another. The transition zones of the theoretical maps were based on analytical models and/or dimensionless correlations which explore relationships between fluid properties, pipe size and flow rates (McQuillan & Whalley, 1985).

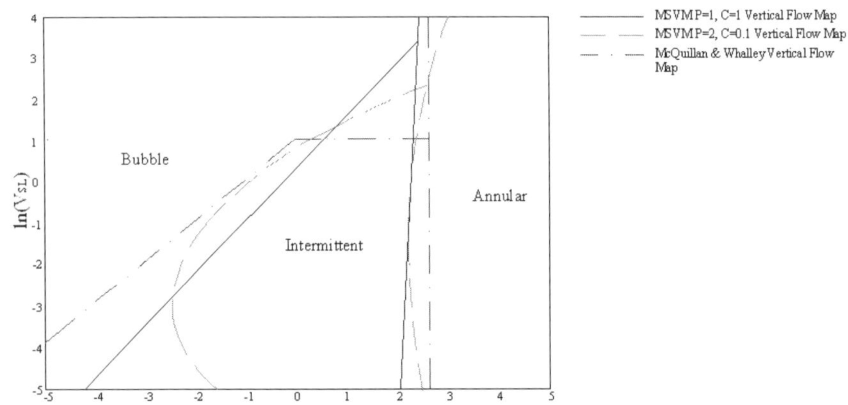

Figure 8. Vertical two-phase flow regime map that results from a 2D multi-class SVM model using polynomial kernel (p = 1, C = 1, solid lines; p = 2, C = 0.1, curved dashed lines) and the theoretical McQuillan & Whalley[4] correlation (dot-dashed lines) for an air-water system. (The transition boundaries were determined on the basis of the logarithm of the superficial gas, V_{SG}, and superficial liquid velocity, V_{SL}).

There is a noticeable difference between the maps with polynomial kernels of degrees 1 and 2. A polynomial of degree 1 is an indication that the flow patterns might actually be linearly separable, i.e., separation of flow patterns can be accomplished with linear equations, while degree 2 clearly implies a nonlinear transition boundary between flow patterns. The MSVM maps had very good prediction capability, outperforming the theoretical model maps in terms of accurately classifying a data point. For the 2-D vertical flow classification test and whole dataset (i.e., combined training and testing datasets), the MSVM accuracies were between 93 – 99 %.

6. Conclusions

In this chapter we have reviewed the theory of SVMs from the perspective of the binary and multiclass classification. Our description was based on optimization and regularization.

Several applications have also been discussed. The implementation of data mining models such as neural networks and Bayesian networks have found success in the application to credit card fraud detection problem (Maes et al., 2002). In future applications of such detection problems, the use of support vector machines or kernel based machines should be employed. Unlike NNs, SVMs have better generalization properties. They solve convex optimization problems providing a global optimal solution in contrast to NNs where the resulting training optimization problem is nonconvex and therefore the solution is a local minimum. SVMs problems have long training time for large scale problems, and problems of parameter tuning. However, researchers are now employing genetic algorithms and pattern search algorithms for the selection of SVM parameters.

Another application area of SVMs is in electronic commerce. In electronic commerce an interesting question would be trying to identify the most valuable clients so as to increase market share. The successful identification of a valuable client aids the decision regarding retaining of such a client or target of new clients with similar features.

Many approaches have not been discussed such as SVMs with noisy data (Trafalis and Gilbert, 2006ab, Santosa and Trafalis, 2006) and SVM clustering. Robustness is important because it can account for uncertainties in seasonal patterns which might exist for example, in the detection of credit card fraud and other applications with seasonal data. The subject is still very much under development, but it can be expected to develop an important tool for data mining, machine learning, and applications in business, engineering and science.

SVMs and kernel methods have been found to work well in practice. The subject is still very much under development but it can be expected to develop an important tool for data mining, machine learning, and applications.

References

Ahn, H., Kim, K-J, Han, I. (2006). Hybrid genetic algorithms and case-based reasoning systems for customer classification. *Expert Systems*, **23**(3), 127 – 144.

Alenezi, A., Moses, S., Trafalis, T.B. (2005). Flowtime estimation for multi-resource production systems using support vector regression., In *Intelligent Engineering Systems Through Artificial Neural Networks*, C.H. Dagli, A.L. Buczak, M.J. Embrechts, O. Ersoy, and D.L. Enke (Eds.), ASME Press, **15**, 699-702.

Baesens B., Viane, S., Van Gestel, T., Suykens, J.A.K., Dedene, G.,K., De Moor, B., Vanthiennen, J. (2000). An empirical assessment of kernel type performance for least squares support vector machine classifiers, *Proceedings of the 4th International Conference on Knowledge-Based Intelligent Engineering System and Allied Technologies (KES2000)*, Brighton, UK.

Bazaraa, M.S., Sherali, H.D., Shetty, C.M. (1993). *Nonlinear Programming – Theory and Algorithms*. John Wiley & Sons, Inc.

Beardslee, E.A., Trafalis, T.B. (2005). Data mining methods in a metrics-deprived inventory transactions environment, In *Data Mining VI: Data Mining, Text Mining and their Business Applications*, A. Zanasi, C.A. Brebbia, and N.F.F. Ebecken (Eds.) MIT Press: Southhampton, UK, 5132-522.

Bennet, K.P., Mangasarian O.L. (1994). Multicategory discrimination via linear programming, *Optimization Methods and Software*, **3**, 27-39.

Bredensteiner E. J.; Bennet, K. P. (1999). Multicategory classification by support vector machines, *Computational Optimization and Applications*, **12**, 53–79.

Brierley, P., Batty B. (1999). Data mining with neural networks—an applied example in understanding electricity consumption patterns, In *Knowledge Discovery and Data Mining*, M.A. Bramer (Ed.), pp. 182-188 (The Institute of Electrical Engineers, London).

Burges, C.J.C. (1998). A tutorial on support vector machines for pattern classification, *Data Mining and Knowledge Discovery*, 2(2):121-167.

Chang, C-C., Lin, C-J. (2001). LIBSVM: A Library for Support Vector Machines (http://www.csie.ntu.edu.tw/~cjlin/libsvm).

Chinnam, R.B. (2002). Support vector machines for recognizing shifts in correlated and other manufacturing processes, *International Journal of Production Research*, **40**(17), 4449 – 4466.

Chung, W.S., Trafalis, T.B., Guenwald, L. (2002). Support vector clustering for web usage mining, In *Intelligent Engineering Systems Through Artificial Neural Networks*, C.H. Dagli, A.L. Buczak, J. Ghösh, M.J. Embrechts, O.Ersoy, and S.W. Kercel (Eds.), ASME Press, **12**, 385-390.

Cristianini, N., Shawe-Taylor, J., (2000). *Support Vector Machines and Other Kernel-based Learning Methods*. Cambridge University Press, Oxford, UK.

Dhond, A., Gupta, A., and Vadhavkar, S., (2000). Data mining techniques for optimizing inventories for electronic commerce, In *Proc. of the 6th ACM SIGKDD Int. Conf. on Knowledge Discovery and Data Mining*.

Ding, C. H. Q., Dubchak, I. (2001). Multi-class protein fold recognition using support vector machines and neural networks, *Bioinformatics*,**17**, 349-358.

Evgeniou, T.; Pontil, M.; Poggio, T. (2000). Regularization networks and support vector machines, *Advances in Computational Mathematics*, **13**, 1-50.

Fung, G., Mangasarian, O.L. (2005). Multicategory proximal support vector machine classifiers. Data Mining Institute Technical Report 01-06, July 2001; *Machine Learning*, 59, 77-97.

Fung, G., Mangasarian, O.L. (2001). Proximal support vector machine classifiers, In *Proceedings KDD2001: Knowledge Discovery and Data Mining*, August 26-29, San Francisco, CA, U.S.A., 64-70. ftp://ftp.cs.wisc.edu/pub/dmi/tech-reports/01-02.ps.

Girosi, F. (1998). An equivalence between sparse approximation and support vector machines, *Neural Computation*, **10**(6), 1455-1480.

Guyon, I. and Elisseeff, A. (2005). An introduction to variable and feature selection, *Journal of Machine Learning Research*, **3**, 1157-1182.

Herbrich, R., Graepel, TH., Campbell, C. (2001). Bayes point machines, *Journal of Machine Learning Research*, **1**, 245–279.

Herbrich, R., Graepel, TH., Campbell, C. (2000). Robust Bayes point machines, *Proceedings of ESANN2000*. D-Facto Publications: Bruges, Belgium, 49-54.

Hsu, C-W., Chang, C-C., Lin, C-J. (2003). A practical guide to support vector classification, Technical Report, Department of Computer Science and Information Engineering, National Taiwan University, Taipei 106, Taiwan.

Hsu, C-W., Lin, C-J. (2002). A comparison of methods for multi-class support vector machines, *IEEE Transactions on Neural Networks*, **13**, 415 – 425.

Ince, H., Trafalis, T.B. (2007). Kernel principal component analysis and support vector machines for stock price prediction, *IIE Transactions,* Special Issue on Data Mining and Web Mining, 39(6), 629-637.

Ince, H., Trafalis, T. B. (2006). A hybrid model for exchange rate prediction. Decision Support Systems, 42(2), 1054-1062.

Ince, H., Trafalis, T.B. (2006a). Kernel methods for short term portfolio management, *Expert Systems and Its Applications*, **30**(3), 535-542.

Ince, H., Trafalis, T.B. (2003). Short Term Forecasting with Support Vector Machines and Application to Stock Price Prediction, in *Intelligent Engineering Systems Through Artificial Networks*, C.H. Dagli, A.L. Buezak, J. Ghösh, M.J. Embrechts, O. Ersoy, and S.W. Kercel, eds. ASME Press, **13**, 737-742.

Ivanov, V.V. (1976). *The Theory of Approximate Methods and Their Application to the Numerical Solution of Singular Integral Equations*, Nordhoff International, Leyden, The Netherlands.

Lee, Y-J., Mangasarian, O.L., Wolberg, W.H. (2003). Survival-time classification of breast cancer patients, *Computational Optimization and Applications*, 25, 151-166.

Lee, Y.-J., Mangasarian, O.L., Wolberg, W.H. (1999). Breast cancer survival analysis and chemotherapy via generalized support vector machines. Center for Discrete Mathematics and Theoretical Computer Science at Rutgers University (DIMACS), Workshop on Discrete Mathematical Problems with Medical Applications; 1999 December 8-10.

Liu, H., Yu, L. (2005). Toward integrating feature selection algorithms for classification and clustering, *IEEE Transactions on Knowledge and Data Engineering*, **17**(4), 491-502.

Maes, S., Tuyls, K., Vanschoenwinkel, B., Manderick, B. (2002). Credit card fraud detection using Bayesian and neural networks. In *Proceedings of the 1st International NAISO Congress on Neuro Fuzzy Technologies*, Havana, Cuba.

Malyscheff, A.M., Trafalis, T.B., Raman, S. (2002). From support vector machine learning to the determination of the minimum enclosing zone, *Computers and Industrial Engineering*, 42, 59-74.

Malyscheff, A. M., Trafalis, T.B. (2003). Support vector machines and the electoral college, *Proceedings of the International Joint Conference on Neural Networks*, Portland, Oregon, USA, IEEE Press, 2345-2348.

Mangasarian, O.L. (2001, 2003). Data mining via support vector machines, Data Mining Institute Technical Report 01-05, May 2001. IFIP Conference on System Modeling and Optimization, July 23-27, 2001; Trier, Germany. System Modeling and Optimization XX, E. W. Sachs and R. Tichatschke, eds. Boston:Kluwer Academic Publishers, 2003, 91-112.

McQuillan, K.W., Whalley, P.B. (1985). Flow patterns in vertical two-phase flow, *International Journal of Multiphase Flow*, **11**, 161–175.

Morozov, V.A. (1984). *Methods for Solving Incorrectly Posed Problems.* Springer-Verlag: Boston, MA, U.S.A.

Oladunni, O., Trafalis, T.B. (2005). Least square multi-classification support vector machines: pairwise (P_ALS-MSVM) & piecewise (P_ILS-MSVM) formulations, *WSEAS Transactions on Circuits and Systems*, 4(4), 363-368.

Opper, M., Haussler, D. (1991). Generalization performance of Bayes optimal classification algorithm for learning a perceptron, *Physical Review Letters*, **66**, 2677-2680.

Pelckmans, K., Suykens, J.A.K., De Moor, B. Morozov, Ivanov and Tikhonov. (2004). Regularization based LS-SVMs, *Proceedings of the International Conference On Neural Information Processing (ICONIP)*, November 22-25, Calcutta, India.

Platt, J.C., Cristianini, N., Shawe-Taylor, J. (2000). Large margin DAGs for multiclass classification, *Advances in Neural Information Processing Systems*, MIT Press, **12**, 547-553.

Piramuthu, S. (1999). The Hausdorff distance measure for feature selection in learning applications. In *Proc. of the 32nd Annual Hawaii Int. Conf. on System Sciences (HICSS-32).*

Poggio, T., Rifkin. R., Mukherjee, S., and Niyogi, P. (2004). General conditions for predictivity in learning theory. *Nature*, **428**, 419-422.

Prakasvudhisarn, C., Trafalis, T.B. and Raman, S. (2003). Support Vector regression for determination of minimum zone, *Transactions of ASME, Journal of Manufacturing Science and Engineering*, **125**(4), 736-739.

Reklaitis, G.V., Ravindran, A., Ragsdell, K.M.B. (1983). *Engineering Optimization: Methods and Applications.* John Wiley & Sons, Inc.

Santosa, B., Conway, T., Trafalis, T.B. (2002). Knowledge based-clustering and application of multi-class SVM for genes expression analysis, *Intelligent Engineering Systems through Artificial Neural Networks,* **12**, 391–395.

Schőlkopf, B., Smola, A. Learning with Kernels. (2002). *Support Vector Machines, Regularization, Optimization, and Beyond*, Bernhard Schölkopf and Alexander J. Smola (Eds.), The MIT Press, Cambridge, MA, U.S.A.

Schölkopf, B., Smola, A., Müller, K.-R. (1999). Kernel principal component analysis. In *Advances in Kernel Methods - Support Vector Learning*, B. Schölkopf, C. J. C. Burges, and A. J. Smola (Eds.) MIT Press: Cambridge, MA, U.S.A., 327-352.

Schőlkopf, B., Burges, C., Smola, A. (1998). *Advances in Kernel Methods: Support Vector Machines.* MIT Press: Cambridge, MA, U.S.A.

Smola, A., Barlett, P., Schőlkopf, B., Schuurmans, C., eds. (2001). *Advances in Large Margin Classifiers.* MIT Press: Cambridge, MA, U.S.A.

Suykens, J.A.K., Lukas, L., Vandewalle, J. (2000). Sparse approximation using least squares support vector machines. In *Proceedings of the IEEE*

International Symposium on Circuits and Systems (ISCAS'00), May 2000, Geneva, Switzerland, II 757-II 760.

Suykens, J.A.K., Lukas, L., Vandewalle, J. (2000). Sparse least squares support vector machine classifiers. *Proceedings of the European Symposium on Artificial Neural Networks (ESANN'00)*, Bruges, Belgium, 37-42.

Suykens, J. A. K., Vandewalle, J. (1999c). Multiclass least squares support vector machine classifiers. *Proceedings of the Joint Conference on Neural Networks (IJCNN'99)*, Washington D. C., U. S. A.

Suykens, J. A. K., Vandewalle, J. (1999b). Least squares support vector machine classifiers, *Neural Processing Letters*, **9**, 293-300.

Suykens, J. A. K., Lukas, L., Van Dooren, P., De Moor, B., Vandewalle, J. (1999). Least squares support vector machine classifiers: A large scale algorithm. *Proceedings of the European Conference on Circuit Theory and Design (ECCTD'99)*, 839-842.

Szedmak, S., Shawe-Taylor, J., Saunders, C.J., Hardoon, D.R. (2004). Multiclass classification by L_1 norm support vector machine. In *Pattern Recognition and Machine Learning in Computer Vision Workshop*, May 2-4, Grenoble, France.

Tax, D., Duin, R. (1999). Data domain description by support vectors. *Proceedings of ESANN99*, M Verleysen, D. Facto (Eds.), Press, Brussels, Belgium, 251-256.

Tax, D., Ypma, A., Duin, R. (1999). Support vector data description applied to machine vibration analysis, *Proceedings of the 5th Annual Conference of the Advanced School for Computing and Imaging*, M. Boasson, J. Kaandorp, J.Tonino, M. Vosselman, (Eds.) Heijen, NL, June 15-17, 398-405.

Tikhonov, A.N., Arsenin, V.Y. (1977). *Solution of Ill-Posed Problems*. Winston, Washington D. C., U. S. A.

Tipping, M. The Relevance Vector Machine. (2000). In Advances in Neural Information Processing Systems 12, Sara A Solla, Todd K Leen, and Klaus-Robert Muller (Eds.), MIT Press: Cambridge, MA, U.S.A.

Trafalis, T.B. (2006). Special Issue on Support Vector Machines and Applications, *Computational Management Science*, 3(2), 101-174.

Trafalis, T.B., Gilbert, R.C. (2007). Robust support vector machines for classification and computational issues, *Optimization Methods and Software*, 22(1), 187-198.

Trafalis, T.B., Gilbert, R.C. (2006). Robust classification and regression using support vector machines, *European Journal of Operational Research*, 173(3), 893-909.

Trafalis, T., Santosa, B., Richman, M. (2005). Learning networks for tornado forecasting: a Bayesian perspective. *Proceedings of the 6th International Conference on Data Mining, Text Mining and their Business Applications*. Skiathos, Greece.

Trafalis, T.B., Oladunni, O., Papavassiliou, D.V. (2005). Two-phase flow regime identification with a multi-classification SVM model. *Industrial & Engineering Chemistry Research*, **44**, 4414–4426.

Trafalis, T.B., Oladunni, O. (2005). Pairwise multi-classification support vector machine: quadratic programming (QP-P_AMSVM) formulations. *WSEAS Transactions on Systems*, **4**(4), 349-354.

Trafalis, T., Santosa, B., Richman, M. (2004). Bayesian neural networks for tornado detection. *WSEAS Transactions on Systems*, **3**, 3211–3216.

Trafalis, T.B., Oladunni, O. (2004). Single Phase Fluid Flow Classification via Neural Networks & Support Vector Machine. *Intelligent Engineering Systems Through Artificial Neural Networks*, C.H. Dagli, A.L. Buczak, D. L. Enke, M.J. Embrechts, and O. Ersoy (Eds.), ASME Press, **14**, 427-432.

Trafalis, T., Ince, H., Richman, M. (2003). Tornado detection with support vector machines. In *Computational Science -ICCS 2003*, P. M. Sloot, D. Abramson, A. Bogdanov, J. J. Dongarra, A. Zomaya, and Y. Gorbachev (Eds.), 202 – 211.

Trafalis, T.B., Malyscheff, A.M. (2002). An Analytic Center Machine, *Machine Learning*, 46, 203-223.

Trafalis, T.B., Ince, H. (2000). Support vector machine for regression and applications to financial forecasting, *IEEE-INNS-ENNS International Joint Conference on Neural Networks*, July 24-27, Como, Italy.

Van Gestel, T., Suykens, J. A. K., Baesens B., Viane, S., Vanthiennen, J., Dedene, G., De Moor, B., Vandewalle, J. (2004). Benchmarking least squares support vector machine classifiers, *Machine Learning*, **54**(1), 5–32.

Vapnik, V. (1998). *Statistical Learning Theory*. John Wiley & Sons, Inc..

Vapnik, V. (1995). *The Nature of Statistical Learning Theory*. Springer-Verlag, New York, NY, U.S.A.

Wai-Ho Au, Chan, Keith C.C., Yao, X. (2003). A novel evolutionary data mining algorithm with applications to churn prediction, *IEEE Transactions on Evolutionary Computation*, **7**(6),532-545.

Wang, J., Zhong, W., Zhang, J. (2004). Support vector machine approach for partner selection of virtual enterprises. J. Zhang et al. (Eds.): *CIS 2004, Lecture notes in Computer Science*, LNCS 3314, Springer-Verlag: Berlin Heidelberg, Germany, 1247-1253.

Watkin, T., Rau, A. (1993). The statistical mechanics of learning a rule. *Reviews of Modern Physics*, 65, 499-556.

Weston, J., Gammerman, A., Stitson, M., Vapnik, V., Vovk, V., Watkins, C. "Support Vector Density Estimation." (1999). In *Advances in Kernel Methods, Support Vector Learning*, B. Scholkopf, C.J.C. Burges, A.J. Smola, (Eds.) MIT Press: Cambridge, MA, U.S.A., 293-305.

Weston, J., Watkins, C. (1999). Multi-class Support Vector Machines. In Proceedings of ESANN99, M. Verleysen, (Ed). D. Facto Press: Brussels, Belgium.

Witten, I.H. and Frank, E., (2005). *Data Mining: Practical Machine Learning Tools and Techniques* -2nd ed., Morgan Kaufmann: San Francisco, CA, U.S.A.

Yohda, M., Saito-Arita, M., Okada, A., Suzuki, R., Kakemoto, Y. (2002). Demand forecasting by the neural network with discrete Fourier transform. In *Proc. of the ICDM 2002 and 2002 IEEE International Conference*, 9-12 December 2002, pp.779 – 782.

Authors' Biographical Statements

Dr. Theodore B. Trafalis is a Professor and Director of the Optimization Intelligent Systems Laboratory in the School of Industrial Engineering at the University of Oklahoma. He earned his BS in Mathematics from the University of Athens, Greece, his MS in Applied Mathematics, MSIE, and PhD in Operations Research from Purdue University. He is a member of INFORMS, SIAM, Institute of Industrial Engineers, and a few other professional societies.

He was a visiting Assistant Professor at Purdue University (1989–1990), an invited Research Fellow at Delft University of Technology, Netherlands (1996), and a visiting Associate Professor at Blaise Pascal University, France, and at the Technical University of Crete (1998). He was also an invited visiting Associate Professor at Akita Prefectural University, Japan (2001). His research interests include operations research/management science, mathematical programming, interior point methods, multiobjective optimization, control theory, artificial neural networks, kernel methods, evolutionary programming, data mining, and global optimization. He has published more than 100 articles in journals, conference proceedings, edited books, made over 100 technical presentations and received several awards for his papers. He has been continuously funded through National Science Foundation (NSF) and received the NSF research initiation award in 1991. He is an Associate Editor of *Computational Management Science* and *The Journal of Heuristics* and has been on the Program Committee of several international conferences in the field of intelligent systems and optimization.

Dr. Olutayo O. Oladunni is a Post-Doctoral Research Associate in the Department of Engineering Education at Purdue University in West Lafayette, Indiana. He earned his BS in Systems Engineering and Management from Richmond the American International University in London, and his MS and PhD in Industrial Engineering from the University of Oklahoma, Norman, Oklahoma. He is a member of NSBE, IIE, and INFORMS. His research interests include support vector machines, kernel methods, engineering optimization, optimization data mining, scientific computing, applied statistics and quality engineering. He has authored and coauthored 12 published articles in journals, conference proceedings, and edited books. His current research is in the modeling of student success and effectiveness of teams.

Chapter 15[1]

A Survey of Manifold-Based Learning Methods

Xiaoming Huo[1], Xuelei (Sherry) Ni[2], and Andrew K. Smith[1]
[1]School of Industrial Engineering, Georgia Institute of Technology, Atlanta, GA, U.S.A.
Email: xiaoming@isye.gatech.edu
[2]Department of Mathematics and Statistics, Kennesaw State University, GA, U.S.A.
Email: xni2@kennesaw.edu

Abstract: We review the ideas, algorithms, and numerical performance of manifold-based machine learning and dimension reduction methods. The representative methods include locally linear embedding (LLE), ISOMAP, Laplacian eigenmaps, Hessian eigenmaps, local tangent space alignment (LTSA), and charting. We describe the insights from these developments, as well as new opportunities for both researchers and practitioners. Potential applications in image and sensor data are illustrated. This chapter is based on an invited survey presentation that was delivered by Huo at the 2004 INFORMS Annual Meeting, which was held in Denver, CO, U.S.A.

***Key Words*:** Manifold, Statistical earning, Nonparametric methods, Dimension reduction.

---

[1] Liao, T.W. and E. Triantaphyllou, (Eds.), **Recent Advances in Data Mining of Enterprise Data: Algorithms and Applications**, *World Scientific*, Singapore, pp. 691-745, 2007.

1. Introduction

Manifold-based learning is an emerging and promising approach in nonparametric dimension reduction. In this chapter, we review the state-of-the-art mathematical developments, as well as some interesting applications.

A manifold is a topological space that is locally Euclidean (i.e., around every point, there is a neighborhood that is topologically the same as the open unit ball in $\Re^n$). A good example of a manifold is the Earth (Figure 1). Locally, at each point on the surface of the Earth, we have a 3-D coordinate system: two for location and the last one for the altitude. Globally, it is a 2-D sphere in a 3-D space.

Manifolds offer a powerful framework for dimension reduction. The key idea of dimension reduction is to find the most succinct low dimensional structure that is embedded in a higher dimensional space. Historically, Occam's razor has been used to justify dimension reduction. The key idea of Occam's razor is to choose the simplest model from a set of equivalent models to explain a given phenomenon. It is easy to see that a manifold gives a dimension reduction. Moreover, if the data are indeed generated according to a manifold, then a manifold-based learning is, in some sense, optimal.

This chapter is organized as follows. Section 2 surveys existing methods, including principal components analysis (PCA), multidimensional scaling (MDS), generative topological mapping (GTM), locally linear embedding (LLE), ISOMAP, Laplacian eigenmaps, Hessian eigenmaps, and local tangent space alignment (LTSA). Section 3 stresses an important common point among some recent methods: their numerical solutions are based on searching for null spaces under certain situations. We choose LLE and LTSA as our illustrative examples. Such a common point is likely to be the key to unifying the theoretical analysis of many manifold-based methods. Section 4 presents some desirable performance properties of a learning method. Some preliminary thoughts in problem formulations and properties are described. For example, we establish the consistency of LTSA in Section 4.3.2. Section 5 gives some examples and potential applications, including examples of feature extraction in Section 5.1, an example of clustering in Section 5.2, a potential application in image detection in Section 5.3, and an application in sensor localization in Section 5.4. We provide some final thoughts on the future of the field in Section 6. Some additional useful resources are described in the Appendix.

Figure 1. An example of a manifold.

Relation to enterprise data mining (DM). This chapter does not directly address the DM in enterprise database. However, it provides powerful nonlinear dimension reduction methods, which are essentially useful in enterprise DM. One possible link is as follows (which is pointed out by an anonymous referee). Sensors are often used to monitor processes in a manufacturing enterprise. To inspect the product quality, images of the product are often captured and then processed to detect flaws. The image detection technique in Section 5.3 can potentially be applied. A second possible link is through object recognition in enterprise data. Manifold-based dimension reduction has potential to be applied there. The sensor location problem that is described in Section 5.4 is another potential application in enterprise data mining.

A generic 'prescription?' This chapter provides a comprehensive survey on existing manifold learning methods. For readers who are looking for a quick (and possibly dirty) solution, we suggest to experiment with local tangent space alignment (LTSA), which in our experience gives the most satisfactory performance in many cases. There are numerous software packages, which realize LTSA and are available freely on the internet. We refer to the URLs given at the end of this chapter. Scientifically speaking, each problem has to be analyzed before one can decide which method is optimal. Keeping this in mind, one should only take the above as a suggestion (not a rule) – there are always situations under which a method outperforms every other method, as reflected in the following detailed survey.

2. Survey of Existing Methods

We organize our presentation of methodologies into five groups.

Group 1: classical methods, including principal component analysis (PCA). We mention other methods that are related, such as factor analysis and other techniques in multivariate analysis.

Group 2: semi-classical methods, including multidimensional scaling (MDS), as described in Kruskal (1964) and Borg and Groenen (1997).

Group 3: manifold searching methods, including generative topographic mapping (GTM), referring to Bishop, Svensen, and Williams (1998), local linear embedding (LLE), referring to Roweis and Saul (2000), and ISOMAP, referring to Tenenbaum, de Silva, and Langford (2000).

Group 4: methods rooted in continuum spectral theory, including the Laplacian eigenmaps (Belkin and Niyogi, 2001) and Hessian eigenmaps (Donoho and Grimes, 2003), which are based on elegant theory in spectral analysis, and then discretize the results in the continuum to generate numerical approaches.

Group 5: advanced manifold methods, including charting (Brand, 2003) and local tangent space alignment (Zhang and Zha, 2004). These methods are based on global alignment. The key insight in these methods is the realization that the global alignment can be achieved via an eigenvalue computation.

Each group is described in its own subsection below.

2.1 Group 1: Principal Component Analysis (PCA)

Principal Component Analysis (PCA) is one of the most classical methods in dimension reduction. PCA is also known as the Karhunen-Loève transform, or singular value decomposition (SVD). The key idea of PCA is to find the low-dimensional linear subspace which captures the maximum proportion of the variation within the data.

PCA considers the second order statistics of a random vector $\mathbf{X} \in \Re^n$. Let X_1, X_2, ..., X_N denote N samples from such a random vector. Let Ω denote the variance-covariance matrix of the random vector $\mathbf{X}$, i.e., $\mathrm{Var}(\mathbf{X}) = \mathrm{E}\{[\mathbf{X} - \mathrm{E}(\mathbf{X})][\mathbf{X} - \mathrm{E}(\mathbf{X})]^{\mathrm{T}}\} = \Omega$. Assume the symmetric and positive-semidefinite matrix Ω has the following eigen-decomposition:

$$\Omega = UDU^T,$$

where $U \in \Re^{n \times n}$ is an orthogonal matrix ($U^T U = I_n$), and D is a diagonal matrix,

$$D = \begin{pmatrix} \lambda_1 & 0 & \cdots & 0 \\ 0 & \lambda_2 & \cdots & 0 \\ & & \ddots & \\ 0 & 0 & \cdots & \lambda_n \end{pmatrix}.$$

The diagonal entries of D, $0 \le \lambda_n \le \lambda_{n-1} \le \cdots \le \lambda_1$, are the ordered eigenvalues of Ω. The columns of U, $U = [U_1, U_2, \ldots, U_n]$, are the associated eigenvectors. From the following matrix computation, we can see that λ_1, λ_2, …, and λ_k are the variances of the transformed random variables $U_1{}^T\mathbf{X}$, $U_2{}^T\mathbf{X}$, …, and $U_k{}^T\mathbf{X}$:

$$\begin{aligned}\mathrm{Cov}\left([U_1^T X, U_2^T X, ..., U_n^T X]\right) &= \mathrm{Cov}(U^T X) \\ &= U^T \,\mathrm{Cov}(X) U \\ &= D.\end{aligned}$$

It is possible to prove that the projection $X \to [U_1, ..., U_k]^T X$ from $\Re^n$ to $\Re^k$ ($k<n$) keeps the greatest possible proportion of the variation in the data. If only the samples are available, the variance-covariance matrix can be estimated as

$$\sum_{i=1}^{N}(X_i - \overline{X})(X_i - \overline{X})^T \text{, where } \overline{X} = \frac{1}{N}\sum_{i=1}^{N} X_i .$$

PCA gives a natural dimension reduction. Consider an extreme case: if all the data lie in a low-dimensional linear subspace of a very high dimensional space, then PCA will find such a linear subspace, because the variations in the directions that are orthogonal to the embedded linear subspace will be equal to zero. An evident disadvantage of PCA is that the embedded subspace has to be linear. For example, if the data are located on a circle in 3-D, PCA will not be able to identify such a structure.

Mathematically speaking, PCA is a problem of finding the largest eigenvalues. We will demonstrate later that many algorithms ultimately lead to a matrix problem that is associated with eigenvalues, including MDS, LLE, Laplacian eigenmaps, and LTSA (Sections 2.2.1, 3.1, and 3.2).

2.2 *Group 2: Semi-Classical Method: Multidimensional Scaling (MDS)*

MDS is the name of a group of methods that have found a wide range of applications. The key idea is to find a mapping from a high-dimensional space to a low-dimensional space, such that the pairwise distances between the observed points are preserved the best. An intuitive example is to recover the relative positions of cities from the inter-city distances. Imagine that the exact locations (coordinates) of N cities are lost. However, we have the driving distances between pairs of them. These distances form an $N \times N$ matrix. Based on this matrix, MDS can recover a 2-D coordinate system that includes the locations of theses cities, subject to a rigid motion (a combination of rotation, shifting, and reflection), such that the distances among the points on this 2-D plane are close to the driving distances among those cities.

The above in fact gives an example of metric MDS (Torgerson, 1952; Young and Householder, 1938), which is related to nonmetric MDS (Kruskal, 1964; Shepard, 1962) that will be explained later.

For metric MDS, consider some points X_i in a metric space Ω, $X_i \in \Omega$. For $1 \leq l \neq m \leq N$, let $d(l,m)$ denote the distance between X_l and X_m. We want to find $X_i^{'} \in \Re^k$, $i = 1,2,...,N$, with k a fixed integer, such that the following optimization problem is solved:

$$\min_{X_i^{'} \in \Re^k} \sum_{l \neq m} [d(l,m) - d'(l,m)]^2 ,$$

where $d'(l,m)$ denotes the distance between $X_l^{'}$ and $X_m^{'}$ in $\Re^k$.

In metric MDS, the numerical values of the inter-distances are to be preserved. Sometimes it makes more sense to preserve the order of these distances. It is even possible that the available distances are ordinal data. In order to map $X_i \in \Omega$ to $X_i^{'} \in \Re^k$, in the case of ordinal data, the following optimization problem is adopted,

$$\min_{X_i^{'};f} \frac{\sum_{l \neq m} [f(d(l,m)) - d'(l,m)]^2}{\sum_{l \neq m} [d'(l,m)]^2} ,$$

where *f* is a monotone increasing function. For any fixed set of X_i's, the *f* is specified. The technical details can be found in Kruskal (1964) and Shepard (1962).

MDS is a very useful tool when the inter-point distances need to be preserved. In most existing MDS algorithms, a linear subspace is still the ultimate result. In ISOMAP, which is a method that will be described later, MDS is applied to geodesic distances, which results in a nonlinear dimension reduction method. We will give more details in Section 2.3.3.

2.2.1 Solving MDS as an Eigenvalue Problem

We present an eigenvalue-based approach to solving the MDS problem approximately. Consider observations $X_1, X_2, \ldots, X_N \in \Re^D$, where *N* and *D* are two positive integers. Let $X=[X_1, X_2, \ldots, X_N]$. Without loss of generality, we assume that the X_i's are centered at the origin, i.e., $X \cdot \mathbf{1}_N^T = O_D$, where $\mathbf{1}_N^T$ is the *N*-dimensional vector made by all ones, while O_D is the *D*-dimensional vector made by all zeroes. It is easy to see that

$$d^2(l,m) = \|X_l\|_2^2 + \|X_m\|_2^2 - 2 < X_l, X_m >, \quad \forall l, m,$$

where $< X_l, X_m >$ denotes the inner project of two vectors. Let $B = \left(\|X_1\|_2^2, \|X_2\|_2^2, \ldots, \|X_N\|_2^2\right)^T \in \Re^{N\times 1}$. Denote $E = \left(d^2(l,m)\right)_{l,m} \in \Re^{N\times N}$. We have $E = B \cdot 1_N^T + 1_N \cdot B^T - 2X^T X$.

From the above, we can easily verify the following:

$$X^T X = -\frac{1}{2}\left(I - \frac{1}{N}\mathbf{1}_N\mathbf{1}_N^T\right)E\left(I - \frac{1}{N}\mathbf{1}_N\mathbf{1}_N^T\right),$$

where *I* is the $N \times N$ identity matrix.

To find low-dimensional Y_i, i=1, 2, …, N, $Y_i \in \Re^d$, $d<D$, such that the matrix $\left(\|Y_l - Y_m\|_2^2\right)_{l,m}$ is a close approximation to *E*, we can find

$Y = [Y_1, \ldots, Y_N] \in \Re^{d \times N}$, such that $Y^T Y$ is close to $X^T X$. Note this approximately solves the original MDS problem, but not exactly. Suppose the eigen-decomposition of matrix $X^T X$ is

$$X^T X = \sum_{i=1}^{N} \lambda_i U_i U_i^T,$$

where $\lambda_1 \geq \lambda_2 \geq \cdots \geq \lambda_N \geq 0$ are the eigenvalues of $X^T X$ and $U_1, U_2, \ldots, U_N \in \Re^N$ are the corresponding eigenvectors. We can assign

$$Y = \mathrm{diag}\left(\sqrt{\lambda_1}, \ldots, \sqrt{\lambda_d}\right)\left[U_{1,} U_2, \ldots, U_d\right]^T.$$

We can verify that $Y^T Y$ is the best approximation to $X^T X$.

2.3 *Group 3: Manifold Searching Methods*

In this group, we review generative topological mapping (GTM), locally linear embedding (LLE), and ISOMAP.

2.3.1 Generative Topological Mapping (GTM)

Generative topological mapping (GTM) is an inspiring nonlinear dimension reduction method. Compared to the methods that will be introduced later, GTM does not contain the same sophisticated numerical approaches. But its formulation highlights some key components in modern dimension reduction.

Let *x* be a point in a latent space and *t* be a point in the data space. Let $t_1, t_2, \ldots, t_N$ denote the observed points (realizations of *t*). Point t_i is generated according to the following:

- First of all, there is a quantity x_i associated with t_i in the latent space. Note that the x_i's are not observable. The latent space has a much lower dimension than the data space does.

- There is a mapping, $x \to y(x, W)$, from the latent space to the data space. This mapping is continuously differentiable and has full column rank in its Jacobian. Notation W denotes the parameters of this mapping. In fact, one can assume that the images $y(x, W)$ for all x form a low-dimensional manifold in the data space.
- Suppose that the observation t_i is generated according to the model

$$t_i = y(x_i; W) + \varepsilon_i, \quad i=1, 2, \ldots, N,$$

where ε_i satisfies a multivariate normal distribution with zero mean and variance-covariance matrix β.

Thus, GTM assumes the existence of an implicit manifold. There are unknown parameters W and β. The latent variables x_i exist, but are also unknown.

By assuming a special distribution for the x_i's and placing the problem in a Bayesian model estimation framework, the authors of GTM introduced an expectation-maximization (EM) based method to estimate the above model (Bishop, Svensen, and Williams, 1998). The dimension reduction is achieved by finding a maximum a posteriori (MAP) estimate.

GTM considers a prior $p(x)$ for the x_i's. This prior is a sum of a finite number of Dirac functions, i.e.,

$$p(x) = \sum_{i=1}^{k} \delta(x - \bar{x}_i),$$

where $\bar{x}_1$, $\bar{x}_2$, …, $\bar{x}_k$ are k given points in the latent space. According to the previous way of generating t_i, there is a probability density function for t: $p(t \mid x; W, \beta)$. The density function on the data space is simply

$$p(t \mid W, \beta) = \int p(t \mid x, W, \beta) p(x) \, \mathrm{d}x .$$

Given that $p(x)$ is a sum of k Dirac functions, we have

$$p(t \mid W, \beta) = \sum_{i=1}^{k} p(t \mid \bar{x}_i, W, \beta) .$$

The principle of maximum likelihood estimation (MLE) is to find W and β such that the log-likelihood function,

$$\sum_{j=1}^{N} \ln p(t_j \mid W, \beta),$$

is maximized. The authors of GTM (Bishop, Svensen, and Williams, 1998) proposed an EM approach to estimate W and β. Here we omit some of the technical details regarding how to choose the functional classes in the nonlinear mapping.

The numerical solution of GTM is based on a strong assumption on the prior. The application of the EM algorithm seems *ad-hoc*. It is also hard to justify the performance of GTM. As a matter of fact, GTM can only be established in some special cases, like clustering, as an alternative to self-organizing maps (SOM). However, the probabilistic model is consistent with other models in data analysis.

2.3.2 Locally Linear Embedding (LLE)

Locally linear embedding (LLE) and ISOMAP comprise a new generation of dimension reduction methods. They have been successfully applied to both synthetic and "real" datasets. We review the LLE in this section, and ISOMAP in the next.

Again, we consider a data space with a very high dimension D. Let $\vec{X}_i$, i=1, 2, ..., N, be N vectors in such a data space. LLE starts with finding the k nearest neighbors (based on the Euclidean distance) for each vector $\vec{X}_i$, $1 \le i \le N$. Let N_i denote the indices of the k nearest neighbors of the vector $\vec{X}_i$. LLE finds the optimal local convex combinations of the k-nearest neighbors to represent each original vector. It is equivalent to minimizing the objective

$$\varepsilon(W) = \sum_i \left| \vec{X}_i - \sum_{j \in N_i} W_{ij} \vec{X}_j \right|^2,$$

where $\sum_j W_{ij} = 1$. It can be shown that the above can be solved as a least-squares problem.

Next, LLE considers a projection space. A projection space plays a role similar to that of the latent space in GTM. Let $\vec{Y}_i$ be the projection of $\vec{X}_i$ in the projection space. The projection space has a dimension much smaller than D. The projections $\vec{Y}_i$ are chosen such that the following objective function is minimized:

$$\Phi(Y) = \sum_i \left| \vec{Y}_i - \sum_{j \in N_i} W_{ij} \vec{Y}_j \right|^2 .$$

Note that the above is equivalent to finding a lower dimensional representation, such that the local convex representations are preserved. It can be shown that with some additional conditions, which make the problem well defined, the minimization task can be accomplished by solving a sparse $N \times N$ eigenvector problem. More specifically, the d eigenvectors associated with the d smallest non-zero eigenvalues provide an ordered set of orthogonal coordinates centered on the origin.

We summarize the LLE algorithm in Table 1. The LLE authors suggest that *k-b* trees can be used to compute the *k*-nearest neighbors efficiently (Friedman, Bentley, and Finkel, 1977). The sparse eigenvector problem can be solved by fast algorithms as well, e.g., Bai, Demmel, Dongarra, et al. (2000).

Table 1. The LLE Algorithm.

LLE Algorithm
1. Compute the k nearest neighbors of each point $\vec{X}_i$.
2. Compute the weights W_{ij} of a convex combination of the k nearest neighbors that best represent the point $\vec{X}_i$.
3. Find a low-dimensional projection $\vec{Y}_i$ such that the above local representations are best preserved.

Note that unlike GTM, LLE does not have a probabilistic model imposed on the data. In fact, the authors of LLE predicted the integration of probabilistic models in their future research.

One disadvantage of LLE is that it implicitly assumes that the manifold is convex. The methods that will be described later can overcome such a disadvantage.

2.3.3 ISOMAP

ISOMAP is another nonlinear dimension reduction method. It can be viewed as an extension of metric MDS, by replacing the Euclidean distance with another type of distance.

ISOMAP works as follows. Consider N points, $\vec{X}_i$, i=1, 2, ..., N, in the data space. First of all, for each data point $\vec{X}_i$, consider its neighbors. There are two possibilities:

- k-nearest neighbors of each point $\vec{X}_i$; or
- an ε-neighborhood, which includes all the points that are no more than ε-distance away from $\vec{X}_i$.

Let N_i denote the index set of the points that are the neighbors of $\vec{X}_i$. We construct a graph, in which each $\vec{X}_i$ is a vertex, and two vertices are connected if and only if $i \in N_j$ or $j \in N_i$. Define the distance between two points, $\vec{X}_i$ and $\vec{X}_j$, to be the sum of the arc lengths of the shortest chain connecting $\vec{X}_i$ and $\vec{X}_j$. The shortest chain can be computed via dynamic programming (e.g., Dijkstra, 1959). The above is called a graphical distance. The geodesic distance between two points on a manifold is the length of the shortest curve that is on the manifold and connects the two points. Bernstein, de Silva, Langford, and Tenenbaum (2000) show that the graphical distance is in some sense a good substitute for the geodesic distance. Note that a graphical distance is computable from data, while the geodesic distance is not computable. A low dimensional projection is then generated by calling a metric MDS.

2.4 *Group 4: Methods from Spectral Theory*

Both Laplacian eigenmaps (Belkin and Niyogi, 2001) and Hessian eigenmaps (Donoho and Grimes, 2004) are motivated by spectral theory in the continuum. The numerical approaches are discretizations of the continuum theory.

2.4.1 Laplacian Eigenmaps

Laplacian eigenmaps are proposed in Belkin and Niyogi (2001). This work establishes both a unified approach to dimension reduction and a new connection to spectral theory. Laplacian eigenmaps are the predecessor of the next method – Hessian eigenmaps, which overcome the convexity limitation.

We first describe the Laplacian eigenmap for discrete data. Its relevant theorem in the continuum will follow. Again, we consider *N* points, $\vec{X}_i$, *i*=1, 2, …, *N*, in the *D*-dimensional data space. For each point $\vec{X}_i$, $1 \le i \le N$, suppose a neighbor set N_i is computed. A graph identical with the graph in ISOMAP can be defined. For any pair of connected points $\vec{X}_i$ and $\vec{X}_j$, we define a weight function

$$W_{ij} = \exp\left\{-\frac{1}{t}\left\|\vec{X}_i - \vec{X}_j\right\|_2^2\right\}.$$

Let *D* denote a diagonal matrix such that $D_{ii} = \sum_j W_{ji}$. Let *W* denote the symmetric matrix with entries W_{ij}, $1 \le i, j \le N$. Finally, let *L* denote the matrix *L*=*D*-*W*. Consider the solutions to the problem:

$$Lf = \lambda Df, \tag{1}$$

where $f \in \Re^N$. Let f_0, f_1, …, f_{k-1} be the solution vectors with corresponding eigenvalues $0 = \lambda_0 \le \lambda_1 \le \cdots \le \lambda_{k-1}$; i.e.,

$$\begin{aligned} Lf_0 &= \lambda_0 Df_0, \\ Lf_1 &= \lambda_1 Df_1, \\ &\vdots \\ Lf_{k-1} &= \lambda_{k-1} Df_{k-1}. \end{aligned}$$

The eigenvectors associated with zeros eigenvectors is left out and the next m eigenvectors are used for the embedding in an m-dimensional Euclidean space

$$\vec{X}_i \to (f_1(i), f_2(i), \ldots, f_m(i)).$$

An intuitive justification for solving the eigenvalue and eigenvector problem (1) is to consider minimizing the objective,

$$\sum_{i,j} (y_i - y_j)^2 W_{ij}, \tag{2}$$

where $y = (y_1, y_2, \ldots, y_N)$ consists of N maps from a point to $\Re$. It is shown in Belkin and Niyogi (2001) that Equation (2) is equivalent to finding

$$\begin{aligned} &\text{argmin} && y^T Ly, \\ &\text{subject to} && y^T Dy = 1. \end{aligned}$$

Minimizing the objective in (2) is equivalent to finding an optimal embedding. By generalizing it to an embedding in $\Re^m$, we have the described eigenvector and eigenvalue problem. We refer the reader to Belkin and Niyogi (2001) for the details.

The above approach uses the Laplacian of a graph, which is analogous to the Laplace Beltrami operator on manifolds. Chung (1997) serves as a good reference. Let M be a smooth, compact, m-dimensional Riemannian manifold. Let f be a map from the manifold to $\Re$. Assume that $f: M \to \Re$ is twice differentiable. Belkin and Niyogi (2001) explain how

$$\int_f L(f)f$$

serves as the weighted sum in Equation (1). Suppose ∇f is the gradient of f and $L(f)$ is the Laplace Beltrami operator. It is known that the $\hat{f}$, which minimizes $\int_M \|\nabla f\|^2$, is an eigenvector of the Laplace Beltrami operator. The spectrum of L on a compact manifold M is known to be discrete. The rest of the dimension reduction is identical with the approach in the discrete case.

The connection between spectral theory and dimension reduction, which is established in Laplacian eigenmaps, is very inspiring.

2.4.2 Hessian Eigenmaps

In all the aforementioned methods, it is required that the embedded manifold is sampled on a convex region. Hessian eigenmaps, as proposed by Donoho and Grimes (2004), relax the convexity condition.

We explain the motivation of Hessian eigenmaps (HLLE) in the continuum. Recall that in Laplacian eigenmaps, the following functional $H_1(f)$ is considered:

$$H_1(f) = \int_M L(f)f \, .$$

In Hessian eigenmaps, the above functional is replaced with

$$H_2(f) = \int_M \|H_f(m)\|_F^2 \, dm \, ,$$

where $H_f(m)$ is the Hessian of the function f. $\|\cdot\|_F^2$ denotes the square of the Frobenius norm of a matrix. Donoho and Grimes prove that by minimizing $H_2(f)$, the convexity condition in the previous approaches can be relaxed.

Donoho and Grimes (2004) then propose a discrete algorithm, which is based on a discrete approximation to the Hessian on a manifold.

2.5 Group 5: Methods Based on Global Alignment

We review the local tangent space alignment (LTSA) method that is proposed in Zhang and Zha (2004). There is another similar method, charting (Brand, 2003), which is not as well-developed mathematically.

The following derivation can be divided into two stages. In the first stage, a local parametrization is established for each data point. In the second stage, a global alignment is computed. Suppose that the *i*th observation is generated according to $x_i = f(\theta_i) + \varepsilon_i$, where θ_i is a natural parameter of x_i, and the ε_i's are random and i.i.d. Let $x_{i,j}$ denote the *j*th nearest neighbor of x_i. Similarly, we have $x_{i,j} = f(\theta_{i,j}) + \varepsilon_{i,j}$. We assume that $\theta_{i,j} \approx \theta_i$, because they are neighbors. Assume *f* is smooth enough so that

$$
\begin{aligned}
x_{i,j} - x_i &= f(\theta_{i,j}) - f(\theta_i) + \varepsilon_{i,j} - \varepsilon_i \\
&= \mathrm{g}\, f(\theta_i)(\theta_{i,j} - \theta_i) + \mathrm{O}(\|\theta_{i,j} - \theta_i\|^2) + \varepsilon_{i,j} - \varepsilon_i .
\end{aligned}
$$

Here $\mathrm{g}\, f(\theta_i)$ is the gradient of function *f* whose variable is θ_i. The above is merely a Taylor expansion. Let $X_i = [x_{i,1}, x_{i,2}, \ldots, x_{i,k}] - x_i \mathbf{1}_k^T \in \Re^{D\times k}$, where $x_{i,1}, \ldots, x_{i,k}$ are the *k* nearest neighbors of x_i, $\mathbf{1}_k^T = (1,1,\ldots,1)^T \in \Re^k$. Let $L_i = \mathrm{g}\, f(\theta_i) \in \Re^{D\times k}$. Let α_i, $\alpha_{i,1}$, …, $\alpha_{i,k}$ denote the temporary local parameterizations of observations x_i, $x_{i,1}$, …, $x_{i,k}$. Similarly, let $A_i = [\alpha_{i,1}, \alpha_{i,2}, \ldots, \alpha_{i,k}] - \alpha_i \mathbf{1}_k^T$. If the ε_i's satisfy a multivariate normal distribution with zero mean and constant variance, and if the second order term $\|\alpha_{i,j} - \alpha_i\|_2^2$ is negligible, the local parameterization and the tangent space can be computed by solving the following optimization problem:

$$
\min_{L_i, A_i} \|X_i - L_i A_i\|_F^2 .
$$

Note that in order to make the solution well defined, we impose the constraint $L_i^T L_i = I_d$. The above is solved via a singular value decomposition (SVD). L_i is made by the singular vectors that are associated with the d largest singular values of X_i. A_i is also computable, and is the only quantity that will be conveyed to the next stage.

In the second stage, a global parameterization that is locally identical to A_i up to a rigid transform is computed. Let

$$\Theta_i = [\theta_{i,1}, \theta_{i,2}, \ldots, \theta_{i,k}] - \theta_i \mathbf{1}_k^T .$$

Let $T_i \in \Re^{d \times d}$ be an orthogonal matrix. We solve

$$\min_{\text{all } \theta_i\text{'s}, T_i\text{'s}} \sum_{i=1}^{N} \left\| \Theta_i - T_i A_i \right\|_F^2 .$$

By following a derivation in Zhang and Zha (2004), it is possible to show that the problem eventually becomes that of finding the 2nd to the *(k+1)*st smallest eigenvalues and eigenvectors of an $N \times N$ matrix. Due to space limitations, the specific form of this matrix is omitted.

3. Unification via the Null-Space Methods

We have presented a large set of methods, all having the flavor of finding the embedded geometric structure, i.e., a manifold. Different methods are based on different ideas. It seems like each method should be analyzed individually in order to determine its performance. In this section, we will demonstrate that many of them eventually become null-space searching algorithms. (Recall that null-spaces are spanned by the solutions of a system of linear equations corresponding to a predetermined matrix.) Hence, if we can characterize the behavior of null-spaces under uncertainty, we can provide a unified analysis of these methods. We show that LLE and LTSA are null space-based methods in Sections 3.1 and 3.2, respectively. We describe the matrices that are used in these methods as a way to compare them on a common ground.

3.1 LLE as a Null-space-based Method

The content of this subsection extends the description in Section 2.3.2. Recall that LLE contains two steps. In the first step, a linear representation of each observation (point) based on its k nearest neighbors is computed. The second step computes a low-dimensional representation that best preserves these local linear representations.

The first step is achieved by solving the following problem:

$$\min_{\substack{\omega\in\Re^k \\ \omega^T\mathbf{1}_k=1}} \|X_i - M_i\omega\|_2^2,$$

where $X_i \in \Re^D$, $i = 1,2,\ldots,N$, are the observed points, $M_i = [X_{i1}, X_{i2}, \ldots, X_{ik}]$ is formed by taking the k nearest neighbors of X_i as its columns, and $\mathbf{1}_k \in \Re^k$ is an all one vector. It is shown in an online introduction of LLE (Saul and Roweis, 2001) that the above is equivalent to solving

$$\min_{\omega^T\mathbf{1}_k=1} \omega^T\left(X_i\mathbf{1}_k^T - M_i\right)^T\left(X_i\mathbf{1}_k^T - M_i\right)\omega.$$

Let $\Omega_i = \left(X_i\mathbf{1}_k^T - M_i\right)^T\left(X_i\mathbf{1}_k^T - M_i\right)$. Using a Lagrange multiplier approach, one can show that

$$\omega_i = \Omega_i^{-1}\mathbf{1}_k \big/ \mathbf{1}_k^T\Omega_i^{-1}\mathbf{1}_k,$$

provided that Ω_i is invertible.

As demonstrated in the original LLE paper, the second step can be achieved by solving

$$\min_{\substack{Y\in\Re^{d\times N} \\ YY^T=I_d}} \sum_i \|Y_i - N_i\omega_i\|_2^2, \tag{3}$$

where $d<D$, $Y = [Y_1, Y_2, \ldots, Y_N]$, matrix $N_i = [Y_{i1}, Y_{i2}, \ldots, Y_{ik}]$, which is made by k Y_i's that correspond to the k nearest neighbors of X_i. I_d is the d-by-d identity matrix. The above objective function can be rewritten as

$$\text{obj(LLE)} = \sum_i \left\| Y(e_i - S_i \omega_i) \right\|_2^2 ,$$

where e_i is an N-dimensional column vector taking one at the ith position and zeros elsewhere, S_i is the selection matrix associated with the k nearest neighbors of X_i, and ω_i is computed in the first step. Moreover, we have

$$\text{obj(LLE)} = \sum_i (e_i - S_i \omega_i)^T Y^T Y (e_i - S_i \omega_i) .$$

Minimizing the above objective function with the constraints in Equation (3) is equivalent to finding the eigenvectors associated with the 2nd to the *(d+1)*st smallest eigenvalues of the matrix

$$\begin{aligned} \text{M(LLE)} &= \sum_i (e_i - S_i \omega_i)(e_i - S_i \omega_i)^T \\ &= I_N - \sum_i S_i \omega_i e_i^T - \sum_i e_i \omega_i^T S_i^T + \sum_i S_i \omega_i \omega_i^T S_i^T . \end{aligned}$$

Let

$$\begin{aligned} W &= [S_1\omega_1, S_2\omega_2, \ldots, S_N\omega_N] \\ &= [S_1\, S_2 \cdots S_N]_{N\times kN} \begin{bmatrix} \omega_1 & & & \\ & \omega_2 & & \\ & & \ddots & \\ & & & \omega_N \end{bmatrix}_{kN\times N} . \end{aligned}$$

We can simplify M(LLE) as

$$M(LLE) = (I_N - W)(I_N - W)^T .$$

Note that M(LLE) is an $N \times N$ symmetric matrix. Because $\mathbf{1}_k^T \omega_i = 1$, $\forall i$, it is evident that the all one vector $\mathbf{1}_N$ belongs to the null-space of matrix M(LLE). The choice of the second to the *(d+1)*st smallest eigenvalues is to exclude such a special case.

3.2 LTSA as a Null-space-based Method

We review LTSA, emphasizing that LTSA is another null-space method, and compare it with LLE. Recall LTSA includes two steps: local parameterization and global alignment.

In the local parameterization step, the following is solved.

$$\min_{\substack{\Theta_i \in \Re^{d\times k} \\ Q^T Q = I_d}} \left\| X_i \overline{P} - Q\Theta_i \right\|_2^2,$$

where $X_i \in \Re^{D\times k}$ is a matrix whose columns are the k nearest neighbors of the ith point including the ith point, $\overline{P} = (I_k - \mathbf{1}_k \mathbf{1}_k^T / k)$, which is a projection matrix projecting $\Re^k$ to a k-1 dimensional linear subspace that is orthogonal to the all one vector $\mathbf{1}_k \in \Re^k$, $Q \in \Re^{D\times d}$ satisfies $Q^T Q = I_d$, and we assume $d <$ min(D, k). Let $X_i \overline{P} = \sum_i \lambda_i u_i v_i^T$ be the singular value decomposition of matrix $X_i \overline{P}$, where $\lambda_1 \geq \lambda_2 \geq \cdots \geq \lambda_{\min(D,k)} \geq 0$, column vectors $u_i \in \Re^D$ are the left singular vectors, and column vectors $v_i \in \Re^k$ are the right singular vectors. Zhang and Zha (2004) demonstrate that the solutions are $Q = [u_1, u_2, \ldots, u_d]$ and

$$\begin{aligned}\Theta_i &= Q^T X_i \overline{P} \\ &= \text{diag}(\lambda_1, \lambda_2, \ldots, \lambda_d) \begin{bmatrix} v_1^T \\ \vdots \\ v_d^T \end{bmatrix}.\end{aligned} \tag{4}$$

In the global alignment, Zhang and Zha (2004) show that the optimal low-dimensional representation is given by the eigenvectors associated with the d+1 smallest eigenvalues of the matrix

$$\text{M(LTSA)} = SWW^T S^T,$$

excluding the zero eigenvalue associated with a constant-valued eigenvector. A detailed explanation can be found in Zhang and Zha

(2004). Here $S = [S_1, S_2, \ldots, S_N]$, where S_i is a selection matrix associated with X_i that is defined in the foregoing subsection (Section 3.1). Moreover,

$$W = \text{diag}(W_1, W_2, \ldots, W_n),$$

where $W_i = \overline{P}(I_k - \Theta_i^+ \Theta_i)$, and Θ_i^+ is the generalized inverse of matrix Θ_i.

Recalling Equation (4), we have

$$W_i = \overline{P}\left(I_k - [v_1, \cdots, v_d] \begin{bmatrix} v_1^T \\ \vdots \\ v_d^T \end{bmatrix} \right).$$

Letting $P_i = W_i W_i^T$, we have

$$P_i = \overline{P}\left(I_k - [v_1, \cdots, v_d] \begin{bmatrix} v_1^T \\ \vdots \\ v_d^T \end{bmatrix} \right)\overline{P},$$

which is a projection matrix that projects to a $\min(D,k) - d - 1$ dimensional subspace of $\Re^k$. The subspace is spanned by the right singular vectors of $X_i \overline{P}$ associated with the $\min(D,k) - d$ smallest singular values and is orthogonal to vector $\mathbf{1}_k$. It is easy to see that

$$\text{M(LTSA)} = SBB^T S^T, \tag{5}$$

where $B = \text{diag}(P_1, P_2, \ldots, P_N)$.
Once again, LTSA is a null-space problem.

3.3 Comparison between LTSA and LLE

Recall M(LLE)=$(I - W)(I - W)^T$, which is formally different from M(LTSA). If we want to write M(LLE) in a format that is similar to the expression of M(LTSA), we can take

$$I_n = [S_1, S_2, \ldots, S_N] \begin{bmatrix} S_1^T \\ \vdots \\ S_N^T \end{bmatrix} \operatorname{diag}(c_1^{-1}, c_2^{-1}, \ldots, c_N^{-1}),$$

where c_i is the number of times that point $\vec{X}_i$ is included in a k nearest neighbor set. One can verify that

$$\mathrm{M(LLE)} = STT^{\mathrm{T}}S^T,$$

$$\text{where: } T = \begin{bmatrix} S_1^T \\ \vdots \\ S_N^T \end{bmatrix} \operatorname{diag}(c_1^{-1}, c_2^{-1}, \ldots, c_N^{-1}) - \begin{bmatrix} \omega_1 & & & \\ & \omega_2 & & \\ & & \ddots & \\ & & & \omega_N \end{bmatrix}.$$

Comparing with Equation (5), we find that TT^T is no longer a block diagonal matrix. Such a difference between LTSA and LLE may lead to different performance. The detailed analysis is left for future research.

4. Principles Guiding the Methodological Developments

4.1 Sufficient Dimension Reduction

We review the general principle of dimension reduction. We start with the concept of *sufficiency* in classical mathematical statistics. Let $x \in \Re^D$ denote an observation. Imagine another quantity $\theta \in \Re^d$, which is an implicit (simpler) representation of x. For instance, θ could be a parameter in classical mathematical statistics. Let $p(x,\theta)$ denote their joint distribution. The parameter θ can be thought of as the meaningful part of x. If there exists a function of x, denoted as $\phi(x)$, such that $p(x,\theta) = p_1(\phi(x),\theta) \cdot p_2(x)$, then $\phi(x)$ is a sufficient statistic of θ. Here $p_1(\cdot)$ and $p_2(\cdot)$ are two functions. We assume that θ resides on one (or a few) simple manifold(s), and $p_1(\phi(x),\theta)$ is approximately

$p_3(\theta)$, a distribution of θ, if and only if $\phi(x)$ is close to θ. It is easy to see that when the previous factorization holds, the conditional probability $p(x \mid \phi(x))$ does not depend on θ. We say that $\phi(x)$ is an *ideal* dimension reduction of x. The idealness is based on the fact that this data description takes the simplest possible form.

The above describes an abstract principle. A lot of specifications are needed to make it concrete. There are many existing studies in dimension reduction, both for supervised learning (Globerson and Tishby, 2003; Fukumizu et al., 2004) and unsupervised learning. We described an unsupervised learning framework. We will describe a manifold-based dimension reduction framework with assumptions on the conditional distribution of $x \mid \phi(x)$.

4.2 *Desired Statistical Properties*

There are more criteria that are commonly adopted in evaluating the fundamental performance of dimension reduction algorithms. Note that nearly all of them take an asymptotic perspective (i.e., assuming the sample size n goes to ∞).

4.2.1 Consistency

For any estimate, the first requirement typically is statistical consistency. In our case, assume that each time course x_i is a combination of a structural component $f(\tau_i)$ and i.i.d. random errors ε_i, where $i = 1, 2, \ldots, n$, and τ_i is a natural parameterization of a compact manifold, or a concatenation of several compact manifolds. Let x denote all the available data: $x = \{x_1, \ldots, x_n\}$. The estimated parameter value at point x_i is denoted by $\hat{\phi}_n(x_i; x)$. An estimate $\hat{\phi}_n$ is consistent if and only if the following holds:

$$\hat{\phi}_n(x_i; x) \Rightarrow T(\tau_i), \qquad \text{as } n \to \infty,$$

where T is an one-to-one rigid transform. In words, a consistent estimate gives the theoretically true estimate when the sample size goes to infinity.

4.2.2 Rate of Convergence

There could be many estimates that are statistically consistent. The rate of convergence is a quantity to further evaluate them. Let std(·) denote the standard deviation of an estimate. Let $f_1(n) \asymp f_2(n)$ denote that $\lim_{n\to\infty} f_1(n)/f_2(n) = \text{constant}$. There exists a constant $\rho > 0$ such that

$$\text{std}(\hat{\phi}_n) \asymp n^{-\rho}.$$

When $\rho = 1/2$, $\hat{\phi}_n$ is $\sqrt{n}$-consistent. If $-\rho$ achieves the smallest possible value, the optimal rate of convergence is achieved. The optimal rate of convergence can be computed via the Fisher information – a well-established technique in statistics.

4.2.3 Exhaustiveness

We hope to have $\hat{\phi}_n(x_i;x) \Rightarrow T(\tau_i)$. It is possible that $\hat{\phi}_n(x_i;x)$ converges to a function (not invertible) of $T(\tau_i)$. On the other hand, it might be possible that $T(\tau_i)$ is a function of the limit of $\hat{\phi}_n(x_i;x)$. In both cases, the estimate $\hat{\phi}_n$ does not converge to the true natural parameterization. When $\hat{\phi}_n(x_i;x)$ converges exactly to a $T(\tau_i)$, the estimate $\hat{\phi}_n$ is called *exhaustive*. This concept has been developed in statistics, such as searching for *central subspaces* in regression. See the introduction of Li et al. (2004) for more related information. Examining whether a manifold learning algorithm leads to an exhaustive estimate is a future task.

4.2.4 Robustness

The last requirement is robustness – namely, if the data are generated according to the model $x_i = f(\tau_i) + \varepsilon_i$, except for a small proportion of them, one should still expect that a *robust* manifold learning algorithm will recover the embedded structure *f*. The threshold of the proportion that can mislead a manifold learning algorithm is called the *breakdown point* of this method. This is an indicator of the robustness of a learning algorithm. Calculating the robustness properties of some manifold learning algorithms will be a future task.

4.3 Initial Results

4.3.1 Formulation and Related Open Questions

We propose a framework to analyze the consistency of a dimension reduction method, especially for those methods that are intended to learn an embedded manifold. The solution to this problem and the technical details will appear in a future publication. We propose this framework to illustrate the necessary components for a theoretical analysis.

We consider a compact subset Ω in the Euclidean space $\Re^d$, $\Omega \subset \Re^d$. Let μ_1 denote a probability measure on Ω. We assume $\mu_1(x) > 0$, $\forall x \in \Omega$, i.e., μ_1 is always positive. We assume that there is an isometric mapping $f : \Omega \to \Re^D$, where $d < D$, and $f \in C^2$, i.e., *f* has continuous (partial) derivatives. It is easy to see that $f(\Omega)$ is a manifold in $\Re^D$ with intrinsic dimension *d*. More specifically, $f(\Omega)$ is a chart, and *x* (as in $f(x)$) is a parameterization of this manifold.

Now we consider a sample version. Assume points X_1, X_2, ..., X_N are i.i.d. sampled from Ω according to μ_1. Because *f* is an isometric mapping, we have $\| X_i - X_j \|_E = \mathrm{d}(f(X_i), f(X_j))$, where $\| X_i - X_j \|_E$ is the Euclidean distance between points X_i and X_j, and $\mathrm{d}(f(X_i), f(X_j))$ is the geodesic distance on the manifold between points $f(X_i)$ and $f(X_j)$. We can consider the following questions:

Question 1: Given the observed points $Y_i = f(X_i)$, $i = 1, 2, ..., N$, as $N \to \infty$, can we use a manifold learning method to recover the X_i's up to a rigid motion?

If we consider sampling noise, we may ask the following question:

Question 2: Given the observed points $Y_i = f(X_i) + \varepsilon_i$, $i = 1,2,...,N$, where $\varepsilon_i \overset{i.i.d.}{\sim} \mu_2$, as $N \to \infty$, what are the necessary and sufficient conditions on μ_2, under which a manifold learning algorithm will recover the X_i's up to a rigid motion?

Moreover, in the above setting, we can consider the rate of convergence to the true parameterization as $N \to \infty$.

Our formulation is different from the consistency that has been addressed by the authors of ISOMAP (Tenenbaum, de Silva, and Langford, 2000). They show that as the sample density goes to zero, the graphical distance converges to the geodesic distance. It follows that a subsequent application of MDS will recover the true parameterization (i.e., the true values of X_i). Their approach is different from a traditional way of data analysis.

Laplacian and Hessian eigenmaps in some sense address the problem of consistency. Both Laplacian eigenmaps and Hessian eigenmaps are discrete approximations of the algorithms that have proven consistency in the continuum. Given that a discrete algorithm converges to the continuum version asymptotically, they will have the same property. It is easy to see that this approach cannot provide an analysis of the rate of convergence.

Comprehensive error analysis is given in Zhang and Zha (2004) regarding LTSA. Their pioneering work is very inspiring to us. However, their analysis focuses on an upper bound, which is equivalent to a worst case study. Our formulation can lead to a more detailed statistical analysis, which we believe in many situations is more meaningful than the worst case study.

4.3.2 Consistency of LTSA

In this section, we establish the consistency of the LTSA algorithm under some mild conditions. The purpose of doing so is to demonstrate some key ingredients in the theoretical analysis.

Recall that Ω is a subset of the feature space $\Re^d$. The function f maps Ω into the data space $\Re^D$, with $d < D$, i.e., $f : \Omega \to \Re^D$. When f satisfies some regularity conditions, the range $f(\Omega)$ forms a manifold. We assume that Ω is bounded, which is formalized in the following:

Condition 1: The domain Ω is bounded, i.e., $|\Omega| < \infty$, where $|\Omega|$ is the Lebesgue measure of Ω in $\Re^d$.

The following notation is needed later. For $x_0 \in \Omega$, an ε-neighborhood of x_0, denoted by $N_\varepsilon(x_0)$, is defined as

$$N_\varepsilon(x_0) = \{x : x \in \Omega, \|x - x_0\|_2 < \varepsilon\}.$$

A function $f : \Omega \to \Re^D$ can be written as

$$f = \begin{bmatrix} f_1 \\ f_2 \\ \vdots \\ f_D \end{bmatrix}_{D\times 1},$$

where each $f_i(x) = f_i(x_1, x_2, \ldots, x_d)$ is a real-valued function of d variables. The Jacobian of f at the point x_0 $(x_0 \in \Omega)$ is

$$\mathrm{J}\,f(x_0)=\begin{pmatrix} \frac{\partial f_1(x_0)}{\partial x_1} & \cdots & \frac{\partial f_1(x_0)}{\partial x_d} \\ \frac{\partial f_2(x_0)}{\partial x_1} & \cdots & \frac{\partial f_2(x_0)}{\partial x_d} \\ \vdots & \ddots & \vdots \\ \frac{\partial f_D(x_0)}{\partial x_1} & \cdots & \frac{\partial f_D(x_0)}{\partial x_d} \end{pmatrix}_{D\times d}.$$

The Hessian of $f_i, 1 \le i \le D$, is

$$\{\mathrm{H}\,f_i(x_0)\}_{s,t} = \frac{\partial^2 f_i(x_0)}{\partial x_s \partial x_t},\ 1 \le s,\ t \le d\,.$$

Another regularity condition on f is the assumption that its Hessians are bounded:

Condition 2: There exists a constant C_1 such that for any $1 \le s$, $t \le d$, $1 \le i \le D$, and $x_0 \in \Omega$, we have $\left|\{\mathrm{H}\,f_i(x_0)\}_{s,t}\right| < C_1$.

The next condition assumes that the mapping f is *locally isometric*.

Condition 3: For any $x_0 \in \Omega$ and $\bar{x}_0 \in N_\varepsilon(x_0)$, $\|\bar{x}_0 - x\| \to 0$ implies that

$$\|f(\bar{x}_0) - f(x_0)\|_2 = \|\bar{x}_0 - x_0\|_2 + O\left(\|\bar{x}_0 - x_0\|_2^2\right).$$

Recall $O(x)$ is a quantity that has the same asymptotic order as x when x goes to the positive infinity.

The following argument demonstrates that when f is locally isometric, its Jacobian $\mathrm{J}\,f(x_0)$ has to be orthonormal for every $x_0 \in \Omega$. To see this, we consider the Taylor expansion at the point x_0. For $\bar{x}_0 \in N_\varepsilon(x_0)$, we have

$$f(\bar{x}_0) = f(x_0) + \mathrm{J}\,f(x_0)(\bar{x}_0 - x_0) + O\left(\|\bar{x}_0 - x_0\|_2^2\right).$$

If f is locally isometric, we have

$$\|\bar{x}_0 - x_0\|_2 = \|f(\bar{x}_0 - f(x_0)\| = \|\mathrm{J}\, f(x_0)(\bar{x}_0 - x_0)\|.$$

The above is true for any $\bar{x}_0 \in N_\varepsilon(x_0)$. Hence $\mathrm{J}\, f(x_0)$ is made by a subset of columns of an orthogonal matrix, i.e., $\mathrm{J}\, f(x_0)$ is orthonormal. Mathematically, we can write

$$[\mathrm{J}\, f(x_0)]^T [\mathrm{J}\, f(x_0)] = I_d.$$

In LTSA, it is assumed that the k nearest neighbors in the data space correspond to the k nearest neighbors in the feature space. The following introduces a sufficient condition for this neighbor-preserving property. Consider points $X_1, X_2, \ldots, X_N$ that are sampled in Ω. Their images in the data space are $f(X_1), f(X_2), \ldots, f(X_N)$. For each $f(X_t)$, $1 \le t \le N$, let $f(X_{t,1}), f(X_{t,2}), \ldots, f(X_{t,k})$ denote the k nearest neighbors of $f(X_t)$ in $\Re^D$. The following is a neighbor-preserving condition:

Condition 4: For any $\delta > 0$, there exist integers $N(\delta)$ and $K(\delta)$ such that for any t, $1 \le t \le N$, $X_{t,j} \in N_\delta(X_t), j = 1, 2, \ldots, k = K(\delta)$.

In fact, the reader may verify that if f^{-1} exists and is absolutely continuous, and if the distribution of random points is dense everywhere on $f(\Omega)$, then Condition 4 holds.

Under Conditions 1, 2, 3, and 4, we show that the LTSA algorithm provides a consistent estimate. Recall that LTSA solves the following optimization problem:

$$\min_{\substack{X_t, L(X_t) \\ 1 \le t \le n}} \frac{1}{N} \sum_{t=1}^{N} \frac{1}{k} \sum_{j=1}^{k} \left\| X_{t,j} - X_t - L(X_t)[f(X_{t,j}) - f(X_t)] \right\|_2^2,$$

where $L(X_t)$ is a $d \times D$ orthonormal matrix, i.e., $L(X_t)[L(X_t)]^T = I_d$. Recall that $X_t, X_{t,j} \in \Re^d$. Note that the objective function, which is also the objective function in LTSA, is nonnegative. Under conditions 1, 2, 3, and 4, we will show that by taking the original parameterization of the manifold, the above objective goes to zero, which is the smallest possible value of the objective function. Moreover, considering the local solution, for $1 \le t \le N$, we have

$$\left\| X_{t,j} - X_t - L(X_t)[f(X_{t,j}) - f(X_t)] \right\|_2^2 \approx 0 .$$

We can see that the solution is unique up to a rigid motion, i.e., $X_t' = UX_t + V$ is another solution if and only if U is a $d \times d$ orthogonal matrix and V is a d-dimensional vector. Combining the above two, the consistency of LTSA is proved.

We now show that the value of the objective function of LTSA goes to zero under the above four conditions. Recall that for $1 \le t \le N$ and $1 \le j \le k$, we have

$$\begin{aligned} &\left\| f(X_{t,j}) - f(X_t) - Jf(X_t)(X_{t,j} - X_t) \right\|_2 \\ &\le \sqrt{D} \frac{1}{2} C_1 d^2 \left\| X_{t,j} - X_t \right\|_2^2 \le \frac{1}{2} C_1 \sqrt{D} d^2 \delta^2 . \end{aligned}$$

The above is derived directly from the Taylor expansion at the X_t. Moreover, we have

$$\begin{aligned} &\min_{L(X_t)} \left\| X_{t,j} - X_t - L(X_t)[f(X_{t,j}) - f(X_t)] \right\| \\ &\le \left\| X_{t,j} - X_t - [Jf(X_t)]^T [f(X_{t,j}) - f(X_t)] \right\| \\ &\le \frac{1}{2} C_1 \sqrt{D} d^2 \delta^2 . \end{aligned}$$

From the above, it is easy to see that the value of the objective function of LTSA is less than or equal to $C_2 \times \delta^2$, where C_2 is a constant. In fact, we can take $C_2 = 1/2\, C_1 \sqrt{D} d^2$. When $\delta \to 0$, the objective of LTSA converges to zero. From all of the above, we have established the consistency of LTSA.

5. Examples and Potential Applications

5.1 Successes of Manifold Based Methods on Synthetic Data

We give some numerical examples to demonstrate the effectiveness of manifold learning approaches.

5.1.1 Examples of LTSA Recovering Implicit Parameterization

The following examples show that LTSA can successfully recover hidden low dimensional parameterization from high dimensional datasets. In Figure 2(a, top), data points are sampled from a 1-D curve in a 2-D (or 3-D) space. For each curve, starting from one end of it, its distance to any point on the curve gives a natural parameterization. Obviously, these datasets are intrinsically one-dimensional. In Figure 2(a, bottom), the recovered parameter values are plotted against the true distance parameter values (mentioned above). When the recovered values are consistent with the true parameterization, the bottom figures should be diagonals (i.e., $y = x$ or $y = -x$). Such a pattern is clearly observed.

We would also like to see how LTSA behaves with noise. In Figure 2(b, top), data are sampled with noise around 1-D curves. In Figure 2(b, bottom), we see that LTSA still reliably recovers the implicit parameterization, because of the observable diagonal patterns. More real-world applications can be found in Zhang and Zha (2004).

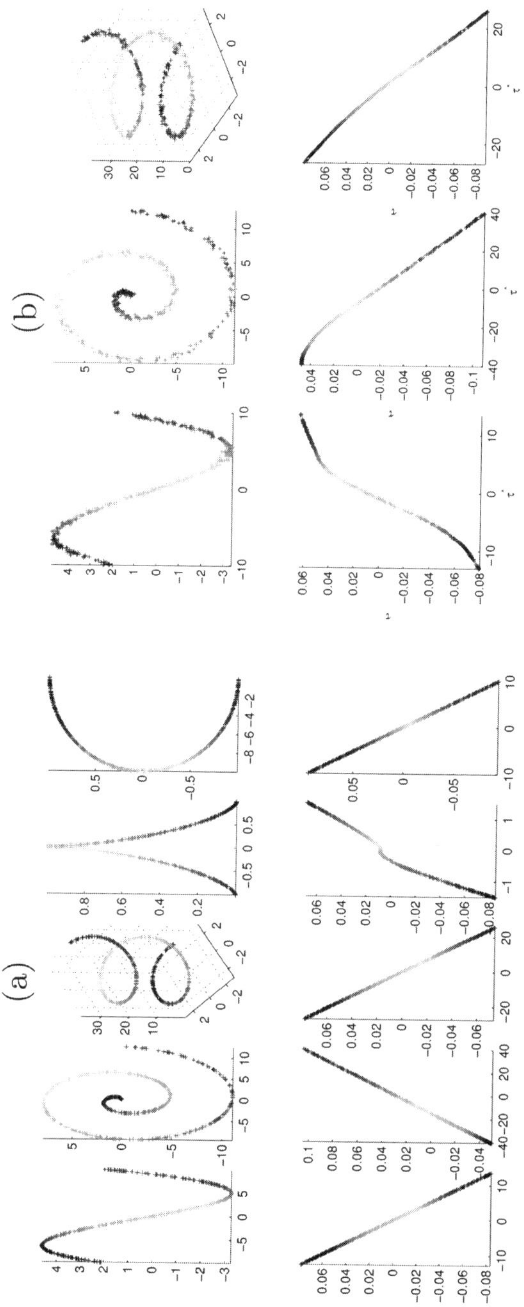

Figure 2. Examples of LTSA recovering the intrinsic parameters from (a) noiseless and (b) noisy data.

5.1.2 Examples of Locally Linear Projection (LLP) in Denoising

An LLP (Huo, 2003; Huo and Chen, 2002) can be applied to extract the local low-dimensional structure. In the first step, neighbor observations are identified. In the second step, singular value decomposition (SVD) or principal components analysis (PCA) is used to estimate the local linear subspace. Finally, the observation is projected into this subspace. An illustration of LLP in 2-D with local dimension 1 (i.e., linear) and 15 nearest neighbors is provided in Figure 3. A detailed description of the algorithm is given in the following.

ALGORITHM: LLP

for each observation y_i, $i = 1, 2, 3, \ldots, N$,

a) Find the K-nearest neighbors of y_i. The neighboring points are denoted by $\tilde{y}_1$, $\tilde{y}_2$, …, $\tilde{y}_K$. Use PCA or SVD to identify the linear subspace that contains most of the information in the vectors $\tilde{y}_1$, $\tilde{y}_2$, …, $\tilde{y}_K$. Suppose the linear subspace is A_i, and let $P_{\mathrm{A}_i}(x)$ denote the projection of a vector x into this subspace.

b) Let k_0 denote the assumed dimension of the embedded manifold. Then subspace A_i can be viewed as a linear subspace spanned by the vectors associated with the first k_0 singular values.

c) Project y_i into the linear subspace A_i and let $\hat{y}_i$ denote this projection: $\hat{y}_i = P_{\mathrm{A}_i}(x)$.

end.

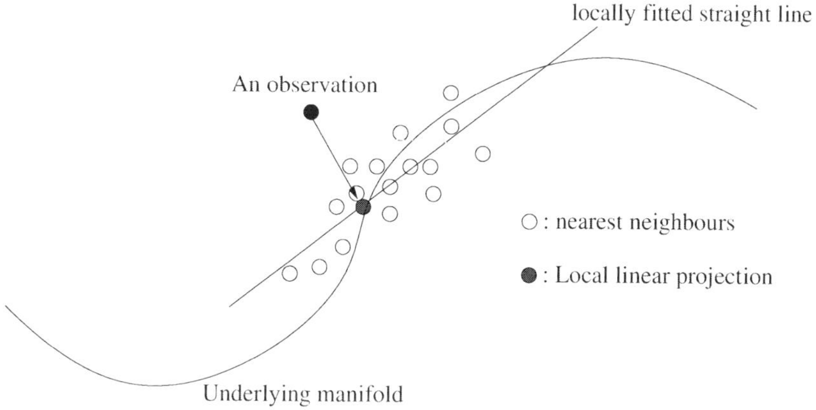

Figure 3. An illustration of Local Linear Projection in a 2-D space with local dimension 1 and 15 nearest neighbors.

In Figure 4 a denoising example via LLP is provided. The noisy data are presented in the left panel, while the denoised data are presented in the right panel. It is clear that the LLP reveals the true underlying structure in the dataset.

5.2 *Curve Clustering*

Clustering is an important technique in data processing. We consider a dataset containing $N = 512$ time series. Each series has dimension $p = 64$. The time series are generated according to the following rule:

$$y_i(t) = \sin\left(\frac{2\pi t}{64} + I(i)\frac{\pi}{2}\right) + \frac{1}{2}\varepsilon_{i,t}, \qquad i = 1,2,\ldots,512; \quad t = 1,2,\ldots,64,$$

where $\varepsilon_{i,t} \sim N(0,1)$ and the function $I(\cdot)$ is defined as

$$I(i) = \begin{cases} 0, & \text{if } 1 \le i \le 128, & \text{type - I signal,} \\ 1, & \text{if } 129 \le i \le 256, & \text{type - II signal,} \\ 2, & \text{if } 257 \le i \le 384, & \text{type - III signal,} \\ 3, & \text{if } 385 \le i \le 512, & \text{type - IV signal.} \end{cases}$$

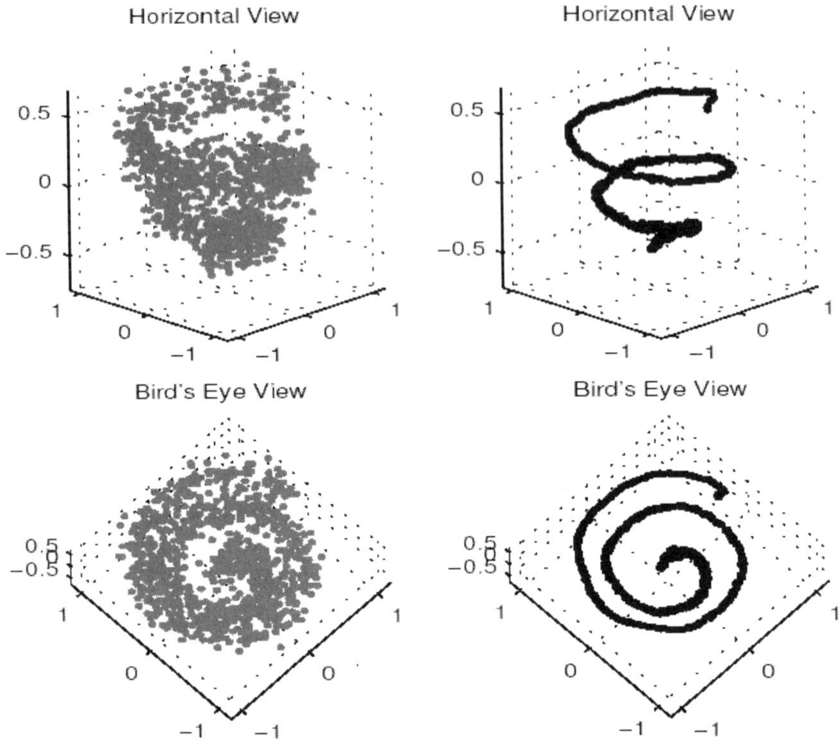

Figure 4. Denoising via LLP.

In words, there are *4* trigonometric time series with different phases. One quarter of these time series belong to each type. Figure 5 provides an illustration of all the time series. Each plot contains 128 time series belonging to one of the four types. The result of LLP-based denoising is shown in Figure 6. Note that the information on how the time series are generated is not used in applying LLP. One can observe that the LLP recovers the underlying patterns of this set of data.

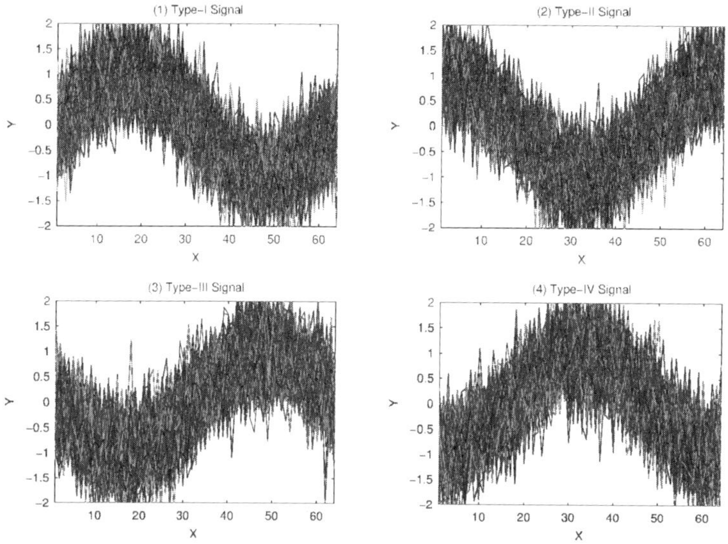

Figure 5. Noisy time series dataset.

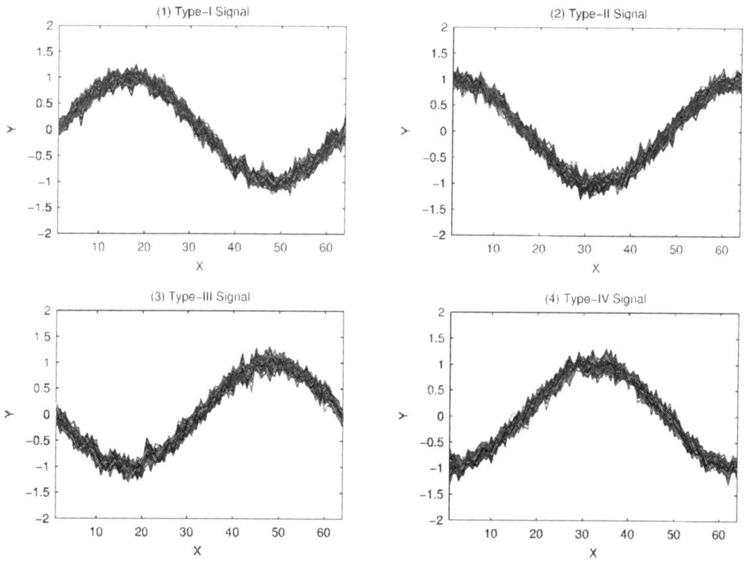

Figure 6. Denoised time series via LLP.

5.3 Image Detection

We now consider the detection of inhomogeneous regions in a homogeneous background (e.g., textures). The underlying assumption is that the samples from the homogeneous background reside on an underlying manifold, while the samples that intersect with the embedded object (i.e., the inhomogeneous region) are 'away' from this manifold.

The empirical distance from each sample to the manifold is a quantity to determine the likelihood of a sample's overlapping with an embedded object. This result can consequently be integrated with the 'Significance Run Algorithm' to predict the presence of the embedded structures. A 'local projection' algorithm is designed to estimate the distances between the samples and the manifold. Simulation results for the features embedded in the textural images show promise. This work can be extended to a formal theoretical framework for underlying feature detection. It is particularly well-suited to textural images.

We consider detecting objects in a homogeneous background. The *objects* are the regions within which the distributional properties of these image pixels are different from those in the rest of the image. Two example cases are given in Figures 7 and 8.

In each case, there is a textural image, a trigonometric-function-shaped slim region with contents different from the texture, and a combination of both of them. The detection problem is (1) to determine the presence of an object region, and furthermore (2) to infer the location and the shape of the object region. This problem is a fundamental one in many applications, such as target recognition, satellite image processing, and so on.

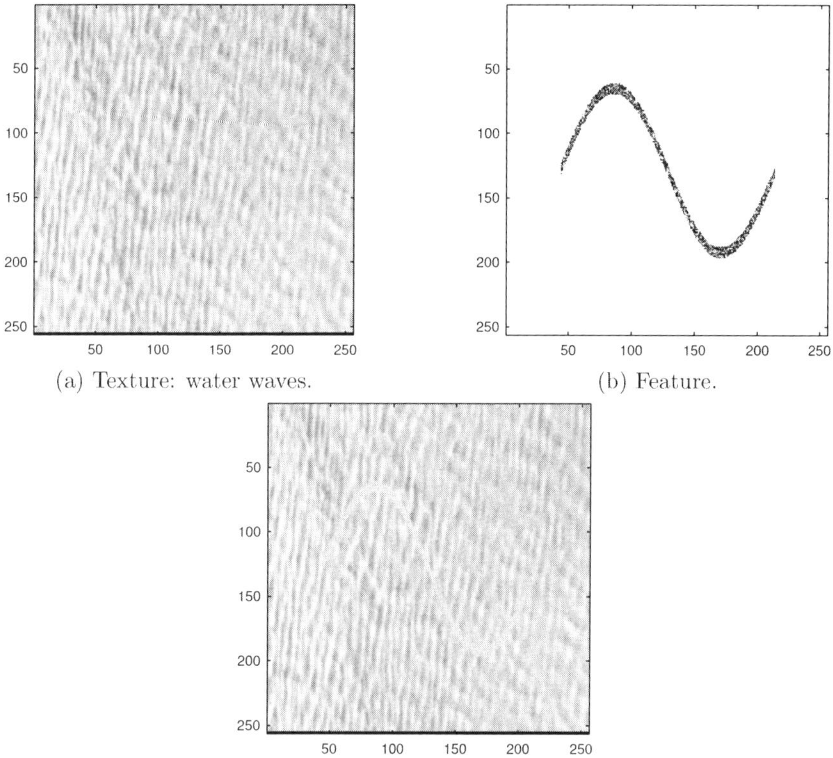

(a) Texture: water waves.

(b) Feature.

(c) Combined.

Figure 7. Example of an object (shaped like a trigonometric function, with its own textural distribution, as depicted in (b)) that is embedded in a textural image ((a)). Panel (c) is a combination: (c)=(a)+(b).

We explore the following idea: (1) the background makes the majority of an image, while an object region is the 'minority'; (2) In addition, the majority of the images (from the homogeneous background), if appropriately sampled, are located on a low-dimensional manifold; (3) The samples that overlap with the embedded region are 'far' from the manifold. Given that the above three conjectures are true, the distance from a sampled patch to the underlying manifold gives the probability that the sample overlaps with the embedded object. If all the *high probability samples* are relatively concentrated, then one has evidence for the presence of an embedded object; otherwise there may not be an embedded object. An illustration of an underlying manifold for samples (e.g., patches) from a homogeneous background is given in Figure 9.

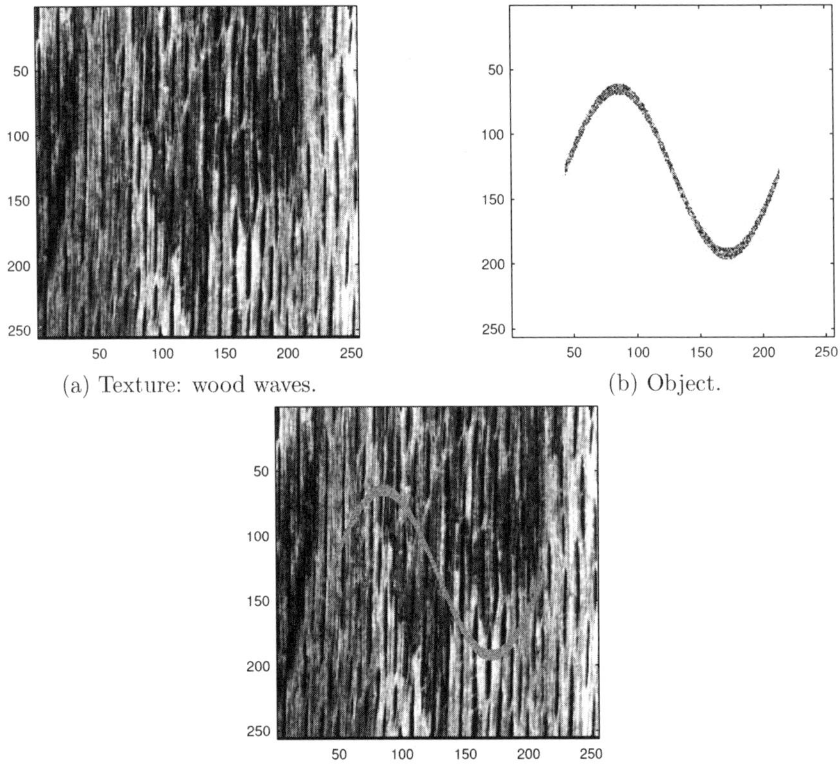

(a) Texture: wood waves.

(b) Object.

(c) Combined.

Figure 8. Another example of an embedded object.

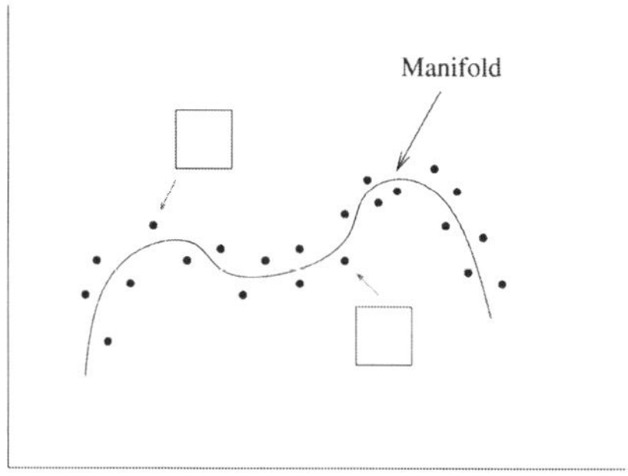

Figure 9. Illustration of an underlying manifold. Each square represents a sample patch from the image.

A previously developed framework named *significance run algorithm* (Arias-Castro, Donoho, and Huo, 2003; Huo, Chen, and Donoho, 2003a, b) can be used to process the patterns of the high probability samples. The distance from a sample to an underlying manifold can be estimated by LLP. Simulations demonstrate the effectiveness of this approach, which will be shown in Section 5.3.5.

The rest of this subsection is organized as follows. In Section 5.3.1, the formulation of the problem is given. In Section 5.3.2, the distance to a manifold is defined. Section 5.3.3 describes the Significance Run Algorithm (SRA). In Section 5.3.4, some issues in parameter estimation are discussed. In Section 5.3.5, we present the simulation results. Some conclusions are presented in Section 5.3.6.

5.3.1 Formulation

For an $N \times N$ image, let y_i, $i \in \mathrm{I}$, denote all of the 8×8 sampled patches (or windows) with two diagonal corners being $(4a+1, 4b+1)$ and $(4a+8, 4b+8)$, where $0 \le a, b \le (N-8)/4$. The patch size 8×8 is chosen for computational convenience. We assume that if patch y_i is sampled in the background, then

$$y_i = f(t_i) + \varepsilon_i, \qquad i \in \mathrm{I},$$

where $f(\cdot)$ is a locally smooth function that determines the underlying manifold, the t_i's denote the underlying parameters for the manifold, and the ε_i's are random errors.

5.3.2 Distance to Manifold

For any patch y_i, the distance from this patch to its original image on the manifold $f(t_i)$ is

$$\|y_i - f(t_i)\|_2 .$$

As explained earlier, this distance measures how likely the patch is in the background. The larger the above distance is, the less likely this patch is on the background.

An illustration of the distance from a patch to the manifold is given in Figure 10. Note that the function $f(\cdot)$ is not available.

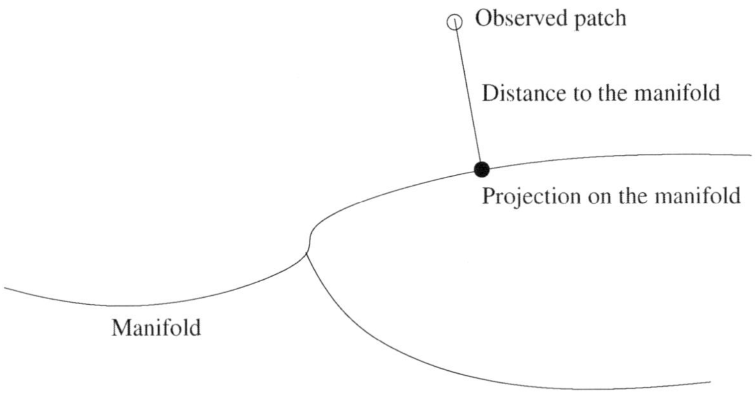

Figure 10. Illustration of the distance from an observed patch to the manifold.

The distance between y_i, $i \in \mathrm{I}$ and $f(t_i)$ can be estimated by $\|y_i - \hat{y}_i\|_2$, as described in Section 5.1.2.

5.3.3 SRA: the Significance Run Algorithm

Even though the distance to a manifold can be estimated, it still remains unclear when the distance is *significantly* large. Instead of studying the distribution of the distances themselves, we study their spatial patterns by using SRA, which was introduced in Arias-Castro, Donoho, and Huo (2003), and was later used in Huo, Chen, and Donoho (2003a) and Huo, Chen, and Donoho (2003b).

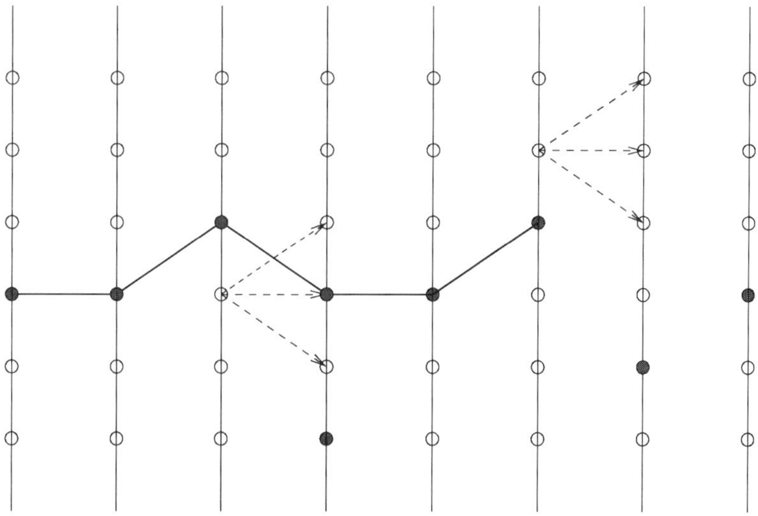

Figure 11. An illustration of a Significance Graph and a Significance Run.

A summary of SRA is as follows. Each patch is associated with a node. Because patches are equally spaced, they form a table as in Figure 11. (See detailed interpretation on this figure in Chen and Huo (2006).)

There is an edge between two nodes if and only if the corresponding patches are spatially connected. A node is significant if and only if the corresponding distance $\|y_i - \hat{y}_i\|_2$ is above a prescribed threshold (denoted by T_1). A *significance run* is a chain of the connected significant nodes. The length of the longest significance run is the test statistic: an embedded object is claimed to be present if and only if this length is above a constant (denoted by T_2). It has been shown (e.g., Arias-Castro, Donoho, and Huo (2003); Huo, Chen, and Donoho (2003b)) that SRA leads to a powerful test.

Note that both T_1 and T_2 can be determined numerically. T_1 can be a given percentile of the empirical estimates of the distances: $\|y_i - \hat{y}_i\|_2$, and T_2 can be derived from simulations.

5.3.4 Parameter Estimation

In LLP, one needs to specify the number of the nearest neighbors and the local dimension. This can be done by studying the empirical distribution of the distances and the total residual sum of squares.

5.3.4.1 Number of nearest neighbors

An illustration of the percentiles of the distances to the nearest neighbors is given in Figure 12. We choose 50 nearest neighbors, because it is approximately a kink point in this figure. It is possible to choose the number of the nearest neighbors by studying the distances to the nearest neighbors. Here we do not pursue this problem further.

5.3.4.2 Local Dimension

The problem of estimating the local dimension has been analyzed in Roweis and Saul (2000) and Tenenbaum, de Silva, and Langford (2000). There are follow-up works in this line. Due to space limitations, we omit the details. Figure 13 gives the plot of the residual sum of squares $\sum_{i \in \mathrm{I}} \|y_i - \hat{y}_i\|_2^2$ versus the local dimension (as k_0 in the LLP). An approximate kink point is at $k_0 = 15$, which is our choice of the local dimension in the simulations.

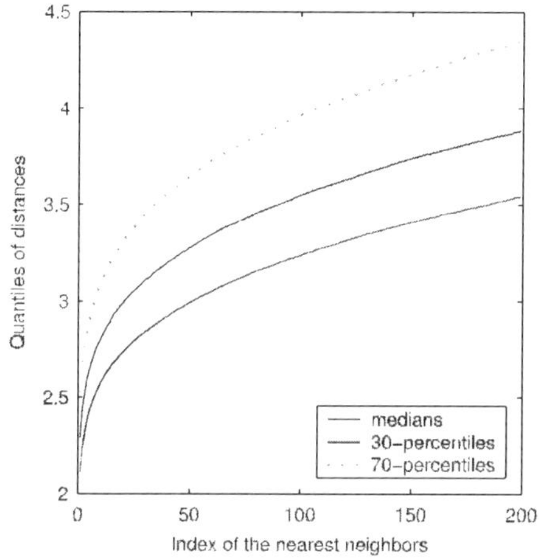

Figure 12. Percentiles of the distances from the nearest neighbors.

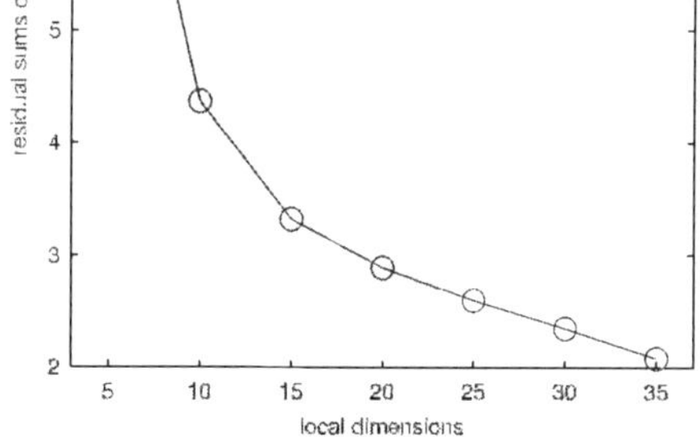

Figure 13. Residual sum of squares versus local dimension.

5.3.5 Simulations

We apply the above approach to the two images in Figure 7(c) and Figure 8(c). The positions of the significant patches are displayed in Figure 14 (for the water image) and in Figure 15 (for the wood image), respectively. In both cases, the constant T_1 is chosen to be the 95th percentile of the squared distances: $\|y_i - \hat{y}_i\|_2^2$, $\forall i \in I$. Obviously, the significant patches are concentrated around the embedded object, which is the trigonometric shape. Hence SRA will unveil the presence of the object.

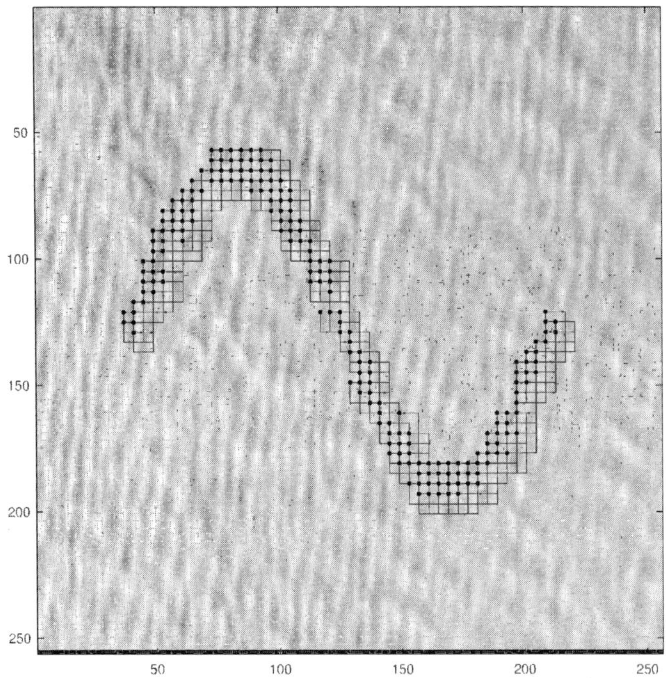

Figure 14. Pattern of significant patches for the water image. Northwestern corners of the significant patches are marked by dark dots.

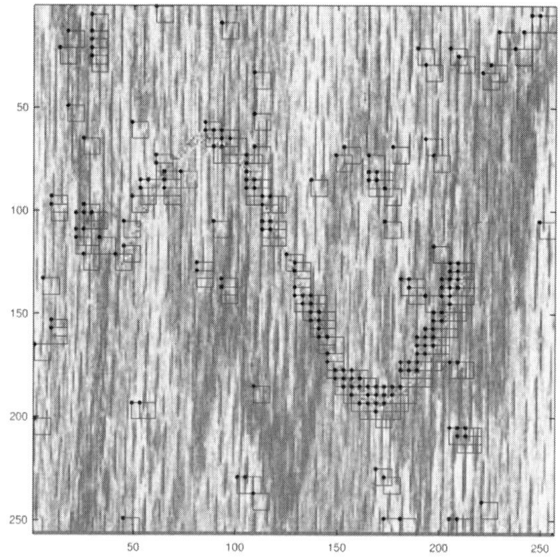

Figure 15. Pattern of significant patches for the wood image. Northwestern corners of the significant patches are again marked by dark dots.

For comparison, Figure 16 gives the patterns of significant patches when there is no embedded object.

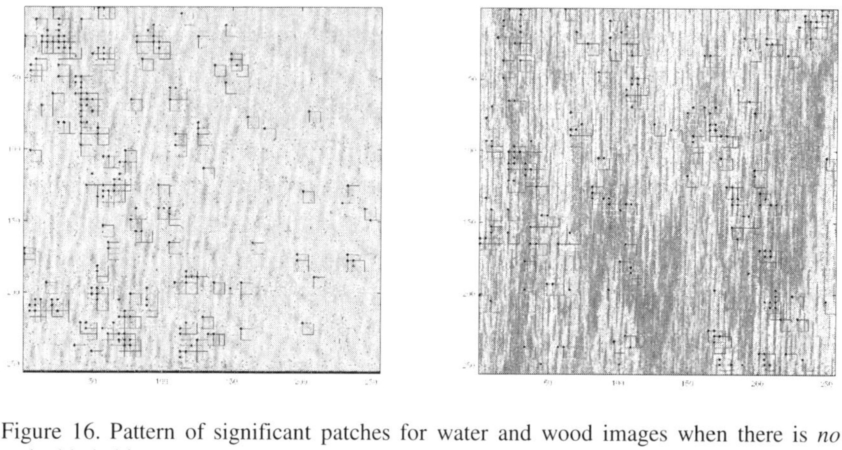

Figure 16. Pattern of significant patches for water and wood images when there is *no* embedded object.

5.3.6 Discussion

By modifying the structure of the significance graph, the above approach can be applied to more general objects, e.g., instead of graphs, one can consider curves, or even non-filamentary objects. We leave this as a future research topic.

If the background is non-homogeneous, which is true in many cases, the above approach will fail. The proposed framework can be used to derive a general theory on when an embedded object is detectable, and when it is not. This will be another topic for future research.

5.4 Applications on the Localization of Sensor Networks

One area in which manifold-based learning methods can be applied is sensor positioning in wireless networks. This type of application is of interest in, for example, military surveillance. We typically assume that there are a large number of sensors randomly deployed over an area. Each sensor contains a simple radio transmitter, and from this we know the pairwise distances between the sensors. Based on this information, we would like to compute the relative positions of all the sensors. Furthermore, we may know the true global positions of a few sensors (called "anchor nodes"), and based on this we may wish to compute the global positions of all the sensors. An example of the situation, in which we may need to compute the global positions, is given in Figure 17.

The solution to the first problem depends on whether we have all the pairwise distances available. Of course this may or may not be true in practice. If all the distances are available, the method is known as classical multidimensional scaling (MDS), which as mentioned earlier is a variation on the idea of principal components. Let $T = [t_{ij}]_{n\times 2}$ be the matrix of the true locations of the set of n sensor nodes in the 2-dimensional Euclidean space, and let $d_{ij}(T)$ denote the true distance between sensors *i* and *j*. We assume that we know the true distances d_{ij}. Then the classical MDS algorithm is as follows:

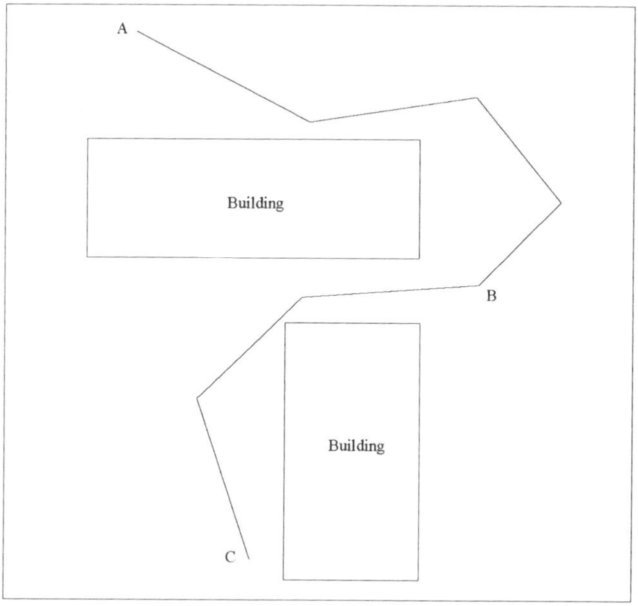

Figure 17. Illustration of the sensor localization problem.

- Compute the matrix of squared distances D^2, where $D=[d_{ij}]_{n\times n}$.
- Compute the matrix *J* with $J = I - \frac{\mathbf{1}\mathbf{1}^T}{n}$, where $\mathbf{1}=(1,1,\ldots,1)$.
- Apply double centering to this matrix: $H = -\frac{1}{2}JD^2J$.
- Compute the eigen-decomposition $H = UVU^T$.
- To recover the solution in *i* dimensions, the coordinate matrix is $X = U_i V_i^{\frac{1}{2}}$, where U_i is formed by the first *i* columns of *U*, and V_i is the diagonal matrix containing the largest *i* eigenvalues of H.

If there are missing distances, we can use a more complicated iterative MDS optimization algorithm to minimize the sum of residual errors of our estimated positions. Such a solution has been presented in Ji and Zha (2004).

The second case is more interesting. Recall that the relative positions of the sensors are assumed to be known, and we wish to compute the global positions based on some knowledge of the exact positions of a few sensors. Intuitively, since the *relative* positions that are computed will be unaltered under rigid motions, the problem is to find the optimal isometric mapping of the local positions to match the known global positions of the anchors. In this sense it can be thought of as a variant of the Local Tangent Space Alignment (LTSA) idea presented above. For simplicity we assume that our measured pairwise distances are all equal to the corresponding true distances to ensure that a solution exists. As it turns out, we need to know the exact global positions of at least 3 anchor nodes in order to have a feasible problem. The requirement that we need at least 3 anchor nodes is also intuitively explained by viewing the optimal isometry as 3 separate functions – a shifting, a rotation, and a reflection. Then the first anchor node can be thought of as determining the optimal shift, the second determines the optimal rotation, and the third determines the reflection.

6. Conclusions

We have given a broad survey of manifold-based learning methods, emphasizing their mathematical formulations. By doing so, we hope to give new insight into the similarities between the various methods, and their underlying unified theoretical framework, which we believe will be the focus of future research in this area. It is our hope that this chapter will attract more researchers to work in this area and stimulate a new direction for work in the theoretical analysis of manifold-based methods and related applied problems.

Appendix: Some related and useful URLs

The following websites provided useful information while this chapter was written.

- MSU: http://www.cse.msu.edu/~lawhiu/manifold/
- MIT: http://www.ai.mit.edu/courses/6.899/doneClasses.html
- UBC: http://www.cs.ubc.ca/~mwill/dimreduct.htm
- Penn: http://www.seas.upenn.edu/%7Ekilianw/workpage/drg/
- Fudan, China: http://www.iipl.fudan.edu.cn/people/zhangjp/literatures/MLF/INDEX.HTM

References

Abdullaev, Y. G. and Posner, M. I. (1998). Event-related brain potential imaging of semantic encoding during processing single words. *NeuroImage*, **7**, 1-13.

Arias-Castro E., Donoho, D. L., and Huo, X. (2006). Adaptive multiscale detection of filamentary structures embedded in a background of uniform random points. *Annals of Statistics*, **34**(1), 326-349, February.

Bai, Z., Demmel, J., Dongarra, J., Ruhe, A., and van der Vorst, H. (2000). Templates for the solution of algebraic eigenvalue problems: a practical guide. Society for Industrial and Applied Mathematics, Philadelphia, PA, U.S.A.

Belkin, M. and Niyogi, P. (2001). Laplacian eigenmaps and spectral techniques for embedding and clustering. In Dietterich, T. G., Becker, S., and Ghahramani, Z. (Eds.), *Advances in Neural Information Processing Systems*, **14**, 585-591.

Belkin, M. and Niyogi, P. (2003). Laplacian Eigenmaps for dimensionality reduction and data representation. *Neural Computation*, **15**(6), 1373-1396.

Bernstein, M., de Silva, V., Langford, J. C., and Tenenbaum, J. B. (2000). Graph approximations to geodesics on embedded manifolds. Technical report, Stanford University, Stanford, CT, U.S.A., December.

Bishop, C. M., Svensen, M., and Williams, C. K. I. (1998). GTM: The generative topographic mapping. *Neural Computation*, **10**(1), 215-234.

Borg, I. and Groenen, P. (1997). *Modern Multidimensional Scaling: Theory and Applications*. Springer-Verlag, New York, NY, U.S.A.

Brand, M. (2003). Charting a manifold. In Proceedings, Neural Information Processing Systems, Volume 15. Mitsubishi Electric Research Lab: MIT Press. TR-2003-13 March 2003, http://www.merl.com, Presented at NIPS-15, December 2002.

Chen, J. and Huo, X. (2004a). Sparse representations for multiple measurement vectors (MMV) in an over-complete dictionary. *ICASSP* 2005, Philadelphia, PA, U.S.A.

Chen, J. and Huo, X. (2006). Distribution of the length of the longest significance run on a Bernoulli net, and its applications. *Journal of the American Statistical Association*, **101**(473), 321-331.

Chen, J. and Huo, X. (2006). Theoretical results on sparse representations of multiple measurement vectors. *IEEE Trans. Signal Processing*, **54**(12), 4634-4643.

Costa, J.A., Patwari, N., and Hero, A. O. (2006). Distributed multi-dimensional scaling with adaptive weighting for node localization in sensor networks. *ACM Trans. on Sensor Networks.*, **2**(1), 39-64.

Dijkstra, E. W. (1959). A note on two problems in connection with graphs. *Numerical Mathematics*, **1**, 269-271.

Donoho, D. L. and Grimes, C. E. (2003). Hessian eigenmaps: new locally linear embedding techniques for high-dimensional data. *Proceedings of the National Academy of Arts and Sciences*; **100**, 5591-5596.

Friedman, J. H., Bentley, J. L., and Finkel, R. A. (1977). An algorithm for finding best matches in logarithmic expected time. *ACM Transactions on Mathematical Software*, **3**(3), 290-226.

Fukumizu, K., Bach, F. R., and Jordan, M. I. (2004). Dimensionality reduction for supervised learning with reproducing kernel Hilbert spaces. *Journal of Machine Learning Research*, **5**, 73-79.

Globerson, A. and Tishby, N. (2003). Sufficient dimensionality reduction. *Journal of Machine Learning Research*, **3**, 1307-1331.

Haase, A. (1990). Snapshot flash MRI: Application to T1, T2, and chemical shift imaging. *Magn. Reson. Med.* **13**, 77-89.

Hero, A. O., Costa, J., and Ma, B. (2003). Convergence rates of minimal graphs with random vertices.
URL: http://www.eecs.umich.edu/~hero/Preprints/convergence_rates_paper_2.pdf

Huo, X. (2003). A geodesic distance and local smoothing based clustering algorithm to utilize embedded geometric structures in high dimensional noisy data. In *SIAM International Conference on Data Mining, Workshop on Clustering High Dimensional Data and its Applications*, San Francisco, CA, U.S.A., May.

Huo, X. and Chen, J. (2002). Local linear projection (LLP). In First IEEE Workshop on Genomic Signal Processing and Statistics (GENSIPS), Raleigh, NC. U.S.A., http://www.gensips.gatech.edu/proceedings.

Huo, X., Chen, J., and Donoho, D. L. (2003a). Multiscale detection of filamentary features in image data. In *SPIE Wavelet-X*, San Diego, CA, U.S.A., August.

Huo, X., Chen, J., and Donoho D. L. (2003b). Multiscale significance run: Realizing the 'most powerful' detection in noisy images. *Asilomar Conference on Signals, Systems, and Computers.*

Huo, X. and Ni, X. (2004b). Counting the number of convex sets in digital image. Technical Report, Downloadable at the URL address given below. http://www2.isye.gatech.edu/statistics/papers/.

Ni, X. S. and Huo, X. (2007). Statistical interpretation of the importance of phase information in signal and image reconstruction. *Statistics and Probability Letters*, 77(4), 447-454.

Ji, X. and Zha, H. (2004). Sensor positioning in wireless ad-hoc sensor networks with multidimensional scaling. *Proceedings of IEEE INFOCOM*, pp. 2652-2661.

Kohonen, T. ((1995, 1997,) 2001). *Self-organizing maps* (3rd edition Ed.). Springer-Verlag, New York, NY, U.S.A.

Kruskal, J. B. (1964). Multidimensional scaling by optimizing goodness of fit to a nonmetric hypothesis. *Psychometrika*, **29**, 1-27.

Li, B. Zha, H., and Chiaromonte, F. (2005). Counter regression: a general approach to dimension reduction. *Annals of Statistics*, 33.

Petersen, S. E., Fox, P. T., Posner, M. I., Mintun, M., and Raichle, M. E. (1990). Positron emission tomographic studies of the processing of single words. *J. Cognitive Neurosci.* **1**(2), 154-170.

Petersen, S. E., Fox, P. T., Posner, M. I., Mintun, M., and Raichle, M. E. (1988). Positron emission tomographic studies of the cortical anatomy of single word processing. *Nature*, **331**, 585-589.

Raichle, M. E., Fiez, J. A., Videen, T. O., MacLeod, A. -M. K., Pardo, J. V., Fox, P. T., and Petersen, S. E. (1994). Practice-related changes in human brain functional anatomy during non-motor learning. *Cereb Cortex*, **4**, 8-26.

Roweis, S. T. and Saul, L. K. (2000). Nonlinear dimensionality reduction by locally linear embedding. *Science*, **290**, 2323-2326.

Saul, L. K. and Roweis, S. T. (2001). An introduction to Locally Linear Embedding. URL: http://www.cs.toronto.edu/~roweis/lle/publications.html.

Shepard, R. N. (1962) The analysis of proximities: multidimensional scaling with an unknown distance function: I & II. *Psychometrika*, **27**, 125-140 & 219-246.

Snyder, A. Z., Abdullaev, Y. G., Posner, M. I., and Raichle, M. E. (1995). Scalp electrical potentials reflect regional cerebral blood flow responses during processing of written words. *Proc. Natl. Acad. Sci.*, Washington D. C., U.S.A., **92**, 1689-1693.

Tamayo, P., Slonim, D., Mesirov, J., Zhu, Q., Kitareewan, S., Dmitrovsky, E., Lander, E. S., and Golub, T. R. (1999). Interpreting patterns of gene expression with self-organizing maps: methods and application to hematopoietic differentiation. *Proc. Natl Acad. Sci.*, Washington D. C., U.S.A. **96**(6), 2907-2912.

Tenenbaum, J. B., de Silva, V., and Langford, J. C. (2000). A global geometric framework for nonlinear dimensionality reduction. *Science*, **290**, 2319-2323.

Torgerson, W. S. (1952). Multidimensional scaling: I. Theory and method. *Psychometrika*, **17**, 401-419.

Wu, Y. N., Zhu, S. C., and Liu, X. W. (2000). Equivalence of Julesz ensemble and FRAME models. *International Journal of Computer Vision*, **38**(3), 247-265.

Young, G. and Householder, A. S. (1938). Discussion of a set of points in terms of their mutual distances. *Psychometrika*, **3**, 19-22.

Yuille, A. L., Coughlan, J. M., Wu, Y. N., and Zhu, S. C. (2001). Order parameter for detecting target curves in images: how does high level knowledge helps? *International Journal of Computer Vision*, **41**(1/2), 9-33.

Zhang, Z. and Zha, H. (2004). Principal manifolds and nonlinear dimension reduction via local tangent space alignment. *SIAM Scientific Computing,* **26**(1), 313-338.

Authors' Biographical Statements

Xiaoming Huo received the B.S. degree in mathematics from the University of Science and Technology, China and the M.S. degree in electrical engineering and the Ph.D. degree in statistics from Stanford University. He is an Associate Professor in the School of Industrial and Systems Engineering, Georgia Institute of Technology, Atlanta. His research interests include dimension reduction and nonlinear methods, and their applications in signal/image processing, data mining. Dr. Huo received first prize in the Thirtieth International Mathematical Olympiad (IMO), which was held in Braunschweig, Germany. He is a senior member of IEEE. His work has been featured in Emerging Research Fronts in Essential Science Indicators.

Xuelei (Sherry) Ni received her B.S. in mathematics from Nanjing University in 2000 and M.S. in statistics from Georgia Tech in 2004. She was awarded the Ph.D. in applied statistics from Georgia Institute of Technology in 2006. Dr. Ni is now an Assistant Professor in the Department of Mathematics and Statistics at Kennesaw State University, and a member of IMS and ASA. Her research interests are geometric statistics, signal representative, and dimension reduction.

Andrew Smith received a B.S. in mathematics from UNC-Chapel Hill in 2003, and is currently pursuing a Ph.D. in Statistics at the Georgia Institute of Technology, where he is a President's Fellow and ARCS Scholar. His research interests are in nonlinear dimension reduction and model selection. Andrew's honors include the individual second prize in the ASA Stat Bowl, held at the 2004 Joint Statistical Meetings in Toronto.

Chapter 16[1]

Predictive Regression Modeling for Small Enterprise Datasets with Bootstrap, Clustering and Bagging

C. Jack Feng and Krishna Erla
Department of Industrial and Manufacturing Engineering
Bradley University, Peoria, Illinois 61625, U.S.A.
Email: cfeng@bradley.edu

Abstract: Most enterprise datasets are large, but some are very small for predictive purposes due to expensive experiments, reduced budget or tight schedule required to generate them. The bootstrap approach is a method used frequently for small datasets in data mining. Numerous theoretical studies have been done on bootstrap in the past two decades but few have applied it to solve real world manufacturing problems. Bootstrap methods provide an attractive option when model selection becomes complex due to small sample sizes and unknown distributions. In principle, bootstrap methods are more widely applicable than the jackknife method, and also more dependable. In this chapter we focus on selecting the best model based on prediction errors computed using the revised bootstrap method, known as the *0.632 bootstrap*. Models developed and selected are then clustered and the best cluster of models is next bagged to provide the minimum prediction errors. Numerical examples based on a small enterprise dataset illustrate how to use this procedure in selecting, validating, clustering, and bagging predictive regression models when sample sizes are small compared to the number of parameters in the model.

***Key Words*:** Bootstrap sampling; Predictive regression; Subset selection; Bagging; Cluster analysis.

---

[1] Liao, T.W. and E. Triantaphyllou, (Eds.), **Recent Advances in Data Mining of Enterprise Data: Algorithms and Applications**, *World Scientific*, Singapore, pp. 747-774, 2007.

1. Introduction

A large variety of models may be used to fit enterprise data and predict a manufacturing or service process: linear, nonlinear, artificial neural networks, and many others. It is thus necessary to compare the various models (for example with regard to their performances and complexity) and choose the best one. The ranking of the models is made according to some criterion such as the prediction error, usually defined as the average prediction error that a model would make over an infinite-size and unknown test set independent from the training one. In practice the prediction error can only be estimated, and some methods are available to provide such estimation. Notable statistical techniques for this purpose include the v-fold cross-validation (Feng *et al.* 2006, Feng *et al.* 2005, Ljung 1999, Kohavi 1995), the leave-one-out (Ljung 1999, Kohavi 1995), and the bootstrap (Efron and Tibshirani 1993, Kohavi 1995) and its unbiased extensions.

Although these methods are roughly asymptotically equivalent (see, for example, Stone 1977 and Kohavi 1995) and despite the fact that the use of the bootstrap is not an irrefutable question, it seems that using the bootstrap can be advantageous in many "real world" modeling cases, i.e., when the number of samples is limited (Kohavi 1995). The bootstrap method is a type of Monte Carlo sampling approach with replacement. Numerous theoretical studies have been done on bootstrap in the past two decades (see, e.g., Davison and Hinkley 1997 and Efron and Tibshirani 1993), but few have applied it in solving real world problems in manufacturing. The main limitation of applying bootstrap in practice is the computation time required for assessing an approximation of sufficient reliability (or *accuracy*). A second limitation, in our context of model selection, is the fact that the selected best model is selected from a set of a priori chosen models, leading to a restricted choice.

Most enterprise datasets are large, but some are very small for predictive data mining purposes due to expensive experiments, reduced budget or tight schedule required to generate such data. In this chapter, we prove experimentally the validity of the sample using 0.632 bootstrap sampling, based on regression analysis and show how to use this approximation to perform efficient bootstrap simulations with reasonable computational complexity. Models developed and selected are then clustered and the best cluster of models is next bagged to provide the minimum prediction errors. Numerical examples based on a small enterprise dataset will illustrate how to use this procedure in selecting, validating, clustering, and bagging predictive regression models when sample sizes are small compared to the number of parameters in the model.

This chapter deals with the estimation of the error rate of a prediction rule constructed from a training dataset. The training set $x = (x_1, x_2, \ldots, x_n)$ consists of n observations $x_i = (t_i, y_i)$, with t_i being the predictors or future vector and y_i the response on the basis of x. We construct a prediction rule $rx(t)$ and wish to estimate the error rate of this rule when it is needed to predict future responses from their predictor vectors.

Cross-validation, the traditional method of choice for this problem, provides a nearly unbiased estimate of the future error rate. However, the low bias of cross-validation is often paid for by high variability. Here we show that suitably defined bootstrap procedures can substantially reduce the variability of the error rates in prediction. The bootstrap procedures are nothing more than smoothed versions of cross-validation, with some adjustments made to correct for bias. The bootstrap method of prediction error gives an upward bias because the test point is chosen randomly from the F distribution without reference to the training sample X called *extra-sample error* (Efron 1979). Efron (1983) investigated a more restrictive definition of prediction error designated to correct the upward bias in error by averaging it with the downwardly biased estimate $\text{Err}_{0.632}$. The 0.632 estimator is

$$E_{pred} = 0.368 E_{learn} + 0.632 E_{validation} \tag{1}$$

The coefficients 0.368 = e - 1 and 0.632 were suggested by an argument based on the fact that the bootstrap samples are supported on approximately $0.632n$ of the original data points. Wang and Liao (2002) used the 0.632 estimator in classifying six types of welding defects for a set of 147 imbalanced examples.

2. Literature Review

Bootstrapping seems to work better than cross-validation in many cases (Efron 1983). In the simplest form of bootstrapping, instead of repeatedly analyzing subsets of the data, one repeatedly analyzes sub samples of the data. Each sub sample is a random sample with replacement from the full sample. Depending on what one wants to do, anywhere from 50 to 200 sub samples might be used. Many more sophisticated bootstrap methods can be used not only for estimating prediction errors but also for estimating confidence bounds for network outputs (Efron and Tibshirani 1993). Producing the simplest classification model with the smallest prediction error on new observations requires to optimally balancing reduction of error on the training data with control of overfitting. An improved bootstrap scheme has been recently proposed for model selection in classification problems (Efron and Tibshirani 1995).

2.1 *Tree-Based Classifiers and the Bootstrap 0.632 Rule*

Tree-based classifiers are potentially prone to over-fitting, thus training must focus on estimates of out-of-sample error to obtain regularized models that will generalize well on novel data. Cross-validation and bootstrap over the training set are typically applied for error estimation and model selection (Breiman *et al.* 1984). Cross-validation provides a low bias solution, at the cost of significant variability for discontinuous error functions (Efron and Tibshirani 1995, Ripley 1996). Bootstrap methods may smooth over possible discontinuity of the error function, but the standard bootstrap is upwardly biased.

Suppose indeed that values $x_1, \ldots, x_n \sim F$ are observed and let the empirical distribution function F be defined assigning probability $1/n$ to each value $x_1, x_2, \ldots, x_n$. Let F be the true error rate and $\overline{err}$ the resubstitution error; the idea is to estimate the parameter Err from the expected value $E_F[\overline{err}\{x_1, x_2, \ldots, x_n\}]$ considering expectation over *bootstrap replicates* of the original sample, i.e., samples $x^* = \{x_1^*, x_2^*, \ldots, x_n^*\}$ of size n extracted *with replacement* from F. In practice, B bootstrap samples X^{*b} are generated from the original data and for each of them a misclassification error E^{*^b} is computed over the data points *not* included in X^{*b}. The bootstrap estimate is finally obtained by averaging over the replicate samples:

$$E^{(\text{boot})} = \frac{1}{B}\sum_{b=1}^{B} E^{*^b} \tag{2}$$

The probability that a data point appears in the bootstrap sample is 1 - $(1 - 1/n)^n \approx 0.632$ for any integer $n > 0$. Thus, for sufficiently large sample size, approximately a fraction of $0.368n$ data will be replaced by duplicate data. Given a prediction rule constructed over the bootstrap sample, the prediction error will likely be larger for points that are not extracted by the replication procedure and the bootstrap estimate will result in an upward bias (Efron and Tibshirani 1995). An adjustment was proposed in Efron (1983) with the *bootstrap 0.632* estimate:

$$E^{(0.632)} = 0.368\ \overline{err} + 0.632\ E^{(\text{boot})} \tag{3}$$

where the weighted contribution of the training set error $\overline{err}$ was introduced to correct the upward bias in $E^{(\text{boot})}$.

2.2 *Bagging*

Bagging is a method of obtaining more robust predictions when the model class under consideration is unstable with respect to the data, i.e., small changes in the data can cause the predicted values to change significantly. In a typical prediction problem, there is a trade-off between bias and variance, in that after a certain amount of fitting, any increase in the precision of the fit will cause an increase in the prediction variance on future observations. Similarly, any reduction in the prediction variance causes an increase in the expected bias for future predictions. Breiman (1996) introduced bagging as a method of reducing the prediction variance without affecting the prediction bias. As a result, the predictive performance can be significantly improved.

Bagging, standing for "Bootstrap Aggregating", is an ensemble learning method. Instead of making predictions from a single model fitted on the observed data, bootstrap samples are taken from the data, the model is fitted on each sample, and the predictions are averaged over all of the fitted models to get the bagged prediction. Breiman (1996) explains that bagging works well for unstable modeling procedures, i.e., those for which the conclusions are sensitive to small changes in the data. He also gives a theoretical explanation of how bagging works, demonstrating the reduction in mean-squared prediction error for unstable procedures. Breiman (1994) demonstrated that tree models, among others, are empirically unstable.

In ordinary (batch) bagging, bootstrap resampling is used to reduce the variability of an unstable estimator. A particular model or algorithm, such as a classification tree, is specified for learning from a set of data and producing predictions. For a particular dataset X_b, denote the vector of predictions (at the observed sites or at new locations) by $G(X_b)$. Denote the observed data by $X = (x_1, x_2, ..., x_n)$. A bootstrap sample of the data is a sample with replacement, so that $X_b = (x_{b1}, ..., x_{bn})$, where $b_i \in \{1, \ldots\ldots, n\}$ with repetitions allowed. X_b can also be thought of as a re-weighted version of X, where the weights $w_i^{(b)}$ are drawn from the set $\{0, \frac{1}{n}, \frac{2}{n}, \ldots, 1\}$ and correspond to the number of times that x_i appears in the bootstrap sample. We denote the weighted sample as $(X, w^{(b)})$. For each bootstrap sample, the model produces predictions $G(X_b)_1, \ldots, G(X_b)_B$. A total of B bootstrap samples are used. The bagged predictor for the jth element $(1 \leq j \leq B)$ is then

$$\frac{1}{B}\sum_{b=1}^{B} G(X_b)_j = \frac{1}{B}\sum_{b=1}^{B} G\left(X, w^b\right)_j \tag{4}$$

or in the case of classification, the jth element is predicted to belong to the most frequently predicted category by $G(X_1)_j, \ldots, G(X_B)_j$.

A version of the pseudocode for implementing bagging is

1. For $b \in \{1, \ldots, B\}$,
   (a) Draw a bootstrap sample, X_b, from X.
   (b) Find the predicted values $G(X_b)$.
2. The bagging predictor is $\frac{1}{B}\sum_{b=1}^{B} G(X_b)$.

or equivalently:

1. For $b \in \{1, \ldots, B\}$,
   (a) Draw random weights $w^{(b)}$ from $\{0, \frac{1}{n}, \frac{2}{n}, \ldots, 1\}$ that sum to 1.
   (b) Find the predicted values $G(X, w^{(b)})$.
2. The bagging predictor is $\frac{1}{B}\sum_{b=1}^{B} G\left(X_b, w^b\right)$.

For classification, the bagging predictor is a plurality vote.

3. Methodology

3.1 *The Data Modeling Procedure*

Various methods have been proposed to select the best predictive model. The bootstrap sampling method is a good and unbiased method to predict the best model especially when the sample size is small, i.e., between 10 ~ 20 and no distribution assumptions can be made. Model selection is entirely based on predictive errors (i.e., the sum of the learning error and the testing error). The proposed procedure for predictive regression modeling of small enterprise datasets is presented in Figure 1. We will detail the above procedure next.

3.2 *Bootstrap Sampling*

The foundation of the bootstrap approach is the plug-in principle (Efron and Tibshirani 1993). This general principle allows for obtaining an estimator of a statistic according to an empirical distribution. In our context of model selection, our statistic of interest is the prediction error. We thus use the bootstrap to estimate the prediction error in order to rank the models and choose the best one. The bootstrap estimator of the prediction error is computed according to the bootstrap resampling approach. Given an original sample (or dataset) X, we generate B new samples, denoted by X^b. The new samples X^b are obtained from the original sample X by drawing with replacement. For each bootstrap sample X^b, we compute a bootstrap estimator of our statistic of interest.

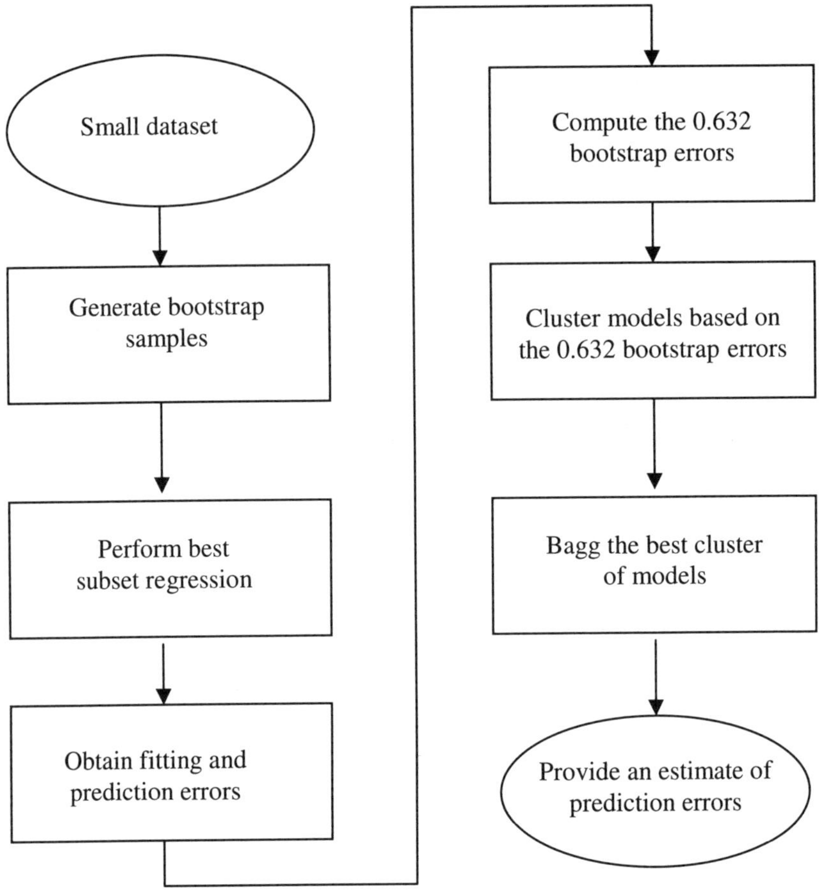

Figure 1. A flowchart for the proposed predictive regression modeling of small datasets.

The consecutive steps of the bootstrap method developed by Efron (1979) are stated as follows. Given dataset *X*, one draws randomly *N* samples with replacement. These new samples form a new learning set x_{learn} of the same size as the original one. The validation set x_{val} is the original learning set *X*. This process is called re-sampling. Figure 2 illustrates the above procedure used in bootstrap sampling. As shown in Section 2.2, X^{*b} is the new samples generated by Monte Carlo simulation, and $G(X^{*b})$ are the predictions.

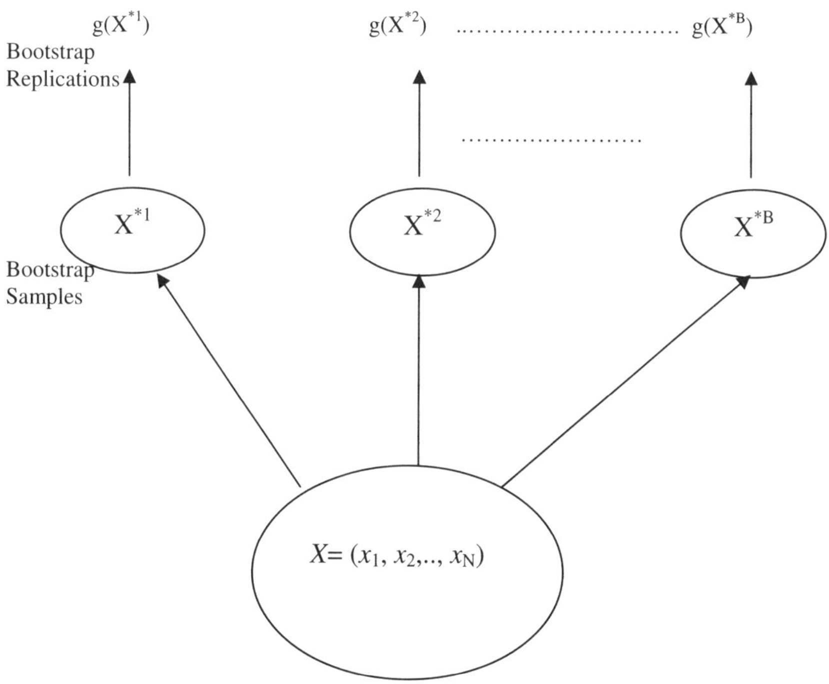

Figure 2. Sampling and resampling components.

3.3 *Selecting the Best Subset Regression Model*

Classic texts on regression analysis outline the following criteria for selecting the best subset regression models: (1) the value of the coefficient of multiple determination R^2, (2) the value of the residual mean square s^2, (3) Mallows' C_p-statistic (Montgomery *et al.* 2001, Draper and Smith 1998, and Myers 1990), and (4) Akaike's information criterion or AIC (Burnham and Anderson 2002, Miller 2002, and McQuarrie and Tsai 1998). An excellent and more comprehensive treatment of criterion (4) is given in Burnham and Anderson (2002), Miller (2002), and McQuarrie and Tsai (1998). Let R_p^2 denote the coefficient of multiple determination for a subset regression model with p terms, which is $p - 1$ regressors and an intercept term β_0. Then

$$R_p^2 = \frac{SS_R(p)}{SS_T} = 1 - \frac{RSS_p}{SS_T} \tag{5}$$

where: $SS_R(p)$, RSS_p and SS_T denote the regression sum of squares, the residual sum of squares and the total sum of squares of the model, respectively, for a p-term subset model.

Although the general consideration in applying the above statistic to subset selection is the larger the better, a subset with a large R_p^2 value does not guarantee the best model. This is true because the value of R_p^2 increases if more regressors are added to the subset. To avoid the latter, some authors prefer to use an adjusted R^2 statistic (e.g., see Ezekiel 1930) defined by a p-term equation as

$$\text{Adjusted } R_p^2 = 1 - \left(\frac{n-1}{n-p}\right)\left(1 - R_p^2\right) \tag{6}$$

where n is the number of data used for fitting the subset regression model. The idea behind this adjustment is that the above statistic can be used to compare equations fitted not only to a specific set of data but also to two or more entirely different sets of data. Draper and Smith (1998) argued that the value of this statistic for the latter purpose is not high; it might be useful as an initial gross indicator. As pointed out by Kennard

(1971), the adjusted R_p^2 is closely related to Mallows's C_p statistic that will be discussed in this subsection. Furthermore, Montgomery *et al.* (2001) pointed out that the adjusted R_p^2 is also closely related to another model evaluation criterion - the residual mean square $s^2(p)$ for a subset as defined next.

The residual mean square $s^2(p)$ for a subset takes the following form:

$$s^2(p) = \frac{RSS_p}{n-p} \tag{7}$$

This criterion for selecting the best subset requires that the smaller the value of $s^2(p)$, the better it is. Montgomery *et al.* (2001) derived the following computational relationship between $s^2(p)$ and the adjusted R_p^2:

$$\text{Adjusted } R_p^2 = 1 - \frac{n-1}{SS_T} s^2(p) \tag{8}$$

Thus the criterion minimum $s^2(p)$ and maximum adjusted R_p^2 are equivalent.

Mallows (1973, 1995, and 1997) proposed a criterion that is related to the mean square error of a fitted value as follows:

$$C_p = \frac{RSS_p}{s^2(p)} - n + 2p \tag{9}$$

Assuming that $E[s^2(p)] = \sigma^2$, the ratio RSS_p/s^2 has expected value $(n - p)\sigma^2/\sigma^2 = n - p$. Thus approximately, $E(C_p) = p$. The best subset model is chosen after inspecting the C_p vs. the p plot. Using the C_p-statistic to best subset selection, we would look for a regression with a low C_p value about equal to p. Draper and Smith (1998) advised caution in using the C_p-statistic. Some modifications of the Mallows C_p-statistic have been made over the years (e.g., see Gilmour 1996). For an in-depth treatment of this topic, see Miller (2002) and McQuarrie and Tsai (1998). Modern statistics software packages, including MINITAB and SAS, report the value of R_p^2, adjusted R_p^2, $s^2(p)$, and C_p vs. p under the best subset regression option.

3.4 Evaluation of Prediction Errors

3.4.1 Prediction Error Evaluation

Regression has four possible uses, including (1) data description, (2) prediction, (3) parameter estimation, and (4) control (Montgomery *et al.* 2001 and Myers 1990). Since the focus of this chapter is to construct and select the best model(s) for prediction of future observations, we would like to select the regressors such that the mean square error of prediction is minimized. The *PRESS* (prediction sum of squares) statistic suggested by Miller (1974) is essentially a leave-one-out cross-validation statistic for model selection based on this consideration. Denote $\hat{y}_{ip}$ as the predicted value for y_i. Computationally (Montgomery *et al.* 2001, p. 301),

$$PRESS_p = \sum_{i=1}^{n} \left[y_i - \hat{y}_{ip} \right]^2 = \sum_{i=1}^{n} \left(\frac{e_i}{1 - h_{ii}} \right)^2 \tag{10}$$

where h_{ii} is the diagonal elements of the hat matrix $\mathbf{H} = \mathbf{X}\,(\mathbf{X'X})^{-1}\mathbf{X'}$. Modern statistics software packages usually report the above value. If $n >> p$, then according to (Miller 2002, p. 146)

$$\begin{aligned} PRESS_p &\approx \sum_{i=1}^{n} \frac{e_i^2}{(1 - p/n)^2} \\ &= \frac{RSS_p}{(1 - p/n)^2} = RSS_p \frac{n^2}{(n-p)^2} \end{aligned} \tag{11}$$

A related criterion is the prediction R^2-like statistic (Montgomery *et al.* 2001, p. 535)

$$R^2_{\text{Prediction}} = 1 - \frac{PRESS_p}{SS_T} \tag{12}$$

that measures, in an approximate sense, how much of the variability in new observations the model might be expected to explain.

3.4.2 The 0.632 Prediction Error

The training of the model g is done using x_{learn} and the errors E_{val}(g) and E_{learn}(g) obtained with this model are calculated according to the following equations:

Step 1:

$$E_{learn}(g) = \frac{\sum_{i=1}^{N}(g(x_i^{learn}) - y_i^{learn})^2}{N} \tag{13}$$

with $(x_i^{learn}, y_i^{learn})$ the elements of x_{learn} and $g(x_i^{learn})$ the approximation of y_i^{learn} obtained by model g.

Step 2:

$$E_{val}(g) = \frac{\sum_{i=1}^{N}(g(x_i^{val}) - y_i^{val})^2}{N} \tag{14}$$

with remaining samples of X_i and Y_i for each bootstrap sample (x_i^{val}, y_i^{val}) the elements of X_{val} and g(x_i^{val}) the approximation of y_i^{val} by model g.

Step 3: Steps 1 and 2 are repeated K times, where K is as large as possible.

Step 4: The prediction error is calculated according to the error equation for each and every bootstrap sample

$$E_{pred} = 0.368\, E_{learn} + 0.632\, E_{val} \tag{15}$$

3.5 Cluster Analysis

Clustering is the process of grouping the data into classes or clusters so that objects within a cluster have high similarity in comparison to one another, but are very dissimilar to objects in other clusters (Han and Kamber, 2006). Dissimilarities are assessed based on the attribute values describing the objects. Often, some distance measures are used. The process of grouping a set of physical or abstract objects into classes of similar objects is called clustering. A cluster of data objects can be treated collectively as one group in many applications.

Cluster analysis can be used as a stand-alone tool to gain insight into the distribution of data, to observe the characteristics of each cluster, and to focus on a particular set of clusters for further analysis. Clustering is a form of learning by observation, rather than learning by classified examples (also known as supervised learning). Conceptual clustering consists of two components: (1) it discovers the appropriate classes, and (2) it forms descriptions for each class, as in classification. Using cluster analysis we can find the best models, which consist of mixed numerical and categorical data in complex datasets.

3.6 Bagging

Bagging frequently improves the predictive performance of a model. In this bootstrap sampling we use simple bagging, i.e., bootstrap aggregating, where we average the prediction errors for the best class of models that come from cluster analysis and compare that error with prediction errors from other methods.

4. A Computational Study

4.1 The experimental data

Usually bootstrap sampling is used for small sets of data where we are not able to collect a large sample. In this chapter, a classic dataset of 13 samples is chosen from Montgomery *et al.* (2001). This set of data was also used in Draper and Smith (1998) and Daniel and Wood (1980). The dataset is small and suitable for bootstrap sampling. It follows the criterion of sample sizes between 10 ~ 20 as laid out in Efron and Tibshirani (1993). This dataset was originally presented in Hald (1952) concerning the heat evolved in calories per gram of cement (Y) as a function of the amount of each of four ingredients in the mix: tricalcium , aluminate (X_1), tricalcium silicate (X_2), tetracalcium alumino ferrite (X_3), and dicalcium silicate (X_4). We will use this dataset to illustrate bootstrap sampling, subset selection, predictive regression modeling and bagging in the selection and validation of predictive models. Table 1 shows the original dataset.

4.2 Computational Results

Taking the cement data as the original sample, 100 bootstrap samples were obtained by using the MINITAB resampling option with replacement and the remaining data are taken as the testing sample. For each learning sample the best subset regression was performed to construct a model by using the C_p statistic. Using these models we calculated the prediction error for each learning sample and the validation error for each testing sample. The same procedure was used to calculate the prediction errors for all 100 samples. Finally, the 0.632 prediction error was obtained by using the learning and validation errors for all 100 samples.

Table 1. The Hald cement design and manufacturing dataset.

X_1	X_2	X_3	X_4	Y
7	26	6	60	78.5
1	29	15	52	74.3
11	56	8	20	104.3
11	31	8	47	87.6
7	52	6	33	95.9
11	55	9	22	109.2
3	71	17	6	102.7
1	31	22	44	72.5
2	54	18	22	93.1
21	47	4	26	115.9
1	40	23	34	83.8
11	66	9	12	113.3

The 100 models were grouped based on prediction errors in order to bagg the best cluster of models with comparable prediction errors. Clustering analysis was conducted by using the Statistica Data Miner (Anon, 2003). Using the *k*-median clustering algorithm, five clusters were considered to provide the best grouping of prediction errors after a number of trial-and-error applications by ranging the number of clusters between 3 and 6. A summary of the key statistics from clustering is presented in Table 2. Table 2 shows that cluster 1 had the smallest mean prediction error, the smallest minimum and maximum prediction errors, and the second smallest standard deviation as compared to other clusters. Summary of the key statistics from cluster analysis of the five clusters along with the prediction errors calculated using equation (1), PRESS, and the predicted R^2 are given in Tables 3, 4, 5, 6, and 7, respectively.

Table 2. Summary of key statistics from cluster analysis.

Prediction error	Cluster 1	Cluster 2	Cluster 3	Cluster 4	Cluster 5	Overall
Min	1.2937	6.2374	2.2114	1.8729	2.8600	1.2937
Max	1.8372	7.9705	2.6506	2.1918	4.2385	7.9705
Mean	**1.6941**	7.1039	2.4041	2.0132	3.3136	2.2300
Std Dev	0.1137	1.2254	0.1434	**0.1024**	0.4343	0.7488

Table 3. Summary of key statistics from cluster analysis for Cluster 1.

Model No.	Prediction Error	PRESS	R^2(Prediction)	Distance from Center
07	1.740480	155.870	94.57	0.006938
08	1.535520	98.253	96.74	0.023759
13	1.837280	56.5161	97.59	0.021436
14	1.780700	67.0309	97.79	0.012962
20	1.775010	60.3798	96.85	0.012110
22	1.618600	73.1053	96.09	0.011316
26	1.769070	87.9342	92.43	0.011220
28	1.674590	115.323	93.89	0.002930
37	1.293700	168.837	94.29	0.059977
38	1.586230	93.5797	96.26	0.016164
40	1.740620	88.8519	97.39	0.006959
42	1.707830	42.4344	98.74	0.002048
43	1.791750	65.1065	98.12	0.014617
49	1.641770	79.2139	96.66	0.007846
51	1.655700	54.7692	98.12	0.005760
52	1.572510	93.7589	94.57	0.018219
54	1.776190	152.415	94.16	0.012286
59	1.735780	80.3219	97.28	0.006234
66	1.776510	119.299	94.94	0.012334
67	1.692470	96.6109	96.89	0.000253
68	1.707660	73.8306	95.18	0.002023
76	1.788140	110.898	94.35	0.014076
82	1.816989	134.972	95.15	0.018397
86	1.673669	41.5959	97.07	0.003068
90	1.646703	130.472	95.30	0.007107
92	1.757817	45.0379	98.04	0.009535
94	1.558863	81.5902	96.77	0.020263
96	1.784216	71.6009	97.58	0.013489

Cluster 1 has twenty-eight models with the smallest prediction error. The average prediction error of all the twenty-eight models is 1.69416. Cluster 1 is categorized based on predictors. Some parameters are critical for all these twenty-eight models. For example, X_1 showed up in each of these models. Others showed up in some of these twenty-eight models, e.g., X_2 showed up in twenty-two models, X_3 in sixteen models, and X_4 in sixteen models. Among the twenty-eight models in cluster 1, eleven models included parameters X_1, X_2, X_3, eleven models included X_1, X_2, X_4, five models included X_1, X_3 and X_4, and one model had X_1 and X_2 as its parameters. All of these models are categorized based on critical parameters in the following.

Table 4. Summary of key statistics from cluster analysis for Cluster 2.

Model No.	Prediction Error	PRESS	R^2(Pred.)	Distance from Center
21	6.237410	40.2132	98.85	0.129784
41	7.970500	16.1218	99.40	0.129784

Table 5. Summary of key statistics from cluster analysis for Cluster 3.

Model No.	Prediction Error	PRESS	R^2 (Pred.)	Distance from Center
02	3.094470	29.3060	98.97	0.032819
05	2.962560	1.17048	99.96	0.052575
10	4.238470	21.5953	99.39	0.138521
15	3.409590	70.9637	97.67	0.014377
33	2.860050	53.3027	97.97	0.067928
34	3.095740	56.8901	97.75	0.032629
46	3.524110	4.75468	99.84	0.031529
71	3.309570	67.1500	97.29	0.000603
74	3.747260	85.0780	95.96	0.064951
93	2.894128	52.6424	98.18	0.062825

Table 6. Summary of key statistics from cluster analysis for Cluster 4.

Model No.	Prediction Error	PRESS	R^2 (Pred.)	Distance from Center
01	1.886870	113.170	96.87	0.018925
03	2.167880	44.570	98.73	0.023163
04	1.901150	75.0944	97.87	0.016786
06	1.984400	29.1847	98.54	0.004317
09	1.885590	77.1561	97.07	0.019116
11	1.978340	45.8987	97.11	0.005225
12	1.908070	76.0413	96.84	0.015750
19	2.109500	87.5981	95.81	0.014419
24	1.943920	78.2737	96.96	0.010380
27	2.128240	342.394	89.97	0.017226
29	2.159850	25.8559	98.68	0.021960
30	2.074890	76.8333	97.08	0.009235
31	1.904630	130.190	95.32	0.016265
44	2.149320	74.3604	96.99	0.020383
45	1.872870	65.4233	96.11	0.021022
47	1.931280	114.091	95.87	0.012273
48	1.890620	46.1885	97.78	0.018363
53	2.004890	119.374	95.90	0.001249
57	1.905970	45.8995	98.01	0.016064
58	1.907650	111.212	96.55	0.015813
60	2.003840	73.4512	97.44	0.001406
62	2.145840	38.0387	98.62	0.019862
63	1.899470	134.569	95.45	0.017038
64	2.062200	49.0651	98.48	0.007335
65	2.191760	36.0407	98.38	0.026739
69	2.153820	51.3715	95.94	0.021057
70	2.008530	113.285	95.04	0.000703
72	2.044970	100.140	96.76	0.004754
77	1.994860	81.4639	96.76	0.002751
78	2.076132	50.4934	96.81	0.009421
79	1.935498	88.0147	97.23	0.011642
80	2.012919	58.2577	97.30	0.000046
81	2.178151	52.7739	98.38	0.024701
84	1.925959	104.559	96.74	0.013070
87	1.948192	49.6866	96.71	0.009740
89	2.167495	101.861	93.37	0.023105
91	2.081194	18.0682	99.47	0.010180
97	1.980658	23.2598	99.21	0.004878

Table 6. Summary of key statistics from cluster analysis for Cluster 4 (cont'd).

Model No.	Prediction Error	PRESS	R^2 (Pred.)	Distance from Center
98	1.881033	66.5390	97.29	0.019799
99	2.080085	46.5860	97.79	0.010013
100	2.073772	42.4631	98.12	0.009068

Table 7. Summary of key statistics from cluster analysis for Cluster 5.

Model No.	Prediction Error	PRESS	R^2(Pred.)	Distance from Center
16	2.334730	76.5553	96.95	0.010395
17	2.445760	56.6143	98.47	0.006234
18	2.608100	60.0768	95.00	0.030548
23	2.536870	39.0046	98.47	0.019880
25	2.327190	55.9534	92.66	0.011524
32	2.450430	35.8701	98.05	0.006934
35	2.229980	70.3773	97.01	0.026084
36	2.623780	115.301	94.15	0.032897
39	2.241890	70.6345	97.56	0.024300
50	2.332880	33.6934	98.88	0.010672
55	2.383790	28.4216	98.72	0.003047
56	2.372040	81.9095	97.34	0.004807
61	2.292760	89.6397	96.97	0.016681
73	2.211400	46.5405	98.70	0.028866
75	2.286120	69.2361	98.07	0.017675
83	2.472022	62.1157	96.30	0.010168
85	2.602940	37.6509	97.88	0.029775
89	2.650637	101.861	93.37	0.036919
95	2.275254	69.2857	96.78	0.019303

The results are shown, respectively, in Tables 8, 9, 10, 11 and 12 with the calculated averages of the predicted error, PRESS, the R^2 predicted values and the C_p-statistics. In these tables, the column $|C_p - p|$ should be the smallest but not zero, while the column "min," "max," "average," and "St Dev" stand for the minimum, the maximum, the average 0.632

bootstrap prediction error, and the standard deviation of the 0.632 bootstrap prediction errors, respectively.

Table 8. A summary of key statistics for models with X_1 (28 models).

Sample	e(pred.)	PRESS	R^2 (pred.)	C_p	$\|C_p\text{-}p\|$
S-07	1.74048	155.8700	94.57	4.1	0.1
S-08	1.53552	98.2530	96.74	3.1	0.9
S-13	1.83728	56.5161	97.59	3.1	0.9
S-14	1.78070	67.0309	97.79	4.5	0.5
S-20	1.77501	60.3798	96.85	3.1	0.9
S-22	1.61860	73.1053	96.09	4.2	0.2
S-26	1.76907	87.9342	92.43	4.4	0.4
S-28	1.67459	115.3230	93.89	3.9	0.1
S-37	1.29370	168.8370	94.29	3.4	0.6
S-38	1.58623	93.5797	96.26	3.2	0.8
S-40	1.74062	88.8519	97.39	4.6	0.6
S-42	1.70783	42.4344	98.74	4.5	0.5
S-43	1.79175	65.1065	98.12	3.0	1.0
S-49	1.64177	79.2139	96.66	3.2	0.8
S-51	1.65570	54.7692	98.12	3.1	0.9
S-52	1.57251	93.7589	94.57	3.6	0.4
S-54	1.77619	152.4150	94.16	4.9	0.9
S-59	1.73578	80.3219	97.28	4.9	0.9
S-66	1.77651	119.2990	94.94	3.2	0.8
S-67	1.69247	96.6109	96.89	3.4	0.6
S-68	1.70766	73.8306	95.18	3.9	0.1
S-76	1.78814	110.8980	94.35	5.3	1.3
S-82	1.81699	134.9720	95.15	4.7	0.7
S-86	1.67367	41.5959	97.07	5.2	1.2
S-90	1.64670	130.4720	95.30	2.8	0.2
S-92	1.75782	45.0379	98.04	3.2	0.8
S-94	1.55886	81.5902	96.77	4.8	0.8
S-96	1.78422	71.6009	97.58	4.6	0.6
Total	47.43634	2539.6080	2692.81	109.9	18.5
Average	1.6940	90.7000	96.17	3.925	0.661
Min	1.2937	41.5960	92.43	2.8	0.1
Max	1.8370	168.8370	98.74	5.3	1.3
St Dev	0.1140	34.6180	1.60	0.777	0.324

Table 9. A summary of key statistics for models with X_1, X_2, X_3 (11 models).

Sample No.	e(pred.)	PRESS	R^2 (pred.)	C_p	$\lvert C_p\text{-}p\rvert$
S-07	1.74048	155.870	94.57	4.1	0.1
S-08	1.53552	98.2530	96.74	3.1	0.9
S-13	1.83728	56.5161	97.59	3.1	0.9
S-20	1.77501	60.3798	96.85	3.1	0.9
S-37	1.29370	168.837	94.29	3.4	0.6
S-43	1.79175	65.1065	98.12	3.0	1.0
S-49	1.64177	79.2139	96.66	3.2	0.8
S-51	1.65570	54.7692	98.12	3.1	0.9
S-54	1.77619	152.415	94.16	4.9	0.9
S-82	1.81699	134.972	95.15	4.7	0.7
S-92	1.75782	45.0379	98.04	3.1	0.9
Total	18.62221	1071.37	1060.29	38.8	8.6
Average	1.693	97.397	96.39	3.527	0.782
Min	1.294	45.038	94.16	3	0.1
Max	1.837	168.837	98.12	4.9	1
St Dev	0.159	46.836	1.574	0.70	0.252

Table 10. A summary of key statistics for models with X_1, X_2, X_4 (11 models).

Sample No.	e(pred.)	PRESS	R^2 (pred.)	C_p	$\lvert C_p\text{-}p\rvert$
S-14	1.78070	67.0309	97.79	4.5	0.5
S-22	1.61860	73.1053	96.09	4.2	0.2
S-26	1.76907	87.9342	92.43	4.4	0.4
S-28	1.67459	115.323	93.89	3.6	0.4
S-38	1.58623	93.5797	96.26	3.2	0.8
S-42	1.70783	42.4344	98.74	4.5	0.5
S-52	1.57251	93.7589	94.57	3.6	0.4
S-59	1.73578	80.3219	97.28	4.9	0.9
S-66	1.77651	119.299	94.94	3.2	0.8
S-76	1.78814	110.898	94.35	5.3	1.3
S-86	1.67367	41.5959	97.07	5.2	1.2
Total	18.68363	925.2812	1053.41	46.6	7.4
Average	1.699	84.116	95.765	4.236	0.673
Min	1.573	41.596	92.43	3.2	0.2
Max	1.788	119.299	98.74	5.3	1.3
St Dev	0.080	26.644	1.899	0.750	0.355

Table 11. A summary of key statistics for models with X_1, X_3, X_4 (5 models).

Sampling No.	e(pred.)	PRESS	R^2 (pred.)	C_p	$\|C_p\text{-}p\|$
S-40	1.74062	88.8519	97.39	4.6	0.6
S-67	1.69247	96.6109	96.89	3.4	0.6
S-68	1.70766	73.8306	95.18	3.9	0.1
S-94	1.55886	81.5902	96.77	4.8	0.8
S-96	1.78422	71.6009	97.58	4.6	0.6
Total	8.483829	412.4845	483.81	21.3	2.7
Average	1.697	82.497	96.762	4.26	0.54
Min	1.559	71.601	95.18	3.4	0.1
Max	1.784	96.611	97.58	4.8	0.8
St Dev	0.085	10.419	0.947	0.590	0.261

Table 12. A summary of key statistics for models with X_1 and X_2 (8 models).

Sample No.	e(pred.)	PRESS	R^2 (pred.)	C_p	$\|C_p\text{-}p\|$
S-15	3.13405	70.9637	97.67	4	1
S-53	2.00489	119.374	95.9	3.8	0.8
S-65	2.19176	36.0407	98.38	3.3	0.3
S-70	1.84146	113.285	95.04	3.6	0.6
S-78	2.07613	50.4934	96.81	1.5	1.5
S-89	2.0667	101.861	93.37	4.1	1.1
S-90	1.6467	130.472	95.3	2.8	0.2
S-93	2.89413	52.6424	98.18	2.2	0.8
Total	17.8558	675.132	770.65	25.3	6.3
Average	2.2320	84.3920	96.331	3.163	0.788
Min	1.6467	36.0407	93.370	1.500	0.200
Max	3.1340	130.4720	98.380	4.100	1.500
St Dev	0.5140	36.1790	1.745	0.927	0.426

All these three category models have almost the same R^2 and PRESS statistics. Considering the prediction error, we chose the model, with X_1, X_2 and X_3 as predictors, which has the smallest prediction error compared to the other models. For example, to compare with the results of Montgomery *et al.* (2001) that were constructed with the parameters of X_1 and X_2, we calculated the predicted error, PRESS, the R^2 predicted values and the C_p statistic for those models having X_1 and X_2 as parameters.

The eight models had X_1 and X_2 as their predictors and the R^2 predicted and PRESS statistics were calculated for samples with parameters X_1 and X_2. The results are provided in Table 13.

Table 13. Comparison of the two best subset models.

	e(pred)	PRESS	R^2 (pred)	C_p	$\lvert C_p\text{-}p\rvert$
Our Models					
Total	18.622	1071.370	1060.290	38.800	8.600
Average	**1.693**	97.397	96.390	3.527	**0.780**
Min	**1.294**	45.038	94.160	3.000	**0.100**
Max	**1.837**	168.837	98.120	4.900	**1.000**
St Dev	**0.159**	46.836	1.5740	0.700	0.250
Models with X_1 and X_2 based on Montgomery *et al.* (2001)					
Total	17.856	675.132	770.650	25.300	6.300
Average	**2.232**	84.392	96.331	3.163	**0.790**
Min	**1.647**	36.041	93.370	1.500	**0.200**
Max	**3.134**	130.472	98.380	4.100	**1.500**
St Dev	**0.514**	36.179	1.745	0.927	0.430

5. Conclusions

The 0.632 bootstrap prediction errors were larger in the cluster of models based on the selection from Montgomery *et al.* (2001) that included predictors X_1 and X_2. It shows that using the 0.632 bootstrap method resulted in models with better prediction performance for small datasets than the traditional best subset regression.

The cluster of models based on our selection is also better than that based on selection by Montgomery's simple best subset approach in terms of $|C_p - p|$, which is preferred in selecting predictive models. However, there was little difference in the R^2 (prediction) and the PRESS statistics between our best models and the best models based on the selection by Montgomery *et al.* (2001) as shown in Table 13. Since the R^2 (prediction) and the PRESS statistics are computed based on the leave-one-out cross-validation (CV) method and Breiman and Spector (1992) and Zhang (1993) have concluded that they are among the worst CV methods, this comparison does not appear to be valuable.

Next is a list of the contributions described in this chapter:

1) The 0.632 bootstrap sampling works better than the simple subset selection when the sample size is small and no distribution can be assumed. However, it involves more computational effort.
2) On the average, bootstrap sampling gives better prediction error than the v fold cross- validation.
3) 0.632 bootstrap sampling gives better prediction errors than bootstrap sampling.

Next is a list of some potential future directions in this area of research:

1) The 0.632-bootstrap sampling method was used to correct upward bias. What if the samples are downwardly biased?
2) What if there is no relationship between the independent and the dependent variables?
3) How to deal with cases when training errors are zero (which is rare)? The 0.632 bootstrap method will give a prediction error of $0.632 \times 0.5 + 0.368 \times 0 = 0.316$. What should have been the true error?

References

Anonymous (2003). *Statistica Data Miner User's Manual.* StatSoft, Tulsa, OK, U.S.A.

Breiman, L. (1994). *Heuristics of Instability in Model Selection.* Technical Report, University of California at Berkeley, Berkeley, CA, U.S.A.

Breiman, L. (1996). Bagging predictors. *Machine Learning*, **26**(2), 123-140.

Breiman, L. and Spector, P. (1992). Submodel selection and evaluation in regression: the *X*-random case. *International Statistics Review*, **60**(3), 291-319.

Breiman, L., Friedman, J., Olshen, R., and Stone, C. (1984). *Classification and Regression Trees*. Wadsworth and Brooks/Cole, Pacific Grove, CA, U.S.A.

Burnham, K. P. and Anderson, D. R. (2002). *Model Selection and Inference: A Practical Information – Theoretic Approach*, 2nd Edition. Springer-Verlag, New York, NY, U.S.A.

Clyde, M. A. and Lee, H. K. H. (2001). "Bagging and the Bayesian bootstrap." *Artificial Intelligence and Statistics*, T. Richardson and T. Jaakkola (Eds.), pp. 169-174.

Daniel, C. and Wood, F. S. (1980). *Fitting Equations to Data*, 2nd Edition. Wiley, New York, NY, U.S.A.

Davison, A. C. and Hinkley, D. V. (1997). *Bootstrap Methods and their Applications*. Cambridge University Press, Cambridge, UK.

Draper, N. R. and Smith, H. (1998). *Applied Regression Analysis*, 3rd Edition. John Wiley & Sons, New York, NY, U.S.A.

Efron, B. (1983). *Estimating the error rate of a prediction rule: some improvements on cross-validation. J. Amer. Stat. Assoc.* 78:316–331.

Efron, B. (1979). Bootstrap methods: another look at the jackknife. *Ann. Statist.* **7**, 1-26.

Efron, B. and Tibshirani, R. J. (1993). *An Introduction to the Bootstrap*. Chapman & Hall, London, UK.

Efron, B. and Tibshirani. R.J (1995). *Cross-Validation and the Bootstrap: Estimating the Error Rate of a Prediction Rule*. Technical Report 176, Stanford University, Stanford, CA, U.S.A.

Ezekiel, M. (1930). *Methods of Correlation Analysis*. Wiley, New York, NY, U.S.A.

Feng, C-X. and Kusiak, A. (2006). Data mining applications in engineering design, manufacturing and logistics. *International Journal of Production Research*, **44**(14), 2689-2694 (July).

Feng, C-X., Yu, Z-G. and Kusiak, A. (2006). Selection and validation of predictive regression and neural networks models based on designed experiments. *IIE Transactions*, **38**(1), 13-24.

Feng, C-X., Yu, Z-G., Kingi, U., and Baig, M. P. (2005). Threefold vs. fivefold cross validation in one-hidden-layer and two-hidden-layer predictive neural networks modeling of machining surface roughness data. SME *Journal of Manufacturing Systems*, **24**(2), 93-107.

Gilmour, S. G. (1996) The interpretation of Mallows C_p-statistic. *The Statistician*, **45**(1): 49-56.

Hald, A. (1952) *Statistical Theory with Engineering Applications*. Wiley, New York, NY, U.S.A.

Han, J. and Kamber, M. (2006). *Data Mining: Concepts and Techniques*, 2nd Edition. Morgan Kaufmann, San Francisco, CA, U.S.A.

Kennard, R. W. (1971) A note on the C_p statistic. *Technometrics*, **13**, 899-900.

Kohavi, R. (1995). A study of cross-validation and bootstrap for accuracy estimation and model selection. *Proc. of the 14th Int. Joint Conf. on A.I.*, Vol. 2, Canada.

Ljung, L. (1999). *System Identification - Theory for the User*, 2nd Edition. Prentice Hall, Upper Saddle River, NJ, U.S.A.

McQuarrie, A. D. R. and Tsai, C-L. (1998). *Regression and Time Series Model Selection*. World Scientific, Singapore.

Mallows, C. L. (1997). C_p and prediction with many regressors: comments on Mallows (1995). *Technometrics*, **39**(1), 115-116.

Mallows, C. L. (1995). More comments on C_p. *Technometrics*, **37**(4), 362-372.

Mallows, C. L. (1973). Some comments on C_p. *Technometrics*, **15**(4), 661-675.

Miller, A. J. (2002). *Subset Selection in Regression*, 2nd Edition. Chapman & Hall, Boca Raton, FL, U.S.A.

Miller, R. G. (1974). The jackknife – A review. *Biometrika*, **61**(1), 1-15.

Montgomery, D. C., Peck, E. A., and Vining, G. G. (2001). *Introduction to Linear Regression Analysis,* 3rd Edition. Wiley, New York, NY, U.S.A.

Myers, R. H. (1990). *Classical and Modern Regression with Applications*, 2nd Edition. Duxbury Press, Boston, MA, U.S.A.

Oza, N. C. and Russell, S. (2001). Online Bagging and Boosting. *Artificial Intelligence and Statistics 2001*, T. Richardson and T. Jaakkola (Eds.), pp. 105-112

Ripley, B.D. (1996). *Pattern Recognition and Neural Networks.* Cambridge University Press, Cambridge, UK.

Rubin, D. B. (1981). The Bayesian bootstrap. *Ann. Stat.* **9**, 130-134.

Stone, M. (1977). An asymptotic equivalence of choice of model by cross-validation and Akaike's criterion. *J. Royal. Statist. Soc.,* **B39**, 44-7.

Wang, G. and Liao, T. W. (2002). Automatic identification of different types of welding defects in radiographic images, *NDT&E International*, **35**, 519-528.

Witten, I. H. and Frank, E. (2000). *Data Mining: Practical Machine Learning Tools and Techniques with Java Implementations.* Morgan Kaufmann Publishers, San Francisco, CA, U.S.A.

Zhang, P. (1993). Model selection via multifold cross-validation. *Annals of Statistics,* **21**(1), 299-31.

Authors' Biographical Statements

Dr. Chang-Xue Jack Feng is a Professor of Industrial and Manufacturing Engineering at Bradley University. He was a Visiting Engineering Fellow with a focus in lean assembly to the Caterpillar Production System Division of Caterpillar Inc. in Peoria, Illinois between May 206 and August 2007. He has been the President of the Institute of Industrial Engineers (IIE) Central Illinois Chapter since 1999 and the President of Feng Consulting since 1995. Before joining Bradley in 1998, he was on the engineering faculty of Penn State University between 1995 and 1998. During this period, he developed, named and directed the William and Mary Hintz Manufacturing Technology Lab.

He received his PHD and MS degrees in industrial engineering, MS degree in manufacturing engineering, and BS degree in mechanical engineering. He has applied computation tools, including statistics, optimization, computational neural networks, and fuzzy logic in integrated product and process development, lean/agile manufacturing, and quality and precision engineering. Dr. Feng serves on the editorial board of the International Journal of Production Research and the Open Operations Research Journal. He is a senior member of ASQ, IIE, and SME and a member of ASA and INFORMS. He has published more than 75 technical papers, three books and three book chapters.

Erla Krishna is the owner of his consulting business in training and support of the ERP software SAP. He was a senior supply quality engineer in Caterpillar's Building and Construction Products Division located in North Carolina after getting his MS IE degree from Bradley University in 2004.

Subject Index

D

E

F

G

H

I

R

S

T

U

V

W

List of Contributors

Nikolaos M. Avouris
Department of Electrical and Computer Engineering
University of Patras
Petras, Greece
Email: avouris@upatras.gr

Pei-Chann Chang
Department of Information Management
Yuan Ze University
No. 135, Yuan-Tung Rd.
Chung-li, Tao-Yuan 32026, Taiwan, R.O.C.
E-mail: *iepchang@saturn.yzu.edu.tw*

Guoqing Chen
School of Economics and Management
Research Center for Contemporary Management
Tsinghua University
Beijing 100084, China
Email: chengq@em.tsinghua.edu.cn

Chen-Fu Chien
Department of Industrial Engineering and Engineering Management
National Tsing Hua University
Hsin Chu, Taiwan
Email: cfchien@mx.nthu.edu.tw

Sophia Daskalaki
Department of Engineering Sciences
University of Patras
Petra, Greece
Email: sdask@upatras.gr

Sigal Elnekave
Department of Information Systems Engineering
Ben-Gurion University of the Negev
Beer-Sheva 84105, Israel
E-mail: elnekave@bgu.ac.il

C. Jack Feng
Department of Industrial and Manufacturing Engineering
Bradley University
Peoria, Illinois 61625, USA
Email: cfeng@bradley.edu

Dimitrios Gunopulos
Department of Computer Science and Engineering
University of California at Riverside
Riverside, CA, USA
Email: dg@cs.ucr.edu

Xunhua Guo
School of Economics and Management
Tsinghua University
Beijing 100084, China

Shao-Chung Hsu
Department of Industrial Engineering and Engineering Management
National Tsing Hua University
Hsin Chu, Taiwan

Xiaoming Huo
School of Industrial Engineering
Georgia Institute of Technology
Atlanta, GA, U.S.A.
Email: xiaoming@isye.gatech.edu

Myong K. Jeong
Department of Industrial & Information Engineering
University of Tennessee
Knoxville, TN 37996-0700, USA
Email: mjeong@utk.edu

Jianxin (Roger) Jiao
School of Mechanical and Aerospace Engineering
Nanyang Technological University
Nanyang Avenue, Singapore 639798
Email: jiao@pmail.ntu.edu.sg

L. P. Khoo
School of Mechanical and Aerospace Engineering
Nanyang Technological University
North Spine (N3) Level 2, 50 Nanyang Avenue, Singapore 639798
Emails: mlpkhoo@ntu.edu.sg

Seong G. Kong
Department of Electrical and Computer Engineering
University of Tennessee
Knoxville, TN 37996-2100, USA.

Ioannis Kopanas
OTE S.A, Hellenic Telecommunications Organization
Patras, Greece
Email: ikopanas@ote.gr

Andy Koronios
School of Computer and Information Science
University of South Australia, Australia

Mark Last
Dept. of Information Systems Engineering
Ben-Gurion University of the Negev
Beer-Sheva 84105, Israel
E-mail: mlast@bgu.ac.il

T. Warren Liao
Industrial Engineering Department
Louisiana State University
CEBA Building, No. 3128, Baton Rouge, LA 70803, U.S.A.
Email: ieliao@lsu.edu

H. Y. Lim
Fabristeel Pte Ltd, 9, Tuas Avenue 10
Singapore 639133

Hyeung-Sik Min
Sandia National Laboratories
Albuquerque, New Mexico, USA
Email: hjmin@sandia.gov

Amos Naor
Golan Research Institute
University of Haifa
P.O. Box 97, Kazrin 12900, Israel
E-mail: amosnaor@research.haifa.ac.il

Xuelei (Sherry) Ni
Department of Mathematics and Statistics
Kennesaw State University
Kennesaw, GA, USA
Email: xni2@kennesaw.edu

Olutayo O. Oladunni
Department of Engineering Education
Purdue University
West Lafayette, IN, USA

Olufemi A. Omitaomu
Department of Industrial & Information Engineering
University of Tennessee
Knoxville, TN 37996-0700, USA

Petra Perner
Institute of Computer Vision and Applied Computer Sciences, IBaI
Leipzig, Germany
Email: www.ibai-institut.de

Giovanni C. Porzio
Department of Economics
University of Cassino
Via S.Angelo I-03043 Cassino (FR), Italy
Email: porzio@eco.unicas.it

Giancarlo Ragozini
Department of Sociology
Federico II University of Naples
Vico Monte di Pietà 1, I-80132 Naples, Italy
Email: giragoz@unina.it

Victor Schoenfeld
Yarden - Golan Heights Winery
Katzrin, Israel
E-mail: victor@golanwines.co.il

Andrew K. Smith
School of Industrial Engineering
Georgia Institute of Technology
Atlanta, GA, USA

Sharmila Subramaniam
Google Inc.
Mountain View, CA, USA
Email: sharmi@cs.ucr.edu

Theodore B. Trafalis
School of Industrial Engineering
University of Oklahoma
Norman, OK, USA
Email: ttrafalis@ok.edu

Yen-Wen Wang
Department of Industrial Engineering and Management
Ching-Yun University
No. 229 Chien-Hsin Rd.
Taoyuan 320, Taiwan
E-mail: ywwang@cyu.edu.tw

Yuehwern Yih
School of Industrial Engineering
Purdue University
West Lafayette, Indiana, USA
Email: yih@purdue.edu

Lan Yu
Department of Computer Science and Technology
Tsinghua University
Beijing 100084, China

Lianfeng Zhang
School of Mechanical and Aerospace Engineering
Nanyang Technological University
Nanyang Avenue, Singapore 639798

Z. W. Zhong
School of Mechanical and Aerospace Engineering
Nanyang Technological University
North Spine (N3) Level 2, 50 Nanyang Avenue, Singapore 639798
http://www.ntu.edu.sg/home/mzwzhong/

Shiwu Zhu
School of Economics and Management
Tsinghua University, Beijing 100084, China

About the Editors

Dr. T. Warren Liao received his MS and Ph.D. both in Industrial Engineering from Lehigh University, Bethlehem, PA, USA, in 1984 and 1990, respectively. The concentration area of his MS study was in Information Systems and his Ph.D. concentraction was in Manufacturing Engineering with dissertation titled "Creep Feed Grinding of Ceramics with Diamond Wheels."

Before that, he had five years work experience. He first worked in the area of Production Planning and Control for two years for an electronics company in Taiwan. He then worked in the area of Manufacturing Engineering for two years and one year as an IE Project Engineer for a TV producer, RCA - Taiwan. This industrial experience has directly or indirectly shaped Dr. Liao's problem oriented research in the years to come.

Since 1990, Dr. Liao has been with the Louisiana State University (LSU) in the U.S.A. He is currently a Full Professor in the Construction Management and Industrial Engineering Department at LSU. His research interest covers three major areas: manufacturing processes, manufacturing systems, and artificial intelligence. More specifically, he has carried out research related to grinding processes, cellular manufacturing systems, automated inspection, intelligent systems, and applied soft computing.

At the turn of this century, he started working together with Dr. E. Triantaphyllou in the area of data mining and knowledge discovery. He decided to devote this particular research effort to enterprise systems at the outset. With the support of National Science Foundation, he together with Dr. Triantaphyllou organized the International Workshop on Mining of Enterprise Data, held on June 23, 2004 at Como, Italy, as part of the Mathematics and Machine Learning (MML) Conference. This edited book is a product evolved from this Workshop. For his individual research effort in data mining and knowledge discovery, Dr. Liao is particularly interested in the mining of time series and images related to the operation of an enterprise system. He welcomes any opportunity for collaboration in this area as well as in others.

Dr. Evangelos Triantaphyllou did all his graduate studies at Penn State University. While at Penn State, he earned a Dual M.S. in Environment and Operations Research (O.R.) (in 1985), an M.S. in Computer Science (in 1988) and a Dual Ph.D. in Industrial Engineering and O.R. (in 1990). His Ph.D. dissertation was related to data mining by means of optimization approaches. Since the spring of 2005 he is a Professor in the Computer Science Department at the Louisiana State University (LSU) in Baton Rouge, LA, U.S. Before that, he had served for 11 years as an Assistant, Associate, and Full Professor in the Industrial Engineering Department at LSU. He has also served for one year as an Interim Associate Dean for the College of Engineering at LSU.

His research is focused on decision-making, data mining, and the interface of O.R. and computer science. He has developed new methods for data mining and knowledge discovery and has also explored some of the most fundamental and intriguing subjects in decision making. In 1999 he has received the prestigious IIE (Institute of Industrial Engineers), OR Division, Research Award. In 2005 he received an LSU Distinguished Faculty Award as recognition of his research, teaching, and service accomplishments. Some of his graduate students have also received awards and distinctions including the Best Dissertation Award at LSU for science, engineering and technology (2003). In 2000 Dr. Triantaphyllou published a bestseller book on multi-criteria decision-making. He has also co-edited a book on data mining by means of induction (2006) and this one on the mining of enterprise data (2007). He has also written a monograph on the use of a new logic method for data mining (to be published by Springer in 2007).

He always enjoys doing research with his students. He has received teaching awards and distinctions. His research has been funded by federal and state agencies, and the private sector. He has extensively published in the above areas. Dr. Triantaphyllou has a strong inter-disciplinary background. He is a strong believer of the premise that the next round of major scientific and engineering discoveries will come from the work of inter-disciplinary groups. More details of his work can be found in his web site (***http://www.csc.lsu.edu/trianta***).